G000135396

Literacy in Context

Language of
pre-1914 literature

Pauline Buckley
Celeste Flower

General editors	**Joan Ward** *and* **John O'Connor**
Literacy consultant	**Lyn Ranson**
General consultant	**Frances Findlay**

PUBLISHED BY THE PRESS SYNDICATE OF THE UNIVERSITY OF CAMBRIDGE
The Pitt Building, Trumpington Street, Cambridge, United Kingdom

CAMBRIDGE UNIVERSITY PRESS
The Edinburgh Building, Cambridge CB2 2RU, UK
40 West 20th Street, New York, NY 10011-4211, USA
10 Stamford Road, Oakleigh, VIC 3166, Australia
Ruiz de Alarcón 13, 28014 Madrid, Spain
Dock House, The Waterfront, Cape Town 8001, South Africa

http://www.cambridge.org

First published 2001

Printed in Italy by Graphicom

Typeface Delima MT 10.5pt on 12.5pt leading   *System* QuarkXPress®

A catalogue record for this book is available from the British Library

ISBN 0 521 80556 2 paperback

Prepared for publication by Pentacor PLC

Cover photograph © BBC 2001

Illustrations by Phil Garner (pp.14, 15), Judy Stevens (p.20), Linda Worrall (pp. 21, 67), Paul Cox (p.27), Peter Massey (p.33), Stephen May (p.39, 65), David Shenton (p.46, 70), Mark Duffin (p.68).

ACKNOWLEDGEMENTS

The publishers gratefully acknowledge the following for permission to reproduce copyright material.

Textual material Extracts from 'The Way Through the Woods' (pp.8, 9) by Rudyard Kipling from *The New Oxford Book of English Verse*, ed. Helen Garner (Book Club Associates 1984), by permission of A P Watt Ltd on behalf of The National Trust for Places of Historical Interest or Natural Beauty; *The Wind in the Willows* (p.27) by Kenneth Grahame copyright © The University Chest, Oxford, by permission of Curtis Brown Ltd, London; *The Natural History of Selborne* (pp.32, 33) by Gilbert White, edited with an introduction by Paul Foster (World's Classics 1993) editorial matter © Paul Foster 1993 (Oxford University Press), by permission of Oxford University Press; *Pygmalion* (pp.44, 45) by George Bernard Shaw (Penguin Books) by permission of the Society of Authors, on behalf of the Bernard Shaw Estate; *Maria Marten*, or *Murder in the Red Barn* (pp.50, 51) by Constance Cox (Samuel French Ltd), by permission of Samuel French Ltd; *Roget's Thesaurus* (p.10) (Pearson Education Ltd), by permission of Pearson Education Ltd.

Photographs Assorted images (p.24), by permission of GettyOne Stone.

Every effort has been made to trace copyright holders, but in some cases this has proved impossible. The publishers would be happy to hear from any copyright holder that has not been acknowledged.

Introduction

- Read a piece of text
- Read it again to discover what makes it special
- Check that you understand it
- Focus on key features
- Learn about these language features and practise using them
- Improve your spelling
- Plan and write your own similar piece
- Check it and redraft

Each unit in this book helps you to understand more about a particular kind of writing, learn about its language features and work towards your own piece of writing in a similar style.

Grammar, spelling and punctuation activities, based on the extract, will improve your language skills and take your writing to a higher level.

 The book at a glance

The texts

The extracts cover a range of texts from the English literary heritage. Each part of the book contains two or three units of extracts and activities at different levels to help you measure your progress.

Each unit includes these sections:

Purpose

This explains exactly what you will read, learn about and write.

Key features

These are the main points to note about the way the extract is written.

Language skills

These activities will improve your grammar, punctuation and spelling. They are all based on the extracts. They are organised using the Word, Sentence and Text Level Objectives of the *National Literacy Strategy Framework for Teaching English.*

Planning your own writing

This structured, step-by-step guide will help you to get started, use writing frames and then redraft and improve your work.

Teacher's Portfolio

The Teacher's Portfolio includes worksheets for more language practice, revision and homework. Self-assessment charts help you to judge and record what level you have reached and to set your own targets for improvement!

Contents

Contents

Plays

Word	Spelling	Sentence	Text	Activities
• Apostrophe for omission and contraction	• of, have and 've	• Exclamation marks • Colon	• Scriptwriting convention and layout	Writing a short dramatic extract involving two characters in conflict
• Adjectives	• Suffix -ful	• Exclamatory sentences	• Melodrama • Asides • Dramatic irony • Stage directions	Continuing a script
• Language change • Prepositions	• y becomes -ies • ey becomes -eys	• Proverbs	• Line endings • Caesura	Writing a script where a character makes a choice including a proverb

• Verbs • Abstract nouns	• Syllables	• Commas for lists and parenthesis	• Personification • Rhyme and rhyme scheme • Rhythm	Writing a poem
• Adjectives	• Adding -ed	• Dialect • Standard and non-standard forms of English	• First-person narrator • Cliffhanger	Writing the opening to a story which gives a sense of tension

Familiar places

In this unit you will:
- read a poem about a place
- explore what the poem is about
- write your own poem about a place

►► Subject links: *science*

2 ► **20th-century poetry**

The Way through the Woods

*T*hey shut the road through the woods
Seventy years ago.
Weather and rain have undone it again,
And now you would never know
5   There was once a road through the woods
Before they planted the trees.
It is underneath the coppice and heath   *undergrowth*
And the thin anemones.   *bright flowers*
Only the keeper sees
10   That, where the ring-dove broods,   *bird*

And the badgers roll at ease,
There was once a road through the woods.

Yet, if you enter the woods
Of a summer evening late,
15   When the night-air cools on the trout-ringed pools
Where the otter whistles his mate,
(They fear not men in the woods,
Because they see so few.)
You will hear the beat of a horse's feet,
20   And the swish of a skirt in the dew,
Steadily cantering through
The misty **solitudes**,   *peace and quiet*
As though they perfectly knew
The old lost road through the woods...
25   But there is no road through the woods.

Rudyard Kipling 1865–1936

3 ▷ Key features

The writer:
- uses interesting vocabulary to give detail
- uses words that sound like their meaning
- uses repetition to create a sense of mystery

- Why was the road closed?
- The pronoun *they* is used a number of times in the poem. Who is meant by *they* each time it is used?
- What suggests that the horse and the woman might be ghosts?

4 ⟩ Language skills

Word

A **hyphen** is a punctuation mark (-)
that can be used to join words or parts
of words together to make a new word:

scrap-book, well-known, home-made

❶ Line 15 has two hyphenated
words which help to create vivid
images. Draw the picture that is
described by this line and write
the line underneath as a caption.

A **thesaurus** is a book that lists words
in related groups. If you have an idea,
but cannot think of the right word for
it, a thesaurus will help you.

❷ If you want another word for
solitudes (line 22) look up the
word in the index of the
thesaurus. It will give you a
number reference for that word
or for similar words:

solitude

seclusion 883 n.

> n. tells you that
> the word is a noun

Turn to the page in the thesaurus
that has 883 as a column heading.
Find the number in that column.
Next to that number you will find
a list of words associated with
seclusion. You will find *peace and
quiet* listed here:

883. **Unsociability. Seclusion – N.**

seclusion, privacy, private world, world
on its own; peace and quiet 266 n.
quietude; home life, domesticity;
loneliness, solitude; retirement,
withdrawal; confinement…

From *Roget's Thesaurus*

❸ Use a thesaurus to find words with
similar meanings to *keeper* (line 9).
Which word do you think best
describes who the keeper is in the
poem? Write down the reasons for
your answer.

Spelling

The vowel sound 'way', can be made
with different spellings. It can be made
on its own when followed by a
consonant and the letter -*e*:

plate

or by adding -*y* or -*i*:

play, plain

❶ Write down the examples of *a-e*,
-*ai* and -*ay* spellings of the same
vowel sound from the poem.

Sentence

If we add a word or phrase to a sentence, using commas, brackets or dashes, we say that the word or phrase is in **parenthesis**. (To pronounce it, put the stress on the *-ren-*.)

Bill was going to the shops with Tracey (Tracey is his sister).

1 From the poem, write down the extra information the sentence in parenthesis provides about the woods.

Ellipsis is the omission of an element in language. The three dots (...) are called **ellipsis points**. They tell us that something has been missed out.

'I don't believe you said that! Now you're in trouble...'

2 Why do you think Kipling uses ellipsis points on line 24? Discuss your own and the following suggestions and write down the one you think fits best.

- to make the lady and the horse sound more mysterious
- to remind you that the lady and the horse are not real
- to emphasise that there is no road through the woods
- to leave us thinking about the mystery of the road

Text

Onomatopoeia is the name given to a word that sounds like its meaning:

Bang! Splash! Crash!

Letters that are sounded with a hiss are called **sibilant** letters.

As you say the word *sizzle* you will hear a hissing sound.

1 Copy out lines 15 and 20. Underline the onomatopoeic words in these lines.

2 Look up the word *hiss* in a thesaurus and write down the other onomatopoeic words that are listed. An example is *buzz*.

Repetition of words is sometimes used for emphasis:

Don't you ever, ever walk through the woods alone!

3 The poet repeats *the woods* in seven lines throughout the poem. Write down each line in which *the woods* appears.

Read these lines out loud to another student. Each time you read out a line, make it sound more mysterious than the one before.

5 ▶ Planning your own writing

Kipling describes the woods and how something about them has changed: he describes what you would see and hear if you were to visit the woods. He uses detail and gives the woods a mysterious feeling.

Imagine you are returning to a place you know well. You find that it has changed in a particular way. Try to make the change a mysterious one… The place can be real or a place that you make up. Write a poem about this place.

▶ STARTING POINTS

- Your school – you remember when the bicycle sheds were there. Can you still hear the chattering of children as they lock up their bicycles?

- A place you visited on holiday – before they built a hotel by the beach. Do the waves whisper the name of an old fisherman as they splash against the rocks?

- Your nearest town centre – where the cinema is now a bar and the little unusual shops have given way to estate agents. Can you hear the music from old film-titles?

- Your local park before it was redeveloped – where the pond used to be is now a car park. Can you hear squeals of laughter as children play on the swings?

▶ CLUES FOR SUCCESS

- Use a thesaurus to help you find words to describe your place.

- Include as much detail as you can: animals, birds, landscape, weather, people – even the ghost of a teacher past!

- Repeat important ideas but use parenthesis for extra information.

- Include onomatopoeia.

- Use ellipsis points to add mystery.

▶ REDRAFTING AND IMPROVING

Work with another student. Read each other's writing out loud.

- Make a list of the vocabulary about your place. Use a thesaurus to check spellings and help you to change or add words that will give the poem detail.

- Is the atmosphere at the end of your poem different from the atmosphere at the start of the poem?

- Underline any onomatopoeic words or phrases and then read them aloud.

- Check spelling and punctuation carefully, especially -a sounding vowels.

WRITING FRAME

The following frame uses the same structure as Kipling's poem.
You might find it helpful in writing your poem.

They shut the	Lane to the bicycle shed?
.... years / months / weeks ago	How long?
....	How has it all been covered and hidden?
And now you would never know	
There was once a	As line 1
Before they	What did they do? Planted or built something?
It is	Where? Under the new science block?
And	Something else? Next to the car park?
Only the caretaker sees	
That, where the children hide,	
And	Who or what else would go there?
There was once	As line 1
Yet, if you enter	As line 1
Of a	What time of the year? Winter's morning?
When	What happens at this time of the year?
Where the	Describe the sound of a bird
(They fear not children in the	As line 1
Because they see so few)	
You will hear	A noise associated with school. A bell?
And the	More school noises. Try to use onomatopoeia.
Steadily unlocking the chains	
For the bike's journey home.	
As though they perfectly knew	
The old lost	As line 1 — remember to use ellipsis points.
But there is no	As line 1

6 ❯ **Looking back**

- **Vocabulary** has to be chosen carefully if you want to describe places in detail.
- **Onomatopoeia** brings words to life by making them sound like their meaning.
- **Repetition** of words and ideas can give them emphasis and different shades of meaning.

Making a splash!

1 ▷ Purpose

In this unit you will:

- enjoy reading a poem from the 18th century
- explore the form and content of the poem
- write a story which teaches a moral

≫ **Subject links:** *art, PSHE, science*

2 ▷ An 18th-century poem which teaches a moral

On a Favourite Cat, Drowned in a Tub of Goldfishes

This poem tells the story of a cat who is so eager to get at a goldfish that she fails to see the danger she is in. In the final verse (or stanza) the poet points out a warning, known as a moral, which also applies to humans.

'Twas on a lofty vase's side,
Where China's **gayest art had dyed**
   The **azure flowers** that blow;
Demurest of the tabby kind,
5 The **pensive Selima reclined**,
   Gazed on the lake below.

the vase is decorated with blue flowers

thoughtful; lying on her side

Her conscious tail her joy declared;
The fair round face, the snowy beard,
   The velvet of her paws,
10 Her coat that with the tortoise **vies**,
Her ears of jet, and emerald eyes,
   She saw; and purr'd applause.

competes

Still had she gazed; but 'midst the tide
Two angel **forms** were seen to glide,
15 The **Genii** of the stream:
Their scaly armour's **Tyrian hue**
Thro' richest purple to the view
   Betray'd a golden gleam.

she might have gone on watching
shapes
spirits
reddish-purple colour

The **hapless Nymph** with wonder saw: *unlucky young female*
20 A whisker first and then a claw,
   With many an **ardent** wish,   *passionate*
She stretch'd in vain to reach the prize.
What female heart can gold despise?
   What **cat's averse to fish**?   *What cat dislikes fish?*

25 **Presumptuous** Maid! with looks intent   *too bold*
Again she stretch'd, again she bent,
   Nor **knew** the gulf between.   *realised, noticed*
(**Malignant** Fate sat by, and smiled)   *evil*
The slipp'ry verge her feet **beguiled**.   *tricked*
30   She tumbled headlong in.

Eight times emerging from the flood
She mew'd to ev'ry wat'ry god,
   Some speedy aid to send.
No Dolphin came, no **Nereid** stirr'd: *a kind of mermaid*
35 Nor cruel Tom, nor Susan heard.
   A Fav'rite has no friend!

From **hence, ye** Beauties, undeceived,   *now on; you*
Know, one false step is ne'er retrieved,
   And be with caution bold.
40 Not all that tempts your wand'ring eyes
And **heedless** hearts, is lawful prize;   *incautious, not listening*
   Nor all that glisters, gold.   *to advice*

Thomas Gray, 1716–1771

3 **Key features**

The writer:

- tells a story in verse, with a touch of humour
- uses a regular pattern of lines and rhymes for the poem
- comments on the events and on what we can learn from them by ending with a moral

» - Retell the story in seven sentences, using one sentence for each stanza.
- How does the poet give the idea that Selima is pampered (lines 7–11)?
- Why does the cat comes up for air eight times (lines 31–32).

4 Language skills

Word

Good writers develop a wide **vocabulary**. This allows them to describe something exactly and also adds variety to their writing.

In the poem, the vocabulary used to describe colours is unusual. In most cases the words suggest richness as well as colour. At line 16 the fish's scales are of *Tyrian hue*. This means that they are a very deep red, with a hint of purple, like the dye of a very expensive type of cloth.

1 Find as many different words as you can for common colours such as red and yellow. Make a colour chart with a column for each of these colours too:

> *blue, white, black, green, purple*

Find the colour vocabulary used in the poem for each one, at lines 3, 8, 11 and 16. Write them in the correct columns.

Now, using a thesaurus, find alternative colour vocabulary and list the words in appropriate columns. Add more columns for other colours.

Spelling

A spelling rule you may have heard is: *i* before *e*, except after *c*, when the sound is *ee*.

Words which contain the letters *ei* or *ie* are often misspelt. The rule above can help you remember the correct ways to spell words such as:

> *retrieved* – *i* before *e*
> *deceived* – except after *c*.

There are some exceptions to this rule. If you are unsure about spelling, it is always better to check in a dictionary or word book and learn each one individually.

1 Create your own vocabulary lists of *-ei-* and *-ie-* words. Begin with those from the poem and continue with these:

> *ceiling, receive, science...*

Add more as you meet them.

2 Look out for words with *-ie-* and *-ei-* which do not have the *-ee-* sound

> *ancient, conscience.*

Keep a separate vocabulary list for these words.

Sentence

The **apostrophe** is a punctuation mark (') which can be used in two different ways.

Ben's homework: this apostrophe shows that the homework belongs to Ben. It shows **possession**.

1 The poem contains only three examples of the apostrophe for possession, at lines 1, 2 and 16. Write out all three and, next to them, complete these statements:

a The cat is lying on the side of a _____

b The pattern of the vase looked as if it came from _____

c The _____ were a deep purple colour.

I can't tell: This apostrophe shows that the two words *can* and *not* have been made into one, with some letters dropped. It shows **omission**.

2 Each stanza of the poem contains at least one example of the apostrophe used to show omission. List them all. For each example write down the complete word with all its letters in.

Text

The poem is written in regular **stanzas**. Some people call them verses. They are regular because:

- each stanza contains the same number of lines
- each stanza has the same **rhyme scheme** or pattern of rhymes

This is how you can work out a poem's rhyme scheme.

1 The first two lines of each stanza rhyme with one another. We can call the rhyme sound 'a':

*'Twas on a lofty vase's **side**,*	a
Where China's gayest art had ***dyed***	a

The third line has a different rhyme sound. Call it 'b':

*The azure flowers that **blow**;*	b

The next two lines also rhyme with one another, but it is a different rhyme sound again, so call it 'c':

*Demurest of the tabby **kind**,*	c
*The pensive Selima re**clined**,*	c

The final line has a sound that rhymes with line 3, so it can be given the same letter:

*Gazed on the lake **below**.*	b

The rhyme scheme for this stanza is known as 'a a b c c b'.

2 Check the rhyme scheme for the other stanzas, writing out the patterns using letters as you have been shown.

5 ▶ Planning your own writing

The poet has used the cat's behaviour to show how foolish humans can be. At lines 40–42, a moral is given. A moral is a piece of advice or wisdom which makes you think about your own behaviour. In this case, the poet suggests that if you are as greedy and reckless as the cat, you too will come to a sticky end.

List some stories you have read where animals behave like human beings.

Write a short story which has an animal as the main character. The story must have a moral, message or warning to humans within it. It can be humorous.

▶ STARTING POINTS

- Proverbs could help you choose an idea for a story, such as *A stitch in time saves nine* or *Never put all your eggs in one basket*.

- The goldfishes' tale – how would the goldfish have narrated what happened to Selima?

- Retell an old fable with a twist. Set it in modern times or change to a different animal. You could base it on *The Hare and the Tortoise*, or *The Fox who wanted the grapes*.

- The pet's tale – everyone's pet has been up to mischief at some time or other!

- Decide on the animal's mistake or downfall at the start of your planning.

- You could tell your story from the animal's point of view.

▶ CLUES FOR SUCCESS

- Draw a cartoon strip or prepare a plan of no more than seven frames or seven sentences before you begin.

- Use one paragraph for each of your pictures or sentences.

- Don't write too much at first. Concentrate on unfolding the story clearly.

- Foxes are thought to be cunning or sly. Elephants are said to have long memories. Think of human elements found in other animals. Aim to show something of this human character when you describe the actions of your animal.

- When you reach the end of the story, remember to include the moral. Be sure to explain how it affects not only the animal in your story, but your reader too.

WRITING FRAME

 REDRAFTING AND IMPROVING

- Share your story with a friend. Ask them to write out seven sentences which summarise the story.

Paragraph 1
Where is the animal? What is it doing at the start of the tale?
Asleep on his perch, at the break of day, sat...

Paragraph 2
Describe the animal, its appearance and characteristics.
With a beady black eye...feathers fine...

Paragraph 3
Explain what catches its eye or sets it off on the adventure.
Suddenly a sound, from the open window...

Paragraph 4
Continue the action.
The latch sprang open...

Paragraph 5
Continue and bring the action to a dramatic climax. This is where you tell your reader the terrible fate of the animal.
Held fast in the claws of...

Paragraph 6
How is the animal saved? Or describe its sticky end.
Alerted by squawks, Judy rushed out...

Paragraph 7
Set out the moral or warning and say how humans can learn from it.
'The perch is always greener on the other side of the blind.'
Beware of...

6 > Looking back

- Writers use unusual words to make their descriptions vivid. Their **vocabulary** is always chosen with care.

- The apostrophe used for **possession** tells us where something belongs to something or someone else. The apostrophe used for **omission** shows where two words have been contracted into a single word or where letters have been dropped from a word.

- A poem written in a regular form may have **stanzas** with a distinct number of lines in each, and a rhyme scheme.

- Look back through your story and underline any colour vocabulary. Use your colour chart to vary the words you use for different effects. You could use rich colours, like chocolate brown, or dull ones like mud to change the impact of your story.

- Read through your story for *ie* and *ei* words. Double check the spellings.

- Check through your work to make sure you have used apostrophes correctly.

Travelling companions

1 ▷ Purpose

In this unit you will:
- read some poetry written over 600 years ago
- compare Middle English and Modern English
- write a description of a person

▷▷ **Subject links:** *history, art, religious studies*

2 ▷ Middle English poetry

The Squire from *The General Prologue* to *The Canterbury Tales*

> *At the start of the book of tales, Chaucer introduces us to his fellow travellers. The first pilgrim we hear of is a knight and then...*

With hym ther was his sone, a yong Squier,
A lovyere and a lusty bacheler,
With lokkes crulle as they were leyd in presse.
Of twenty yeer of age he was, I gesse,
5   Of his stature he was of evene lengthe,
And wonderly delyvere, and of greet strengthe,
And he hadde been somtyme in chyvachie
In Flaundres, in Artoys, and Pycardie,
And born hym weel, as of so litel space,
10   In hope to stonden in his lady grace.
Embrouded was he, as it were a meede
Al ful of fresshe floures, whyte and reede.
Syngynge he was, or floytynge, al the day;
He was as fressh as is the month of May.
15   Short was his gowne, with sleves longe and wyde.
Wel koude he sitte on hors and faire ryde.
He koude songes make and wel endite,
Juste and eek daunce, and weel purtreye and write.
So hoote he lovede that by nyghtertale
20   He sleep namoore than dooth a nyghtyngale.
Curteis he was, lowely, and servysable,
And carf biforn his fader at the table.

Geoffrey Chaucer, c. 1345–1400

How we might describe the Squire today

The knight had with him his son, who was training to be a knight himself.
He was a handsome and likeable lad
With such curly hair that it looked as if he'd permed it.
I reckon he was about twenty years old.
5   He was fairly tall,
Extremely fit and very strong.
He'd spent some time with the Armed Forces
In different parts of Europe,
And in just a short time shown what he was made of,
10   Hoping to impress his girlfriend.
His clothes were embroidered in red and white
Like a meadow full of fresh flowers.
You could hear him singing or whistling all day long,
As brightly as the month of May.
15   He wore a fashionable short jacket, with long
    wide sleeves.
He rode well and looked good on horseback.
He wrote his own songs, both the music and
    the lyrics.
20   He could joust, dance, draw well and write poetry.
And he was so much in love that at night
He hardly slept, just like the nightingale.
He was always polite, obedient and helpful
And he did all his chores at home without
25   complaining.

3 ▶ Key features

The writer:
- describes the Squire using rhyming couplets
- emphasises the Squire's characteristics using simple comparisons and similes
- contrasts the two sides of the Squire's character

- Which characteristics of the Squire would make him a good soldier?
- What other things is the Squire good at?
- What can you tell about the relationship between the Squire and his father?

4 > Language skills

Word

Language changes over time. Some words which were once used in English are rarely, if at all, found today.

Chaucer would never have heard of the words *television, computer, tea* or *coffee*. They were not part of his world. In the same way he used words which we may not have heard or seen.

❶ Look for these words from Chaucer's poem which we no longer use:

eek	*chyvachie*
meede	*nyghtertale*
endite	*dooth*
wonderly	*juste*

❷ Match each of the words in the list above to one of these meanings:

does	*also*
meadow	*night-time*
cavalry raids	*write words*
joust	*wondrously*

❸ Over the last 600 years, some of the words Chaucer used have not been lost. Instead they have changed their meanings.

Here are some words we use today. What they meant in Chaucer's time appears in brackets beside them. Find out what the words mean now:

lusty (lively)
bacheler/bachelor (young knight)
fresh (bright, bold)
lowely/lowly (humble)
faire/fair (well)

Now use the modern words you have found in five of your own sentences.

Spelling

When Chaucer was writing, the printing press had not been invented. Spelling rules existed but were not as hard and fast as they are today. Chaucer's English was also pronounced very differently from ours.

❶ Read the text through, looking out for words which look like modern words, apart from one or two letters. Note the spelling differences under the following headings. Some line references are given to help you begin.

● words with an extra final *-e* – 1, 3, 4…

● words using *y* where we would now write *i* – 1, 7, 12…

● words where *k* is used for *c*, or *f* for *v*, or *d* for *th* – 3, 16, 22…

● words appearing with two different spellings – 12, 14…

Sentence

The order of words in a sentence or phrase is also known as the **syntax**. Chaucer's syntax was sometimes different from ours today. In line 17 of the text we read that the Squire could *songes make*. Today we would say that he could make up songs.

❶ Change the following phrases to modern syntax:

faire ryde	*(line 16)*
weel purtreye	*(line 18)*
lokkes crulle	*(line 3)*

Text

A writer may use a **simple comparison** to help us imagine how a character or thing looks or behaves. If Ebeneezer's snores were louder than thunder, we will have an idea of how loud that is. We will never have heard Ebeneezer's snores, but we have heard thunder. We can, therefore, imagine the sound of the snoring by comparison.

1 In Chaucer's poem, the Squire is said to *sleep namoore than dooth a nyghtyngale.*

What does the simple comparison with the nightingale tell us about the Squire's night-time habits?

A **simile** is a way of making an unusual or unexpected comparison. The writer uses the words like or as to make the comparison:

Her eyes were black as coal, her skin like milk.

2 Write some similes of your own to describe these things:

> a hedgehog   eggs
> a windmill   roller skates

Make the simile as unusual as you can.

3 Find the two similes in the description of the Squire at lines 11–12 and 14. What do they tell you about the way he looks and behaves?

Chaucer's early readers had clear ideas about the ways in which lovers or soldiers were meant to look and behave. Chaucer uses the characteristics of both 'types' in his description of the Squire, setting up a **contrast** between them.

4 Write down the words and phrases from the poem which tell you that the Squire is: in love, a good soldier.

In your view, does he seem to be a better lover or a better soldier?

When two lines of poetry next to each other have the same rhyme at the end, they are known as a **rhyming couplet:**

Embrouded was he, as it were a meede

Al ful of fresshe floures, whyte and reede.

The General Prologue to Chaucer's *Canterbury Tales* **is written in rhyming couplets.**

5 Complete these lines as rhyming couplets:

Sir Fergus was a fearsome tabby cat.
He always _____

But if he met the next door neighbour's pet,
Then _____

5 ▷ Planning your own writing

Write a description of a person.

1 They can be real or an invention of your own, male or female.

2 You may choose to write in prose or poetry.

3 Write between 14 and 20 lines of poetry or up to 200 words of prose.

4 If you can draft your writing on a word processor, you will find it easier to edit and change later. This is particularly important when you are aiming to keep to a word or line limit.

5 If you choose to write a poem, include some rhyming couplets.

▷▷ STARTING POINTS

- Describe a modern day squire, a combination of soldier and young lover.

- Describe a 21st-century hero from sport, music, film or TV, or any part of life.

- Describe your millennium hero, someone from the 20th century who made history.

- Describe a person whom you know and admire personally.

▷▷ CLUES FOR SUCCESS

- Begin with a context: Chaucer's pilgrims are on a journey. What is your character doing?

- Plan two contrasting sides to your character. For example, perhaps a champion skier might spend their spare time helping on local hospital radio as a DJ.

- Don't be too ambitious. We don't need to know everything about your character. A few key ideas for each aspect of their personality will be enough.

- Keep the language simple, but look for good accurate adjectives. Using a thesaurus may help.

- You might find it useful to include some comparisons and similes.

WRITING FRAMES

This frame will work for prose and poetry versions.

- In one sentence, set the context (what your character is doing).

- Introduce your character by name or occupation.

- Describe their physical appearance (age, hairstyle, height, build).

- Explain what experience they have had in their main occupation.

- In contrast, describe what they prefer to wear, and what their hobby or other activity is.

- Describe some things that they are really good at.

- Explain how they get on with other people or a little bit about their personality.

REDRAFTING AND IMPROVING

- Share your character description with another person.

- You might ask them to make a sketch of your character, or describe it again in their own words. The clearer your description, the easier they should find this.

- Ask them to suggest changes which would help them get a better image. Now redraft your writing.

- If you are writing a poem, check that any changes do not upset your rhyming couplet pattern.

6 > Looking back

- **Language changes** over time. Some words which were in everyday use in past centuries are no longer used. Others have simply taken on a new meaning. New words are constantly being invented.

- When two lines of poetry next to each other have the same rhyme at the end, they are known as a **rhyming couplet**. Couplets have been a favourite form for poetry down through the ages.

- **Similes** are unusual comparisons using *like* or *as*.

Alone in the wild wood

In this unit you will:

- read an extract from a novel written for children at the beginning of the 20th century
- think about how to create atmosphere and tension in writing
- continue writing where the story breaks off

▶▶ **Subject links:** *drama, science*

2 ▸ 20th-century narrative fiction

The Wind in the Willows

Mole has spent most of his life underground. One fine spring morning he meets the water rat and discovers the joys of the river bank. He longs to see what is beyond in the wild wood, in spite of Ratty's warnings.

Everything was very still now. The dusk advanced on him steadily, rapidly, gathering in behind and before; and the light seemed to be draining away like flood-water.

Then the faces began.

5 It was over his shoulder, and indistinctly, that he first thought he saw a face: a little evil wedge-shaped face, looking out at him from a hole. When he turned and confronted it, the thing had vanished.

He quickened his pace, telling himself cheerfully not to begin imagining things, or there would be simply no end to it. He passed
10 another hole, and another, and another; and then – yes! – no! – yes! certainly a little narrow face, with hard eyes, had flashed up for an instant from a hole, and was gone. He hesitated – braced himself up for an effort and strode on. Then suddenly, and as if it had been so all the time, every hole, far and near, and there were hundreds of them, seemed
15 to possess its face, coming and going rapidly, all fixing on him glances of malice and hatred: all hard-eyed and evil and sharp.

If he could only get away from the holes in the banks, he thought, there would be no more faces. He swung off the path and plunged into the untrodden places of the wood.

20   Then the whistling began.

Very faint and shrill it was, and far behind him, when first he heard it; but somehow it made him hurry forward. Then, still very faint and shrill, it sounded far ahead of him, and made him hesitate and want to go back. As he halted in indecision it broke out on either side, and
25   seemed to be caught up and passed on throughout the whole length of the wood to its furthest limit. They were up and alert and ready, evidently, whoever they were! And he – he was alone, and unarmed, and far from any help; and the night was closing in.

Then the pattering began.

Kenneth Grahame, 1859–1932

3 ▶ Key features

The writer:

- creates atmosphere by choosing words carefully
- uses commas to give information and make meanings clear
- gives a sense of action and time passing by using time adverbials

- Do you think Mole is a brave character or a foolish one? Explain your choice.
- *– yes! – no! – yes!* How do you think Mole moves at this point in the extract (line 10)?
- To whom or to what do you think 'the faces' belong?

27

4 ▷ Language skills

Word

An **antonym** is a word which has the opposite meaning to another word. The term comes from *anti-*, a prefix which means *against*.

❶ There are several pairs of words with opposite meanings in the extract. *Far* and *near* appear in line 14. Find two more pairs: one is in line 15 and the other in lines 21 and 26.

❷ Find antonyms for the following words from the extract:

furthest	*shrill*
indistinct	*sharp*
faint	*evil*

A **synonym** is a word which means the same, or almost the same, as another word. *Malice* and *hatred* are two words in the extract with very similar meanings.

❸ Using a thesaurus, find as many other synonyms as you can for *malice* and *hatred*.

Spelling

-ly

Many English adverbs are formed simply by adding *-ly* to the end of an adjective:

adjective	adverb	
rapid	*rapidly*	in line 2.

This rule applies even when the adjective ends in a single *-l*.

❶ Find six more adverbs ending with *-ly* in the extract. Which two of these have to change their spelling before adding *-ly*? Learn them using the Look–Say–Cover–Write–Check system.

Sentence

Commas are punctuation marks which can have several uses.

They can be used to separate items in a list. The last item in the list usually follows the word *and*, instead of another comma:

letter-paper, bacon, ham, cards and dominoes.

❶ Unscramble the contents of Ratty's picnic hamper and write the sentence out correctly using commas in the list.

> *There's cold chicken inside it, coldtonguecoldhamcoldbeefpickledg herkinssaladfrenchrollscresssandwic hespottedmeatgingerbeerlemonades odawater.*

Text

Time adverbials are words and phrases which tell you *when* something happened.

Then the faces began.
When he turned and confronted it...
Everything was very still *now*.

There are a lot of words and phrases relating to time which can tell you *when* something happens in a story and help move the story on. A few of these are:

> on Thursday
> for several minutes
> each week
> last month
> later
> before

❶ Pick out four time adverbials from this paragraph and write them down:

> *Meantime the Rat, warm and comfortable, dozed by his fireside. His paper of half-finished verses slipped from his knee. Then a coal slipped, the fire crackled and sent up a spurt of flame, and he woke with a start. He reached down to the floor for his verses, pored over them for a minute and then looked round for the Mole...*

The writer uses the time adverbial *then* over and over again in the text.

❷ Find each example of the word *then* in the text and write down the line number where it appears.

Write out the complete sentences for lines 4, 20 and 29. Look at these three sentences and at where they are found in the text. You should see a pattern. Discuss with another student why the writer chose to repeat *then* so often.

❸ Each time you see the time adverbial *then* in the text, change it to another word or phrase. It must be another time adverbial that will move the action forward.

Write out the sentences which contain your new time adverbials.

Then compare your new words with those that someone else used in the same exercise. Explain the slightly different meanings that you have created with the new time adverbials.

29

5 ▷ Planning your own writing

Continue the story from where the study text finishes.

❶ Begin with the sentence: 'Then the pattering began.'

❷ What must it be like alone in a wood as night falls? Write down your thoughts and feelings.

❸ List all the sounds you might hear as the darkness falls.

❹ Cold and hunger will bother you. Make a note of any other worries you may have.

❺ What strengths do you think a mole might have which will help in this situation? Compare your ideas with those of another person.

❻ What about weaknesses?

❼ Follow the writing frame below to structure your story.

❽ If you prefer not to use the writing frame, use the starting points as paragraph topics.

▷▷ STARTING POINTS

- Mole tries to decide where the pattering is coming from.

- He puzzles over what is making the pattering noise.

- Another sound reaches his ears. What is it this time?

- Something rushes out of the undergrowth and heads straight towards him.

- Mole tries to escape from the creature.

- He finds safety. Where and how?

▷▷ CLUES FOR SUCCESS

- Use simple sentences in your first draft.

- When you have a story you like, add more detail using commas for lists.

- Use time adverbials to move the story on, saying when things happen to Mole.

WRITING FRAMES

He thought it was only falling leaves at first.
The sound of it was…
Then as it grew…
Was it in front or behind? It seemed to be …
As he stood still…
He waited, expecting…

Paragraph 1: describe the pattering in more detail, as it gets louder or closer. Write about the direction it comes from. How does Mole react? What is he expecting?

The pattering increased till it sounded like…
The whole wood seemed…

Paragraph 2: the pattering is now very loud and close. Describe its effect on the whole wood.

Then the mumbling began.
Then the laughter began.
Then the screaming began.

Paragraph 3: choose one of these ideas, and write about it as you did in paragraph 1. You could, instead, write a paragraph for each of these ideas, or use some sounds of your own.

In panic, he began to run… he darted …and dodged…
At last he…
Anyhow, he was too tired to run any further, and could only…
And as he lay there panting…

Final paragraph: write about the way Mole tries to escape from the noises he hears.

He knew, at last, the Terror of the Wild Wood!

Finish with this sentence.

REDRAFTING AND IMPROVING

- Read through your story, or ask someone else to read it with you and make comments.
- If you have used a single time adverbial (phrase or word) several times, you may want to make changes.
- Introduce some adverbs to describe Mole's actions – *He ran* aimlessly, *he listened* anxiously.
- Make a final copy of your story ending.

6 ⟩ Looking back

- A **synonym** is a word which means the same, or almost the same, as another word. When a word with an opposite meaning is used, we call it an **antonym**.
- **Commas** are punctuation marks. One of their uses is to separate items in a list.
- **Time adverbials** are words and phrases which tell you *when* something happened. Using a variety of time adverbials makes the writing clearer and helps to keep the reader interested.

Gazing into the goldfish bowl

1 Purpose

In this unit you will:
- read a letter written in the 18th century
- think about how observations can be presented clearly to readers
- write a description of a creature you have observed

» **Subject links:** *science*

2 An 18th-century letter

The Natural History of Selborne

Gilbert White was a clergyman in Selborne, Hampshire. He walked in the parish daily, taking note of everything he saw around him. He was fascinated by natural history and observed animals, birds and fish closely. He wrote down what he saw in letters. Part of one of these letters is about the habits of goldfish. Notice that some of the rules for punctuation were different when White was writing.

As soon as the creature sickens, the head sinks lower and lower, and it stands as it were on it's head; till, getting weaker, and losing all poise, the tail turns over, and at last it floats on the surface of the water with it's belly uppermost. The reason
5 why fishes, when dead, swim in that manner is very obvious; because, when the body is no longer balanced by the fins of the belly, the broad muscular back **preponderates** by it's own   *weighs more* gravity, and turns the belly uppermost, as lighter from it's being a cavity, and because it contains the swimming-bladders,
10 which contribute to render it buoyant.

Some that delight in gold and silver fishes have adopted a notion that they need no **aliment**. True it is that they will   *food* subsist for a long time without any apparent food but what they can collect from pure water frequently changed; yet they

15   must draw some support from **animalcula**, and other
nourishment supplied by the water; because, though they seem
to eat nothing, yet the consequences of eating often drop
from them. That they are best pleased with such **jejune** diet
may easily be confuted, since if you toss them crumbs they
20   will seize them with great readiness, not to say greediness:
however, bread should be given sparingly, lest, turning sour, it
corrupt the water. They will also feed on the water-plant
called lemna (duck's meat), and also on small **fry**.

When they want to move a little they gently protrude
25   themselves with **pinnae pectorales**; but it is with their strong
muscular tails only that they and all fishes shoot along with
such inconceivable rapidity.

It has been said that the eyes of fishes are immoveable: but
these apparently turn them forward or backward in their
30   sockets as their occasions require. They take little notice of a
lighted candle, though applied close to their heads, but
flounce and seem much frightened by a sudden stroke of the
hand against the support whereon the bowl is hung; especially
when they have been motionless, and are perhaps asleep. As
35   fishes have no eyelids, it is not easy to **discern** when they are
sleeping or not, because their eyes are always open.

Gilbert White, 1720–1793

animals too small to be seen with the naked eye

sparse, thin

young fish

chest fins

judge

3 ▷ Key features

The writer:

- chooses accurate descriptive words and specialist terms
- uses a simple but formal style to report what he has seen and heard
- uses facts to support his ideas and to show how other opinions may be false

- What is the first sign that a goldfish is feeling unwell?
- According to the writer, what do goldfish eat, exactly?
- What makes the fish move slowly and what makes them move quickly?

4 Language skills

Word

Jargon is the name we give to the special words and phrases used by groups of people who share the same job or interest. Jargon words can also be called **specialist terms**. The writer of the letter uses both specialist terms and everyday descriptions to record what he has observed.

1 Draw up two columns:

Specialist terms   *Everyday vocabulary*

Find all of the words below in the text and make a note of their line numbers. Then place the words in the specialist terms column:

gravity	*cavity*
swimming-bladders	
buoyant	*aliment*
subsist	*animalcula*
nourishment	*diet*
corrupt	*lemna*
fry	*protrude*
pinnae pectorales	
sockets	

For each of these terms, find an everyday definition and write it in the second column. Some are given in the gloss alongside the extract, but you will need to look some up for yourself.

2 Take four sentences from the extract which contain words in the specialist terms column. Rewrite them replacing the words with everyday vocabulary.

Spelling

An apostrophe can be used to shorten the phrases *it is* or *it has*. The phrases are then written **it's**:

> *It's pouring with rain and it's been raining all day.*

This is different from **its** which shows possession: *The cat lapped up all of its milk.*

1 Re-read the first paragraph of the letter and you will notice that the rules about *its* and *it's* were different in the 18th century.

Find four examples of *it's* in the paragraph and rewrite the sentences following the modern rule.

Sentence

A **semi-colon (;)** can be used in place of a full stop. It shows that the sentences on either side of it are connected:

> *We've had a disappointing winter; it's only snowed once.*

In the 18th-century text the writer sometimes uses a colon (:) where today we would use a semi-colon or a full stop.

1 Find two colons in the extract. Re-write the sentences, changing to modern punctuation of semi-colons or full stops

2 Find examples of the semi-colon in the text. Which of these do not follow the modern use? What punctuation could you use in their place?

Text

Factual writing, especially when it is on a scientific topic, deals with true phenomena – that is, events that have actually taken place. If a writer wants to prove the truth of what he or she says, then there must be some evidence. Factual writing includes information about what the writer has observed or demonstrated, in experiments, to be true.

In the text you have read, the writer explains exactly how he has seen the goldfish behave:

> … *at last it floats on the surface of the water with it's belly uppermost.*

From this observed fact he is able to suggest a scientific reason for the behaviour:

> … *because, when the body is no longer balanced...*

1 Make a note of the facts from the text. Use a separate list for each paragraph. Next turn over the sheet of text and write a summary of the facts in your own words.

Without evidence, what a writer says will only be his or her **opinion**.

At line 28 the writer of the letter sets out an opinion held by other people:

It has been said that the eyes of fishes are immoveable

By the end of line 30 he has given evidence to show that the opinion is false. The facts are quite different, because he has seen these fish:

> *turn them forward or backward in their sockets*

2 Lines 11 and 12 give an opinion about the fishes' diet. Rewrite the opinion in your own words.

3 Two sets of facts (line 12 and lines 18-22) disprove that opinion. Find and rewrite those facts.

Naturalists record their observations and develop their ideas over a period of time in a diary, journal or research log

4 You are Gilbert White's assistant. He observes and comments on what he sees. Make notes for him.

Ask another student to read the text aloud to you, as if they are watching the goldfish. As they are speaking, make brief notes. Just record the important facts.

5 Use your notes to write a final summary about the behaviour of goldfish.

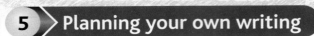

5 ▷ Planning your own writing

You are a naturalist reporting on what you have seen in your fieldwork.

Present your report as:

- either a letter to another scientist
- or a section for a manual for keeping pets or watching wildlife.
- write for readers of your own age.
- Write in clear, descriptive language. Use specialist terms only if they will help your reader.

▶ STARTING POINTS

- Dogs making friends with one another.
- A cat who can make its owner do what it wants.
- A tame bird which has learnt to talk or whistle imitations.
- Reptiles devouring their prey.
- A hamster with its activity toys.
- A spider spinning a web.
- A caterpillar building its cocoon.
- Wild birds feeding or nest-building.

▶ CLUES FOR SUCCESS

- Decide what you want to watch the creature doing.
- Observe your creature, taking very careful and detailed notes of what you see.
- Keep asking yourself questions: How do they do this? Why do they do it?
- Be patient. You may have to watch several times.

▶ WRITING FRAMES

Letter or report of observations

I have been observing the
    behaviour of…
To a casual observer…
Looking more closely I noted that…
…this is because…
I also saw that… …the reason
    seems to be…
Some people have seen…
They have been seen to…
Most … but when …

**Owner's or Spotter's manual:
    an example**

How to have a healthy goldfish
Look out for
What to do
When to seek help
Preventing disease
A healthy diet

This frame is based on the goldfish passage. You can use the same headings for any pet. Other headings might include:

When to look
Where to find out more etc.

Introduce your creature and say when or why you watched it.
Give a brief description of the creature.
Describe some of the behaviour.
Give a reason why the creature behaves in that way.
Continue with describing what you saw. Add more information.
Finally you can describe something your creature did which might seem out of the ordinary.

Use a heading and then write your observations under sub-headings, e.g. in the goldfish's case, symptoms of illness. Suggest remedies or first aid.

When your fish is in a really bad way, who to turn to

How to provide a fish with a healthy habitat

Tips on feeding your fish

➤➤ REDRAFTING AND IMPROVING

- Ask another student or teacher to read your draft. What more do they want to know about your creature and observations? Add it in.

- Include photographs or diagrams to liven your text up.

- If you have written a guide rather than a report you could use bullet points for sub-headings.

- Extra material could appear in boxes. Look at some modern non-fiction books to give you ideas about layout.

6 ▷ Looking back

- **Specialist terms** give authority to the style of writing. When writers are aiming at a young audience, or beginners to a subject, they will use more everyday vocabulary.

- A **semi-colon (;)** can show a link between two sentences. It replaces a full stop.

- **Factual writing** must include evidence that the writer is reporting the truth.

The face at the window

1 ▷ Purpose

In this unit you will:
- read an extract from a famous 19th-century novel
- learn about some features of first-person narrative fiction
- write about a supernatural encounter or dream

▶▶ **Subject links:** *art, media studies*

2 ▷ 19th-century gothic fiction: the first-person narrative

Wuthering Heights

When Mr Lockwood visits Wuthering Heights in the Yorkshire Moors, a heavy snowfall prevents him returning home. The mysterious Mr Heathcliff is reluctant to let Lockwood stay overnight at the Heights but a kindly servant leads Lockwood upstairs. He finds a large enclosed oak bed next to a window ledge in a room that no one uses. His sleep that night is disturbed by bad dreams and a tapping at the window.

This time, I remembered I was lying in the oak closet, and I heard distinctly the gusty wind, and the driving of the snow; I heard also, the fir-bough repeat its teasing sound, and **ascribed** it to the right *put it down to* cause: but it annoyed me so much, that I resolved to silence it, if

5 possible; and, I thought, I rose and endeavoured to **unhasp the** *unlatch the window* **casement**. The hook was soldered into the staple: a circumstance observed by me when awake, but forgotten.

'I must stop it, nevertheless!' I muttered, knocking my knuckles through the glass, and stretching an arm out to seize the **importunate** *persistently troublesome*

10 branch; instead of which, my fingers closed on the fingers of a little, ice-cold hand!

The intense horror of nightmare came over me: I tried to draw back my arm, but the hand clung to it, and a most melancholy voice sobbed, 'Let me in – let me in!'

15 'Who are you?' I asked, struggling, meanwhile, to disengage myself.

3 **Key features**

The writer:

- tells the story from the point of view of the main character
- uses vocabulary which brings to mind ghosts and the supernatural
- uses dialogue full of exclamations to add to the excitement and tension

'Catherine Linton,' it replied. 'I'm come home: I'd lost my way on the moor!' As it spoke, I **discerned**, **obscurely**, a child's face looking through the window.

saw indistinctly, vaguely

20 Terror made me cruel; and, finding it useless to attempt shaking the creature off, I pulled its wrist on to the broken pane, and rubbed it to and fro till the blood ran down and soaked the bedclothes: still it wailed, 'Let me in!' and maintained its **tenacious grip**, almost maddening me with fear.

strong, stubborn grasp

'How can I?' I said at length. 'Let me go, if you want me to let you in!'

25 The fingers relaxed, I snatched mine through the hole, hurriedly piled the books up in a pyramid against it, and stopped my ears to exclude the **lamentable** prayer. I seemed to keep them closed above a quarter of an hour; yet, the instant I listened again, there was the **doleful** cry moaning on!

sorrowful, sad

full of grief

30 'Begone!' I shouted, 'I'll never let you in, not if you beg for twenty years.'

'It is twenty years,' mourned the voice: 'twenty years. I've been a **waif** for twenty years!'

wandering, homeless person

Emily Brontë, 1818–1848

- What does the narrator, Mr Lockwood, think has woken him?
- Who or what do you think is really outside the window?
- Can you list all the words and phrases that give a ghostly atmosphere to the extract, for example, *ice-cold hand, melancholy, nightmare*?

4 ▶ Language skills

Word

A **pronoun** is a word used instead of a noun or a noun phrase. It helps avoid repetitions.

*John went to the shop. **He** bought chocolate. (Not – John bought chocolate.)*

The personal pronouns are: *I, me, you, she, her, he, him, it, we, us, they* and *them*.

❶ Read lines 12–23 of the extract again. Pick out the pronouns that the writer uses for Catherine Linton. Hint – you would expect the writer to use the personal pronouns *she* and *her*. Give a reason why the writer does not use the obvious pronouns.

In the same section of the extract, the writer uses *a* and *the* where she could have used *its hand* or *her hand*:

a most melancholy voice

and later:

the fingers
the voice

❷ What does this tell you about the way Lockwood thinks about the *child* or *creature*? Which of these words would you use to describe his thoughts or feelings about her:

angry, afraid, benevolent, cautious, cruel, incensed, indifferent, indignant, terrified, repulsed, uncaring?

With another student, discuss why Lockwood shows no sympathy towards the child.

Spelling

-ough is a combination of letters which appears in many words. Take care!
-ough has lots of different pronunciations:

through   ('oo')
bough   ('ow')
thought   ('or')

The three examples above can all be found in the extract. Other pronunciations are:

though   ('oh')
enough   ('uf')
trough   ('off')
hiccough ('up')!

❶ Learn all of these spellings using the Look – Say – Cover – Write – Check method. Write a sentence of your own using each one, to show that you understand how to use it.

❷ Find at least one further example for each way of pronouncing *-ough*:

thought – sought.

Turn each pair of words you find into a sentence:

I thought that he sought a new girlfriend!

Sentence

Statements are sentences which give information. They end with full stops:

I'll never let you in, not if you beg for twenty years.

Questions are sentences which are asking for information to be given. They end with question marks:

Who are you?

Exclamatory sentences show emotions such as anger, surprise, joy, shock, pain or urgency. They can also be commands. They end with exclamation marks:

Let me in!
Begone!

❶ Rewrite each of the three sentences below, adding the correct punctuation:

> *I'm sorry I disturbed you*
>
> *What do you mean and what are you doing here*
>
> *It is swarming with ghosts and goblins*

❷ Find all the exclamatory sentences in the novel extract. There are nine. Take just four of these and think of an adverb or phrase to describe how each exclamation is made: in shock, or surprise, or urgently. To help you, the first one might be:

> *I must stop it, nevertheless!*

Lockwood has just been woken by the noise so he would probably exclaim this *angrily*.

Text

A **narrator** is a storyteller.

A **first-person narrator** is a teller who is also one of the characters in the story. They tell the story from their point of view, as a witness involved in events. You can spot a first-person narrative because the narrator uses first-person pronouns, *I*, *me*, *we*, *us*, *myself*, etc. (see **Word**) frequently.

A first-person narrator can tell the reader about their feelings and reactions to the events, in the way that an outside observer (or third-person narrator) could not. In this extract the narrator is able to explain his actions:

> *Terror made me cruel*
> (line 19).

❶ Change part of the extract from first-person narrative to third-person. You will need to change the pronouns as you write.

Begin at line 24 and go on to the end:

> *'How can I?' he said at length…*

Notice that you do not need to change the dialogue sections at all. With another student, compare the two versions and discuss the differences.

5 Planning your own writing

Write about a mysterious experience.

- Imagine that the experience happened to you.
- Jot down the events as you imagine they happened.
- For each event, note down what you heard, saw or smelled.
- Make a note of what your emotions and thoughts would be.
- Imagine what physical reactions you might have – dry mouth, hair standing on end.
- Plan any snippets of conversation or other communications.
- Be clear about how the encounter ends. Is it a real experience or a dream?
- Using your notes and the writing frame as a paragraph plan, write a first person narrative.

STARTING POINTS

- You wake up in an unfamiliar bed, in an unfamiliar room. What has woken you?
- You are driving alone at night along a road you do not recognise. Your engine suddenly dies.
- In a large shopping centre, you find that you have taken a wrong turning and are lost.
- In deep space, you wake from suspended animation before reaching your destination planet. The rest of the crew cannot be revived.
- You have taken a dare to spend the night in a haunted building. It is midnight.

CLUES FOR SUCCESS

- Give some detail about the setting of the story to help the reader imagine it.
- Imagine that you are describing the event to someone you know; this will help with writing in the first person.
- Describe your emotions and explain the motives for your actions.
- Add some dialogue. Mix it with the action to move the story along.
- Questions and explanations in the dialogue will create tension and excitement, and will also keep the story moving.
- Choose your vocabulary carefully. Use words that will create a mysterious atmosphere.

WRITING FRAMES

Locate yourself and your action. Describe sights and sounds around you.	I found myself... I could see only... I heard...
What is the first thing you do?	I must...
What do you find or meet? Explain your feelings and reactions. Describe any physical effects.	My fingers met with... The intense horror of nightmare came over me...
Begin a conversation, or some other form of communication.	'Who...? What...? Where...? How can I? If you want me to... you must...' Suddenly I was able to...
Describe your struggle to resist the being you have encountered. Is it a mental struggle or physically violent? Or is the creature gentle and persuasive?	
How do you make your escape? What are your final words? Is there a reply?	I shouted, '...!'

 REDRAFTING AND IMPROVING

- Read your story aloud to another person. Do they believe any of it?

- Ask your listener which parts of the story they found least convincing. Rewrite those sections.

- Check that you have used correct sentence punctuation for statements, questions and exclamations.

6 ▷ Looking back

- **Pronouns** are words used instead of nouns or noun phrases to avoid repetition.

- **Exclamatory sentences** end with exclamation marks. They show emotions or urgency. They can also be commands.

- A **first-person narrator** tells a story from his or her own point of view, as they experienced it. Characters in novels such as *Wuthering Heights* can be narrators. An autobiography is also a first-person narrative.

Comedy and conflict

1 ▶ **Purpose**

In this unit you will:

● read an extract from a comedy written before 1914
● explore the form and content of the play extract
● write your own script based on conflict

▶▶ **Subject links:** *design and technology, drama*

2 ▶ **20th-century comedy**

Pygmalion

Eliza Doolittle is a flower seller working in Covent Garden. One evening she meets Henry Higgins, a gentleman who studies the science of speech. He says that, despite her poor speech and grammar, he could pass her off as a duchess at an ambassador's garden party in three months. She turns up on his doorstep, demanding lessons in how to talk more formally. She is allowed to stay but Higgins suggests that she first takes a bath. In this extract Higgins' housekeeper, Mrs Pearce, introduces Eliza to the importance of bathing!

*Eliza is taken upstairs to the third floor greatly to her surprise; for she expected to be taken down to the **scullery**. Then Mrs Pearce opens the door and takes her into a spare bedroom.*

back kitchen where the dishes would be washed

MRS PEARCE I will have to put you here. This will be your bedroom.

LIZA O-h, I couldnt sleep here, missus. It's too good for the likes of me. I should be afraid to touch anything. I aint a duchess yet, you know.

5 **MRS PEARCE** You have got to make yourself as clean as the room: then you wont be afraid of it. And you must call me Mrs Pearce, not missus [*She throws open the door of the dressing room, now modernized as a bathroom*].

LIZA Gawd! whats this? Is this where you wash clothes? Funny sort of **copper** I call it.

copper hot-water boiler used for washing clothes

10 **MRS PEARCE** It is not a copper. This is where we wash ourselves, Eliza, and where I am going to wash you.

LIZA You expect me to get into that and wet myself all over! Not me. I should catch my death. I knew a woman did it every Saturday night; and she died of it.

15 **MRS PEARCE** Mr Higgins has the gentlemen's bathroom downstairs; and he has a bath every morning, in cold water.

LIZA Ugh! He's made of iron, that man.

MRS PEARCE If you are to sit with him and the Colonel and be taught you will have to do the same. They wont like the smell of
20 you if you dont. But you can have the water as hot as you like. There are two taps: hot and cold.

LIZA [*weeping*] I couldnt. I dursnt. Its not natural: it would kill me. Ive never had a bath in my life: not what youd call a proper one.

MRS PEARCE Well, dont you want to be clean and sweet and decent,
25 like a lady?

LIZA Boohoo!!!!

MRS PEARCE Now stop crying and go back into your room and take off all your clothes. Then wrap yourself in this [*taking down a gown from its peg and handing it to her*] and come back to me. I will get the
30 bath ready.

LIZA [*all tears*] I cant. I wont. I'm not used to it. Ive never took off all my clothes before. It's not right: it's not decent.

MRS PEARCE Nonsense, child. Dont you take off all your clothes every night when you go to bed?

35 **LIZA** [*amazed*] No. Why should I? I should catch my death. Of course I take off my skirt.

MRS PEARCE Do you mean that you sleep in the underclothes you wear in the daytime?

LIZA What else have I to sleep in?

40 **MRS PEARCE** You will never do that again as long as you live here. I will get you a proper nightdress.

LIZA Do you mean change into cold things and lie awake shivering half the night? You want to kill me, you do.

George Bernard
Shaw, 1856–1950

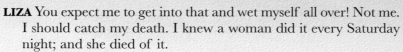

3 Key features

The writer:

- decides how their characters should say their lines.
- has characters speak using formal and informal English.
- gives plays a different layout from prose and poetry.

- Why do you think Eliza is surprised to be taken upstairs to the bedroom instead of downstairs to the scullery?

- What three reasons does Eliza give for not wanting to take a bath?

- What do you think is Mrs Pearce's opinion of Eliza's behaviour?

4 ⟩ Language skills

Word

An **apostrophe** (') can be used to show that a letter or a group of letters has been missed out.

A **contraction** is when you join two words together to form one word:

I did not like the film

becomes

I didn't like the film

❶ Often Shaw does not use apostrophes. Find three examples where letters have been missed out and write them down. Then, write the words out again putting the apostrophe in the correct place.

❷ When we speak, we often use contractions in a similar way to Eliza.

Find three examples of contractions in the extract. Then write out in full the two words that have been joined together, for example:

ELIZA I couldn't sleep
ELIZA I could not sleep

Spelling

We often use *'ve* as a contraction after *would* instead of *have*:

I would've been on time

❶ Write a short paragraph where Mrs Pearce describes Eliza's reactions to her new surroundings. Use the contraction *would've* three times:

I would've thought she'd be glad to get out of those filthy clothes…

Sentence

Exclamatory sentences show emotions such as anger, surprise, joy, shock, pain or urgency. They can also be commands. They end with exclamation marks (!)

Watch out!

In a play, when we see an exclamation mark, it helps us to understand how the spoken words might sound.

❶ Eliza is shocked when she first sees the bath because she has never seen anything like it. Say Eliza's line out loud,

Gawd! What's this?

Write down the advice you would give to the actress playing Eliza, about saying this line.

2 Find two other lines where Eliza's words or sentences end with exclamation marks. Note them down. Write down the advice you would give to the actress playing the part of Eliza about how to say these lines. For example, is she shocked, amused... ?

A **colon (:)** is a punctuation mark which shows that there is something else to follow in the sentence. It can lead you from the first part of the sentence to the second:

He was a natural leader: brave and courageous.

or it can introduce an example:

You need three ingredients: eggs, milk and flour.

3 From the extract, write down an example of a colon used to divide a sentence followed by an example of a colon used to introduce a list.

4 Re-read your last piece of extended writing. Are there any places in your writing where you could use colons instead of full stops or commas? Put them in and ask your teacher to check them.

Text

When we write a playscript, we follow certain **conventions**:

A space separates the character's name from the speech.

Speech marks are not needed.

MRS PEARCE Now stop crying and go back into your room and take off all your clothes. Then wrap yourself in this [*taking down a gown from its peg and handing it to her*] and come back to me. I will get the bath ready.

Stage directions are in italics.

Stage directions are in brackets.

Plays are to be performed to an audience, not just read aloud. If you are playing a part in a play, you have to think about how the character speaks and what they are doing when they speak.

1 Pick out four lines that Eliza speaks and write them down.

Write a stage direction for each line to help an actress playing the part of Eliza to understand how to say the line.

What would she do when she is saying the line? Ask another student to act out the lines using your stage directions.

Remember, the play is a comedy, so the more scared Eliza appears to be, the more the audience will laugh.

You might begin:

LIZA [*she is shocked as she looks round the room*] O-h, I couldn't sleep here, missus. It's too good for the likes of me...

5 ▷ Planning your own writing

The extract is based on the idea of conflict: Mrs Pearce wants Eliza to have a bath but Eliza is determined that she is not going to have one. The conflict is made more interesting because it is between two people who have different points of view.

Your task is to write a short play extract in which two characters are in conflict with each other.

⫸ STARTING POINTS

- A teenager argues that they do not want to go to school. The parent is determined that they will go.

- A customer takes an item of clothing back to a shop. The shop assistant is determined that they will not take it back.

- A student does not see why they should have to do their homework. The teacher is determined that they will.

- A neighbour accuses a teenager of breaking their window. The teenager is determined that they did not do it.

- A child wants their parent to take them to an adventure park for the day. The parent wants to go to a museum.

⫸ CLUES FOR SUCCESS

- Make a list of the reasons given by the characters to support their points of view.

- Remember to set your work out using the layout for a play.

- Write the play extract first and put in the stage directions in your second draft. You do not need a stage direction for every line.

- You need to show that the two characters are different from each other. One character might use more contractions than the other character.

- Begin with an opening paragraph that tells the audience who the characters are, where they are and what is about to happen.

WRITING FRAMES

You might find it helpful to use the following structure:

What happens	Example of what they might say	Language	Layout
The first character should explain what the conflict is about	I don't want to go to school today. I've been awake all night.	apostrophe (don't) makes it sound natural	A space separates the name of the character from the speech
The second character should disagree with the first	You were perfectly all right when you were out playing with your friends.		
The first character should give a list of reasons to support their argument	I know, but I think I stayed out in the sun too long. I've got a terrible headache.	use of contraction 've	
The second character should give a list of reasons to support their argument	Rubbish! This has got more to do with not having done your homework because you were out so late.	use of exclamation mark	
The first character should argue in return	How could you think such a thing? [*his mouth drops open as he is horrified*]	Stage direction in brackets	Stage direction in *italics*

 REDRAFTING AND IMPROVING

- Talk about your play script with another student. In what ways is the argument convincing? Suggest ways in which the argument could be extended.

- Talk about the way the lines should be spoken.

- Act out the extract with another student. Ask a third student to watch the performance and suggest improvements before writing your second draft.

- Remember to put in your stage directions.

6 ⟩ **Looking back**

- **Contractions** are often used when we speak informally but should be avoided when writing formally.

- **Exclamation marks** help actors and actresses to think more carefully about how to deliver their lines in order to make plays convincing.

- Plays have a special **layout** to explain who is speaking and what the characters are doing.

Murder most horrid!

In this unit you will:
- read an extract from a play popular in the 19th century
- explore the form and content of the play
- write a continuation of the extract

▷▷ **Subject links:** *drama*

2 ▷ **19th-century melodrama**

Maria Marten or Murder in the Red Barn

The title of the extract was given to a series of anonymous plays based on a real murder case. Here we meet Maria Marten, a simple country girl, who has been seduced by the handsome, well-to-do William Corder. Although promising to marry Maria, William abandoned her. Alone and with his baby, she returns to her village to seek the help of her parents.

[*The music **swells**. Maria enters from the fields, carrying a baby. She*   *grows louder*
moves slowly to the bench and sits, putting the baby down beside her.
The music fades.]

MARIA Oh, I am so weary! I must sit down before I go and
see my parents. What will they say to me? A ruined daughter
with an **ailing** child? Perhaps they'll not be hard on me. I was   *sick*
deceived and foolish, but not wicked.
   [*Voices are heard off towards the high road*]
5 **MARIA** But who comes here?
   [*William enters, smiling into the face of Dora Mannering, a pretty,
   fashionably dressed girl, who is on his arm. They are followed by
   Jenny, a maid. They stop up C, William pointing towards the fields.*]
MARIA It's William! He forbade me to return here! I must not
   let him see me! [*She pulls her shawl over her head and sits with her
   back to the others*]

WILLIAM Look yonder, dearest. There you can see the
church where we'll be married.

10 **MARIA** [*aside*] Married!

DORA Oh, how pretty it is, William! [*Moves L, looking off*]

WILLIAM Pretty for a pretty bride. [*He takes her hand*] How I
long for the day to come when I can call you mine.

DORA And will you love me always, William?

15 **WILLIAM** Always, my dearest Dora. You will find in me the
faithfullest of husbands.

MARIA [*aside*] Ah, wretched me!

DORA And you have never loved another woman? [*Moving
downstage*]

WILLIAM Never, upon my honour. [*Following her*]

20 **MARIA** [*aside*] I can stand no more! [*She rises, throws back her
shawl, and turns*] You lie, William Corder, you lie! Look upon
me, then talk about your honour!

WILLIAM [*aside*] The devil – Maria! [*To Dora*] Dora, go back
to the house and await me there.

25 **DORA** But who is this?

WILLIAM A beggar woman who **plagues** me. Jenny, tell   *pesters*
them to bring the carriage to the path. Go quickly!

JENNY Yes, sir. Will you come with me, madam?

DORA No! William, I want to know …

30 **WILLIAM** [*passing her towards the high road exit*] Please, my
beloved, do as I say.

JENNY Come, madam, this is no place for you.
[*Dora exits to the high road, looking curiously at Maria. Jenny follows
her off*]

WILLIAM [*to Maria; angrily*] What are you doing in this
village? Didn't I tell you never to come here again?

*Adapted by Constance Cox, c. 1830
(based very closely on the original)*

3 ❯ **Key features**

The writer uses:

- language features which are typical of a melodrama
- stage directions to provide information for the actors and the audience
- dramatic irony to involve the audience

- What are the lies that William tells?
- How does Maria feel about William's marriage to Dora?
- How does Dora feel about William?

4 ▷ Language skills

Word

Adjectives are words which describe somebody or something. They help give more information about a noun or pronoun:

Maria is poor.

❶ The following adjectives are taken from the extract:

fashionable	ruined
wretched	pretty
foolish	wicked
weary	

Make a table with three columns headed Maria, Dora and William. Place each adjective in one of the columns, to match the character it describes. Then add some more of your own adjectives to describe each character.

Spelling

When you add *-full* to a word, it only needs one *-l*:

Hope + full = hopeful

❶ Match the following words to Dora, Maria or William, and place each in a sentence (or two) which helps to explain its meaning. For example:

*Maria is **hopeful**. She thinks her parents will look after her.*

deceitful	beautiful
sorrowful	fearful
disgraceful	regretful

Sentence

Exclamatory sentences show emotions such as anger, surprise, joy, shock, pain or urgency. They can also be commands. They end with exclamation marks (!):

Watch out!

Characters in melodramas often have their speech punctuated by exclamation marks. Exclamations can be used for each of the following:

- strong commands   *Come here!*
- sharp statements   *No!*
- urgency   *Quick!*
- forceful statements   *You will go!*
- surprise / disbelief   *It can't be!*
- decisive statements   *I've got it!*
- powerful emotion   *I hate you!*
- amusement   *He's fallen in!*
- a loud noise   *Crash!*

❶ Write down some examples from the extract for these uses of exclamation marks. Begin with:

Strong command   *Go quickly!*

Then add some examples of your own.

Text

Some plays written in the 19th century are known as **melodramas**. They have the following features:

- heroes and heroines are innocent and virtuous
- villains are without pity
- the language and acting are exaggerated
- the characters often speak directly to the audience using asides (see below)
- the plot is full of sensational action and intrigue
- music accompanies the emotional scenes

1 Read the extract again and write down an example of each of these features.

Asides are words in a play spoken for the audience to hear but not the other characters on stage.

2 Asides would be spoken in an exaggerated way. Find the asides in the extract and say them aloud so that they sound exaggerated or melodramatic.

Dramatic irony is a situation in which the audience is aware of things that the characters in the play are not aware of.

3 When William enters the stage with Dora, he is unaware that Maria can hear what he is saying.

Write down three of his lines which are examples of dramatic irony. After each line, write down what it is that we know, but other characters do not.

Play scripts use special terms to describe parts of the stage, such as *up left [up L]* and *down right [down R]*.

To understand them, it helps to remember two things:

- many stages used to be sloped up towards the back, so that the audience could see the actors more clearly
- the different parts of the stage (left and right) are described from the actors' point of view, not the audience's.

4 The stage direction on line 18 gets Dora to move away from William. Note down why you think she distances herself from him at this point.

5 Look again at the extract and write down an example of each of these five uses for stage directions:

- to describe whereabouts a character should move on stage
- to introduce music
- to describe what characters are doing
- to indicate sounds off stage
- to describe what characters look like

5 Planning your own writing

Continue the extract from:

WILLIAM *Didn't I tell you never to come here again?*

STARTING POINTS

- Begin with Maria's answer. Why did she come?

- William explains why he left Maria. Does he ask about his baby?

- Maria asks about Dora. How does she feel about what she has just seen?

- William explains his relationship with Dora. Does he tell the truth?

- Maria wants to know what William is going to do? What does he tell her?

- The scene ends with William persuading Maria to meet him at the Red Barn...

CLUES FOR SUCCESS

- Make sure you include some of the features of melodrama.

- Keep the dialogue short and simple. Use exclamation marks to show the range of emotions.

- Asides will tell the audience how the characters are really feeling.

- Try to include dramatic irony – the audience knows that William is lying.

- Put some background music into the stage directions for an emotional scene. Which of today's songs might be appropriate?

- Use stage directions to give the characters information about movements on stage.

- Set out your writing like a play script (see Comedy and conflict).

WRITING FRAMES

Clues for directions

Maria is upset.
William moves away.
Maria moves to him.
William shows his panic in an aside to the audience.
Maria presses for a commitment from William.
William says he will meet Maria at the Red Barn and elope with her.
The audience is aware of the play's title!

Line starters

I had no choice but to come home...
Nonsense! You should have waited for me...
I heard you promise to marry that woman!
How can I get rid of this woman?

You are the father of my child...

Think of the happiness that awaits you at the Red Barn!

REDRAFTING AND IMPROVING

- Read and check your writing carefully. Does your punctuation reflect the exaggerated language? Check exclamation marks against the list of uses you looked at earlier.

- With another student act out your scene to some other members of your group. Which actions or speeches are exaggerated? Which could be more exaggerated?

- Think about the asides. What will one character be doing whilst the other character is delivering the aside to the audience?

- Have you made William appear to be a real villain? Does the audience feel sorry for Maria?

- Think about what the scenery on the stage will look like. How will the characters be dressed?

6 > Looking back

- **Melodramas** are popular plays from the 19th-century with very dramatic and emotional plots.

- **Stage directions** help people performing in plays to understand how to act out their lines and where to move about the stage.

- **Asides** allow characters to speak directly to the audience and involve them in the action.

Dramatic choices

1 **Purpose**

In this unit you will:
- read an extract from a work by Shakespeare
- explore how to read aloud Shakespeare's verse
- write your own script involving making a choice

» **Subject links:** *history, geography*

2 **Elizabethan drama**

The Merchant of Venice (written between 1596 and 1597)

Portia is a rich and much-desired young lady. Her father died before she found a husband. He had devised a test for any man who should ask for her hand in marriage. Suitors must find her picture, hidden in one of three caskets.

MOROCCO The first, of gold, who this inscription **bears**:	*carries*
Who chooseth me shall gain what many men desire.	
The second, silver, which this promise carries:	
Who chooseth me shall get as much as he deserves.	
5 This third, dull lead, with warning all as blunt:	
*Who chooseth me must give and **hazard** all he hath.*	*risk*
How shall I know if I do choose the right?	
PORTIA The one of them contains my picture, prince:	
If you choose that, then I am yours **withal**.	*with it*
10 **MOROCCO** What says this leaden casket?	
Who chooseth me must give and hazard all he hath.	
Must give: for what? For lead? Hazard for lead?	
This casket threatens. Men that hazard all	
Do it in hope of fair advantages:	
15 A golden mind stoops not to shows of **dross**;	
I'll then nor give nor hazard **aught** for lead.	*rubbish*
What says the silver with her virgin **hue**?	*anything*
Who chooseth me shall get as much as he deserves.	*colour*
As much as he deserves! Pause there, Morocco,	
20 And weigh thy value with an even hand.	

If thou be'st rated by thy estimation,
Thou dost deserve enough; and yet enough
May not extend so far as to the lady:...
As much as I deserve! Why, that's the lady:
25   I do in birth deserve her, and in fortunes,
In graces, and in qualities of breeding;
But more than these, in love I do deserve.
What if I stray'd no further, but chose here?
Let's see once more this saying graved in gold:
30   *Who chooseth me shall gain what many men desire.*
Why, that's the lady: all the world desires her;
From the four corners of the earth they come,
To kiss this shrine, this mortal-breathing saint...
One of these three contains her heavenly picture.
35   Is't like that lead contains her? 'T were damnation
To think so **base** a thought: it were too gross   *rotten*
To rib her **cerecloth** in the obscure grave.   *burial clothes*
Or shall I think in silver she's **immured**,   *walled up*
Being ten times undervalued to tried gold?
40   O sinful thought! Never so rich a gem
Was set in worse than gold...
... Here an angel in a golden bed
Lies all within. Deliver me the key:
Here do I choose, and thrive I as I may!
45 **PORTIA** There, take it, prince; and if my form lie there,
Then I am yours. [*He unlocks the golden casket*]
MOROCCO O hell! What have we here?
A **carrion Death**, within whose empty eye   *skull*
There is a written scroll. I'll read the writing.
50   *All that glisters is not gold;*
Often have you heard that told:
Many a man his life hath sold
But my outside to behold:
*Gilded tombs do worms **infold**.*   *enclose*
55   *Had you been as wise as bold,*
Young in limbs, in judgement old,
Your answer had not been inscroll'd:
Fare you well; your suit is cold.

William Shakespeare, 1564–1616

3 ▶ Key features

The writer:
- uses a proverb to get across a message
- shows the audience how a character makes a choice
- uses pauses to break up lines in different places

- Why did the prince choose the golden casket?
- What does his choice tell you about him?
- What is meant by the saying *all that glisters is not gold*?

4 > Language skills

Word

Language changes over time. Shakespeare used words that we no longer use today. Verbs could have *-th*, following *he*, *she* or *it*; or *-st*, following *thou* (*you*):

> *does* could be *doth* or *dost*

❶ Look again at line 6.

> *Who chooseth me must give and hazard all he hath*

Write out this line, as we would say it today; you can rearrange the word order. What message does the inscription give to the reader?

❷ Read lines 21 and 22 again. Which words would you not be likely to find in English today? Write them down, together with the modern words which have taken their place.

A **preposition** is a word used with a noun or pronoun, usually to make phrases to do with position:

> *Good for nothing.*
> *He's behind you.*
> *Walk round the grass, not over it.*

❸ Find the following phrases in the extract and fill in the gaps using prepositions:

> *silver ... her virgin hue*
> *Hazard ... lead*
> *angel .. a golden bed*

❹ Write a paragraph in which the prince describes his encounter with Portia and the caskets. Include five prepositions from this list:

> *across, during, until, into, in, on, inside*

Spelling

When there is a consonant before *-y* at the end of a word, to make a plural, change the *-y* to *-ies*.

If the letter before the *-y* is a vowel, add the letter *-s*.

> *one library*   *two libraries*
> *one monkey*   *two monkeys*

❶ Find an example of the consonant +*y* rule in the extract. Then find an example of the vowel +*y* rule. Write them down.

Write down the plural of these words. Write down two more examples of your own for each of the rules.

Sentence

A **proverb** is a short, well-known sentence that gets across a message or a moral:

> *A friend in need is a friend in deed.*

❶ Write down the proverb on line 50. Discuss with another student what you think it means at this point in the play.

2 The proverb on line 50 is important in helping us to understand one of the major themes of the play. A proverb can also tell us something about the character who utters it. Rephrase Morocco's proverbial saying (line 15) in your own words. What does it tell you about the kind of character he is?

Text

An **end-stopped** line is a line of verse which ends at a point where a natural pause is likely in speech:

> *What says the silver with her virgin hue?*

Enjambement is an arrangement of the verse in which the sentence runs over the end of one line and comes to a pause in the next line:

> *Thou dost deserve enough; and yet enough*
> *May not extend so far as to the lady.*

A pause or break in the line caused by the rhythm or the meaning or the syntax, is called a **caesura**:

> *As much as I deserve! Why, that's the lady:*

1 Copy out lines 34–41. Decide where the lines are end-stopped, where they run on into each other and where there is a strong pause in the middle of a line.

Underline the examples you have found. Write down whether the pause is end-stopped, enjambement or a caesura.

2 The prince is making a difficult choice here. The pauses help to show his mind working and give us time to think about which choice we would make.

Look again at your underlining. Discuss with another student the feelings that may be going through the prince's mind when he pauses.

Use the following ideas to get you started.

Read line 34 aloud:
One of these three contains her heavenly picture
as though he is thinking things over carefully.

Try line 35:
Is't like that lead contains her?
as though he has serious doubts.

Read lines 35– 36:
…'T were damnation
To think so base a thought…
as though he is angry.

Think of other emotions that the prince might have when reading these lines aloud and try them out.

3 Write down some suggestions for what the prince might be doing during these pauses. Who or what might he be looking at? What could he be pointing to? What facial expressions might he use?

5 ▷ Planning your own writing

In the extract a character is making a choice: the prince needs to decide which casket to choose. He shares his thoughts with us by speaking aloud the options available to him. The extract is interesting because he has so many different options.

Write your own play where a character has to make a choice. In your script you should try to include a proverb.

▶▶ STARTING POINTS

- It is bank holiday and your character has a choice of going out for the day with his parents, his friends or his girlfriend.

- A girl has been asked to go to the school disco by three different boys or a boy asked by three different girls!

- A contestant has to choose which of three possible prizes to take having won a TV competition.

- Your character has won the opportunity to meet his favourite pop group. He can take only one person with him. Should he take his brother, sister or best friend? They are all equally mad about the group!

- Your character finds £100. Should she keep it, hand it in to the police or give it back to the person whose name and address is in the wallet?

▶▶ CLUES FOR SUCCESS

- Set out your writing like a play (see **Unit 1**).

- The main character should think aloud the three options available. They should also think aloud about the reasons for refusing two of the choices but choosing the third option.

- Use a variety of sentence lengths and punctuation to give your character pauses in which to think through the choices.

- Make sure your characters draw out different feelings from different lines. You might include stage directions for how some of the lines should be spoken, for example [*angrily*].

- Include a proverb at the end of the scene, for example: *time and tide wait for no man*.

WRITING FRAMES

You might find it helpful to use the following structure:

The first character should explain what the choice is e.g.	**KEVIN:** *I can't believe it. I don't ever have anything to do on bank holidays. They're usually so boring! And now I've got three things to choose from.*
The second character should get Kevin to explain what the choices are.	*Where does his girlfriend want to go? Where do his parents want to go?*
Kevin should explain what are the advantages and disadvantages of each choice.	**KEVIN:** *I could go to the theme park with my mates but it always rains on bank holidays.*
He should develop points in as much detail as he can.	**KEVIN:** *... and you get wet and miserable standing in the rain.*
Remember there are three choices and you can break each choice with questions from the second character.	**JAMES:** *But there are some great rides. Which is your favourite?*
Your second character might offer helpful advice/or unhelpful advice	**JAMES:** *You could toss a coin.*
	JAMES: *I wouldn't be seen dead at the seaside with my parents.*
Continue to discuss all the options until you make a decision.	
At the end of the scene, one of your characters should include a proverb	**JAMES:** *Well, I hope you have a good time with your mates and don't worry about your girlfriend. There are plenty more fish in the sea.*

 REDRAFTING AND IMPROVING

Read out your script with another student. Check that you have:

- developed the choices you have introduced
- used punctuation to create pauses
- included a proverb

6 ▶ Looking back

- When you want to get across a short, clear message you can use a **proverb**. It can tell us about the theme or about the person who speaks it.

- **End-stopped lines** and **enjambement** can be used to create different emphasis in a section of verse.

- A **caesura** can be used to emphasise a strong pause within a line.

Words of war

1 Purpose

In this unit you will:

- explore poetry written about war
- discuss the imagery used by poets
- write your own poem about an issue that interests you

>> **Subject links:** *history, ICT, art*

2 Poems about war

The Drum

I hate that drum's **discordant** sound,   *harsh noise*
Parading round, and round, and round:
To thoughtless youth it pleasure **yields**,   *gives*
And **lures** from cities and from fields,   *tempts*
5   To sell their **liberty** for charms   *freedom*
Of **tawdry** lace, and glittering arms;   *cheap and tasteless*
And when Ambition's voice commands,
To march, and fight, and fall, in foreign lands.

I hate that drum's discordant sound,
10 Parading round, and round, and round:
To me it talks of **ravaged** plains,   *destroyed*
And burning towns, and ruined **swains**,   *young men*
And mangled limbs, and dying groans,
And widows' tears, and orphans' moans;
15 And all that Misery's hand bestows,
To fill the catalogue of human **woes**.   *sorrows*

John Scott of Amwell, 1730–1783

The Shield of War

Lastly, stood War, in glittering arms **yclad**,   *clothed*
With **visage** grim, stern looks, and blackly hued;   *face*
In his right hand a naked sword he had,
That to the hilts was all with blood **imbrued**;   *stained*
5   And in his left, that kings and kingdoms **rued**,   *regretted*
Famine and fire he held, and **therewithal**   *with those*
He **razed** towns and threw down towers and all.   *completely destroyed*

Cities he **sacked** and realms, that **whilom** flowered   *plundered; formerly*
In honour, glory, and rule above the best,
He overwhelmed and all their fame devoured,
10 Consumed, destroyed, wasted, and never ceased,
Till he their wealth, their name, and all **oppressed**;   *defeated*
His face **forhewed** with wounds, and by his side   *cut*
There hung his **targe**, with gashes deep and wide.   *shield*

Thomas Sackville, Earl of Dorset, 1536–1608
(First two verses only)

3 ▸ Key features

The writers use:
- interesting vocabulary
- personification to create vivid pictures
- rhyme and rhythm to create different effects

- In the first poem, what does the sound of the drum tempt young men to do?
- What purpose does War have in the second poem?
- In both poems, War is described as bloody and brutal. Which poem do you think creates the most vivid image of War? Write down a reason for your choice.

Words of war

4 ⟩ Language skills

Word

A **verb** is a word in a sentence which can tell us what people or things are doing:

Lastly, stood War
I hate that drum

1 Use a dictionary to help you write your own definition of each of these verbs as they are used in the poems:

The Drum
commands	(line 7)
fall	(line 8)
bestows	(line 15)

The Shield of War
hued	(line 2)
flowered	(line 8)
devoured	(line 10)

Nouns that actually name people or places are called proper nouns. They always begin with a capital letter.

Abstract nouns are the labels we give to things we cannot touch, such as emotions, feelings or ideas.

People's qualities, such as cleverness or impatience, are all labelled by abstract nouns.

2 Make a list of the abstract nouns used in both poems.

Ambition is an abstract noun, but the poet has made it into a proper noun by using a capital letter. Write down the other abstract nouns that have been made into proper nouns. What effect do you think this has?

Spelling

Breaking down words into **syllables** or sounds can help you remember how to spell them.

When you say a word, carefully pronounce each syllable:

dis cord ant has three syllables.

Each syllable must have a vowel:

glitt er ing

1 Break down the following words into syllables. Write the words down and underline the syllables as in the example above. Remember that -*y* is a part-time vowel!

parading
overwhelmed
ambition
blackly
burning

Learn the spellings.

Note that there is more than one way to break these words up into syllables.

cap it al
ca pit al

64

Sentence

A **comma (,)** can be used to separate items in a list: *I need to buy tea, coffee, sugar and milk.*

❶ Read lines 10 and 11 of *The shield of war* aloud.

Where there is a comma, take a brief pause. The pauses give you a chance to think about the meaning of each of the words.

What picture of war is created by the words separated with commas?

A comma can also be used as parenthesis to separate extra information in a sentence:

The king, who was wealthy, could not buy peace.

❷ Reread lines 5 and 6 of *The shield of war* to *he held*.

What extra information about *famine and fire* is given inside the commas? Write it down in your own words.

Why do kings and kingdoms regret that War also brings famine and fire?

Text

Personification is a type of metaphor in which an object or idea is described as though it were a person:

> *The litter danced in the breeze.*

In *The Shield of War*, *War* is made to sound like a person because it stands and it is dressed in glittering armour.

1 Write down the other ways in which *War* is described as if it were human.

2 In *The Drum* how does the poet get across the idea that *Ambition*, (line 7) and *Misery* (line 15) are people?

Write down the human things that they do. For example:

> *Greed looked with envy*

Here, Greed has eyes that can see and Greed is jealous, a human quality.

Words ending with the same (or similar) sounds are said to **rhyme**.

Both poems are written with a regular **rhyme scheme** throughout.

3 Look back at **Unit 2** of the **Poetry section**. Use the method described there to work out the rhyme scheme used in both poems.

Write down any ways in which you think the rhyme scheme contributes to the meaning of the poems.

You can rhyme lines 11 and 12 of *The Shield of War* with each other as the words sound so similar. This is called a half-rhyme.

When two lines rhyme with each other it is called a rhyming couplet.

4 What is the effect of beginning each stanza of *The Drum* with the same rhyming couplet?

In all speech and poetry we feel a beat or **rhythm**.

5 Read lines 1 and 2 of *The Drum* aloud placing emphasis on the words or syllables in bold:

> *I **hate** that **drum's** dis**cord**ant*
> *   **sound**,*
> *Pa**rad**ing **round**, and **round**,*
> *   and **round***

There are four beats in these lines. Copy out lines 5–7 and underline the syllables with the heavy beats. Always begin the first beat on the second syllable of the line. Here are the next two lines to get you started:

> *To **thought**less **youth** it **plea**sure*
> *   **yields***
> *And **lures** from **cities** and from **fields***

6 What do you notice about the rhythm of the last line of each stanza?

7 What is the effect of making these lines different from the rest of the lines in the stanzas? What meaning does it help to get across?

5 > Planning your own writing

Write your own poem about an issue that interests you: Peace, Death, Love, Loneliness, Friendship…

- Your poem should have no more than two verses or 16 lines.
- Your poem does not have to rhyme.

>> **STARTING POINTS**

- Use a spider diagram to brainstorm images and sounds that are associated with Peace.

- Think of Peace as if it were a person. List what it would look like and how it would behave.

- Discuss with another student how people who live in countries in conflict would feel if, suddenly, there was Peace.

>> **CLUES FOR SUCCESS**

- Use the vocabulary from your brainstorming session.

- Remember to put a capital letter on your proper noun, Peace, and any others that you choose to emphasise.

- Use personification to create the kind of person you think Peace would be.

- Use a consistent rhyme and rhythm in your poem.

- Use repetition for emphasis.

WRITING FRAMES

Use the following questions to provide you with a plan:

- War has the sound of an angry drum. What sound will Peace have?
- War gives pleasure to thoughtless youth. Who will Peace give pleasure to?
- War makes false promises. What promises will Peace make to people?
- War ends in death and separated families. What will Peace give to people?
- War has a terrible landscape. What landscape does Peace have?
- War makes ruined towns, orphans, widows and sadness. What does Peace make?
- War makes a catalogue of sorrow. What catalogue does Peace make?

Use the following line openers to get you started:

- I love the comfort Peace provides.
- To me Peace talks of happy hearts.
- Firstly stood Peace in billowing robes of white.
- Cities she rescued from the grip of War.

⟫ REDRAFTING AND IMPROVING

Read your poem to another student.

Divide your page into two columns. Put two headings: War and the heading of your poem. Choose one of the two poems you have looked at in this unit and write in the column the words that are associated with War.

When you have finished, look at your own poem and in the second column write in the words that are associated with your poem. Add some more words to your column that you could include in a second draft of your poem. For example:

War	*Peace*
Ambition	*liberty*
marching	*freedom*
fighting	*happiness*
dying	*friendship*

Work out the rhyme scheme of your poem if you have one (see **Unit 2** of the **Poetry section**).

6 ⟩ Looking back

- Writers make careful **vocabulary choices** to create vivid images in poems.

- **Personification** can be used to give physical qualities to abstract ideas.

- **Rhyme** and **rhythm** can reflect the content of a poem and emphasise certain words.

Novel starters

1 ▷ **Purpose**

In this unit you will:

- learn about the features that make good stories
- explore how atmosphere can be created within texts
- write your own narrative creating a sense of tension

≫ **Subject links:** *history, PHSE*

2 ▷ **The 19th-century novel**

Great Expectations – 1861

O urs was the marsh country, down by the river, within, as the river wound, twenty miles of the sea. My first most vivid and broad impression of the identity of things, seems to me to have been gained on a memorable raw
5   afternoon towards evening. At such a time I found out for certain, that this bleak place overgrown with nettles was the churchyard; and that Philip Pirrip, late of this parish, and also Georgiana wife of the above, were dead and buried; ... and that the dark flat wilderness beyond the churchyard, intersected
10   with **dykes** and mounds and gates, with scattered cattle feeding   *ditches* on it, was the marshes; and that the low leaden line beyond, was the river; and that the distant savage lair from which the wind was rushing, was the sea; and that the small bundle of shivers growing afraid of it all and beginning to cry, was Pip.
15   'Hold your noise!' cried a terrible voice, as a man started up from among the graves at the side of the church porch. 'Keep still, you little devil, or I'll cut your throat!'

A fearful man, all in coarse grey, with a great iron on his leg. A man with no hat, and with broken shoes, and with an
20 old rag tied round his head. A man who had been soaked in water, and smothered in mud, and lamed by stones, and cut by flints, and stung by nettles, and torn by briars; who limped, and shivered, and glared and growled; and whose teeth chattered in his head as he seized me by the chin.

25 'O! Don't cut my throat, sir,' I pleaded in terror. 'Pray don't do it, sir.'

'Tell us your name!' said the man. 'Quick!'

'Pip, sir.'

'Once more,' said the man, staring at me. 'Give it mouth!'

30 'Pip. Pip, sir.'

'Show us where you live,' said the man. 'Pint out the place!'   *Point*

I pointed to where our village lay, on the flat in-shore among the alder-trees and pollards, a mile or more from the church, and then…

The man continues to threaten Pip and eventually discovers that Pip lives with a blacksmith…

35 'Blacksmith, eh?' said he. And looked down at his leg.

After darkly looking at his leg and me several times, he came closer to my tombstone, took me by both arms, and tilted me back as far as he could hold me; so that his eyes looked most powerfully down into mine, and mine looked
40 most helplessly up into his.

He threatens Pip with another man if Pip does not fetch him a file…

'There's a young man hid with me, in comparison with which young man I am a Angel. That young man hears the
45 words I speak. That young man has a secret way pecooliar to himself, of getting at a boy, and at his heart, and at his liver. It is in wain for a boy to attempt to hide himself from that   *useless* young man… I am a keeping that young man from harming of you at the present moment, with great difficulty…'

Charles Dickens, 1812–1870

Treasure Island – 1881

I remember him as if it were yesterday, as he came
plodding to the inn door, his sea-chest following
behind him in a hand-barrow; a tall, strong, heavy,
nut-brown man; his tarry pigtail falling over the shoulders — covered with tar
5 of his soiled blue coat; his hands ragged and scarred, with
black, broken nails; and the sabre cut across one cheek,
a dirty, livid white. I remember him looking round the cove — leaden colour –
and whistling to himself as he did so, and then breaking — bluish grey
out in that old sea-song that he sang so often afterwards:
10 'Fifteen men on The Dead Man's Chest –
Yo-ho-ho, and a bottle of rum!'
in the high, old tottering voice that seemed to have been
tuned and broken at the capstan bars… — equipment to
— raise anchor
'This is a handy cove,' says he at length; 'and a pleasant
15 sittyated grog-shop. Much company, mate?' — drink, usually rum

My father told him no, very little company, the more
was the pity.

'Well, then,' said he, 'this is the berth for me. Here you, — place where a ship
matey,' he cried to the man who trundled the barrow; — is moored
20 'bring up alongside and help up my chest. I'll stay here a
bit,' he continued. 'I'm a plain man; rum and bacon and
eggs is what I want, and that head up there for to watch
ships off. What you mought call me? You mought call me
captain. Oh, I see what you're at – there,' – and he threw
25 down three or four gold pieces on the threshold. 'You can
tell me when I've worked through that,' says he, looking as
fierce as a commander.

And, indeed, bad as his clothes were, and coarsely as he
spoke, he had none of the appearance of a man who sailed
30 before the mast; but seemed like a mate or a skipper,
accustomed to be obeyed or to strike…

*The captain continues to make a great impression on
the boy and offers him a silver fourpenny every month if he
will look out for a seafaring man with one leg...*

How that personage [*the seafaring man*] haunted my
dreams, I need scarcely tell you. On stormy nights, when
the wind shook the four corners of the house, and the surf

35 roared along the cove and up the cliffs, I would see him in
a thousand forms, and with a thousand diabolical
expressions...

But it is the captain who scares the others at the inn...

His stories were what frightened people worst of all.
Dreadful stories they were; about hanging, and walking the

40 plank, and storms at sea, and the *Dry Tortugas*, and wild   islands between
deeds and places on the Spanish Main... My father was   Florida and Cuba
always saying the inn would be ruined, for people would
soon cease coming there to be tyrannised over and put
down, and sent shivering to their beds; but I really believe

45 his presence did us good. People were frightened at the
time, but on looking back they rather liked it; ...

Robert Louis Stevenson, 1850–1894

3 ▶ Key features

The writers:
- choose words carefully to create atmosphere
- use non-standard forms of English in dialogue
- use the first-person narrative

- At which point in the stories would you expect to see these extracts?
  Give reasons for your answers.
- Write down the things that make you feel sorry for Pip.
- What evidence is there that the man in the first extract is a convict?
- What evidence is there that the man in the second extract is a sailor?
- Which man do you think is described most clearly? Give reasons.
- For each extract list the things that make both men frightening.

73

4 > Language skills

Word

Adjectives are words which describe somebody or something. They help to give more information about a noun or pronoun.

Great Expectations is set on a *raw afternoon*. The adjective *raw* describes the weather.

1 Use a dictionary to look up the meanings of the word *raw* and discuss with another student why Dickens chooses that particular adjective.

Find the following adjectives:

leaden, savage, bleak, dark

They all appear in the first paragraph of the extract. Copy out the adjective and the noun to which it refers.

2 Using appropriate words from the list below, write a sentence describing the atmosphere created by each of the adjectives used above. You can add some of your own words:

spooky, mysterious, cheerful, sinister, happy, frightening

3 Take out the adjectives from the first paragraph and replace them with others to create a pleasant, friendly atmosphere.

A *raw afternoon* might become a *sunny afternoon*.

4 Copy out the opening paragraph of *Treasure Island*. Underline the adjectives that describe the captain.

What do we learn about the captain's lifestyle from his appearance?

Spelling

Add *-ed* to a word to form the past tense when the word ends in a consonant:

limp + -ed = limped

When a word ends in *-e*, you simply add the letter *-d*:

glare + -ed = glared

1 Write down a list of words from both extracts that follow these rules. Write down what happens to the words that end in *-y* when you add *-ed*.

Sentence

A **dialect** is a variety of language used by a particular group of people which has its own set of expressions and grammatical rules.

Standard English is the most common dialect in English. It is the dialect used in nearly all writing. Non-standard dialects, on the other hand, make our language varied and interesting.

Look at the following examples:

Standard English	Non-standard English
I did it	I done it
You saw her	You seen her
I would have gone	I would of gone

❶ Write down some examples of non-standard dialect either from your own area or another part of the country.

In both extracts, the men speak using non-standard dialect. This is effective because it gives more interest and realism to their characters.

❷ The following non-standard speeches are from the extracts. Write down the standard English versions:

I am a keeping that young man from harming of you at the present moment…

… and that head up there for to watch ships off. What you mought call me? You mought call me captain.

❸ Read aloud the dialogue spoken by both men and discuss with another student what part of England you think they come from.

Text

When a story is told from the point of view of one of the characters, we say that it has a **first-person narrator**.

The first-person narrator uses first person pronouns, *I, me, we, us, myself.*

Dickens and Stevenson tell us their stories through the eyes of first person narrators, Pip Pirrip: *My most vivid and broad impression...*

and Jim Hawkins: *I remember him as if it were yesterday...*

Using the first-person narrator enables us, when we read, to experience the character's emotions as if they were our own.

❶ Copy out the sentence where Pip is grabbed by the man, beginning *After darkly looking at his leg...* (line 36). Underline all the pronouns.

Explain, using your own words, how Pip feels at this moment.

❷ Imagine that the convict is the first-person narrator. Rewrite this sentence from his point of view.

Discuss with another student how he would feel as he spoke his words.

A **cliffhanger** is when a writer gives an ending to an episode that leaves the reader expecting more.

Great Expectations and *Treasure Island* were both published as serials, *Great Expectations* in a weekly magazine started by Dickens himself called *All the Year Round* and *Treasure Island* in a publication called *Young Folks*.

In order to get people really involved in the stories, and to buy the next issue, chapters had to end on a cliffhanger.

❸ What are you left wondering about at the end of the extracts?

Make a list of questions that will have to be answered. You might begin with *Great Expectations: Who is the young man?*

Compare your list of questions with that of another student and talk about the differences. Write the answers for each other's questions.

❹ Imagine you are asked to read one of the complete books. Which book would you choose to read and why? Write down some reasons for your choice and then state whether you think the books would appeal to boys or girls or both equally.

5 ▶ Planning your own writing

Write the opening to a mysterious story which creates a sense of tension.

 STARTING POINT

- You are late leaving a friend's house one evening and take a short cut home through the woods...

- You are walking home when you hear a noise coming from the deserted house at the end of your street...

- You are sent to the attic in your school to collect some costumes for the school play...

- Closing your bedroom curtains for the night you see a bright light descending on your garden...

- It is raining heavily on your way home from work. You decide to stop and offer a hitch-hiker a lift...

▶ **CLUES FOR SUCCESS**

- Write using a first-person narrator.

- Think about the setting – try to make it scary.

- Use adjectives to help create a sinister atmosphere.

- Introduce a threatening character.

- Use non-standard forms of English in your dialogue.

- End your extract on a cliffhanger.

- What questions will readers ask themselves at the end of the story?

⟫ WRITING FRAME

Begin by introducing your narrator. Create sympathy for your narrator.

I was at that time a confident and cheerful girl, but a little too young to be walking home through the woods on my own in the dark.

Introduce the setting for the story. Use adjectives that create a dark atmosphere.

The crooked branches of the black trees appeared to be reaching down to me.

Introduce your second character. Use non-standard English forms in their dialogue.

A shadowy figure appeared from out of the darkness. 'Where d'ye think yer heading to?' he demanded.

Explain what the narrator wants from you – use adverbs to make their actions more threatening.

'I want you to deliver this package for me,' he whispered as his eyes looked menacingly into mine.

Describe how both characters part, but remember to create the idea that they will meet again…

'I'll expect an answer from you!' hissed the man towering over my trembling shape.

REDRAFTING AND IMPROVING

When you have finished your first draft, with another student look closely at your own writing and compare your partner's attempts. Can you spot any errors in their work or make any suggestions for improving the characters or atmosphere?

Your final draft should have tension, so:

- have you created a sinister atmosphere?
- have you used adjectives carefully?
- have you created characters that are different from each other?
- have you used interesting dialogue?
- have you left the reader wanting to find out more about characters and events?

6 ▷ Looking back

- **Adjectives** have to be chosen carefully to give a clear picture to the reader.
- Writers use **non-standard forms** of English to add interest and variety.
- A **first-person narrator** tells the story from their point of view. We can see things clearly through their eyes.

Glossary

Abstract nouns The label we give to something we cannot touch, such as an emotion, a feeling or an idea.

Antonym A word which has the opposite meaning to another word.

Apostrophe A punctuation mark (') with two different uses:

1 to show that a letter or group of letters has been missed out (omission)

2 to show possession or ownership.

Caesura A strong pause in a line of poetry.

Cliffhanger An ending to an episode that leaves the reader expecting more.

Contraction Joining two words together to form one word.

Dramatic irony A situation in which the audience is aware of something but the characters in the play are not aware of it.

Ellipsis The omission of an element in language. The three dots (...) are called ellipsis points. They tell us that something has been missed out.

Hyphen A punctuation mark (-) that joins words or parts of words together to make a new word.

Internal rhyme The effect of having two or more words on the same line rhyming with each other.

Onomatopoeia A word whose sound echoes its meaning.

Parenthesis A word or phrase inserted into a sentence to provide additional information, placed between commas, brackets or dashes.

Personification A special kind of metaphor in which a thing or an idea is spoken about as though it were a person.

Prepositions A word which shows the relationship between a noun, a pronoun, or a noun and a pronoun.

Proper nouns The name of a person or place. It always begins with a capital letter.

Pronoun A word used instead of a noun or noun phrase.

Proverb A short, well-known sentence that gets across a message or a moral.

Simile A way of comparing things in an unusual or unexpected way, in which the writer creates an image in the reader's mind. A simile uses words 'like' or 'as'.

Synonym A word which means the same, or almost the same, as another word.

Syntax The order of words in a sentence or phrase.

Time adverbials A word or phrase which tells you when something happens.

WEBER'S™
BARBECUE
BIBLE

Step-by-step advice and over 150 delicious barbecue recipes

BY JAMIE PURVIANCE

PHOTOGRAPHY BY TIM TURNER

MURDOCH BOOKS
SYDNEY · LONDON

Published in 2016 by Murdoch Books, an imprint of Allen & Unwin

First published by Weber-Stephen Products Co, 2008

Murdoch Books Australia
83 Alexander Street
Crows Nest NSW 2065
Phone: +61 (0) 2 8425 0100
Fax: +61 (0) 2 9906 2218
murdochbooks.com.au
info@murdochbooks.com.au

Murdoch Books UK
Ormond House
26–27 Boswell Street
London WC1N 3JZ
Phone: +44 (0) 20 8785 5995
murdochbooks.co.uk
info@murdochbooks.co.uk

For Corporate Orders & Custom Publishing, contact our Business Development Team
at salesenquiries@murdochbooks.com.au.

Weber, the kettle configuration, 🔲 , RapidFire, and the kettle silhouette are registered trademarks;
Smokey Mountain Cooker is a trademark; all of Weber-Stephen Products Co, 200 East Daniels Road,
Palatine, Illinois 60067 USA.

Dr. Pepper® is a registered trademark of Dr. Pepper/Seven Up, Inc, Plano, Texas.

A cataloguing-in-publication entry is available from the catalogue of the National Library of Australia
at nla.gov.au.

ISBN 978 1 74336 900 5

Colour reproduction by Splitting Image Colour Studio Pty Ltd, Clayton, Victoria
Printed by 1010 Printing International Limited, China
Reprinted in 2016, 2017

www.weber.com®

www.sunset.com

acknowledgements

The idea for this book emerged from the agile publishing minds of Mike Kempster, Susan Maruyama and Christina Schroeder. With the help of Jim Childs and Bob Doyle, they outlined an ambitious project and honoured me with the job of tackling it. I am grateful to each of them for their confidence and support.

When it came down to managing all the words and pictures here, Marsha Capen was a thoughtful and remarkably hard-working editor. She always found a gracious way to herd the flock of pigeons involved in this creative process.

The sheer quantity of photographs required for this book would strike fear into the hearts of many photographers, but Tim Turner, who is a master of light and lens (and quite a good griller, too), thrived on the challenge. He was assisted by a particularly talented crew, which included food stylists Lynn Gagné, Nina Albazi and Christina Zerkis, as well as photo assistants Takamasa Ota, Christy Clow, David Garcia and Justin Lundquist.

There is another excellent reason why the meat in this book looks so irresistibly fabulous. Almost all of it came from Lobel's of New York (www.lobels.com). Evan, Stanley, Mark and David Lobel, along with David Richards and all their colleagues, maintain standards so high for meat quality and customer service that whenever I open a box with Lobel's on the label, I am always delighted.

For the recipes, I relied on a sharp team of culinary minds. Many thanks to April Cooper, who handled most of the testing and tweaking, and thank goodness for the many other barbecuers involved, too. I especially want to acknowledge Patty Ada, Emily Baird, Gary Bramley, Neal Corman, Jerry DiVecchio, Ryan Gardner, John Gerald Gleeson, Joyce Goldstein, Gary Hafer, Jay Harlow, Rita Held, Susan Hoss, Ellen Jackson, Elaine Johnson, Carolyn Jung, Alison Lewis, James McNair, Andrew Moore, Merrilee Olson, Jeff Parker, David Pazimo, Craig Priebe, Anne-marie Ramo, Justin Roche, Rick Rodgers, James Schend, David Shalleck and Bob and Coleen Simmons.

I love what Shum Prats and Elaine Chow did with the design of this book, managing to strike a gorgeous balance between clear instructions and imaginative aesthetics.

I want to thank Weber's Creative Services department for improving the look of every last page. Thank you, Becky LaBrum, for a very useful index.

For lots of good advice and generous support all along, I offer special thanks to Sherry Bale, Brooke Jones, Nancy Misch and Sydney Webber.

While working on this book, I referred to many other books for solid culinary information. I found the following ones very helpful: *The Complete Meat Cookbook*, by Bruce Aidells and Denis Kelly; *The Cook's Illustrated Guide to Grilling and Barbecue*, by the editors of *Cook's Illustrated*; *The New Food Lover's Companion*, by Sharon Tyler Herbst; *The Barbecue Bible*, by Steven Raichlen; and *How to Cook Meat*, by Chris Schlesinger and John Willoughby.

In the final weeks of production, I had impeccable editing help from Sarah Putman Clegg and Carolyn Jung.

This book took me out of town for many days and nights, away from my wife, Fran, and our children, Julia, James and Peter. I missed some family holidays and quite a few weekends with the people that matter most to me. I owe them a lot for remaining patient and supportive throughout the whole process.

Finally, I want to thank a few mentors who gave a great deal of themselves to me early in my culinary career, Antonia Allegra, Esther McManus and Becky and David Sinkler. With selfless generosity, each one of them set me on the right course and encouraged me to get going.

CONTENTS

5

INTRODUCTION

I wasn't born with a complete understanding and mastery of barbecue techniques. As a kid growing up in suburban America, I had to pick up the basics from my dad and other weekend barbecuers. Eventually, when it was my turn to barbecue, I had to imitate what I'd seen and I had to develop my own style by doing what so many other barbecuers do. I had to experiment. I had to wing it. Sometimes it worked, and other times…well, it did not.

To be honest, I didn't really learn to barbecue until I was about thirty years old. That's when I tackled the subject in a much more methodical way. Obsessed with good food and frustrated by the limitations of winging it, I enrolled at the Culinary Institute of America. There I immersed myself in a rigorous curriculum of the hows and whys of topics like meat butchering, food chemistry, sauce making and charcuterie. Under the supervision of demanding chefs, I learned serious science-based lessons like how heat affects the structure of meats and fats, how sauces are held together and how marinades can unravel proteins.

Since my graduation about fifteen years ago, I've focused my attention on how advanced culinary ideas relate to barbecuing. With the help of many experts at Weber, I've done extensive research on this particular way of cooking and I've written five books on the subject. Each book was an opportunity to learn more about what works on the barbecue and why some techniques work better than others. This book is a culmination of all the lessons I've learnt.

So what is the right way to barbecue? Well, first of all, there's not just one way to do it. It is not about absolute right and wrong when it comes to issues like gas versus charcoal, direct versus indirect heat, or barbecuing with the lid on or off. This book includes and embraces any way to barbecue – so long as it works. And what works best, I've learned, is paying attention to culinary details. There is a big difference between winging it and paying attention.

Let me share a couple of examples of what paying attention can do. The first deals with the reason why most steaks turn out beautifully when barbecued over direct high heat but most pork chops do not. Why should this be? High heat, of course, can char the surface of meat long before the centre is fully cooked. For a steak, that's a fine result, because you are left with a nicely caramelised outer crust and an interior that is dripping with rosy red juices. A pork chop is another matter. We don't like our pork chops raw in the middle, but if we barbecued most pork chops over direct high heat until the centres were properly cooked, the surfaces would be badly burned. That's why using medium heat is a better way to cook most pork chops. It allows the centres to reach an ideal degree of doneness without overcooking the surfaces. Simple enough, right? But back in my early days, when I was winging it, I threw every kind of meat over the same high heat. That's one reason things did not always work out.

Successful barbecuing is about paying attention to details as basic and significant as salt.

A second example about the importance of paying attention deals with something quite fundamental: salt. Many of you might not give salt much thought, but did you know that, teaspoon for teaspoon, common table salt has about twice the sodium as some types of sea salt? So if you happened to use common table salt instead of the sea salt that I call for in almost every recipe in this book, I'm afraid your food will taste awfully salty (and a little metallic from calcium silicate found in common table salt). To take

this topic one step further, I suggest that you pay attention to which brand of sea salt you use. They are not all the same.

So, yes, culinary details matter. They explain why you would want to wrap barbecued ribs in foil during the final stages of cooking. They explain why you would barbecue fish fillets longer on the first side than the second. They explain why you would smoke a turkey with the breast side down.

That's why this book includes so many how-to photographs and explanatory captions and detailed recipes. The emphasis here is on paying close attention. It's about learning how and why certain methods work well, so you can move beyond the limits of winging it. Great taste lies in the details. Just pay attention and enjoy a new level of barbecuing success.

Jamie Purviance

BARBECUE

Barbecuing is so woven into the culture when the sun is shining that almost everyone has something to say about how to do it. All of us have had experiences that help us to be better barbecuers. I think what separates the master barbecuers from the beginners is really an understanding of the fundamentals. What follows here are the questions I hear again and again during my barbecuing classes. The answers make the biggest difference in anyone's ability to barbecue.

STARTING A CHARCOAL FIRE

Q: WHAT'S THE DIFFERENCE BETWEEN COOKING OVER A WOOD FIRE VERSUS A CHARCOAL FIRE? IS ONE BETTER THAN THE OTHER?

A: It's all about ease and time management. Barbecuing began over a wood fire, which imparts a wonderful flavour, but has its drawbacks. A wood-log fire tends to create huge amounts of smoke and often requires waiting up to an hour or more for the flames to settle down and the embers to reach a manageable level of heat.

With many barbecuers, barbecue briquettes are more popular than lump charcoal. They are inexpensive and available practically everywhere. Most commonly, barbecue briquettes are a blend of hardwood charcoal and mineral carbon, along with a binder, filler and oxidising agent. They are safe, non-toxic and do not leave a trace of kerosene odour on your food.

Q: WHAT ABOUT LUMP CHARCOAL? HOW'S IT DIFFERENT FROM BARBECUE BRIQUETTES?

A: Charcoal is essentially pre-burned wood, which means it reaches ideal barbecuing temperatures faster than wood and with much less smoke. It is made by slowly burning hardwood logs in an oxygen-deprived environment, like an underground pit or kiln. Over time, the water and resins are burned out of the logs, leaving behind big chunks of combustible carbon. These chunks are then broken into smaller lumps, hence the name, lump charcoal. It's also known as 'charwood'.

Standard barbecue briquettes don't burn as hot as lump charcoal and the amount of smoke produced is minimal at best. But they do produce predictable, even heat over a long period of time. A batch of 50–64 briquettes will last for about 3 to 4 hours, which is plenty of time to barbecue most foods without having to replenish the fire, whereas a pure lump-charcoal fire may provide only a quarter as much barbecuing time before it requires more coals.

Q: WHAT ARE CHARCOAL BRIQUETTES?

A: Most commonly, they are compressed black bundles of sawdust and coal, along with binders and fillers like clay and sodium nitrate. Some are presoaked in lighter fluid so they start easier, but these can impart a chemical taste to food if you don't completely burn off the lighter fluid before you begin cooking. A batch of 80 to 100 briquettes will last for about an hour.

Q: ARE THERE ANY OTHER CHOICES?

A: Pure hardwood (or 'all-natural') briquettes are a great option, if you can find them. They have the same pillow shape of standard briquettes, but they burn at higher temperatures, and with none of the fillers and binders. Usually they are made of crushed hardwoods bound together with nothing but natural starches. You'll probably pay more for these coals, but many serious barbecuers and barbecue competitors consider them the gold standard of charcoal.

Q: IF SOMEONE IS ENTIRELY NEW TO CHARCOAL BARBECUING (AND MAYBE A LITTLE INTIMIDATED), WHAT'S THE BEST WAY TO GET STARTED?

A: My advice is to start by learning to light the barbecue briquettes safely and reliably using a chimney starter. This simple device consists of a metal cylinder with holes cut along the bottom, a wire rack inside and two handles attached to the outside. Here's how to use the chimney. First, fill the chimney with the required amount of barbecue briquettes. Remove the top grate, or cooking grill, from your barbecue and place three fire lighters on the charcoal grate below. Next, light the fire lighters and place the chimney directly over the fire lighters. The beauty of this method is that the chimney sucks the hot air up from the bottom and makes it circulate through the briquettes, lighting them much faster and more evenly than if you spread the briquettes out.

Lump charcoal will burn strong and be ready for barbecuing in about 15 minutes. Barbecue briquettes will take a little longer to light fully, generally 20 to 30 minutes.

When the briquettes are lightly coated all over with white ash (or lump charcoal is lit round the edges of all the pieces), it's ready to go. To empty it on to the charcoal grate, put on two insulated barbecue mitts or oven gloves. Grab hold of the heatproof handle in one hand and the swinging handle in the other. The swinging handle is there to help you lift the chimney and safely aim the contents just where you want them. For safety's sake, always wear insulated barbecue mitts or oven gloves when doing this. And never place a hot, empty chimney starter on the grass or a deck. Be sure to put it on a heatproof surface away from children and pets.

If you don't have a chimney starter, for indirect cooking fill your charcoal baskets with the required amount of barbecue briquettes. Place four fire

BARBECUE BASICS

lighters (two on each side) in the cavities provided in your charcoal 'V' grate, then light the cubes. Once the fire lighters are alight move the metal baskets to the centre of the charcoal grate over the flames. When all the coals are glowing bright orange and covered with ash, separate the charcoal baskets to either side of the bowl.

Alternatively for direct cooking, build a pyramid of barbecue briquettes on top of a few fire lighters, then light the cubes. When the coals in the middle are lit, use tongs to pile the unlit coals on top. When all the coals are glowing bright orange and covered with ash, arrange them the way you want them on the charcoal grate.

Q: ARE YOU SAYING I SHOULDN'T USE LIGHTER FLUID?

A: That's right. Lighter fluid is a petroleum-based product that can really ruin the flavour of your food. I know there are some people who grew up with the stuff and still think a hamburger is supposed to taste like petrol, but for the rest of us we would never think of using it.

Q: HOW DO I KNOW HOW MUCH CHARCOAL TO USE?

A: That depends on the size of your barbecue and how much food you want to cook. Let's assume you have a classic 57 cm (22½ inch) diameter kettle barbecue and you are cooking for four to six people. The simplest way to measure the right amount of barbecue briquettes is to count them. After a while, you will become familiar with the various quantities required and you will be able to judge them visually. Approximately 64 barbecue briquettes (32 in each charcoal basket) will provide enough charcoal to create a hot indirect fire. As a rule of thumb, after approximately 2 hours of cooking with the lid on, a hot fire will become the equivalent of a normal fire, and a normal fire will become the equivalent of a low fire after the same period of time. That's usually enough to cook a couple of courses for four to six people.

Q: WHY WOULDN'T I FILL THE WHOLE CHARCOAL GRATE WITH BURNING COALS?

A: If you covered the entire grate with coals, then you would have only direct heat available to you. Everything on the cooking grill would be right on top of burning coals. That's fine for some foods like burgers and hot dogs, but a lot of other foods do best barbecued over both direct and indirect heat. Bone-in chicken pieces are a good example. Have you ever seen what happens to them when they cook only over direct heat? They burn. The outsides turn black before the meat along the bone has a chance to cook properly. The correct way to barbecue foods like this is to brown them for a while over direct heat and then move them over indirect heat to finish the cooking process.

Also, if the food being cooked over direct heat causes flare-ups, you have a convenient place to put the food while you figure out what to do next. At the very least, you can just close the lid and let the food finish cooking over indirect heat.

ARRANGING THE COALS

Q: WHAT EXACTLY IS THE DIFFERENCE BETWEEN DIRECT AND INDIRECT HEAT?

A: With direct heat, the fire is right below the food. With indirect heat the fire is off to one side of the barbecue, or on both sides of the barbecue, and the food sits over an unlit part.

Direct heat works great for small, tender pieces of food that cook quickly, such as hamburgers, steaks, chops, boneless chicken pieces, fish fillets, shellfish and sliced vegetables. It sears the surfaces of the food, developing flavours, texture and delicious caramelisation while it also cooks the food all the way to the centre.

Indirect heat works better for larger, tougher foods that require longer cooking times, such as whole joints, whole chickens and ribs. As I mentioned, it is also just the right method for finishing thicker foods or bone-in cuts that have been seared or browned first over direct heat.

Q: DOES THE DIRECT METHOD COOK MY FOOD DIFFERENTLY FROM THE INDIRECT METHOD?

A: Yes. A direct fire creates both radiant heat and conductive heat. Radiant heat from the coals quickly cooks the surface of the food closest to it. At the same time, the fire heats the cooking grill rods, which conducts heat directly to the surface of the food and creates those unmistakable and lovely grill marks.

If the food is off to the side of the fire, or over indirect heat, the radiant heat and the conductive heat are still factors, but they are not as intense. If the lid of the barbecue is closed however, as it should be, there is another kind of heat generated: convective heat. It radiates off the coals, bounces off the lid and goes round and round the food. Convection heat doesn't sear the surface of the food the way radiant and conductive heat do. It cooks it more gently all the way to the centre, like the heat in an oven, which lets you cook joints, whole birds and other large foods to the centre without burning them.

Q: WHERE DO I POSITION MY CHARCOAL BASKETS FOR INDIRECT COOKING?

A: For indirect heat, put on two insulated barbecue mitts or oven gloves and, using long handled tongs, move them as far as possible out to the sides. Place the cooking grill on the barbecue with the grill handles directly over the fires. These are to facilitate the addition of either smoking wood chunks or, should the need arise, extra barbecue fuel. The centre of the cooking grill has transformed into the indirect cooking zone with the same level of heat on either side.

Q: HOW DO I ARRANGE MY CHARCOAL FOR DIRECT COOKING?

A: The straightforward way to create a direct cooking zone is to pour the lit coals from the chimney starter in the centre of the charcoal grate. If the barbecue briquettes were lit using the pyramid technique they will already be in the correct position for direct cooking. The bed of coals should be layered approximately two to three briquettes high and extend at least 10 cm (4 inches) beyond every piece of food on the cooking grill above, to ensure that every piece of food cooks evenly.

Q: ARE THERE ANY OTHER GOOD WAYS TO ARRANGE THE COALS?

A: Another great configuration that provides both direct and indirect heat, is a two-zone fire. The coals are to one side of the barbecue, one zone of direct heat and one zone of indirect heat. Once the barbecue briquettes have ashed over in the chimney starter simply pour the coals directly onto the charcoal grate on one side of the kettle. The temperature of a two-zone fire can be high, medium or low, depending on how many briquettes are burning and how long it has been burning. Remember briquettes lose heat over time.

You can also create a three-zone fire, which provides even more flexibility. On one side of the barbecue, pile coals two or three briquettes deep. Then, slope the coals down to a single layer across the centre of the barbecue, and place no coals on the opposite side. When the coals are completely ashen and have burnt down for 10 to 20 minutes longer, after being emptied from the chimney – *voila*! – you have direct high heat on one side, medium heat in the centre and indirect heat on the opposite side.

There are also times when you might prefer a three-zone 'split' fire, where the coals are separated into two equal piles on opposite sides of the charcoal grate. This gives you two zones for direct heat (high, medium or low) and one zone between them for indirect heat. This works nicely for cooking a joint over indirect heat, such as pork loin or beef fillet, because you have the same level of heat on either side of the meat.

BARBECUE BASICS

13

Q: WHAT'S THE RING OF FIRE?

A: It's another way of arranging charcoal for both direct and indirect heat. The ring of coals around the perimeter provides direct heat while the empty centre of the ring provides an area of indirect heat.

Q: WHAT'S THE BULL'S-EYE?

A: The bull's-eye is the flip side of the ring of fire. With the coals piled in the centre of the charcoal grate, you have a small area of direct heat, but a lot of area around the perimeter for indirect heat. This is a convenient arrangement for slow cooking or warming several small pieces of food, such as bone-in chicken pieces.

Q: WHAT'S THE SNAKE METHOD? WHAT'S ITS BENEFIT?

A: The snake method is perfect for low and slow cooking as it allows for fully controlled, consistent and steady low heat temperature throughout the cook. To start, arrange two rows of barbecue briquettes on a 45° angle around the edge of the kettle (approximately 20 briquettes will make up the outer row). Then place a singular line of barbecue briquettes on top of the double lined row. Place a drip pan filled with hot water in the centre of the charcoal grill, and position with any wood chunks on the outer edge on top of the briquettes. When ready to light the snake, pour approximately 15 lit barbecue briquettes on one end of the snake, ensuring it is the correct end so the lit beads will 'fall' onto the next bead. This method will create a consistent low indirect burn for up to approximately 12 hours.

Q: WHAT'S THE PURPOSE OF A DRIP PAN ON A CHARCOAL GRATE?

A: The pan catches drippings, so it extends the life of your barbecue by keeping it clean. If you fill the pan with water, the water will absorb and release heat slowly, adding a bit of moisture to the cooking process.

JUDGING THE HEAT LEVEL

Q: HOW DO I KNOW I HAVE THE RIGHT LEVEL OF HEAT?

A: As soon as briquettes are lightly covered with grey ash (or lump charcoal is lit round the edges of all the pieces), and you've poured the coals on to the charcoal grate, you have very high heat, actually too high for almost any food to handle without burning quickly.

Spread the coals out the way you like, set the cooking grill in place and close the lid. It's important now to preheat the barbecue. You should do this for 10 to 15 minutes, to make the cooking grill hot enough for searing and to make it easier to clean. The heat will loosen all the little bits and pieces clinging to the cooking grill, left over from the last time you barbecued, and a barbecue brush will easily remove them.

There are two reliable ways to judge how hot a charcoal fire is. One is to use the thermometer in the lid of your barbecue, if there is one. With the lid closed, the temperature should climb past 260°C (500°F) initially. Then, once it has reached its peak, the temperature will begin to fall. You can begin barbecuing whenever the temperature has fallen into the desired range.

HEAT	TEMPERATURE RANGE	WHEN YOU WILL NEED TO PULL YOUR HAND AWAY
High	230° to 290°C (450° to 550°F)	2 to 4 seconds
Medium	180° to 230°C (350° to 450°F)	5 to 7 seconds
Low	120° to 180°C (250° to 350°F)	8 to 10 seconds

The second way is less technical but surprisingly reliable. It involves extending the palm of your hand over the barbecue at a safe distance above the charcoal grate. Imagine a soft drink can standing on the cooking grill, right over the coals. If your palm were resting on top of the can, it would be about 12 cm (5 inches) from the cooking grill. That's where you should measure the heat of coals.

If you need to pull your hand away after 2 to 4 seconds, the heat is high. If you need to pull your hand away after 5 to 7 seconds, the heat is medium. If you need to pull it away after 8 to 10 seconds, the heat is low. Use common sense and always pull your hand away from the heat before it hurts – you don't want to get burned.

Q: WHAT SHOULD I DO TO MAINTAIN THE HEAT FOR A LONG PERIOD OF TIME?

A: As mentioned earlier, a typical barbecue briquette fire will slowly lose heat over time. The temperature will start higher at the beginning of cooking, and as the barbecue briquettes gradually burn away the temperature will fall. If you started with a hot fire, after approximately 2 hours of cooking with the lid on, it will drop to the temperature of a normal fire, and a normal fire will become the equivalent of a low fire after the same period of time. If you need to add more briquettes to the fire to cook a second course, you must leave the lid off the barbecue until the additional briquettes have ashed over before you resume cooking. This will take approximately 20 to 30 minutes.

Alternatively, you can light the barbecue briquettes ahead of time in a chimney starter, keep them burning in a safe place and add them when you need instant results. For a fairly even fire, add about 10 to 15 briquettes, every 3 to 4 hours.

Under normal circumstances, a charcoal briquette fire will lose about 38°C (100°F) of heat over 40 to 60 minutes. A typical lump charcoal fire will lose even faster. Lump charcoal and all-natural briquettes light faster than most standard briquettes so they require less lead time. Add them just 5 to 10 minutes before you need to raise the heat. Smaller pieces of lump charcoal will burn out quickly, so you will need to add them more often. Larger lumps will take a little more time to get hot, but they will last longer. Fortunately, lump and all-natural briquettes don't produce any unwanted aromas in the early stages of their burning.

Q: HOW SHOULD I WORK THE AIR VENTS ON MY BARBECUE?

A: The vents on the top and bottom of the barbecue control the airflow inside the barbecue. The more air flowing into the barbecue, the hotter the fire will grow and the more frequently you will have to replenish it. To slow the rate of your fire's burn, close the top vent as much as halfway and keep the lid on as much as possible. The bottom vent should be left open whenever you are barbecuing so you don't kill your fire.

All kinds of charcoal, especially briquettes made with fillers, will leave behind some ash after all the combustible carbon has burned. If you allow the ashes to accumulate on the bottom of the barbecue, they will cover the vent and starve the coals of air, eventually extinguishing them. So, every hour or so, give the vent a gentle sweep, to clear them of ashes, by opening and closing the bottom vent several times in a row.

STARTING A GAS BARBECUE

**WHAT'S THE PROCESS FOR LIGHTING
A GAS BARBECUE?**

Q: **A:** There's nothing complicated about lighting
a gas barbecue. However, gas barbecue
operation does vary, so be sure to consult the
owner's manual that came with your barbecue. To
light a Weber® gas barbecue, first open the lid so
unlit gas fumes don't collect in the cooking box.
Next, slowly open the valve on your propane tank (or
natural gas line) all the way and wait a minute for the
gas to travel through the gas line. Then turn on the
burners, setting them all to high. Close the lid and
preheat the barbecue for 10 to 15 minutes.

Q: WHAT IF I SMELL GAS?

A: That might indicate a leak around the connection or in the hose. Turn off all the burners. Close the valve
on your propane tank (or natural gas line) and disconnect the hose. Wait a few minutes and then reconnect the
hose. Try lighting the barbecue again. If you still smell gas, shut the barbecue down and call the manufacturer.

DIRECT AND INDIRECT HEAT ON A GAS BARBECUE

HOW DO I SET UP MY GAS BARBECUE TO COOK WITH DIRECT HEAT?

A: On a gas barbecue, simply leave all the burners on and adjust them for the heat level you want. For example, if you want direct medium heat, turn all the burners down to medium, close the lid and wait until the thermometer indicates that the temperature is in the range of 180° to 230°C (350° to 450°F). Then set your food on the cooking grill right over the burners. If your gas barbecue does not have a thermometer, use the 'hand test' (see page 15).

Q: WHAT'S THE SETUP FOR INDIRECT HEAT?

A: On a gas barbecue, you can switch from direct to indirect heat almost immediately. Just turn off one or more of the burners and place the food over an unlit burner. If your barbecue has more than two burners, turn off the one(s) in the middle. The burners that are left on can be set to high, medium or low heat, as desired. Whenever the food is over an unlit burner and the lid is closed, you're cooking over indirect heat.

BARBECUE KNOW-HOW

Q: DO I NEED TO CLEAN THE COOKING GRILLS EVERY TIME I USE THE BARBECUE?

A: You really should clean the grills every time, not only to be tidy, but also because any residue left on the cooking grills may cause your food to stick. You will find that food releases from the grills much more easily, and with more impressive grill marks, if the grills are clean.

The easiest way to clean your cooking grills is to preheat the barbecue, with the lid down, to about 260°C (500°F). Then, while wearing an insulated barbecue mitt or oven glove, use a long-handled grill brush to scrape off any bits and pieces that may be stuck to the grills.

Q: WHAT ABOUT CLEANING THE REST OF THE BARBECUE?

A: Once a month or so, you should do a more thorough cleaning of your barbecue. Be sure to read the instructions in your owner's manual beforehand. Wipe down the barbecue with a sponge and warm, soapy water. Scrape off any debris that has accumulated under the lid. Remove the cooking grills, brush the burners and clean out the bottom of the cooking box and the drip pan. For full care and upkeep instructions, consult your owner's manual. With charcoal barbecues, remember that ash naturally has a small amount of water in it. Don't leave it sitting in your barbecue for a long period of time; it can rust some parts of your barbecue.

Q: DO I NEED TO OIL THE COOKING GRILLS BEFORE I BARBECUE?

A: I do not recommend it. Many barbecuers do, and that's fine, but keep in mind that oil will drip though the cooking grills and may cause flare-ups on both charcoal and gas barbecues. You can avoid wasting oil and improve your chances of a food releasing more easily by oiling the food, not the grills.

Q: WHAT SHOULD I DO IF FLARE-UPS HAPPEN?

A: A certain number of flare-ups are to be expected. When oil and fat drip into a hot barbecue, especially a charcoal barbecue, they tend to produce flames. If the flames are barely reaching the surface of the food and then they subside, don't worry about it. If, however, the flames are rising through the cooking grills and surrounding your food, you need to act quickly. Otherwise, the foods will pick up a sooty taste and colour, and could burn.

On a charcoal barbecue, most flare-ups begin within a few seconds of putting food on the barbecue, or right after you turn food over. Your first reaction should be to put the lid on the barbecue and close the top vent about halfway. By decreasing the amount of air getting to the fire, you may extinguish a flare-up. You can check the status of the flare-up by carefully looking through the partially open vent. If the flames are still threatening, open the lid and move the food over indirect heat. That's one very important reason why you should always have an indirect heat zone available. After a few seconds, the oil and fat will usually burn off and the flare-up will subside. When the flare-up dies down, resume cooking your food over direct heat.

You are less likely to have flare-ups with a gas barbecue because many of them have a system that prevents fat and oil from falling directly onto the burners. For example, most Weber® gas barbecues have angled steel bars on top of the burners. Not only do they prevent almost all flare-ups, they also transform dripping juices and fat into wonderfully aromatic smoke. The solutions to flare-ups on a gas barbecue are the same as they are on a charcoal barbecue. First, make sure the lid is closed. Then, if necessary, move the food over indirect heat.

Q: WHEN SHOULD I BARBECUE WITH THE LID ON?

A: As often as possible. Whether using a charcoal barbecue or a gas barbecue, the lid is really important. It limits the amount of air getting to the fire, thus preventing flare-ups, and it helps to cook food on the top and bottom simultaneously. While the bottom of the food is almost always exposed to more intense heat, the lid reflects some heat down and speeds up the overall cooking time. Without the lid, the fire would lose heat more quickly and many foods would take much longer to cook, possibly drying out. Plus, using the lid keeps the cooking grill at a

higher temperature, giving you more conductive heat, which creates better searing and caramelisation. Finally, the lid traps all those good smoky aromas inside the barbecue and surrounds your food with them. Otherwise, the smoke will drift away and serve no real purpose. One exception to this rule occurs when you are barbecuing very thin pieces of food, like bread slices and tortillas. They cook (and potentially burn) so quickly that it's wise to leave the lid off and watch them carefully.

Q: IS IT WORTH GETTING A ROTISSERIE ATTACHMENT FOR MY BARBECUE?

A: If you want to cook large hunks of meat – like pork loins, whole chickens, turkey, duck and beef joints – a rotisserie attachment is a good investment. Any of those meats can be barbecued right on the cooking grill over indirect heat, but the advantage of a rotisserie is that the food slowly self-bastes as it rotates and absorbs the flavours of the fire.

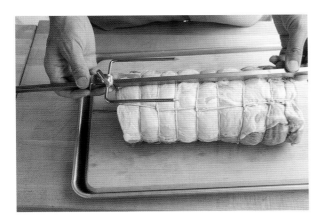
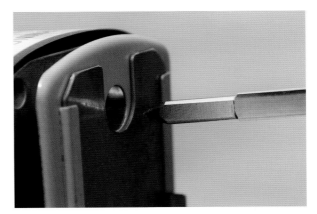

To ensure that the meat stays in place as it turns and cooks uniformly, use butcher's string to truss your food into a compact shape. Then secure the food on the spit, making sure it is centred as evenly as possible. This will put less strain on the motor. Always preheat the barbecue first. When ready to cook, set the spit in place, put a disposable foil tin underneath the roast to catch the grease, turn on the motor and close the lid.

Q: SO WHAT SHOULD I BUY: A CHARCOAL OR GAS BARBECUE?

A: That decision depends a lot on what kind of barbecuer you are. There are some barbecuers who put a high priority on enjoying the food as quickly, cleanly and conveniently as possible. For them, a gas barbecue makes the most sense. The fire is ready in 10 to 15 minutes. The temperature stays right where you need it for as long as you need it, and clean-up is minimal. Then there are some barbecuers who relish the opportunity to build their own fires and tend the coals. Glowing embers and wood smoke thrill them so much that charcoal barbecuing is well worth the extra time and cleanup required. They believe with every last taste bud that the flavour of food cooked over a live fire is better. So, you tell me: which type of barbecuer are you?

SMOKING AND BARBECUING

A: Congratulations, you get a gold star. Every barbecuer ought to try smoking with hardwoods. Done right, it lends food an irresistible flavour.

Smoking on a kettle barbecue is really easy to do, especially if you are already comfortable barbecuing with indirect heat. Begin by filling a chimney starter about one-quarter full with briquettes. When they are fully lit, pour all of the charcoal on one side of the cooking grill (if desired, use a charcoal basket, which holds the coals close together so they burn more slowly) and place an aluminium foil tin on the other side. Then, carefully add about 600 ml (21 fl oz) of water to the tin. The water in the tin is important because it helps to maintain a low cooking temperature. It also adds some moisture to the food, which in many cases will cook for hours and hours, so it could dry out otherwise. Allow 30 minutes to 1 hour for the coals to burn down to the correct temperature and the water to heat up. Next, drop damp wood chips or dry wood chunks directly onto the coals. Then place your food on top of the cooking grill over the water pan and cover your barbecue. Expect to add more coals every 2 hours or so to maintain the heat.

Wood chips, even when they have been soaked in liquid, will smoke sooner than wood chunks, but they often burn out in a matter of minutes. Wood chunks tend to burn for an hour or more. I suggest using chunks and positioning them on the outer edge of a charcoal fire to prolong and extend smoking times even further.

You've got a lot of options in the hardwoods category, including the most popular ones: oak, hickory and mesquite. Of those, mesquite has the strongest aroma, so be careful about using too much of it for too long. In fact, be careful about using too much of any kind of wood. A common rookie mistake is to keep adding wood throughout hours and hours of cooking. The aromas of the smoke can eventually overpower the food, so start with just a few handfuls, then stop. Next time, if you want a little more smokiness, add an additional handful or two.

In my opinion, oak and hickory complement beef, lamb and pork really well. Milder woods pair nicely with milder foods, for example, apple wood, pecan and cherry with chicken and fish. Don't worry about using the 'wrong' wood for any kind of food. It's almost impossible to make a mistake here. Some people latch on to a favourite kind of wood and use it to smoke almost anything. That's fine. The differences between the hardwoods are pretty subtle.

But please don't add soft, resinous woods like pine, cedar and aspen to your fire. They create an acrid (and sometimes toxic) smoke. And never use any wood that has been treated with chemicals.

Q: IF SMOKING IS USUALLY DONE WITH LOW TEMPERATURES, HOW DO I GET MY KETTLE BARBECUE TO DO THAT?

A: Many foods are smoked and simultaneously cooked in the temperature range of 120° to 180°C (250° to 350°F). You can maintain the correct level of heat by controlling the amount of charcoal and the airflow. This is why you begin with 36 barbecue briquettes in a chimney starter. Adding 10 to 15 barbecue briquettes every 2 hours or so will help to maintain the temperature. So will opening and closing the vents on the lid. Opening the vents will help the fire burn faster and hotter. Closing them partially (not all the way, or you might put out the fire) will restrict the airflow and drop the temperature. Having a thermometer on the lid is very helpful here. Alternatively, refer to the snake method on page 14 for another great set up.

Q: CAN I SMOKE FOOD WITH A GAS BARBECUE?

A: Yes, some of today's gas barbecues come equipped with a metal smoker box that sits on top of a dedicated burner. Just turn on the burner and add as many wood chips as you like. You can control how quickly they smoke by turning the knob of the burner higher or lower. Some of the boxes have a separate compartment for water, which will provide a steaming effect on the food, too.

A: A water smoker allows you to smoke meat at temperatures well below 150°C (300°F) for many hours. The Weber version is basically an upright bullet-shaped unit with three sections. The barbecue briquettes burn in the bottom section. For smoky barbecue aromas, add a few fist-sized chunks of hardwood to the coals right from the beginning. The meat will absorb the smoke best when it is uncooked.

The water sits in a pan in the middle section, preventing any fat from dripping on to the coals and, more importantly, keeping the temperature nice and low. The meat sits on one or two racks in the top section.

The following instructions and quantities are designed for use with barbecue briquettes. When building your fire, I suggest you use a combination of lit and unlit fuel. Unlit fuel is placed around the outside of the charcoal ring on the charcoal grate. The lit fuel should be prepared using a chimney starter. The lit fuel will provide the heat to start cooking and smoking, while the unlit fuel provides a reserve that will slowly burn and maintain heat over the duration of cooking time.

Suggested fuel quantities:

	37 CM SMOKER	47 CM SMOKER	57 CM SMOKER
UNLIT FUEL	40 briquettes	40 briquettes	110 briquettes
LIT FUEL	35 briquettes	55 briquettes	55 briquettes

A water smoker has vents on both the bottom and top sections. Generally, it's a good idea to leave the top vent open so that smoke can escape. Use the bottom vents as your primary way of regulating the temperature. The less air you allow into the smoker, the lower the temperature will go.

Generally speaking, if the ring in the bottom section of the smoker is filled with lit briquettes, and the water pan is nearly filled, the temperature will stay in the range of 110°C to 130°C (225° to 250°F) for 6 to 8 hours. This is an ideal range for barbecuing food like pork ribs, turkeys and large beef joints.

When you see that very little smoke is coming out of the top vent, add another chunk or two through the door on the side. Wood chunks burn slowly and evenly, so they are a better choice than wood chips in this situation. For cooking sessions lasting longer than 6 to 8 hours, you will probably need to add more unlit barbecue briquettes occasionally. Start with 5 to 10 briquettes and recheck the temperature in 15 minutes.

During long cooking times, also be sure to replenish the water pan every few hours with warm water. But keep the lid on the smoker as much as possible. That's critical for maintaining even heat.

MUST-HAVE TOOLS

Once you have a good barbecue that allows you to control the fire easily and cook your food over both direct and indirect heat, it's time to equip yourself with the right tools. I've broken down my recommendations into two groups. The first ten tools are essential for most tasks. The other ten will make many jobs a lot easier.

TONGS

Oh, the tongs. Definitely the hardest working tool of all. You will need one pair to load raw food on the barbecue and move it around. You will need another pair (clean tongs that haven't touched any raw meat, fish or poultry) to remove the barbecued food. Dedicate a third pair for rearranging charcoal.

BARBECUE BRUSH

Spring for a solid, long-handled model with stainless-steel bristles. Use the brush to clean off the grills before and after barbecuing, and you will eliminate many problems with food sticking to the grills. And your food won't taste like last night's dinner. Replace the brush when the bristles wear down to about one-half their original length.

GRILL PAN

At first I didn't see the wisdom of a grill pan, but I came around on the issue when I saw (and tasted) how well a perforated grill pan can handle delicate fish fillets and small foods like chopped vegetables that might otherwise fall through the cooking grill. If you preheat a stainless-steel grill pan properly, it will brown the food nicely and allow the smokiness from the barbecue to flavour the food.

CHIMNEY STARTER

Brilliantly simple, a chimney starter lets you start the coals faster and more evenly than you could with lighter fluid. And who needs all those chemicals in lighter fluid? Look for a chimney starter with a capacity of at least 5 litres (175 fl oz/20 cups) of barbecue briquettes, roughly 80 pieces. Also, it should have two handles: a heatproof side handle for lifting the chimney and a hinged top handle to provide support when dumping hot coals onto the charcoal grate.

INSTANT-READ THERMOMETER

You only have to overcook a fine cut of meat once to learn the importance of a good digital thermometer. Small and relatively inexpensive, an instant-read thermometer is essential for quickly gauging the internal temperature of the meat. To get the most accurate read, insert it into the thickest part of the cut and avoid touching any bone, because the bone conducts heat.

ROASTING TRAY

I learned the value of a sturdy roasting tray when I was in culinary school, where there were dozens within reach in every kitchen. A shallow tray, like the one pictured here, is a great portable work surface for oiling and seasoning food, and there's nothing better to use as a landing pad for food coming off the barbecue.

BASTING BRUSH

In the past, basting brushes were made of wooden/plastic handles and synthetic/natural-boar bristles. Today you can find them made of stainless steel with silicone bristles that have beads at the tips to help load the brush with a sauce or marinade. While most old-style brushes had to be hand washed, this new high-tech style can go right into the dishwasher. Nice.

BARBECUE MITTS

You'll need these to shield your hand and forearm when managing a charcoal fire or reaching towards the back of any hot barbecue. You will probably put them through the wash a lot, so invest in mitts or oven gloves of good-quality materials and workmanship. Silicone barbecue mitts are easy to care for because you can just wipe them off when they get dirty, but insulated cloth mitts will give better dexterity.

SPATULA

Look for a long-handled spatula designed with a bent (offset) neck so that the blade is set lower than the handle. This will make it easier to lift food off the barbecue without hitting your knuckles. The blade should be at least 10 cm (4 inches) wide.

SKEWERS

Bamboo skewers are simple and inexpensive, though they need to be soaked in water for at least 30 minutes prior to loading, in order to keep the wood from burning. If you don't want the hassle, use metal skewers, or freeze bamboo skewers in a bag after soaking them (see page 155). The flat metal skewers and double-pronged ones are nice because they prevent the food from spinning when you turn the skewers.

NICE TO HAVE TOOLS

TIMER

As the old saying goes, timing is everything. It's never truer than when you are trying to pull off a perfect meal at the barbecue. A rotary kitchen timer is adequate, but you can also ante up for a more elaborate digital timer, preferably one that lets you track a couple of barbecuing times simultaneously.

WIRELESS MEAT THERMOMETER

While an instant-read thermometer is a must-have, a wireless thermometer is a cool little luxury. It's a high-tech gadget that monitors the temperature of meat using a wireless probe. You can walk away from the barbecue and a remote beeper will tell you when your food is ready.

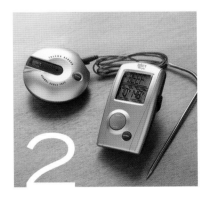

SMALL SHOVEL

Seeing this tool on the list might surprise you, but a small shovel is really helpful for pushing charcoal around. You can buy a shovel specifically for the task at a barbecue retailer, or buy a small shovel (one with no plastic parts) from a hardware, DIY or garden shop.

ROTISSERIE

It's true that you can roast a chicken, turkey or pork loin on the barbecue without a rotisserie, but there is something wonderfully medieval about food spinning over a fire. Many people also argue that the rotisserie causes the meat to self-baste while cooking. I agree that food comes out juicier, so I am pro-rotisserie.

DISPOSABLE PANS

Available in large and small sizes, disposable foil tins offer many conveniences. Use them to move food to and from the barbecue, keep food warm on the cooking grill, soak wood chunks in them or set them under the grill to catch drippings and keep a charcoal barbecue clean.

CAST-IRON FRYING PAN

A big cast-iron frying pan allows you to make favourites in this book, like paella, gingerbread and a stunning pineapple upside-down cake. Once it gets hot on the barbecue, you can sauté, stew or pan-roast just about anything in it without ever worrying that the pan will discolour or deteriorate. It will last you forever.

RESEALABLE PLASTIC BAGS

Marinating foods in plastic bags allows you to force some of the marinade up and over the food, particularly when you set a bag snugly in a bowl, giving you better coverage and faster marinating times. Resealable bags also avoid dreaded spills in your refrigerator.

RIB RACK

This wire rack holds multiple slabs of ribs upright so that heat circulates around the ribs, cooking them evenly, and it encourages the pork fat to drip down and away from the ribs. Plus, it frees up space on the cooking grills for barbecuing other food at the same time.

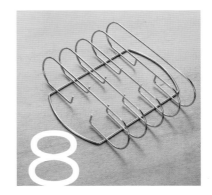

FISH BASKET

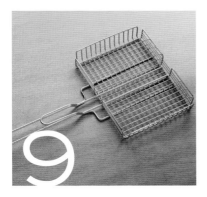

Many people resist barbecuing fish, especially whole fish, for fear that it will stick and fall apart on the cooking grill. For them, there are hinged baskets that provide one degree of separation from the grill, which makes turning a cinch. Using one of these sure beats the alternative of cooking the fish inside the house and smelling it for days.

MICROPLANE GRATER

This is terrific at grating garlic, whole nutmeg and hard cheeses. It's even better used to zest citrus fruits. You'll see Microplane graters in several shapes and sizes. I prefer the long, thin one shaped like a paint brush.

RED MEAT

TECHNIQUES

RECIPES

HOW TO BARBECUE BURGERS

5 THINGS YOU NEED TO KNOW

1 WHAT MAKES THEM JUICY

Fat makes burgers juicy. That's a big reason why minced (ground) chuck (from the shoulder) is better for burgers than minced round (from the rump). Chuck is typically about 18 per cent fat, whereas round is often down around 12 per cent fat. The reality is that most minced beef in supermarkets comes from all kinds of parts of the animal, but that shouldn't stop you from asking the person behind the counter to mince some chuck just for you, maybe mixing in some sirloin for extra flavour.

2 SEASONING WORKS

Minced beef alone makes a pretty dull-tasting hamburger, so make sure that the meat is, at least, mixed with salt and pepper. Other ingredients, like worcestershire sauce, hot sauce or grated onions, will improve not only the taste but also the juiciness of your hamburgers.

SHAPING UP

3

The ideal thickness for a raw burger is 1.5 cm (¾ inch). If it's any thinner, it's likely to overcook and dry out before a nice crust develops on the outside. If it's much thicker, the crust might turn black and unappetising before the centre reaches the safe internal doneness level of medium.

4 LEVELING OFF

Burgers tend to puff up in the centre as they cook, making the tops rounded and awkward for piling on the toppings. A good trick for avoiding this problem is pressing a little indentation into the top of each raw burger with your thumb or the back of a spoon. Then, when the centre pushes up, the top of each burger will be relatively level.

5 FLIPPING ONLY ONCE

You should flip each burger only once, and only when it's ready to flip. You'll know when by slipping the edge of a spatula or spatula underneath the edge of the burger and lifting up very gently. If the meat is sticking to the cooking grill, back off and try again a minute later. When you can lift the edge of the burger without sticking, it's ready to flip.

CLASSIC PATTY MELTS ON RYE

SERVES: 6
PREP TIME: 25 MINUTES

HEAT: DIRECT HIGH HEAT 230° TO 290°C (450° TO 550°F)
AND DIRECT MEDIUM HEAT 180° TO 230°C
(350° TO 450°F)
COOKING TIME: 11 TO 13 MINUTES

3 tablespoons canola or other vegetable oil
2 large brown onions, halved and thinly sliced
½ teaspoon sugar
Sea salt
50 g (2 oz) unsalted butter, softened
12 slices crusty rye bread, each about 8 mm (⅓ inch) thick
1 kg (2 lb) minced (ground) chuck
2 tablespoons worcestershire sauce
½ teaspoon freshly ground black pepper
125 g (4 oz) havarti or Swiss cheese, grated
Dijon or French mustard, optional

1. Warm the oil in a large frying pan over a medium heat.
Add the onions, sprinkle with the sugar, cover and cook for
15 to 20 minutes, stirring occasionally, until the onions are
tender and golden brown. Season to taste with salt, then
remove from the heat.

2. Butter the bread on each side and set aside.

3. Prepare the barbecue for direct cooking over a high heat. Mix
the minced chuck with the worcestershire sauce, 1 teaspoon
of salt and the pepper in a large bowl, incorporating the spices
evenly. Gently shape into 6 equal-sized burgers, each about
1.5 cm (¾ inch) thick. With your thumb or the back of a spoon,
make a shallow indentation about 2.5 cm (1 inch) wide in the
centre of each burger.

4. Brush the cooking grills clean. Cook the burgers over **direct
high heat** for 8 to 10 minutes, with the lid closed as much as
possible but turning once. Transfer the burgers to a work surface.

5. Lower the temperature of the barbecue to medium. Barbecue
the bread slices over **direct medium heat** for about 1 minute
until toasted on one side only. Transfer the bread, toasted sides
up, to a work surface.

6. Evenly divide the caramelised onions on 6 of the toasted bread
slices and top each with a burger. Scatter the cheese over the
tops and place the remaining bread slices, toasted sides down,
on top of the burgers. Using a spatula, carefully place the burger
melts back on to the grill and barbecue over **direct medium heat**
for about 1 minute until the bread on the bottom is toasted, and
then carefully turn the sandwiches and toast the other side. Serve
the burger melts warm with mustard, if desired.

*The sturdy texture
of crusty rye bread
holds up well under
the weight of all the
wonderfully messy
ingredients in a
burger melt.*

HOW TO SPICE UP MAYONNAISE

1. Tame the sharp flavour and crunch of raw onion in your mayonnaise by grating the onion on the medium-sized holes of a grater, then rinse the grated onion in a sieve for a mild taste.

2. A Microplane grater with tiny holes will quickly make a paste out of fresh garlic.

3. Swipe the paste right off the back side of the grater and into your mayonnaise.

CALIFORNIA BURGERS WITH GUACAMOLE MAYONNAISE

SERVES: 4
PREP TIME: 25 MINUTES

HEAT: DIRECT HIGH HEAT 230° TO 290°C (450° TO 550°F)
COOKING TIME: 18 TO 20 MINUTES

MAYONNAISE
2 tablespoons grated white onion
1 ripe haas avocado, stoned and peeled
2 tablespoons mayonnaise
2 roma tomatoes, cored, deseeded and chopped
1 tablespoon finely chopped coriander
2 teaspoons fresh lime juice
1 small garlic clove, grated
Sea salt

2 poblano chillies or other mild chillies
750 g (1½ lb) minced (ground) chuck
1½ teaspoons sea salt
1 teaspoon freshly ground black pepper

4 hamburger buns

1. Rinse the grated onion in a sieve under cold water and allow the excess water to drain off. Mash the avocado and mayonnaise together in a bowl with a fork. Stir in the onion, tomatoes, coriander, lime juice and garlic, then season generously with salt. Cover with plastic wrap, pressing the plastic directly on to the surface, and set aside. (The mayonnaise can be prepared up to 8 hours ahead.)

2. Prepare the barbecue for direct cooking over high heat. Brush the cooking grills clean. Barbecue the chillies over ***direct high heat*** for about 10 minutes, with the lid closed as much as possible but turning occasionally, until the skin has blackened on all sides. Remove them from the barbecue and set aside to cool completely. Peel off and discard the blackened skin, and then remove and discard the stem, seeds and ribs. Chop the chillies into 1-cm (½-inch) dice.

3. Mix the minced chuck, chillies, salt and pepper together in a large bowl, then shape into 4 equal-sized burgers, each about 1.5 cm (¾ inch) thick. With your thumb or the back of a spoon, make a shallow indentation about 2.5 cm (1 inch) wide in the centre of each burger so the centres are about 1 cm (½ inch) thick. This will help the burgers cook evenly and prevent them from puffing on the barbecue.

4. Barbecue the burgers over ***direct high heat*** for 8 to 10 minutes, with the lid closed as much as possible, turning once when the burgers release easily from the grill without sticking, until cooked to medium. During the last minute of cooking time, toast the buns, cut sides down, over a direct heat. Top the burgers with the mayonnaise and serve warm.

CABERNET BURGERS WITH ROSEMARY FOCACCIA

SERVES: 4
PREP TIME: 25 MINUTES

HEAT: DIRECT HIGH HEAT 230° TO 290°C (450° TO 550°F)
    AND DIRECT MEDIUM HEAT 180° TO 230°C
    (350° TO 450°F)
COOKING TIME: 10 TO 14 MINUTES

CABERNET GLAZE
500 ml (17 fl oz/2 cups) cabernet sauvignon wine
1 tablespoon light brown sugar

BUTTER
50 g (2 oz) unsalted butter, softened
1 tablespoon very finely chopped rosemary leaves

BURGERS
750 g (1½ lb) minced (ground) chuck
4 tablespoons Cabernet glaze (above)
2 teaspoons sea salt
½ teaspoon freshly ground black pepper

4 slices cheddar cheese
8 slices ripe tomato, each about 1 cm (½ inch) thick
Extra-virgin olive oil
Sea salt
4 focaccia squares, each about 11 cm (4¼ inches),
    sliced in half horizontally, or 4 focaccia buns, split
100 g (3½ oz) rocket leaves

4 thick rashers cooked, crisp bacon

Thanks to a red wine reduction, the burger on the left has improved dramatically in flavour, moisture and appearance.

1. Combine the wine and brown sugar in a heavy-based saucepan over a medium heat and cook for 20 to 25 minutes until reduced to 125 ml (4 fl oz/½ cup). Set aside to cool.

2. Mix the butter and rosemary together in a small bowl.

3. Prepare the barbecue for direct cooking over a high heat. Combine the burger ingredients in a large bowl and shape into 4 equal-sized burgers, each about 1.5 cm (¾ inch) thick. With your thumb or the back of a spoon, make a shallow indentation about 2.5 cm (1 inch) wide in the centre of each burger.

4. Brush the cooking grills clean. Barbecue the burgers over **direct high heat** for 8 to 10 minutes with the lid closed as much as possible. Brush with the glaze every 2 minutes and turn them once when the burgers release easily from the grill without sticking, until cooked to medium. During the last minute of cooking, place a slice of cheese on each burger to melt.

5. Lower the temperature of the barbecue to medium. Brush the tomato slices with oil, season to taste with salt and cook over **direct medium heat** for 2 to 4 minutes, turning once, until soft. Spread the cut sides of the focaccia with the rosemary butter and heat over **direct medium heat** for about 1 minute, cut sides down, until lightly toasted. Assemble each burger with rocket, a cooked burger, a rasher of bacon and 2 slices of tomato. Serve warm.

BRIE AND SHALLOT PARISIAN BURGERS

SERVES: 4
PREP TIME: 30 MINUTES

HEAT: DIRECT HIGH HEAT 230° TO 290°C (450° TO 550°F)
COOKING TIME: 8 TO 10 MINUTES

150 g (5 oz) shallots, thinly sliced
2 tablespoons extra-virgin olive oil

BURGERS
750 g (1½ lb) minced (ground) chuck
3 tablespoons fine dried breadcrumbs
3 tablespoons beef or chicken stock
1 teaspoon sea salt
½ teaspoon freshly ground black pepper

50 g (2 oz) brie cheese (not the triple cream variety)
4 round crusty rolls, each about 10 cm (4 inches)
    in diameter
75 g (3 oz) wholegrain mustard
100 g (3½ oz) rocket leaves, to serve

1. Combine the shallots with the oil in a frying pan
over low heat and cook for about 20 minutes, stirring often
until the shallots are browned but not scorched. Allow to cool
to room temperature.

2. Prepare the barbecue for direct cooking over a high heat. Mix
the burger ingredients together in a large bowl, then shape into
4 equal-sized burgers, each about 1.5 cm (¾ inch) thick. Make
a hole in the centre of each burger for the cheese.

3. Trim away the rind of the brie and bury the cheese, about
15 g (½ oz) for each burger, into the hole of each. Close the
opening to seal the cheese inside. It's important that there is

8 mm (⅓ inch) of meat on the top and bottom of the cheese so
it doesn't seep out during barbecuing.

4. Brush the cooking grills clean. Barbecue the burgers over
direct high heat for 8 to 10 minutes, with the lid closed as
much as possible, until cooked to medium, but turning once
when the burgers release easily from the grate without sticking.
During the last minute of cooking time, toast the buns, cut sides
down, over a direct heat.

5. Assemble the burgers with shallots, mustard and rocket.
Serve warm.

HOW TO MAKE 'OUTSIDE-IN' CHEESEBURGERS

A fun way to turn a cheeseburger outside-in is by nestling a little knob of cheese in the centre and letting it soften slowly while the
burger barbecues.

1. Trim off any unwanted rind.

2. Cut the pieces small enough so
that the cheese won't seep out of
the burger.

3. Nestle each piece right in the
centre of each burger.

4. Seal each burger tightly to
enclose the cheese completely.

KOFTA IN PITTA POCKETS WITH CUCUMBER AND TOMATO SALAD

SERVES: 6
PREP TIME: 25 MINUTES

HEAT: DIRECT AND INDIRECT HIGH HEAT
    230° TO 290°C (450° TO 550°F)
COOKING TIME: 8 TO 10 MINUTES

DRESSING
125 g (4 oz) Greek-style yogurt
125 g (4 oz) sesame tahini
15 g (½ oz) coriander or mint leaves,
    or a combination, finely chopped
3 tablespoons fresh lemon juice
2 tablespoons extra-virgin olive oil
½ teaspoon sea salt

SALAD
175 g (6 oz) cherry tomatoes, quartered
100 g (3½ oz) cucumber, chopped
40 g (1½ oz) red onion, finely chopped
Sea salt

KOFTA
750 g (1½ lb) minced (ground) chuck
25 g (1 oz) flat-leaf parsley, very finely chopped
1 tablespoon very finely chopped garlic
2 teaspoons ground coriander
1½ teaspoons ground cumin
1½ teaspoons sea salt
½ teaspoon freshly ground black pepper
½ teaspoon ground allspice
¼ teaspoon ground cardamom
¼ teaspoon ground turmeric

Extra-virgin olive oil
3 wholegrain or wholemeal pitta breads

1. Combine the dressing ingredients in a small bowl. If the dressing is too thick, whisk in up to 3 tablespoons of water until your desired consistency is reached.

2. Combine the salad ingredients in another bowl, including salt to taste.

3. Prepare the barbecue for direct and indirect cooking over a high heat. Combine the kofta ingredients in a large bowl and shape into 6 equal-sized koftas, each about 1.5 cm (¾ inch) thick. With your thumb or the back of a spoon, make a shallow indentation about 2.5 cm (1 inch) wide in the centre of each kofta, then brush them with oil.

4. Sprinkle the pittas with water and wrap them in foil.

5. Brush the cooking grills clean. Barbecue the koftas over **direct high heat** for 8 to 10 minutes, with the lid closed as much as possible but turning once when they release easily

from the grill without sticking, until medium. While they cook, warm the pitta pockets over **indirect high heat** for 4 to 5 minutes, turning once.

6. Cut each pitta in half. Scoop about 3 tablespoons of the salad into each pitta. Spoon some of the dressing over the salad. Place a kofta into each pitta pocket and spoon in more dressing, if desired. Serve warm.

HOW TO SEASON KOFTA

1. The bold flavours of this dish rely on a panoply of international ingredients.

2. Kofta refers to any kind of ground meat mixed with grains, vegetables or spices.

3. Pressing a shallow indentation in each kofta prevents the meat from puffing up like a meatball during cooking.

As with any type of burger, the key to keeping this one flat instead of puffed up is to make a shallow indentation in the meat while it is raw. During the last minute of barbecuing, scatter crumbled goats' cheese on top so that it oozes a little into the burger.

LAMB BURGERS WITH TAPENADE AND GOATS' CHEESE

SERVES: 6
PREP TIME: 25 MINUTES

HEAT: DIRECT HIGH HEAT 230° TO 290°C (450° TO 550°F)
COOKING TIME: 8 TO 10 MINUTES

TAPENADE
1 garlic clove
75 g (3 oz) pitted kalamata olives
75 g (3 oz) pitted green olives
2 tablespoons small capers, rinsed
2 tablespoons extra-virgin olive oil
½ teaspoon dijon mustard
½ teaspoon dried herbes de provence

1.1 kg (2¼ lb) minced (ground) lamb
½ teaspoon dried herbes de provence
½ teaspoon sea salt
½ teaspoon freshly ground black pepper
150 g (5 oz) goats' cheese, crumbled
6 hamburger buns
3 roma tomatoes, thinly sliced

1. Fit a food processor with the metal chopping blade. With the machine running, drop the garlic through the feed tube and very finely chop. Add the rest of the tapenade ingredients and pulse until coarsely chopped. (The tapenade can be made, and then covered and refrigerated, for up to 1 week ahead. Bring to room temperature before serving.)

2. Prepare the barbecue for direct cooking over a high heat. Mix the lamb, herbs, salt and pepper together in a large bowl, then shape in to 6 equal-sized burgers, each about 10 cm (4 inches) across and 1.5 cm (¾ inch) thick. With your thumb or the back of a spoon, make a shallow indentation about 2.5 cm (1 inch) wide in the centre of each burger.

3. Brush the cooking grills clean. Barbecue the burgers over **direct high heat** for 8 to 10 minutes, with the lid closed as much as possible but turning once until medium. During the last minute of cooking, top each burger with the cheese to allow the cheese to soften, and toast the buns.

4. Assemble the burgers with tomato slices and tapenade. Serve warm.

LAMB MEATBALLS WITH CHOPPED SALAD AND MINTED YOGURT

SERVES: 6
PREP TIME: 30 MINUTES

HEAT: DIRECT MEDIUM-HIGH HEAT
    ABOUT 200°C (400°F)
COOKING TIME: 4 TO 6 MINUTES
SPECIAL EQUIPMENT: METAL OR BAMBOO SKEWERS (IF
    BAMBOO, SOAK IN WATER FOR AT LEAST 30 MINUTES)

SALAD
4 tablespoons extra-virgin olive oil
2 tablespoons red wine vinegar
1 teaspoon finely grated lemon rind
2 teaspoons very finely chopped garlic
3 large roma tomatoes, deseeded and diced
½ cucumber, deseeded and diced
½ small red onion, finely diced
40 g (1½ oz) feta cheese, crumbled
15 g (½ oz) flat-leaf parsley, chopped
½ teaspoon sea salt
¼ teaspoon freshly ground black pepper

MEATBALLS
750 g (1½ lb) minced (ground) lamb
1 tablespoon very finely chopped garlic
2 teaspoons ground cumin
1 teaspoon sea salt
½ teaspoon freshly ground black pepper

Extra-virgin olive oil

SAUCE
375 g (13 oz) Greek-style yogurt
2 tablespoons fresh lemon juice
15 g (½ oz) mint leaves, coarsely chopped
½ teaspoon sea salt

4–6 naan breads

1. Whisk the oil, vinegar, lemon rind and garlic together in a large non-metallic bowl. Add in the rest of the salad ingredients and gently toss with the dressing.

2. Mix all the meatball ingredients in a bowl. Do not overwork the mixture or the meatballs will be tough. Shape about 24 meatballs. Thread 4 meatballs on to each skewer and lightly brush with oil.

3. Prepare the barbecue for direct cooking over a medium-high heat.

4. Combine the yogurt and lemon juice in a small bowl. Fold in the mint and season with the salt.

5. Brush the cooking grills clean. Barbecue the meatballs over *direct medium-high heat* for 4 to 6 minutes, with the lid closed as much as possible but turning occasionally, until they have browned but are still slightly pink in the centre. During the last 30 seconds of barbecuing time, heat the naan over a direct heat.

6. Cut the naan in half, or into pieces large enough to hold 4 meatballs. Top with a generous spoonful of sauce and some salad.

Skewering these meatballs allows you to turn 4 of them at a time, rather than having to turn them individually. Skewers are ready to turn only when the meat releases from the cooking grill without any sticking.

HOW TO BARBECUE MEAT LOAF

1. Light panko breadcrumbs hold these meat loaves together without making them dense.

2. Check the internal temperature near the top because that part takes the longest to cook.

3. To remove each meat loaf in one whole piece, support both ends with spatulas.

BARBECUED MEAT LOAF

SERVES: 8 TO 10
PREP TIME: 20 MINUTES

HEAT: INDIRECT MEDIUM-LOW HEAT
    ABOUT 150°C (300°F)
COOKING TIME: 50 TO 60 MINUTES
SPECIAL EQUIPMENT: INSTANT-READ THERMOMETER

MEAT LOAF
625 g (1¼ lb) minced (ground) beef
625 g (1¼ lb) minced (ground) pork
125 g (4 oz) panko breadcrumbs
150 g (5 oz) brown onion, finely chopped
1 egg
1 teaspoon worcestershire sauce
1 teaspoon garlic granules
1 teaspoon dried tarragon
1 teaspoon sea salt
1 teaspoon freshly ground black pepper

SAUCE
125 ml (4 oz/½ cup) barbecue sauce
65 g (2½ lb) tomato sauce

1. Gently combine the meat loaf ingredients using your hands in a large bowl.

2. Divide the meat loaf mixture in half and form into 2 loaves, each about 10 cm (4 inches) wide and 15 to 18 cm (6 to 7 inches) long. Place the loaves on a roasting tray. Prepare the barbecue for indirect cooking over a medium-low heat.

3. Mix the sauce ingredients in a small bowl. Set aside half of the sauce to serve with the meat loaf. Top each meat loaf with 3 tablespoons of the remaining sauce and coat thoroughly.

4. Brush the cooking grills clean. Pick up each loaf from the roasting tray with a metal spatula, and place directly on the grill. Barbecue the meat loaves over *indirect medium-low heat* for 50 to 60 minutes, with the lid closed, until a thermometer inserted horizontally through the top of each loaf registers 68°C (155°F). Remove the loaves from the barbecue and allow to rest for 10 to 15 minutes. Once removed from the barbecue, the loaves will continue to cook, allowing them to reach the 70°C (160°F) recommended for minced beef and pork. Cut the loaves into 1-cm (½-inch) slices and serve with the reserved sauce.

TO MAKE MEAT LOAF SANDWICHES
Cut the meat loaf into 1-cm (½-inch) slices and slather both sides with some of the reserved sauce. Barbecue over *direct low heat*, 130° to 180°C (250° to 350°F), with the lid closed as much as possible but turning once, for 4 to 6 minutes. Serve on sourdough bread. This is also great with melted provolone cheese.

'TUBE STEAKS' WITH PICKLED ONIONS

SERVES: 8
PREP TIME: 15 MINUTES
MARINATING TIME: 2 TO 3 HOURS

HEAT: DIRECT MEDIUM HEAT 180° TO 230°C
(350° TO 450°F)
COOKING TIME: 5 TO 7 MINUTES

PICKLED ONIONS
1 small white or brown onion
1 small red onion
125 ml (4 fl oz/½ cup) apple cider vinegar
125 ml (4 fl oz/½ cup) white vinegar
100 g (3½ oz) sugar
1 tablespoon sea salt
2 teaspoons celery seeds
1 teaspoon crushed red chilli flakes

8 all-beef hot dogs, about 125 g (4 oz) each
8 hot dog buns
Mustard
Tomato sauce

1. Trim off the ends of the onions. Cut each onion in half lengthways, then with a very sharp knife cut the onions into paper-thin slices and place in a shallow, non-metallic dish. Combine the remaining onion ingredients in a bowl and whisk thoroughly until the sugar and salt have dissolved. Pour the vinegar mixture over the onions and stir to coat them evenly. Set aside at room temperature for about 3 hours, stirring occasionally. Drain the pickled onions and set aside.

2. Using a sharp knife, cut a few shallow slashes in each hot dog.

3. Prepare the barbecue for direct cooking over a medium heat. Brush the cooking grills clean. Barbecue the hot dogs over **direct medium heat**, with the lid closed as much as possible, until lightly marked on the outside and hot all the way to the centre, for 5 to 7 minutes, turning occasionally.

4. Place the hot dogs in buns. Squeeze your condiment of choice alongside each hot dog and top with pickled onions. Serve warm.

HOW TO PICKLE ONIONS

1. Peel and halve the onions, and make sure the root and stem ends are completely removed.

2. Cut the onions into paper-thin slices, place them in a shallow glass dish and pour the pickling liquid over them.

3. Stir to coat them evenly and set aside to marinate for about 3 hours.

HOW TO BARBECUE STEAK
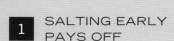THINGS YOU NEED TO KNOW

1 SALTING EARLY PAYS OFF

You might have heard the warning that you shouldn't salt meat too far ahead of cooking because it can draw out moisture. It's true that salt draws moisture towards itself, but over the course of 20 to 30 minutes that's a good thing, because the salt begins to dissolve into that little bit of moisture. When the steak hits the hot cooking grill, the sugars and proteins in the moisture combine with the salt and other seasonings to create a delicious crust. Any moisture you might lose is well worth the flavour of that crust.

2 TAKING OFF THE CHILL SPEEDS UP COOKING

The goal of barbecuing a steak is to brown and lightly char the surface while also cooking the interior to a perfectly juicy doneness, right? If the steak is too cold, the interior might require so much cooking time to reach that perfect doneness that the steak overcooks deep below the surface, turning grey and dry. Allow your steaks to stand at room temperature for 20 to 30 minutes before barbecuing. They will cook faster all the way to the centre and stay juicier.

3 SEARING EQUALS FLAVOUR

One good habit that separates professional chefs from many home cooks is that chefs spend more time searing their steaks. They understand that searing develops literally hundreds of flavours and aromas on the surface of steak, so they allow their steaks to sizzle over a direct heat until the surfaces are dark, dark brown. Don't allow anyone to tell you that searing 'locks in the juices'. That's a myth. But searing does make steak tasty.

4 THICKER STEAKS SHOULD SLIDE OVER

Most steaks barbecue beautifully over direct high heat alone. The only time you might need to move them is if/when they cause flare-ups. Some steaks, however, are so thick that if you left them over a direct heat alone, they would burn on the outside before they reached the internal doneness you like. If your steaks are much thicker than 2.5 cm (1 inch), consider the sear-and-slide approach. After you have seared both sides nicely over direct high heat, slide the steaks to a part of the barbecue that is not so hot, perhaps over indirect heat, and finish cooking them safely there.

5 YOU CAN'T PUT MOISTURE BACK INSIDE A STEAK

As steaks cook over a high heat, they lose moisture. Fat and juices are literally pushed out of the meat. That's the price we pay for making the steaks easier to digest. Perhaps the most important part of barbecuing a steak is taking it off the heat before it has lost too much moisture. There is a short window of time, usually just a minute or two, when steaks go from medium rare to medium, or from medium to medium well. Catching that window requires vigilance. Don't walk away from a steak on the barbecue. And remember, it's always better to take it off when it's underdone and then return it to the barbecue than it is to let a steak overcook.

HOW TO BUTCHER A WHOLE PORTERHOUSE

1. Buying a whole porterhouse is a great way to save money on steaks.

2. You'll need to trim away most of the thick 'fat cap' on the top side.

3. Next, remove the long section of scraggy meat and fat on the thinnest edge.

4. Cutting the porterhouse yourself allows you to make the steaks just the right thickness.

5. After cutting the steaks, go back and trim the fat around the outer edges to about 5 mm (¼ inch).

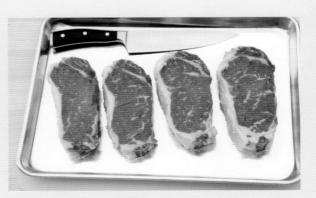

6. Barbecue some of the steaks now and freeze the remaining ones for another day. (For how to freeze steaks, see page 294.)

HOW TO PREP AND BARBECUE PORTERHOUSE STEAKS

1. Lean porterhouse benefits from the rich flavour and slickness of extra-virgin olive oil.

2. Rub the oil evenly all over the steaks to prevent them from sticking to the cooking grill.

3. The oil also helps the seasonings adhere to the meat.

4. Sometimes coarse salt and freshly ground pepper are all you need for a great-tasting steak.

5. Bring the barbecue temperature to 260°C (500°F). A hot cooking grill will sear the steaks quickly.

6. Once the cooking grills are smoking hot, they are easy to clean with a stainless-steel bristle brush.

7. Lay each steak on the cooking grill over a high heat as if it were the small hand of a clock pointing to 10 o'clock, then close the lid.

8. After a couple of minutes, lift each steak with tongs – not a fork! Piercing the steaks would mean losing delicious juices.

9. Rotate the steaks so that they point to 2 o'clock, close the lid and allow them to sear for another minute or two.

10. Flip each steak and check out those handsome cross-hatch grill marks.

11. Putting cross-hatches on the second side is optional. The key now is to finish the steaks, with the lid down, without overcooking them. An internal doneness of 52°C (125°F) will give you a medium-rare steak.

12. As the steaks rest for a few minutes after barbecuing, the internal temperature will climb several degrees and the juices will redistribute evenly.

Occasionally the fat and juices dripping from a steak will cause flare-ups on the barbecue. Don't panic. Simply slide the steak to a cooler area of the grill. If your steak already has good charring on both sides, finish cooking it over indirect heat, with the lid closed. If you want more charring, slide the steak back over a high heat once the flare-ups have died out.

PORTERHOUSE STEAKS WITH RED-EYE BARBECUE SAUCE

SERVES: 4
PREP TIME: 20 MINUTES

HEAT: DIRECT HIGH HEAT 230° TO 290°C (450° TO 550°F)
COOKING TIME: 6 TO 8 MINUTES

SAUCE
15 g (½ g) unsalted butter
2 teaspoons very finely chopped Shallot
1 teaspoon very finely chopped garlic
125 g (4 oz) tomato sauce
4 tablespoons brewed dark-roast coffee or espresso
1 tablespoon balsamic vinegar
1 tablespoon light brown sugar
2 teaspoons ground ancho chilli powder

4 porterhouse steaks, each 300 to 375 g (10 oz to 13 oz) and
    about 2.5 cm (1 inch) thick, trimmed of excess fat
2 tablespoons extra-virgin olive oil
¾ teaspoon sea salt
¾ teaspoon freshly ground black pepper

1. Melt the butter in a saucepan over a medium heat. Add the shallot and cook for about 3 minutes, stirring often, until it begins to brown. Add the garlic and cook for about 1 minute until fragrant. Stir in the rest of the sauce ingredients and bring to a simmer. Reduce the heat to low and simmer for about 10 minutes, stirring often, until slightly reduced. Transfer to a bowl to cool.

2. Lightly brush the steaks on both sides with the oil and season evenly with the salt and pepper. Allow the steaks to stand at room temperature for 20 to 30 minutes before barbecuing. Prepare the barbecue for direct cooking over a high heat.

3. Brush the cooking grills clean. Barbecue the steaks over ***direct high heat***, with the lid closed as much as possible but turning once, until cooked to your desired doneness, 6 to 8 minutes for medium rare. Remove from the barbecue and allow the steaks to rest for 3 to 5 minutes. Serve the steaks warm with the sauce on the side.

Barbecued red onions make a great addition to a steak sandwich, and here they benefit from soaking twice in a bold sweet-and-sour marinade: once before barbecuing and once afterwards.

STEAK SANDWICHES WITH BARBECUED ONIONS AND CREAMY HORSERADISH SAUCE

SERVES: 4
PREP TIME: 15 MINUTES
MARINATING TIME: 30 MINUTES

HEAT: DIRECT HIGH HEAT 230° TO 290°C (450° TO 550°F)
    AND DIRECT MEDIUM HEAT 180° TO 230°C (350° TO 450°F)
COOKING TIME: 7 TO 9 MINUTES

MARINADE
500 ml (17 fl oz/2 cups) red wine
200 ml (7 fl oz) soy sauce
4 tablespoons balsamic vinegar
3 tablespoons dark brown sugar
1 tablespoon finely chopped garlic
1 teaspoon freshly ground black pepper
125 ml (4 fl oz/½ cup) extra-virgin olive oil

½ teaspoon bicarbonate of soda

4 porterhouse steaks, each about 375 g (13 oz) and about
    2.5 cm (1 inch) thick
2 red onions, sliced into 5-mm (¼-inch) rings

125 ml (4 fl oz/½ cup) sour cream
4 tablespoons prepared horseradish
1 teaspoon finely chopped thyme
Sea salt
Freshly ground black pepper

4 crusty bread rolls
2 bunches watercress, trimmed and rinsed

1. Combine the marinade ingredients in a large bowl, whisking in the oil until blended. Divide the marinade, pouring 750 ml (26 fl oz/3 cups) into a non-metallic ovenproof dish and leaving the rest in the bowl. Add the bicarbonate of soda to the marinade in the dish for a tenderising effect (the mixture may fizz a little).

2. Put the steaks into the dish with the marinade and turn to completely coat them. Allow them to marinate at room temperature for 30 minutes, turning once.

3. Place the sliced onions in the bowl with the marinade and gently stir to coat them evenly. Set aside and allow them to marinate alongside the steaks.

4. Mix the sour cream and horseradish in a bowl, then stir in the thyme and season to taste with salt and pepper. Cover and refrigerate until ready to use.

5. Prepare the barbecue for direct cooking over a high heat on one side of the barbecue and a medium heat on the other. Brush the cooking grills clean. Remove the steaks from the dish, allowing most of the marinade to drip back into the dish. Discard the marinade. Barbecue the steaks over *direct high heat*, with the lid closed as much as possible but turning once, until cooked to your desired doneness, 6 to 8 minutes for medium rare. While the steaks are cooking, carefully remove the onions from the marinade, keeping the bowl of marinade close by, and barbecue over *direct medium heat* for 6 to 8 minutes, turning once. Remove the onions from the barbecue and plunge back into the bowl of marinade. Toss to coat and allow the onions to soak up the marinade while the steaks rest for 3 to 5 minutes. Slice and toast the cut sides of the rolls over *direct medium heat*, for about 1 minute.

6. To assemble the sandwiches, slice the steaks on the bias into thin strips. Pile the bottom of a bread roll with onions and layer with strips of steak. Top with horseradish sauce and watercress.

HOW TO CHECK STEAKS FOR DONENESS

1. Because steaks get firmer as they cook, one way to judge their doneness is by lightly squeezing the sides with tongs. It takes time to learn just how firm each type of steak will feel at each level of doneness, but this is how many restaurant chefs work, and it's a technique worth practising.

2. Another popular method is to press the surface of a steak with your fingertip. When the meat is no longer soft, but is not yet firm either, you know a steak has reached medium-rare doneness. See below for more hints on judging doneness by touch.

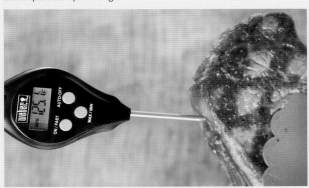

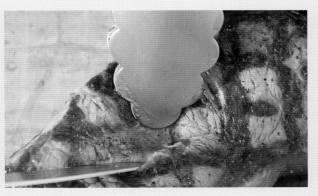

3. A more scientific approach is to use an instant-read thermometer. If you are sure to position the thermometer sensor right in the middle of the steak, you'll have a perfectly accurate reading of doneness.

4. Perhaps the most straightforward approach is to have a look at the colour of the meat inside the steak. On the underside of the steak (the side that will face the plate), cut a little slit down to the centre of the meat and peek inside. When it's cooked just the way you want it, turn the steak over and press the surface with your fingertip. Note how it feels so that next time you won't need to cut into your steak.

HOW TO CHECK DONENESS BY TOUCH

1. Most raw steaks are as soft as the base of your thumb when your hand is relaxed.

2. If you touch your index finger and thumb together, and then press the base of your thumb, that's how most steaks feel when they are rare.

3. If you touch your middle finger and thumb together, and then press the base of your thumb, that's how most steaks feel when they are medium rare.

PANZANELLA STEAK SALAD

SERVES: 4 TO 6
PREP TIME: 20 MINUTES

HEAT: DIRECT AND INDIRECT HIGH HEAT 230° TO 290°C
　　　(450° TO 550°F)
COOKING TIME: 12 TO 16 MINUTES
SPECIAL EQUIPMENT: BAMBOO SKEWERS,
　　　SOAKED IN WATER FOR AT LEAST 30 MINUTES

DRESSING
3 tablespoons red wine vinegar
1 teaspoon sea salt
1 teaspoon freshly ground black pepper
2 teaspoons very finely chopped garlic
125 ml (4 fl oz/½ cup) extra-virgin olive oil

2 porterhouse steaks, each about 375 g (13 oz) and 2.5 cm
　　　(1 inch) thick, trimmed of excess fat
275 g (9 oz) crusty bread, cut into 3.5-cm (1½-inch) cubes
6 roma tomatoes, about 750 g (1½ lb), cut in half
　　　lengthways and deseeded
1 brown onion, cut into 1-cm (½-inch) slices
150 g (5 oz) black olives, pitted
50 g (2 oz) basil leaves, torn into pieces

1. Combine the dressing ingredients in a small bowl, gradually whisking in the oil until it has emulsified.

2. Put the steaks in a shallow dish, pour 3 tablespoons of the dressing on top, and turn to coat them evenly. Allow them to stand at room temperature for 20 to 30 minutes before barbecuing. Set aside the remaining dressing.

3. Put the bread cubes into a large bowl, add 2 tablespoons of the dressing and toss to coat them evenly. Thread the bread cubes on to skewers. Brush the cut sides of the tomatoes and the onion slices with 2 tablespoons of the dressing.

4. Prepare the barbecue for direct and indirect cooking over a high heat.

5. Brush the cooking grills clean. Barbecue the tomatoes and onions over **direct high heat** and the bread skewers over **indirect high heat**, with the lid closed as much as possible, but turning as needed, until the tomatoes are lightly charred, the onions are browned and the bread is toasted. The tomatoes will take 2 to 4 minutes and the onions and bread skewers will take 6 to 8 minutes. Remove the food from the barbecue as it is done.

6. Brush the cooking grills clean. Barbecue the steaks over **direct high heat**, with the lid closed as much as possible but turning once, until cooked to your desired doneness, 6 to 8 minutes for medium rare. Remove from the barbecue and let rest for 3 to 5 minutes.

7. Pull off and discard the tomato skins. Cut the onion, tomatoes and steak into bite-sized chunks, then place in a large serving bowl. Add the remaining dressing, olives, bread cubes and basil and gently mix. Serve immediately.

HOW TO PREP PANZANELLA STEAK SALAD

1. Toss big cubes of dense bread in salad dressing for flavour and even browning.

2. Skewer the bread cubes to make them easier to handle on the barbecue.

3. Firm but ripe roma tomatoes maintain their shape even when you lightly char them.

4. Barbecuing the bread cubes over an indirect heat allows you to brown them slowly, with little risk of burning.

PORTERHOUSE STEAK PAILLARDS

SERVES: 4
PREP TIME: 20 MINUTES

HEAT: DIRECT HIGH HEAT 230° TO 290°C (450° TO 550°F)
COOKING TIME: ABOUT 3 MINUTES

4 porterhouse steaks, each 200 to 250 g (7 to 8 oz) and
  1 to 1.5 cm (½ to ¾ inch) thick, trimmed of all fat
  and silver skin
Extra-virgin olive oil
Sea salt
Freshly ground black pepper

DRESSING
4 tablespoons sour cream
4 tablespoons mayonnaise
2 tablespoons dijon mustard
½ teaspoon worcestershire sauce

1 tomato, about 375 g (13 oz), cut into 4 even slices
4 thin slices red onion
50 g (2 oz) triple cream cheese, cut into thin wedges,
  at room temperature

1. One at a time, place each steak between 2 sheets of plastic wrap and pound to an even 5-mm (¼-inch) thickness. Lightly brush the paillards with oil and season them evenly with salt and pepper.

2. Combine the dressing ingredients in a small bowl, including salt to taste.

3. Prepare the barbecue for direct cooking over a high heat.

4. Lightly brush each tomato slice with oil and season to taste with salt and pepper. Brush the cooking grills clean. Barbecue the tomatoes over *direct high heat* for 2 to 3 minutes until slightly charred on one side. Transfer to a roasting tray, barbecued sides up.

5. Barbecue the paillards over *direct high heat* for 1½ to 2 minutes, with the lid open and turning when the first side is nicely marked. The second side will only take 10 to 15 seconds for medium-rare doneness (the paillards will continue to cook as they rest).

6. Transfer the paillards, with the first barbecued sides facing up, to a serving platter or individual plates. Place a slice of tomato in the centre of each paillard.

7. Evenly divide the dressing over the tomatoes. Separate the slices of onion into rings and place a small mound on the tomatoes. Finish with a piece of cheese and a grinding of pepper on top of each.

Three stages of a steak paillard. On the left, a porterhouse just as you find it at the butcher's. In the centre, a steak trimmed of all the fat around the edges, to make it easier to pound. On the right, an evenly pounded paillard ready for greasing, seasoning and barbecuing.

RED MEAT

HOW TO BUTCHER A BONE-IN RIB JOINT

Many chefs and carnivores will tell you that their favourite steak for barbecuing is a rib-eye. The meat is magnificently tender and flavourful, due in large part to the generous interior marbling of milky white fat. Sadly, though, many supermarket butchers cut rib-eyes too thin, so the steaks tend to overcook rather quickly, squandering some of their magnificence. One solution is to cut your own rib-eyes from a bone-in rib roast, also known as a prime rib.

1. Use a long, sharp knife to cut right along the ribs, separating them from the meat.

2. Now cut along the bone at the base of the joint to separate the meat from the bones completely.

3. Don't throw away those ribs. Barbecue them! See page 85.

4. Trim off most of the surface fat from your boneless rib roast.

5. At this point, you could barbecue the whole boneless joint in one piece for a big event (see page 91), or you can slice it into thick steaks and freeze the ones you don't use right away. (For how to freeze steaks, see page 294.)

6. Use the blade of a carving knife to measure a consistent thickness for each steak.

7. Make a shallow slit at each point where you plan to slice.

8. Slice the steaks as evenly as possible. Avoid sawing back and forth, which tears the surface of the meat and gives the steaks a ragged appearance.

HOW TO PREP RIB-EYE STEAKS

1. As with any steak, trim off any sections along the edges that include more fat than meat.

2. A flavourful cut like rib-eye requires no marinade or elaborate sauce, but consider using a bold blend of dry seasonings as a complement to the meat's richness.

3. With so much marbling in the steak, just a light coating of oil is all you'll need to prevent sticking on the barbecue.

4. Allow your seasoned steaks to stand at room temperature for 20 to 30 minutes before cooking to take the chill off. They will cook a little faster and stay juicier.

RIB-EYE STEAKS
WITH ESPRESSO-CHILLI RUB

SERVES: 4
PREP TIME: 10 MINUTES

HEAT: DIRECT HIGH HEAT 230° TO 290°C (450° TO 550°F)
COOKING TIME: 6 TO 8 MINUTES
SPECIAL EQUIPMENT: SPICE MILL

RUB
2 teaspoons cumin seeds, toasted
2 tablespoons dark-roast coffee or espresso beans
1 tablespoon ground ancho chilli
1 teaspoon sweet paprika
1 teaspoon sea salt
1 teaspoon freshly ground black pepper

4 rib-eye steaks, each about 250 g (8 oz) and 2.5 cm (1 inch) thick
Extra-virgin olive oil

1. Grind the cumin seeds and coffee beans together in a spice mill. Transfer to a small bowl, add the remaining rub ingredients and stir to combine.

2. Lightly brush the steaks with oil and season evenly with the rub, pressing the rub into the meat. Cover and allow to stand at room temperature for 20 to 30 minutes before barbecuing. Prepare the barbecue for direct cooking over a high heat.

3. Brush the cooking grills clean. Barbecue the steaks over *direct high heat*, with the lid closed as much as possible but turning once, until cooked to your desired doneness, 6 to 8 minutes for medium rare. (If flare-ups occur, move the steaks temporarily over indirect high heat.) Remove from the barbecue and allow to rest for 3 to 5 minutes. Serve warm.

HOW TO PREP ESPRESSO-CHILLI RUB

1. A coffee grinder works well for grinding spices, too. Clean it out later by whirling raw white rice in it to absorb the spice residue.

2. Grind your cumin and coffee to a coarse texture, similar to that of sea salt.

HOW TO MAKE PAN-ROASTED CHILLI SALSA

1. The distinctive flavour of the salsa on the opposite page comes mostly from an ancho chilli, which is a dried poblano chilli. It is not terribly spicy, but it has a brilliant sweet heat, especially when it is toasted first.

2. Cut off and discard the stem of the chilli, then slice open the chilli so that you can lay it flat like a book.

3. A lot of the heat is in the seeds, so tap the chilli on a board or use a knife to remove them, if you like.

4. Use a spatula to flatten the chilli in a hot, dry frying pan. This step brings out big flavour. Next, soak the chilli in hot water for 20 to 30 minutes.

5. You can blacken and blister tomatoes, onions, a jalapeño chilli and garlic in the same pan. Don't be afraid to get them dark and caramelised.

6. Puréeing all the ingredients with some fresh lime juice, salt and oregano gives you an exciting salsa to serve with steaks. If it seems a little thick, thin it out with a touch of the water used to soak the ancho chilli.

RIB-EYE STEAKS WITH PAN-ROASTED CHILLI SALSA

SERVES: 4
PREP TIME: 20 MINUTES

HEAT: DIRECT HIGH HEAT 230° TO 290°C (450° TO 550°F)
COOKING TIME: 6 TO 8 MINUTES
SPECIAL EQUIPMENT: 30-CM (12-INCH) CAST-IRON PAN

SALSA
1 dried ancho chilli
1 tablespoon extra-virgin olive oil
4 ripe tomatoes, quartered, with stalks and seeds removed
1 slice white onion, about 1.5 cm (¾ inch) thick
1 jalapeño chilli, stem removed
1 large garlic clove (do not peel)
1 teaspoon fresh lime juice
½ teaspoon sea salt
¼ teaspoon dried oregano

RUB
1 tablespoon sea salt
2 teaspoons paprika
1 teaspoon onion granules
1 teaspoon freshly ground black pepper

4 rib-eye steaks, each about 250 g (8 oz) and 2.5 cm
    (1 inch) thick
Extra-virgin olive oil

1. Bring 500 ml (17 fl oz/2 cups) of water to a simmer in a small saucepan. Preheat a 30-cm (12-inch) cast-iron or ovenproof frying pan over a medium heat on your side burner or stove top.

2. Remove and discard the stem from the ancho chilli, then open like a book and discard the seeds. Flatten the chilli and place it in the hot, dry pan. Press down on the chilli with a spatula to flatten it and dry fry until the aroma is obvious and you begin to see wisps of smoke. Transfer the chilli to the pan of hot water and soak for 20 to 30 minutes until it is very soft. Reserve the water; you may need a little to thin out the salsa.

3. Meanwhile, add the oil, tomatoes, onion, jalapeño and garlic to the pan and fry over a medium heat for 10 to 15 minutes, turning occasionally, until the vegetables have blackened and blistered in spots. Remove the vegetables as they are finished cooking (they may not finish cooking at the same time). Allow them to cool until you can handle the garlic, then squeeze the garlic out of its skin into a blender or food processor. Add the ancho chilli, tomatoes, onion, jalapeño, lime juice, salt and oregano and process to make a salsa. For a thinner consistency, add a little of the water used to soak the ancho chilli.

4. Mix the rub ingredients together in a small bowl. Lightly brush the steaks on both sides with oil. Season evenly with the rub. Allow the steaks to stand at room temperature for 20 to 30 minutes before barbecuing. Prepare the barbecue for direct cooking over a high heat.

5. Brush the cooking grills clean. Barbecue the steaks over **direct high heat**, with the lid closed as much as possible but turning once until cooked to your desired doneness, 6 to 8 minutes for medium rare. (If flare-ups occur, move the steaks temporarily over indirect high heat.) Remove from the barbecue and allow to rest for 3 to 5 minutes. Serve warm with the salsa.

HOW TO BARBECUE PIADINI

1. Your dough should be at room temperature and you should have flour on both your board and your rolling pin.

2. Roll each piece of dough to a diameter of 20 to 25 cm (8 to 10 inches) and a thickness of about 8 mm (⅓ inch). Stack the dough rounds between sheets of baking paper.

3. Barbecue the dough rounds over direct medium heat, with the lid closed, until they bubble on top and turn gold brown on the bottom. Then turn them over with a spatula to toast the other side.

4. While the second side grills, distribute the cheese on top so that it begins to melt. Rotate each dough round and move it around the barbecue as needed for even cooking.

STEAK AND GORGONZOLA PIADINI

SERVES: 4
PREP TIME: 30 MINUTES
RISING TIME: 1½ TO 2 HOURS

HEAT: DIRECT HIGH HEAT 230° TO 290°C (450° TO 550°F) AND DIRECT MEDIUM HEAT 180° TO 230°C (350° TO 450°F)
COOKING TIME: 14 TO 18 MINUTES
SPECIAL EQUIPMENT: ELECTRIC STAND MIXER

DOUGH
350 ml (12 fl oz) warm water (40° to 45°C/100° to 110°F)
1 sachet instant dry yeast
½ teaspoon sugar
625 g (1¼ lb) strong plain white flour, plus more for rolling the dough
3 tablespoons extra-virgin olive oil
2 teaspoons sea salt

DRESSING
2 tablespoons extra-virgin olive oil
2 teaspoons balsamic vinegar
½ teaspoon very finely chopped garlic
½ teaspoon dijon mustard
¼ teaspoon sea salt
⅛ teaspoon freshly ground black pepper

2 rib-eye steaks, each 175 g to 250 g (6 to 8 oz) and about 2.5 cm (1 inch) thick
Extra-virgin olive oil
Sea salt
Freshly ground black pepper
250 g (8 oz) gorgonzola dolce or other soft, mild blue cheese, broken into small pieces
75 g (3 oz) baby rocket or spinach

1. Combine the water, yeast and sugar in the bowl of an electric stand mixer. Stir briefly and allow to stand for 5 minutes, or until the top surface has a thin, frothy layer. (This indicates that the yeast is active.) Add the flour, the oil and salt. Fit the mixer with the dough hook and mix on low speed for about 1 minute or until the dough begins to come together. Increase the speed to medium and continue to mix for about 10 minutes until the dough is slightly sticky, smooth and elastic. Form the dough into a ball and place in a lightly greased bowl. Turn it over to coat all sides and tightly cover the bowl with plastic wrap. Allow the dough to rise in a warm place for 1½ to 2 hours until it has doubled in size.

2. Whisk the dressing ingredients together in a small bowl.

3. Trim most of the exterior fat from the steaks and then allow to stand at room temperature for 20 to 30 minutes before barbecuing. Prepare the barbecue for direct cooking over a high heat.

Piadini are thin folded flat breads with a long history in Romagna, Italy. Filled with meat, cheeses and vegetables, they make a fun snack or not-so-ordinary sandwiches.

4. Knock back the dough in the bowl. Transfer to a lightly floured surface and cut into 4 equal-sized pieces. Cut baking paper into 25-cm (10-inch) squares and lightly grease each sheet on one side. Roll each piece of dough flat into rounds 20 to 25 cm (8 to 10 inches) in diameter. Lay each dough round on a greased sheet of paper and lightly grease the top of each round. Stack the dough rounds between the sheets of paper and set aside on a roasting tray.

5. Lightly brush both sides of the steaks with oil and season them evenly with salt and pepper. Brush the cooking grills clean. Barbecue the steaks over **direct high heat**, with the lid closed as much as possible but turning once, until cooked to your desired doneness, 6 to 8 minutes for medium rare. (If flare-ups occur, move the steaks temporarily over indirect high heat.) Remove from the barbecue, cover and keep warm.

6. Reduce the temperature of the barbecue to a medium heat. Lay 2 dough rounds over **direct medium heat**, with the paper sides facing up. Grab one corner of the paper with tongs and peel it off. Barbecue the rounds for 2 to 3 minutes, rotating them occasionally for even cooking, until they are golden and marked on the underside.

7. Turn the crusts over and distribute one quarter of the cheese over each crust, leaving a 1-cm (½-inch) border round the edges. Continue cooking over **direct medium heat** for about 2 minutes, rotating the crusts occasionally for even cooking, until the crusts are crisp and the cheese has melted. Transfer the barbecued crusts to a work surface. Repeat with the remaining crusts.

8. Place the greens in a salad bowl, pour the dressing over the greens and toss to combine.

9. Cut the steaks into thin slices, removing any pockets of fat, and distribute evenly over the crusts, then top with equal portions of the salad. Fold each piadini in half and eat it like a sandwich or, for easier eating or sharing, cut each piadini in half with a serrated knife after folding.

HOW TO CUT BONE-IN STEAKS FROM A RIB JOINT

You can tell a lot about the taste and tenderness of a cut of meat by where it comes from on the animal. The parts of the animal that get a lot of exercise, like the shoulder and the back end (the topside), develop more tough connective tissue than the parts of the animal that don't work so hard, like the porterhouse and rib sections. From the T-bone, we get tender steaks like the porterhouse and the eye fillet. The rib section, pictured below, is where you'll find incredibly tender and succulent rib steaks.

1. Stand the rib joint on end so that you can clearly see the tips of the bones.

2. The advantage of barbecuing rib-eye steaks with the bones attached is that the bones will add mouthwatering flavour to the steaks and help keep the meat moist during cooking.

3. Using a very sharp knife, slice between the bones, trying not to saw back and forth too much. A hollow-ground knife will give the cleanest cut and best appearance.

4. What you have now is a big, brawny masterpiece called a bone-in rib-eye steak.

HOW TO MAKE GARLIC PASTE

Fresh garlic on a steak lights up all the endorphins in my brain. When time is short and I'm craving a full-throttled steak experience, I always turn to chopped garlic. The only problem is, I often barbecue my steak over very high heat, and so the bits and pieces of garlic sometimes burn, turning them bitter. I avoid this problem by making a garlic paste instead. The paste melts into the surface of the meat, and all the fat and juices collected there prevent it from burning.

1. Begin by thinly slicing the garlic with a chef's knife.

2. Finely chop the garlic, keeping the knife tip on the board and moving the blade from side to side.

3. Add some sea salt for flavour, crumbling it between your fingers if it is very coarse.

4. The salt will also hold the garlic together while you chop it very finely.

5. Now, drag the side of the knife over the garlic, putting extra pressure near the tip, to smash the garlic into a paste.

6. Keep swishing the knife back and forth until the garlic is so thin it's almost transparent. Now it's ready to smear on your steaks.

GARLIC-CRUSTED RIB-EYE STEAKS WITH BARBECUED BROCCOLINI

SERVES: 4
PREP TIME: 15 MINUTES

HEAT: DIRECT AND INDIRECT HIGH HEAT
    230° to 290°C (450° to 550°F)
COOKING TIME: 11 TO 15 MINUTES

PASTE
4 large garlic cloves
1 tablespoon sea salt
15 g (½ oz) flat-leaf parsley, finely chopped
4 tablespoons extra-virgin olive oil
2 teaspoons balsamic vinegar
1 teaspoon freshly ground black pepper

4 bone-in rib-eye steaks, 280 to 350 g (10 to 12 oz) each and
    about 2.5 cm (1 inch) thick, trimmed of excess fat
175 g (6 oz) broccolini, with stalks no wider than 1 cm (½ inch)
Extra-virgin olive oil
Sea salt

1. Finely chop the garlic on a chopping board, then sprinkle with the salt. Use the side of a knife to smash the garlic into a paste. Put the garlic paste into a small bowl and add the remaining paste ingredients.

2. Smear the paste evenly over both sides of each steak. Allow the steaks to stand at room temperature for 20 to 30 minutes before barbecuing.

3. Meanwhile, soak the broccolini in a large bowl of water for 20 to 30 minutes so that they absorb the water. This will help them to steam a little on the barbecue.

4. Prepare your grill for direct and indirect cooking over high heat.

5. Pour off the water from the bowl of broccolini. Lightly drizzle some oil over the broccolini and season with ½ teaspoon salt. Toss to coat them evenly with oil and salt.

6. Brush the cooking grills clean. Barbecue the steaks over **direct high heat**, with the lid closed as much as possible but turning once, until cooked to your desired doneness, 6 to 8 minutes for medium rare. (If flare-ups occur, move the steaks temporarily over indirect high heat.) Remove from the barbecue and allow to rest while you cook the broccolini.

7. Use tongs to lift the broccolini and allow any excess oil to drip back into the bowl. Barbecue the broccolini over **direct high heat** for 3 to 4 minutes, with the lid closed as much as possible but turning occasionally, until lightly charred. Finish cooking the broccolini over **indirect high heat** for 2 to 3 minutes. Serve warm with the steaks.

HOW TO MAKE TEA PASTE

1. A bit of earl grey tea leaves adds a deep, unexpected fragrance to this spice rub.

2. To get the best peppery zing, grind whole black peppercorns in a spice mill with the other seasonings. As with other spices, whole peppercorns retain more aromatic flavour than pre-ground pepper.

3. Pulse all the seasonings into a coarse blend to release their flavours, then mix them in a bowl with oil to make a paste.

TEA-RUBBED FILLET STEAKS WITH BUTTERY MUSHROOMS

SERVES: 4
PREP TIME: 25 MINUTES

HEAT: DIRECT MEDIUM HEAT 180° TO 230°C
(350° TO 450°F)
COOKING TIME: ABOUT 8 MINUTES
SPECIAL EQUIPMENT: SPICE MILL, 30-CM (12-INCH)
CAST-IRON FRYING PAN

PASTE
2 teaspoons (about 2 tea bags) earl grey tea leaves
1 teaspoon whole black peppercorns
1 teaspoon dried tarragon
1 teaspoon sea salt
½ teaspoon dried thyme
3 tablespoons extra-virgin olive oil

4 eye fillet steaks, each about 250 g (8 oz) and
3.5 cm (1½ inches) thick

MUSHROOMS
250 g (8 oz) button mushrooms
25 g (1 oz) unsalted butter
2 tablespoons extra-virgin olive oil
4 large garlic cloves, thinly sliced
¼ teaspoon sea salt
⅛ teaspoon freshly ground black pepper
15 g (½ oz) flat-leaf parsley, roughly chopped
1 teaspoon sherry or red wine vinegar

1. Whirl the tea leaves, peppercorns, tarragon, salt and thyme in a spice mill until finely ground. Pour the spice mix into a bowl, add the oil and stir to make a paste.

2. Brush all sides of each fillet with the paste, then allow to stand at room temperature for 20 to 30 minutes before barbecuing.

3. Before you cook the steaks, prepare the mushrooms and have all the other ingredients in place. Lay the mushrooms on their sides and cut off a 5-mm (¼-inch) slice lengthways, then roll the mushrooms over so the flat sides are on your chopping board and the mushrooms no longer roll around. Cut the mushrooms lengthways into 5-mm (¼-inch) slices.

4. Prepare the barbecue for direct cooking over a medium heat.

5. Brush the cooking grills clean. Barbecue the steaks over **direct medium heat**, with the lid closed as much as possible but turning once, until cooked to your desired doneness, about 8 minutes for medium rare. Remove from the barbecue and allow the steaks to rest while you sauté the mushrooms.

6. Melt the butter with the oil in a 30-cm (12-inch) cast-iron frying pan over a high heat on your barbecue's side burner or your stove top. Add the mushrooms and spread them out so that most are touching the bottom of the pan. Cook the

mushrooms without moving them for 2 minutes, then stir and add the garlic, salt and pepper and cook for a further 2 to 3 minutes, stirring 2 or 3 times, until the mushrooms are barely tender. Add the parsley and vinegar and mix well. Season to taste with salt and pepper, if needed. Spoon the hot mushrooms over the steaks.

HOW TO BROWN MUSHROOMS

1. Cut off one round edge to make a flat, stable surface.

2. Then cut into 5-mm (¼-inch) slices.

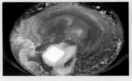

3. Melt the butter with a little oil, which helps to prevent the butter from burning.

4. Spread the mushrooms in a single layer and don't touch them for 2 minutes.

5. Add the salt towards the end of cooking because it draws moisture out of the mushrooms and hinders browning.

6. A little sherry vinegar near the end of cooking cuts the richness of the butter.

7. By resisting the urge to stir the mushrooms often, you will brown them better and create deeper flavours.

HOW TO MAKE FLAVOURED BUTTER

If you like to barbecue steaks – or any kind of meat, fish or poultry for that matter – I think you should have at least one flavoured butter waiting for you at all times in the refrigerator or freezer. One of the surest ways to please your palate and delight your guests is to crown each barbecued steak with a savoury slice of butter blended with the flavours of your choice. The heat of the steak will melt the butter and send the flavours running to mingle with the meat juices for a luxurious sauce.

1. Start by mixing softened butter with fresh herbs and other seasonings, along with Shallots that have been simmered in red wine.

2. Shape the butter into a little log on baking paper.

3. Wrap the log tightly in the paper and squeeze both ends to compact it.

4. Twist the ends of the baking paper in opposite directions and store the flavoured butter in the refrigerator or freezer.

5. When it's time to serve, trim off one end. Remember to remove the frozen butter from the freezer in enough time to thaw.

6. Cut as many slices as you need and pull off the paper. Re-wrap any that is left over and return to the refrigerator or freezer.

HOW TO MAKE CROSS-HATCH MARKS

1. For a nice diamond pattern on your steaks, position them at a 45-degree angle to the bars of the cooking grill.

2. After searing for a couple of minutes, rotate your steaks 90 degrees.

3. Turn the steaks over and, if you like, mark the other side in the same way.

RED MEAT

T-BONE STEAKS WITH RED WINE-SHALLOT BUTTER

SERVES: 4 TO 6
PREP TIME: 15 MINUTES

HEAT: DIRECT HIGH HEAT 230° TO 290°C (450° TO 550°F)
COOKING TIME: 8 TO 10 MINUTES

BUTTER
3 tablespoons hearty red wine
2 tablespoons very finely chopped shallot
125 g (4 oz) unsalted butter, softened
1 tablespoon very finely chopped flat-leaf parsley,
1 tablespoon very finely chopped tarragon
½ teaspoon sea salt
¼ teaspoon freshly ground black pepper

4 T-bone steaks, each about 500 g (1 lb)
    and 2.5 cm (1 inch) thick
2 tablespoons extra-virgin olive oil
2 teaspoons sea salt
½ teaspoon freshly ground black pepper

1. Bring the wine and shallot to the boil in a small, heavy-based saucepan over a high heat. Boil for 3 to 5 minutes until the wine

is reduced to a glaze and is absorbed mostly by the shallots. Transfer to a bowl and allow to cool completely.

2. Add the butter, parsley, tarragon, salt and pepper to the shallot-wine reduction and mix to combine. Scoop the mixture out of the bowl on to a sheet of baking paper. Loosely shape the mixture into a log about 2.5 cm (1 inch) in diameter. Roll the log in the paper and twist the ends in opposite directions to form an even cylinder. Refrigerate until about 1 hour before serving. (The butter can be made up to 1 week ahead.)

3. Allow the steaks to stand at room temperature for 20 to 30 minutes before barbecuing. Prepare the barbecue for direct cooking over a high heat.

4. Lightly brush the steaks with the oil and season evenly with the salt and pepper. Brush the cooking grills clean. Barbecue the steaks over **direct high heat**, with the lid closed as much as possible but turning once, until cooked to your desired doneness, 8 to 10 minutes for medium rare. (If flare-ups occur, move the steaks temporarily over indirect high heat.) Remove the steaks from the barbecue and allow to rest for 3 to 5 minutes. Serve the steaks hot with the butter smeared over the top.

HOW TO BARBECUE REALLY THICK STEAKS

One of the noblest dishes in the pantheon of international barbecued steaks is Bistecca alla Fiorentina, an enormous T-bone steak jockeyed over and beside the hot coals until the outside is crisply charred and the interior is just rosy red and deliciously tender. The seasonings are pure and simple – nothing more than coarse salt, preferably sea salt, and freshly ground black pepper. The finishing touches are a squeeze of lemon juice and a drizzle of the best olive oil in the house.

1. Whereas most steaks do best when you don't fiddle with them on the barbecue, this one is so thick and monstrous that you will need to move it every few minutes.

2. Charcoal fires are inherently uneven, so don't be surprised if one part of the steak browns faster than another. Move the steak around to compensate for the unevenness.

3. This is a case where the charcoal is as much an ingredient in the recipe as the seasonings. The smokiness permeates the meat and delivers great primordial flavours.

BISTECCA ALLA FIORENTINA

SERVES: 4
PREP TIME: 5 MINUTES

HEAT: DIRECT AND INDIRECT MEDIUM HEAT
   180° TO 230°C (350° TO 450°F)
COOKING TIME: 25 TO 27 MINUTES

1 T-bone steak, about 1.25 kg (2½ lb) and
   5.5 cm (2¼ inches) thick
Grey or coarse sea salt
Freshly ground black pepper
2 lemons
Extra-virgin olive oil

1. Allow the steak to rest at room temperature for 1 hour
before cooking. During this hour, you can prepare and cook
the barbecue-baked beans, and then keep them warm.

2. Prepare the barbecue for direct and indirect cooking over a
medium heat.

3. Liberally season the steak on both sides with salt and pepper.
Rub the seasoning into the meat.

4. Barbecue the steak over **direct medium heat** for 10 to
12 minutes, rotating the steak 45 degrees about every 3 minutes
to create a nice crust and turning once. Move the steak over
indirect medium heat and continue to cook until the internal
temperature reaches 52°C (125°F) for rare, about 15 minutes,
rotating the steak as needed for even cooking. Allow the steak to
rest for about 10 minutes before carving.

5. To carve the steak, cut the fillet side first as close to the bone
as possible. Repeat the procedure for the sirloin. Slice each
piece crossways into 1-cm (½-inch) slices, keeping the slices
intact. Transfer to a serving platter and reassemble the steak
with the bone. Drizzle some extra-virgin olive oil over the slices
and serve with lemon and barbecue-baked beans.

BARBECUE-BAKED BEANS ALLA CONTADINA
PREP TIME: 10 MINUTES

HEAT: INDIRECT MEDIUM HEAT 180° TO 230°C
   (350° TO 450°F)
COOKING TIME: ABOUT 15 MINUTES

2 tins (425 g/14 oz each) cannellini beans, rinsed
175 g (6 oz) vegetable stock
4 tablespoons tomato sauce
1 tablespoon extra-virgin olive oil
1 teaspoon very finely chopped thyme
½ teaspoon sea salt
1 teaspoon very finely chopped garlic
1 tablespoon plus 1 teaspoon very finely chopped
   flat-leaf parsley

1. Prepare the barbecue for indirect cooking over a medium
heat.

2. Place the beans in a 23-cm (9-inch) square ovenproof dish.

3. Combine the stock, tomato sauce, oil, thyme and salt in a
small bowl, then pour over the beans. Lightly press the beans
so they are all immersed in the liquid. Bake the beans over
indirect medium heat for about 15 minutes, with the lid closed,
until they are bubbling and most of the liquid has reduced.

4. Blend the garlic with the parsley and scatter over the beans.
Serve with the steak.

HOW TO CARVE BISTECCA

1. The T-bone is a large cut that
includes a T-shaped bone, with
meat from the sirloin on one side
and the fillet on the other.

2. The traditional way to serve
it is to cut all the meat from the
bone in 2 big sections and then
slice it.

3. Cut the sirloin crossways in
nice thick slices.

4. Also cut the fillet section in
thick slices, and then arrange all
the slices back along the bone.

SKIRT STEAKS WITH DESIREE POTATOES AND FETA

SERVES: 4
PREP TIME: 15 MINUTES

HEAT: INDIRECT AND DIRECT HIGH HEAT
    230° TO 290°C (450° TO 550°F)
COOKING TIME: 34 TO 46 MINUTES
SPECIAL EQUIPMENT: PERFORATED GRILL PAN, LARGE
    DISPOSABLE FOIL TIN

RUB
1 teaspoon sea salt
1 teaspoon ground cumin
½ teaspoon granulated garlic
¼ teaspoon freshly ground black pepper

750 g (1½ lb) small desiree potatoes, 3.5 cm to 5 cm
    (1½ to 2 inches) in diameter, cut into quarters
2 tablespoons extra-virgin olive oil
½ teaspoon sea salt
2 skirt steaks, about 375 g (13 oz) each, trimmed of
    excess surface fat
65 g (2½ lb) feta cheese, crumbled
2 tablespoons chopped flat-leaf parsley
Sea salt
Freshly ground black pepper

1. Prepare the barbecue for indirect and direct cooking over a high heat.

2. Combine the rub ingredients in a small bowl.

3. Combine the potatoes, oil and salt in a large bowl and stir to coat them evenly.

4. Preheat a grill pan over **_indirect high heat_** for about 10 minutes. Add the potatoes to the pan and barbecue them for 30 to 40 minutes, with the lid closed as much as possible but turning them 2 or 3 times, until the potatoes are golden brown and tender.

5. After the potatoes have cooked for about 10 minutes, season the steaks evenly with the rub, pressing the spices into the meat. Allow the meat to stand at room temperature for 20 to 30 minutes before barbecuing.

6. When the potatoes are fully cooked, transfer them to a large disposable foil tin. Add the cheese and parsley and mix well, then season to taste with salt and pepper. To keep the potatoes warm, place the pan over indirect heat while the steaks cook.

7. Barbecue the steaks over **_direct high heat_**, with the lid closed as much as possible but turning once, until cooked to your desired doneness, 4 to 6 minutes for medium rare. Transfer the steaks to a chopping board and allow to rest for 3 to 5 minutes. Keep the potatoes warm on the barbecue. Cut the meat across the grain into thin slices. Serve warm with the potatoes.

HOW TO PREP SKIRT STEAK

1. Trim away most of the fat that clings to both sides of the skirt steaks with a sharp knife.

2. Thoroughly trimming the fat will help prevent flare-ups.

3. Working with lengths of about 30 cm (12 inches) makes steaks easier to handle on the barbecue.

4. Season the meat generously with the rub, patting and massaging it in with your fingertips so it won't fall off during barbecuing.

RED MEAT

CARNE ASADA WITH BLACK BEAN AND AVOCADO SALSA

SERVES: 4 TO 6
PREP TIME: 20 MINUTES

HEAT: DIRECT HIGH HEAT 230° TO 290°C (450° TO 550°F)
COOKING TIME: 4 TO 6 MINUTES

SALSA
1 can (425 g/14 oz) black beans, rinsed
1 ripe haas avocado, finely chopped
150 g (5 oz) white onion, finely chopped and rinsed in a sieve
175 g (6 oz) ripe tomato, finely chopped
2 tablespoons roughly chopped coriander
1 tablespoon fresh lime juice
½ teaspoon sea salt
¼ teaspoon chipotle chilli powder
¼ teaspoon ground cumin
⅛ teaspoon freshly ground black pepper

RUB
1 teaspoon chipotle chilli powder
1 teaspoon sea salt
½ teaspoon ground cumin
¼ teaspoon freshly ground black pepper

750 g (1½ lb) skirt steak, trimmed of excess fat
Extra-virgin olive oil

Raw onions can taste a little harsh in a salsa, but a good rinse will take the edge off.

1. Combine the salsa ingredients in a non-metallic bowl. Cover with plastic wrap, pressing the film directly on to the surface and set aside at room temperature for as long as 2 hours before serving.

2. Mix the rub ingredients together in a small bowl. Cut the steak into 30-cm (12-inch) lengths to make them easier to handle on the barbecue. Lightly coat both sides of the steaks with oil. Season evenly with the rub and allow to stand at room temperature for 20 to 30 minutes before barbecuing. Prepare the barbecue for direct cooking over a high heat.

3. Brush the cooking grills clean. Barbecue the steaks over **direct high heat**, with the lid closed as much as possible but turning once, until cooked to your desired doneness, 4 to 6 minutes for medium rare. Remove the steaks from the barbecue and allow them to rest for 3 to 5 minutes.

4. Cut the steaks across the grain into 1-cm (½-inch) slices. Serve warm with the salsa.

HOW TO PREP SHALLOTS

1. Trim off most of each root end.

2. Peel off the papery skin.

3. Spread the shallots on foil and drizzle with oil.

4. Wrap the foil over the shallots to make a neat packet.

HOW TO PREP OYSTER BLADE STEAKS

1. Some oyster blade steaks, like the one on the right, have a tough streak running down the centre.

2. It's more difficult to see it after the steak is cooked.

3. To ensure that every slice is tender, cut away that tough area before serving.

BISTRO STEAKS WITH MUSTARD CREAM SAUCE

SERVES: 4
PREP TIME: 15 MINUTES

HEAT: INDIRECT AND DIRECT MEDIUM HEAT
180° TO 230°C (350° TO 450°F)
COOKING TIME: ABOUT 1 HOUR

8 large shallots, about 375 g (13 oz) total
Extra-virgin olive oil
1¾ teaspoons sea salt
1 teaspoon dried thyme
1 teaspoon paprika
¾ teaspoon freshly ground black pepper
4 oyster blade steaks, each 175 to 250 g (6 to 8 oz) and about
    2.5 cm (1 inch) thick
125 ml (4 fl oz/½ cup) sour cream
1 tablespoon dijon mustard

1. Prepare the barbecue for indirect and direct cooking over a medium heat.

2. Peel and trim the shallots, removing most of each root end. Cut the larger shallots in half lengthways or pull apart the distinct halves. Pile the shallots in the middle of a large square of aluminium foil. Drizzle with 1 tablespoon of oil and season with ¼ teaspoon of the salt. Fold up the sides and seal to make a packet. Barbecue over *indirect medium heat* for 20 to 30 minutes, with the lid closed as much as possible but turning once or twice, until a knife slides easily in and out of the shallots. Open the packet and continue to cook the shallots in the foil for 20 to 30 minutes more, turning the shallots very gently once or twice, until nicely browned. Remove the packet from the barbecue.

3. Mix the remaining 1½ teaspoons of salt with the thyme, paprika and pepper in a small bowl. Lightly coat the steaks on both sides with oil, then season evenly with the spices. Allow the steaks to stand at room temperature for 20 to 30 minutes before barbecuing.

4. Combine the sour cream and mustard in a small bowl.

5. Brush the cooking grills clean. Barbecue the steaks over *direct medium heat*, with the lid closed as much as possible but turning once, until cooked to your desired doneness, 8 to 10 minutes for medium rare. At the same time reheat the packet of shallots over *indirect medium heat*. Remove the steaks from the barbecue and allow them to rest for 3 to 5 minutes before slicing. While the steaks rest, remove any charred outer layers from the shallots.

6. Cut each steak lengthways on either side of the gristle that runs down the middle. Thinly slice the steak against the grain and overlap the slices on serving dishes. Serve the steaks warm with the shallots and sauce.

SESAME-GINGER FLANK STEAK WITH ASPARAGUS AND GOMASHIO

SERVES: 4 TO 6
PREP TIME: 25 MINUTES
MARINATING TIME: 3 TO 4 HOURS

HEAT: DIRECT MEDIUM HEAT 180° TO 230°C
(350° TO 450°F)
COOKING TIME: 12 TO 16 MINUTES
SPECIAL EQUIPMENT: PESTLE AND MORTAR

MARINADE
5 tablespoons soy sauce
2 tablespoons sugar
3 tablespoons rice wine vinegar
2 tablespoons toasted sesame oil
1 tablespoon very finely chopped garlic
1½ tablespoons grated fresh root ginger
1½ teaspoons sambal oelek or other ground fresh chilli paste
150 g (5 oz) spring onions, white and light green parts, finely chopped
15 g (½ oz) coriander, coarsely chopped

1 flank steak, 750 g to 1kg (1½ to 2 lb) and about
1.5 cm (¾ inch) thick

GOMASHIO
40 g (1½ oz) sesame seeds
1 teaspoon sea salt

ASPARAGUS
1 large bunch asparagus, about 500 g (1 lb)
1 tablespoon extra-virgin olive oil
½ teaspoon sea salt

2 tablespoons finely chopped coriander or
flat-leaf parsley

1. Whisk the soy sauce, sugar, vinegar, oil, garlic, ginger and chilli paste together in a small bowl. Add the spring onions and coriander. Place the steak in a glass or stainless-steel dish and pour in the marinade, turning the steak to coat both sides. Cover and refrigerate for 3 to 4 hours, turning the steak once or twice.

2. Toast the sesame seeds in a clean, dry non-stick frying pan over a low heat for 2 to 3 minutes, shaking and stirring until the seeds are golden brown, but before they begin to pop. Turn them out on to a plate and allow to cool for 10 minutes. Add the sea salt and combine in a pestle and mortar. Lightly crush the seeds so that some texture remains; do not make a fine powder. (The unused portion can be stored in a glass jar in the refrigerator for up to 2 months.)

3. Snap or cut off the dry, woody ends from the asparagus spears. Lightly coat them with the oil and season with the salt.

4. Prepare the barbecue for direct cooking over a medium heat.

HOW TO MAKE GOMASHIO

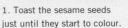

1. Toast the sesame seeds just until they start to colour.

2. Grind coarsely with sea salt to make a delicious seasoning.

HOW TO SLICE FLANK STEAK

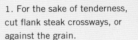

1. For the sake of tenderness, cut flank steak crossways, or against the grain.

2. Keep the slices no thicker than about 8 mm (⅓ inch).

5. Remove the steak from the refrigerator and allow to stand at room temperature for 20 to 30 minutes before barbecuing. Brush the cooking grills clean. Barbecue the steak over **direct medium heat**, with the lid closed as much as possible but turning once, until cooked to your desired doneness, 8 to 10 minutes for medium rare. Transfer to a chopping board and allow to rest while you barbecue the asparagus.

6. Arrange the asparagus perpendicular to the bars on the grill. Barbecue over **direct medium heat** for 4 to 6 minutes, with the lid closed as much as possible but rolling the spears a couple of times, until lightly charred and crisp-tender. Remove them from the barbecue and arrange on one side of a large platter.

7. Thinly slice the steak on the bias, then arrange it next to the asparagus. Sprinkle over the gomashio and coriander. Serve warm.

HOW TO STUFF AND ROLL FLANK STEAK

1. Trim the silver skin and most of the fat from the surface of the meat.

2. Holding your knife parallel to the board, make a shallow cut along the length of the steak.

3. Slice again, making the cut a little deeper.

4. Keep making strokes with the tip of your knife as you open up the meat with your other hand.

5. Continue cutting until you come within about 1 cm (½ inch) from the opposite edge.

6. Now open the steak like a book, laying it flat.

7. Turn the steak over and carefully trim off the seam that sticks up.

8. Turn the steak back over so the cut side is facing up.

9. With the grain of the meat running horizontally, spread the stuffing mixture to within 2.5 cm (1 inch) of the outer edges and a few centimetres (inches) from the top.

10. Roll up the meat from the bottom edge to the top.

11. With no stuffing at the top of the meat, all the ingredients will stay nicely inside the roll.

12. Tie the roll every couple of centimetres (inches) with lengths of butcher's string.

RED MEAT

FLANK STEAK WITH ROASTED CAPSICUM AND FETA STUFFING

SERVES: 6
PREP TIME: 40 MINUTES

HEAT: INDIRECT MEDIUM HEAT 180° TO 230°C
    (350° TO 450°F)
COOKING TIME: 20 TO 30 MINUTES
SPECIAL EQUIPMENT: BUTCHER'S STRING

75 g (3 oz) feta cheese, drained and crumbled
50 g (2 oz) dried breadcrumbs
1 small red capsicum, roasted, peeled, deseeded and diced
1 large garlic clove
25 g (1 oz) flat-leaf parsley
1 tablespoon thyme
½ teaspoon sea salt
¼ teaspoon freshly ground black pepper

2 flank steaks, about 750 g (1½ lb) each
1 tablespoon extra-virgin olive oil
Sea salt
Freshly ground black pepper

1. Combine the cheese, breadcrumbs and diced capsicum in a bowl. Finely chop the garlic and herbs together and add to the bowl, then blend thoroughly with a fork. Season with the salt and pepper.

2. Lay out the flank steak on a chopping board. Starting near one end of the steak, carefully insert a boning knife horizontally into one long edge (the edge parallel to the grain), splitting the steak evenly top to bottom. Continue this cut until the entire steak can be opened up like a book (see directions at left). Repeat with the other flank steak.

3. Prepare your barbecue for indirect cooking over a medium heat.

4. Evenly spread the stuffing mixture over the inside of the butterflied steaks to within 2.5 cm (1 inch) of the edges and a few centimetres (inches) from the top (you may not need all of it). Be careful not to overstuff or it will just fall out and make it more difficult to roll. Roll up the steaks around the filling, with the grain running the length of the roll. Tie the rolls every few centimetres (inches) with butcher's string. Brush the outside of the rolls with oil and lightly season with salt and pepper.

5. Brush the cooking grills clean. Barbecue over **indirect medium heat**, with the lid closed as much as possible but turning once, until cooked to your desired doneness, 20 to 30 minutes for medium rare. Transfer to a carving board, lightly cover with foil, and allow to rest for 10 minutes before slicing.

6. To serve, cut the rolls into 1- to 1.5-cm (½- to ¾-inch) slices. Serve warm.

RED MEAT

71

ARGENTINE BEEF SKEWERS WITH CHIMICHURRI SAUCE

SERVES: 4 TO 6
PREP TIME: 20 MINUTES

HEAT: DIRECT HIGH HEAT 230° TO 290°C (450° TO 550°F)
COOKING TIME: 6 TO 8 MINUTES
SPECIAL EQUIPMENT: BAMBOO SKEWERS,
    SOAKED IN WATER FOR AT LEAST 30 MINUTES

SAUCE
50 g (2 oz) flat-leaf parsley leaves and tender stems
25 g (1 oz) basil leaves
40 g (1½ oz) white onion, finely chopped and rinsed
25 g (1 oz) carrot, finely chopped
1 garlic clove
½ teaspoon sea salt
6 tablespoons extra-virgin olive oil
2 tablespoons rice vinegar

RUB
1½ teaspoons sea salt
½ teaspoon paprika
½ teaspoon ground coriander
½ teaspoon ground cumin
¼ teaspoon freshly ground black pepper

1 kg (2 lb) rump steak, 2.5 to 3 cm (1 to 1¼ inches) thick,
    cut into 2.5-cm (1-inch) cubes
Extra-virgin olive oil
18 large cherry tomatoes

1. Finely chop the parsley, basil, onion, carrot, garlic and salt in a food processor or blender. With the machine running, add the oil and vinegar in a steady stream, using just enough oil to create a fairly thick sauce.

2. Mix the rub ingredients together in a small bowl.

3. Place the meat cubes in a large bowl. Lightly coat the meat with oil and then season with the rub, stirring to coat the meat evenly. Allow the meat to stand at room temperature for 20 to 30 minutes before barbecuing. Prepare the barbecue for direct cooking over a high heat.

4. Thread the meat and tomatoes alternately on to skewers. Brush the cooking grills clean. Barbecue the skewers over **direct high heat,** with the lid closed as much as possible but turning occasionally, until cooked to your desired doneness, 6 to 8 minutes for medium rare. Serve warm with the sauce on the side or drizzled over the top.

HOW TO CUBE RUMP STEAK

When making kebabs, the goal is to create cubes of the same size and thickness so they all cook at the same rate.

1. Start with a nice even piece of steak at least 2.5 cm (1 inch) thick.

2. Cut it down the centre and side to side in whichever way leaves you with 2.5-cm (1-inch) cubes.

3. With so many flat sides, you now have plenty of opportunities to lightly char and flavour the surface of the meat.

4. If some cubes end up a little smaller than most, combine all the small ones on a skewer or two of their own and barbecue them for a shorter time.

The centre-cut section of a beef fillet is almost always the most expensive part. Save that to slice into steaks. To make skewers or kebabs, use the tail ends of the fillet and enjoy all the buttery texture for far less cost. Some folded lemon slices complement the flavours in the finadene, which is a very popular marinade and sauce on the tropical island of Guam.

BEEF KEBABS WITH FINADENE

SERVES: 4 TO 6
PREP TIME: 20 MINUTES
MARINATING TIME: 1 TO 2 HOURS

HEAT: DIRECT HIGH HEAT 230° TO 290°C (450° TO 550°F)
COOKING TIME: 4 TO 6 MINUTES
SPECIAL EQUIPMENT: BAMBOO SKEWERS, SOAKED IN WATER FOR AT LEAST 30 MINUTES

SAUCE
125 ml (4 fl oz/½ cup) soy sauce
40 g (1½ oz) white onion, very finely chopped
3 tablespoons fresh lemon juice
3 tablespoons water
1 teaspoon very finely chopped jalapeño chilli

1 beef scotch fillet roast, about 1.25 kg (2 lb 12 oz)
4 tablespoons extra-virgin olive oil
2 lemons, thinly sliced

1. Mix the sauce ingredients together in a bowl. In a separate small bowl reserve 5 tablespoons of the sauce to spoon over the barbecued meat.

2. Trim any excess fat and sinew from the surface of the meat. Cut it crossways into steaks about 3 cm (1¼ inches) thick, then cut each steak into pieces 2.5 to 3 cm (1 to 1½ inches) thick, cutting away and discarding any clumps of fat and sinew. Place the meat into a large, resealable plastic bag, pour in the remaining sauce and add the oil. Press the air out of the bag, seal tightly and turn the bag several times to incorporate the oil and evenly coat the meat, then refrigerate for 1 to 2 hours.

3. Thread the meat on to skewers, placing a folded slice of lemon between each piece so that the meat cooks evenly. Allow the kebabs to stand at room temperature for 20 to 30 minutes before cooking. Prepare the barbecue for direct cooking over a high heat.

4. Brush the cooking grills clean. Barbecue the skewers over **direct high heat**, with the lid closed as much as possible but turning 2 or 3 times, until the meat is cooked to your desired doneness, 4 to 6 minutes for medium rare. Serve warm with the reserved sauce spooned over the top.

RED MEAT

HOW TO PREP CUCUMBER

1. Grate the cucumber coarsely on the side of a box grater.

2. Arrange the pieces in the middle of a sturdy piece of paper towel.

3. Squeeze gently to remove the water, then mix the cucumbers into the sauce.

LAMB SOUVLAKI WITH CUCUMBER-YOGURT SAUCE

SERVES: 4
PREP TIME: 20 MINUTES
MARINATING TIME: 3 TO 4 HOURS

HEAT: DIRECT HIGH HEAT 230° TO 290°C (450° TO 550°F)
COOKING TIME: 6 TO 7 MINUTES
SPECIAL EQUIPMENT: BAMBOO SKEWERS,
    SOAKED IN WATER FOR AT LEAST 30 MINUTES

MARINADE
125 ml (4 fl oz/½ cup) extra-virgin olive oil
1 tablespoon finely chopped garlic
1 tablespoon very finely chopped oregano leaves, or
    1 teaspoon crumbled dried oregano
1 teaspoon sea salt
¼ teaspoon freshly ground black pepper

1 boneless leg of lamb, about 750 g (1½ lb), trimmed of
    excess fat and cut into 3.5-cm (1½-inch) chunks
2 red or green capsicums, cored, deseeded and cut into
    2.5-cm (1-inch) squares
24 large cherry tomatoes

SAUCE
½ cucumber, coarsely grated
250 g (8 oz) natural Greek yogurt
2 tablespoons very finely chopped red onion
1 teaspoon finely grated lemon rind
1 tablespoon fresh lemon juice
½ teaspoon very finely chopped garlic
Sea salt
Freshly ground black pepper

1. Whisk the marinade ingredients together in a small bowl. Thread the lamb chunks, capsicum squares and tomatoes alternately on to skewers. Place in a shallow dish, pour the marinade over the skewers and turn to coat them evenly. Cover and refrigerate for 3 to 4 hours, turning occasionally. Allow to stand at room temperature for 20 to 30 minutes before barbecuing.

2. Squeeze the grated cucumber to remove as much liquid as possible. Transfer the cucumber to a small bowl and stir in the yogurt, onion, lemon rind, lemon juice and garlic. Season to taste with salt and pepper, cover and refrigerate until serving.

3. Prepare the barbecue for direct cooking over a high heat. Brush the cooking grills clean. Remove the skewers from the dish and discard the marinade. Barbecue the skewers over **direct high heat**, with the lid closed as much as possible but turning occasionally, until the meat is cooked to your desired doneness, 6 to 7 minutes for medium rare. Serve warm with the sauce.

PORCINI-RUBBED VEAL CHOPS WITH HERBED MASCARPONE

SERVES: 4
PREP TIME: 15 MINUTES

HEAT: DIRECT MEDIUM HEAT 180° TO 230°C
(350° TO 450°F)
COOKING TIME: ABOUT 6 MINUTES
SPECIAL EQUIPMENT: SPICE MILL

MASCARPONE
5 tablespoons mascarpone cheese
1 teaspoon very finely chopped sage
¼ teaspoon sea salt
¼ teaspoon freshly ground black pepper

25 g (1 oz) dried porcini mushrooms
2 teaspoons sea salt
1 teaspoon freshly ground black pepper

4 veal rib chops, each about 250 g (8 oz) and
2.5 cm (1 inch) thick
Extra-virgin olive oil

1. Mix the mascarpone ingredients together in a small bowl. Cover and allow to stand at room temperature for 1 hour.

2. Grind the mushrooms into a powder in a spice mill (this should yield 2 tablespoons). Put the powder into a small bowl and mix with the salt and pepper. Pour some oil on to a roasting tray and then sprinkle the seasoning over the oil. Dredge the chops through the oil mixture to coat them evenly. Cover and allow them to stand at room temperature for 20 to 30 minutes before barbecuing. Prepare the barbecue for direct cooking over a medium heat.

3. Brush the cooking grills clean. Barbecue the chops over **direct medium heat**, with the lid closed as much as possible but turning once, until cooked to your desired doneness, about 6 minutes for medium rare. Remove from the barbecue and allow the chops to rest for 3 to 5 minutes. Serve the chops hot with the herbed mascarpone.

■■■

If your impression of veal comes mostly from over-breaded and overcooked schnitzel, you owe it to yourself to try this chop. Quickly grilling a lean, bone-in veal chop over a fragrant fire, Tuscan style, results in a succulent, tender taste experience.

■■■

HOW TO PREP VEAL CHOPS

1. Dried porcini mushrooms star in this veal chop recipe. Pulverise them first in a spice mill or coffee grinder.

2. Brush some good olive oil on to a roasting tray and sprinkle the pulverised mushrooms, salt and pepper over the oil.

3. Press the veal chops into the oil and seasonings.

4. Drag each chop back and forth on both sides to get an even coating.

HOW TO FRENCH A RACK OF LAMB

 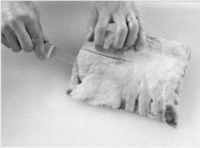 

1. 'Frenching' means removing the fat on the bones extending from a rack (or chop) and cleaning them thoroughly for a nice presentation.

2. Each rack of lamb has a 'fat cap' that runs on top of the rib bones and meat. Make a cut through the fat at the base of the bones.

3. Use the knife to help lift off the fat cap.

4. Use your knife to cut out the rib meat between the bones and to scrape the bones clean.

5. Then trim off the fat clinging to the loin meat, to prevent flare-ups.

6. Ideally the meat will be pinkish red, not purple. A dark colour indicates an older animal.

HOW TO BARBECUE RACK OF LAMB

Lamb chops are a buttery-soft luxury. You can certainly barbecue them individually, but they are likely to be juicier and more succulent if you cook whole racks first and then cut them into chops.

1. Prepare your barbecue by spreading the coals over one-half to three-quarters of the charcoal grate.

2. Barbecue the lamb as much as possible over a direct heat.

3. If flare-ups occur, move the racks to the other side of the barbecue, over indirect heat.

4. Once the internal temperature reaches 52°C (125°F), remove the racks from the barbecue, loosely cover them with foil and allow them to rest for about 5 minutes before cutting into chops.

RACK OF LAMB WITH ORANGE-POMEGRANATE SYRUP

SERVES: 4 TO 6
PREP TIME: 40 MINUTES

HEAT: DIRECT MEDIUM HEAT 180° TO 230°C
   (350° TO 450°F)
COOKING TIME: 15 TO 20 MINUTES

2 lamb racks, 500 to 750 g (1 to 1½ lb) each

PASTE
2 tablespoons extra-virgin olive oil
1 tablespoon very finely chopped garlic
1 tablespoon chilli con carne seasoning
2 teaspoons sea salt
1 teaspoon freshly ground black pepper

SYRUP
125 ml (4 fl oz/½ cup) fresh orange juice
4 tablespoons pomegranate juice
2 tablespoons runny honey
1 tablespoon balsamic vinegar
½ teaspoon sea salt

1. French the lamb racks as shown on the previous page.
2. Mix the paste ingredients in a small bowl. Spread the paste over the lamb racks and allow them to stand at room temperature for 20 to 30 minutes before barbecuing.

3. Combine the orange juice, pomegranate juice, honey and balsamic vinegar in a small saucepan over a high heat and bring to the boil. Once boiling, reduce the heat to medium and simmer for 15 to 20 minutes until the liquid has reduced to about 5 tablespoons. Season the light syrup with the salt and allow to cool. (You can refrigerate the syrup for up to 3 days.)

4. Prepare the barbecue for direct cooking over a medium heat. Brush the cooking grills clean. Barbecue the lamb, bone sides down first, over **_direct medium heat_**, with the lid closed as much as possible but turning once or twice and moving the racks over indirect heat if flare-ups occur, until cooked to your desired doneness, 15 to 20 minutes for medium rare. Remove from the barbecue when the internal temperature reaches 52°C (125°F). Allow the lamb to rest for 5 minutes before carving into chops (the internal temperature will rise during resting).

5. If necessary, warm the syrup over a low heat until it reaches your desired consistency. Serve the lamb warm with the syrup drizzled on top.

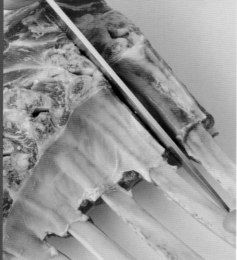

Of course you can buy pre-cut lamb rib chops, but cutting them yourself from a frenched rack of lamb will probably save you some money and assure you that each chop is the same thickness. For a clear look at where the bones are, face the meaty side of each rack down on a chopping board. Cut right between each pair of ribs.

LAMB CUTLETS WITH INDIAN SPICES

SERVES: 4
PREP TIME: 10 MINUTES
MARINATING TIME: 1 TO 2 HOURS

HEAT: DIRECT HIGH HEAT 230° TO 290°C (450° TO 550°F)
COOKING TIME: 4 TO 6 MINUTES

MARINADE
4 tablespoons extra-virgin olive oil
2 tablespoons fresh lime juice
1 tablespoon very finely chopped garlic
1½ teaspoons sea salt
1 teaspoon ground coriander
1 teaspoon ground cumin
½ teaspoon ground ginger
½ teaspoon freshly ground black pepper

16 lamb cutlets, each about 1.5 cm (¾ inch) thick, trimmed of excess fat

Lime wedges, to serve, optional

1. Whisk the marinade ingredients together in a small bowl.

2. Arrange the chops on a large, rimmed plate. Spoon or brush the marinade over the chops, turning to coat them evenly. Cover with plastic wrap and refrigerate for 1 to 2 hours.

3. Remove the cutlets from the refrigerator 20 to 30 minutes before barbecuing. Prepare the barbecue for direct cooking over a high heat.

4. Brush the cooking grills clean. Barbecue the cutlets over **direct high heat**, with the lid closed as much as possible but turning once, until nicely marked on both sides and cooked to your desired doneness, 4 to 6 minutes for medium rare.

5. Remove the chops from the barbecue and allow them to rest for 3 to 5 minutes. Serve warm with lime wedges, if desired, for squeezing over.

LAMB CHOPS IN UZBEK MARINADE

SERVES: 4
PREP TIME: 10 MINUTES
MARINATING TIME: 3 TO 5 HOURS

HEAT: DIRECT HIGH HEAT 230° TO 290°C (450° TO 550°F)
COOKING TIME: ABOUT 8 MINUTES

MARINADE/SAUCE
1 small brown onion, cut into chunks
4 canned roma tomatoes
125 ml (4 fl oz/½ cup) extra-virgin olive oil
4 large garlic cloves
2 tablespoons red wine vinegar
1 tablespoon sweet paprika
1 tablespoon dried thyme
1 tablespoon ground coriander
2 teaspoons ground cumin
2 teaspoons sea salt
½ teaspoon ground cayenne pepper
½ teaspoon freshly ground black pepper

8 lamb loin chops, each about 3.5 cm (1½ inches) thick
Extra-virgin olive oil

1. Process the marinade ingredients in a food processor for 1 to 2 minutes until very smooth.

2. Arrange the chops side by side in a shallow dish. Pour the marinade over the chops and turn to coat them on all sides. Cover with plastic wrap and marinate in the refrigerator for 3 to 5 hours.

3. Remove the chops from the dish and wipe off most of the marinade. Discard the marinade. Lightly brush the chops with oil and allow to stand at room temperature for 20 to 30 minutes before barbecuing. Prepare the barbecue for direct cooking over a high heat.

4. Brush the cooking grills clean. Barbecue the chops over **direct high heat**, with the lid closed as much as possible but rotating and turning the chops once or twice for even cooking, until they are cooked to your desired doneness, about 8 minutes for medium rare. Each time you lift the chops off the grill to rotate them or turn them over, place them down on a clean area of the grill, and brush away the bits of marinade that will cling to the grill as you go.

5. Remove the chops from the barbecue and allow them to rest for 3 to 5 minutes. Serve warm.

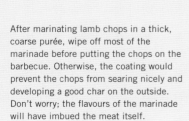

After marinating lamb chops in a thick, coarse purée, wipe off most of the marinade before putting the chops on the barbecue. Otherwise, the coating would prevent the chops from searing nicely and developing a good char on the outside. Don't worry; the flavours of the marinade will have imbued the meat itself.

HOW TO MAKE BASIL-GARLIC OIL

1. Bring a saucepan of salted water to the boil. Add the basil leaves and blanch them for 10 seconds.

2. Immediately remove the basil with a slotted spoon and plunge the leaves into a bowl of iced water to stop them cooking and to retain the green colour.

3. Lay the basil leaves on paper towel and pat them dry.

4. Combine the basil leaves, oil and garlic in a food processor or blender.

5. Process until the basil is puréed, then season the mixture with salt and crushed red chilli flakes.

6. Drizzle the basil-garlic oil over barbecued meats. Save any remaining oil by straining out the solids and storing it in the refrigerator for up to a week.

HOW TO PREP SHOULDER CHOPS

1. Lamb shoulder chops typically cost about one-third the price of loin and rib chops, and their flavour is excellent.

2. First brush them with good-quality olive oil and some bold seasonings like dried herbes de provence.

3. Their texture, though, can be a little tough, so it's best to slow-cook them over indirect heat, which renders them tender.

HERBES DE PROVENCE

Dried herbes de provence is an aromatic blend of dried herbs frequently used in the south of France. It typically includes thyme, marjoram, parsley, tarragon, lavender, celery seeds and bay leaf. Available from specialty grocery stores.

LAMB SHOULDER CHOPS WITH RATATOUILLE SALAD AND BASIL-GARLIC OIL

SERVES: 4
PREP TIME: 25 MINUTES

HEAT: DIRECT AND INDIRECT MEDIUM HEAT
  180° TO 230°C (350° TO 450°F)
COOKING TIME: 51 TO 58 MINUTES

OIL
1 tablespoon plus ½ teaspoon sea salt
50 g (2 oz) basil leaves
175 g (6 fl oz) extra-virgin olive oil
1 medium garlic clove, peeled
¼ teaspoon crushed red chilli flakes

RATATOUILLE
1 large red capsicum
1 eggplant, cut into 1-cm (½-inch) slices
2 small zucchinis, cut in half lengthways
1 brown onion, cut crossways into 4 thick slices
Extra-virgin olive oil
4 roma tomatoes
Sea salt
Freshly ground black pepper

2 teaspoons dried herbes de provence
4 lamb shoulder chops, 300 to 375 g (10 oz to 13 oz) each

1. Bring a small saucepan of water, with 1 tablespoon of the salt, to the boil over a high heat. Add the basil leaves and blanch them for 10 seconds, then immediately remove the basil and plunge them into a bowl of iced water. Transfer to paper towel and pat away the excess water. Process the basil, oil and garlic in a blender or food processor until the basil is puréed. Season with the remaining ½ teaspoon salt and the red chilli flakes, then pour into a small jug and set aside.

2. Prepare the barbecue for direct and indirect cooking over a medium heat.

3. Remove the stalk, ribs and seeds from the capsicum and cut into 4 pieces. Lightly brush the eggplant, zucchini and onion with oil. Brush the cooking grills clean. Barbecue all the vegetables over **direct medium heat** for 6 to 8 minutes, turning occasionally, until the capsicum is charred and blistered, the eggplant, zucchini and onion are tender, and the tomato skins are seared and blistered. Transfer the vegetables to a platter as they are done, and season to taste with salt and pepper. Cut the vegetables into bite-sized pieces and drizzle with 2 tablespoons of basil-garlic oil. Set aside.

4. Mix 2 teaspoons sea salt, ½ teaspoon pepper and the dried herbs together in a bowl. Lightly brush the lamb with oil and season with the spices.

5. Brush the cooking grills clean. Barbecue the lamb over **indirect medium heat** for 45 to 50 minutes, with the lid closed as much as possible but turning once or twice, until the chops are fork tender.

6. Place equal portions of ratatouille on each of 4 dinner plates. Add a chop to each plate and garnish with another drizzle of basil-garlic oil on the plate around the lamb and vegetables.

HOW TO CUT SHORT RIBS

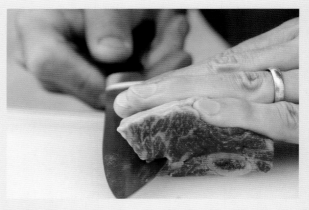

1. Short ribs are cut two different ways for Korean barbecue. You can buy 'Korean-style' short ribs, like what you see towards the bottom of this picture, or you can buy the more-conventional short ribs, like the thicker pieces towards the top of this picture.

2. To prepare the more-conventional short ribs, begin by making a horizontal cut just over the bone of each rib.

3. Stop just before you cut all the way through the meat.

4. Continue to make horizontal cuts and butterfly the meat until it is about 1 cm (½ inch) thick.

5. Next, cut very shallow slits in the meat to tenderise it.

HOW TO BARBECUE KOREAN-STYLE RIBS

1. Korean-style ribs are thin enough that they require no cutting. Simply marinate them for a few hours in the refrigerator. When you lift them, allow the excess liquid to drip back into the bowl before laying them on the barbecue.

2. Barbecue the ribs over direct high heat, leaving the lid off so that you can keep an eye on them and turn them as they char.

KOREAN BEEF BARBECUE

SERVES: 4 TO 6
PREP TIME: 10 MINUTES
MARINATING TIME: 2 TO 4 HOURS

HEAT: DIRECT HIGH HEAT 230° TO 290°C (450° TO 550°F)
COOKING TIME: 3 TO 5 MINUTES

MARINADE
1 nashi pear (baseball size), peeled, cored and
    roughly chopped
3 spring onions, trimmed and roughly chopped
6 large garlic cloves
500 ml (17 fl oz/2 cups) water
175 ml (6 fl oz) soy sauce
75 g (3 oz) sugar
4 tablespoons rice vinegar

12 Korean-style beef ribs, about 2 kg (4 lb) total
    and 1 cm (½ inch) thick
2 tablespoons toasted sesame seeds

1. Finely chop the pear, spring onions and garlic in a food
processor. Add the remaining marinade ingredients and process
until well combined.

2. Put the ribs in a large bowl and pour in the marinade. Mix
well to coat the ribs evenly, then cover and refrigerate for 2 to
4 hours.

3. Prepare the barbecue for direct cooking over a high heat.

4. Brush the cooking grills clean. One at time, lift the ribs and
allow the liquid and solid bits to fall back into the bowl. Discard
the marinade. Barbecue the ribs over **direct high heat** for 3 to
5 minutes, with the lid open and turning occasionally, until
they are nicely charred on both sides and cooked to a medium
or medium-rare doneness. Remove from the barbecue and
sprinkle with the sesame seeds.

The crisp, translucent flesh of nashi pears makes a sweet juice
that is excellent for marinating beef.

RED MEAT

HOW TO BARBECUE BEEF RIBS

1. Look for the meatiest beef ribs you can find and season them generously.

2. Line them up on their sides in a disposable foil tin.

3. Add beef stock to create a moist cooking environment.

4. Cover the tin with foil, which will trap steam and help to tenderise the meat.

5. Seal the edges tightly so that the liquid does not evaporate.

6. The ribs should cook over indirect heat, with the lid closed, for the first hour.

7. It's important to maintain the barbecue's temperature at about 180°C (350°F).

8. Uncover the tin and turn the ribs over so they cook evenly.

9. Wearing barbecue mitts or oven gloves, seal the tin again for the second hour of cooking.

10. Remove the ribs from the tin and brush them with the sauce.

11. Finish them over a direct heat for a beautifully caramelised surface.

BEEF RIBS WITH BARBACOA SAUCE

SERVES: 2 TO 4
PREP TIME: 45 MINUTES

HEAT: INDIRECT AND DIRECT MEDIUM HEAT
    180° TO 230°C (350° TO 450°F)
COOKING TIME: ABOUT 2¼ HOURS
SPECIAL EQUIPMENT: LARGE DISPOSABLE FOIL TIN,
    CAST-IRON FRYING PAN

RUB
2 teaspoons garlic granules
1 teaspoon ground cinnamon
1 teaspoon sea salt
1 teaspoon freshly ground black pepper

½ rack beef ribs (7 ribs), about 2.5 kg (5 lb)
500 ml (17 fl oz/2 cups) beef stock

SAUCE
3 dried ancho chillies
150 g (5 oz) onion, finely chopped
1 teaspoon dried oregano
1 teaspoon ground cumin
1 garlic clove, very finely chopped
2 tablespoons apple cider vinegar
1 tablespoon light brown sugar
¾ teaspoon sea salt
125 g (4 oz) tomato sauce

1. Combine the rub ingredients in a small bowl.

2. Prepare the barbecue for indirect and direct cooking over a medium heat.

3. Cut the rack into individual ribs and arrange them on a roasting tray. Evenly coat each rib with the rub and then place them side by side in a large disposable foil tin, layering a few ribs if necessary. Add the beef stock to the tin and tightly cover with aluminium foil.

4. Place the tin over *indirect medium heat*, close the lid, and cook for 1 hour. After the first hour, using tongs and wearing insulated barbecue mitts, carefully remove the aluminium foil cover and turn the ribs over. Put the foil cover back on the tin and continue to cook over *indirect medium heat* for another hour.

5. While the ribs are cooking, make the sauce. Heat a cast-iron frying pan over a medium-high heat. Add the chillies and cook for 3 to 5 minutes, occasionally pressing the chillies against the bottom of the pan, until they are lightly toasted, pliable and dark brick red in spots. The chillies may start to puff while in the pan. Allow the toasted chillies to cool until easy to handle, then split them open and remove and discard the stems, seeds and ribs. Transfer to a bowl, cover with 600 ml (21 fl oz) hot tap water and allow them to stand for about 20 minutes until they become soft. Strain into a small bowl, reserving the chilli soaking liquid.

6. Combine the soaked chillies, onion, oregano, cumin and garlic in a blender or food processor. Add 125 ml (4 fl oz/½ cup) of the reserved soaking liquid and blend to make a thick paste, adding more reserved liquid, if necessary. Combine the chilli paste, vinegar, brown sugar and salt in a saucepan over a medium heat, and bring to the boil, stirring often. Reduce the heat to medium-low and cook for about 5 minutes until slightly thickened. Remove the pan from the heat and stir in the tomato sauce. Transfer to a bowl and allow the sauce to cool.

7. When the ribs are tender and the meat has visibly shrunk back from the bones, wearing insulated barbecue mitts, carefully remove the tin from the barbecue. Remove the ribs from the tin drippings and place them on a roasting tray. Discard the tin and the drippings. Liberally brush the ribs with the sauce and then barbecue the ribs over *direct medium heat* for 3 to 5 minutes. Brush the ribs again with more sauce, turn them over and barbecue for a further 3 to 5 minutes. Transfer the ribs to a platter and allow to rest for 5 minutes. Serve with the remaining sauce.

LEG OF LAMB
WITH MOROCCAN SPICES

SERVES: 6 TO 8
PREP TIME: 20 MINUTES
MARINATING TIME: 1 HOUR

HEAT: DIRECT AND INDIRECT HIGH HEAT
    230° TO 290°C (450° TO 550°F)
COOKING TIME: 21 TO 27 MINUTES

MARINADE
75 g (3 oz) brown onion, chopped
1 tablespoon grated lemon rind
4 tablespoons fresh lemon juice
3 tablespoons extra-virgin olive oil
2 garlic cloves
1½ teaspoons crushed red chilli flakes
1 teaspoon ground coriander
1 teaspoon ground cumin
1 teaspoon paprika
1 teaspoon ground ginger
1 teaspoon sea salt

1 boneless leg of lamb, about 1.5 kg (3 lb), butterflied
    and trimmed of any excess fat and sinew

1. Combine the marinade ingredients in a food processor and
pulse to make a smooth paste, scraping down the side of the
bowl as necessary. Place the lamb in a large, resealable plastic
bag and pour in the marinade. Press the air out of the bag and
seal tightly. Turn the bag to distribute the marinade and
refrigerate for 1 hour. Allow the lamb to stand at room
temperature for 20 to 30 minutes before barbecuing. Prepare
the barbecue for direct and indirect cooking over a high heat.

2. Remove the lamb from the bag, letting the marinade cling to
the lamb. Discard the marinade in the bag. Brush the cooking
grills clean. Barbecue the lamb over **direct high heat** for about
6 minutes, with the lid closed as much as possible but turning
once, until nicely browned on both sides. Slide the lamb over
indirect high heat and cook, with the lid closed, to your desired
doneness, 15 to 20 minutes for medium rare. Remove the lamb
from the barbecue and allow to rest for about 5 minutes before
carving. Cut the lamb across the grain into thin diagonal slices
and serve warm.

HOW TO BUTTERFLY A LEG OF LAMB

1. A boneless leg of lamb is actually several
muscles held together. The different muscles
have various shapes and thicknesses.

2. In order to barbecue the whole leg evenly, you
need to make the thickest parts thinner.

3. You do that by making angled cuts at the
thickness you want and then spreading the meat
open like a book.

PANIOLO TRI-TIP ROAST WITH ORANGE BARBECUE SAUCE

SERVES: 6
PREP TIME: 20 MINUTES

HEAT: DIRECT AND INDIRECT MEDIUM HEAT
    180° TO 230°C (350° TO 450°F)
COOKING TIME: 23 TO 30 MINUTES

PASTE
2 tablespoons extra-virgin olive oil
2 tablespoons very finely chopped fresh root ginger
2 tablespoons light brown sugar
2 teaspoons coarse sea salt
2 teaspoons very finely chopped garlic
1 teaspoon chilli-garlic sauce, such as sriracha

1 tri-tip roast, about 1 kg (2 lb) and 3.5 cm (1½ inches) thick,
    fat and silver skin removed

SAUCE
250 ml (8 fl oz/1 cup) orange juice
2 tablespoons light brown sugar
2 tablespoons apple cider vinegar
2 tablespoons soy sauce

1. Combine the paste ingredients in a bowl. Coat the joint evenly with the paste and allow the roast to stand at room temperature for 20 to 30 minutes before barbecuing. Prepare the barbecue for direct and indirect cooking over a medium heat.

2. Combine the sauce ingredients in a saucepan over a medium heat and bubble for 10 to 15 minutes, whisking frequently, until thickened and reduced to about 175 ml (6 fl oz). Set aside and reheat just before serving.

3. Brush the cooking grills clean. Barbecue the roast over **direct medium heat** for 8 to 10 minutes, turning once, until well marked on both sides. Move the tri-tip over **indirect medium heat** and cook to your desired doneness, 15 to 20 minutes for medium rare. Keep the lid closed as much as possible during barbecuing but turn the joint over every 5 minutes or so. Remove the joint from the barbecue, cover with foil, and allow it to rest for 5 to 10 minutes. Cut the joint across the grain into thin slices. Serve warm with the sauce.

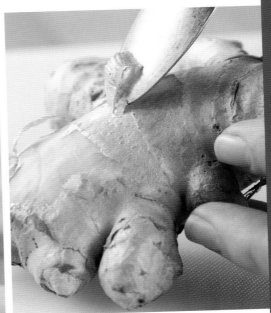

Much of what gives this Hawaiian-style tri-tip roast such great flavour is the paste, which features fresh root ginger. Before very finely chopping the ginger, scrape off the skin with the back of a spoon. Also, be careful not to overcook the joint. It's a very lean cut of meat and it's best served medium rare.

HOW TO PREP BEEF FILLET

1. Slide a sharp knife just under any large clumps of fat, being careful not to cut into the meat. Also remove the strips of silver skin, which are tough and chewy.

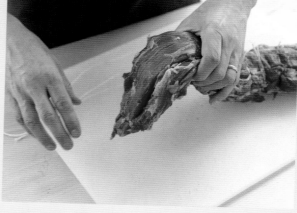

2. Tie the 'cleaned' joint every couple of centimetres to make it even and compact. Because the tail is thinner than the rest of the joint, fold it underneath and tie it snugly for a more even thickness end to end.

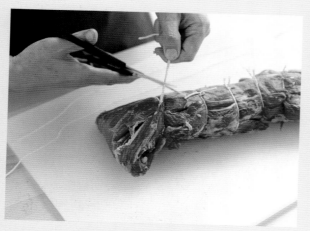

3. Cut off the loose ends of the string.

4. Rub oil all over the joint and season it with herbs and spices.

5. Barbecue the joint first over a direct heat to brown it on all sides.

6. Finish cooking it over indirect heat so that the exterior does not burn before the interior is cooked.

HERB-CRUSTED BEEF FILLET WITH WHITE WINE CREAM SAUCE

SERVES: 10 TO 12
PREP TIME: 40 MINUTES

HEAT: DIRECT AND INDIRECT MEDIUM HEAT
   180° TO 230°C (350° TO 450°F)
COOKING TIME: 35 TO 45 MINUTES
SPECIAL EQUIPMENT: BUTCHER'S STRING

RUB
1½ tablespoons dried tarragon
2½ teaspoons sea salt
2 teaspoons freshly ground black pepper
1½ teaspoons dried thyme
1 teaspoon dried sage, packed

1 whole beef fillet, 3 to 3.5 kg (6 to 7 lb), untrimmed
Extra-virgin olive oil

SAUCE
75 g (3 oz) shallot, very finely chopped
125 ml (4 fl oz/½ cup) rice vinegar
1½ teaspoons dried tarragon
¼ teaspoon dried thyme
125 ml (4 fl oz/½ cup) dry white wine
125 ml (4 fl oz/½ cup) chicken stock
350 ml (12 fl oz) thickened cream
25 g (1 oz) flat-leaf parsley, very finely chopped

Sea salt

1. Mix the rub ingredients together in a small bowl.

2. Trim and discard the excess fat and silver skin from the fillet. Part of the thin 'tail' end of the fillet may separate as it is trimmed, but leave it connected to the main muscle as much as possible. Lay the fillet out flat and straight, with the smoothest side up, aligning the narrow pieces at the tail end. Neatly fold the tail end of the fillet under itself to form an even thickness (one end may be larger). Tie the joint snugly with butcher's string at 5-cm (2-inch) intervals. Secure the folded end with 2 strings. Lightly coat the joint with oil, then season the joint all over with the rub.

3. Allow the joint to stand at room temperature for 30 minutes to 1 hour before barbecuing. Prepare the barbecue for direct and indirect cooking over a medium heat.

4. Combine the shallot, vinegar, tarragon and thyme in a large frying pan over a high heat, and cook for 3 to 4 minutes, stirring often, until the vinegar has evaporated. Add the wine and stock and boil for 3 to 4 minutes until reduced to about 125 ml (4 fl oz). Add the cream and continue boiling for a further 5 to 7 minutes until the surface is covered with large, shiny bubbles and the sauce is reduced to about 375 ml (13 fl oz/ 1½ cups). Remove the pan from the heat, adjust the seasonings and set aside. Reheat and add parsley just before serving.

5. Brush the cooking grills clean. Sear the joint over **direct medium heat** for about 15 minutes, turning a quarter turn once every 3 to 4 minutes. Slide the joint over **indirect medium heat** and cook, turning once, until it reaches your desired doneness, 20 to 30 minutes for medium rare. Keep the lid closed as much as possible during cooking. Remove the joint from the barbecue, loosely cover with foil and allow to rest for 10 to 15 minutes. The internal temperature will rise during this time.

6. Snip and remove all the string from the joint. Cut the meat crossways into 1- to 2.5-cm (½- to 1-inch) slices. Season to taste with salt. Serve warm with the sauce.

HOW TO PREP BONELESS RIB ROAST

1. For a special occasion, consider buying a rib roast a few days before you plan to serve it and dry-ageing it in your refrigerator. (For safety reasons, never do this for more than 4 days.) Patted dry and set on a rack over a roasting tray in the refrigerator, the meat will develop more concentrated flavours and a softer texture.

2. After you have seasoned the meat, allow it to stand at room temperature for 30 to 40 minutes so that the outer ring of the joint won't overcook before the centre reaches your ideal temperature on the barbecue.

HOW TO SMOKE A BONELESS RIB ROAST

1. Spread a layer or two of lit coals on one-half of the charcoal grate. Position some wood chunks alongside the coals. On the opposite side, set up a water pan, which will absorb some heat and release it slowly.

2. Initially position the joint with the thicker end towards the coals.

3. An instant-read thermometer takes all the guesswork out of doneness. For medium rare, remove the joint when it hits the 49° to 52°C (120° to 125°F) range. The internal temperature will climb as the meat rests.

The sweet, haunting aromas of smouldering oak are a distinctive part of this recipe. Bags of wood chunks are pretty easy to find in shops specialising in selling barbecues, but if you happen to have dried oak logs lying around, you can make your own chunks. Saw the logs into smaller sections and use a chisel and hammer to break off most of the bark; it tends to add a bit of bitterness to the smoke. Next split the wood into fist-sized pieces. Unlike wood chips, chunks don't need to be soaked. Alongside the coals, they will burn slowly and permeate the meat with a taste of the great outdoors.

OAK-SMOKED BONELESS RIB ROAST WITH SHIRAZ SAUCE

SERVES: 10
PREP TIME: 30 MINUTES

HEAT: INDIRECT MEDIUM HEAT 180° TO 190°C
    (350° TO 375°F)
COOKING TIME: ABOUT 1½ HOURS
SPECIAL EQUIPMENT: LARGE DISPOSABLE FOIL TIN,
    INSTANT-READ THERMOMETER

1 boneless rib roast, about 2.2 kg (5½ lb), trimmed
    of excess surface fat
Sea salt
Freshly ground black pepper
4 tablespoons dijon mustard
50 g (2 oz) brown onion, coarsely grated
3 garlic cloves, very finely chopped
2 oak wood chunks (not soaked)

SAUCE
40 g (1½ oz) unsalted butter, cold
3 tablespoons very finely chopped shallot
1 garlic clove, very finely chopped
1 litre (35 fl oz/4 cups) beef stock, preferably home-made
375 ml (13 fl oz/1½ cups) shiraz wine
1 tablespoon soy sauce
1½ teaspoons tomato purée
¼ teaspoon dried thyme
½ bay leaf

1. Season the joint with 2 teaspoons salt and 1 teaspoon pepper. Mix the mustard, onion and garlic together in a small bowl. Spread this mixture over the top of the joint and allow it to stand at room temperature for 30 to 40 minutes before barbecuing.

2. Prepare the barbecue for indirect cooking over a medium heat (see instructions at left). Add 2 wood chunks alongside the coals. Brush the cooking grills clean. Position the joint with the thicker end facing the coals. Barbecue over *indirect medium heat* for about 1½ hours, with the lid closed as much as possible but rotating the joint 180 degrees halfway through the cooking time, until the internal temperature reaches 49° to 52°C (120° to 125°F) for medium rare. Keep the barbecue's temperature between 180° and 190°C (350° and 375°F).

3. Melt 15 g (½ oz) of the butter in a medium, heavy-based saucepan over a medium heat (keep the remaining butter refrigerated). Add the shallot and cook for about 2 minutes until softened. Add the garlic and cook for about 1 minute until fragrant. Add the stock, wine, soy sauce, tomato purée, thyme and bay leaf, and bring to the boil over a high heat. Cook for about 30 minutes, uncovered, until reduced to about 500 ml (17 fl oz/2 cups). Season to taste with salt and pepper. Remove the bay leaf and keep the sauce warm.

4. Remove the joint from the barbecue, loosely cover with foil, and rest for 20 to 30 minutes. The internal temperature will rise during this time. Carve the joint into 1-cm (½-inch) slices, reserving the juices. Just before serving, whisk the remaining cold butter into the sauce, and stir in the carving juices. Serve warm with the sauce.

HOW TO BARBECUE BRISKET

1. The first layer of flavour to apply is the sweet heat of a good spice rub and mustard. Next, cook the seasoned brisket on a smoker for 4 to 5 hours so that it absorbs a good amount of flavourful wood smoke. The brisket should be in a large disposable foil tin to catch some of the juices, and the thick layer of fat should be on top so that it bastes the meat below it.

2. When the internal temperature of the meat reaches 70°C (160°F), take it out of the foil tin and double-wrap the brisket in aluminium foil. This will trap some moisture and help to break down the tough fibres in the meat.

3. When the internal temperature reaches 91° to 93°C (195° to 200°F) in the thickest section, remove the brisket from the smoker and allow the precious meat juices to collect in the foil. The brisket will stay warm and continue to cook for an hour or two.

4. Carefully unwrap the foil, set the brisket aside and bend the foil to funnel the juices into a serving bowl.

5. Slice a section of fat from the top side of the brisket so you can see which way the grain of the meat runs. For the sake of tenderness, you want to slice against the grain.

6. Slice the brisket nice and thin with a sharp knife. That beautiful pink ring is a result of the wood smoke. Now spoon those meat juices over the top and enjoy eating it.

TRULY BARBECUED BRISKET

SERVES: 6
PREP TIME: 15 MINUTES
MARINATING TIME: 6 TO 8 HOURS

HEAT: INDIRECT LOW HEAT 110° TO 130°C (225° TO 250°F)
COOKING TIME: 6 TO 8 HOURS, PLUS 1 TO 2 HOURS
RESTING TIME
SPECIAL EQUIPMENT: LARGE DISPOSABLE FOIL TIN,
INSTANT-READ THERMOMETER

RUB
4 teaspoons sea salt
2 teaspoons ancho chilli powder
2 teaspoons light brown sugar
2 teaspoons garlic granules
2 teaspoons smoked paprika
1 teaspoon celery seeds
1 teaspoon coarsely ground black pepper

1 brisket (flat cut), 2.5 to 3 kg (5 to 6 lb), untrimmed
4 tablespoons yellow mustard
6 hickory or oak wood chunks (not soaked)
500 ml (17 fl oz/2 cups) barbecue sauce

1. Mix the rub ingredients together in a small bowl.

2. Lay the brisket, fat side up, on a large chopping board. Trim the layer of fat to a 1-cm (½-inch) thickness. Turn the brisket over and trim any hard fat or thin membrane covering the meat.

3. Season the brisket evenly with the mustard and then the rub. Cover and refrigerate for 6 to 8 hours.

4. Place the brisket, fat side up, in a large disposable foil tin.

5. Prepare your smoker, following manufacturer's instructions, for indirect cooking over a low heat.

6. Place the tin with the brisket on the cooking grill. Smoke the brisket for 4 to 5 hours, starting with 2 chunks of wood, at 110° to 130°C (225° to 250°F), until the internal temperature of the meat reaches 70° to 77°C (160° to 170°F). If necessary, add more coals to maintain the temperature of the smoker at 110° to 130°C (225° to 250°F).

7. When the internal temperature of the meat has reached 70° to 77°C (160° to 170°F), the collagen in the meat will have dissolved. At that point, remove the brisket and tin from the smoker (close the lid to maintain the heat). Baste the brisket with some of the juices and fat collected in the tin, then wrap the joint in 2 large sheets of heavy-duty foil. Discard the tin.

8. Return the brisket to the smoker and cook for 2 to 3 hours, without adding more wood chunks, until the internal temperature of the brisket has reached 91° to 93°C (195° to

200°F) in the thickest section. The probe of the thermometer should slide in and out of the brisket with just a little resistance.

9. Remove the brisket from the smoker and allow it to rest inside the foil at room temperature for 1 to 2 hours. It will stay hot and continue to tenderise.

10. Carefully unwrap the brisket, being careful not to lose any of the juices inside the foil. Move the brisket to a large chopping board and pour the juices into a small bowl.

11. If necessary, cut off a small chunk of brisket to identify the direction of the grain. Cut the brisket across the grain into 3-mm (⅛-inch) slices. Spoon or brush some of the juices over the slices. Serve warm with barbecue sauce on the side.

■ ■ ■

*Brisket is the Mt Everest of barbecue.
Not only is it huge, but it also poses challenges
all along the way. If your first couple of attempts
don't work out exactly as you had hoped, persevere.
The rewards of mastering your own barbecued
brisket are unspeakably good. Among a cadre
of outdoor cooks you will have earned
long-standing respect and admiration.*

■ ■ ■

PORK

TECHNIQUES

RECIPES

HOW TO BARBECUE BRATWURST

1. Before cooking, prick several small holes in each bratwurst to prevent them from bursting open.

2. For the first stage of cooking, you will need a very hot fire on one side of the cooking grill.

3. Arrange the bratwurst in a single layer in a disposable tin with the cider and sliced onions.

4. Simmer the bratwurst for about 20 minutes, turning them occasionally. If the liquid boils, slide the tin over indirect heat.

5. Strain the onions and return them to the tin to caramelise with brown sugar.

6. Finish barbecuing the bratwurst over direct heat to lightly char the surfaces.

CIDER-SIMMERED BRATS WITH APPLES AND ONIONS

SERVES: 5
PREP TIME: 15 MINUTES

HEAT: DIRECT HIGH HEAT 230° TO 290°C
(450° TO 550°F) AND DIRECT MEDIUM HEAT
180° TO 230°C (350° TO 450°F)
COOKING TIME: 6 TO 8 MINUTES
SPECIAL EQUIPMENT: 2 LARGE DISPOSABLE FOIL TINS

MUSTARD
2 tablespoons apple sauce
2 tablespoons dijon mustard
2 tablespoons wholegrain mustard

750 ml (26 fl oz/3 cups) cider
2 brown onions, halved and cut into 5-mm (¼-inch) slices
5 fresh bratwurst, pierced several times
1 tablespoon brown sugar
5 long bread rolls or hot dog buns, halved lengthways
2 granny smith apples, cored and thinly sliced

1. Mix the mustard ingredients together in a small bowl. Cover and let stand at room temperature until ready to serve.

2. Prepare the barbecue for direct and indirect cooking over a high heat. Brush the cooking grills clean. Put the cider, onions and bratwurst into a large disposable foil tin. Place the tin over **direct high heat** and bring the liquid to a simmer. Keep the barbecue lid closed as much as possible but turn the bratwursts occasionally, until they are evenly coloured and have lost their raw look. If the liquid starts to boil, move the tin over indirect heat to prevent the bratwurst from splitting open.

3. Lower the temperature of the barbecue to a medium heat. Transfer the brats to another large disposable aluminium tin. Strain the onions in a colander over the tin with the brats (the liquid will keep the brats warm while you cook the onions). Return the onions to the original tin and stir in the brown sugar. Cook the onions over **direct medium heat** for about 15 minutes, with the lid closed as much as possible but stirring occasionally, until they are golden brown. Move the onions over indirect heat to keep them warm.

4. Remove the brats from the liquid and barbecue them over **direct medium heat** for 6 to 8 minutes, turning once or twice, until browned. During the last minute, place the buns on the barbecue to toast.

5. Place the brats in the buns. Spread each with the mustard, and top with the glazed onions and a few apple slices. Serve hot.

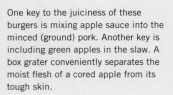

One key to the juiciness of these burgers is mixing apple sauce into the minced (ground) pork. Another key is including green apples in the slaw. A box grater conveniently separates the moist flesh of a cored apple from its tough skin.

PORK BURGERS WITH APPLE-TARRAGON SLAW

SERVES: 4
PREP TIME: 20 MINUTES

HEAT: DIRECT MEDIUM HEAT 180° TO 230°C
   (350° TO 450°F)
COOKING TIME: 12 TO 15 MINUTES

SLAW
175 g (6 oz) green cabbage, thinly sliced
65 g (2½ lb) granny smith apple or other tart green apple, coarsely grated
50 g (2 oz) carrot, coarsely grated
2 tablespoons finely chopped tarragon
2 tablespoons apple cider vinegar
1 tablespoon sugar
½ teaspoon celery seeds
¼ teaspoon sea salt

BURGERS
750 g (1½ lb) minced (ground) pork
75 g (3 oz) apple sauce
1½ teaspoons sea salt
1 teaspoon hot sauce, or to taste
½ teaspoon freshly ground black pepper

4 hamburger buns

1. Mix the slaw ingredients together in a large bowl. Cover and refrigerate until ready to assemble the burgers.

2. Gently mix the burger ingredients together in a large bowl. Gently shape into 4 equal-sized burgers, each about 1.5 cm (¾ inch) thick. With your thumb or the back of a spoon, make a shallow indentation about 2.5 cm (1 inch) wide in the centre of each burger. Prepare the barbecue for direct cooking over a medium heat.

3. Brush the cooking grills clean. Barbecue the burgers over **direct medium heat** for 12 to 15 minutes with the lid closed as much as possible but turning once when the burgers release easily from the grill without sticking, until cooked through. During the last minute of cooking time, toast the buns, cut sides down, over **direct medium heat**. Place the burgers on the buns and top with the slaw. Serve warm.

BUTTERMILK ENGLISH MUFFINS WITH CHILLI JAM–GLAZED HAM

SERVES: 6
PREP TIME: 20 MINUTES

HEAT: INDIRECT HIGH HEAT ABOUT 200°C (400°F) AND DIRECT MEDIUM HEAT 180° TO 230°C (350° TO 450°F)
COOKING TIME: 16 TO 21 MINUTES

BISCUITS
550 g (1 lb 2 oz) plain flour
4 teaspoons baking powder
1 teaspoon bicarbonate of soda
1 teaspoon sea salt
250 g (8 oz) copha, cold
350 ml (12 fl oz) buttermilk, cold
1 tablespoon unsalted butter, melted

250 g (8 oz) chilli jam
1 kg (2 lb) ham steaks, about 1 cm (½ inch) thick

1. Prepare the barbecue for indirect cooking over a high heat.

2. Combine the flour, baking powder, bicarbonate of soda and salt in a large bowl. Cut in the copha with your fingertips or a pastry blender until the mixture resembles coarse breadcrumbs. Add the buttermilk and stir just until the mixture sticks together. Turn the dough out on to a lightly floured surface and knead lightly for 20 to 30 seconds. Lightly dust your hands with flour and gently pat out the dough to a thickness of about 1.5 cm (¾ inch). Dip a 6-cm (2½-inch) round biscuit cutter in flour and cut out rounds of dough. Gather scraps of dough and pat out, using a light touch so you don't overwork the dough. Cut to make a total of 12 muffins. Place the muffins close together on a greased baking sheet. Brush the tops with melted butter.

3. Barbecue the sheet of muffins over **_indirect high heat_** (keeping the barbecue's temperature as close to 200°C/400°F as possible) with the barbecue lid closed as much as possible but checking occasionally and moving or rotating the sheet as needed so the bottoms of the muffins do not burn, until they are lightly browned. Remove the muffins from the barbecue and set aside to keep warm.

4. Prepare the barbecue for direct cooking over medium heat.

5. Warm one-third of the chilli jam in a small saucepan over low heat until it melts. Brush the cooking grills clean. Barbecue the ham steaks over **_direct medium heat_** for 4 to 6 minutes, with the lid closed as much as possible but turning once and basting with chilli jam before and after turning, until the steaks are nicely marked and crispy on the edges.

6. Cut the ham into pieces about the same size as the muffins. Split each muffin horizontally. Serve the ham warm in muffins with the remaining chilli jam on top.

HOW TO MAKE BUTTERMILK ENGLISH MUFFINS

1. Mix the dry ingredients in a medium bowl. Add cold vegetable fat. Use a pastry blender or fork to 'cut in' the fat until the mixture resembles coarse crumbs with a few larger clumps.

2. Add buttermilk and stir just until the mixture comes together.

3. Pat the dough on a floured surface into a round about 1.5 cm (¾ inch) thick. Use a floured biscuit cutter to cut out rounds of dough.

HOW TO BARBECUE PORK CHOPS
5 THINGS YOU NEED TO KNOW

1 NOT YOUR GRANDFATHER'S PORK

Today's pigs come to market younger and smaller than the pigs of yesteryear. They have had less time to develop much collagen and connective tissue – that is, the stuff that can make pork chewy. Pork chops, therefore, are definitely tender enough for barbecuing. That's the good news.

2 IT'S BRINE TIME

The bad news is that today's pigs are also much leaner than the pigs of yesteryear. In fact, pork chops are about as lean as chicken today, which means it doesn't take long for them to dry out on the barbecue. So it is always a good idea to brine pork chops first. Brining means soaking them in a flavourful salty liquid that the meat can absorb, giving them more moisture (and flavour) from the start.

3 CHOOSE YOUR CHOP WELL

Pork chops are cut from a pig's loin, which runs from the shoulder to the hip. The chops from the shoulder (blade chops and country-style ribs) are the most marbled and flavourful, but also the chewiest. The chops from the mid-section of the loin (rib chops and loin chops) can be quite tender and juicy, if you cook them right.

4 EASY DOES IT

We don't serve pork chops charred on the outside and rare or medium rare in the middle, like steaks. We serve them with a relatively even doneness from top to bottom. This means a gentler heat on the barbecue so that the centres of the chops can reach the right degree of doneness well before the outsides are overdone.

5 THAT TOUCH OF PINK

There is really only one correct doneness level for pork chops. You'll know it when you see it and when you taste it. As the chop cooks, the colour of the meat inside will turn from reddish-pink to a very light pink. That's it. Stop there. If you cook pork chops any further than that, the meat will be grey and bland.

Good barbecuing is all about layering flavours from the inside out. In this recipe, pork chops benefit dramatically from a cider brine that penetrates right to the centre of the meat, plus an apple-brandy glaze that coats the outside.

CIDER-BRINED PORK CHOPS WITH GRILLED APPLES

SERVES: 4
PREP TIME: 15 MINUTES
BRINING TIME: 1 TO 1½ HOURS

HEAT: DIRECT MEDIUM HEAT 180° TO 230°C
(350° TO 450°F)
COOKING TIME: ABOUT 12 MINUTES

BRINE
350 ml (12 fl oz) cider
100 g (3½ oz) sea salt
1 tablespoon dried rosemary
1 tablespoon dried sage
1½ teaspoons dried thyme
½ teaspoon whole black peppercorns

4 boneless pork loin chops, each about 350 g (12 oz) and 3.5 cm (1½ inches) thick, bone out and trimmed of excess fat
Extra-virgin olive oil

GLAZE
6 tablespoons apple sauce
2 tablespoons unsalted butter
2 tablespoons Calvados or other apple brandy

4 granny smith apples or other tart green apples, each cut into 6 wedges with the cores removed

1. Mix the brine ingredients together in a large bowl. Put the chops in a large, resealable plastic bag and pour in the brine. Press the air out of the bag and seal tightly. Place the bag in a bowl or a rimmed dish and refrigerate for 1 to 1½ hours, turning the bag every 30 minutes.

2. Remove the chops from the bag and discard the brine. Rinse the chops under cold water and pat dry with paper towel. Lightly brush the chops with oil and let stand at room temperature for 20 to 30 minutes before cooking. Prepare the barbecue for direct cooking over a medium heat.

3. Warm the apple sauce and butter in a small saucepan over a medium-low heat, stirring to combine. Remove the pan from the heat and stir in the Calvados. If the glaze cools, reheat gently until fluid. Set aside half of the glaze to serve as a sauce with the barbecued pork. Brush the remaining glaze all over the apple slices and then the chops.

4. Brush the cooking grills clean. Barbecue the chops over **direct medium heat** for about 10 minutes, with the lid closed as much as possible, but turning then once, until they are slightly pink in the centre. Remove the chops from the barbecue and allow to rest for 3 to 5 minutes. While they rest, cook the apples over **direct medium heat**, about 2 minutes, turning once, until crisp-tender. Serve the chops and apples warm with the reserved glaze.

HOW TO PREP LEEKS

1. Remove the tough green tops from small, slender leeks and trim off just enough of the root end to get rid of the stringy parts.

2. Cut each leek in half lengthways to expose the many layers inside, making sure to leave some root end intact so the layers remain attached.

3. Because leeks grow underground, you will often find dirt and sand trapped between the layers. Spread the layers open under running water to clean them before barbecuing.

HOW TO MAKE BUTTERFLIED PORK

1. Begin with boneless pork loin chops at least 2.5 cm (1 inch) thick. Cut into the centre of the fat side to within about 1 cm (½ inch) of the other side, so that each chop opens up like a butterfly.

2. Flatten the meat with the palm of your hand and trim off any excess fat around the perimeter.

3. Lay each chop between 2 large sheets of plastic wrap. Use the flat side of a meat tenderiser (or the bottom of a small, heavy frying pan) to flatten the meat to an even thickness of about 5 mm (¼ inch).

HOW TO BARBECUE BUTTERFLIED PORK

1. While thick pork chops do best over a medium heat, thinly-pounded pork should be barbecued quickly over a very high heat.

2. Barbecue the first side of each pork piece with the lid closed until it has nice grill marks, usually about 3 minutes.

3. The second side should need no more than 1 minute to finish cooking.

BUTTERFLIED PORK
WITH ROMESCO SAUCE

SERVES: 4
PREP TIME: 25 MINUTES

HEAT: DIRECT LOW HEAT 130° TO 180°C (250° TO 350°F)
AND DIRECT HIGH HEAT 230° TO 290°C (450° TO 550°F)
COOKING TIME: 19 TO 24 MINUTES

4 boneless pork loin chops, 175 to 200 g (6 to 7 oz) each and
    about 2.5 cm (1 inch) thick
Extra-virgin olive oil
Sea salt
Freshly ground black pepper
8 small leeks, no wider than 2.5 cm (1 inch) in diameter,
    optional

SAUCE
100 g (3½ oz) roasted red capsicum, roughly chopped
25 g (1 oz) flaked almonds, toasted
1 tablespoon tomato sauce
1 tablespoon extra-virgin olive oil
1 tablespoon fresh lemon juice
1 teaspoon roughly chopped garlic
½ teaspoon paprika
⅛ teaspoon ground cayenne pepper

1 tablespoon flat-leaf parsley, finely chopped

1. Butterfly each chop from the fat side and trim them of
excess fat. One at a time, place each chop between 2 sheets of
plastic wrap and pound to an even 5-mm (¼-inch) thickness.
Lightly brush the pork with oil and season all sides with salt
and pepper.

2. Remove the dark green tops off of each leek, cutting about
5 cm (2 inches) above the point where the leaves begin to
darken. Trim just enough of each root end to remove the stringy
parts, but leave enough of each root end so the layers remain
attached. Cut each leek in half lengthways. Remove the tough
outer leaves on each leek. Rinse the leeks under water, opening
up the layers to remove any dirt, then pat dry. Lightly coat the
leeks with oil and season to taste with salt and pepper.

3. Prepare the barbecue for direct cooking over a low heat.

4. Brush the cooking grills clean. Barbecue the leeks over **direct
low heat** for 15 to 20 minutes, with the lid closed as much as
possible but turning every couple of minutes for even cooking,
and moving over indirect heat if the leeks become too dark
before they are tender, until softened and slightly charred on
all sides.

5. Combine the sauce ingredients in a food processor. Pulse
until you get a semi-smooth consistency, then season to taste
with salt.

6. Increase the temperature of the barbecue to a high heat.
Brush the cooking grills clean. Barbecue the pork over **direct
high heat** for about 3 minutes on the first side, turning when the
meat is nicely marked. The second side will need only a minute
to finish cooking.

7. Transfer the pork, with the first barbecued side facing up, to
a serving platter or individual plates. Divide the sauce evenly
and spoon over the meat. Arrange 2 leeks on top of each pork
piece. Garnish with some parsley over the top.

Once the sandwiches are assembled, you can reheat the meat and melt the cheese by wrapping each sandwich in baking paper or aluminium foil and barbecuing them over direct medium heat, turning them occasionally.

PORK, ROASTED CAPSICUM AND CHEESE SANDWICHES

SERVES: 4
PREP TIME: 30 MINUTES
MARINATING TIME: 30 MINUTES

HEAT: DIRECT HIGH HEAT 230° TO 290°C (450° TO 550°F) AND DIRECT MEDIUM HEAT 180° TO 230°C (350° TO 450°F)
COOKING TIME: 18 TO 22 MINUTES

MARINADE
2 tablespoons fresh lemon juice
1 teaspoon dried oregano
1 teaspoon finely chopped rosemary
1 teaspoon very finely chopped garlic
1 teaspoon sea salt
¼ teaspoon crushed red chilli flakes
5 tablespoons extra-virgin olive oil

6 boneless pork loin chops, each 50 to 125 g (2 oz to 4 oz) and about 1 cm (½ inch) thick, trimmed of excess fat
2 red capsicums
4 crusty bread rolls, split in half crossways
4 slices pepper jack or cheddar cheese
65 g (2½ lb) baby spinach leaves, rinsed and dried

1. Combine the lemon juice, oregano, rosemary, garlic, salt and chilli flakes in a small bowl, then whisk in the oil. Reserve 2 tablespoons of the marinade to use as a dressing.

2. Working with 1 chop at a time, place each chop between 2 sheets of plastic wrap. Using a flat meat tenderiser, pound the chop until it is an even 5 mm (¼ inch) thick. When all the chops are pounded, place them in a large, resealable plastic bag, arrange them flat and pour in the marinade. Press the air out of the bag and seal tightly. Turn the bag to distribute the marinade, place the bag on a plate and allow to marinate at room temperature for 30 minutes. Prepare the barbecue for direct cooking over a high heat.

3. Brush the cooking grills clean. Barbecue the capsicums over **direct high heat** for 10 to 12 minutes, with the lid closed as much as possible but turning every 3 to 5 minutes, until blackened and blistered all over. Place the capsicums in a bowl, cover with plastic wrap and allow to stand for 10 to 15 minutes. Remove the capsicums from the bowl and peel away and discard the charred skins. Cut off the tops and remove the seeds. Cut lengthways into 1-cm (½-inch) wide strips.

4. Remove the chops from the bag and discard the marinade. Sear the chops over **direct high heat** for about 4 minutes, with the lid closed as much as possible but turning once. During the last minute of cooking, toast the cut sides of the rolls over direct heat.

5. Toss the spinach with the 2 tablespoons of reserved marinade in a bowl. Build the sandwiches with a slice of cheese, 1 to 1½ pork chops, cut to fit the roll, strips of roasted capsicum and spinach.

6. Lower the temperature of the barbecue to a medium heat. Completely wrap each sandwich in a 30 by 30-cm (12 by 12-inch) sheet of baking paper, twisting the ends in opposite directions to enclose the sandwiches. Barbecue over **direct medium heat** for 4 to 6 minutes, until the cheese melts and the sandwiches are hot.

PORK LOIN CHOPS
WITH SOFRITO BARBECUE SAUCE

SERVES: 4
PREP TIME: 30 MINUTES

HEAT: DIRECT MEDIUM HEAT 180° TO 230°C
(350° TO 450°F)
COOKING TIME: 7 TO 9 MINUTES

SAUCE
250 g (8 oz) brown onion, cut into 5 mm (¼ inch) dice
3 tablespoons extra-virgin olive oil
1 small bay leaf
1 tablespoon finely chopped garlic
1 tablespoon sherry vinegar
125 ml (4 fl oz/½ cup) apple juice
1 can (425 g/14 oz) diced tomatoes
1 teaspoon paprika
½ teaspoon dried oregano
¼ teaspoon crushed red chilli flakes
¼ teaspoon sea salt
¼ teaspoon freshly ground black pepper

RUB
1 teaspoon sea salt
½ teaspoon paprika
½ teaspoon dried oregano
½ teaspoon freshly ground black pepper

4 bone-in pork loin rib chops, each 2.5 cm (1 inch) thick
Extra-virgin olive oil

1. Combine the onion, oil and bay leaf in a frying pan over a medium heat. When the onion starts to sizzle, adjust the heat to medium-low and cook for about 30 minutes, stirring frequently and adding the garlic to the pan after 15 minutes, until the onions are evenly browned. Add the vinegar and cook until it has almost evaporated. Add the apple juice and simmer until

the liquid in the pan has reduced by half. Add the rest of the sauce ingredients and continue to simmer for about 5 minutes.

2. Remove the bay leaf. Transfer the sauce to a food processor or blender and purée until smooth. Reserve 125 ml (4 fl oz/½ cup) of the sauce for basting and the rest to serve with the chops.

3. Combine the rub ingredients in a small bowl. Lightly coat the chops with oil and season with the rub. Allow the chops to stand at room temperature for 20 to 30 minutes before barbecuing. Prepare the barbecue for direct cooking over a high heat.

4. Brush the cooking grills clean. Barbecue the chops over ***direct medium heat*** for 4 to 5 minutes, with the lid closed as much as possible but turning once, until they are nicely marked on each side. Then brush both sides with the reserved sauce and continue cooking for 3 to 4 minutes, turning once or twice, until the sauce cooks into the meat a bit and the centres are barely pink. Remove the chops from the barbecue and allow to rest for 2 to 3 minutes. Serve warm with the reserved sauce.

HOW TO BARBECUE PORK CHOPS WITH SOFRITO BARBECUE SAUCE

1. In Spain and throughout much of Latin America, it is common to begin sauces with a sofrito, which is slowly browned onions and garlic followed by tomatoes.

2. Combined with apple juice and spices, this sofrito becomes a barbecue sauce. Use it for brushing onto the chops and as a dipping sauce.

3. Mark the pork chops well on both sides before brushing on the sauce, then let the sauce flavours cook into the meat.

PORK

To remove the tough silver skin from the surface, slip the tip of a narrow, sharp knife under a piece of silver skin, then grab the loosened end and stretch it taut. Slide the knife just over the pinkish meat below, angling it upwards to avoid cutting into the meat. The goal is to 'clean' the fillets without losing any more meat than necessary.

PORK FILLETS WITH CREAMY CORN

SERVES: 4 TO 6
PREP TIME: 25 MINUTES
MARINATING TIME: 1 TO 3 HOURS

HEAT: DIRECT MEDIUM HEAT 180° TO 230°C
    (350° TO 450°F)
COOKING TIME: 25 TO 30 MINUTES

PASTE
3 large garlic cloves
15 g (½ oz) oregano leaves and tender stems
1 teaspoon sea salt
4 tablespoons extra-virgin olive oil
2 tablespoons apple cider vinegar
½ teaspoon freshly ground black pepper

2 pork fillets, about 500 g (1 lb) each
5 ears corn, husked
Extra-virgin olive oil
50 g (2 oz) red onion, finely chopped
3 spring onions, thinly sliced crossways
250 ml (8 fl oz/1 cup) double cream
¼ teaspoon sea salt
⅛ teaspoon freshly ground black pepper
1 tablespoon finely chopped oregano
Hot chilli sauce, such as sriracha, optional

1. Roughly chop the garlic, then sprinkle the oregano and salt over the garlic. Continue to chop until the garlic and oregano are very finely chopped. Periodically use the side of your knife blade to press the garlic on the cutting board and create a paste. Transfer the garlic paste to a bowl and mix in the oil, vinegar and pepper.

2. Trim the pork fillets of surface fat and silver skin. Brush the paste all over the surface of the meat. Cover and refrigerate for 1 to 3 hours. Allow the meat to stand at room temperature for 20 to 30 minutes before barbecuing. Prepare the barbecue for direct cooking over a medium heat.

3. Lightly brush the ears of corn with oil. Brush the cooking grills clean. Barbecue the corn over **direct medium heat** for about 10 minutes, with the lid closed as much as possible but turning occasionally, until browned in spots and barely tender. Using a sharp knife, cut the corn kernels off the cobs.

4. Warm 2 tablespoons of olive oil in a frying pan over a medium heat. Add the onion and spring onions; cook for 3 to 4 minutes, stirring occasionally. Add the corn kernels, cream, salt and pepper and mix well. Reduce the heat to low and simmer for 5 to 7 minutes until about half of the cream has evaporated. Add the oregano and a couple dashes of hot sauce, if desired. Set aside.

5. Barbecue the pork over **direct medium heat** for 15 to 20 minutes, with the lid closed as much as possible but turning about every 5 minutes, until the outsides are evenly seared and the centres are barely pink. The internal temperature of the tenderloins should be 65°C (150°F) when fully cooked.

6. Remove the pork from the barbecue and allow it to rest for 3 to 5 minutes before slicing. Meanwhile, warm the corn mixture over a medium heat. Cut each fillet crossways into slices about 1 cm (½ inch) thick. Arrange the slices on a platter or individual plates. Serve warm with the creamy corn.

PORK FILLETS WITH SMOKED PAPRIKA ROUILLE

SERVES: 6
PREP TIME: 15 MINUTES

HEAT: DIRECT MEDIUM HEAT 180° TO 230°C
(350° TO 450°F)
COOKING TIME: 27 TO 35 MINUTES

ROUILLE
2 red capsicums
2–3 small garlic cloves
¾ teaspoon sea salt
100 g (3½ oz) dried breadcrumbs
3 tablespoons fresh lemon juice
¾ teaspoon smoked paprika
150 ml (5 fl oz) extra-virgin olive oil

2 pork fillets, about 500 g (1 lb) each
Extra-virgin olive oil
½ teaspoon sea salt
¼ teaspoon freshly ground black pepper

1. Prepare the barbecue for direct cooking over medium heat. Brush the cooking grills clean. Barbecue the capsicums over **direct medium heat** for 12 to 15 minutes, with the lid closed as much as possible but turning every 3 to 5 minutes, until blackened and blistered all over. Place the capsicums in a bowl, cover with plastic wrap and allow to stand for 10 to 15 minutes. Remove the capsicums from the bowl and peel away and discard the charred skins, tops and seeds.

2. Very finely chop the garlic in a blender or food processor, then add the roasted capsicums, salt and breadcrumbs. Add the lemon juice and paprika and, with the motor running, slowly add the oil. Blend until very smooth and orangey-red in colour. If the rouille is too thick, add about 1 tablespoon of water. Season to taste with more salt, if needed.

3. Trim the fillets of any surface fat and silver skin. Lightly brush with oil and season evenly with the salt and pepper. Allow the meat to stand at room temperature for 20 to 30 minutes before barbecuing.

4. Barbecue the fillets over **direct medium heat** for 15 to 20 minutes, with the lid closed as much as possible but turning about every 5 minutes, until the outsides are evenly seared and the centres are barely pink. The internal temperature of the fillets should be 65°C (150°F) when fully cooked.

5. Remove the pork from the barbecue and allow it to rest for 3 to 5 minutes. Cut each fillet crossways into thin slices. Serve warm or at room temperature with the rouille.

A rouille is a rust-coloured garlicky paste that it is traditionally added to bouillabaisse (fish stew), but if you thin out a rouille with a bit more extra-virgin olive oil, it also makes a very nice sauce. The key to a smooth texture is adding the oil very slowly while the paste whirls in a food processor or blender. Some food processors have a handy little hole in the feed tube that prevents too much oil from pouring into the emulsion all at once.

Cut each pork fillet crossways into pieces about 3.5 cm (1½ inches) thick. Use the heel of your hand to flatten each piece into a medallion about 2.5 cm (1 inch) thick. For juicy results, marinate the medallions for at least 1 hour and then grill them gently over a medium heat until barely pink in the centre.

PORK MEDALLIONS WITH ASIAN BLACK BEAN SAUCE

SERVES: 4
PREP TIME: 25 MINUTES
MARINATING TIME: 1 HOUR

HEAT: DIRECT MEDIUM HEAT 180° TO 230°C
   (350° TO 450°F)
COOKING TIME: 4 TO 5 MINUTES

MARINADE
½ teaspoon grated orange rind
4 tablespoons fresh orange juice
4 tablespoons Chinese rice wine or dry sherry
2 tablespoons soy sauce
1 tablespoon hoisin sauce
1 tablespoon very finely chopped fresh root ginger
1 tablespoon toasted sesame oil
¼ teaspoon crushed red chilli flakes

2 pork fillets, about 500 g (1 lb) each,
   trimmed of silver skin

SAUCE
2 tablespoons Chinese fermented black beans
125 ml (4 fl oz/½ cup) chicken stock
2 tablespoons Chinese rice wine or dry sherry
1 tablespoon soy sauce
1 teaspoon sugar
1½ teaspoons cornflour
1 tablespoon canola or other vegetable oil
2 teaspoons peeled and very finely chopped fresh root ginger
1 garlic clove, very finely chopped
2 tablespoons fresh orange juice

1. Whisk the marinade ingredients together in a bowl.

2. Cut off the thin, tapered end from each fillet and reserve for another use, or marinate and barbecue along with the medallions. Cut each fillet crossways into 6 equal-sized pieces, each about 3.5 cm (1½ inches) thick. One at a time, stand the pork rounds on a work surface and, using the heel of your hand, slightly flatten into a round medallion about 2.5 cm (1 inch) thick. Place the medallions in a large, resealable plastic bag and pour in the marinade. Press the air out of the bag and seal tightly. Turn the bag several times to distribute the marinade and refrigerate for at least 1 hour, turning the bag occasionally.

3. Soak the fermented black beans in a small bowl filled with warm water for 10 to 20 minutes, then drain well. Coarsely chop the beans and set aside. Whisk the stock, rice wine, soy sauce and sugar together in a bowl until the sugar has dissolved. Sprinkle in the cornflour and stir to dissolve. Set aside.

4. Warm the oil in a small saucepan over a medium-high heat. Add the ginger and garlic and stir for about 20 seconds, until softened. Stir in the beans, then add the stock mixture and bring to the boil, stirring constantly, until the sauce has slightly thickened. Remove from the heat and stir in the orange juice.

5. Prepare the barbecue for direct cooking over a medium heat. Brush the cooking grills clean. Remove the pork from the bag and discard the marinade. Barbecue the medallions over **direct medium heat** for 4 to 5 minutes, with the lid closed as much as possible but turning once, until the outsides are evenly seared and the centres are barely pink. Remove from the barbecue and allow to rest for 2 to 3 minutes. Serve hot with the black bean sauce.

AMERICAN-STYLE SOFT DRINK-BRINED PORK LOIN WITH CHERRY-CHIPOTLE GLAZE

SERVES: 4 TO 6
PREP TIME: 25 MINUTES
BRINING TIME: 1 TO 2 HOURS

HEAT: DIRECT AND INDIRECT HIGH HEAT 230° TO 290°C
(450° TO 550°F)
COOKING TIME: 33 TO 42 MINUTES
SPECIAL EQUIPMENT: LARGE DISPOSABLE FOIL TIN

1 litre (35 fl oz/4 cups) Dr. Pepper® (not diet)
100 g (3½ oz) sea salt
1 boneless pork loin, 750 g to 2 kg (1 lb 10 oz to 4 lb 8 oz)

GLAZE
275 g (9 oz) tart cherry preserve
125 ml (4 fl oz/½ cup) Dr. Pepper®
125 ml (4 fl oz/½ cup) water
1–2 tablespoons very finely chopped tinned chipotle in adobo
(or chipotle salsa)
4 teaspoons dijon mustard

Canola or other vegetable oil

1. Pour the soda into a large bowl and slowly add the salt (the mixture will foam up quite a bit so be sure to use a bowl large enough to prevent overflowing). Stir for 1 to 2 minutes until the salt has dissolved completely. Place a large, disposable plastic bag inside a large bowl, and carefully pour the brine into the bag.

2. Trim excess fat and silver skin from the pork. Submerge the pork in the brine, seal the bag and refrigerate for 1 to 2 hours.

3. Combine the glaze ingredients in a small bowl.

4. Remove the pork from the bag and discard the brine. Pat dry with paper towel. Lightly coat the pork with oil and allow to stand at room temperature for 20 to 30 minutes before barbecuing. Prepare the barbecue for direct and indirect cooking over a high heat.

5. Brush the cooking grills clean. Sear the pork over ***direct high heat*** for 8 to 12 minutes, with the lid closed as much as possible but turning once, until the surface is well marked but not burned.

6. Place a large disposable tin over ***indirect high heat*** and pour the glaze into the tin. Transfer the pork to the tin and turn to coat with the glaze. Barbecue the pork over ***indirect high heat*** for 25 to 30 minutes, with the lid closed as much as possible but turning in the glaze every 8 to 10 minutes, until barely pink in the centre and the internal temperature reaches 63° to 65°C (145° to 150°F). If the glaze gets too thick or starts to scorch, add a little water or more soda to the tin. Transfer the pork to a chopping board and allow it to rest for about 5 minutes. Cut the pork crossways into 1-cm (½-inch) slices and serve with the remaining tin sauce on the side.

If it's not treated correctly, pork loin can dry out all too quickly on the barbecue. The surest way to prevent this is to brine it first in a sweet-and-savoury solution, swelling the meat with moisture and flavour. Next, brown the joint over direct heat and finish cooking it over indirect heat, glazing it periodically.

HOW TO MAKE ROTISSERIE PORK LOIN

1. Large, thick pieces of meat will almost always be juicier after cooking than small narrow ones will, so improve your chances of wonderfully moist results by tying 2 sections of pork loin together.

2. Place one joint on top of the other, with the fat sides on the outside, and tie them together crossways with individual lengths of butcher's string separated by 2.5 cm (1 inch) or so.

3. Cut 2 very long pieces of string, each about 1.2 m (4 feet). Tie one end of each piece to a crossways piece at one end of the roast. Weave the long pieces of string lengthways in and out of the crossways pieces and all the way around the length of the joint.

4. Tie off each lengthways piece of string at the knot where it began, on the first crossways piece. The twine will hold the meat in place as it shrinks a little on the rotisserie.

5. Slide the centre rod (spit) of the rotisserie between the sections of pork loin, making sure to imbed the fork prongs well inside the meat.

6. Allow the meat to rest at room temperature for 1 hour before cooking. Brush it with oil and season it evenly with salt and pepper before putting the rotisserie in position.

7. Natural juices baste the meat inside and out as the joint turns slowly on the rotisserie. Place a foil tin underneath to prevent grease from falling into the barbecue.

8. Check the internal temperature of the meat at the centre of the joint. When it reaches 63° to 65°C (145° to 150°F), turn off the rotisserie and, wearing insulated barbecue mitts or oven gloves, remove it from the barbecue. While the meat rests at room temperature, it will continue to cook.

PORK

ROTISSERIE PORK LOIN AGRO DOLCE

SERVES: 12 TO 14
PREP TIME: 45 MINUTES

HEAT: INDIRECT HEAT ABOUT 200°C (400°F)
COOKING TIME: 1 TO 1¼ HOURS
SPECIAL EQUIPMENT: BUTCHER'S STRING, ROTISSERIE,
    LARGE DISPOSABLE FOIL TIN

SAUCE
2 tablespoons extra-virgin olive oil
375 g (13 oz) brown onions, finely diced
½ teaspoon sea salt
750 ml (26 fl oz/3 cups) red wine
150 g (5 oz) raisins
125 g (4 oz) pitted prunes, finely diced
1 tablespoon finely grated orange rind
175 ml (6 fl oz) fresh orange juice
1/8 teaspoon ground cloves
Sea salt
Freshly ground black pepper

2 boneless pork loin joints, 1.5 to 1.75 kg (3 to 3½ lb) each
2 tablespoons extra-virgin olive oil
1½ teaspoons sea salt
1 teaspoon freshly ground black pepper

1. Warm the oil in a saucepan over a medium heat. Add the onions and salt and cook for about 15 minutes, stirring often, until the onions are quite soft. Increase the heat to high, add the wine and boil for about 8 minutes until it has reduced by half. Stir in the raisins, prunes and orange rind, reduce the heat to medium and cook for 5 to 10 minutes, stirring occasionally, until the fruit is tender. Add the orange juice and cloves and season to taste with salt and pepper. Keep warm.

2. Trim the pork loins to match in size and then place one joint on top of the other, making sure the sides of the joint with the layers of fat are facing outwards. This fatty layer will help protect the meat while it cooks. Tie the 2 joints together to make one large cylindrical joint. Allow the roast to stand at room temperature for 1 hour before barbecuing. Brush the roast with the oil and season with the salt and pepper.

3. Prepare the barbecue for rotisserie cooking over indirect heat. If your gas barbecue has one, turn on the infrared burner to **low** and set the outer burner control knobs to **low heat**. The temperature of the barbecue should be around 200°C (400°F). You may need to adjust the outer burners to medium heat.

4. Carefully slide one pronged fork on to the spit, with the fork facing inwards, about 25 cm (10 inches) from the end of the spit. Secure the fork but do not tighten at this time. Slide the spit through the centre of the joint and gently push the joint

on to the fork so that they are deep inside the joint. Add the other pronged fork to the spit with the tines facing inwards and slide down until they are firmly imbedded into the joint. Secure the fork, but do not completely tighten at this time. Wearing barbecue mitts or oven gloves, place the pointed end of the spit into the rotisserie motor. If necessary, adjust the joint so that it is centred on the spit and tighten the forks into place. Place the foil tin under the joint to catch any grease. Turn on the motor to begin the rotisserie.

5. Barbecue the joint for 1 to 1¼ hours, until the internal temperature reaches 63° to 65°C (145° to 150°F). To check the temperature, turn off the rotisserie motor and insert a thermometer down the centre of one of the joints. Wearing barbecue mitts or oven gloves, carefully remove the spit from the barbecue. Gently loosen the forks and slide the joint off of the spit. Transfer the pork to a carving board, tent with foil and allow to rest for 15 to 30 minutes (the roast will continue to cook during this time).

6. Slice the joint and serve with the sauce.

HOW TO BARBECUE BONE-IN PORK LOIN

1. A moderately hot fire of about 180°C (350°F) is just right for roasting a bone-in pork loin. Begin with a chimney starter filled about half full with barbecue briquettes. Let the coals burn down until they are completely covered with ash, and then dump them on to the charcoal grate.

2. Spread the briquettes in a single layer over one side of the charcoal grate and lay an oak log beside them. It will smolder and smoke, filling the pork with haunting outdoorsy aromas.

3. Cook the joint on the cooler side of the barbecue opposite the bed of briquettes, with the bone side facing down and the thick meaty side facing the coals. If the log catches fire, use a spray bottle filled with water to douse the flames.

4. After cooking with the lid on for 45 minutes, rotate the joint 180 degrees so the tips of the bones are facing the coals.

5. Remove the joint from the barbecue when the internal temperature reaches the range of 63° to 65°C (145° to 150°F). Loosely cover the joint with foil and allow it to rest for 15 minutes, which allows the juices to stay in the meat when you slice it.

6. The easiest way to carve the joint is to turn it over so the bone side is facing up. That way you can see exactly where the bones are and slice right between them.

When you buy a bone-in pork loin, make sure the butcher has removed the chine bone (backbone), which runs along the top of all the rib bones. Otherwise it will be nearly impossible to slice between the ribs and serve individual chops. Also, don't be afraid to season the meat generously before cooking. It is a thick joint that can handle plenty of salt and pepper.

SMOKE-ROASTED PORK LOIN WITH REDCURRANT SAUCE

SERVES: 8
PREP TIME: 20 MINUTES

HEAT: INDIRECT MEDIUM HEAT 150° TO 180°C
(300° TO 350°F)
COOKING TIME: 1½ TO 2 HOURS

1 bone-in pork loin joint, 3.5 to 4 kg (7 lb 14 oz to 8 lb 12 oz)
3 tablespoons extra-virgin olive oil
2 teaspoons sea salt
1 teaspoon freshly ground black pepper

1 oak log, about 45 cm (18 inches) long and 10 cm (4 inches) in diameter

SAUCE
175 g (6 oz) redcurrant jelly
125 g (4 oz) tomato sauce
125 ml (4 fl oz/½ cup) apple juice
2 tablespoons apple cider vinegar
1 tablespoon soy sauce
1 tablespoon whisky
½ teaspoon crushed red chilli flakes

1. Lightly coat the pork with the oil and season with the salt and pepper. Allow the pork to stand at room temperature for 30 minutes while you prepare the barbecue.

2. Starting with about half of a chimney of lit coals, arrange them on one-third of the charcoal grate. Place the log alongside the outer edge of the coals; do not place it directly on top of the coals. The log should slowly start to smolder but should not catch on fire. If it does catch on fire, use a spray bottle filled with water to douse the flames. Put the cooking grill in place and set the pork joint, bone side down and with the meaty section facing the fire, over *indirect medium heat* (about 180°C/350°F), and cook for 45 minutes with the lid closed.

3. After 45 minutes, rotate the meat 180 degrees so the bone section is facing the heat. Continue to cook over *indirect medium heat* for 45 minutes to 1¼ hours with the lid closed, until the internal temperature reaches 63° to 65°C (145° to 150°F).

4. Combine the sauce ingredients in a saucepan over a medium heat. Let the sauce come to a simmer and cook, stirring occasionally until the preserves have melted and the sauce is well combined. Remove the pan from the heat.

5. Transfer the joint to a chopping board, loosely cover with foil and allow to rest 15 to 30 minutes. Slice between each bone. Serve warm with the sauce.

HOW TO BARBECUE PORK SHOULDER

1. A water smoker can maintain temperatures between 110°C (225°F) and 130°C (250°F) for several hours, which is just what you need to break down the connective tissue in pork shoulder joints.

2. Fill the water pan in the middle section of the smoker. It will absorb some of the charcoal's heat and release it slowly with some humidity.

3. After 8 to 10 hours of barbecuing, the meat will be so tender that you can slide the bone out cleanly.

4. Ideally you will need both a spatula and a pair of tongs to remove the shoulders without the meat falling apart.

5. Shred the meat with your fingers or 2 forks. Discard any clumps of fat, but hold onto the crispy bits of 'bark' that have developed on the outside of the meat.

6. The pinkish colour of the meat is a good sign that smoke has penetrated the surface and filled the pork with authentic barbecue flavour.

PULLED PORK SANDWICHES

SERVES: 10 TO 12
PREP TIME: 25 MINUTES

HEAT: INDIRECT LOW HEAT 110° TO 130°C (225° TO 250°F)
COOKING TIME: 8 TO 10 HOURS

RUB
2 tablespoons pure chilli powder
2 tablespoons sea salt
4 teaspoons garlic granules
2 teaspoons freshly ground black pepper
1 teaspoon mustard powder

2 bone-in pork shoulder joints, 2.5 to 3 kg (5 to 6 lb) each
3 large handfuls hickory wood chips, soaked in water for at least
    30 minutes

SAUCE
275 g (9 oz) tomato sauce
175 ml (6 fl oz) apple cider vinegar
50 g (2 oz) light brown sugar
1½ teaspoons worcestershire sauce
1 teaspoon hot chilli sauce, such as sriracha, or to taste
1 teaspoon sea salt
½ teaspoon mustard powder
¼ teaspoon freshly ground black pepper

12 hamburger buns

1. Prepare your smoker, following manufacturer's instructions, for indirect cooking over a low heat.

2. Mix the rub ingredients together in a small bowl. Season the pork shoulders all over with the rub and press the spices into the meat.

3. Smoke the pork over *indirect low heat*, with the lid closed but adding a handful of drained wood chips to the coals every hour for the first 3 hours, until the internal temperature of the meat reaches 88°C (190°F). At this point the bone should easily slip out of the meat, and the meat should be falling apart in some areas. The total cooking time will be 8 to 10 hours. Maintain the heat of the smoker at 110° to 130°C (225° to 250°F).

4. Whisk the sauce ingredients together in a large, heavy-based saucepan. Bring to a simmer over a medium heat and cook for about 5 minutes, stirring occasionally. Taste and adjust the seasonings, if necessary. It should be spicy and tangy.

5. Transfer the pork joints to a roasting tray and tightly cover them with aluminium foil. Allow the pork to rest for 30 minutes.

6. Pull the warm meat apart with your fingers, or use 2 forks to shred the meat. Discard any large pieces of fat or sinew. Put the pork into a large bowl and moisten with as much sauce as you like (you may not need all of the sauce). Pile the pork on hamburger buns.

HOW TO MAKE PORCHETTA

1. Trim off the relatively thin pieces of meat on the ends of the pork shoulder joint. Also trim the thick sections of the joint to create a fairly even thickness from end to end.

2. Ideally you will have 250 to 300 g (8 to 10 oz) of trimmed meat and fat to mix with delicious herbs, spices, garlic and olive oil. This will be the porchetta filling.

3. Pulse the ingredients in a food processor 20 to 25 times until they have the look and texture of minced (ground) sausage meat. Then spread the filling over the interior of the joint.

4. Leave a border along the edges of the pork joint so the filling does not spill out when you roll the meat. Press the filling into any grooves in the meat.

5. Now roll up the meat from one short end to the other, creating an evenly shaped and compact cylinder.

6. Use several long pieces of butcher's string to tie the joint both crossways and lengthways. Allow the joint to stand at room temperature for 20 to 30 minutes before cooking.

PORCHETTA-STYLE PORK SHOULDER

SERVES: 6 TO 8
PREP TIME: 30 MINUTES

HEAT: INDIRECT MEDIUM HEAT 180° TO 200°C
    (350° TO 400°F)
COOKING TIME: 2 TO 2½ HOURS
SPECIAL EQUIPMENT: BUTCHER'S STRING

FILLING
125 ml (4 fl oz/½ cup) extra-virgin olive oil
3 sprigs rosemary leaves
16 large sage leaves
1 tablespoon finely grated lemon rind
1 tablespoon chopped garlic
1 teaspoon sea salt
½ teaspoon whole fennel seeds
½ teaspoon crushed red chilli flakes

1 boneless pork shoulder joint, about 2.5 kg (5 lb), butterflied,
    ends trimmed to produce 250 to 300 g (8 to 10 oz) meat
    and fat
1 tablespoon extra-virgin olive oil
½ teaspoon sea salt
½ teaspoon freshly ground black pepper

1. Combine the filling ingredients in a food processor and
process until they form a smooth purée. Add the trimmed
meat and fat and pulse for 20 to 25 pulses, until it resembles
sausagemeat.

2. Place the joint, skin side down, on a work surface. Evenly
distribute the filling over the pork, leaving a border round the
edges of the joint. Roll up the meat and tie with butcher's string
in 5 or 6 places. Rub the outside of the joint with the oil, salt
and pepper, then allow the joint to stand at room temperature
for 20 to 30 minutes before barbecuing. Prepare the barbecue
for indirect cooking over a medium heat.

3. Brush the cooking grills clean. Barbecue the joint over
indirect medium heat for 2 to 2½ hours, with the lid closed,
until the internal temperature reaches 82° to 85°C (180° to
185°F).

4. Transfer the joint to a chopping board, loosely cover with foil
and allow to rest for 20 to 30 minutes. Remove the string and
carve the meat into thin slices. Serve warm.

■ ■ ■

*In and around Rome, Italy, porchetta is a
bacchanalian dish that involves stuffing a whole pig
with wild fennel, garlic and spices, and then cooking
it on a rotisserie spit. Assuming that you may not be
inclined to tackle such a huge project, here's a simpler
version that calls for a pork shoulder filled with the
authentic flavours.*

■ ■ ■

PORK

HOW TO SEASON PORK ROAST

1. Grate the garlic finely.

2. Make shallow cross-hatch slashes about 5 cm (2 inches) apart through the fat but not into the flesh.

3. Smear the garlic-and-herb paste all over the joint, pressing it into the slashes and crevices.

4. Cover the joint and refrigerate for 12 to 24 hours.

HOW TO BARBECUE PORK ROAST

1. Cook a bone-in pork shoulder over indirect low heat (about 130°C/250°F) so that its collagen and fat will melt and make the meat succulent before the outside burns.

2. When the meat's internal temperature reaches 85° to 88°C (185° to 190°F), remove the joint from the barbecue, wrap it in foil and let the meat rest and juices redistribute for a full hour.

3. Cut the joint into 1-cm (½-inch) slices or tear the meat into bite-sized chucks. Serve with a bold garlic-citrus sauce called mojo (pronounced 'mo-ho').

LATINO PORK ROAST

SERVES: 6 TO 8
PREP TIME: 30 MINUTES
MARINATING TIME: 12 TO 24 HOURS

HEAT: INDIRECT LOW HEAT ABOUT 130°C (250°F)
COOKING TIME: 5 TO 7 HOURS, PLUS 1 HOUR
    RESTING TIME

PASTE
5 large garlic cloves, very finely grated
3 tablespoons extra-virgin olive oil
3 tablespoons apple cider vinegar
2 tablespoons dried oregano
1 tablespoon plus 2 teaspoons sea salt
1 tablespoon freshly ground black pepper

1 bone-in pork shoulder joint, with an outer layer of fat,
    3 to 3.5 kg (6 to 7 lb)
4 handfuls oak or hickory wood chips, soaked in water for at least
    30 minutes

MOJO
Finely grated rind of 1 orange
250 ml (8 fl oz/1 cup) fresh orange juice
125 ml (4 fl oz/½ cup) fresh grapefruit juice
50 g (2 oz) white onion, finely chopped
2 tablespoons distilled white vinegar
1 small serrano chilli, very finely chopped
1 garlic clove, finely chopped
1 teaspoon sugar
Sea salt

3 tablespoons coriander, finely chopped

1. Combine the paste ingredients in a small bowl.

2. Score the fat on the joint in a cross-hatch pattern, about 5 cm
(2 inches) apart, cutting through the fat just to the flesh. Rub
the paste all over the joint, then place it in a bowl, cover and
refrigerate for 12 to 24 hours. Allow the joint to stand at room
temperature for 1 hour before barbecuing.

3. Prepare the barbecue for indirect cooking over a low heat.
Brush the cooking grills clean. Drain 1 handful of the wood
chips and scatter them over the coals or in the smoker box
of a gas barbecue, following the manufacturer's instructions.
Barbecue the pork, fat side down, over **indirect low heat** for
5 to 7 hours, with the lid closed as much as possible but turning
once after about 3 hours and adding 1 handful of drained wood
chips each hour until they are gone, until the meat is so tender
that it gives no resistance when pierced with a meat fork and
the internal temperature registers 85° to 88°C (185° to 190°F).
Transfer the joint to a platter and loosely cover with aluminium
foil, then allow to rest for about 1 hour.

4. Combine the mojo ingredients, including salt to taste, in a
small serving bowl, stirring to dissolve the sugar and salt. Cover
and set aside. Just before serving, stir in the coriander.

5. Cut the joint into 1-cm (½-inch) slices (it may fall apart into
chunks and not carve neatly, but that's okay). Serve warm with
the mojo.

HOW TO BARBECUE PORK RIBS
5 THINGS YOU NEED TO KNOW

1 STRIKE THE BALANCE
A perfectly barbecued rack of ribs achieves a seamless harmony of effects. The slightly crisp texture of a handsome, glossy surface gives way to morsels of luscious meat with a fragrant wood-smoke flavour. At each step of cooking your goal is to balance the spices, sauce and smoke with the inherently beautiful flavour of slow-roasted pork, never allowing one effect to outdo the others.

2 USE WHAT YOU HAVE
You can make satisfying barbecued ribs on a gas barbecue, charcoal barbecue or smoker. Each one is capable of slowly tenderising the rib meat and scenting it with wood smoke, although with a gas barbecue you will need a smoker box attachment.

3 WATCH THAT HEAT
The key to tender ribs is maintaining a low temperature for several hours. Spikes and valleys of heat will tighten and dry out the meat, but consistently low temperatures will produce soft and succulent meat.

4 ALL IN GOOD TIME
It's one thing to wait the required 3 to 4 hours for baby back ribs or 5 to 6 hours for spareribs, but that's not the only timing issue. You must not sauce any ribs too early, especially if you are using a sweet sauce, as the sugars will burn and threaten your precious ribs. Sauce them during the final 30 minutes of cooking, or just before you wrap them in foil.

5 WRAP 'EM UP
Wrapping ribs in foil during the final stages of cooking holds in some moisture and helps to tenderise the meat. This is a little trick that some barbecue professionals dismiss as 'the Texas crutch', but you know what? It works.

HOW TO PREP BABY BACK RIBS

1. At one end of the rack, slide a dinner knife under the membrane and over a bone.

2. Lift and loosen the membrane until it tears.

3. Grab the edge of the membrane with paper towel and pull it off.

4. The membrane may come off in one whole piece, or you may need to remove it in smaller pieces.

5. Season the ribs mostly on the meaty side and press the spices into the meat so they don't fall off.

6. Stand the ribs in a rib rack to double the number of ribs you can cook in a limited cooking space.

HOW TO SET UP A CHARCOAL BARBECUE FOR SMOKING

1. If you are using wood chips, soak them first in water for at least 30 minutes so that they smolder and smoke slowly rather than flame up.

2. Dump the barbecue briquettes on one side of the charcoal grate. A charcoal basket holds the coals together in a compact bunch and slows down the burning. Tap the edge of the basket with tongs every hour or so to knock the ashes through the basket holes.

3. Place a foil tin on the other side of the charcoal grate and fill it at least halfway with water to create a little steam inside the barbecue. The ribs will cook on the cooking grill directly above the water pan.

4. Drain some wood chips and lay them right on the coals. Replenish them after the first hour of cooking.

HOW TO BARBECUE BABY BACK RIBS

1. To protect the meat, begin with the bone side of the ribs facing the coals.

2. After the first hour of cooking, baste the ribs with a vinegar 'mop'.

3. Periodically swap the positions of the ribs in the rib rack for even cooking.

4. Towards the end of cooking, face the meaty sides of the ribs towards the coals to brown and crisp the surface.

5. The meat should be tender enough that it tears when you bend a rack backwards.

6. Lightly brush each rack of ribs with sauce as it comes off the barbecue.

7. Wrap each rack individually in aluminium foil.

8. The ribs will stay warm and continue to cook a bit for at least 30 minutes.

SLOW GOOD BABY BACK RIBS WITH SOO-WEE SAUCE

SERVES: 4 TO 6
PREP TIME: 20 MINUTES

HEAT: INDIRECT LOW HEAT 130° TO 150°C (250° TO 300°F)
COOKING TIME: 3 TO 4 HOURS
SPECIAL EQUIPMENT: RIB RACK

RUB
2 tablespoons sea salt
2 tablespoons paprika
4 teaspoons garlic granules
4 teaspoons pure chilli powder
2 teaspoons mustard powder
2 teaspoons freshly ground black pepper

4 racks baby back ribs, 1 to 1½ kg (2 to 2½ lb) each

SAUCE
250 ml (8 fl oz/1 cup) apple juice
137 ml (4½ fl oz) tomato sauce
3 tablespoons apple cider vinegar
1 tablespoon soy sauce
2 teaspoons molasses
½ teaspoon pure chilli powder
½ teaspoon garlic granules
½ teaspoon mustard powder
¼ teaspoon sea salt
¼ teaspoon freshly ground black pepper

MOP
175 ml (6 fl oz) red wine vinegar
175 ml (6 fl oz) water
2 tablespoons soy sauce

4 handfuls hickory wood chips, soaked in water for at least 30 minutes

1. Prepare a charcoal barbecue for indirect cooking over a low heat (see page 121).

2. Mix the rub ingredients together in a small bowl.

3. Slide a dull dinner knife tip under the membrane covering the back of each rack of ribs. Lift and loosen the membrane until it breaks, and then grab a corner of it with paper towel and pull it off. Season the ribs all over with the rub, putting more of it on the meaty sides than the bone sides. Arrange the ribs in a rib rack, all facing the same direction. The ribs should stand at room temperature for 30 minutes to 1 hour before cooking.

4. When the fire has burned down to about 180°C (350°F), drain 2 handfuls of hickory wood chips and place them on top of the coals. The damp wood will lower the temperature a bit. Put the cooking grill in place. Place the ribs in the rack over **indirect low heat** (positioned over the foil tin) as far from the coals as possible, with the bone sides facing toward the coals. Close the lid. Close the top vent about halfway. Allow the ribs to cook and smoke for 1 hour. During this time, maintain the temperature at 130° to 150°C (250° to 300°F) by opening and closing the top vent. Meanwhile, make the sauce and the mop.

5. Mix the sauce ingredients together in a small saucepan over a medium heat. Simmer for about 5 minutes, then remove the pan from the heat. Taste and add more salt and pepper, if desired.

6. Mix the mop ingredients together in a small bowl.

7. After the first hour of cooking the ribs, add the remaining 2 handfuls of wood chips (drained) to the lit coals. Move the ribs from the rack and spread them out on 2 roasting trays. Brush them generously on both sides with some of the mop. Return the ribs to the rack, all facing the same direction, now with the bone sides facing away from the coals.

8. Close the lid and cook for another hour. During this time, maintain the temperature at 130° to 150°C (250° to 300°F) by opening and closing the top vent.

9. Move the ribs from the rack and spread them out on 2 baking trays. Brush them generously on both sides with some of the mop. Return the ribs to the rack, all facing the same direction, but this time turned over so that the ends facing down before now face up. Also position any ribs that appear to be cooking faster then others toward the back of the rib rack, further away from the coals. This time the bone sides should face the coals.

10. Close the lid and let the ribs cook for a third hour. During this time, maintain the temperature at 130° to 150°C (250° to 300°F) by opening and closing the top vent.

11. After 3 hours of cooking, check to see if any rack is ready to come off the barbecue. They are done when the meat has shrunk back from most of the bones by 5 mm (¼ inch) or more. When you lift a rack by picking up one end with tongs, the rack should bend in the middle and the meat should tear easily. If the meat does not tear easily, continue to cook the ribs. The total cooking time could be anywhere between 3 to 4 hours. Not all racks will cook in the same amount of time. Lightly brush the ribs with some sauce. Transfer the racks to a clean roasting tray and brush the ribs on both sides with some sauce. Wrap each rack individually in aluminium foil and allow to rest for about 30 minutes. Serve warm with the remaining sauce on the side.

HOW TO COOK STACKED RIBS

1. One space-saving solution, whether you are cooking with charcoal or gas, is to stack the racks of ribs on top of each other in the centre of the barbecue.

2. Cook the ribs for about 45 minutes, with the lid closed and low heat radiating from both sides of the barbecue.

3. Then undo the stack of ribs on the cooking grill.

4. Baste the ribs on both sides with some reserved marinade.

5. Stack them again, swapping the positions of the ribs by moving the top rack to the bottom, the bottom rack to the centre, and the middle rack to the top.

6. Continue to cook the ribs, basting and swapping positions of the racks occasionally, until the meat has shrunk back at least 5 mm (¼ inch) from the ends of the bones.

STACKED BABY BACK RIBS

SERVES: 6 TO 8
PREP TIME: 20 MINUTES
MARINATING TIME: 30 MINUTES

HEAT: INDIRECT AND DIRECT LOW HEAT 150° TO 170°C
(300° TO 340°F)
COOKING TIME: 2¾ TO 3¼ HOURS

MARINADE
250 g (8 oz) sweet chilli sauce
250 ml (8 fl oz/1 cup) water
Grated rind of 3 limes
5 tablespoons fresh lime juice
4 large garlic cloves
4 tablespoons soy sauce
3 tablespoons roughly chopped fresh root ginger

3 racks baby back ribs, 1 to 1.5 kg (2 to 2½ lb) each
1 tablespoon sea salt

1. Combine the marinade ingredients in a blender or food
processor and process for about 1 minute to purée. Set aside
250 ml (8 fl oz/1 cup) of the marinade to use as a basting
sauce.

2. Remove the thin membrane from the back of each rack of
ribs (see page 121). Season the ribs on the meaty sides with
salt. Brush the remaining marinade over all the ribs. Allow
the ribs to stand at room temperature for 30 minutes before
cooking. Prepare the barbecue for indirect cooking over a
low heat.

3. Brush the cooking grills clean. Stack the ribs on top of each
other, with the bone sides facing down, and barbecue over
indirect low heat for 45 minutes, with the lid closed.

4. Undo the stack of ribs on the barbecue. Brush the meaty
sides with some of the reserved marinade. Stack the ribs, with
the bone sides facing down, moving the top rack to the bottom,
the bottom rack to the centre, and the middle rack to the top.
Cook over *indirect low heat* for another 45 minutes, with the
lid closed.

5. Undo the stack of ribs on the barbecue again. Brush the meaty
sides with some of the reserved marinade. Stack the ribs, with the
bone sides facing down, moving the top rack to the bottom, the
bottom rack to the centre, and the middle rack to the top. Cook
over *indirect low heat* for 1 to 1½ hours, with the lid closed.
During this third round of cooking, move the relative positions of
the ribs occasionally so that the racks that are browning a little
faster cook in the centre of the stack and the racks that are not as
brown cook at the top of the stack. As you move the ribs, brush
the meaty sides with the reserved marinade.

6. Undo the stack of ribs and place them side by side, with
the bone sides facing down, over *direct low heat* for 10 to
15 minutes, turning occasionally to prevent burning. Brush with
a little more of the reserved marinade and continue cooking
until the meat is very tender and has shrunk back from the ends
of the bones.

7. Transfer the racks to a roasting tray, cover with foil and allow to
rest for 15 minutes before cutting into individual ribs. Serve warm.

HOW TO PREP ST LOUIS–STYLE RIBS

1. There is a tough flap of meat, called the skirt, hanging from the bone side of a full rack of spareribs. The first step for converting 'regular' spareribs to the St Louis-style cut is to remove that flap.

2. The next step is to cut off the long strip of cartilaginous meat, called the brisket, which runs along the bottom of the rack.

3. Then trim off any meat dangling from either end of each rack. The goal is to make a handsome rectangular rack of ribs.

4. Use a dinner knife or some other dull instrument to get under the membrane and lift it so that you can grab an edge with paper towel. Then peel off and discard the membrane.

5. The rack on top is a St Louis-style cut. It is about the same length as the rack of baby back ribs, shown on the bottom, but the St Louis-style cut is obviously wide and meatier. It's also tougher, so it requires longer cooking.

6. You can bump up the flavour and give the ribs a crispy surface by marinating them in a sweet-and-savoury marinade for a few hours before cooking.

HOW TO USE 'THE TEXAS CRUTCH'

1. In the world of competition barbecue, 'the Texas crutch' refers to the technique of wrapping ribs in foil during the final stages of cooking, often with some liquid trapped inside.

2. The theory is that the humidity inside the foil moistens and tenderises the meat. Some purists shun this approach – hence the mocking sobriquet. It's unclear why the technique is associated with Texas.

3. Many barbecue teams and home cooks use the technique with great success, either finishing their ribs in foil on their smoker or just allowing their ribs to 'rest' in foil after they have been removed from the smoker.

SWEET GINGER-AND-SOY-GLAZED SPARERIBS

SERVES: 6
PREP TIME: 30 MINUTES
MARINATING TIME: 3 HOURS

HEAT: INDIRECT LOW HEAT ABOUT 150°C (300°F)
COOKING TIME: 4 TO 5 HOURS

MARINADE
100 g (3½ oz) brown sugar
125 ml (4 fl oz/½ cup) soy sauce
125 g (4 oz) tomato sauce
125 ml (4 fl oz/½ cup) dry sherry
2 tablespoons very finely chopped fresh root ginger
1½ teaspoons very finely chopped garlic

2 racks pork spareribs, about 2 kg (4 lb 8 oz) each

1. Combine the marinade ingredients in a large bowl.

2. Prepare the racks of spareribs as detailed at left. Put the spareribs, meaty side up, on a chopping board. Follow the line of fat that separates the meaty ribs from the much tougher tips at the base of each rack, and cut off the tips. Turn each rack over. Cut off the flap of meat attached in the centre of each rack. Also cut off the flap of meat that hangs below the shorter end of the ribs. (The flaps and tips may be barbecued separately, but they will not be as tender as the ribs.) Remove the thin membrane from the back of each rack of ribs.

3. Place the ribs in one layer on a large roasting tray. Pour the marinade over the ribs and turn to coat them evenly. Cover and refrigerate for 3 hours, turning occasionally. Remove the ribs from the tray and reserve the marinade. Allow the ribs to stand at room temperature for 30 minutes before barbecuing. Prepare the barbecue for indirect cooking over a low heat.

4. Brush the cooking grills clean. Barbecue the ribs over **_indirect low heat_** for 2 hours, with the lid closed. Remove the ribs from the barbecue, brush them on both sides with the reserved marinade, wrap them in aluminium foil and continue cooking the ribs for 2 to 3 hours, until the meat has shrunk back about 1 cm (½ inch) from the ends of the rib bones and the meat is tender enough to tear with your fingers.

5. Transfer the ribs (keep them wrapped in foil) to a large tray and allow them to rest for 30 minutes. Serve warm.

HOW TO COOK SPARERIBS ON A SMOKER

1. Fill the ring in the bottom section of the smoker with a combination of lit and unlit barbecue briquettes as per the recommendations on page 25. Barbecue briquettes will burn much longer than lump charcoal, so they are a good choice for meats like pork spareribs, which require long, slow smoking.

2. Toss a few chunks of hardwood on the coals right at the start. Don't bother soaking the chunks first. They won't absorb much water, and they are large enough that they will smoke for quite a while. Put the middle section in place and immediately fill the water pan three-fourths of the way with water. The water pan gets hot fast, so don't wait to fill the pan or water will splatter all over!

3. The vent on the lid should be open right from the start. It allows much of the smoke to escape. Otherwise, the meat would be overpowered. Also, the vent keeps the air flowing so the coals stay lit.

4. Regulate the temperature in the smoker by adjusting the bottom vents. If the temperature begins to fall, open the bottom vents a bit more to allow more airflow. If the temperature begins to rise, close the bottom vents to restrict airflow.

5. After the first few chunks of hardwood have burned out, open the side door and drop one or two more on the burning coals. Work quickly when the door is open so you don't allow too much air into the smoker and create havoc with the cooking temperatures.

6. If necessary, for really long cooking times, add a few more handfuls of barbecue briquettes to the coals.

SLOW-SMOKED SPARERIBS WITH SWEET-AND-SOUR BARBECUE SAUCE

SERVES: 8
PREP TIME: 30 MINUTES

HEAT: INDIRECT LOW HEAT 110° TO 130°C (225° TO 250°F)
COOKING TIME: 5 TO 6 HOURS

RUB
3 tablespoons sea salt
2 tablespoons pure chilli powder
2 tablespoons light brown sugar
2 tablespoons garlic granules
2 tablespoons paprika
4 teaspoons dried thyme
4 teaspoons ground cumin
4 teaspoons celery seeds
2 teaspoons freshly ground black pepper

4 racks St Louis-style spareribs (see page 126)

MOP
250 ml (8 fl oz/1 cup) apple juice
125 ml (4 fl oz/½ cup) apple cider vinegar
2 tablespoons worcestershire sauce

5 fist-sized chunks hickory or apple wood (not soaked)

SAUCE
550 g (1 lb 2 oz) tomato sauce
250 ml (8 fl oz/1 cup) apple juice
150 ml (5 fl oz) apple cider vinegar
2 tablespoons worcestershire sauce
2 tablespoons runny honey
2 tablespoons reserved rub

1. Prepare your smoker, following manufacturer's instructions, for indirect cooking over a low heat.

2. Mix the rub ingredients together in a medium bowl. Set aside 2 tablespoons for the sauce.

3. See the top of page 126, steps 1 to 4, for how to prep St Louis-style ribs. Season the ribs all over with the rub, putting more of it on the meaty sides than the bone sides.

4. Mix the mop ingredients together in a small bowl.

5. Smoke the spareribs, adding 2 wood chunks at the start of cooking and 1 chunk each hour after that, until the chunks are gone. Cook until the meat has shrunk back from the bones at least 1 cm (½ inch) in several places and the meat tears easily when you lift each rack, basting the ribs on both sides with the mop every 2 hours. The total cooking time could be anywhere between 5 to 6 hours. Not all racks will cook in the same amount of time. Maintain the temperature of the smoker between 110° to 130°C (225° to 250°F) by opening and closing the vents.

6. Mix the sauce ingredients together in a saucepan over a medium heat and cook for about 5 minutes. Remove the pan from the heat.

7. When the meat has shrunk back at least 1 cm (½ inch) in several places, lightly brush the ribs on both sides with sauce.

8. Cook the ribs for a further 30 to 60 minutes. Remove them from the smoker and, if desired, lightly brush the ribs on both sides with sauce again, then cut the racks into individual ribs. Serve warm with the remaining sauce on the side.

Tamarind pods (top) provide a pulp that is responsible for an addictive sour flavour in many South-east Asian dishes. Finding the pods can be a challenge, but Asian food shops and many supermarkets stock tamarind paste (bottom). It needs to be diluted in a liquid to use in a marinade or glaze.

TAMARIND-GLAZED COUNTRY-STYLE RIBS

SERVES: 6
PREP TIME: 10 MINUTES
MARINATING TIME: 20 TO 30 MINUTES

HEAT: INDIRECT MEDIUM HEAT 180° TO 230°C
    (350° TO 400°F)
COOKING TIME: 45 TO 50 MINUTES

MARINADE
150 g (5 oz) tamarind paste
5 tablespoons soy sauce
75 g (3 oz) light brown sugar
4 tablespoons water
½ teaspoon freshly ground black pepper
½ teaspoon garlic granules
¼ teaspoon ground cayenne pepper

12 country-style pork ribs, 1.5 to 1.75 kg (3 to 3½ lb) total

1. Whisk the marinade ingredients together in a bowl. Set aside 4 tablespoons for brushing on the ribs during barbecuing.

2. Liberally brush the ribs with the marinade. Allow the ribs to marinate at room temperature for 20 to 30 minutes before cooking. Prepare the barbecue for indirect cooking over a medium heat.

3. Brush the cooking grills clean. Barbecue the ribs over *indirect medium heat* for 20 minutes with the lid closed. Turn the ribs over, brush with the reserved marinade and continue to cook for a further 25 to 30 minutes.

4. Remove the ribs from the barbecue, tightly wrap with foil and allow them to rest for 30 minutes. Serve warm.

CHILLI VERDE COUNTRY-STYLE RIBS

SERVES: 6 TO 8
PREP TIME: 30 MINUTES

HEAT: DIRECT MEDIUM HEAT 180° TO 230°C
    (350° TO 450°F)
COOKING TIME: 30 MINUTES
SPECIAL EQUIPMENT: LARGE DISPOSABLE FOIL TIN

1.5 kg (3 lb) boneless country-style pork ribs, 1.5 to 2.5 cm
    (¾ to 1 inch) thick and trimmed of fat
1 medium white onion, cut into 1-cm (½-inch) slices
2 jalapeño chillies
Canola or other vegetable oil

RUB
1 tablespoon ground cumin
1 tablespoon brown sugar
2 teaspoons sea salt
1 teaspoon pasilla or pure chilli powder
1 teaspoon ground coriander
1 teaspoon dried oregano

SAUCE
425 g (14 oz) jarred jalapeño chillies with juice, diced
1 can (425 g/14 oz) diced tomatoes with juice
400 ml (14 fl oz) chicken stock
1 tablespoon finely chopped garlic
1 teaspoon ground cumin
1 teaspoon dried oregano

12 corn or flour tortillas (18 to 20 cm/7 to 8 inches)
250 ml (8 fl oz/1 cup) sour cream
1 ripe haas avocado, peeled, stoned and diced
100 g (3½ oz) Cheddar cheese, grated
25 g (1 oz) coriander, finely chopped
2 limes, cut into wedges

1. Lightly brush the ribs, onion slices and chillies with oil.

2. Mix the rub ingredients together in a small bowl. Generously coat the ribs on both sides with the rub. Allow the ribs to stand at room temperature for 20 to 30 minutes before barbecuing. Prepare the barbecue for direct cooking over a medium heat.

3. Brush the cooking grills clean. Barbecue the ribs, onion slices and chillies over **direct medium heat** for 10 to 12 minutes, with the lid closed as much as possible but turning once, until the meat is well browned but still a little pink and the onions and chillies are lightly charred and softened.

4. Remove the meat and vegetables from the barbecue and allow them to cool for a few minutes. Cut the pork into 1.5-cm (¾-inch) cubes. Coarsely chop the onions. Remove and discard the skins, seeds and stems from the chillies and then finely chop them.

5. Combine the sauce ingredients in a large disposable foil tin. Place the pan over **direct medium heat** and bring the sauce to a simmer. Add the meat and vegetables to the sauce. Keep the sauce at a simmer and cook for 15 to 20 minutes, with the lid closed, until the pork is tender when tested with a fork (if the liquid is cooking too fast, move the tin to indirect medium heat). Carefully slide the foil tin on to a roasting tray and remove from the barbecue.

6. Barbecue the tortillas in a single layer over **direct medium heat** for about 1 minute, turning once, just long enough to warm and soften them. Stack the tortillas and wrap them in a tea towel.

7. Spoon the pork and a generous amount of sauce into warm bowls. Top with sour cream, avocado, cheese and coriander. Serve with warm tortillas and lime wedges.

Looking more like pork chops than ribs, country-style ribs are cut from the upper shoulder. You can buy them with or without bones. Either way, the meat is a little tough, but simmering it in a spicy chilli verde sauce makes it tender.

POULTRY

TECHNIQUES

RECIPES

HOW TO BARBECUE CHICKEN INVOLTINI

1. The brilliance of involtini, an Italian dish of stuffed and rolled meat, is that it allows you to fill fairly bland pieces of meat like chicken breasts with gorgeous flavours like fresh basil, prosciutto and provolone cheese.

2. First flatten the chicken breasts, smooth side down, between layers of plastic wrap. Next, season each one with sea salt, garlic granules and freshly ground black pepper.

3. Lay a slice of prosciutto on each piece of chicken, then top with a couple pieces of cheese and a couple basil leaves.

4. Roll up the chicken lengthways, keeping it as compact as you can.

5. Tie each piece of chicken with 2 pieces of butcher's string, then lightly brush the surface with olive oil.

6. Barbecue for about 12 minutes, turning the rolls every few minutes, over direct medium heat until the chicken is fully cooked through and the cheese has begun to melt.

CHICKEN INVOLTINI WITH PROSCIUTTO AND BASIL

SERVES: 4
PREP TIME: 20 MINUTES

HEAT: DIRECT MEDIUM HEAT 180° TO 230°C (350° TO 450°F)
COOKING TIME: ABOUT 12 MINUTES
SPECIAL EQUIPMENT: BUTCHER'S STRING

4 boneless, skinless chicken breasts, about
   250 g (8 oz) each, with the fillets removed
1 teaspoon sea salt
1 teaspoon garlic granules
½ teaspoon freshly ground black pepper
4 very thin slices prosciutto
4 thin slices provolone cheese, halved
8 large basil leaves, plus more for garnish
Extra-virgin olive oil
450 ml (16 fl oz) good-quality tomato sauce

1. Prepare the barbecue for direct cooking over a medium heat.

2. For each piece of chicken, use about 30 cm (12 inches) of plastic wrap. Place the chicken, smooth side down, to one side of the plastic, about 5 cm (2 inches) from the edge. Fold the remaining plastic wrap over the chicken leaving an inch or so from the folded edge. This will allow the chicken to spread out as it gets thinner. Starting from the thick side, gently pound the chicken with the flat side of a tenderiser or the bottom of a small, heavy frying pan, moving to different areas with every stroke until it is about 5 mm (¼ inch) thick and doubles in size. Do not pound too hard or the chicken might break apart.

3. Season each piece of chicken on both sides with the salt, garlic granules and pepper. Arrange the chicken with the smooth side down on a work surface.

4. Lay a slice of prosciutto on each piece of chicken, then top with 2 halves of the provolone and then 2 basil leaves. Carefully roll up the chicken, keeping it snug as you work. Tie 2 pieces of butcher's string around each piece to keep it together, then trim the loose ends of string. Lightly brush each rolled piece of chicken with oil.

5. Brush the cooking grills clean. Barbecue the chicken over **direct medium heat** for 12 minutes, with the lid closed as much as possible but giving a quarter turn every 3 minutes, until golden on all sides. Remove from the barbecue and allow to rest for 3 to 5 minutes. Meanwhile, warm the tomato sauce in a small saucepan over a medium-high heat.

6. Remove the string from the chicken pieces, cut into slices, and serve warm on a pool of sauce. Garnish with torn pieces of basil.

HOW TO BARBECUE BUTTERFLIED CHICKEN BREASTS

1. On the underside of some shop-bought chicken breast halves is a thin strip of meat called the tenderloin. To pound the chicken breasts thinly for this recipe, remove each fillet first and save it for another use.

2. Holding each breast steady with one hand, use your other hand to grab the tenderloin near the thick end of each breast and pull it off.

3. Place each chicken breast, smooth side down, between 2 sheets of plastic wrap and pound it to a thickness of about 5 mm (¼ inch).

4. For an even thickness, aim the back of a small, heavy frying pan at the centre of each breast and push the pan towards the thinner edges as you make contact.

5. Barbecue each chicken breast over a direct high heat mostly on the first side. When the perimeter of the second side is turning opaque, it's time to turn the breast.

6. Check the doneness by firmness. The chicken should yield just a little to pressure. It should not be soft or firm.

BUTTERFLIED CHICKEN BREASTS WITH TOMATO AND OLIVE RELISH

SERVES: 4
PREP TIME: 30 MINUTES

HEAT: DIRECT MEDIUM HEAT 180° TO 230°C (350° TO 450°F)
COOKING TIME: 4 TO 5 MINUTES

RUB
1 tablespoon ground fennel seeds
1½ teaspoons sea salt
½ teaspoon garlic granules
½ teaspoon freshly ground black pepper

4 boneless, skinless chicken breasts, about 175 g (6 oz) each
Extra-virgin olive oil

RELISH
125 g (4 oz) cored and deseeded tomato, cut into 5-mm (¼-inch) dice
75 g (3 oz) trimmed celery heart, cut into 5-mm (¼-inch) dice
75 g (3 oz) kalamata olives, rinsed, pitted and cut into 5-mm (¼-inch) dice
75 g (3 oz) green olives, rinsed, pitted and cut into 5-mm (¼-inch) dice
2 tablespoons extra-virgin olive oil
2 teaspoons very finely chopped thyme or ½ teaspoon dried thyme leaves
Sea salt
1 lemon

1. Combine the rub ingredients in a small bowl.

2. Remove the tenderloins from the underside of each breast (save for another use). One at a time, place each breast, smooth side down, between 2 sheets of plastic wrap and pound to an even 5-mm (¼-inch) thickness. Lightly brush the chicken with oil and season both sides with the rub.

3. Prepare the barbecue for direct cooking over a medium heat.

4. Combine the relish ingredients, including salt to taste, in a large bowl.

5. Brush the cooking grills clean. Barbecue the chicken, smooth side down, over **direct medium heat** for 3 to 4 minutes, with the lid closed as much as possible, until no longer pink. Turn over and barbecue just to sear the surface for about 1 minute. Transfer the chicken, with the first cooked sides facing up, to a serving platter or individual plates. Spoon the relish over each piece and squeeze fresh lemon juice on top just before serving.

LEMON-OREGANO CHICKEN BREASTS

SERVES: 6
PREP TIME: 15 MINUTES
MARINATING TIME: 1 TO 2 HOURS

HEAT: DIRECT MEDIUM HEAT 180° TO 230°C (350° TO 450°F)
COOKING TIME: 8 TO 12 MINUTES

MARINADE
6 tablespoons extra-virgin olive oil
Finely grated rind and juice of 2 lemons
1 tablespoon dried oregano
1 tablespoon very finely chopped garlic
2 teaspoons paprika
1½ teaspoons sea salt
½ teaspoon freshly ground black pepper

6 boneless, skinless chicken breasts, about
175 g (6 oz) each

1. Whisk the marinade ingredients together in a bowl.

2. Place the breasts on a large, rimmed plate. Spoon or brush the marinade over the breasts, turning to coat them evenly. Cover with plastic wrap and refrigerate for 1 to 2 hours.

3. Prepare the barbecue for direct cooking over a medium heat.

4. Brush the cooking grills clean. Barbecue the chicken, smooth side down, over **direct medium heat** for 8 to 12 minutes, with the lid closed as much as possible but turning once or twice, until the meat is firm to the touch and opaque all the way to the centre. Serve warm.

HOW TO GRATE LEMON RIND

1. A Microplane grater can quickly remove the outermost skin of a lemon.

2. The oil-rich rind holds a wealth of flavour, but avoid the bitter, white pith.

HOW TO JUICE LEMON

1. Cut off each end of the lemon to expose a small amount of fruit, then cut the lemon in half.

2. This makes the lemon much easier to juice.

TANDOORI CHICKEN BREASTS WITH MANGO-MINT CHUTNEY

SERVES: 4
PREP TIME: 20 MINUTES
MARINATING TIME: 2 HOURS

HEAT: DIRECT MEDIUM HEAT 180° TO 230°C (350° TO 450°F)
COOKING TIME: 10 TO 14 MINUTES

MARINADE
250 g (8 oz) natural yogurt
3 tablespoons fresh lemon juice
1 tablespoon chopped garlic
1 tablespoon chopped fresh root ginger
2 teaspoons garam masala
2 teaspoons sea salt
1 teaspoon sweet paprika

4 boneless, skinless chicken breasts, about 175 g (6 oz) each

CHUTNEY
2 firm ripe mangoes, sides cut from stone
½ tablespoon canola or other vegetable oil
2 tablespoons finely chopped mint
2 tablespoons apple cider vinegar
½ teaspoon sugar
¼ teaspoon sea salt
¼ teaspoon freshly ground black pepper

Canola or other vegetable oil

1. Blend the marinade ingredients together in a food processor until uniform in consistency, adding 1 or 2 tablespoons of water, if needed. Place the chicken in a large, resealable plastic bag and pour in the marinade. Press the air out of the bag and seal it tightly. Turn the bag several times to distribute the marinade, then refrigerate for 2 hours, turning occasionally.

2. Prepare the barbecue for direct cooking over a medium heat.

3. Lightly brush the mango sides with the oil. Brush the cooking grills clean. Barbecue over **direct medium heat** for about 2 minutes, flat sides down, with the lid closed, until they brown. Remove the mango from the barbecue and cut cross-hatch marks in the flesh down to the skin, then scoop out the little pieces. Combine the mango with the remaining chutney ingredients in a small bowl.

4. Remove the chicken from the bag and discard the marinade. Wipe off most of the marinade clinging to the chicken and then brush the chicken with oil. Barbecue over **direct medium heat** for 8 to 12 minutes, with the lid closed as much as possible but turning once, until the meat is firm to the touch and no longer pink in the centre. Serve warm with the chutney.

HOW TO CUT A MANGO

1. Inside each mango is a flat stone that runs from side to side.

2. To cut around the stone, rotate the mango so that the stone runs parallel to the blade of your knife.

3. Cut each mango lengthways along each side of the stone.

HOW TO MAKE PLUM SAUCE

1. For the sauce, barbecue halved red plums until they are soft and sweet.

2. Simmer the grilled plums with port, sugar and shallots. Strain the sauce through a coarse sieve, pressing the solids to extract as much flavour as possible.

HOW TO PREP DUCK BREASTS

1. The skin of a duck breast is very fatty. To avoid flare-ups on the barbecue, one good option is to remove the skin before barbecuing.

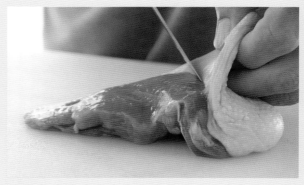

2. Lift the edge of the skin and use the sharp tip of a paring knife to separate the skin from the flesh as you pull back the skin.

3. The secret ingredient used in both the rub and the sauce is smoked sea salt. Look for it in speciality food shops.

4. The salt in the rub not only adds flavour, it also breaks down some muscle fibres, making the duck meat more tender.

DUCK BREASTS WITH PORT-PLUM SAUCE

SERVES: 4
PREP TIME: 30 MINUTES

HEAT: DIRECT MEDIUM HEAT 180° TO 230°C (350° TO 450°F)
COOKING TIME: ABOUT 12 MINUTES

SAUCE
500 g (1 lb) red plums, halved and stoned
1 tablespoon extra-virgin olive oil
125 ml (4 fl oz/½ cup) port wine
3 tablespoons sugar
1 shallot, thinly sliced
Smoked sea salt
Freshly ground black pepper

RUB
1 tablespoon smoked sea salt
1 tablespoon sea salt
1 tablespoon light brown sugar

4 duck breasts, 125 to 175 g (4 to 6 oz) each, skinned
1 tablespoon extra-virgin olive oil

1. Prepare the barbecue for direct cooking over a medium heat. Brush the cooking grills clean.

2. Lightly brush the plums with the oil. Barbecue the plums over **direct medium heat** for about 4 minutes, with the lid closed as much as possible but turning once, until they have light grill marks and are starting to soften. Remove them from the barbecue and place in a saucepan with the port, sugar and shallot. Bring the mixture to the boil, then reduce the heat to medium, cover and simmer for about 10 minutes, stirring occasionally. After the sauce has cooked, use a wooden spoon to gently crush the plums into the sauce. Strain the sauce through a coarse sieve into a bowl, pushing as much plum pulp as possible through the sieve. Discard the remaining plum skin and pulp. Season to taste with smoked salt and pepper. Warm the sauce just before serving.

3. Combine the rub ingredients in a small bowl. Place the duck in a large, resealable plastic bag and add the rub. Seal the bag and toss to coat the duck thoroughly with the rub. Allow to stand at room temperature for 10 minutes, then remove the duck from the bag, pat dry with paper towel and brush with the oil.

4. Brush the cooking grills clean. Barbecue the duck over **direct medium heat** for about 8 minutes for medium rare, with the lid closed as much as possible but turning once. Let the duck rest for 5 minutes before serving. Slice the duck crossways into 5-mm (¼-inch) slices and serve warm with the sauce.

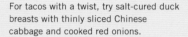

For tacos with a twist, try salt-cured duck breasts with thinly sliced Chinese cabbage and cooked red onions.

DUCK BREAST TACOS WITH SOUR ORANGE-ONION SALSA

SERVES: 4 TO 6
PREP TIME: 30 MINUTES

HEAT: DIRECT MEDIUM HEAT 180° TO 230°C (350° TO 450°F)
COOKING TIME: ABOUT 9 MINUTES

4 boneless duck breasts, 125 to 175 g (4 to 6 oz) each
2 tablespoons sea salt
2 tablespoons sugar

SALSA
300 g (10 oz) red onion, thinly sliced
125 ml (4 fl oz/½ cup) fresh orange juice
4 tablespoons fresh lime juice
4 tablespoons poblano chillies or other mild chillies, finely
    chopped
1 tablespoon sugar
¼ teaspoon sea salt
15 g (½ oz) chopped coriander

Extra-virgin olive oil

16 corn tortillas (18 cm/7 inches in diameter)
1 ripe haas avocado, peeled, stoned and sliced
125 g (4 oz) red radishes, thinly sliced
100 g (3½ oz) Chinese cabbage, finely sliced

1. Remove and discard the thick layer of fat and skin from the duck breasts (see page 140).

2. Mix the salt and sugar together in a large bowl, then add the duck breasts and turn to coat them. Allow the breasts to stand at room temperature for 20 to 30 minutes before barbecuing, turning them over once or twice.

3. Combine the onion, orange and lime juices, chilli, sugar and salt in a large frying pan and boil over a medium-high heat for 15 to 18 minutes, stirring occasionally to avoid burning, until most of the liquid has evaporated. Remove the pan from the heat and stir in the coriander.

4. Prepare the barbecue for direct cooking over a medium heat.

5. Pat the breasts dry and generously coat them on both sides with oil.

6. Brush the cooking grills clean. Barbecue the breasts over **direct medium heat** for about 8 minutes, with the lid closed as much as possible but turning once, until lightly browned on each side and still rosy pink in the centre. Transfer to a chopping board and, while the duck rests, grill the tortillas.

7. Brush the grills clean. Barbecue the tortillas over **direct medium heat** for about 10 seconds on each side. Stack the hot tortillas and wrap them in a thick tea towel (or put them in an insulated tortilla server).

8. Thinly slice the duck and serve with the warm tortillas, salsa, avocado, radish and cabbage.

JERK CHICKEN SKEWERS
WITH HONEY-LIME CREAM

SERVES: 4 TO 6
PREP TIME: 30 MINUTES
MARINATING TIME: 2 TO 3 HOURS

HEAT: DIRECT MEDIUM HEAT 180° TO 230°C (350° TO 450°F)
COOKING TIME: 6 TO 8 MINUTES
SPECIAL EQUIPMENT: RUBBER OR PLASTIC GLOVES;
    8 TO 12 BAMBOO SKEWERS, SOAKED IN WATER FOR
    AT LEAST 30 MINUTES

PASTE
1 habanero or scotch bonnet chilli
50 g (2 oz) coriander leaves and tender stems
125 ml (4 fl oz/½ cup) extra-virgin olive oil
4 spring onions, white and light green parts, roughly chopped
6 garlic cloves
2 tablespoons finely chopped fresh root ginger
2 tablespoons sugar
1 tablespoon fresh lime juice
1 tablespoon ground allspice
2 teaspoons sea salt
1 teaspoon freshly ground black pepper

6 boneless, skinless chicken breasts, 175 to 250 g (6 to 8 oz) each

SAUCE
125 ml (4 fl oz/½ cup) sour cream
½ teaspoon finely grated lime rind
1 tablespoon fresh lime juice
1 tablespoon extra-virgin olive oil
2 teaspoons runny honey
¼ teaspoon sea salt
⅛ teaspoon freshly ground black pepper

1. To avoid burning your skin, wear rubber or plastic gloves when you handle the chilli. After handling the chilli, do not touch your face or any other part of your body, as that may cause a burning sensation. Remove and discard the stem of the chilli, then cut away and discard the hot whitish veins and seeds. Put the rest of the chilli in a food processor. Add the remaining paste ingredients and process until smooth.

2. Trim the chicken of any fat and remove the tenderloins. Cut it lengthways into even strips, 1 to 1.5 cm (½ to ¾ inch) thick.

3. Place the chicken strips and tenderloins into a large, resealable plastic bag and spoon in the paste. Work the paste into the chicken, press out the air in the bag and seal tightly. Place in the refrigerator and allow to marinate for 2 to 3 hours.

4. Whisk the sauce ingredients together in a small bowl, then cover with plastic wrap and refrigerate. Allow the sauce to stand at room temperature for about 30 minutes before serving. Prepare the barbecue for direct cooking over a medium heat.

5. Wearing rubber or plastic gloves, thread the chicken strips on to the skewers, being sure to keep each skewer well within the flesh of the chicken. If you don't have rubber gloves, be sure to wash your hands thoroughly after this step.

6. Brush the cooking grills clean. Barbecue the skewers over **direct medium heat** for 6 to 8 minutes, with the lid closed as much as possible but turning once or twice, until the meat is firm and the juices run clear. Serve warm with the sauce.

HOW TO MAKE CHICKEN SKEWERS

1. Wearing rubber or plastic gloves, remove and discard the incredibly spicy seeds and whitish veins in habanero chilli.

2. Marinate the chicken pieces in the puréed chilli paste, then thread them on to skewers. Make sure that the skewers run through the centre of the chicken pieces.

3. When you are done, you should see wood only at the tip and base of each skewer.

HOW TO PREP CHICKEN BREASTS

1. For the puréed parsley sauce with olive oil, nuts and garlic, you can use all but the tough stalks of parsley. Hold the tough stalks in one hand and use the other to shave off the leaves and tender stalks.

2. This Tunisian-inspired spice paste will be particularly aromatic if you cook the spices first in a dry frying pan over a medium heat.

3. Crush the toasted spices with a pestle and mortar, or use a clean coffee mill or spice mill to grind them to a powder.

4. To get the spices right on to the meat, very gently work your fingertips under the skin at the thin end and lift the skin, but leave it attached at the other end.

5. Spread the spice paste all over the exposed meat.

6. Lay the skin back in place and spread a bit more of the spice paste on top.

TUNISIAN CHICKEN WITH PARSLEY SAUCE

SERVES: 4
PREP TIME: 20 MINUTES

HEAT: DIRECT AND INDIRECT MEDIUM HEAT
    180° TO 230°C (350° TO 450°F)
COOKING TIME: 23 TO 35 MINUTES
SPECIAL EQUIPMENT: PESTLE AND MORTAR OR
    SPICE MILL

SAUCE
75 g (3 oz) flat leaf Italian parsley leaves and
    tender stalks
40 g (1½ oz) whole unsalted almonds
1 garlic clove
125 ml (4 fl oz/½ cup) extra-virgin olive oil
2 teaspoons dijon mustard
1 teaspoon runny honey
¼ teaspoon sea salt

PASTE
4 teaspoons coriander seeds
2 teaspoons caraway seeds
2 teaspoons cumin seeds
2 teaspoons crushed red chilli flakes
2 tablespoons extra-virgin olive oil
1 teaspoon sea salt

4 chicken breasts (with bone and skin), 300 to 375 g
    (10 oz to 13 oz) each

1. Pulse the parsley, almonds and garlic together in a food processor until finely chopped. With the motor running, slowing add the oil to create an emulsion. Stir in the mustard, honey and salt and emulsify the sauce again just before serving.

2. Toast the seeds and chilli flakes in a frying pan over a medium heat for 2 to 3 minutes, until fragrant, then put into a pestle and mortar or spice mill and grind to a powder. Transfer to a bowl, add the oil and salt and stir to make a paste.

3. Using your fingertips, carefully lift the skin from the chicken breasts, leaving the skin closest to the breastbone attached. Rub 1 teaspoon of the paste under the skin of each chicken breast, then lay the skin back in place and rub the remaining paste evenly over all the pieces of chicken. Place the chicken on a plate and cover with plastic wrap. Allow the chicken to stand at room temperature for 20 to 30 minutes before barbecuing. Prepare the barbecue for direct and indirect cooking over a medium heat.

4. Brush the cooking grills clean. Barbecue the chicken, skin side down, over **_direct medium heat_** for 3 to 5 minutes, until the skin is browned. Turn over the chicken and continue to cook over **_indirect medium heat_** for 20 to 30 minutes, with the lid closed, until the meat is opaque all the way to the bone. Transfer to a platter and allow to rest for 5 to 10 minutes. Serve the chicken warm with the sauce.

HOW TO BARBECUE CHICKEN WINGS

1. You don't have to use skewers to barbecue chicken wings. You'll get great results without them, but skewers are helpful for spreading the wings flat, as if they were 'in flight'.

2. The flatter the wings, the more contact they have with the cooking grill. That means crispier skins and more flavour.

3. Brushing the wings with a honey-garlic glaze just before serving helps add flavour, too.

HONEY-GARLIC CHICKEN WINGS

SERVES: 4 TO 6 AS A STARTER
PREP TIME: 20 MINUTES
MARINATING TIME: UP TO 4 HOURS

HEAT: DIRECT AND INDIRECT MEDIUM HEAT
180° TO 230°C (350° TO 450°F)
COOKING TIME: 19 TO 25 MINUTES
SPECIAL EQUIPMENT: 12 BAMBOO SKEWERS,
SOAKED IN WATER FOR AT LEAST 30 MINUTES

MARINADE
6 tablespoons fresh lemon juice
1 tablespoon finely chopped garlic
1 teaspoon sea salt
½ teaspoon freshly ground black pepper

1 kg (2 lb) chicken wings
175 g (6 oz) runny honey
1 tablespoon hot chilli sauce, such as sriracha, or to taste

1. Combine 3 tablespoons of the lemon juice, the garlic, salt and pepper in a large non-metallic bowl. Add the wings and toss to coat them evenly, then cover and refrigerate for up to 4 hours.

2. Combine the remaining 3 tablespoons of lemon juice with the honey and hot sauce in a small bowl.

3. Prepare the barbecue for direct and indirect cooking over a medium heat.

4. Thread each wing on to a bamboo skewer, being sure to skewer each portion of the wing all the way up into the cartilage in the wingtip and then spreading it out as if it were 'in flight'.

5. Brush the cooking grills clean. Brown the wings over **direct medium heat** for 4 to 5 minutes, with the lid closed as much as possible, turning once. Move the wings over **indirect medium heat** and barbecue for 15 to 20 minutes, basting with the honey mixture once or twice during the last 10 minutes of cooking time, until the meat is no longer pink at the bone. Keep the lid closed as much as possible during cooking. Remove the wings from the barbecue, brush once more with the glaze and serve warm.

HICKORY 'DRUMETTES' WITH BOURBON-MOLASSES GLAZE

SERVES: 6 TO 8 AS A STARTER
PREP TIME: 20 MINUTES

HEAT: INDIRECT MEDIUM HEAT 180° TO 230°C
   (350° TO 450°F)
COOKING TIME: 20 TO 30 MINUTES

RUB
1 tablespoon smoked paprika
2 teaspoons mustard powder
1 teaspoon sea salt
½ teaspoon garlic granules
½ teaspoon onion granules
¼ teaspoon ground chipotle chilli

20 chicken wing drumettes, about 1.5 kg (3 lb)

GLAZE
2 tablespoons soy sauce
2 tablespoons bourbon
1 tablespoon molasses
15 g (½ oz) unsalted butter

2 handfuls hickory wood chips, soaked in water for at
   least 30 minutes

1. Mix the rub ingredients together in a large bowl. Add the
drumettes and toss to coat them evenly.

2. Prepare the barbecue for indirect cooking over a
medium heat.

3. Bring the glaze ingredients to the boil in a small, heavy-
based saucepan over a high heat and cook just until the butter
melts. Transfer to a small bowl and allow the glaze to cool.

4. Drain and scatter the wood chips over lit barbecue briquettes
or put them in the smoker box of a gas barbecue, following
manufacturer's instructions. Brush the cooking grills clean.
Barbecue the wings over *indirect medium heat* for 20 to
30 minutes with the lid closed as much as possible but turning
and basting with the glaze once or twice during the last
20 minutes of cooking, until the meat is no longer pink at
the bone.

HOW TO BARBECUE CHICKEN DRUMETTES

1. Each chicken wing has three parts: a
wingtip (left); a 2-bone middle section
(middle); and an upper wing (right).

2. The upper wing is called the 'drumette'
because it looks like a little drumstick.

3. Barbecue drumettes over indirect heat to
break down some of the chewy characteristic
of the meat, and give them some good hickory
smoke and a sweet boozy glaze.

HOW TO PREP WHOLE CHICKEN LEGS

1. Turn each chicken leg skin-side down and trim off the excess skin. The fat under that skin tends to melt into the barbecue and pose a threat of flare-ups.

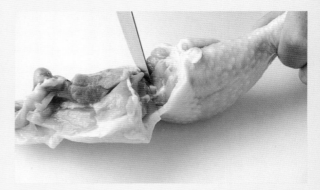

2. The meat near the joint of a chicken leg will take the longest to cook. So cut an opening between the drumstick and thigh to expose that innermost meat and speed up its cooking time.

3. Making some slashes on the outside of the leg will allow the marinade to penetrate faster and deeper.

4. The provençal flavours in this recipe come primarily from a blend of dried herbs that usually includes thyme, marjoram, parsley, tarragon and bay leaf, as well as lavender and celery seeds. It is sold as dried herbes de provence, available from specialty food stores.

5. Pour the marinade over the chicken in a large, resealable plastic bag. Press the air out of the bag, seal it tightly and turn it several times, making sure to coat all of the pieces evenly.

6. When you are dealing with raw chicken and a messy marinade, it's always a good idea to avoid spills by putting the bag in a bowl before refrigerating it.

POULTRY

PROVENÇAL MARINATED CHICKEN LEGS

SERVES: 6
PREP TIME: 15 MINUTES
MARINATING TIME: 4 TO 8 HOURS

HEAT: INDIRECT MEDIUM HEAT 180° TO 230°C
   (350° TO 450°F)
COOKING TIME: 50 MINUTES TO 1 HOUR

MARINADE
250 ml (8 fl oz/1 cup) dry white wine
5 tablespoons extra-virgin olive oil
3 tablespoons wholegrain mustard
3 tablespoons white wine vinegar
2 tablespoons dried herbes de provence
3 garlic cloves, very finely chopped
2 teaspoons sea salt
½ teaspoon crushed red chilli flakes

6 whole chicken legs, 300 to 375 g (10 to 13 oz) each

1. Whisk the marinade ingredients together in a bowl.

2. Cut a few deep slashes into the meaty parts of each chicken leg. Place them in a large, resealable plastic bag and pour in the marinade. Press the air out of the bag and seal tightly. Turn the bag to distribute the marinade and refrigerate for 4 to 8 hours, turning occasionally.

3. Prepare the barbecue for indirect cooking over a medium heat.

4. Remove the chicken from the bag, letting the herbs cling to the chicken. Discard the marinade. Brush the cooking grills clean. Barbecue the chicken over ***indirect medium heat*** for 50 minutes to 1 hour with the lid closed as much as possible but turning once, until the juices run clear and the internal temperature reaches 77°C (170°F) in the thickest part of the thigh (not touching the bone). If desired, to crisp the skin, barbecue the chicken over ***direct medium heat*** during the last 5 minutes of cooking time, turning once. Remove from the barbecue and cut into thighs and drumsticks.

Boneless chicken pieces do well barbecued quickly over direct heat, but bone-in pieces take longer and direct heat alone would burn them, so use indirect heat (or both direct and indirect) for bone-in pieces.

HOW TO ROAST DUCK LEGS

1. Duck legs have so much fat under their skins that they are prone to flare-ups if you try barbecuing them over direct heat, but the 'ring of fire' gives you ample room in the centre of the cooking grill to smoke-roast them safely over indirect heat.

2. While the barbecue briquettes burn down to the right temperature and the wood chunks begin smoking, trim any fat hanging from the edges of the duck legs.

3. Cook the duck legs, skin side up, until dark brown and crisp. Brush on the orange-hoisin glaze near the end of the cooking time so that it does not burn.

SLOW-ROASTED DUCK LEGS WITH HOISIN-ORANGE GLAZE

SERVES: 4
PREP TIME: 10 MINUTES

HEAT: INDIRECT MEDIUM HEAT ABOUT 160°C (315°F)
COOKING TIME: ABOUT 1 HOUR

GLAZE
4 tablespoons orange marmalade
4 tablespoons fresh orange juice
4 tablespoons mirin (rice wine)
2 tablespoons hoisin sauce
½ teaspoon crushed red chilli flakes

RUB
2 teaspoons sea salt
¾ teaspoon freshly ground black pepper
¾ teaspoon Chinese five-spice powder

8 whole duck legs, 175 to 250 g (6 to 8 oz) each, trimmed of excess fat
5 apple wood chunks (not soaked)

1. Prepare the barbecue for indirect cooking over a medium heat using the 'ring-of-fire' configuration (see photo above).

2. Combine the glaze ingredients in a small saucepan over a medium-high heat. Bring to a simmer to melt the marmalade, then remove the pan from the heat.

3. Combine the rub ingredients in a small bowl, then season the duck evenly with the rub.

4. Add the wood chunks directly on to burning coals. As soon as the wood starts to smoke, barbecue the duck, skin side up, over **_indirect medium heat_** for about 1 hour, with the lid closed as much as possible but turning and basting with the glaze during the last 15 to 20 minutes of cooking time, until the duck is evenly browned and crisp and is fully cooked through. Serve warm.

HOW TO BARBECUE CHICKEN

1. Season the chicken thighs and drumsticks with the spices.

2. After browning the chicken first over direct heat, move it to indirect heat to smoke and finish cooking.

3. A couple handfuls of damp wood chips should provide smoke for 20 to 30 minutes.

4. Spices, smoke and finally a light coating of sauce. That's a triple-play of flavour.

TRIPLE-PLAY BARBECUED CHICKEN

SERVES: 4
PREP TIME: 30 MINUTES

HEAT: DIRECT AND INDIRECT MEDIUM HEAT 180° TO 230°C (350° TO 450°F)
COOKING TIME: 43 TO 45 MINUTES

SAUCE
75 g (3 oz) brown onion, finely chopped
2 teaspoons very finely chopped garlic
2 tablespoons extra-virgin olive oil
275 g (8 oz) tomato sauce
125 ml (4 fl oz/½ cup) lemon-lime carbonated beverage (not diet)
4 tablespoons fresh lemon juice
50 g (2 oz) light brown sugar
2 tablespoons wholegrain mustard

RUB
2 teaspoons smoked paprika
2 teaspoons sea salt
Finely grated rind of 1 lemon
½ teaspoon garlic granules
½ teaspoon freshly ground black pepper

4 whole chicken legs, 300 to 375 g (10 to 13 oz) each, cut into thighs and drumsticks
2 handfuls hickory wood chips, soaked in water for at least 30 minutes

1. Cook the onion and garlic in the oil in a saucepan over a medium heat for about 10 minutes, stirring often, until golden. Add the rest of the sauce ingredients and stir to combine. Bring the sauce to a simmer, reduce the heat to low and cook for 10 to 15 minutes, stirring often, until slightly thickened.

2. Mix the rub ingredients together in a bowl. Sprinkle the rub evenly over the chicken pieces and allow to stand at room temperature for 20 to 30 minutes before barbecuing. Prepare the barbecue for direct and indirect cooking over a medium heat.

3. Brush the cooking grills clean. Barbecue the chicken, skin side down, over **direct medium heat** for 8 to 10 minutes, with the lid closed as much as possible but turning occasionally, until golden brown. Move the chicken pieces over **indirect medium heat**. Drain and scatter the wood chips over the lit barbecue briquettes or put them in the smoker box of a gas barbecue, following manufacturer's instructions. Continue to cook the chicken, with the lid closed, for about 20 minutes. Then brush both sides with a thin layer of the sauce and cook for a further 15 minutes, turning occasionally and brushing with the sauce, until the juices run clear and the meat is no longer pink at the bone. Serve warm or at room temperature with the remaining sauce on the side.

HOW TO CEDAR-PLANK BONE-IN CHICKEN THIGHS

1. Soak the cedar plank in beer or water for at least 1 hour.

2. Weight the plank down with something heavy so it doesn't float.

3. Place the soaked plank over direct medium heat and close the lid to start the plank smoking.

4. When the plank starts smoking, turn it over and arrange the marinated chicken thighs on top.

5. Finish cooking the chicken thighs with the plank over indirect heat, basting them occasionally with the reserved marinade. If you left the plank over direct heat for too long, it would ignite.

6. To check for doneness, pull one of the thickest thighs from the barbecue and cut into the underside. If the colour of the meat near the bone is still pink, put it back on the plank until it is fully cooked.

7. Using 2 pairs of tongs, carefully remove the plank and chicken thighs to a heatproof surface.

8. Before serving, glaze the chicken thighs one more time.

CEDAR-PLANKED CHICKEN THIGHS WITH SOY-GINGER GLAZE

SERVES: 4 TO 6
PREP TIME: 30 MINUTES

HEAT: DIRECT AND INDIRECT MEDIUM HEAT 180° TO
230°C (350° TO 450°F)
COOKING TIME: 40 TO 50 MINUTES
SPECIAL EQUIPMENT: 1 UNTREATED CEDAR PLANK, 30
TO 45 CM (12 TO 15 INCHES) LONG AND 1 TO 1.5 CM
(½ TO ¾ INCH) THICK, SOAKED IN BEER OR WATER
FOR AT LEAST 1 HOUR

GLAZE
175 g (6 oz) soy sauce
125 ml (4 fl oz/½ cup) balsamic vinegar
100 g (1½ oz) light brown sugar
1 tablespoon very finely chopped garlic
1 tablespoon very finely chopped fresh root ginger
1 teaspoon crushed red chilli flakes
4 tablespoons toasted sesame oil

10 skinless chicken thighs (with bone), 150 to 175 g
(5 to 6 oz) each

1. Combine the soy sauce, vinegar and sugar in a small,
saucepan over a medium-low heat and simmer for about
20 minutes until reduced by half. Remove the pan from the
heat and add the garlic, ginger and red chilli flakes. Cool slightly
and then whisk in the oil. Reserve 125 ml (4 fl oz/½ cup) of the
glaze for basting the chicken.

2. Put the thighs in a large bowl, pour in the remaining glaze
and toss to coat. Cover and refrigerate until you are ready
to barbecue.

3. Prepare the barbecue for direct and indirect cooking over a
medium heat. Place the soaked plank over **direct medium heat**
and close the lid. After 5 to 10 minutes, when the plank begins
to smoke and char, turn the plank over.

4. Remove the thighs from the bowl and discard the glaze.
Arrange the thighs on the smoking plank and cook over **direct
medium heat**, with the lid closed, for 5 to 10 minutes. Move
the plank over **indirect medium heat** and continue cooking for
35 to 40 minutes, with the lid closed as much as possible but
basting occasionally with the reserved glaze during the last
10 to 15 minutes of cooking time, until the juices run clear.
Remove the chicken plank and thighs from the barbecue and
baste with the reserved glaze once more before serving.

DRESSING
1 large poblano chilli or other mild chilli
125 ml (4 fl oz/½ cup) sour cream
25 g (1 oz) coriander leaves and tender stems
1 tablespoon fresh lime juice
1 tablespoon extra-virgin olive oil
1 large garlic clove
½ teaspoon ground cumin
½ teaspoon sea salt
¼ teaspoon freshly ground black pepper

SALAD
250 g (8 oz) cos lettuce, thinly sliced or shredded
175 g (6 oz) corn tortilla chips, crushed
175 g (6 oz) ripe tomato, diced
2 haas avocados, diced
1 can (425 g/14 oz) pinto or black beans, rinsed

1. Whisk the marinade ingredients together in a medium bowl. Add the chicken thighs, turning several times to coat them evenly, then cover and refrigerate for 30 minutes to 1 hour.

2. Prepare the barbecue for direct cooking over a medium heat. Brush the cooking grills clean. Barbecue the chilli over **direct medium heat** for 8 to 10 minutes, with the lid closed as much as possible but turning occasionally, until the skin is blackened and blistered. Transfer the chilli to a small bowl, cover with plastic wrap and let steam for about 10 minutes. Gently peel the skin from the chilli and remove the seeds. Put the chilli in a blender with the remaining dressing ingredients and process until smooth. Refrigerate until ready to serve.

3. Arrange a bed of lettuce on a large platter and then add the chips, tomato, avocado and beans in separate sections on top.

4. Barbecue the chicken over **direct medium heat** for 8 to 10 minutes, with the lid closed as much as possible but turning once or twice, until the meat is firm and the juices run clear. Transfer the chicken to a chopping board and cut into 1-cm (½-inch) strips. Place the chicken on a separate section of the platter. Serve the dressing alongside.

LAYERED MEXICAN CHICKEN SALAD

SERVES: 4 TO 6
PREP TIME: 35 MINUTES
MARINATING TIME: 30 MINUTES TO 1 HOUR

HEAT: DIRECT MEDIUM HEAT 180° TO 230°C
(350° TO 450°F)
COOKING TIME: 16 TO 20 MINUTES

MARINADE
4 tablespoons extra-virgin olive oil
2 tablespoons fresh lime juice
1 teaspoon dried thyme
1 teaspoon dried marjoram
½ teaspoon sea salt
¼ teaspoon freshly ground black pepper

6 boneless, skinless chicken thighs, about 125 g (4 oz) each

HOW TO BARBECUE CHICKEN THIGHS

1. Lay chicken thighs, smooth side down first, over direct heat and resist the urge to turn them for at least 4 minutes. Otherwise, you might rip the meat.

2. However, if the meat is bunched on top of itself, unfold it so that it lies at flat as possible on the barbecue for better charred flavour.

3. You can check the doneness by bending back a thigh and opening up the meat. If there is no trace of pink, it's done.

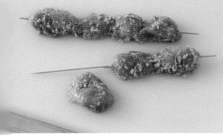

KEEPING FROZEN SKEWERS ON HAND

To avoid soaking bamboo skewers each time you need them, soak a big batch once for an hour or so, then drain them and freeze them in a plastic bag. When it's time to barbecue, pull out as many skewers as you need.

Ingredients like chicken pieces will stay juicier longer if they are touching (but not crammed) on the skewers.

PERSIAN CHICKEN KEBABS

SERVES: 4 TO 6
PREP TIME: 15 MINUTES
MARINATING TIME: 30 MINUTES

HEAT: DIRECT MEDIUM HEAT 180° TO 230°C
(350° TO 450°F)
COOKING TIME: 8 TO 10 MINUTES
SPECIAL EQUIPMENT: BAMBOO SKEWERS,
SOAKED IN WATER FOR AT LEAST 30 MINUTES

MARINADE
1 large onion, coarsely chopped
125 ml (4 fl oz/½ cup) fresh lemon juice
2 tablespoons dried oregano
2 teaspoons sweet paprika
2 teaspoons very finely chopped garlic
250 ml (8 fl oz/1 cup) extra-virgin olive oil

10 boneless, skinless chicken thighs, about 125 g (4 oz) each,
cut into 3.5-cm (1½-inch) pieces

1. Purée the onion, lemon juice, oregano, paprika and garlic together in a food processor or blender. With the motor running, slowly add the oil.

2. Place the chicken pieces in a large, resealable plastic bag and pour in the marinade. Press the air out of the bag and seal tightly. Turn the bag to distribute the marinade and allow the chicken to marinate at room temperature for 30 minutes.

3. Prepare the barbecue for direct cooking over a medium heat.

4. Remove the chicken from the marinade and thread on to skewers, so that the pieces are touching (but not crammed together). Discard the marinade.

5. Brush the cooking grills clean. Barbecue the kebabs over **direct medium heat** for 8 to 10 minutes, with the lid closed as much as possible but turning once, until the meat is fully cooked but not dry. Serve warm.

HOW TO BARBECUE QUESADILLAS

1. Of course most great quesadillas involve guacamole, and that means avocado. To stone one, cut lengthways around the stone and then twist the halves in opposite directions.

2. Tap the exposed stone with the heel of your knife. It will pull out easily from the avocado.

3. You can chop the avocado right in the skin by cross-hatching it and then scooping the little pieces into a bowl with a spoon. Next, mash the avocado pieces with lime juice, garlic and salt.

4. Load up one side of each tortilla with barbecued chicken, vegetables and some grated cheese, but don't add so much that the filling may spill out the sides.

5. Fold the other half of the tortilla on top and firmly press down on it. At this point, you can set the quesadillas aside for a couple hours before barbecuing them.

6. Barbecue the quesadillas over direct medium heat until toasted on each side. This is one of the few times when it's best to leave the barbecue lid open, so you can keep an eye on the quesadillas and prevent them from burning.

CHICKEN AND VEGETABLE QUESADILLAS WITH GUACAMOLE

SERVES: 4 TO 6
PREP TIME: 30 MINUTES

HEAT: DIRECT MEDIUM HEAT 180° TO 230°C
(350° TO 450°F)
COOKING TIME: 10 TO 13 MINUTES

RUB
1 teaspoon pure chilli powder
1 teaspoon sea salt
½ teaspoon dried oregano
¼ teaspoon garlic granules
¼ teaspoon onion granules
¼ teaspoon freshly ground black pepper

4 boneless, skinless chicken thighs, about 125 g (4 oz) each
2 zucchinis, trimmed and halved lengthways
2 ears corn, husked
Extra-virgin olive oil
2 teaspoons chopped oregano
1 teaspoon very finely chopped garlic
1 tablespoon fresh lime juice
Sea salt
Freshly ground black pepper

GUACAMOLE
2 haas avocados, diced
2 teaspoons fresh lime juice
1 teaspoon very finely chopped garlic
¼ teaspoon sea salt

10 flour tortillas (25 cm/10 inches in diameter)
400 g (13 oz) pepper jack or cheddar cheese, grated

1. Prepare the barbecue for direct cooking over a medium heat.

2. Combine the rub ingredients in a small bowl. Lightly brush the chicken, zucchinis and corn with oil. Season the chicken with the rub.

3. Brush the cooking grills clean. Barbecue the chicken and vegetables over ***direct medium heat***, with the lid closed as much as possible but turning the chicken once and the vegetables occasionally, until the meat is firm and the juices run clear, the zucchinis are just tender and the corn kernels are golden brown in spots. The chicken will take 8 to 10 minutes and the vegetables will take 6 to 8 minutes. Remove the chicken and vegetables from the barbecue as they are cooked and allow them to cool.

4. Cut the chicken and zucchinis into 5-mm (¼-inch) chunks. Cut the kernels from the cobs. Combine the zucchinis and corn with the oregano, garlic and lime juice in a large bowl, then season to taste with salt and pepper. Add the chicken to the vegetable mixture and stir to combine.

5. Mash together the guacamole ingredients In a small bowl.

6. Lay the tortillas in a single layer on a work surface. Evenly divide the chicken and vegetable mixture, and then the cheese, over half of each tortilla. Fold the empty half of each tortilla over the filling, creating a half circle, and press down firmly.

7. Barbecue the quesadillas over ***direct medium heat*** for 2 to 3 minutes with the lid open, turning once. Transfer the quesadillas from the barbecue to a chopping board and cut into wedges. Serve warm with the guacamole.

HOW TO SPLIT SPATCHCOCKS

1. Use poultry shears to cut along both sides of the backbone, then discard it.

2. Cut through the centre of the breast.

3. The breastbone will stay attached to one of the halves.

4. Spatchcocks cut into halves will absorb marinades more easily and cook faster than whole ones.

SPATCHCOCKS MARINATED IN BOURBON, HONEY AND SOY

SERVES: 4
PREP TIME: 30 MINUTES
MARINATING TIME: 4 TO 8 HOURS

HEAT: INDIRECT MEDIUM HEAT 180° TO 230°C
   (350° TO 450°F)
COOKING TIME: ABOUT 30 MINUTES

MARINADE
350 ml (12 fl oz) soy sauce
175 ml (6 fl oz) bourbon or other whisky
6 garlic cloves, very finely chopped
2 tablespoons runny honey
1½ tablespoons grated fresh root ginger

4 spatchcocks, 500 to 625 g (1 to 1¼ lb) each
Extra-virgin olive oil
½ teaspoon freshly ground black pepper

1. Combine the marinade ingredients in a medium bowl.

2. Remove and discard the giblets from each spatchcock. Using poultry shears, cut along both sides of each backbone and discard it, then cut through the centre of each breast.

3. Place the birds side by side in a shallow, non-metallic dish and cover with the marinade. Turn to coat the birds evenly, then cover and refrigerate for 4 to 8 hours. (Do not marinate overnight or the ginger will cause the meat to break down and become mushy.)

4. Remove the spatchcocks from the dish and reserve the marinade. Lightly brush the hens with oil and season with the pepper. Allow them to stand at room temperature for 20 to 30 minutes before barbecuing. Prepare the barbecue for indirect cooking over medium heat.

5. Pour the reserved marinade into a small saucepan and bring to the boil over a high heat for about 30 seconds. Set aside to use as a basting sauce.

6. Brush the cooking grills clean. Barbecue the spatchcocks, skin side up, over **indirect medium heat** for about 30 minutes, with the lid closed but basting the birds with the sauce a couple of times during the last 10 minutes of cooking, until the skin is golden brown and the internal temperature in the thickest part of the thigh reaches 77°C (170°F). Remove the birds from the barbecue and serve warm.

HULI-HULI CHICKEN

SERVES: 4 TO 6
PREP TIME: 15 MINUTES
MARINATING TIME: ABOUT 4 HOURS

HEAT: INDIRECT MEDIUM HEAT 180° TO 230°C
    (350° TO 450°F)
COOKING TIME: 45 MINUTES TO 1 HOUR

MARINADE
250 ml (8 fl oz/1 cup) pineapple juice
125 ml (4 fl oz/½ cup) soy sauce
65 g (2½ lb) tomato sauce
2 tablespoons very finely chopped fresh root ginger
2 teaspoons very finely chopped garlic

2 whole chickens, 1.5 to 2 kg (3 to 4 lb) each
4 handfuls mesquite wood chips, soaked in water for at
    least 30 minutes

1. Whisk the marinade ingredients together in a bowl.

2. Place one of the chickens, breast side down, on a
chopping board. Using poultry shears, cut along each side of
the backbone and discard it. Open the chicken like a book, and
then cut the chicken in half lengthways along one side of the
breastbone. Pull off and discard any lumps of fat. Remove and
discard the wingtips. Repeat the process with the other chicken.
Place the chicken halves in a large, resealable plastic bag and
pour in the marinade. Press the air out of the bag and seal it
tightly. Turn the bag several times to coat the chicken evenly
with the marinade. Place the bag in a bowl and refrigerate for
about 4 hours, turning the bag occasionally.

3. Remove the chicken from the bag and discard the marinade.

4. Prepare the barbecue for indirect cooking over a medium heat.

5. Drain half of the wood chips and toss them on to burning
coals or into the smoker box of a gas barbecue, following
manufacturer's instructions. Begin cooking the chicken when
the wood starts to smoke.

6. Brush the cooking grills clean. Barbecue the chicken, skin
side up first, over ***indirect medium heat*** for 45 minutes to
1 hour, with the lid closed as much as possible but turning the
chicken every 15 minutes, until the juices run clear and the
internal temperature reaches 77°C (170°F) in the thickest part
of the thigh (not touching the bone). Drain and add the rest of
the wood chips after the first 15 minutes of cooking.

7. Remove from the barbecue and allow the chicken to rest for
about 10 minutes before serving.

Huli-Huli is a Hawaiian term meaning 'turn-turn', which is
exactly what you need to do here to prevent the sweet marinade
from burning. That said, turn the chicken halves carefully with
a spatula so they hold together. And don't forget the wood
smoke. It is as important as any ingredient in the recipe.

HOW TO SMOKE BEER CAN CHICKEN

1. Blanketing a chicken with salt and refrigerating it for a couple hours will draw out some moisture and strengthen the chicken flavours. Don't worry; the chicken will not be salty. The next step is to rinse off the salt.

2. After you have rinsed and seasoned the chicken, open a beer can and pour out half of it (into a cold mug). With a can opener, make 2 more holes in the top to allow steam to escape.

3. Fold the wingtips behind the back of the chicken to shield the tips from the heat.

4. Working with a solid surface underneath, slide the chicken over the beer can as far as it will go.

5. Set up the barbecue with a water pan in the middle and coals on either side. Add a couple handfuls of damp chips to each pile of coals.

6. When the wood starts to smoke, place the chicken in the centre of the cooking grill. Position the chicken legs towards the front so they balance the chicken with the can like a tripod.

7. When the chicken is fully cooked (77°C/170°F in the thickest part of the thigh), grab the back with tongs and slide a spatula under the can to lift it. Be careful; the beer will be very hot. Allow the chicken to cool for about 10 minutes before sliding it off the can.

SMOKED BEER CAN CHICKEN

SERVES: 4
PREP TIME: 10 MINUTES
SALT-CURING TIME: 1½ TO 2 HOURS

HEAT: INDIRECT MEDIUM HEAT 180° TO 230°C
   (350° TO 450°F)
COOKING TIME: 1¼ TO 1½ HOURS

1 whole chicken, about 2.5 kg (5 lb)
65 g (2½ lb) sea salt

RUB
2 teaspoons onion granules
2 teaspoons garlic granules
1 teaspoon chili con carne seasoning
½ teaspoon freshly ground black pepper

1 can (425 ml/14 fl oz) beer, at room temperature
4 handfuls hickory wood chips, soaked in water for at
   least 30 minutes

1. Remove and discard the neck, giblets and any excess fat
from the chicken. Sprinkle the salt over the entire surface and
inside the cavity of the chicken, covering it all like a light blanket
of snow. Cover the chicken with plastic wrap and refrigerate for
1½ to 2 hours.

2. Mix the rub ingredients together in a small bowl.

3. Rinse the chicken inside and out with cold water. Gently
pat the chicken dry with paper towel. Season it all over with
the rub. Fold the wingtips behind the chicken's back. Allow
the chicken to stand at room temperature for 20 to 30 minutes
before barbecuing. Prepare the barbecue for indirect cooking
over a medium heat.

4. Open the beer can and pour out about half the beer. Using a
can opener, make 2 more holes in the top of the can. Place the
beer can on a solid surface. Ease the chicken cavity over the
beer can.

5. Drain and add the wood chips directly on to burning
coals or to the smoker box of a gas barbecue, following
manufacturer's instructions. When the wood chips begin to
smoke, transfer the bird-on-a-can to the barbecue, balancing
the bird on its two legs and the can, like a tripod. Barbecue over
indirect medium heat for 1¼ to 1½ hours, with the lid closed,
until the juices run clear and the internal temperature registers
77°C (170°F) in the thickest part of the thigh (not touching the
bone). Carefully remove the chicken and can from the barbecue
(do not spill contents of the beer can, as it will be very hot).
Allow the chicken to rest for about 10 minutes before lifting it
from the beer can and cutting into serving pieces. Serve warm.

HOW TO COOK ROTISSERIE CHICKEN

1. To truss the chicken, remove the wingtips and slide a 1.2-metre (4-feet) length of string under the legs and back.

2. Lift both ends of the string and cross it between the legs, then run one end under one drumstick.

3. Run the other end under the other drumstick and pull both ends to draw the drumsticks together.

4. Bring the string along both sides of the chicken so that it holds the legs and wings against the body.

5. Tie a knot in the ends between the neck and the top of the breast. If necessary, push the breast down a little to expose more of the neck.

6. Marinate the chicken in a bag with the buttermilk mixture for 2 to 4 hours in the refrigerator.

7. Position one set of fork prongs on the far end of the centre rod (spit) and slide the spit into the opening between the neck and the knotted string, though the chicken, and out the other side, just underneath the drumsticks. Slide the other set of fork prongs on the spit and drive the prongs into the back of the chicken. Make sure the chicken is centred on the spit before tightening the fork prongs into place.

8. Position the chicken over a drip pan of water. Turn on the motor and let the chicken cook over indirect heat. Adjust the burners as necessary to maintain a cooking temperature of about 200°C (400°F). Brush the chicken a few times with the glaze during the last 30 minutes of cooking, but keep the lid closed as much as possible. For a crispier skin, turn on the infrared burner at the back of the barbecue during the final minutes of cooking.

SERVES: 4
PREP TIME: 25 MINUTES
MARINATING TIME: 2 TO 4 HOURS

HEAT: INDIRECT MEDIUM HEAT ABOUT 200°C (400°F)
COOKING TIME: 1 TO 1¼ HOURS
SPECIAL EQUIPMENT: BUTCHER'S STRING,
    ROTISSERIE, LARGE DISPOSABLE FOIL TIN,
    INSTANT-READ THERMOMETER

MARINADE
500 ml (17 fl oz/2 cups) buttermilk
15 g (½ oz) roughly chopped rosemary leaves
4 large garlic cloves, finely chopped
2 tablespoons sea salt
1 teaspoon freshly ground black pepper

1 whole chicken, 4.4 to 5 kg (4½ to 5 lb)

GLAZE
250 ml (8 fl oz/1 cup) apricot nectar
3 tablespoons maple syrup
1 tablespoon dijon mustard
1 tablespoon white wine vinegar

1. Combine the marinade ingredients in a large bowl.

2. Truss the chicken with butcher's string (see preceding page). Place the chicken in a large, resealable plastic bag and pour in the marinade. Press the air out of the bag and seal it tightly. Turn the bag several times to coat the chicken evenly, place in a large bowl, starting with the breast side facing down, and marinate in the refrigerator for 2 to 4 hours, turning the bag once or twice. Allow the chicken to stand at room temperature for about 30 minutes before barbecuing. Prepare the barbecue for indirect cooking at 200°C (400°F), with the outside burners on medium to high and the middle burners turned off.

3. Whisk the glaze ingredients together in a small saucepan over a medium-high heat, then bring to the boil, reduce the heat and simmer for about 5 minutes until you have about 250 ml (8 fl oz) remaining. Reserve half of the glaze to use as a sauce.

4. Remove the chicken from the bag. Wipe off most of the marinade and discard the marinade. Following the barbecue's instructions, secure the chicken in the middle of a rotisserie spit, put the spit in place and turn on the motor. Place a large disposable foil tin under the chicken to catch drippings and pour about 250 ml (8 fl oz/1 cup) of warm water into the tin. Barbecue the chicken over **indirect medium heat** for 1 to 1¼ hours, with the lid closed but brushing the chicken with the glaze a few times during the last 30 minutes of cooking, until the internal temperature reaches 77°C (170°F) in the thickest part of the thigh (not touching the bone).

5. When the chicken is fully cooked, turn off the rotisserie motor and, wearing insulated mitts, carefully remove the spit from the barbecue. Tilt the chicken upright over the disposable foil tin so that the liquid that has accumulated in the chicken's cavity pours into the tin. Slide the chicken from the spit on to a chopping board. Allow it to rest for about 10 minutes before carving into serving pieces. Serve warm with the reserved sauce.

HOW TO ROAST CHICKEN

Most chickens in supermarkets today have been bred primarily for their appearance. Large-scale farmers select their breeds for plump breast meat and raise the chickens in cramped cages, feeding them cheap diets that promote quick growth but contribute very little to flavour. One way around the blandness problem is to buy old-fashioned breeds instead. They might be a little more difficult to find, and they will cost you more, but they do taste better. Another way around the blandness problem is to roast mass-market chickens with plenty of butter, fresh herbs and seasonings under the skin.

1. Starting at the bottom of the breast, work your fingertips gently under the skin and over the meat. Try not to tear the skin.

2. Use just one finger to reach down each drumstick and along the thigh meat.

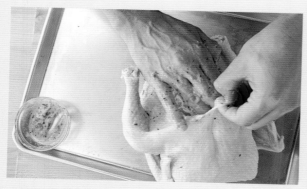

3. Smear the flavoured butter over the breast meat and cover as much of the thigh meat as possible without tearing the skin. Use the remaining flavoured butter to coat the outside of the chicken evenly.

4. Wrap a piece of butcher's string under and around the drumsticks, cross it in the centre and pull the ends to draw the drumsticks together.

5. Cross the string above the drumsticks and tie a knot. This will hold the chicken in a compact shape and help the meat cook more evenly.

6. Roast the chicken inside a disposable foil tin to catch the melted butter and drippings. Baste the chicken occasionally with what's in the tin and rotate the tin as necessary for even browning.

ORANGE-TARRAGON ROASTED CHICKEN

SERVES: 4
PREP TIME: 15 MINUTES

HEAT: INDIRECT MEDIUM HEAT 180° TO 230°C
    (350° TO 450°F)
COOKING TIME: 1¼ TO 1½ HOURS
SPECIAL EQUIPMENT: LARGE DISPOSABLE FOIL TIN,
    BUTCHER'S STRING

BUTTER
50 g (2 oz) unsalted butter, softened
1 tablespoon finely chopped tarragon
2 teaspoons finely grated orange rind
½ teaspoon sea salt
¼ teaspoon freshly ground black pepper

1 whole chicken, 2.5 to 2.75 kg (5 to 5½ lb)
1 teaspoon sea salt
½ teaspoon freshly ground black pepper

1. Use the back of a fork to mix and mash the butter ingredients together in a small bowl.

2. Remove and discard the neck, giblets and any excess fat from the chicken. Loosen the chicken skin gently with your fingertips and spread the butter under the skin on to the breast meat and as much as you can reach on the drumsticks and thighs.

3. Season the chicken inside and out with the salt and pepper. Truss the chicken legs with butcher's string. Place the chicken, breast side up, in a large disposable foil tin. Allow the chicken to stand at room temperature for 20 to 30 minutes before barbecuing. Prepare the barbecue for indirect cooking over a medium heat.

4. Brush the cooking grills clean. Barbecue the chicken over **_indirect medium heat_** for 1¼ to 1½ hours, with the lid closed but rotating the tin as needed for even browning and occasionally basting the chicken with the melted butter collected in the bottom of the tin, until the juices run clear and the internal temperature in the thickest part of the thigh reaches 77°C (170°F). When fully cooked, transfer the chicken to a platter and loosely cover with aluminium foil. Allow to rest for about 10 minutes. Remove the string and carve the chicken. Serve warm.

HOW TO BARBECUE BUTTERFLIED CHICKEN

1. Pull out and discard the loose clumps of fat that are typically just inside the chicken. Otherwise they might drip into the barbecue and cause flare-ups.

2. Turn the chicken over so that the back is facing up and the neck end is closest to you. Use poultry shears to cut along both sides of the backbone, then discard it.

3. Open the chicken like a butterfly spreading its wings, and press down to flatten it.

4. Run your fingertips along both sides of the breastbone to expose it.

5. Dig your fingers down along the breastbone until it comes loose from the meat, then pull it out and discard it.

6. Fold the wingtips behind the chicken's back to prevent them from burning.

7. Now you have overcome one of the key cooking challenges of a whole chicken: an uneven shape. By butterflying (or spatchcocking) the bird, you have created a relatively even shape.

8. Barbecue the chicken, bone side down first, with a heavy weight on top. Use a medium-low heat to gently cook the meat.

9. After about 25 minutes, carefully turn the chicken over with a spatula and put the weight back on top. With the skin side down, flare-ups are more likely. If necessary, turn off the middle burners or move the chicken to finish cooking over indirect heat.

POULTRY

166

NUTMEG CHICKEN UNDER A CAST-IRON FRYING PAN

SERVES: 4
PREP TIME: 30 MINUTES
MARINATING TIME: 2 HOURS

HEAT: DIRECT MEDIUM-LOW HEAT ABOUT 180°C (350°F)
COOKING TIME: 40 MINUTES TO 1 HOUR
SPECIAL EQUIPMENT: CAST-IRON FRYING PAN OR
    SHALLOW ROASTING TIN AND 2 FOIL-WRAPPED
    BRICKS, INSTANT-READ THERMOMETER

MARINADE
4 tablespoons extra-virgin olive oil
2 tablespoons very finely chopped rosemary
1 tablespoon very finely chopped garlic
1 tablespoon freshly grated nutmeg
1 tablespoon sea salt
1 tablespoon sugar
1 teaspoon freshly ground black pepper

1 whole chicken, about 2.5 kg (5 lb)

1. Combine the marinade ingredients in a large, shallow bowl.

2. Place the chicken, breast side down, on a chopping board. Using sturdy poultry shears or a very sharp knife, cut from the neck to the tail end, along either side of the backbone, to remove it. Take special care if you are using a knife; you'll be cutting through small bones and will have to use some force.

3. Once the backbone is out, you'll be able to see the interior of the chicken. Make a small slit in the cartilage at the bottom end of the breastbone. Then, placing both hands on the rib cage, crack the chicken open like a book. Run your fingers along either side of the cartilage in between the breasts to loosen it from the flesh. Grab the bone and pull up on it to remove it along with the attached cartilage. The chicken should now lay flat.

4. Place the chicken inside the bowl or a roasting tin and turn to coat it evenly with the marinade. Cover with plastic wrap and refrigerate for about 2 hours.

5. Prepare the barbecue for direct cooking over a medium-low heat.

6. Brush the cooking grills clean. Place the chicken, bone side down, over ***direct medium-low heat*** for 20 to 30 minutes, with the lid closed, and put a heavy cast-iron frying pan or a roasting tin weighted down with 2 foil-wrapped bricks, directly on top. Remove the pan, turn the chicken over, replace the weight, close the lid and cook for a further 20 to 30 minutes until the juices run clear and an instant-read thermometer inserted into the thigh (not touching the bone) registers 77°C (170°F). Remove from the barbecue and allow to rest for 3 to 5 minutes. Serve warm.

HOW TO BARBECUE BACON-WRAPPED TURKEY BREAST

1. With the smooth side facing the board, open up the breast and cut down the centre (but not all the way through) to make the breast as flat and even as possible.

2. Lay the butterflied turkey breast between 2 large sheets of plastic wrap and pound it to a thickness of 1.5 to 2.5 cm (¾ to 1 inch).

3. Spread the stuffing evenly over the turkey breast, but leave a margin all the way round the perimeter. Don't over-stuff the breast.

4. Roll up the breast lengthways to create a cylinder. If any excess stuffing falls out, discard it.

5. Arrange the bacon slices on a work surface in 6 tightly spaced parallel rows, overlapping the ends of 2 slices to make each row.

6. Place the rolled turkey breast in the centre of the bacon and then criss-cross the bacon around the turkey.

7. Tie the turkey crossways with butcher's string at 2.5-cm (1-inch) intervals.

8. Thread a long piece of string lengthways, in and out of the crossways pieces, and tie the ends together to create a uniform roast and to secure the bacon.

9. Set a disposable foil tin under the cooking grill to catch the bacon grease. Barbecue the roast over the tin, using indirect heat, until the internal temperature of the meat and stuffing reaches 74°C (165°F), turning to ensure even cooking.

BACON-WRAPPED TURKEY BREAST WITH HERB STUFFING

SERVES: 4 TO 6
PREP TIME: 30 MINUTES

HEAT: INDIRECT HIGH HEAT 230° TO 290°C (450° TO 550°F)
COOKING TIME: 1 TO 1¼ HOURS
SPECIAL EQUIPMENT: BUTCHER'S STRING, LARGE
    DISPOSABLE FOIL TIN, INSTANT-READ THERMOMETER

STUFFING
75 g (3 oz) fresh breadcrumbs
4 tablespoons chicken stock
1 tablespoon finely chopped garlic
2 teaspoons finely chopped rosemary
2 teaspoons finely chopped oregano
1 teaspoon finely grated lemon rind
½ teaspoon sea salt
½ teaspoon freshly ground black pepper

500 g (1 lb) bacon rashers
1 boneless, skinless turkey breast, about 1 kg
    (2 lb), butterflied

1. Combine the stuffing ingredients in a bowl. The stuffing should be moist, mounding nicely on a spoon, but should not be sopping wet. Add more stock if needed.

2. Carefully place a large disposable foil tin underneath the cooking grill to catch the bacon grease. Prepare the barbecue for indirect cooking over a high heat.

3. Place the butterflied turkey breast on a work surface between 2 sheets of plastic wrap and pound to an even thickness. Spread the stuffing evenly over the turkey breast and then roll up the breast lengthways to create a cylinder. Arrange the bacon slices on a work surface in 6 tightly spaced, parallel rows, overlapping the ends of 2 slices to make each row. Place the rolled turkey breast in the centre of the bacon and then criss-cross the bacon around the turkey. Tie the turkey with butcher's string to create a uniform roast and to secure the bacon.

4. Brush the cooking grills clean. Centre the turkey over the drip tin and barbecue over ***indirect high heat*** for 1 to 1¼ hours, with the lid closed as much as possible but turning occasionally to ensure the bacon gets crisp on all sides, until the internal temperature reaches 77°C (170°F). Transfer to a carving board and allow to rest for 10 minutes (the internal temperature will rise during this time). Remove the string and carve into 2.5-cm (1-inch) slices.

HOW TO COOK TURKEY
5 THINGS YOU NEED TO KNOW

Every December millions of cooks tighten up with stress at the thought of how to cook a golden, succulent turkey for Christmas. Let me tell you; it's not that difficult. Focus on a handful of critical elements.

1 BRINING A DAY AHEAD

Because turkey meat is so lean and bland, some kind of brining is important. In the following recipe I call for a dry brine, which just means coating the turkey with sea salt the day before cooking. Overnight, in the refrigerator, the salt will draw out some moisture, which will mix with the salt, and then the meat will reabsorb much of that flavourful moisture.

2 MAINTAINING AN EVEN TEMPERATURE

An even temperature in the range of 180 to 200°C (350° to 400°F) is also key here. That's easy enough to achieve on a gas barbecue, assuming there is plenty of gas in the tank. It's a bit more challenging with a charcoal barbecue. Before cooking your first turkey with charcoal, make sure you have had some good experiences maintaining a live fire over the course of several hours.

3 SHIELDING THE BREAST MEAT

Because the breast meat cooks faster than the leg meat, you should protect the breast and slow down its rate of cooking. I do that by facing the breast down inside a stock-and-vegetable-filled pan for the first hour of cooking.

4 CATCHING THE PERFECT DONENESS

In a very short period of time, a turkey can turn from moist and fabulous to dry and stringy, so it's imperative that you use an instant-read thermometer and remove the turkey from the barbecue when the internal temperature in the thickest part of the thigh reaches 77°C (170°F).

5 GETTING ENOUGH REST

Finally, don't skip the resting step after your turkey comes off the barbecue. During that period, the turkey will finish cooking and the juices will redistribute nicely.

HOW TO PREP TURKEY THE DAY BEFORE

1. Generously season the turkey, inside and out, with sea salt and freshly ground black pepper.

2. Refrigerate the seasoned turkey on a roasting tray, uncovered, for 12 hours. It's okay if the skin looks dry and tightened at the end of the time.

HOW TO SMOKE TURKEY

1. Remove the turkey from the refrigerator and allow it sit at room temperature for 1 hour. Brush the legs, breast and wings with butter.

2. Place 1 large disposable foil tin inside the other and add the vegetables, herbs and 450 ml (16 fl oz) of chicken stock.

3. Arrange the barbecue briquettes in a half circle on one side of the charcoal grate. A drip tin filled with warm water will help you maintain the temperature of the fire.

4. Place the turkey, breast side down, over the vegetables, inside the foil tins.

5. Add wood chips to the barbecue briquettes and set the pan over the water tin, with the legs facing the hottest side of the barbecue.

6. Keep the barbecue temperature inside the range of 180 to 200°C (350° to 400°F).

7. After barbecuing for 1 hour, flip over the turkey so that the breast side is facing up.

8. Continue cooking and smoking the turkey, occasionally adding damp wood chips.

9. After the turkey has been cooking for 1½ hours, cover any parts that are getting too dark.

HOW TO CARVE TURKEY

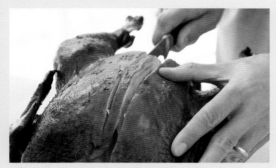

1. Remove each half of the turkey breast by cutting lengthways along each side of the breastbone.

2. Pull the first half of the breast away from the breastbone, using a sharp knife to carefully release the meat from the rib cage.

3. It is much easier to carve a half of a turkey breast into crossways slices than it is to carve the breast while it is still attached to the body.

HICKORY-SMOKED TURKEY WITH BOURBON GRAVY

SERVES: 8 TO 12
PREP TIME: 20 MINUTES
DRY BRINING TIME: 12 HOURS

HEAT: INDIRECT MEDIUM HEAT 180° TO 230°C
   (350° TO 400°F)
COOKING TIME: ABOUT 2½ HOURS
SPECIAL EQUIPMENT: 3 LARGE DISPOSABLE FOIL TINS,
   INSTANT-READ THERMOMETER, FAT SEPARATOR

1 turkey, about 6 kg (12 lb)
2 tablespoons sea salt
2 teaspoons freshly ground black pepper
40 g (1½ oz) unsalted butter, softened

AROMATICS
150 g (5 oz) brown onion, chopped
65 g (2½ lb) carrot, chopped
50 g (2 oz) celery, chopped
1 teaspoon dried rosemary
1 teaspoon dried thyme
1 teaspoon dried sage

450 ml (16 fl oz) chicken stock, plus more for the gravy
4 handfuls hickory wood chips, soaked in water for at least
   30 minutes

GRAVY
75 g (3 oz) plain flour
3 tablespoons bourbon or whisky
½ teaspoon sea salt
¼ teaspoon freshly ground black pepper

1. The day before cooking, prepare the turkey. Remove the giblets from the turkey and set aside for another use. Rinse the turkey with cold water, then shake off the excess water, but do not pat dry. Combine the salt and pepper and rub it all over the turkey, inside and out. Place the turkey on a roasting tray and refrigerate, uncovered, for 12 hours.

2. Remove the turkey from the refrigerator. The skin may look dry, and that's okay. Do not rinse the turkey. Allow the turkey to stand at room temperature for 1 hour. Brush the legs, breast and wings with the butter.

3. Place one foil tin inside the other and combine the aromatics in the top tin. (Do not use a high-quality metal roasting tin, as the smoke may discolour it.) Add 500 ml (17 fl oz/2 cups) of the chicken stock. Place the turkey, breast side down, inside the foil tins and over the aromatics.

4. Drain and add 2 handfuls of the wood chips directly on to burning coals or to the smoker box of a gas barbecue, following manufacturer's instructions. Barbecue the turkey over **indirect medium heat** for 1 hour, with the lid closed, keeping the barbecue 's temperature between 180 to 200°C (350° to 400°F).

5. After barbecuing for 1 hour, wearing barbecue mitts or an oven glove and using a pair of tongs, flip over the turkey so that the breast side is facing up. Add the remaining 2 handfuls of the wood chips. Continue barbecuing and smoking the turkey for 1½ hours, until it is golden brown and a thermometer inserted in the thickest part of the thigh (not touching the bone) reaches 77°C (170°F). After the turkey has been on the barbecue for 1½ hours, check to see if the wing tips or the ends of the drumsticks are getting too dark. If so, wrap them with foil.

6. Carefully remove the turkey and roasting tins from the barbecue. Transfer the turkey to a carving board and allow to rest for 20 to 30 minutes. Save the juices and vegetables to make the gravy.

7. Strain the tin juices into a fat separator, pressing the vegetables firmly with a wooden spoon to extract as much liquid as possible. Discard the vegetables left in the sieve. Allow the tin juices to stand until the fat rises to the surface, about 2 minutes. Pour the tin juices into a 1-litre (35-fl oz/ 4 cup) measuring jug. Add more chicken stock, if needed, to make 750 ml (26 fl oz/3 cups). Measure the turkey fat; you should have 125 ml (4 fl oz/½ cup). Add melted butter, if needed.

8. Warm the fat in a heavy-based saucepan over a medium heat, for about 2 minutes. Whisk in the flour and let it bubble until golden brown. Whisk in the stock mixture and the bourbon. Gently heat until lightly thickened, stirring often. Season with the salt and pepper.

9. Carve the turkey and serve with the gravy.

MAPLE-PLANKED TURKEY BURGERS

SERVES: 6
PREP TIME: 20 MINUTES

HEAT: DIRECT MEDIUM HEAT 180° TO 230°C (350° TO 450°F)
COOKING TIME: 20 TO 30 MINUTES
SPECIAL EQUIPMENT: 2 UNTREATED MAPLE PLANKS,
    EACH 30 TO 45 CM (12 TO 15 INCHES) LONG AND
    1 TO 1.5 CM (½ TO ¾ INCH) THICK, SOAKED IN BEER
    OR WATER FOR AT LEAST 1 HOUR

SAUCE
125 g (4 oz) tomato sauce
5 tablespoons worcestershire sauce
3 tablespoons soy sauce
1 tablespoon apple cider vinegar
1 tablespoon light brown sugar
1½ teaspoons mustard powder
1½ teaspoons ground cumin
1 teaspoon hot sauce, or to taste

1 kg (2 lb) minced (ground) turkey thigh meat
40 g (1½ oz) shallot, finely chopped
65 g (2½ lb) old-fashioned porridge oats
1 teaspoon sea salt
½ teaspoon freshly ground black pepper

6 hamburger buns
18 sweet pickle slices
18 red onion slices

1. Combine the sauce ingredients in a bowl. Set aside about
125 ml (4 fl oz/½ cup) of the sauce to serve with the burgers.

2. Mix the minced turkey with the shallot, oats, salt and pepper
and form into 6 burgers, each about 2 cm (¾ inch) thick. With
your thumb or the back of a spoon, make a shallow indentation
about 2.5 cm (1 inch) wide in the centre of each burger so the
centres are about 1 cm (½ inch) thick.

3. Prepare the barbecue for direct cooking over a medium heat.

4. Brush the cooking grills clean. Drain the planks and heat
them over ***direct medium heat*** for 5 to 10 minutes with the
lid closed, until they begin to char and lightly smoke. Turn
the planks over and place 3 burgers on each plank. Barbecue
the burgers over ***direct medium heat*** for 15 to 20 minutes, with
the lid closed as much as possible, turning and basting with the
sauce once after 10 minutes.

5. During the last minute of cooking time, lightly toast the cut
sides of the buns over ***direct medium heat***. Serve the burgers
on buns with pickles, the reserved sauce and slices of onion.

HOW TO SMOKE TURKEY BURGERS ON PLANKS

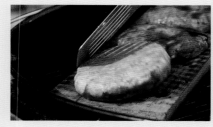

1. Cook the burgers for about 10 minutes
on the planks, then begin basting them with
sauce and turn them over.

2. Cook for 5 to 10 minutes, basting now and
again, until there's no red left in the centre and
the internal temperature registers 74°C (165°F).

3. You will find that burgers made with dark
thigh meat give you much juicer results than
those made with light breast meat.

HOW TO REMOVE CORN KERNELS

1. Cut off the stem end of an ear of corn to create a flat surface.

2. Stand the ear of corn, stem side down, in a dish or bowl. Cut from top to bottom so the kernels fall into the dish or bowl.

HOW TO SHRED CABBAGE

1. Split a head of cabbage in half lengthways and cut out the tough, triangular core of each half.

2. Lay each half flat on a chopping board and slice as thinly as you can.

SOUTHWESTERN TURKEY BURGERS WITH SALSA SLAW

SERVES: 4
PREP TIME: 20 MINUTES

HEAT: DIRECT MEDIUM HEAT 180° TO 230°C (350° TO 450°F)
COOKING TIME: 8 TO 10 MINUTES

SLAW
150 g (5 oz) savoy cabbage, finely shredded
250 g (8 oz) fresh tomato salsa (see page 291), drained
15 g (½ oz) coriander, finely chopped
3 tablespoons sour cream

BURGERS
750 g (1½ lb) minced (ground) turkey thigh meat
50 g (2 oz) corn kernels
4 tablespoons finely chopped pickled jalapeño chilli, or to taste
1 tablespoon pure chilli powder
2 teaspoons very finely chopped garlic
1½ teaspoons sea salt
1 teaspoon ground cumin

4 wholegrain hamburger buns

1. Mix the slaw ingredients together in a bowl. Cover and refrigerate. Stir and then drain well just before serving.

2. Prepare the barbecue for direct cooking over a medium heat.

3. Gently mix the burger ingredients together, then shape into 4 burgers, each about 2 cm (¾ inch) thick. With your thumb or the back of a spoon, make a shallow indentation about 2.5 cm (1 inch) wide in the centre of each burger so the centres are about 1 cm (½ inch) thick. This will help the burgers cook evenly and prevent them from puffing on the barbecue.

4. Brush the cooking grills clean. Barbecue the burgers over **direct medium heat** for 8 to 10 minutes, with the lid closed as much as possible but turning once, until fully cooked but still juicy. During the last minute of cooking time, lightly toast the cut sides of the buns over **direct medium heat**. Top the burgers with slaw and serve on the toasted buns.

SEAFOOD

TECHNIQUES

RECIPES

Before barbecuing, remove any tough little side muscles still attached to the scallops (top photo). After barbecuing, the interior of the scallops should be barely opaque, like the one in the centre. The scallop on the left is a little underdone and the scallop on the right is overdone (bottom photo).

SCALLOPS WITH BARBECUE-ROASTED TOMATO SAUCE

SERVES: 4
PREP TIME: 25 MINUTES
MARINATING TIME: 10 TO 15 MINUTES

HEAT: DIRECT MEDIUM HEAT 180° TO 230°C
     (350° TO 450°F)
COOKING TIME: 14 TO 16 MINUTES

SAUCE
500 g (1 lb) roma tomatoes
3 spring onions, tops and root ends trimmed
1 teaspoon finely grated lemon rind
2 tablespoons fresh lemon juice
1 tablespoon sugar
1 teaspoon yellow mustard seeds, ground
1 teaspoon fennel seeds
½ teaspoon sea salt

12 jumbo sea scallops, about 50 g (2 oz) each

MARINADE
15 g (½ oz) unsalted butter, melted
1 tablespoon extra-virgin olive oil
1 teaspoon grated lemon rind
1 tablespoon fresh lemon juice
½ teaspoon sea salt
¼ teaspoon freshly ground black pepper

1 tablespoon finely chopped basil or flat-leaf parsley

1. Prepare the barbecue for direct cooking over a medium heat. Brush the cooking grills clean.

2. Barbecue the tomatoes and spring onions over **direct medium heat**, with the lid closed as much as possible, until the

tomato skins blister and brown and the spring onions are lightly browned, turning as needed. The tomatoes will take about 10 minutes and the spring onions will take 4 to 5 minutes. Transfer the vegetables to a chopping board. Carefully pull off and discard the tomato skins and trim and discard the stem ends. Chop the tomatoes into 5-mm (¼-inch) pieces, and then transfer the tomatoes with their juices to a large frying pan. Thinly slice the spring onions, including the tops, and add to the tomatoes along with the rest of the sauce ingredients. Simmer the sauce over medium heat for 5 to 6 minutes, stirring occasionally, until the flavors blend. Keep warm. (The sauce can be made a day ahead and reheated.)

3. Remove the small, tough side muscle that may be left on each scallop. Combine the marinade ingredients in a small bowl. Toss the scallops in the marinade and allow them to stand at room temperature for 10 to 15 minutes.

4. Brush the cooking grills clean. Lift the scallops from the bowl and lay slightly apart on the cooking grill. Discard the marinade. Barbecue over **direct medium heat** for 4 to 6 minutes with the lid closed as much as possible but turning once, until lightly browned and just opaque in the centre (check one by cutting it open).

5. Add the basil to the tomato sauce. Divide the sauce evenly on 4 warmed plates and top with hot scallops.

PROSCIUTTO-BELTED SCALLOPS WITH LENTIL SALAD

SERVES: 4
PREP TIME: 25 MINUTES
MARINATING TIME: 1 HOUR

HEAT: DIRECT MEDIUM HEAT 180° TO 230°C
   (350° TO 450°F)
COOKING TIME: 4 TO 6 MINUTES

12 jumbo sea scallops, about 50 g (2 oz) each
6 thin slices prosciutto, cut in half lengthways

MARINADE
3 tablespoons very finely chopped shallot
3 tablespoons fresh lemon juice
2 tablespoons extra-virgin olive oil
1½ tablespoons dijon mustard
¾ teaspoon dried tarragon
¼ teaspoon freshly ground black pepper

LENTILS
6 thin slices prosciutto, finely chopped
2 tablespoons extra-virgin olive oil
75 g (3 oz) button mushrooms, finely chopped
50 g (2 oz) very finely chopped shallot
½ teaspoon dried tarragon
200 g (7 oz) green lentils
750 ml (26 fl oz/3 cups) chicken or vegetable stock
1 teaspoon finely grated lemon rind
15 g (½ oz) flat-leaf parsley, finely chopped
Sea salt
Freshly ground black pepper

1. Remove the small, tough side muscle that may be left on each scallop.

2. Wrap one slice of prosciutto around each scallop and secure with a small skewer.

3. Mix the marinade ingredients together in a shallow non-metallic dish. Gently turn the scallops in the marinade and then lay them flat in the dish. Cover with plastic wrap and refrigerate for 1 hour. Meanwhile, prepare the lentils.

4. Combine the chopped prosciutto, oil, mushrooms, shallot and tarragon in a large saucepan over a medium-high heat. Stir often for 5 to 7 minutes until the vegetables are limp and slightly browned.

5. Sort through the lentils and discard any debris. Rinse and drain the lentils and add them to the pan along with the stock and bring to the boil. Reduce the heat, cover and simmer for 40 to 55 minutes until the lentils are tender. Stir in the lemon rind and parsley, then season to taste with salt and pepper. Keep warm.

6. Prepare the barbecue for direct cooking over a medium heat. Brush the cooking grills clean. Barbecue the scallops, unwrapped sides down, over *direct medium heat* for 4 to 6 minutes, with the lid closed as much as possible but turning them once, until they are lightly browned and opaque in the centre. Remove from the barbecue and serve warm with the lentils.

HOW TO PREP SCALLOPS

1. Cut each prosciutto slice to fit the scallops.

2. Wrap a strip of prosciutto around each scallop and secure it with a small skewer.

3. Barbecue the scallops for 2 or 3 minutes until they can easily lift off the grill without sticking.

4. Turn the scallops over and finish cooking. Barbecue so the flat sides of each lie flat on the grill.

CEDAR-PLANKED SCALLOPS WITH BARBECUED CORN SALAD

SERVES: 4 TO 6
PREP TIME: 25 MINUTES

HEAT: DIRECT MEDIUM HEAT 180° TO 230°C
(350° TO 450°F)
COOKING TIME: 23 TO 32 MINUTES
SPECIAL EQUIPMENT: 1 UNTREATED CEDAR PLANK,
30 TO 32 CM (12 TO 15 INCHES) LONG AND
1 TO 1.5 CM (½ TO ¾ INCH) THICK, SOAKED IN
WATER FOR AT LEAST 1 HOUR

MARINADE
5 tablespoons extra-virgin olive oil
5 tablespoons fresh lime juice
1 tablespoon honey
1 teaspoon sea salt

20 large sea scallops, each about 3 cm (1¼ inches) in diameter

SALAD
½ small red onion, cut into 3 wedges
3 ears sweet corn, shucked
1 red capsicum
Extra-virgin olive oil
Sea salt
Freshly ground black pepper
½ teaspoon ground cumin
1 teaspoon hot sauce, or to taste

1. Whisk the marinade ingredients together in a bowl. Transfer 3 tablespoons of the marinade to a large bowl to use for dressing the salad. Set the 2 bowls aside.

2. Remove the small, tough side muscle that may be left on each scallop. Refrigerate until ready to cook.

3. Prepare the barbecue for direct cooking over a medium heat. Lightly brush the onion, corn, and capsicum with oil and season evenly with salt and pepper. Brush the cooking grills clean. Barbecue the vegetables over **direct medium heat**, with the lid closed as much as possible but turning the vegetables as needed, until the onion has softened and started to collapse, the corn kernels are mostly brown, with some beginning to char and the capsicum is blackened and blistered all over. The onion will take about 4 minutes, the corn will take 6 to 8 minutes and the capsicum, 10 to 12 minutes. Place the capsicum in a bowl, cover with plastic wrap and allow it to cool.

4. When the vegetables are cool enough to handle, cut the onion into a small dice, cut the kernels off the cobs and remove and discard the charred skin, stem, ribs and seeds from the capsicum. Cut the capsicum into a medium dice, saving the juice. Combine the onion, corn, capsicum with juice, cumin and hot sauce into the large bowl with the 3 tablespoons of reserved marinade.

5. Place the soaked plank over **direct medium heat** and close the lid. After 5 to 10 minutes, when the plank begins to smoke and char, turn the plank over. Put the scallops in the bowl with the marinade and toss to coat. Place the scallops in a single layer on the plank. Close the barbecue lid and cook for 8 to 10 minutes, until they are slightly firm on the surface and opaque in the centre. Serve the scallops warm with the salad.

HOW TO CUT ONION WEDGES

1. The layers of the onion wedges will hold together on the barbecue if you leave part of the root end attached.

2. After you have cut your wedges, peel off the papery skin.

CHECKING DONENESS

When smoked scallops are done, they will feel slightly firm on top and look lightly coloured all over by the smoke.

THAI PRAWNS
WITH WATERMELON SALSA

SERVES: 4
PREP TIME: 25 MINUTES
MARINATING TIME: 30 MINUTES

HEAT: DIRECT HIGH HEAT 230° TO 290°C (450° TO 550°F)
COOKING TIME: 3 TO 5 MINUTES
SPECIAL EQUIPMENT: 8 BAMBOO SKEWERS,
    SOAKED IN WATER FOR AT LEAST 30 MINUTES

SALSA
2 tablespoons very finely chopped shallot
2 teaspoons rice vinegar
1 teaspoon sugar
1–2 tablespoons very finely chopped jalapeño chilli
325 g (11 oz) seedless watermelon, cut into 1-cm (½-inch) cubes
1 7.5-cm (3-inch) piece cucumber, halved lengthways,
    deseeded and thinly sliced into half-moons
1 teaspoon very finely chopped mint
¼ teaspoon sea salt

MARINADE
25 g (1 oz) coriander leaves and tender stems
15 g (½ oz) mint leaves
3 garlic cloves
2 tablespoons coarsely chopped fresh root ginger
2 tablespoons rice vinegar
2 tablespoons sunflower or other vegetable oil
2 teaspoons sugar
1 teaspoon Thai red curry paste
¼ teaspoon sea salt

625 g (1¼ lb) extra-large prawns, peeled and deveined but with
    tails left on

1. Mix the shallot, vinegar, sugar and jalapeño together in a
large bowl. Add the watermelon, cucumber, mint and salt and
toss gently to combine. To fully incorporate the flavours, allow
the salsa to sit at room temperature for 30 to 60 minutes.

2. Combine the marinade ingredients in a food processor.
Process to create a coarse purée, occasionally scraping down
the side of the bowl to incorporate the ingredients evenly.

3. Transfer the marinade to a bowl. Add the prawns, and toss to
coat them evenly. Cover the bowl and refrigerate for 30 minutes,
turning the prawns after 15 minutes. Prepare the barbecue for
direct cooking over a high heat.

4. Remove the prawns from the bowl and discard the marinade.
Thread the prawns on to skewers. Brush the cooking grills
clean. Barbecue the skewers over **direct high heat** for 3 to
5 minutes, with the lid closed as much as possible but turning
once, until the prawns are firm to the touch, lightly charred and
just turning opaque in the centre. Serve the prawns warm or at
room temperature with the salsa.

Fresh and frozen prawns can range from very small, less than
2.5 cm (1 inch) to 33 cm (13 inches) for Black Tiger prawns,
and the terms 'standard', 'medium', 'large', 'king' and 'jumbo' are
used inconsistently, with the very smallest prawns called 'shrimp'.
To add to the confusion, large and jumbo warm-water prawns
(freshwater or seawater) can both be sold as 'kings'. Supermarkets
and fishmongers generally sell all prawns by weight and you have
to make your choice based on sight. Choose the size most suitable
for your recipe raw or cooked. Prawns the size of the two largest
examples above are the best choice for barbecuing, because
they are easy to peel and they don't dry out as quickly as smaller
prawns would.

PRAWN PO'BOYS WITH CREOLE RÉMOULADE

SERVES: 6
PREP TIME: 20 MINUTES

HEAT: DIRECT HIGH HEAT 230° TO 290°C (450° TO 550°F)
COOKING TIME: 3 TO 5 MINUTES
SPECIAL EQUIPMENT: PERFORATED GRILL PAN

RÉMOULADE
125 g (4 oz) mayonnaise
2 tablespoons creole or dijon mustard
2 tablespoons sweet pickle relish
1 tablespoon prepared horseradish
2 teaspoons very finely chopped tarragon
1 teaspoon very finely chopped garlic
½ teaspoon hot sauce, or to taste
½ teaspoon sweet paprika
½ teaspoon sea salt
¼ teaspoon freshly ground black pepper

1 kg (2 lb) large prawns, peeled and deveined with
    tails removed
2 tablespoons extra-virgin olive oil
1 tablespoon creole seasoning
6 soft bread rolls, split horizontally
Lettuce, chopped
18 ripe tomato slices

Rémoulade is a mayonnaise-based spread flavoured with mustard and other condiments. Among mustards, creole is one of the spiciest, thanks to its horseradish and vinegar-marinated brown mustard seeds.

1. Combine the rémoulade ingredients in a small bowl. Cover and refrigerate until serving.

2. Prepare the barbecue for direct cooking over a high heat. Preheat the grill pan for about 10 minutes.

3. Toss the prawns with the oil and then evenly coat with the creole seasoning. Spread the prawns on the grill pan and cook over **direct high heat** for 2 to 4 minutes, with the lid closed as much as possible but turning once, until firm to the touch and just turning opaque in the centre. Remove from the barbecue and keep warm.

4. Barbecue the rolls, cut sides down, over **direct high heat** for 30 seconds to 1 minute, until lightly toasted. Spread the rémoulade on the cut sides of the rolls and add lettuce, tomatoes and prawns. Serve warm.

ORANGE-FENNEL PRAWNS OVER WATERCRESS

SERVES: 4
PREP TIME: 25 MINUTES
MARINATING TIME: 1 HOUR

HEAT: DIRECT HIGH HEAT 230° TO 290°C (450° TO 550°F)
COOKING TIME: 2 TO 4 MINUTES
SPECIAL EQUIPMENT: PERFORATED GRILL PAN

MARINADE
Grated rind of 2 oranges
125 ml (4 fl oz/½ cup) fresh orange juice
5 tablespoons extra-virgin olive oil
2 tablespoons fresh lime juice
1 tablespoon very finely chopped garlic
1 teaspoon ground fennel
1 teaspoon sea salt
½ teaspoon ground cayenne pepper

750 g (1½ lb) large prawns, peeled and deveined with tails
     left on
100 g (3½ oz) watercress leaves and tender stems

1. Mix the marinade ingredients together in a bowl. Set aside
125 ml (4 fl oz/½ cup) of the marinade to use as a dressing for
the salad.

2. Place the prawns in a large, resealable plastic bag and pour
in the marinade. Press the air out of the bag and seal tightly.
Turn the bag several times to distribute the marinade, lay the
bag flat on a plate and refrigerate for 1 hour.

3. Prepare the barbecue for direct cooking over high heat.
Preheat the grill pan for about 10 minutes.

4. Drain the prawns in a sieve. Spread the prawns in a single
layer on the grill pan and cook over **direct high heat** for 2 to
4 minutes, with the lid closed as much as possible but

shaking the pan once or twice and turning the prawns over for
even cooking, until they are slightly firm on the surface and
completely opaque in the centres. Remove the pan from the
barbecue and rest it on a baking tray. Transfer the prawns to
a large bowl to stop the cooking.

5. Add the watercress to the prawns in the large bowl. Spoon
the reserved dressing over the watercress and prawns (you
may not need all of it). Toss to coat the ingredients evenly.
Serve right away.

HOW TO PEEL AND DEVEIN PRAWNS

1. Grab the shell just above the
tail and break it loose.

2. Peel off the shell along with all
the little legs.

3. With a sharp paring knife,
make a shallow slit along the back
of each prawn.

4. Lift any black vein out of the
slit and discard it.

HOW TO BARBECUE PRAWN POPS

1. By using 2 spoons moving in opposite directions, you can make little oval-shaped mixtures called quenelles.

2. Move the top spoon over and behind the prawn mixture while moving the bottom spoon under and in front.

3. Continue to move the spoons over the surface of the mixture a few times to smooth it out and shape it.

4. Slide a short bamboo skewer through the centre of each quenelle, and turn the prawn mixture on a greased roasting tray.

5. Barbecue the pops over a high heat, with the bare ends of the skewers shielded by a folded sheet of aluminium foil.

6. Cook them long enough on the first side so that you can roll them over without any sticking, rather than picking them up with tongs and squeezing them.

VIETNAMESE PRAWN POPS WITH PEANUT SAUCE

SERVES: 4 TO 6
PREP TIME: 30 MINUTES
CHILLING TIME: 30 MINUTES TO 1 HOUR

HEAT: DIRECT HIGH HEAT 230° TO 290°C (450° TO 550°F)
COOKING TIME: 4 TO 6 MINUTES
SPECIAL EQUIPMENT: BAMBOO SKEWERS,
    SOAKED IN WATER FOR AT LEAST 30 MINUTES

SAUCE
250 ml (8 fl oz/1 cup) unsweetened coconut milk, stirred
125 g (4 oz) peanut butter, stirred
1 teaspoon finely grated lime rind
3 tablespoons fresh lime juice
1 tablespoon soy sauce
1 tablespoon brown sugar
1 teaspoon hot chilli sauce, such as sriracha
½ teaspoon grated fresh root ginger

PRAWN POPS
500 g (1 lb) minced (ground) pork
375 g (13 oz) prawns, peeled and deveined
25 g (1 oz) basil, coarsely chopped
15 g (½ oz) panko breadcrumbs
2 large garlic cloves
1 tablespoon soy sauce
½ teaspoon freshly ground black pepper

4 tablespoons sunflower or other vegetable oil

1. Combine the sauce ingredients in a heavy-based saucepan over a medium heat. Cook (but do not simmer) for 2 to 3 minutes, whisking constantly, just until the sauce is smooth and slightly thickened (the sauce will thicken further as it cools). Remove the pan from the heat.

2. Put the prawn pop ingredients in a food processor or blender and process until a chunky paste is formed. Pour the vegetable oil on to a baking tray and brush it evenly all over the surface. Using 2 spoons, shape the mixture into small quenelles or ovals, placing them on the greased tray as you make them. Turn them, making sure they are well coated with oil. Refrigerate the quenelles for 30 minutes to 1 hour to firm up the texture.

3. Prepare the barbecue for direct cooking over a high heat.

4. Place a quenelle on the end of each skewer. Brush the cooking grills clean. Barbecue the prawn pops over *direct high heat* for 4 to 6 minutes, with the lid closed as much as possible but turning once or twice, until they are opaque throughout, (cut one open with a sharp knife to test for doneness). Arrange the prawn pops on a serving platter. Serve warm with the dipping sauce.

HOW TO MAKE ROASTED CHILLI AND AVOCADO SAUCE

1. Roast the anaheim chillies over direct medium heat until the skins are blackened and blistered.

2. Discard the chilli stems, skins and seeds. Then combine the roasted chillies in a food processor with sour cream, mayonnaise, dill, garlic, salt and pepper.

3. Give the sauce a good whizz, stopping occasionally to scrape down the sides of the bowl.

4. If the sauce seems a little thick, add a touch of water to thin it out. The sauce will keep well in the refrigerator for a couple of days.

HOW TO PREP THE PRAWNS

1. Choose prawns that are the same size so that you can nestle them together with no empty spaces between them.

2. Begin by skewering one prawn through both the head and tail ends. Skewer the next prawn through the head end only, with the tail end pointing in the opposite direction. Skewer the remaining prawn just like the second one, with all their tails facing the same way.

3. The prawns are nestled closely together on the skewers, without spaces in between. This means they will stay juicy on the barbecue a little bit longer.

JUICY PRAWNS WITH ROASTED CHILLI AND AVOCADO SAUCE

SERVES: 4 TO 6
PREP TIME: 20 MINUTES

HEAT: DIRECT MEDIUM HEAT 180° TO 230°C
(350° TO 450°F) AND DIRECT HIGH HEAT
230° TO 290°C (450° TO 550°F)
COOKING TIME: 10 TO 16 MINUTES
SPECIAL EQUIPMENT: 8 TO 10 FLAT-SIDED OR ROUND
BAMBOO SKEWERS, SOAKED IN WATER FOR AT
LEAST 30 MINUTES

SAUCE
3 anaheim chillies or other mild chillies, each about 15 cm
(6 inches) long
1 haas avocado
4 tablespoons sour cream
4 tablespoons mayonnaise
2 tablespoons roughly chopped dill
1 large garlic clove
½ teaspoon sea salt
¼ teaspoon freshly ground black pepper

RUB
1 teaspoon garlic granules
1 teaspoon paprika
¾ teaspoon sea salt
½ teaspoon ground cumin
¼ teaspoon freshly ground black pepper

500 g (1 lb) large prawns, peeled and deveined, with tails left on
Extra-virgin olive oil

1. Prepare the barbecue for direct cooking over a medium heat. Brush the cooking grills clean. Barbecue the chillies over **direct medium heat** for 8 to 12 minutes, with the lid closed as much as possible but turning occasionally, until they are blackened and blistered in spots all over. Put the chillies in a bowl, cover with plastic wrap, and allow to steam for 10 minutes. When cool enough to handle, remove and discard the stem ends, skins and seeds. Drop the chillies into a food processor or blender and add the remaining sauce ingredients. Process to create a smooth dipping sauce. If the sauce seems too thick, add a little water. Spoon the sauce into a serving bowl.

2. Mix the rub ingredients together in a small bowl.

3. Lay 5 to 7 prawns on a work surface and arrange them so that the prawns on one end lays one way and all the rest lay in the same direction (see photo at left). Choose prawns that are the same size so that you can nestle them together with no empty spaces between them. This will help to keep the prawns from spinning, when you turn them, and prevent them from drying out on the barbecue. Pick up and skewer each prawn through the centre, pushing the prawns together on each

skewer. Repeat the process with the remaining prawns and skewers. Lightly brush the skewers with oil and then season them evenly with the rub.

4. Increase the temperature of the barbecue to a high heat. Brush the cooking grills clean. Barbecue the prawns over **direct high heat** for 2 to 4 minutes, with the lid closed as much as possible but turning once, until slightly firm on the surface and opaque in the centre. Remove from the barbecue and serve warm with the dipping sauce.

The 'fresh' prawns glistening on a bed of shaved ice at the market were almost certainly frozen previously, on the boat or at the harbour, and then they were thawed at the market. In fact, prawns will be closer to 'fresh' if you buy them frozen and thaw them yourself just before cooking.

HOW TO MAKE PAELLA

Paella is a rice dish that is traditionally cooked outdoors in a wide, shallow pan of the same name. Spreading the rice out in such a wide pan helps it to absorb the aromas of burning logs or charcoal. A big cast-iron frying pan substitutes well for the traditional paella pan, but there is no substitute for paella's quintessential spice: saffron.

1. Heat the stock with prawn shells, white wine, bay leaves, smoked paprika, salt, red chilli flakes and saffron.

2. Barbecue the prawns over direct high heat, but cook them only about halfway. They will finish cooking in the rice.

3. Cook the prosciutto in the pan until it releases its fat and begins to crisp.

4. Cook the onions, capsicum and garlic with the prosciutto to create an aromatic base of flavours.

5. Add a short- or round-grain rice, such as arborio, not a long-grain rice.

6. Stir to cook the rice lightly and to coat all the grains in the pan juices.

7. Add the hot, strained stock and close the lid of the barbecue so that the liquid gently simmers and the wood smoke does not escape.

8. At some point you may need to rotate the pan or move it to another part of the barbecue to even out the cooking.

9. The rice is done when it has absorbed most of the stock and the texture is tender but not mushy.

PAELLA

SERVES: 6 TO 8
PREP TIME: 40 MINUTES
SOAKING TIME FOR WILD MUSSELS: 30 MINUTES TO
    1 HOUR (SEE AUTHOR'S NOTE ON PAGE 190)

HEAT: DIRECT HIGH HEAT 230° TO 290°C (450° TO 550°F)
    AND DIRECT MEDIUM HEAT 180° TO 230°C
    (350° TO 450°F)
COOKING TIME: 35 TO 37 MINUTES
SPECIAL EQUIPMENT: 30-CM (12-INCH) CAST-IRON
    FRYING PAN

250 g (8 oz) large prawns, tails left on and shells reserved
    for the stock
2 teaspoons extra-virgin olive oil
Sea salt
Freshly ground black pepper

STOCK
Shells from peeled prawns
1 litre (35 fl oz/4 cups) chicken stock
175 ml (6 fl oz) dry white wine
2 bay leaves
1½ teaspoons smoked paprika
1 teaspoon sea salt
½ teaspoon dried red chilli flakes
¼ teaspoon crushed saffron threads

12 live mussels, scrubbed and beards removed
3 tablespoons extra-virgin olive oil
125 g (4 oz) thick-sliced prosciutto, cut into 5-mm
    (¼-inch) dice
150 g (5 oz) red onion, finely chopped
75 g (3 oz) red capsicum, finely chopped
1 tablespoon very finely chopped garlic
400 g (14 oz) short- or round-grain rice, such as arborio
175 g (6 oz) frozen baby peas

1. Peel and devein the prawns, reserving the shells to make
the stock. Toss the prawns with the oil in a large bowl and
season evenly with salt and pepper. Cover and refrigerate
until ready to grill.

2. Bring the prawn shells and the stock ingredients to a simmer
in a saucepan over a high heat. Strain, discarding the shells
and bay leaves, and reserve the stock. (The stock can be made
up to 2 hours ahead.)

3. Check each mussel and discard those with broken shells,
any that don't close up when you lightly tap on their shells
and any others that feel unusually heavy because of sand
trapped inside.

4. Prepare the barbecue for direct cooking over a high heat on
one side and medium heat on the other side. Brush the cooking
grills clean. Barbecue the prawns over **direct high heat** for
about 2 minutes until cooked halfway, turning once (the prawns
will finish cooking in the stock). Remove from the barbecue and
set aside to cool.

5. Place a 30-cm (12-inch) cast-iron frying pan on the cooking
grill over **direct high heat.** Heat the oil in the skillet. Add the
prosciutto and cook for about 3 minutes, stirring occasionally,
until it begins to crisp. Add the onion, capsicum and garlic and
cook for about 5 minutes, stirring occasionally and rotating the
pan for even cooking, until the onion is translucent. Slide the
pan away from the fire.

6. Place the pan over **direct medium heat**, stir in the rice and
cook for about 2 minutes until well coated with the pan juices.
Stir in the prawn stock and the frozen peas. Close the barbecue
lid and let the rice cook at a brisk simmer for about 15 minutes,
until the rice is al dente. Nestle the prawns into the rice. Add
the mussels, hinged sides down. Cook, with the barbecue lid
closed, for 8 to 10 minutes until the mussels open.

7. Remove the pan from the heat, cover with aluminium foil
and allow to stand for 5 minutes. Remove and discard any
unopened mussels. Serve hot straight from the pan.

WILD VERSUS FARM-RAISED MUSSELS

Check each mussel and discard those with broken shells, any that don't close up when you lightly tap on their shells and any others that feel unusually heavy because of sand trapped inside. Soak the mussels in cold, salted water for 30 minutes to 1 hour, then drain. The soaking is to remove sand, but that's only an issue with wild mussels (pictured at left) that grow in sandy places. If you use farm-raised mussels (pictured at right), you can skip the soaking step.

COCONUT-CURRY MUSSELS

SERVES: 4
PREP TIME: 15 MINUTES
SOAKING TIME FOR WILD MUSSELS: 30 MINUTES
    TO 1 HOUR

HEAT: DIRECT MEDIUM HEAT 180° TO 230°C
    (350° TO 450°F)
COOKING TIME: 17 TO 22 MINUTES
SPECIAL EQUIPMENT: LARGE DISPOSABLE FOIL TIN

SAUCE
1 can (425 ml/14 fl oz) coconut milk, light or regular
1 tablespoon Thai green curry paste
1 tablespoon fresh lime juice
2 teaspoons light brown sugar
2 teaspoons fish sauce
2 tablespoons peanut oil
1 tablespoon finely chopped fresh root ginger
1 tablespoon finely chopped garlic

1 kg (2 lb) live mussels, scrubbed and beards removed
15 g (½ oz) coriander leaves, finely chopped

Crusty bread, to serve (optional)

1. Prepare the barbecue for direct and indirect cooking over a medium heat.

2. Whisk the coconut milk, curry paste, lime juice, brown sugar and fish sauce together in a bowl.

3. Combine the peanut oil, ginger and garlic in a large disposable foil tin. Place the tin over **direct medium heat**, close the barbecue lid and let the aromatics cook for about 1 minute. Add the coconut milk mixture to the foil tin and gently stir to combine. Cook for 5 to 6 minutes to bring the sauce to the boil.

4. Add the mussels to the sauce. Cover the foil tin with a roasting tray (to trap the steam and cook the mussels), close the barbecue lid, and cook for 8 to 10 minutes. Check the mussels to see if they are open. If not, continue to cook for a further 3 to 5 minutes. Wearing barbecue mitts or oven gloves, carefully remove the roasting tray from the foil tin and carefully remove the foil tin from the barbecue. Remove and discard any unopened mussels. Sprinkle the coriander on top. Serve the mussels and sauce in bowls with crusty bread, if desired.

CAJUN-STYLE CLAMBAKE

SERVES: 4
PREP TIME: 45 MINUTES

HEAT: DIRECT MEDIUM HEAT 180° TO 230°C
   (350° TO 450°F)
COOKING TIME: 20 TO 25 MINUTES

125 g (4 oz) unsalted butter, melted
5 tablespoons fresh lemon juice
1 tablespoon cajun seasoning
1 tablespoon very finely chopped garlic
2 teaspoons chopped thyme leaves
4 desiree potatoes, halved and sliced into 2.5 mm (⅛-inch)
   half-moons
375 g (13 oz) jumbo prawns, peeled and deveined with
   tails left on, cold
1 kg (2 lb) littleneck clams, rinsed and scrubbed
375 g (13 oz) chorizo sausage, thinly sliced
2 ears sweet corn, each shucked and cut into
   4 pieces

1. Combine the butter, lemon juice, seasoning, garlic and thyme in a small bowl.

2. Prepare the barbecue for direct cooking over a medium heat.

3. Cut 8 sheets of aluminium foil, each about 30 by 50 cm (12 by 20 inches). Line a 20- by 20-cm (8- by 8-inch) cake tin with 2 sheets of aluminium foil, arranged in a criss-cross pattern. Layer the bottom of the foil-lined tin with the sliced potatoes. (This will help insulate the shellfish and keep them from overcooking.) Top the potatoes evenly with the prawns, clams, sausage and corn pieces. Drizzle each packet evenly with the butter mixture. Close the packet by bringing the ends of the 2 inner sheets together, folding them on top of the filling and then bringing the ends of the 2 outer sheets together, folding them down. Repeat this procedure to make 3 more packets.

4. Barbecue the packets over **direct medium heat** for 20 to 25 minutes, with the lid closed, until the clams have opened, the prawns have turned opaque and the potatoes are cooked. To check for doneness, using tongs, gently unfold one of the packets and carefully remove a potato, being careful not to puncture the bottom of the foil. Gently pierce the potato with a knife to ensure doneness. When everything is cooked, remove the packets from the barbecue. Carefully open each packet to let the steam escape and then pour the contents into warmed bowls and serve immediately.

HOW TO PREP FOR A CLAMBAKE

1. Rinse and scrub the clams under cold water. To remove sand and grit from inside the shells, soak them in iced water mixed with salt (1 teaspoon of salt per 250 ml/8 fl oz of water) for a few hours.

2. You can peel and devein the prawns ahead of time.

3. In a foil-lined tin, arrange the sliced potatoes on the bottom so that they will protect the other ingredients from the heat.

4. Be generous with the butter mixture.

5. Fold up the ends of the foil tightly to prevent any liquid from escaping.

6. You will remove each packet from its tin and cook it directly on the barbecue so that all the ingredients steam and simmer inside.

HOW TO CHAR-GRILL OYSTERS

1. For barbecuing, choose oysters like these, with deep rounded shells to hold in their juices.

2. Holding each oyster in a towel with the flat side facing up, push the tip of an oyster knife into the small opening at the hinge of the shell.

3. Twist the knife and wiggle it back and forth to pop open the shell.

4. Drag the knife along the seam between the top and bottom shells.

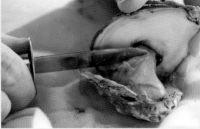

5. Use the side of the knife to cut the oyster meat loose from the top shell.

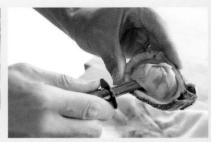

6. Slide the knife under the oyster meat to release it from the bottom shell.

7. As you finish shucking each oyster, lay it flat on a roasting tray, keeping as much liquid as possible in the shells.

8. The grilling goes quickly, so have all your sauces and serving platters ready.

9. Spoon the sauces into the raw oysters, but don't overfill the shells.

10. A very hot charcoal fire is crucial for cooking oysters in just a few minutes. As soon as the juices start to bubble, remove the oysters from the barbecue.

11. The meat of the oyster should be warm but not cooked all the way through.

SEAFOOD

CHAR-GRILLED OYSTERS

SERVES: 4 TO 6
PREP TIME: 30 MINUTES

HEAT: DIRECT HIGH HEAT 230° TO 290°C (450° TO 550°F)
COOKING TIME: 2 TO 4 MINUTES
SPECIAL EQUIPMENT: OYSTER KNIFE

24 large, oysters
Lemon wedges
Hot sauce
Cocktail sauce

1. Grip each oyster, flat side up, in a folded tea towel. Find the small opening between the shells near the hinge and pry it open with an oyster knife. Try not to spill the delicious juices, known as the 'oyster liqueur', in the bottom shell. Cut the oyster meat loose from the top shell and then loosen the oyster from the bottom shell by running the oyster knife carefully underneath the body. Discard the top, flatter shell, keeping the oyster and juices in the bottom, deeper shell.

2. Prepare the barbecue for direct cooking over a high heat.

3. Spoon some of your favourite dipping sauce on top of each oyster (recipes follow).

4. Brush the cooking grills clean. Barbecue the oysters, shell sides down, over **direct high heat** for 2 to 4 minutes, with the lid closed as much as possible, until the oyster juices start to bubble and the edges curl. Using tongs, carefully remove the oysters from the barbecue. Serve with lemon wedges, hot sauce, cocktail sauce and your favourite dipping sauce.

GARLIC-THYME BUTTER
MAKES: ENOUGH FOR 24 OYSTERS

50 g (2 oz) unsalted butter, divided
1 tablespoon very finely chopped garlic
2 teaspoons sherry vinegar
4 tablespoons dry white wine
2 teaspoons very finely chopped thyme
¼ teaspoon sea salt

1. Melt 15 g (½ oz) of the butter in a small frying pan over a medium heat. Add the garlic and sauté for about 2 minutes until it starts to brown. Add the vinegar and wine and simmer for about 2 minutes until the sauce reduces by half. Remove from the heat, whisk in the remaining butter and stir in the thyme and salt.

GRAPEFRUIT-BASIL AÏOLI
MAKES: ENOUGH FOR 24 OYSTERS

4 tablespoons mayonnaise
1 tablespoon chopped basil
1½ teaspoons finely grated grapefruit rind
2 teaspoons fresh grapefruit juice
1 teaspoon very finely chopped garlic
¼ teaspoon sea salt

1. Combine the ingredients in a small bowl and mix thoroughly.

ASIAN BUTTER SAUCE
MAKES: ENOUGH FOR 24 OYSTERS

1 tablespoon sesame oil
2 teaspoons very finely chopped fresh root ginger
2 tablespoons oyster sauce
1 teaspoon soy sauce
¼ teaspoon mustard powder
50 g (2 oz) unsalted butter, cut into small chunks

1. Combine the oil and ginger in a small frying pan over a medium heat and cook until the oil begins to foam. Remove from the heat and stir in the oyster sauce, soy sauce and mustard. Whisk in the butter a few chunks at a time until incorporated.

GORGONZOLA-TOMATO SAUCE
MAKES: ENOUGH FOR 24 OYSTERS

15 g (½ oz) unsalted butter
1 tablespoon very finely chopped shallot
1 teaspoon very finely chopped garlic
125 ml (4 fl oz/½ cup) vegetable juice
2 teaspoons prepared horseradish
½ teaspoon sea salt
40 g (1½ oz) gorgonzola cheese, crumbled

1. Melt the butter in a small saucepan over a medium heat. Add the shallot and garlic and sauté for about 2 minutes. Add the vegetable juice, horseradish and salt. Bring the sauce to a simmer. Remove the pan from the heat. After you've added the sauce to the oysters, sprinkle the cheese on top and then cook.

HOW TO PREP AND BARBECUE LOBSTER TAILS

1. Different varieties and sizes of lobster tail are available. Shown here, left to right, are New Zealand, 175 to 250 g (6 to 8 oz); Maine, 150 to 175 g (5 oz to 6 oz); West Australian, 250 to 300 g (8 to 10 oz); and South African, 135 to 150 g (4½ oz to 5 oz). Adjust cooking times according to size.

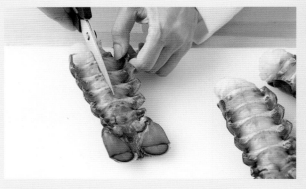

2. Use kitchen shears to cut through the centre of the shell on the underside of each tail.

3. Turn each tail over and cut through the harder back shell all the way to the fins.

4. Use a sharp, heavy knife to cut each tail in half lengthways, passing through the openings you have already made.

5. Barbecue the tails, meat side down, until the surface of the meat turns opaque.

6. Then turn the tails over on to their shells and brush with garlic butter while the meat turns opaque all the way to the centre.

SEAFOOD

LOBSTER ROLLS

SERVES: 4
PREP TIME: 25 MINUTES

HEAT: DIRECT MEDIUM HEAT 180° TO 230°C
(350° TO 450°F)
COOKING TIME: 6 TO 7 MINUTES

3 large garlic cloves, lightly crushed
75 g (3 oz) salted butter
4 lobster tails, about 175 g (6 oz) each
Sea salt
4 tablespoons mayonnaise
75 g (3 oz) roma tomato, cut into 5-mm (¼-inch) dice
2 tablespoons very finely chopped spring onion, white and light
green parts
2 teaspoons fresh lemon juice
Hot sauce
2 teaspoons chopped chervil
4 hot dog buns, sliced vertically from the top
75 g (3 oz) cos lettuce heart, shredded

1. Warm the garlic and butter in a small saucepan over
a medium-low heat until the butter melts. Set aside about
2 tablespoons for brushing on the buns.

2. Prepare the barbecue for direct cooking over a medium heat.
Carefully cut the lobster tails in half lengthways. Season the meat

with a little salt and brush some of the garlic butter over the
surface of each one. Brush the cooking grills clean. Barbecue the
tails, meat side down, over ***direct medium heat*** for 2 to 3 minutes,
with the lid open, until the meat is opaque. Turn the tails over,
brush with more garlic butter and continue to grill for about a
further 3 minutes, until the meat is slightly firm. Set aside to cool.

3. Combine the mayonnaise, tomato, spring onion and lemon
juice in a bowl and season to taste with salt and hot sauce.
Remove the lobster meat from the shells and cut into 1-cm
(½-inch) pieces. Add the lobster meat to the mayonnaise
mixture. For best flavour, chill for at least 1 hour. Mix in the
chervil just before serving.

4. Using a serrated knife, trim
some of the crust from the
sides of the buns. Brush the
remaining garlic butter on the
cut sides (outside only) of the
buns and toast over ***direct
medium heat*** for about
1 minute, turning once, until
golden brown on both sides.

5. Place cos lettuce on the bottom of each roll and then top with
the lobster mixture.

HOW TO PREP AND BARBECUE CRAB

1. Lay each uncooked crab flat on its back. Use a cleaver and mallet to cut right down the centre and all the way through.

2. Cut off the dangling tail flap attached to the underside of one half.

3. Also cut off the tail flap dangling on the other half.

4. Find the parts of the mouth that protrude from the front of each half and cut those off.

5. Turn each half over and pull off the top shell.

6. Remove the feathery gills, known as 'dead man's fingers'.

7. Rinse out the brownish viscera in a bowl of cold water.

8. The half on the left is cleaned. The one on the right is not.

9. Cut through the shell between each leg with the cleaver or a sharp knife.

10. You should have five legs from each half crab.

11. Use a clean hammer or a nutcracker to crack the shells prior to barbecuing.

12. Barbecue the crab legs over direct high heat for a couple of minutes on each side to absorb the charcoal aromas.

13. Move the crab legs to a frying pan with butter, garlic, wine, lemon and chillies.

14. Turn and coat the crab legs in the buttery mixture as they finish cooking.

CRAB WITH WHITE WINE-GARLIC BUTTER

SERVES: 2 AS A MAIN COURSE OR 4 STARTERS
PREP TIME: 30 MINUTES

HEAT: DIRECT HIGH HEAT 230° TO 290°C (450° TO 550°F)
COOKING TIME: 9 TO 11 MINUTES
SPECIAL EQUIPMENT: 30-CM (12-INCH) CAST-IRON
 FRYING PAN

2 large uncooked crabs, such as blue swimmer
125 g (4 oz) unsalted butter, cut into 8 equal-sized pieces
2 tablespoon very finely chopped garlic
Finely grated rind and juice of 1 lemon
½ teaspoon dried red chilli flakes
½ teaspoon sea salt
¼ teaspoon freshly ground black pepper
150 ml (5 fl oz) dry white wine
1 baguette, torn into bite-sized pieces, to serve

1. Prepare the barbecue for direct cooking over a high heat.

2. To kill each crab, place it on its back and hold it down with a large cleaver. Use a hammer to tap the top edge of the cleaver and cut the crab in half lengthways all the way through. Remove and discard the dangling tail flaps and mouth parts. Turn the crab over. Pull off and discard the top shell. Remove and discard the gills. Rinse each half of the crab in a bowl of cold water or under cold running water and use your finger to scoop out and discard the dark viscera. Slice each half into 5 pieces by cutting between each leg and through the body. Using the hammer again (or a nutcracker or crab cracker), crack each section of each leg to make eating easier after the crabs are cooked.

3. Combine the butter, garlic, lemon rind, lemon juice, red chilli flakes, salt and pepper in a 30-cm (12-inch) cast-iron frying pan. Mix well.

4. Place the pan over **direct high heat** and cook for 2 to 3 minutes, with the lid open, until the butter has melted and the garlic turned golden. Add the wine and cook until it comes to the boil. Remove the pan from the barbecue and set it down on a heatproof surface.

5. Barbecue the crab pieces over **direct high heat** for about 4 minutes, with the lid open and turning once, then move them to the pan. Return the pan over **direct high heat** and gently turn the crab pieces with tongs to coat them with the sauce. Cook for 2 to 3 minutes, until the liquid boils and the crab is fully cooked. Serve warm with pieces of bread to dip into the liquid remaining in the pan.

The difference in quality between fresh and canned crabmeat is striking. While crabmeat hand-picked from freshly caught, seasonal crabs is sweet and luscious, what you often find in cans is pasteurised and metallic in flavour. Even the crabmeat from previously frozen crabs can't compete with the truly fresh stuff. For this recipe, the variety of crab (such as blue swimmer) is far less important than freshness. However, don't bother spending high prices on 'jumbo' crab, the big unbroken pieces of meat. 'Backfin' or broken pieces of crabmeat will work just great.

CRAB AND AVOCADO QUESADILLAS

SERVES: 4 TO 6
PREP TIME: 20 MINUTES

HEAT: DIRECT MEDIUM HEAT 180° TO 230°C
   (350° TO 450°F)
COOKING TIME: 2 TO 4 MINUTES

500 g (1 lb) fresh crabmeat, such as blue swimmer
20 g (¾ oz) basil, finely chopped
Finely grated rind of 2 lemons
Juice of 2 lemons
1 tablespoon very finely chopped jalapeño chilli
½ teaspoon sea salt
¼ teaspoon freshly ground black pepper
125 ml (4 fl oz/½ cup) sour cream
6 flour tortillas (20 cm/8 inches)
2 ripe haas avocados, deseeded, peeled and cubed
175 g (6 oz) tomatoes, finely diced
200 g (7 oz) cheddar cheese, grated
Extra-virgin olive oil

1. Combine the crabmeat, basil, half of the lemon rind, the lemon juice, jalapeño, salt and pepper in a bowl and mix well.

2. Combine the sour cream with the remaining half of the lemon rind in a separate bowl. Set aside.

3. Prepare the barbecue for direct cooking over a medium heat.

4. Lay the tortillas in a single layer on a work surface. Evenly divide the crabmeat mixture, avocados, tomatoes and cheese over half of each tortilla. Fold the empty half of each tortilla over the filling, creating a half circle, and press down firmly. Lightly brush the tortillas with oil. Brush the cooking grills clean. Barbecue the quesadillas over *direct medium heat* for 2 to 4 minutes, with the lid closed as much as possible but carefully turning over once, until the cheese melts and the tortillas are well marked. Cut each quesadilla into wedges. Serve with the sour cream mixture.

SEAFOOD ZUPPA

SERVES: 4
PREP TIME: 30 MINUTES

HEAT: DIRECT MEDIUM HEAT 180° TO 230°C
(350° TO 450°F) AND DIRECT HIGH HEAT
230° TO 290°C (450° TO 550°F)
COOKING TIME: 17 TO 19 MINUTES
SPECIAL EQUIPMENT: PERFORATED GRILL PAN

ZUPPA
2 small fennel bulbs
1 lemon, ends trimmed and cut in half
2 red capsicums, cut into flat pieces
4–5 shallots, about 250 g (8 oz), peeled
Extra-virgin olive oil
250 ml (8 fl oz/1 cup) fish stock
250 ml (8 fl oz/1 cup) vegetable stock
½ teaspoon paprika
⅛ teaspoon crushed red chilli flakes
⅛ teaspoon saffron threads
Sea salt
Freshly ground black pepper

4 large or jumbo scallops, 40 to 50 g (1½ to 2 oz) each
8 jumbo prawns, peeled and deveined
1 skinless flaky fish fillet, such as barramundi, about 250 g
(8 oz), cut into 4 pieces
1 skinless firm fish fillet, such as swordfish, about 250 g (8 oz),
cut into 4 pieces

4 thick slices bread
15 g (½ oz) flat-leaf parsley, finely chopped

1. Prepare the barbecue for direct cooking over a medium heat.

2. Preheat the grill pan over **direct medium heat** for about 10 minutes. While the pan preheats, prepare the vegetables. Cut off the thick stalks above the fennel bulbs and save for another use.
Cut each fennel bulb into quarters and then remove the thick triangular-shaped core. Slice the fennel vertically into 5-mm (¼-inch) thick slivers. Place the fennel, lemon halves, capsicums and shallots in a bowl, add 4 tablespoons oil, and toss to coat the vegetables evenly. Place the vegetables on the grill pan and barbecue over **direct medium heat** for about 10 minutes, with the lid closed as much as possible but turning as needed, until the vegetables are tender.

3. Place the vegetables in a large bowl, cover the bowl with aluminium foil. Steam for 10 minutes. Remove and discard any charred skin from the shallots. Coarsely chop the shallots along with the capsicums. Combine the fennel, capsicums, shallots and the juice of one grilled lemon half in a blender and purée until smooth. Add the fish stock and vegetable stock and purée again (the blender will be very full). Pour the zuppa through a strainer into a saucepan and discard any bits left in the strainer. Season with the paprika, chilli flakes and saffron. Keep warm over a low heat. Add additional grilled lemon juice, salt and pepper to taste.

4. Increase the temperature of the barbecue to a high heat. Remove the small, tough side muscle that may be left on each scallop. Lightly coat the shellfish and fish fillets with oil and season with salt and pepper. Brush the cooking grills clean. Barbecue the seafood over **direct high heat**, with the lid closed as much as possible but turning the pieces once, until the prawns is lightly charred on the outside and just turning opaque in the centre, the scallops are slightly firm on the surface and opaque in the centre, and the fish fillets are just beginning to separate into layers and the colour is opaque at the centre. The prawns will take 3 to 5 minutes, the scallops will take 4 to 6 minutes and the fillets will take 6 to 8 minutes.

5. Toast the bread over direct heat for about 1 minute, turning once. Evenly divide the shellfish and fish among individual bowls. Ladle the zuppa into each bowl. Garnish with parsley and serve with the bread.

HOW TO BARBECUE FISH
THINGS YOU NEED TO KNOW

1 PRACTICE MAKES PERFECT

Many barbecuers consider fish fillets and steaks their biggest challenge. They remember the times when fish stuck to the grill and fell to pieces when they tried to take it off the barbecue. To greatly improve your chances of success, learn to grill firm fish first, especially the ones that are a bit oily, including salmon, swordfish and tuna.

2 DON'T OVERDO IT

Fish and seafood don't have the muscle structure and firmness that many four-legged creatures have. Therefore marinades work more quickly to break down the structure of fillets and steaks. So, to prevent mushy textures, limit marinating times to just a few hours. And, above all else, don't overcook fillets and steaks.

3 FEED THE FIRE

Don't be afraid of high heat. It creates a bit of a crust on the surface of fish, and the crust helps the fish release from the cooking grill. The thinner the fillets or steaks you have, the higher the heat should be.

4 NO FLIP-FLOPPING

Every time you turn fish on the barbecue, you create a new possibility for sticking, so turn it only once.

5 QUICK FINISH

Barbecue the first side longer than the second. This assures you a nicely developed crust on the first side. Plus, if you are barbecuing with the lid closed (as you should), the second side will begin to cook while the first side is on the grate. So the second side will not need as long on the grate.

SALMON WITH NECTARINE SALSA

SERVES: 4
PREP TIME: 20 MINUTES

HEAT: DIRECT HIGH HEAT 230° TO 290°C (450° TO 550°F)
COOKING TIME: 8 TO 11 MINUTES

SALSA
2 nectarines, about 500 g (1 lb), cut into 1-cm (½-inch) dice
65 g (2½ lb) red capsicum, cut into 5-mm (¼-inch) dice
40 g (1½ oz) red onion, cut into 5-mm (¼-inch) dice
15 g (½ oz) chervil, finely chopped
1 jalapeño chilli, deseeded and finely diced
2 tablespoons finely chopped mint
1 tablespoon honey
1 tablespoon fresh lime juice
¼ teaspoon dried red chilli flakes
¼ teaspoon sea salt

4 salmon fillets (with skin), 175 to 250 g (6 to 8 oz) each and
    about 2.5 cm (1 inch) thick
½ teaspoon sea salt
¼ teaspoon crushed red chilli flakes
2 tablespoons fresh lime juice
1 tablespoon extra-virgin olive oil

1. Combine the salsa ingredients in a non-metallic bowl. Cover
and refrigerate until ready to serve.

2. Prepare the barbecue for direct cooking over a high heat.

3. Season the salmon on both sides with the salt and chilli
flakes and then drizzle with the lime juice and oil. Brush the
cooking grills clean. Barbecue the salmon, flesh side down, over
direct high heat for 6 to 8 minutes, with the lid closed as much
as possible, until you can lift the fillets off the grate with tongs
without sticking. Turn the fillets over and cook them for a further
2 to 3 minutes for medium rare, or longer for more well done.
Slip a spatula between the skin and the flesh, and transfer the
fillets to serving plates. Serve warm with the salsa.

HOW TO BARBECUE SALMON

1. Start with generously greased
fillets, flesh side down, on a clean,
hot grill.

2. Barbecue them over high heat
and roll them over when the flesh
side releases easily.

3. When the salmon is done,
wiggle a spatula into the seam
between the flesh and skin.

4. Scoop the flesh off the skin
and pat yourself on the back.
Serving the skin is optional.

The sauce for this recipe features some classic Thai ingredients, including coconut milk and red curry paste. The cream that rises to the top of chilled coconut milk contains a good amount of oil, so use it to fry the curry paste, releasing its spicy flavours, before adding the rest of the milk and the other sauce ingredients.

SALMON WITH RED CURRY-COCONUT SAUCE

SERVES: 4 TO 6
PREP TIME: 25 MINUTES

HEAT: DIRECT HIGH HEAT 230° TO 290°C (450° TO 550°F)
COOKING TIME: 3 TO 6 MINUTES
SPECIAL EQUIPMENT: 12 BAMBOO SKEWERS,
SOAKED IN WATER FOR AT LEAST 30 MINUTES

300 ml (10½ fl oz) chilled coconut milk
3½ tablespoons Thai red curry paste
1 tablespoon fish sauce
1 tablespoon soy sauce
1½ teaspoons light brown sugar
1 skinless salmon fillet, about 1 kg (2 lb)
2 tablespoons sunflower or other vegetable oil
2 tablespoons finely chopped spring onion

1. Scoop 4 tablespoons of the coconut cream from the top of the chilled coconut milk and transfer it to a small saucepan over a medium heat and bring to the boil. Add 2 tablespoons of the curry paste and cook for 3 to 5 minutes, stirring constantly, until very fragrant. Stir the remaining coconut milk to achieve a smooth consistency, and then slowly incorporate it into the curry paste mixture. Add the fish sauce, soy sauce and sugar and return the mixture to the boil, stirring constantly. Reduce the heat to maintain a steady simmer and cook for 5 to 10 minutes, stirring frequently, until thickened to a thin sauce consistency. Set aside.

2. Prepare the barbecue for direct cooking over a high heat.

3. Remove any remaining pin bones from the salmon fillet. Cut the fillet into 1.5-cm (¾-inch) thick slices. Thread them on to skewers.

4. Combine the remaining 1½ tablespoons curry paste with the oil in a small bowl and generously brush the salmon with the mixture. Brush the cooking grills clean. Barbecue the skewers over **direct high heat** for 2 to 4 minutes, with the lid closed as much as possible, until you can lift them off the grill with tongs without sticking. Turn the skewers over and cook them for a further 1 to 2 minutes for medium, or longer for more well done. Reheat the sauce and spoon it on to a serving dish, or divide evenly among individual plates. Top with the salmon and scatter the spring onion over the top. Serve warm.

CEDAR-PLANKED SALMON WITH TARATOR SAUCE

SERVES: 4
PREP TIME: 20 MINUTES

HEAT: DIRECT MEDIUM HEAT 180° TO 230°C
(350° TO 450°F)
COOKING TIME: 20 TO 30 MINUTES
SPECIAL EQUIPMENT: 1 UNTREATED CEDAR PLANK,
30 TO 38 CM (12 TO 15 INCHES) LONG AND
1 TO 1.5 CM (½ TO ¾ INCH) THICK, SOAKED IN
SALTED WATER FOR AT LEAST 1 HOUR

SAUCE
2 pieces firm white bread, crusts removed
2 garlic cloves
50 g (2 oz) hazelnuts, lightly toasted and skinned
3 tablespoons fresh lemon juice
125 ml (4 fl oz/½ cup) extra-virgin olive oil
15 g (½ oz) flat-leaf parsley leaves
Sea salt
Freshly ground black pepper

1 salmon fillet (skin on), about 1 kg (2 lb)
75 g (3 oz) brown sugar

1. Soak the bread briefly in water, then squeeze dry and set aside. Combine the garlic and hazelnuts in a food processor and process until the nuts are finely ground. Add the bread and lemon juice and process until smooth. With the motor running, add the oil in a slow, steady stream. Add the parsley, ½ teaspoon salt and ¼ teaspoon pepper and pulse quickly. Season to taste with additional salt, pepper and lemon juice, if desired. Cover with plastic wrap and chill until required.

2. Prepare the barbecue for direct cooking over a medium heat. Remove any remaining pin bones from the fillet. Cut the fillet crossways to make 4 servings, but do not cut through the skin. Generously season with salt and pepper.

3. Place the soaked plank over **direct medium heat** and close the lid. After 5 to 10 minutes, when the plank begins to smoke and char, turn the plank over and then lay the fillet on the plank. Carefully sprinkle the brown sugar over the entire surface of the fillet. Close the lid and let the salmon cook for 15 to 20 minutes until lightly browned on the surface for medium rare, or longer for more well done. Cooking time will vary according to the thickness of the fillet. Serve warm with the sauce on the side.

HOW TO PLANK SALMON

Cooking salmon on a cedar plank prevents the fish from sticking to the cooking grill and imbues it with delicious smoky flavours.

1. Run your fingertips over the salmon to feel for any bones. Use needle-nose pliers or tweezers to grab the ends of any tiny pin bones and pull them out.

2. Cut the raw fish into individual portions, right down to the skin but not through it, to make it easier to serve later.

3. Lay the salmon on a lightly charred, smoldering plank and sprinkle brown sugar over the top.

4. The sugar will melt and caramelise on the surface while the cedar smoke permeates the flesh.

HOW TO PREP FENNEL

1. Cut off the thick stalks above the bulb, leaving the root end attached to hold the bulb together, then cut the bulb in half through the root end.

2. Chop some of the flavourful fronds to season the salad.

3. Simmer the fennel halves in salted water until just tender. Immediately plunge the fennel into iced water to stop the cooking.

4. Trim off the root end and thinly slice the fennel.

HOW TO BONE SALMON STEAKS

1. Find any pin bones and remove them with needle-nose pliers.

2. Trim off any thin, dangling flaps of flesh.

3. Starting at the top of the steak, cut alongside the bone.

4. Continue to cut all along the bone and rib sections.

5. Cut along the other side of the bones, too.

6. The goal is to isolate the bones only, without cutting away much of the flesh.

7. Cut the bones free near the top, leaving just a little bit of bone attached to hold the flesh together.

8. Bring the sides together and secure the ends with a shortened bamboo skewer.

SALMON WITH FENNEL AND OLIVE SALAD

SERVES: 4
PREP TIME: 30 MINUTES

HEAT: DIRECT HIGH HEAT 230° TO 290°C (450° TO 550°F)
COOKING TIME: 8 TO 11 MINUTES
SPECIAL EQUIPMENT: 8 BAMBOO SKEWERS,
   SOAKED IN WATER FOR AT LEAST 30 MINUTES

SALAD
1 fennel bulb
75 g (3 oz) green olives with pimentos, quartered
3 spring onions, white and light green parts, finely chopped
2 tablespoons chopped fennel fronds
1 tablespoon extra-virgin olive oil
½ teaspoon finely grated lemon rind

4 salmon steaks or fillets, each 175 to 250 g (6 to 8 oz)
   and 2.5 to 3.5 cm (1 to 1½ inches) thick
2 tablespoons extra-virgin olive oil
½ teaspoon sea salt
¼ teaspoon freshly ground black pepper

1. If the fennel stalks have the fronds attached, trim off the fronds and chop enough to make 2 tablespoons; set aside. Cut off the thick stalks above the bulb and save the stalks for another use. Leave the root end attached to hold the bulb together. Cut the fennel bulb in half. Fill a small saucepan with water. Lightly salt the water and bring to the boil over a medium-high heat. Reduce the heat to medium and gently simmer the fennel bulb for 3 minutes. Remove from the water and immediately plunge into iced water to rapidly cool it. Remove the bulb from the water, trim off the root end and thinly slice.

2. Combine the salad ingredients in a bowl. Toss to coat and set aside to let the flavours marinate while you barbecue the salmon.

3. Prepare the barbecue for direct cooking over a high heat.

4. Prepare the salmon steaks as detailed at left. Brush the salmon with the oil and season with the salt and pepper. Brush the cooking grills clean. Barbecue the salmon over **_direct high heat_** for 6 to 8 minutes, with the lid closed as much as possible, until you can lift the steaks off the grill with tongs without sticking. Turn the steaks over and cook for a further 2 to 3 minutes for medium, or longer for more well done. If using fillets, to easily remove the skin, just slip a spatula between the skin and the flesh, and lift the salmon flesh from the barbecue. Transfer the salmon to plates and top with the salad.

A potent ingredient in any barbecuer's pantry, chipotles are dried and smoked jalapeño chillies. They are often found packed in, which is a tomato-based sauce with vinegar, onions, garlic and spices. How to freeze leftover chillies: spoon one chilli, with a little of the sauce, into each space of an icecube tray. After they have frozen, pop them out of the tray, tightly wrap them with plastic wrap, and place them in a resealable freezer bag.

BAJA FISH WRAPS WITH CHIPOTLE-LIME SLAW

SERVES: 6
PREP TIME: 20 MINUTES

HEAT: DIRECT HIGH HEAT 230° TO 290°C (450° TO 550°F)
COOKING TIME: 7 TO 8 MINUTES

RUB
½ teaspoon pure chilli powder
½ teaspoon ground cumin
½ teaspoon sea salt
¼ teaspoon ground cayenne pepper
¼ teaspoon ground cinnamon

4 halibut, salmon or perch fillets, or a mix (with skin), about 175 g
    (6 oz) each and 2.5 to 3.5 cm (1 to 1½ inches) thick
Sunflower or other vegetable oil

SLAW
275 g (9 oz) green cabbage, very thinly sliced
15 g (½ oz) coriander, coarsely chopped
4 tablespoons mayonnaise
2 tablespoons fresh lime juice
2 teaspoons sugar
1 teaspoon very finely chopped canned chipotle chilli in adobo
    (or chipotle salsa, see above)
½ teaspoon sea salt

6 flour tortillas (10 to 12 inches)

1. Mix the rub ingredients together in a small bowl. Lightly brush the fillets with oil and then apply the rub evenly. Cover and set aside in the refrigerator.

2. Combine the slaw ingredients in a large bowl and toss to coat. Set aside until ready to assemble the wraps. Prepare the barbecue for direct cooking over a high heat.

3. Brush the cooking grills clean. Barbecue the fillets over **direct high heat** for about 4 minutes, with the lid closed as much as possible, until you can lift them with a spatula off the cooking grill without sticking. Turn the fillets over and cook them for a further 2 to 3 minutes, until they are opaque in the centre. Transfer them to a plate. Warm the tortillas over **direct high heat** for 30 seconds to 1 minute, turning once.

4. To assemble the wraps, break a fillet into large chunks and arrange on one half of a warm tortilla, then top with some of the slaw. Roll the tortilla to enclose the fillings, fold in the sides, and continue rolling to the end. Cut the wrap in half. Serve warm or at room temperature.

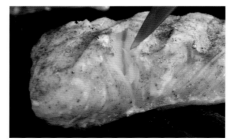

Halibut has a nice, mild, sweet flavour, but the flesh is quite lean, so it dries out quickly if it's overcooked. The key is to remove it from the barbecue before it begins to flake apart. Check each fillet first with a paring knife to make sure the flesh is no longer translucent at the centre.

FISH FILLETS WITH BOMBAY TOMATO SAUCE

SERVES: 4

PREP TIME: 30 MINUTES

HEAT: DIRECT MEDIUM HEAT 180° TO 230°C (350° TO 450°F) AND DIRECT HIGH HEAT 230° TO 290°C (450° TO 550°F)

COOKING TIME: 19 TO 23 MINUTES

SPECIAL EQUIPMENT: 30-CM (12-INCH) CAST-IRON FRYING PAN

SAUCE

3 tablespoons peanut oil
1 brown onion, halved and thinly sliced
1 tablespoon very finely chopped garlic
2 teaspoons finely grated fresh root ginger
1 teaspoon ground coriander
1 teaspoon paprika
½ teaspoon turmeric
½ teaspoon sea salt
¼ teaspoon ground cayenne pepper
2 cans (425 g/14 oz) peeled, chopped tomatoes with juice
175 ml (6 fl oz) unsweetened coconut milk, stirred

4 tablespoons peanut oil
1 teaspoon finely grated fresh root ginger
1 teaspoon sea salt
½ teaspoon freshly ground black pepper
¼ teaspoon turmeric
4 halibut or perch fillets, each 175 to 250 g (6 to 8 oz) and about 2.5 cm (1 inch) thick
2 tablespoons torn basil leaves, optional

1. Prepare the barbecue for direct cooking over a medium heat on one side and high heat on the other side. Brush the cooking grills clean. Warm the oil in a 30-cm (12-inch) cast-iron frying pan over **direct medium heat**. Add the onion and cook for about 5 minutes, stirring often until it softens and begins to brown. Add the garlic, ginger, coriander, paprika, turmeric, salt and cayenne. Mix well and cook for 2 to 3 minutes, stirring often to avoid burning. Add the tomatoes and coconut milk, then taste and adjust the seasoning, if needed. Allow the sauce to simmer for 5 minutes or so while you prepare the fish.

2. Mix the oil, ginger, salt, pepper and turmeric together in a small bowl. Brush the fish on both sides with the oil mixture.

3. Barbecue the fillets over **direct high heat** for 4 to 5 minutes, with the lid closed, until they release easily from the cooking grill. Lift the fillets, one at a time, with a spatula and turn them over into the pan with the sauce, so that the barbecued side is facing up. Nestle the fillets into the sauce, close the lid, and let the fillets cook over **direct medium heat** for 3 to 5 minutes until they have just begun to flake when you poke them with the tip of a knife.

4. Remove from the barbecue. Scatter the basil and serve warm.

HOW TO PREP FISH FILLETS

1. The first step is to skin the fish. Along one end of the fillet, cut a slit all the way through the skin large enough to get your finger though it.

2. Holding the skin steady with your finger in the slit, angle the blade of a large, sharp knife inside the seam between the flesh and skin.

3. Cut away from you and over the top of the skin, always with the knife angled slightly downwards.

4. Barbecue the fillets on one side only until they release easily from the grill.

5. Move the fillets to a frying pan with warm tomato sauce, barbecued sides facing up.

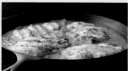

6. The sauce helps to keep the fillets moist as they finish cooking.

HOW TO SKIN MAHI-MAHI FILLETS

  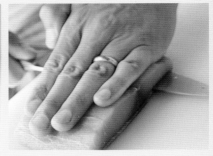

1. Angle the blade of a large, sharp knife into the seam between the flesh and skin on one end of a fillet.

2. Hold the fillet steady with your other hand and slide the knife right over the skin.

3. For safety's sake, cut away from your body, in case the knife slips, and tilt the blade downwards so you don't cut into the flesh of the fillet.

HOW TO MAKE CORN AND MUSHROOM SALSA

1. The cooking goes quickly, so have all your ingredients chopped and weighed beforehand. Chefs refer to this as their 'mise en place'.

2. Cook the corn in a smoking-hot frying pan, stirring occasionally to prevent the kernels from popping right out of the pan.

3. The goal is to caramelise the natural sugars in the corn, turning the kernels golden brown and super sweet.

4. Cook the mushrooms in the same hot pan. The less you stir them, the browner and more delicious they will be.

5. Cook the tomatillos, black beans and garlic just until the garlic begins to brown, too.

6. Combine all the vegetables in the pan, adjust the seasonings and cook just long enough to marry the flavours.

HOW TO CHECK FOR DONENESS

When you insert the end of a metal skewer into the centre of a fillet and then quickly and carefully touch the end of the skewer on the outside of the base of your thumb, it should feel warm. If it feels less than warm, the fish is under-cooked. If it feels hot, the fish is overcooked.

MAHI-MAHI
WITH CORN AND MUSHROOM SALSA

SERVES: 4
PREP TIME: 25 MINUTES
MARINATING TIME: UP TO 1 HOUR

HEAT: DIRECT HIGH HEAT 230° TO 290°C (450° TO 550°F)
COOKING TIME: 13 TO 15 MINUTES
SPECIAL EQUIPMENT: 30-CM (12-INCH) CAST-IRON
FRYING PAN

RUB
1 teaspoon pure chilli powder
1 teaspoon garlic granules
1 teaspoon paprika
1 teaspoon sea salt
½ teaspoon ground coriander
½ teaspoon ground cumin
½ teaspoon freshly ground black pepper

4 skinless mahi-mahi fillets, each about 250 g (8 oz)
and 1.5 mm (¾ inch) thick
4 tablespoons extra-virgin olive oil

SALSA
Kernels cut from 2 ears sweet corn
1 large portabello mushroom, stems removed and the
caps diced
3–4 medium tomatillos, cored and cut into 5-mm to 1-cm
(¼- to ½-inch) pieces
3 tablespoons extra-virgin olive oil
75 g (3 oz) canned black beans, drained
2 teaspoons very finely chopped garlic
2 tablespoons coriander, roughly chopped
2 teaspoons fresh lime juice
½ teaspoon sea salt
¼ teaspoon freshly ground black pepper
Hot chilli sauce, such as sriracha

1. Mix the rub ingredients together in a small bowl. Generously
coat the mahi-mahi fillets on both sides with the oil. Season
evenly with the rub. Cover and refrigerate for up to 1 hour.

2. Assemble all salsa ingredients so that everything is ready for
quick cooking.

3. Prepare the barbecue for direct cooking over a high heat.

4. Warm 1 tablespoon of the oil in a 30-cm (12-inch) cast-iron
frying pan over a **direct high heat**. When it is smoking hot, add
the corn and spread the kernels in an even layer. Cook for about
2 minutes, stirring 2 or 3 times, until most of the kernels have
turned golden brown and crisp-tender, then transfer to a bowl.
Add another tablespoon of oil to the pan, and when the oil
begins to smoke, add the mushrooms and spread them out in

a single layer. Cook without touching them for 30 seconds,
then give them a stir and cook for about 3 minutes, until the
mushrooms are browned and tender. Add the mushrooms to
the bowl with the corn. Add another tablespoon of the oil to
the pan and immediately add the tomatillos, black beans and
garlic. Mix well and cook for about 30 seconds, until the garlic
begins to brown. Add the corn kernels and the mushrooms from
the bowl, the remaining salsa ingredients and heat for about
1 minute. Taste and adjust the seasonings, if necessary. Pour
the salsa into the bowl and let cool while you barbecue the fish.

5. Barbecue the mahi-mahi fillets over **direct high heat** for 6 to
8 minutes, with the lid closed as much as possible but turning
once, until the fish is fully cooked but still moist.

6. Serve the fish fillets warm with the salsa served on the side.

Recipe from the chefs at
Weber Grill® Restaurant, USA

Poke is a beloved Hawaiian dish of finely chopped raw fish tossed with edible seaweed, seeds or nuts and a dressing. In this recipe, the flavour and texture of the fish benefit from a quick sear on the barbecue. If you use dried seaweed, be sure to rehydrate it in water for about 15 minutes.

BARBECUED AHI POKE

SERVES: 4 AS A STARTER
PREP TIME: 15 MINUTES

HEAT: DIRECT HIGH HEAT 230° TO 290°C (450° TO 550°F)
COOKING TIME: ABOUT 2 MINUTES

2 tablespoons dried Japanese arame or other thin
    edible seaweed
40 g (1½ oz) white onion, finely chopped
4 tablespoons spring onion, white and light green parts, thinly
    sliced
2 tablespoons soy sauce
1 tablespoon dark sesame oil
1 teaspoon grated fresh root ginger
½ teaspoon very finely chopped serrano chilli

2 sushi-grade tuna fillets, each about 175 to 250 g
    (6 to 8 oz) and 1.5 to 2.5 cm (¾ to 1 inch) thick
Sunflower or other vegetable oil
Coarse sea salt
Freshly ground black pepper
2 tablespoons toasted sesame seeds
1 lemon, cut into wedges, optional

1. If using dried seaweed, place the seaweed in a small bowl, add enough water to cover and set aside to soften for 15 minutes. Drain and coarsely chop before using.

2. Prepare the barbecue for direct cooking over a high heat.

3. Mix the onion, spring onion, soy sauce, sesame oil, ginger and chilli together in a bowl. Add the seaweed.

4. Brush the tuna with oil and lightly season with salt and pepper, patting the seasoning into the fish. Brush the cooking grills clean. Barbecue the tuna over ***direct high heat*** for about 2 minutes, with the barbecue lid open and turning once, just until seared on both sides but still rare inside.

5. Transfer the tuna to a chopping board and cut into 1- to 1.5-cm (½- to ¾-inch) cubes. Add to the bowl containing the onion mixture and toss to combine. Divide equally into individual bowls. Sprinkle with the sesame seeds. Serve warm with lemon wedges, if desired.

SMOKED TUNA SALAD
WITH BARBECUED MANGO

SERVES: 4 TO 6
PREP TIME: 30 MINUTES

HEAT: DIRECT MEDIUM HEAT 180° TO 230°C
    (350° TO 450°F)
COOKING TIME: ABOUT 10 MINUTES
SPECIAL EQUIPMENT: 4 TO 6 CEDAR PAPERS, SOAKED
    IN WATER FOR 10 MINUTES; BUTCHER'S STRING

DRESSING
125 g (4 oz) runny honey
3 tablespoons dijon mustard
2 tablespoons rice wine vinegar
2 tablespoons mayonnaise
½ teaspoon sea salt
¼ teaspoon chilli con carne seasoning

2 firm but ripe mangoes
Sunflower or other vegetable oil
300 g (10 oz) sugar snap peas
¼ teaspoon sea salt
2 tuna steaks, each about 500 g (1 lb) and 2.5 cm (1 inch) thick
150 g (5 oz) mixed baby greens, rinsed and crisped
125 g (4 oz) roasted and salted cashews
Freshly ground black pepper

1. Whisk the dressing ingredients in a small bowl until thoroughly combined. Set aside 5 tablespoons of the dressing for the tuna.

2. Slice the sides from the mangoes, cutting along either side of the stone. Carefully, without cutting through the skin, slice 3 to 4 short lines along the inside of the flesh. Using the point of the knife, cut 3 to 4 lines in the opposite direction of the first set of cuts to create mango cubes. Brush the mango halves with oil.

3. Place the snap peas just off the centre on a 30 by 30-cm (12 by 12-inch) sheet of aluminium foil and season them with the salt. Fold the foil over the snap peas and seal to create a pouch.

4. Slice each tuna steak to create equal strips that will fit on the cedar papers. Liberally brush the tuna with the reserved dressing and roll up in the cedar paper, tying to keep the paper secure.

5. Prepare the barbecue for direct cooking over a medium heat. Brush the cooking grills clean. Barbecue the cedar bundles over **direct medium heat** for about 6 minutes, with the lid closed as much as possible but turning once, until the tuna is pink but still juicy. Keep an eye on the cedar paper. If it catches on fire, use a spray bottle to mist out the flames. Remove the cedar bundles from the barbecue, cut the string, remove the tuna from the cedar paper and let cool. Gently flake the tuna.

6. Place the mangos and the foil pouch with the snap peas over **direct medium heat** and cook for about 4 minutes, with the lid closed as much as possible but turning once. Remove from the barbecue. Open the foil pouch to let the steam escape so the peas do not overcook. When the mangoes are cool enough to handle, hold each mango slice in both hands and press up on the skin side to expose the cubes. Slice the cubes off the skin.

7. Divide the salad greens evenly on serving plates. Top with barbecued mango, peas, flaked tuna and cashews. Drizzle with some dressing and finish with a grinding of pepper.

HOW TO SMOKE TUNA IN CEDAR PAPERS

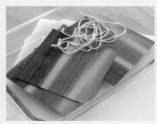

1. Submerge the cedar papers and string in water for 10 minutes.

2. Cut thick tuna steaks into strips that will fit inside the papers. Lay a strip of tuna on each paper parallel to the grain of the wood. Brush the tuna with some of the dressing.

3. Roll up the sides of the paper over the tuna and secure with string.

4. Barbecue for a few minutes on each side to produce some smoke while the fish cooks.

A cardinal rule for grilling seafood is that freshness and firmness always matter more than a particular type of fish. Don't go to the store thinking that only the type of fish suggested in the recipe will work. If the fish you are after is not fresh that day, choose whatever else is firm and fresh. Good options here are swordfish, scallops, prawns and sea bass.

BARBECUED FISH IN A CARIBBEAN CITRUS MARINADE

SERVES: 6
PREP TIME: 15 MINUTES
MARINATING TIME: 3 HOURS

HEAT: DIRECT HIGH HEAT 230° TO 290°C (450° TO 550°F)
COOKING TIME: 8 TO 10 MINUTES (FILLETS) OR
    4 TO 6 MINUTES (SHELLFISH)

MARINADE
2 teaspoons grated orange rind
125 ml (4 fl oz/½ cup) fresh orange juice
1 teaspoon grated lime rind
4 tablespoons fresh lime juice
4 tablespoons extra-virgin olive oil
25 g (1 oz) pure chilli powder
1½ tablespoons very finely chopped garlic
1½ teaspoons ground coriander
1 teaspoon very finely chopped jalapeño chilli
¾ teaspoon ground allspice
¾ teaspoon freshly ground black pepper
¼ teaspoon ground cayenne pepper

6 firm fish fillets, such as grouper, flathead, barramundi, cod or perch (with skin), each 150 to 175 g (5 to 6 oz) and about 2.5 cm (1 inch) thick or 750 g (1½ lb) large prawns or scallops
Extra-virgin olive oil
Sea salt

1. Combine the marinade ingredients in a non-metallic bowl. Reserve 5 tablespoons of the marinade to serve with the barbecued fish.

2. Place the fillets or shellfish side by side in another non-metallic dish, such as an 20 by 20-cm (8 by 8-inch) ovenproof dish. Pour the remaining marinade over the fish or shellfish and turn to coat them. Cover and refrigerate the fish and reserved marinade for 3 hours.

3. Prepare the barbecue for direct cooking over a high heat.

4. Remove the fillets or shellfish from the dish and discard the marinade. Lightly brush with oil and season with some salt.

5. Brush the cooking grills clean. Barbecue the fillets, skin side up, over *direct high heat* for 8 to 10 minutes, with the lid closed as much as possible but turning once after 6 to 7 minutes when they release easily from the grill, until just opaque in the centre. If using prawns or scallops, barbecue over *direct high heat* for 4 to 6 minutes, turning once. Serve with the reserved marinade spooned over the fillets or shellfish.

SWORDFISH ESCABÈCHE

SERVES: 4
PREP TIME: 30 MINUTES
MARINATING TIME: UP TO 2 HOURS

HEAT: DIRECT MEDIUM HEAT 180° TO 230°C
  (350° TO 450°F)
COOKING TIME: 14 TO 18 MINUTES

MARINADE
125 ml (4 fl oz/½ cup) extra-virgin olive oil
3 tablespoons sherry vinegar
1 tablespoon very finely chopped garlic
1 teaspoon dried oregano
¾ teaspoon sea salt
½ teaspoon crushed red chilli flakes
¼ teaspoon freshly ground black pepper

8 button mushrooms
2 roma tomatoes, cored and halved lengthways
1 large anaheim chilli or other mild chilli
1 small yellow summer squash, halved lengthways
4 swordfish steaks, 250 to 300 g (8 to 10) each and about
  2.5 cm (1 inch) thick

ESCABÈCHE
250 ml (8 fl oz/1 cup) chicken stock
1 tablespoon sherry vinegar
¼ teaspoon dried oregano
⅛ teaspoon freshly ground black pepper

1. Whisk the marinade ingredients together in a small bowl. Transfer 4 tablespoons of the marinade to another bowl. Add the vegetables to the second bowl and mix to coat them evenly.

2. Place the swordfish steaks flat on a plate large enough to fit them in a single layer. Spoon the remaining marinade over the steaks, turning them over to coat them evenly. Cover with plastic wrap and refrigerate for as long as 2 hours.

3. Prepare the barbecue for direct cooking over a medium heat. Brush the cooking grills clean. Barbecue the vegetables over **direct medium heat** for 6 to 8 minutes, with the lid closed as much as possible but turning occasionally, until they are lightly marked and tender. Remove the vegetables from the barbecue.

4. Place the chilli in a bowl and cover with plastic wrap. When cool enough to handle, remove and discard the stem, seeds and skin. Roughly chop all the vegetables.

5. In a frying pan over a medium-high heat, combine the escabèche ingredients and bring the liquid to the boil. Add the chopped vegetables and spread them out in the pan. Cook for 3 to 5 minutes until the vegetables are tender. Remove the pan from the heat, cover and keep warm.

6. Lift the swordfish steaks off the plate and let the excess marinade drip on to the plate. Discard the marinade. Brush the cooking grills clean. Barbecue the steaks over **direct medium heat** for 8 to 10 minutes, with the lid closed as much as possible but turning once, until the centre is opaque but the flesh juicy. Serve the swordfish warm with the vegetable mixture.

HOW TO MAKE SWORDFISH ESCABÈCHE

1. Swordfish steaks work well here, as would any firm-flesh fish. Remove the tough outer skin before marinating and barbecue the steaks.

2. Barbecuing the tomatoes and chilli, as well as the squash and mushrooms, will add depth and complexity to the final dish.

3. Escabèche is a preparation involving fish and hot vinegar-based liquid poured over the top. Barbecued vegetables enliven the savoury liquid.

HOW TO BARBECUE FISH FILLETS IN BANANA LEAVES

As you get closer and closer to the equator, you will find more and more barbecuers in the tropics using banana leaves to wrap and steam fish, vegetables, rice and tamales. These inexpensive leaves, which are now available frozen in most Asian and Latino food shops, trap moisture and add a subtle tea-like fragrance to the food. Thaw them in the refrigerator for a few hours, or pour boiling water over them to make them pliable quickly.

1. Cut the leaves into rectangles large enough to wrap around each fish fillet. Leave the sturdy fibrous vein along one edge intact, which holds the leaves together.

2. Wipe both sides with a damp piece of paper towel to clean the leaves, moving in the same direction as the grain so you don't split them open.

3. Fold one side over the marinated fish, and then overlap the first side with the opposite side.

4. Fold down the top and bottom sides so that they overlap in the centre. If the leaf splits, use a second leaf to double-wrap the fish.

5. Thread a small skewer in and out of the overlapping leaves but not into the fish itself.

6. Brush each packet generously with water to prevent it drying out. Assemble the packets on a roasting tray and cover with damp tea towels until ready to barbecue.

8. Barbecue the packets with the small skewers on top most of the time so the wood does not burn.

9. When the fish is fully cooked, you can unwrap the leaves and use them as serving plates.

GINGER AND MISO COD IN BANANA LEAVES

SERVES: 6
PREP TIME: 20 MINUTES
MARINATING TIME: 2 HOURS

HEAT: DIRECT MEDIUM HEAT 180° TO 230°C
   (350° TO 450°F)
COOKING TIME: 8 TO 10 MINUTES

MARINADE
5 tablespoons white miso paste
4 tablespoons unsweetened coconut milk, stirred
2 teaspoons very finely chopped garlic
2 teaspoons sugar
1 teaspoon finely grated fresh root ginger

6 skinless cod fillets, 150 to 175 g (5 oz to 6 oz)
   each and about 1 cm (½ inch) thick
6 banana leaves, each about 30 cm (12 inches) square
6 spring onions, white and light green parts, thinly sliced
1½ teaspoons low-sodium soy sauce
About 1 kg (2 lb) steamed rice, optional

1. Whisk the marinade ingredients into a smooth paste in a
small bowl. Smear the paste all over the fillets. Cover with plastic
wrap and refrigerate for 2 hours.

2. Rinse the banana leaves under cool running water or
carefully wipe them clean with damp paper towel.

3. Prepare the barbecue for direct cooking over a medium heat.

4. Remove the excess marinade from the fillets, then discard
the marinade and place each fillet on the centre of a banana
leaf. Place some spring onions on top. Fold the leaf over to
completely enclose the fillet and make a packet. Secure with a
small skewer, being careful not to pierce the fish. Brush each
packet on both sides with water.

5. Brush the cooking grills clean. Barbecue the packets over
direct medium heat for 8 to 10 minutes, with the lid closed
as much as possible but turning the packet once, until the
leaves are blackened in some parts. (If the leaves begin to
burn through, move the packet[s] over indirect medium heat.)
Remove one of the packets from the barbecue to check the
fish for doneness. If it is opaque all the way through, the fish is
done. If not, return to the barbecue for a few more minutes.

6. Carefully open each packet, remove any pin bones from the
fillets, drizzle each with ¼ teaspoon of soy sauce, or more to
taste, and serve with steamed rice, if desired.

HOW TO FILLET RED SNAPPER

1. Scale the fish, remove the head and make a shallow cut all along one side of the backbone.

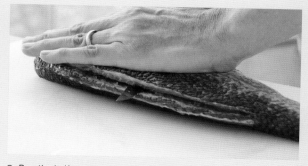

2. Run the knife under the top fillet and over the fish bones.

3. Use your other hand to steady the fish as you slide the knife towards the tail. Remove the top fillet.

4. Turn the fish over and make a second shallow cut, this time on the other side of the backbone.

5. Use the tip of the knife to make deeper and deeper cuts along the tops of the bones.

6. Use your other hand to pull the fillet gently upwards so you can see where to cut.

7. To skin the fillets, hold the end of the skin with your fingertips and run the knife just under the flesh.

8. Cut the fillets into individual portions.

RED SNAPPER IN COCONUT BROTH

SERVES: 8
PREP TIME: 20 MINUTES

HEAT: DIRECT HIGH HEAT 230° TO 290°C (450° TO 550°F)
COOKING TIME: 4 TO 5 MINUTES

STOCK
3 tablespoons peanut oil
125 g (4 oz) carrot, finely diced
40 g (1½ oz) shallot, finely chopped
1 teaspoon freshly grated fresh root ginger
1 teaspoon finely grated lime rind
1 can (400 ml/14 fl oz) unsweetened coconut milk, stirred
125 ml (4 fl oz/½ cup) water
3 tablespoons fresh lime juice
1 tablespoon sugar
2 teaspoons very finely chopped or thinly sliced red birds-eye
     chilli
1 teaspoon fish sauce

8 skinless red snapper fillets, each 125 to 175 g (4 to 6 oz) and
     about 1 cm (½ inch) thick
Peanut or canola oil
Sea salt
Freshly ground black pepper

1. Warm the oil in a small saucepan over a medium heat. Add the carrot, shallot, ginger and lime rind, mix well and cook for 3 to 5 minutes, until the carrots are softened, stirring often. Add the remaining stock ingredients, mix well and allow to simmer for 2 to 3 minutes.

2. Prepare the barbecue for direct cooking over a high heat. Lightly brush each fillet on both sides with oil. Season evenly with salt and pepper. Brush the cooking grills clean. Barbecue over **_direct high heat_** for 4 to 5 minutes, with the lid closed as

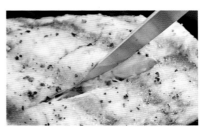

much as possible but turning once with a spatula, until the fish just barely begins to flake when you poke it with the tip of a knife. Meanwhile, warm the stock over a medium heat.

3. Spoon equal portions of the stock into 8 shallow bowls. Lay a fillet in the centre of each bowl. Serve warm.

HOW TO USE A GRILL PAN FOR VEGETABLES AND FISH

1. Coat the fillets generously with the marinade on both sides.

2. Preheat the grill pan over a medium heat for about 10 minutes to prevent food from sticking.

3. Place the vegetables on the grill pan and cook until they soften and begin to brown.

4. Barbecue each fillet flesh side down first, turning with a spatula only when it releases easily from the grill pan.

MEXICAN-STYLE GRILL-PAN FISH

SERVES: 4
PREP TIME: 15 MINUTES
MARINATING TIME: 30 MINUTES

HEAT: DIRECT MEDIUM HEAT 230° TO 290°C
    (450° TO 550°F)
COOKING TIME: 16 TO 20 MINUTES
SPECIAL EQUIPMENT: PERFORATED GRILL PAN

MARINADE
4 tablespoons extra-virgin olive oil
4 teaspoons fresh lime juice
2 teaspoons pure chilli powder
1½ teaspoons sea salt
½ teaspoon ground cumin
½ teaspoon garlic granules
½ teaspoon dried Mexican oregano
½ teaspoon paprika

4 cod, flathead or red snapper fillets (with skin), 175 to 250 g
    (6 to 8 oz) each and about 1.5 cm (¾ inch) thick
Sea salt

2 poblano chillies or other mild chillies, stems and seeds
    removed, and cut into 1-cm (½-inch) rings
4 roma tomatoes, cored and cut into 1-cm (½-inch) slices
8 garlic cloves, peeled
4 large spring onions, rinsed and trimmed

1. Combine the marinade ingredients in a small bowl. Transfer 2 tablespoons of the marinade to a large bowl.

2. Arrange the fillets in a single layer on a platter, pour the marinade from the small bowl over the fillets to coat each piece evenly and season with some salt. Cover with plastic wrap and marinate at room temperature for 30 minutes.

3. Place the chillies, tomatoes, garlic and spring onions in the bowl with the reserved marinade and toss to coat them evenly.

4. Prepare the barbecue for direct cooking over a medium heat. Brush the cooking grills clean. Preheat the grill pan over **direct medium heat** for about 10 minutes. When hot, barbecue the vegetables on the pan for 6 to 8 minutes, with the lid closed as much as possible but turning occasionally, until the chillies and tomatoes are softened and the garlic and spring onions begin to brown. Remove the vegetables from the grill pan and set aside. Barbecue the fish, skin side up, on the grill pan, over **direct medium heat** for 10 to 12 minutes, with the lid closed as much as possible but carefully turning once when the fish releases easily from the grill pan, until the fish is opaque and still juicy.

5. Transfer the fish to a serving platter and arrange the vegetables all around. Serve warm.

SEAFOOD

218

WHOLE FISH IN MOROCCAN MARINADE

SERVES: 4 TO 6
PREP TIME: 10 MINUTES
MARINATING TIME: 2 TO 3 HOURS

HEAT: DIRECT MEDIUM HEAT 180° TO 230°C
    (350° TO 450°F)
COOKING TIME: 12 TO 15 MINUTES

MARINADE
5 tablespoons extra-virgin olive oil
4 tablespoons fresh lemon juice
15 g (½ oz) flat-leaf parsley, chopped
15 g (½ oz) coriander, chopped
1 tablespoon very finely chopped garlic
1½ teaspoons sweet paprika
1 teaspoon ground cumin
1 teaspoon sea salt
½ teaspoon freshly ground black pepper
¼ teaspoon ground cayenne pepper

2 whole sea bass or mackerel, 750 g to 1 kg (1½ lb to 2 lb)
    each, scaled, cleaned and fins removed

1. Combine the marinade ingredients in a bowl. Set aside
5 tablespoons to spoon over the fish after barbecuing.

2. Cut 3 or 4 slashes about 1 cm (½ inch) deep and 2.5 cm
(1 inch) apart on each side of the fish.

3. Place the fish on a roasting tray. Spread over the marinade,
inside and out, working it into the cuts. Cover with plastic wrap
and refrigerate the fish and reserved marinade for 2 to 3 hours.

4. Prepare the barbecue for direct cooking over a medium heat.

5. Remove the fish from the refrigerator and brush with a little
more olive oil. Barbecue over **direct medium heat** for 12 to
15 minutes, with the lid closed as much as possible but carefully

turning once, until the flesh is opaque near the bone but still
juicy. Transfer to a platter and spoon the reserved marinade over
the top. If desired, serve with Roasted Capsicum, Lemon and
Olive Relish (see recipe below).

ROASTED CAPSICUM, LEMON AND OLIVE RELISH
PREP TIME: 10 MINUTES

2 roasted red capsicums, peeled, deseeded and cut into 5-mm
    (¼-inch) dice
1 whole lemon, peeled, white pith removed, segmented,
    deseeded and coarsely chopped
75 g (3 oz) black olives, pitted and coarsely chopped
5 tablespoons extra-virgin olive oil
2 tablespoons fresh lemon juice
2 tablespoons chopped coriander
Sea salt
Freshly ground black pepper

1. Combine the relish ingredients, including salt and pepper to
taste, in a bowl. Keep at room temperature.

HOW TO PREP WHOLE FISH

1. Scale the fish and cut off the
pectoral fins with kitchen shears.

2. Cut the spiny dorsal fins off
the backbone.

3. Also cut off the fins along the
belly (ventral) side of the fish.

4. Cut 3 or 4 slashes about 1 cm
(½ inch) deep and 2.5 cm (1 inch)
apart on each side of the fish.

HOW TO BARBECUE TROUT IN A BASKET

Whole fish can be difficult to barbecue without their skins sticking to the grate. A fish basket allows you to turn the fish easily. Just be sure to grease the basket itself so the skins of the fish pull away cleanly after they are cooked.

1. Lining the fish basket with orange slices, lettuce leaves or thick spring onions prevents the skins of the fish from sticking to the basket.

2. In this recipe, the juice of the orange also complements the sake marinade on the fish.

3. Lower the moveable section of the basket so that it rests snugly on the top layer of orange slices, preventing the ingredients from shifting.

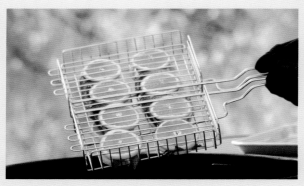

4. You can barbecue the fish without the cooking grill. Just wear barbecue mitts or oven gloves and hold the basket over the coals, turning it over as needed for even cooking.

5. If flare-ups occur, move quickly to rotate the basket away from the flames.

6. The goal is to lightly char the orange and cook the fish all the way to the bone without burning the skins.

SAKE-MARINATED TROUT

SERVES: 4
PREP TIME: 25 MINUTES
MARINATING TIME: 15 TO 30 MINUTES

HEAT: DIRECT MEDIUM HEAT 180° TO 230°C
   (350° TO 450°F)
COOKING TIME: ABOUT 8 MINUTES
SPECIAL EQUIPMENT: FISH BASKET

MARINADE
5 tablespoons sake or dry sherry
4 tablespoons soy sauce
4 tablespoons mirin (sweet rice wine)
2 tablespoons peeled and finely chopped fresh root ginger
2 tablespoons unseasoned rice vinegar
2 garlic cloves, finely chopped
¼ teaspoon crushed red chilli flakes

4 whole boneless trout, each about 375 g (13 oz), cleaned
   and gutted
Sunflower or other vegetable oil
4–6 oranges, cut into 32 slices, each about 5 mm (¼ inch)
   thick

1. Whisk the marinade ingredients together in a bowl. Place the trout in a large, resealable plastic bag and pour in the marinade.

Press out the air and seal the bag tightly. Turn to distribute the marinade. Refrigerate for 15 to 30 minutes. Take care not to over-marinate the fish. (Although this marinade isn't highly acidic, the delicate flesh could become overwhelmed by the sake, soy sauce and mirin.)

2. Remove the trout from the bag and transfer to a roasting tray. Strain the marinade into a saucepan and bring to a boil over medium-high heat. Cook for about 10 minutes, until syrupy and reduced to about 4 tablespoons. Set aside.

3. Prepare the barbecue for direct cooking over a medium heat.

4. Lightly brush the inside of the fish basket with oil. Lay 4 orange slices in the basket and place 1 trout on top of them. Then place 4 more orange slices on top of the fish in the same manner. Repeat with the remaining trout, and then close and secure the fish basket. (If your fish basket is not large enough to hold 4 whole trout, you will need to cook the fish in 2 batches.) Barbecue the trout over ***direct medium heat*** for about 8 minutes, with the barbecue lid open, turning the basket every 2 minutes and rotating when needed for even cooking, until the flesh is opaque in the centre and the skin and oranges are lightly charred. Using a spatula, carefully remove the trout from the fish basket and transfer each fish to a dinner plate. Serve hot with the reduced marinade on the side.

HOW TO TRIM TROUT

1. Trim off the collar bone with scissors and cut off the head.

2. Cut off the dorsal fin.

3. Cut off the fins attached to each side of the belly.

4. Cut off the fin near the tail.

5. Trim the very thin edges of the belly.

6. Remove the bit of backbone between the fillets.

HOW TO SEGMENT AN ORANGE

1. Slice off the ends of each orange and stand it upright. Following the curve of the sides, slice off the peel, leaving as much flesh as possible.

2. Cut out the individual segments by slicing as close as possible to the membrane on both sides of each segment.

3. Squeeze the remaining orange 'skeleton' to capture all the juices.

4. Use the segments for the salad and the juice for the dressing.

Heat the soaked cedar planks by themselves until they begin to smoke and char, then turn them over and set the trout on top to cook and smoke simultaneously.

CEDAR-PLANKED TROUT WITH ROCKET, FENNEL AND ORANGE

SERVES: 4 TO 6

PREP TIME: 20 TO 25 MINUTES

HEAT: DIRECT MEDIUM-HIGH HEAT 190° TO 230°C
(375° TO 450°F)

COOKING TIME: 11 TO 18 MINUTES

SPECIAL EQUIPMENT: 2 UNTREATED CEDAR PLANKS,
EACH 30 TO 38 CM (12 TO 15 INCHES) LONG AND
1 TO 1.5 CM (½ TO ¾ INCH) THICK, SOAKED IN WATER
FOR AT LEAST 1 HOUR

2 tablespoons red wine vinegar
1 small shallot, finely chopped
2 oranges
4 tablespoons grapeseed oil
Sea salt
Freshly ground black pepper

4 whole boneless trout, each about 375 g (13 oz), cleaned
and gutted with head, tails and fins removed
Extra-virgin olive oil

175 g (6 oz) rocket
1 fennel bulb, cored and thinly sliced

1. Combine the vinegar and shallot in a small, non-metallic bowl. Remove the rind of 1 of the oranges, then peel and segment both oranges, reserving the juice. Set aside the orange segments. Whisk the orange juice (there should be about 4 tablespoons) into the vinegar and shallot. Drizzle in the oil, whisking constantly, and then season to taste with salt and pepper.

2. Prepare the barbecue for direct cooking over a medium-high heat. Rinse the trout under cold water and pat dry with paper towel. Lightly brush the inside of the trout with oil and generously season with salt and pepper.

3. Place the soaked planks over *direct medium-high heat* and close the lid. After 5 to 10 minutes, when the planks begin to smoke and char, turn them over and then place 2 trout, slightly overlapping, on each plank. Barbecue over *direct medium-high heat* for 6 to 8 minutes, with the lid closed, until the fish are firm to the touch and cooked through.

4. Use a spatula to carefully lift each fish on to an individual serving plate, skin side down and open like a book.

5. Put the rocket in a bowl and the orange segments and fennel in another. Season both with salt and pepper and toss with vinaigrette. Spoon some of the orange-fennel mixture over each fish, top with the dressed greens and garnish with the remaining orange and fennel mixture.

HOW TO PREP SQUID

1. Cleaning a whole squid (left) will leave you with a tube-like body and separate tentacles (right).

2. To start, pull the tentacles away from the body (tube) of each squid, then reach inside to grab the end of the hard quill.

3. Pull the plastic-like quill out of the tube and discard.

4. Squeeze the tube to push out and discard the mushy innards.

5. Scratch the surface of the brownish skin and peel it off the tubes. Discard the skin.

6. Cut the tentacles from the head just above the eyes. Discard the eyes.

7. Squeeze the hard mouth (beak) from the tentacles and discard it.

8. Slide a knife into each tube.

9. The knife inside the tube allows you to score each tube without cutting all the way through.

10. As you remove the squid from the marinade, shake off the excess liquid to help browning.

11. Barbecue the tubes as quickly as possible over a very high heat.

12. The tentacles will cook a little faster. Be careful not to lose them through the cooking grill.

THAI SQUID

SERVES: 4
PREP TIME: 45 MINUTES
MARINATING TIME: 20 MINUTES

HEAT: DIRECT HIGH HEAT 230° TO 290°C (450° TO 550°F)
COOKING TIME: 2 TO 3 MINUTES

12 whole, small squid

MARINADE
15 g (½ oz) coriander, finely chopped
4 tablespoons fresh lime juice
4 tablespoons fish sauce
2 tablespoons sugar
1 tablespoon very finely chopped garlic
½ teaspoon freshly ground black pepper

1. Hold each squid and gently pull to separate the tube from the tentacles. Pull out and discard any remaining contents from inside each tube, including the plastic-like quill. Peel off the brownish skin that covers the tubes. Rinse the inside of the tubes and set aside. Slice off each tentacles portion just above the eyes and discard everything except the tentacles. Squeeze out and discard the hard beak found at the base of the tentacles. Remove the gritty 'teeth' on the tentacles (you can feel them) by rubbing them between your fingers under cold running water.

2. Combine the marinade ingredients in a large bowl. Add the squid and toss to coat them evenly. Cover and refrigerate for 20 minutes. Prepare the barbecue for direct cooking over a high heat.

3. Remove the squid from the bowl and discard the marinade. Brush the cooking grills clean. Barbecue the squid over **direct high heat** for 2 to 3 minutes, with the lid open and turning once, until they are just turning opaque and no longer look wet. Serve warm.

HOW TO BARBECUE CALAMARI UNDER BRICKS

1. Separate the tubes from the tentacles on a roasting tray. Everything should be well coated with the marinade.

2. Line up the tubes on the barbecue in groups of 4. Immediately set a brick on top of each group, with the smooth side of the foil facing down.

3. Barbecue the tubes for about 2 minutes. Then carefully roll the bricks over on to their sides so you can turn the tubes over.

4. Barbecue the tentacles beside the bricks, turning them once and being careful not to lose them through the grill.

5. For the most flavourful, tender calamari possible, lightly char them over very high heat, then remove them from the barbecue before they overcook.

BRICKYARD CALAMARI SALAD

SERVES: 4
PREP TIME: 25 MINUTES
MARINATING TIME: 30 MINUTES

HEAT: DIRECT HIGH HEAT 230° TO 290°C (450° TO 550°F)
COOKING TIME: ABOUT 4 MINUTES PER BATCH
SPECIAL EQUIPMENT: 2 FOIL-WRAPPED BRICKS

DRESSING
3 tablespoons fresh lemon juice
1 teaspoon very finely chopped garlic
½ teaspoon crushed red chilli flakes
½ teaspoon sea salt
¼ teaspoon freshly ground black pepper
5 tablespoons extra-virgin olive oil

12 whole, small squid, cleaned (see page 224)
¼ teaspoon sea salt
¼ teaspoon freshly ground black pepper
250 g (8 oz) small cherry tomatoes, halved
40 g (1½ oz) red onion, cut into 5-mm (¼-inch) diced
2 large ripe haas avocados, cubed
1½ tablespoons chopped oregano

1. Combine the lemon juice, garlic, chilli flakes, salt and pepper in a bowl. Slowly whisk in the olive oil.

2. Season the calamari with the salt and pepper and place on a roasting tray with 2 tablespoons of the dressing. Toss to coat, then allow to marinate at room temperature for about 30 minutes.

3. Prepare the barbecue for direct cooking over a high heat. Brush the cooking grills clean.

4. Place about 4 calamari tubes in 2 rows over **direct high heat** so they can be weighted under the bricks. Place the bricks on top of the tubes, with the smooth side of the foil facing down, and barbecue for about 2 minutes, with the lid closed as much as possible, until the tubes easily lift off the cooking grill. Wearing insulated barbecue mitts or oven gloves and using tongs, carefully tilt the bricks on to their sides off of the tubes. Turn the tubes over, then set the bricks back in place over the tubes for a further 2 minutes. Transfer the tubes to a platter. Repeat with the remaining tubes, brushing the cooking grills clean after you remove the first batch. Barbecue the tentacles beside the bricks for about 4 minutes, turning once.

5. Put the tomatoes and onion into the bowl with the remaining dressing and toss to coat. Spoon the tomatoes and diced onion over the calamari tubes and add the avocado. Sprinkle with the oregano.

VEGETABLES

TECHNIQUES

RECIPES

HOW TO MAKE POLENTA

1. As soon as the polenta begins to boil, turn the heat to low and stir with a wooden spoon to prevent the hot mixture from splattering out of the saucepan.

2. Cook over a low heat until the polenta is thick and no longer gritty. Continue to stir every few minutes to prevent sticking and scorching on the sides of the saucepan.

3. Scrape the hot polenta into a greased pan and smooth it out with the back of a wet spoon or spatula. Allow the mixture to cool and firm up for a couple hours, then flip it on to a board and cut it into serving pieces.

4. Tomatillos provide really nice tangy and herb-like flavours to the base of the sauce. You will find them at fresh food markets and in Mexican food shops with papery husks still attached. Peel the husks off and rinse each tomatillo under water to remove the sticky coating.

5. Barbecue the tomatillos over direct medium heat until their skins begin to break, turning occasionally. During this cooking time, their flavours will turn richer, sweeter and more concentrated.

6. Barbecue the poblano chilli and onion slices at the same time as the tomatillos. Once the chilli has been peeled and deseeded, purée the vegetables with some olive oil, fresh coriander, brown sugar and salt for a bold vegetarian sauce to serve with grilled polenta.

POLENTA WITH QUESO FRESCO AND ROASTED TOMATILLO SAUCE

SERVES: 4
PREP TIME: 40 MINUTES
COOLING TIME: 2 HOURS

HEAT: DIRECT AND INDIRECT MEDIUM HEAT 180° TO
  230°C (350° TO 450°F)
COOKING TIME: 18 TO 22 MINUTES

POLENTA
25 g (1 oz) unsalted butter
75 g (3 oz) brown onion, finely chopped
1 litre (35 fl oz/4 cups) milk
125 g (4 oz) polenta
1 teaspoon chilli con carne seasoning
¾ teaspoon sea salt
Extra-virgin olive oil

SAUCE
2 slices brown onion, each about 1 cm (½ inch) thick
4 tomatillos, about 250 g (8 oz) total, papery skins
    removed and rinsed
1 small poblano chilli (or other mild chilli), 7.5 to 10 cm
    (3 to 4 inches) long
15 g (½ oz) coriander leaves
½ teaspoon brown sugar
¼ teaspoon sea salt

125 g (4 oz) queso fresco or mild feta cheese, crumbled
1 ripe haas avocado

1. Melt the butter in a large saucepan over a medium heat. Add the onion and cook for 3 to 5 minutes, stirring occasionally until lightly browned. Add the milk, polenta, chilli seasoning and salt, whisking until the mixture begins to boil. Turn the heat to very low and stir with a wooden spoon almost constantly to prevent splattering or burning. Cook and stir for 15 to 20 minutes until the polenta is very thick and no longer gritty to the bite.

2. Brush the inside of a 20-cm (8-inch) square tin with 1 tablespoon of oil. Scrape the hot polenta into the tin and spread into a smooth, even layer. Allow it to cool at room temperature for 2 hours. Prepare the barbecue for direct and indirect cooking over a medium heat.

3. Brush the onion slices, tomatillos and chilli with olive oil. Brush the cooking grills clean. Barbecue the vegetables over **direct medium heat**, with the lid closed as much as possible but turning as necessary, until the onions are lightly charred, the tomatillos soften and begin to collapse and the chilli is slightly softened and lightly charred. The onions will take 8 to 10 minutes, the tomatillos about 10 minutes and the chilli, 10 to 12 minutes. Remove the vegetables from the barbecue as they are done. Place the chilli in a bowl, cover with plastic wrap and allow to steam for 10 to 15 minutes.

4. When the chilli is cool enough to handle, pull off and discard the skin, stem and seeds. Put the vegetables, the coriander, brown sugar and salt in a food processor or blender and whizz until evenly puréed. Add more brown sugar and salt to taste.

5. Invert the tin of polenta on to a chopping board, tapping to release the polenta, if necessary. Cut the polenta into 4 to 8 pieces of whatever size and shape you like.

6. Set the pieces of polenta, smooth and greased side down, over **indirect medium heat**. Carefully pile the crumbed cheese on top of each piece. Barbecue for 8 to 10 minutes, with the lid closed, until the polenta is warmed and the cheese has begun to melt. While the polenta is on the barbecue, peel and thinly slice the avocado.

7. Transfer the polenta to serving plates. Spoon the tomatillo sauce over the polenta and top with avocado slices.

HOW TO BARBECUE CORN

1. Cut off the exposed brownish silk and peel the layers of the husk until you begin to see some kernels showing through the layers. Now the charcoal flavours can penetrate the kernels.

2. Lay the ears of corn on and alongside the embers, turning them as the husks blacken in spots.

3. Let the ears of corn cool a bit and then peel off the remaining layers of the husk. Finish cooking the corn in a tin of melted lemon-curry butter.

EMBER-ROASTED CORN WITH LEMON-CURRY BUTTER

SERVES: 4
PREP TIME: 10 MINUTES

HEAT: DIRECT MEDIUM HEAT 180° TO 230°C
(350° TO 450°F) FOR CHARCOAL BARBECUES ONLY
COOKING TIME: 20 TO 25 MINUTES

BUTTER
50 g (2 oz) unsalted butter, softened
1 tablespoon finely chopped dill
2 teaspoons finely grated lemon rind
1 teaspoon curry powder
½ teaspoon sea salt
⅛ teaspoon freshly ground black pepper

4 ears sweet corn, in husks

1. Prepare the charcoal barbecue as seen on the left. Allow the coals burn down to medium heat.

2. Mash the butter ingredients together in a bowl with the back of a fork, mixing until the ingredients are evenly distributed.

3. Trim the pointed end of each ear of corn, cutting off and discarding the fine silk sticking out of the husk. Remove and discard a layer or two of the tough outer leaves of each husk. If you can see some kernels through the transparent leaves, that's good.

4. Carefully lay the ears of corn in a single layer on the charcoal grate, on and alongside the coals. Cook the ears of corn there for 15 to 20 minutes, with the lid closed as much as possible but swapping the positions of the ears and rolling them over a few times for even cooking, until the husks are blackened all over and the kernels are tender. If any of the kernels are exposed, keep that side away from direct exposure to the coals. If the outer leaves burn, that's okay.

5. Use long-handled tongs to carefully remove the ears of corn from the barbecue. Allow them to cool for a few minutes, or until you can safely hold them in your hands. Carefully peel off and discard the husk and silk from each ear of corn. Leave the stalk ends attached to use as handles.

6. Arrange the corn in a single layer in a tin that will fit on the barbecue. Add the butter to the tin. When ready to serve, place the tin on the cooking grill and barbecue over **direct medium heat** for about 5 minutes, with the lid closed as much as possible but turning occasionally, until the butter has melted and the ears of corn are warmed. If desired, keep the corn warm in the tin over indirect heat while you finish cooking other parts of the meal.

GINGER-AND-LIME-GLAZED CORN ON THE COB

SERVES: 6
PREP TIME: 15 MINUTES

HEAT: DIRECT MEDIUM HEAT 180° TO 230°C (350° TO 450°F)
COOKING TIME: 10 TO 15 MINUTES

GLAZE
5 tablespoons chicken stock
50 g (2 oz) unsalted butter
1 tablespoon sugar
1 teaspoon finely grated lime rind
1 teaspoon sea salt
1 teaspoon grated fresh root ginger

6 ears sweet corn, in husks

1. Prepare the barbecue for direct cooking over a medium heat.

2. Stir the glaze ingredients together in a saucepan over a medium-high heat and bring to the boil. Continue to boil for 5 to 7 minutes until the glaze slightly thickens. Keep the glaze warm.

3. Cut off the top of each ear of corn just above the first row of kernels. Set aside a couple of corn husks to make long strips. Pull the corn husks back, but do not break them off the ears. Remove and discard the corn silk. Gather the husks together on each ear where they narrow towards the ends and use a strip of husk about 1 cm (½ inch) wide to tie the husks together for a handle. Mix and then brush the glaze all over the corn. Brush the cooking grills clean. Barbecue the corn over **direct medium heat** for 10 to 15 minutes, with the lid closed as much as possible and letting the husks extend over indirect heat so they do not burn, but turning several times until they are browned in spots and tender. Transfer to a platter and baste the kernels with the remaining glaze.

HOW TO PREP CORN ON THE COB

1. Pull the husks back, but leave them attached at the stalk end so you have handles. Remove and discard the corn silk.

2. Use a couple of long husks from the outer layers to cut long strips for tying up the handles.

3. Brush the exposed corn kernels with some of the glaze.

4. Barbecue the corn over direct medium heat, with the handles extending over indirect heat so that they do not burn.

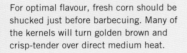

For optimal flavour, fresh corn should be shucked just before barbecuing. Many of the kernels will turn golden brown and crisp-tender over direct medium heat.

BARBECUED CORN AND MUSHROOM RISOTTO

SERVES: 4 TO 6
PREP TIME: 50 MINUTES

HEAT: DIRECT MEDIUM HEAT 180° TO 230°C (350° TO 450°F)
COOKING TIME: 8 TO 10 MINUTES
SPECIAL EQUIPMENT: 30-CM (12-INCH) FRYING PAN

250 g (8 oz) button mushrooms
1 poblano chilli or other mild chilli,
    about 15 cm (6 inches) long
3 ears sweet corn, husked
1 brown onion, cut crossways into 1-cm (½-inch) slices
Extra-virgin olive oil
1.2 litres (41 fl oz) chicken stock
25 g (1 oz) unsalted butter
200 g (7 oz) arborio rice
½ teaspoon sea salt
100 g (3½ oz) chile jack or parmesan cheese, grated
65 g (2½ lb) feta cheese, crumbled
15 g (½ oz) coriander leaves, chopped

1. Prepare the barbecue for direct cooking over a medium heat.

2. Wipe the mushrooms with a damp cloth or paper towel. Remove and discard the discoloured stalk ends. Lightly brush the mushrooms, chilli, corn and onion slices with oil.

3. Barbecue the vegetables over **direct medium heat** for 8 to 10 minutes, with the lid closed as much as possible but turning as needed, until the mushrooms and onion slices are tender, the chilli is blackened and blistered all over and the corn is browned in spots and tender. Remove the vegetables from the barbecue and allow them to cool. Coarsely chop the mushrooms and cut the corn kernels off the cobs. Scrape off the loosened bits of skin from the chilli and discard along with the seeds and stem; finely chop the remaining part of the chilli. Roughly chop the onion. Combine the mushrooms, chilli and corn in a bowl. Set the onion aside. (The vegetables can sit at room temperature for 3 to 4 hours.)

4. Warm the stock until it simmers in a large saucepan over a medium heat.

5. Melt the butter in a 30-cm (12-inch) frying pan over a high heat. Add the onion and rice and cook for 2 to 3 minutes, stirring frequently, until the rice is slightly opaque. Pour in 250 ml (8 fl oz/1 cup) of the hot stock and stir the mixture often until the stock is absorbed.

6. Continue to add the hot stock, 250 ml (8 fl oz/1 cup) at a time, and cook at a simmer for 20 to 30 minutes, stirring frequently, until the stock is absorbed and the rice is tender. When the rice is fully cooked, the mixture should be creamy but not soupy. At this point, add the remaining barbecued vegetables and the salt.

7. Remove the risotto from the heat, add the cheese and stir until melted. Spoon risotto into warm, wide bowls, and top with feta cheese and coriander.

MARINATED BABY BOK CHOY AND SHIITAKES

SERVES: 4
PREP TIME: 15 MINUTES
MARINATING TIME: 1 TO 2 HOURS

HEAT: DIRECT MEDIUM HEAT 180° TO 230°C (350° TO 450°F)
COOKING TIME: ABOUT 5 MINUTES
SPECIAL EQUIPMENT: PERFORATED GRILL PAN

MARINADE
5 tablespoons low-sodium soy sauce
4 tablespoons dry sherry
1 tablespoon light brown sugar
1 tablespoon dark sesame oil
4 slices peeled fresh root ginger, each 8 mm (⅛ inch) thick, crushed
2 garlic cloves, crushed
¼ teaspoon crushed red chilli flakes

4 baby bok choy, larger ones cut in half
20 large shiitake mushrooms

1. Whisk the marinade ingredients together in a bowl until the sugar has dissolved.

2. Plunge the bok choy into a bowl of water and shake to clean off the dirt nestled between the leaves. Wipe the mushrooms clean with a damp cloth or paper towel and then remove and discard the stalks.

3. Place the vegetables into a large, resealable plastic bag and pour in the marinade. Press the air out of the bag and seal tightly. Turn the bag to distribute the marinade and let stand at room temperature for 1 to 2 hours, turning occasionally.

4. Prepare the barbecue for direct cooking over a medium heat. Preheat a grill pan over **_direct medium heat_** for about 10 minutes.

5. Remove the vegetables from the bag and reserve the marinade. When the grill pan is hot, place the bok choy and mushrooms on to the pan, spreading them out in a single layer. Barbecue over **_direct medium heat_** for about 5 minutes, with the lid closed as much as possible but turning once or twice and basting occasionally with the reserved marinade, until the bok choy is crisp-tender and the shiitakes are heated through. Serve hot.

HOW TO BARBECUE BOK CHOY AND SHIITAKE MUSHROOMS

1. Plunge the baby bok choy under water to remove any dirt between the leaves.

2. Remove and discard the tough stalks from the mushrooms.

3. Cut the larger bok choy in half, keeping the root ends intact.

4. Leave the smaller bok choy whole.

5. Coat the vegetables with the marinade in a large plastic bag.

6. Barbecue the vegetables on a preheated grill pan, basting occasionally with the marinade.

PORTABELLO MUSHROOM SANDWICHES WITH BASIL AND BALSAMIC AÏOLI

SERVES: 6
PREP TIME: 20 MINUTES
MARINATING TIME: 15 TO 20 MINUTES

HEAT: DIRECT MEDIUM HEAT 180° TO 230°C (350° TO 450°F)
COOKING TIME: 8 TO 12 MINUTES

AÏOLI
5 tablespoons mayonnaise
2 tablespoons balsamic vinegar
1 teaspoon sea salt
½ teaspoon very finely chopped garlic

MARINADE
175 ml (6 fl oz) extra-virgin olive oil
4 tablespoons red wine vinegar
2 tablespoons very finely chopped shallot
1 teaspoon very finely chopped garlic
1 teaspoon sea salt
½ teaspoon freshly ground black pepper

6 large portabello mushrooms, cleaned, with stalks and black
    gills removed (see photos below)
Sea salt
Freshly ground black pepper

6 hamburger buns, cut in half
50 g (2 oz) basil, trimmed, rinsed and dried

1. Combine the aïoli ingredients in a small bowl. Refrigerate
until ready to assemble the sandwiches.

2. Whisk the marinade ingredients together in another small
bowl. Place the mushroom caps, gill sides down, in a large dish.
Brush the mushroom caps generously with the marinade and
turn the caps over. Spoon the rest of the marinade over the gill
side. Allow the mushrooms to marinate at room temperature for
15 to 20 minutes.

3. Prepare the barbecue for direct cooking over a medium heat.

4. Remove the mushrooms from the dish and reserve the
marinade. Lightly season the mushrooms with salt and pepper.
Brush the cooking grills clean. Barbecue the mushrooms, gill
sides down, over **direct medium heat** for 4 to 6 minutes, with
the lid closed as much as possible, until they begin to soften.
Brush the cap sides of the mushrooms with some of the
remaining marinade from the pan. Turn the mushrooms over
and grill them for a further 4 to 6 minutes until they are tender
when pierced with a knife.

5. Barbecue the buns, cut sides down, over **direct medium
heat** for about 30 seconds until lightly toasted.

6. Spread aïoli on the toasted buns and top each one with a
mushroom and some basil. Serve warm.

HOW TO BARBECUE PORTABELLO MUSHROOMS

1. Cut away the stalks and any curled edges around the rims.

2. With a spoon, gently scrape away the dark gills that might be holding dirt.

3. Use a vinaigrette to marinate and baste the mushrooms.

4. Finish barbecuing the mushrooms with the stalk sides facing up so that the juices are held inside the caps.

MARINATED PORTABELLO MUSHROOMS WITH ASIAGO

SERVES: 6
PREP TIME: 10 MINUTES
MARINATING TIME: 15 TO 20 MINUTES

HEAT: DIRECT MEDIUM HEAT 180° TO 230°C (350° TO 450°F)
COOKING TIME: 8 TO 12 MINUTES

MARINADE
4 tablespoons extra-virgin olive oil
3 tablespoons balsamic vinegar
1 tablespoon soy sauce
1 teaspoon chopped rosemary, or ½ teaspoon dried crushed
    rosemary
½ teaspoon freshly ground black pepper
¼ teaspoon sea salt

6 large portabello mushrooms, each 12 to 15 cm (5 to 6 inches)
    in diameter
40 g (1½ oz) fresh breadcrumbs
1 tablespoon finely chopped flat-leaf parsley
150 g (5 oz) asiago or parmesan cheese, grated
Sea salt
Freshly ground black pepper

1. Whisk the marinade ingredients together in a small bowl.

2. Wipe the mushrooms clean with a damp cloth or paper towel. Remove and discard the stalks. Carefully scrape out and discard the black gills from the mushroom caps with a teaspoon (see photos on opposite page). Place the mushrooms, cap sides up, on a rimmed plate and brush them with the marinade. Turn the mushrooms over and brush again with the marinade. Allow them to stand for 15 to 20 minutes at room temperature. Meanwhile, Prepare the barbecue for direct cooking over a medium heat.

3. Combine the breadcrumbs with the parsley in another small bowl.

4. Brush the cooking grills clean. Barbecue the mushrooms, gill sides down, over ***direct medium heat*** for 4 to 6 minutes, with the lid closed, until the mushrooms begin to soften. Brush the cap sides with some of the remaining marinade from the plate, turn them over, add one-sixth of the cheese on top of each mushroom, close the lid and cook for 4 to 6 minutes until tender when pierced with a knife. During the last minute of cooking, place the breadcrumb mixture evenly on top of each mushroom. Remove from the barbecue, add salt and pepper to taste and serve immediately.

HOW TO BARBECUE PIZZA

1. A grill pan is a convenient tool for barbecuing small pizza toppings such as chopped mushrooms and capsicum slices. Roast the garlic in a foil packet.

2. To flatten and stretch dough easily, without it springing back, it needs to be at room temperature. If you buy refrigerated dough to save time, allow it sit on a work surface for a few hours so it will warm up and relax.

3. A bit of olive oil on your hands and your board will make the dough more pliable. Finish flattening each piece of dough on a sheet of baking paper.

4. The baking paper will help to hold the shape of the dough as you flip it on to the barbecue. After a minute or so of grilling, peel off the paper.

5. The oil will prevent sticking and promote even browning. When the underside is crisp and toasted, transfer the crusts to a work surface, with the barbecued sides facing up.

6. Arrange the toppings on the toasted sides, return the pizzas to the barbecue and cook until the bottoms of the crusts are crisp and the cheese has melted.

PIZZA WITH MUSHROOMS, CAPSICUM, GARLIC AND SMOKED MOZZARELLA

SERVES: 8
PREP TIME: 25 MINUTES
RISING TIME: 1½ TO 2 HOURS

HEAT: DIRECT MEDIUM HEAT 180° TO 230°C (350° TO 450°F)
   AND DIRECT MEDIUM-HIGH HEAT ABOUT 230°C (450°F)
COOKING TIME: 29 TO 46 MINUTES
SPECIAL EQUIPMENT: ELECTRIC STAND MIXER

DOUGH
350 ml (12 fl oz) warm water (40° to 43°C/100° to 110°F)
1 sachet instant dry yeast
½ teaspoon sugar
625 g (1¼ lb) strong white flour
3 tablespoons extra-virgin olive oil
2 teaspoons sea salt

4 tablespoons extra-virgin olive oil
½ teaspoon sea salt
¼ teaspoon freshly ground black pepper
10 garlic cloves, peeled
1 large red capsicum, cored, deseeded and cut into
   5-mm (¼-inch) strips
250 g (8 oz) brown mushrooms, cleaned, stalks removed and
   quartered
225 g (7½ oz) smoked mozzarella cheese, grated

1. Combine the water, yeast and sugar in the bowl of an electric stand mixer. Stir briefly and allow to stand for 5 minutes, or until the top surface has a thin, frothy layer. (This indicates that the yeast is active.) Add the flour, oil and salt. Fit the mixer with the dough hook and mix on low speed for about 1 minute or until the dough begins to come together. Increase the speed to medium, and continue to mix for about 10 minutes until the dough is slightly sticky, smooth and elastic. Form the dough into a ball and place in a lightly greased bowl. Turn it over to coat all sides and tightly cover the bowl with plastic wrap. Allow the dough to rise in a warm place for 1½ to 2 hours until it has doubled in size.

2. Mix 4 tablespoons oil with the salt and pepper in a large bowl. Place the garlic cloves in the middle of a small sheet of aluminium foil, about 20 cm (8 inches) square, and pour 1 tablespoon of the oil mixture over the garlic. Fold up the sides to make a sealed packet, leaving a little room for the expansion of steam.

3. Add all the capsicums and mushrooms to the bowl with the remaining oil mixture. Toss to coat the vegetables evenly.

4. Prepare the barbecue for direct cooking over a medium-high heat. Preheat a perforated grill pan over ***direct medium-high heat*** for about 10 minutes. While the pan is preheating, place the packet of garlic over ***direct medium-high heat*** and cook for 15 to 20 minutes until the cloves are soft and light brown. Remove the packet from the barbecue. When the grill pan is really hot, lift the mushrooms and capsicums from the bowl with

tongs and spread them out in a single layer on the pan. Cook for about 6 minutes, stirring once or twice, until they are nicely browned and tender. Wearing barbecue mitts, remove the pan from the barbecue and set it down on a heatproof surface.

5. Cut the dough into 8 equal-sized pieces. Lightly brush eight, 23-cm (9-inch) squares of baking paper on one side with oil. Using your fingers, flatten each piece of dough on a sheet of baking paper to create 8 rounds. Each round should be about 8 mm (⅓ inch) thick and 15 to 20 cm (6 to 8 inches) in diameter. Lightly brush the tops with oil. Allow the rounds to sit at room temperature for 5 to 10 minutes.

6. Lower the temperature to a medium heat. Brush the cooking grills clean. Working with 4 rounds at a time, place the dough on the grill with the paper sides facing up. Barbecue over ***direct medium heat*** for 2 to 5 minutes, with the lid closed as much as possible but rotating as needed for even cooking, until the dough is well marked and firm on the underside. Peel off and discard the baking paper. Transfer the crusts to a work surface with the barbecued sides facing up. Repeat with the other 4 rounds.

7. Spread the cheese evenly over the crusts and then arrange some garlic, mushrooms and capsicum slices on top. Return the pizzas to the barbecue and cook over ***direct medium heat*** for 2 to 5 minutes, with the lid closed as much as possible but rotating the pizzas occasionally for even cooking, until the cheese has melted and the bottom of the crusts are crisp. Transfer to a chopping board and cut into wedges. Serve warm.

Go ahead and burn them. Roasting capsicums is one technique where it is okay to burn the food… to a degree. Charring the capsicums until black (see above, left) helps to loosen the skin so you can peel it away and enjoy the sweet flesh below (see above, right).

ROASTED CAPSICUM AND BACON BRUSCHETTA

SERVES: 6 AS A STARTER (MAKES 18 PIECES)
PREP TIME: 15 MINUTES

HEAT: DIRECT MEDIUM HEAT 180° TO 230°C (350° TO 450°F)
COOKING TIME: 13 TO 17 MINUTES

3 red capsicums
6 bacon rashers, cooked, drained and finely chopped
2 tablespoons extra-virgin olive oil, divided
1 tablespoon red wine vinegar
Sea salt
1 loaf Italian or French bread, cut in half lengthways
2½ tablespoons freshly grated parmesan cheese
15 g (½ oz) basil, finely chopped

1. Prepare the barbecue for direct cooking over a medium heat. Brush the cooking grills clean. Barbecue the capsicums over *direct medium heat* for 12 to 15 minutes, with the lid closed as much as possible but turning every 3 to 5 minutes, until blackened and blistered all over. Place the capsicums in a bowl and cover with plastic wrap. Allow them to stand for 10 to 15 minutes. Remove the capsicums from the bowl and peel away and discard the charred skins. Cut off and discard the tops and seeds, and then chop the capsicums. Transfer the chopped capsicums to a bowl and toss with the bacon, 2 teaspoons of the oil and the vinegar. Season to taste with salt.

2. Lightly brush or spray the cut sides of the bread with the remaining 4 teaspoons of oil and barbecue over *direct medium heat* for 1 to 2 minutes, until toasted. Remove from the barbecue and cut the bread on the diagonal into 5-cm (2-inch) wide pieces.

3. Just before serving, add the cheese to the capsicum mixture. Spoon the mixture on the toasted pieces of bread. Sprinkle the basil on top and serve at room temperature.

HOW TO BARBECUE ONIONS

1. Cut off the root and stem ends from each onion. Peel off the papery skin.

2. Cut each onion crossways into 1-cm (½-inch) slices.

3. The layers will hold together best if they are evenly sliced.

4. When turning the slices, hold the layers closest to the centre with tongs.

ROASTED CAPSICUM, BARBECUED ONIONS AND FETA CHEESE SALAD

SERVES: 6
PREP TIME: 15 MINUTES

HEAT: DIRECT MEDIUM HEAT 180° TO 230°C (350° TO 450°F)
COOKING TIME: 12 TO 15 MINUTES

VINAIGRETTE
4 tablespoons extra-virgin olive oil
2 tablespoons red wine vinegar
½ tablespoon very finely chopped garlic
½ teaspoon sea salt
¼ teaspoon freshly ground black pepper

2 red onions, cut crossways into 1-cm (½-inch) slices
Extra-virgin olive oil
2 large red capsicums
350 g (12 oz) rocket, rinsed and dried
65 g (2½ lb) toasted walnuts, coarsely chopped
125 g (4 oz) feta cheese, crumbled

1. Prepare the barbecue for direct cooking over a medium heat.

2. Whisk the vinaigrette ingredients together in a small bowl until emulsified.

3. Lightly brush the onion slices with oil. Brush the cooking grills clean. Barbecue the onions and capsicums over **direct medium heat**, with the lid closed as much as possible and turning occasionally, until the onions are tender and the skins of the capsicums are evenly charred and blistered. The onions will take 8 to 12 minutes and the capsicums, 12 to 15 minutes. Remove the veggies from the barbecue. Place the capsicums in a bowl, cover with plastic wrap, and allow them to steam for 10 to 15 minutes. When the capsicums are cool enough to handle, remove and discard the charred skins, stalks and seeds and cut them into strips about 1 cm (½ inch) wide.

4. Place the capsicums and onions in a bowl. Add 2 tablespoons of the vinaigrette and toss to coat.

5. Toss the rocket with the remaining dressing in a salad bowl. Top with the onions and capsicums and then add the walnuts and feta cheese. Serve right away.

BARBECUE-ROASTED TOMATO SOUP WITH PARMESAN CROÛTONS

SERVES: 4
PREP TIME: 30 MINUTES

HEAT: DIRECT LOW HEAT 110° TO 180°C (250° TO 350°F)
COOKING TIME: 8 TO 10 MINUTES
SPECIAL EQUIPMENT: PERFORATED GRILL PAN

1 kg (2 lb) firm but ripe roma tomatoes
1 red onion, quartered through the root end and peeled
10 garlic cloves, peeled
15 g (½ oz) thyme sprigs
4 tablespoons extra-virgin olive oil
1 litre (35 fl oz/4 cups) chicken stock
1 teaspoon sugar
1 teaspoon sea salt
½ teaspoon freshly ground black pepper
25 g (1 oz) unsalted butter, softened
8 slices crusty bread, each about 5 mm (¼ inch) thick
50 g (2 oz) parmesan cheese, grated
2 tablespoons roughly chopped basil

1. Prepare the barbecue for direct cooking over a low heat. Preheat a grill pan over **direct low heat** for about 10 minutes.

2. Combine the tomatoes, onion, garlic, thyme and oil in a bowl and toss to coat. Using tongs, arrange all the vegetables and herbs on the grill pan and cook over **direct low heat** for 20 to 25 minutes, with the lid closed as much as possible but turning the vegetables occasionally, until the tomato skins have wrinkled and started to brown. Transfer the tomatoes to a large saucepan. Continue to cook the onions, garlic and thyme for 5 to 10 minutes until the onions and garlic are lightly charred on all sides. Add the onions and garlic to the pan. Discard the thyme.

3. Add the chicken stock to the pan and bring to the boil. Reduce the heat and simmer for 8 to 10 minutes until the tomatoes have collapsed completely. Transfer the soup to a

blender and purée until very smooth. Pour the soup through a mesh sieve to remove all the tomato seeds and skin. Season with the sugar, salt and pepper.

4. If the barbecue has an infrared burner above the warming rack, preheat the burner on high, with the barbecue lid open. Butter one side of each slice of bread. Top each buttered side with about 1 teaspoon of cheese. Use tongs to position the bread slices on the warming rack (towards the back) just in front of the burner. Cook for about 2 minutes, with the lid open, until the cheese has melted and browned. Watch carefully so the cheese doesn't burn. Remove the croûtons from the warming rack. (If your barbecue does not have an infrared burner, toast the croûtons under a conventional grill.)

5. Just before serving, reheat the soup, if necessary, and add the basil. Ladle the soup into bowls and float the croûtons on top. Garnish with any remaining cheese. Serve warm.

HOW TO BARBECUE-ROAST TOMATOES

1. Coat the tomatoes and other vegetables with oil and spread them out on a preheated grill pan.

2. Cook over direct low heat until the tomato skins are wrinkled and browned.

3. Turn the vegetables occasionally for even caramelisation.

4. Don't be afraid of deep, dark colours on the vegetables. That's where the flavour is.

PANZANELLA SKEWERS
WITH SHERRY VINAIGRETTE

SERVES: 4
PREP TIME: 15 MINUTES

HEAT: DIRECT MEDIUM HEAT 180° TO 230°C (350° TO 450°F)
COOKING TIME: ABOUT 4 MINUTES
SPECIAL EQUIPMENT: 4 BAMBOO SKEWERS,
    SOAKED IN WATER FOR AT LEAST 30 MINUTES

VINAIGRETTE
2 tablespoons sherry vinegar
1 teaspoon dijon mustard
½ teaspoon finely chopped garlic
6 tablespoons extra-virgin olive oil
¼ teaspoon sea salt
¼ teaspoon freshly ground black pepper

1 small loaf focaccia or Italian bread, cut into 2.5-cm (1-inch)
    cubes
12 firm but ripe cherry tomatoes
250 g (8 oz) baby rocket
2 tablespoons coarsely chopped basil leaves
2 tablespoons freshly grated parmesan cheese

1. Prepare the barbecue for direct cooking over a medium heat.

2. Whisk the vinegar, mustard, and garlic together in a small
bowl. Slowly drizzle and whisk in the oil until the vinaigrette has
emulsified. Season with the salt and pepper.

3. Combine the bread cubes and tomatoes in a large bowl with
2 tablespoons of the vinaigrette and toss to coat. Thread the
bread cubes and tomatoes alternately on the skewers.

4. Brush the cooking grills clean. Barbecue the skewers over
direct medium heat for about 4 minutes, with the lid open
but turning every minute (if the bread starts to burn, move
the skewer over indirect heat for the remaining time), until the
tomato skins are browned and the bread is lightly toasted.

5. Toss the rocket and basil in a large bowl with 2 tablespoons
of the vinaigrette. Brush the skewers with the remaining
vinaigrette. To serve, divide the salad greens evenly on to
serving plates and top with a panzanella skewer. Sprinkle with
the cheese.

HOW TO PREP VINAIGRETTE

1. Whisk the vinegar, mustard and garlic first. The mustard
will help to emulsify the oil.

2. Add the extra-virgin olive oil slowly, whisking all the time for
a smooth dressing.

HOW TO PREP SKEWERS

Cut the bread cubes just a little bigger than the tomatoes so
that the cubes will toast nicely before the tomatoes collapse.

HOW TO BARBECUE ARTICHOKE HEARTS

1. Bend back the dark outer leaves of each artichoke, breaking them just above the base. Stop when you see the pale green and yellowish leaves exposed.

2. Trim the stalk of each artichoke, leaving 1.5 cm (¾ inch) or so attached.

3. Remove the pale green and yellowish leaves above the base of each artichoke with a sharp knife.

4. Use a small spoon to scrape out the fuzzy choke from each artichoke heart.

5. Cut each artichoke heart in half lengthways through its stalk.

6. Using a vegetable peeler or paring knife, trim most of the rough edges from the artichoke hearts and trim off a thin layer of the stem to expose the softer interior.

7. After blanching the artichoke hearts in boiling water to make them tender, brush them with oil, season them with salt and barbecue them over direct medium heat until warmed and lightly charred on all sides.

ARTICHOKE HEARTS WITH SMOKED TOMATO AND ROASTED GARLIC AÏOLI

SERVES: 4 TO 6
PREP TIME: 35 MINUTES

HEAT: INDIRECT AND DIRECT MEDIUM HEAT 180°
    TO 230°C (350° TO 450°F)
COOKING TIME: 24 TO 26 MINUTES

3 roma tomatoes, about 125 g (4 oz) each, halved, cored
    and deseeded
Extra-virgin olive oil
3 large garlic cloves
2 handfuls oak or hickory wood chips, soaked in water for
    at least 30 minutes
175 g (6 oz) mayonnaise
1½ teaspoons balsamic vinegar
1 teaspoon sea salt
¼ teaspoon freshly ground black pepper

6 large artichokes, 300 to 350 g (10 to 12 oz) each
Juice of 1 lemon

1. Prepare the barbecue for indirect and direct cooking over a
medium heat.

2. Lightly brush the tomatoes with oil. Cut a sheet of aluminium
foil about 20 by 30 cm (8 by 12 inches). Put the garlic cloves
in the centre of the foil. Drizzle ½ teaspoon of oil over the garlic
cloves and fold up the sides to make a packet.

3. Drain and add the wood chips directly on to burning coals or
to the smoker box of a gas barbecue, following manufacturer's
instructions. Brush the cooking grills clean. As soon as the wood
begins to smoke, place the tomatoes and the packet
of garlic over **indirect medium heat** and cook for about
20 minutes until the tomatoes are lightly smoked and browned
in spots, and the garlic is browned along the edges.

4. Purée the tomatoes and garlic in a food processor until they
are smooth. Add the mayonnaise, vinegar, ½ teaspoon of the
salt and the pepper. Pour the sauce into individual serving
bowls. (Cover and refrigerate if you are not planning to serve
the sauce within the next hour but allow it to stand at room
temperature for about 30 minutes before serving.)

5. Bring a large pot of salted water to the boil.

6. Prepare the artichokes by snapping off the dark outer leaves
until you expose the yellowish leaves with pale green tips. Lay
each artichoke on its side. Cut off the remaining leaves just
above the base. Using a small teaspoon, scoop out the fuzzy
choke. Cut the base of each artichoke in half lengthways,
through the stalk, and then trim the stalk, leaving about 1.5 cm
(¾ inch) attached. Trim and smooth the rough and greenish

areas around the base with a vegetable peeler or small knife.
Trim a very thin strip all the way around the stalk to expose the
tender part of the stalk. After each artichoke heart is trimmed,
place it into a large bowl mixed with lemon juice.

7. Cook the artichokes in the boiling salted water for 10 to
12 minutes until you can pierce them easily with a knife,
being careful not to over-cook them. Drain the artichokes in a
colander and place them in a large bowl. While still warm, add
2 tablespoons of oil and the remaining salt. Toss gently to coat
the artichokes. (The artichokes may be prepared up to this point
and refrigerated for up to 4 hours. Bring to room temperature
before barbecuing.)

8. Lift the artichoke hearts from the bowl letting any excess oil
drip back into the bowl. Barbecue the artichokes over **direct
medium heat** for 4 to 6 minutes, with the lid closed as much as
possible but turning them once or twice, until warmed and lightly
charred. Serve warm or at room temperature with the sauce.

HOW TO BARBECUE ASPARAGUS

1. During springtime, the peak season for asparagus, look for firm spears with smooth skins and tightly closed heads.

2. Spears of medium thickness do better on the barbecue than pencil-thin spears. They are less likely to fall through the cooking grill and they usually have fuller flavours. Both purple and green spears will be green when they are cooked.

3. Coat raw, trimmed asparagus spears with a vinaigrette. The dressing will add flavour and promote even browning on the barbecue; however, the spears should not be dripping wet when you lay them on the barbecue, which would cause flare-ups.

4. So that you don't lose spears through the cooking grill, align them so that they run perpendicular to the bars. Roll the spears over every few minutes with tongs to cook them evenly.

HOW TO BARBECUE PROSCIUTTO

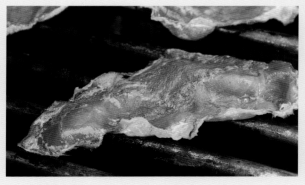

1. While the asparagus is cooking, lay thin slices of prosciutto over direct heat and barbecue them until crisp, turning once or twice.

2. It will take only a minute or two for most of the fat to melt, making the meat golden brown and delicious. Let the slices cool and then break them into bits and pieces for a garnish.

ASPARAGUS AND PROSCIUTTO WITH LEMON VINAIGRETTE

SERVES: 4
PREP TIME: 20 MINUTES

HEAT: DIRECT MEDIUM HEAT 180° TO 230°C (350° TO 450°F)
GRILL TIME: 6 TO 8 MINUTES

VINAIGRETTE
2 tablespoons apple cider vinegar
1 tablespoon finely chopped shallot
2 teaspoons finely grated lemon rind
1 teaspoon dijon mustard
4 tablespoons extra-virgin olive oil
¼ teaspoon sea salt
¼ teaspoon freshly ground black pepper

750 g (1½ lb) asparagus
½ teaspoon sea salt
4 thin slices prosciutto, about 50 g (2 oz) total

1. Prepare the barbecue for direct cooking over a medium heat.

2. Whisk the vinegar, shallot, lemon rind and mustard together in a small bowl. Slowly drizzle and whisk in the oil until the vinaigrette has emulsified. Season with the salt and pepper.

3. Remove and discard the tough bottom of each asparagus spear by grasping each end and bending it gently until it snaps at its natural point of tenderness, usually two-thirds of the way down the spear. If desired, use a vegetable peeler to peel off the outer skin from the bottom half of each spear. Spread the asparagus on a large plate. Drizzle with a few tablespoons of the vinaigrette and season evenly with the salt.

4. Brush the cooking grills clean. Barbecue the asparagus and the prosciutto over **direct medium heat**, with the lid closed as much as possible but turning once or twice, until the asparagus is tender and the prosciutto is crisp. The asparagus will take 6 to 8 minutes and the prosciutto will take 1 to 2 minutes.

5. Arrange the asparagus on a platter, spoon over the vinaigrette and crumble the crisp prosciutto on top.

VEGETABLES

LEMON BROCCOLI

SERVES: 4
PREP TIME: 10 MINUTES

HEAT: DIRECT MEDIUM HEAT 180° TO 230°C (350° TO 450°F)
COOKING TIME: 4 TO 6 MINUTES
SPECIAL EQUIPMENT: PERFORATED GRILL PAN

2½ teaspoons sea salt
500 g (1 lb) broccoli florets
2 tablespoons extra-virgin olive oil
1 tablespoon finely grated lemon rind
40 g (1½ oz) parmesan cheese, grated

1. Fill a large saucepan with water to within a few centimetres (inches) of the top. Add 2 teaspoons of the salt to the water and bring to the boil over a high heat. Add the broccoli to the boiling water and cook for 3 to 5 minutes until crisp-tender. Remove the florets from the pan and plunge them into a bowl of iced water to rapidly cool them, then remove them from the water and drain.

2. Prepare the barbecue for direct cooking over a medium heat. Brush the cooking grills clean. Preheat a grill pan over **direct medium heat** for about 10 minutes.

3. Mix the broccoli, oil, lemon rind and the remaining ½ teaspoon salt together in a large bowl.

4. Spread the broccoli on the grill pan in a single layer. Barbecue over **direct medium heat** for 4 to 6 minutes, with the lid closed as much as possible but turning occasionally, until the broccoli is warmed and just beginning to brown.

5. Remove the broccoli from the barbecue and sprinkle with the cheese. Serve warm.

HOW TO BARBECUE BROCCOLI

1. Cut broccoli florets into even-sized pieces before blanching them.

2. For quick browning, preheat the grill pan before laying out the florets.

3. Turn the florets occasionally with tongs or shake the grill pan wearing an insulated barbecue mitt or oven gloves.

GREEN BEANS WITH LEMON OIL

SERVES: 4
PREP TIME: 20 MINUTES
COOLING TIME: 30 MINUTES TO 1 HOUR

HEAT: DIRECT MEDIUM HEAT 180° TO 230°C (350° TO 450°F)
COOKING TIME: 5 TO 7 MINUTES
SPECIAL EQUIPMENT: PERFORATED GRILL PAN

LEMON OIL
1 lemon
4 tablespoons extra-virgin olive oil
2 large garlic cloves, thinly sliced
¼ teaspoon crushed red chilli flakes

500 g (1 lb) fresh green beans
2 tablets (500 mg each) vitamin C
Sea salt

1. Remove wide strips of yellow rind from the lemon with a vegetable peeler. Put them in a small saucepan with the oil, garlic and chilli flakes. Cook over a low heat until the oil simmers, then allow it to simmer for about 2 minutes. Remove the pan from the heat and allow the oil cool and steep for 30 minutes to 1 hour.

2. Remove and discard the stem ends from the green beans. Pile the beans into a large bowl.

3. Remove and discard the lemon rind and garlic from the oil. Using the sharp blade and the side of a knife, chop and crush the vitamin C tablets into a powder. Add the powder and ½ teaspoon salt to the oil and mix well.

4. Prepare the barbecue for direct cooking over a medium heat. Preheat the grill pan over **direct medium heat** for about 10 minutes.

5. Pour the oil mixture over the green beans and toss the beans over and over again to make sure they are well coated.

6. Lift the green beans from the bowl with tongs and shake off any excess oil, letting it fall back into the bowl. Spread the green beans on the grill pan in a single layer. Barbecue over **direct medium heat** for 5 to 7 minutes, with the lid closed as much as possible but turning occasionally, until browned in spots and crisp-tender.

7. Remove the green beans from the pan. Season to taste with salt and freshly squeezed lemon juice. Serve warm.

HOW TO BARBECUE GREEN BEANS

1. To infuse olive oil with more flavour, heat it with strips of lemon rind, garlic and chilli flakes.

2. Crushed vitamin C (an antioxidant) in the oil will help to keep the beans bright green as they cook.

3. Spread the beans on a preheated grill pan so they cook quickly in direct contact with the pan.

HOW TO BARBECUE CARROTS

1. I once considered carrots too crunchy to barbecue, then I realised that I should just boil them first to make them tender. Now they are one of my favourite side dishes, especially when I find young carrots with their tops still attached. They are so sweet and fabulous.

2. Trim off the tops and leaves 2.5 cm (1 inch) or so above the end of each carrot. Next, peel the carrots and blanch them in boiling salted water until they are barely tender.

3. Stop the cooking by plunging the carrots in a bowl of iced water. At this point, you could drain the carrots and set them aside for several hours before barbecuing them.

4. When you are ready to grill, coat the carrots in a bowl with melted butter, honey, orange rind and a little balsamic vinegar.

5. Arrange the carrots more or less perpendicular to the bars of the cooking grill so that you don't lose any. Barbecue them over direct medium heat until they develop handsome grill stripes.

6. Finally, return the carrots to the bowl with the glaze and coat them again for extra flavour.

ORANGE-GLAZED CARROTS

SERVES: 4 TO 6
PREP TIME: 8 TO 10 MINUTES

HEAT: DIRECT MEDIUM HEAT 180° TO 230°C (350° TO 450°F)
COOKING TIME: 4 TO 6 MINUTES

2¼ teaspoons sea salt
12 carrots, each 15 to 20 cm (6 to 8 inches) long and about
    2.5 cm (1 inch) wide at the top, peeled and trimmed
3 tablespoons unsalted butter, melted
40 g (1½ oz) runny honey or maple syrup
2 teaspoons finely grated orange rind
2 teaspoons balsamic vinegar
2 tablespoons finely chopped flat-leaf parsley
Orange wedges, to serve (optional)

1. Fill a large saucepan with water to within a few centimetres (inches) of the top. Add 2 teaspoons of the salt to the water and bring to the boil over a high heat. Add the carrots to the boiling water and cook for 4 to 6 minutes until tender but still crisp. Remove the carrots from the saucepan and plunge into a bowl of iced water to cool them rapidly, then remove them from the water and drain.

2. Prepare the barbecue for direct cooking over a medium heat.

3. Combine the melted butter, honey, orange rind, vinegar and the remaining ¼ teaspoon of salt in a large bowl. Add the carrots to the bowl and toss to coat them evenly.

4. Brush the cooking grills clean. Remove the carrots from the bowl and let the excess butter mixture drip back into the bowl. Set the bowl aside. Barbecue the carrots over **_direct medium heat_** for 4 to 6 minutes, with the lid closed as much as possible but turning occasionally, until lightly caramelised. Place the carrots back into the bowl with the remaining butter mixture. Toss to coat thoroughly. Sprinkle with the parsley and serve warm with orange wedges for squeezing over, if desired.

HOW TO BARBECUE TOFU

1. 'Steaks' of tofu can be a delicious alternative to meat. Buy extra-firm tofu so that it holds together well on the barbecue.

2. To give tofu some added flavour, coat the steaks in a marinade based on lemon juice, fresh root ginger and soy sauce.

3. Barbecuing tofu steaks on sheets of aluminium foil avoids any risk of sticking. The heat conducted through the foil browns the surfaces nicely.

LEMON-GINGER TOFU STEAKS WITH CARROT AND CASHEW SALAD

SERVES: 4
PREP TIME: 20 MINUTES
MARINATING TIME: 3 TO 4 HOURS

HEAT: DIRECT HIGH HEAT 230° TO 290°C (450° TO 550°F)
COOKING TIME: 6 TO 8 MINUTES

MARINADE
4 tablespoons fresh lemon juice
4 tablespoons canola or other vegetable oil
4 tablespoons soy sauce
2 tablespoons freshly grated root ginger
2 tablespoons light brown sugar
1 teaspoon chilli-garlic sauce, such as sriracha

2 packages (425 g/14 oz each) extra-firm tofu
    (not silken-style)

SALAD
225 g (7½ oz) carrot, coarsely grated
65 g (2½ lb) cashews, roughly chopped
4 tablespoons very finely chopped spring onions, white and light
    green parts
2 tablespoons finely chopped coriander or flat-leaf parsley
2 teaspoons fresh lemon juice
1 teaspoon dark sesame oil
1 teaspoon soy sauce

1. Whisk the marinade ingredients together in a bowl. Remove the blocks of tofu from their containers, leaving the liquid behind. Cut each block lengthways into 4 slices, each about 2.5 cm (1 inch) thick. Arrange the slices in a single layer on a rimmed platter or in an ovenproof dish.

2. Pour the marinade over the tofu slices and brush the marinade on all sides. Cover with plastic wrap and refrigerate for 3 to 4 hours, turning the slices over once or twice.

3. Combine the salad ingredients in a large bowl and mix well. Set aside at room temperature.

4. Prepare the barbecue for direct cooking over a high heat. Brush the cooking grills clean. Lay a large sheet of aluminium foil, about 40 by 30 cm (16 by 12 inches), directly on the cooking grill. Lift the tofu slices from the platter and arrange them in a single layer on the foil, reserving the marinade for glazing. Barbecue the tofu over **direct high heat** for 6 to 8 minutes, with the lid closed as much as possible but turning once and brushing occasionally with some of the reserved marinade, until both sides are nicely caramelised and the slices are warmed. Using a spatula, transfer the slices of tofu to serving plates. Stack the salad on top. Serve warm or at room temperature.

When roasting, peeling and opening the chillies, be careful that you maintain enough structure in the chillies so they can hold the cheese filling.

CHILLIES RELLENOS WITH TOMATO SALSA AND GUACAMOLE

SERVES: 6
PREP TIME: 30 MINUTES

HEAT: DIRECT AND INDIRECT MEDIUM HEAT 180° TO 230°C (350° TO 450°F)
COOKING TIME: 22 TO 31 MINUTES

SALSA
3 firm but ripe tomatoes, halved and cored
1 small white onion, cut crossways into 1-cm (½-inch) slices
Extra-virgin olive oil
2 tablespoons finely chopped coriander leaves
1 tablespoon fresh lime juice
1 teaspoon very finely chopped serrano or jalapeño chilli
1 teaspoon sea salt

GUACAMOLE
3 large ripe haas avocados
40 g (1½ oz) red onion, finely chopped
2 tablespoons fresh lime juice
1 teaspoon sea salt

6 large poblano chillies or other mild chillies
100 g (3½ oz) monterey jack or wensleydale cheese, grated
100 g (3½ oz) cheddar cheese, grated
65 g (2½ lb) goats' cheese, crumbled

1. Prepare the barbecue for direct and indirect cooking over a medium heat. Brush the cooking grills clean.

2. Lightly brush the tomatoes and onion slices with oil. Barbecue over **direct medium heat** for 6 to 8 minutes, with the lid closed as much as possible but turning once, until lightly charred all over. Remove from the barbecue, finely chop and transfer to a bowl. Stir in the remaining salsa ingredients.

3. Using a fork, coarsely mash the avocados in another bowl. Stir in the onion and lime juice, then season with the salt. Cover with plastic wrap, placing the plastic directly on the surface of the guacamole to prevent it from browning, and refrigerate until about 1 hour before serving.

4. Barbecue the chillies over **direct medium heat** for 10 to 15 minutes, with the lid open but turning occasionally, until the skins are blackened and blistered all over. (The goal is to char the skins quickly so that you can peel them without the chillies collapsing. You will need chillies with enough structure, even when roasted, to hold the filling.) Place the chillies in a large bowl, cover with plastic wrap and allow them to steam for about 10 minutes. Gently peel and discard the skin from the chillies, leaving the stems intact. Carefully cut a slit down one side of each chilli and remove and discard the seeds and veins.

5. Combine the cheeses in a bowl and mix together with a fork. Carefully stuff the mixture into the chilli cavities. Brush the chillies with olive oil.

6. Barbecue the stuffed chillies, seam sides up, over **indirect medium heat** for 6 to 8 minutes, with the lid closed, until the cheese has melted. Carefully remove them from the barbecue with a spatula. Serve warm with the salsa and guacamole.

HOW TO ROAST GARLIC

1. Cut off the top of a head of garlic to expose the cloves, and drizzle with some oil.

2. Wrap the head in foil and grill it over indirect heat until the cloves are soft and beginning to brown.

3. Allow the head of garlic to cool at room temperature and then squeeze out the soft, mellow-tasting garlic cloves.

HOW TO PREP EGGPLANT

1. Eggplants should be quite firm, with glossy, unblemished skins. Look for cylindrical shapes that feel heavy for their size.

2. A male eggplant (left) will often have fewer seeds than a female eggplant (right), making the pulp of the male sweeter and less bitter.

3. Prick the whole eggplants several times with a fork and grill them over direct high heat until the skins are charred and beginning to collapse.

4. Cut the cooled eggplants in half lengthways and scoop out the pulp for the dip, but remove and discard any clumps of seeds that could turn the dip bitter.

ROASTED EGGPLANT DIP

SERVES: 8 TO 10 AS A STARTER
PREP TIME: 10 MINUTES

HEAT: INDIRECT AND DIRECT HIGH HEAT 230° TO 290°C
(450° TO 550°F), DIRECT MEDIUM HEAT 180° TO 230°C
(350° TO 450°F)
COOKING TIME: 42 TO 52 MINUTES

1 head garlic
1 teaspoon extra-virgin olive oil
2 large eggplants, about 500 g (1 lb) total
1 tablespoon fresh lemon juice
1 teaspoon oregano leaves
½ teaspoon sea salt
½ teaspoon freshly ground black pepper

BAGEL CHIPS
2 bagels
2 tablespoons extra-virgin olive oil
¼ teaspoon sea salt

1. Prepare the barbecue for indirect and direct cooking over a high heat.

2. Remove the loose, papery outer skin from the head of garlic and cut off the top to expose the cloves. Place the garlic on a large square of aluminium foil and drizzle the oil over the top of the cloves. Fold up the sides to make a sealed packet, leaving a little room for the expansion of steam. Brush the cooking grills clean. Barbecue over **indirect high heat** for 40 to 50 minutes, with the lid closed, until the cloves are soft.

3. Prick the eggplants several times with a fork. Barbecue over **direct high heat** for 15 to 20 minutes, with the lid closed as much as possible but turning occasionally, until the skins are charred and they have begun to collapse. A knife should slide in and out of the flesh without resistance.

4. Once the garlic and eggplants are cool enough to handle, squeeze out the garlic cloves into the large bowl of a food processor fitted with a metal blade. Cut the eggplants in half lengthways and, using a large spoon, scrape away the flesh from the skin. Discard the skin and any large seed pockets. Add the flesh of the eggplants to the food processor and pulse to create a thick paste. Add the lemon juice and oregano and process until the mixture is smooth. Season with the salt and pepper. Decrease the temperature of the barbecue to a medium heat.

5. Slice the bagels in half so you have two half-moons. Slice the bagel halves lengthways into 5-mm (¼-inch) thick slices.

6. Lightly brush the bagel slices with the oil. Sprinkle with salt and barbecue over **direct medium heat** for about 2 minutes, turning once, until the chips begin to brown and get crisp.

7. Serve the dip warm with bagel chips and fresh vegetables.

HOW TO BARBECUE SANDWICHES

1. Cut the zucchinis and eggplants lengthways and evenly into 8-mm (⅓-inch) slices and grill them over direct medium heat before assembling the sandwiches.

2. Coarsely chop the fresh herbs, garlic and sun-dried tomatoes. Distribute the spread on the inside of each bread slice.

 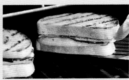

3. Brush the outside of each slice of bread with oil and barbecue the sandwiches until toasted on each side.

VEGETABLE SANDWICHES WITH SUN-DRIED TOMATO SPREAD

SERVES: 4
PREP TIME: 20 MINUTES

HEAT: DIRECT MEDIUM HEAT 180° TO 230°C (350° TO 450°F)
COOKING TIME: 10 TO 14 MINUTES

SPREAD
50 g (2 oz) basil leaves
50 g (2 oz) flat-leaf parsley
1 garlic clove
40 g (1½ oz) oil-packed sun-dried tomatoes, finely chopped
2 tablespoons oil from the jar of oil-packed sun-dried tomatoes
1 teaspoon finely grated lemon rind
1 teaspoon fresh lemon juice
¼ teaspoon sea salt

2 eggplants, about 500 g (1 lb) total, trimmed and cut lengthways into 8-mm (⅓-inch) slices
1–2 yellow zucchinis, about 250 g (8 oz) total, trimmed and cut lengthways into 8-mm (⅓-inch) slices
Extra-virgin olive oil
½ teaspoon sea salt
¼ teaspoon freshly ground black pepper
8 slices country-style sourdough bread, each about 1 cm (½ inch) thick
4 slices provolone cheese, cut to fit the bread

1. Prepare the barbecue for direct cooking over a medium heat.

2. Finely chop the basil and parsley with the garlic. Place the herb mixture in a small bowl. Add the remaining spread ingredients and mix well to form a paste.

3. Lightly brush both sides of the eggplant and zucchini slices with oil. Season with the salt and pepper. Barbecue the vegetable slices over *direct medium heat* for 8 to 10 minutes, with the lid closed as much as possible but turning once or twice, until nicely marked on both sides. The zucchini will cook a little faster than the eggplant. Transfer the vegetables from the barbecue to a platter as they are done.

4. Distribute the spread on the inside of each bread slice. Arrange the cheese and grilled vegetables in layers on half of the bread slices, making sure the cheese is in the centre. Place the top slice of bread on and gently press with your hand to keep the sandwich together. Lightly brush the outsides of the bread with oil.

5. Barbecue over *direct medium heat* for 2 to 4 minutes, with the lid open but turning once, until the bread is toasted and the cheese has melted. Serve warm.

HONEY-AND-CURRY-GLAZED PUMPKIN

SERVES: 4 TO 6
PREP TIME: 15 MINUTES

HEAT: INDIRECT MEDIUM HEAT 180° TO 230°C
(350° TO 450°F)
COOKING TIME: 1 HOUR TO 1 HOUR AND 10 MINUTES

2.5 to 3 kg (5 to 6 lb) butternut pumpkin
4 tablespoons extra-virgin olive oil
Sea salt
Freshly ground black pepper

GLAZE
50 g (2 oz) unsalted butter
75 g (3 oz) runny honey
1 tablespoon apple cider vinegar
2 teaspoons mild curry powder
¼ teaspoon ground chipotle chilli powder

1. Prepare the barbecue for indirect cooking over a
medium heat.

2. Wash the butternut pumpkins under cold water. Cut the
ends off of each pumpkin and then cut each pumpkin into 4 or
6 pieces. Using a tablespoon, scoop out and discard the seeds
and pulp. Place the pumpkin pieces on a baking tray and brush
the flesh with the oil and season to taste with salt and pepper.

3. Brush the cooking grills clean. Barbecue the pumpkin
pieces, skin sides down, over *indirect medium heat* for about
30 minutes, with the lid closed.

4. Meanwhile, combine the glaze ingredients in a small
saucepan over a medium heat and heat for about 2 minutes,
stirring often, until the butter has melted and the glaze is
smooth. Remove the pan from the heat.

5. After the first 30 minutes of cooking, return the pumpkin
pieces to the baking tray. Close the barbecue's lid to maintain
the heat inside. Brush the flesh with the glaze, return the
pumpkin to the barbecue, and continue to roast over *indirect
medium heat* for 30 to 40 minutes, with the lid closed as
much as possible but glazing every 15 to 20 minutes, until the
pumpkin pieces are soft and tender. Season with more salt, if
desired. Drizzle with the remaining glaze and serve warm.

Barbecue the butternut pumpkin pieces over indirect medium
heat for about 30 minutes before glazing them. Applying a
sweet glaze too early could cause burning. During the final
30 to 40 minutes of cooking, glaze the pumpkin every 15
to 20 minutes, but close the lid as quickly as possible to
maintain the correct temperature.

VEGETABLES

After roasting red and golden beetroot over indirect heat, put them in separate bowls so their colours won't run together, and cover the bowls with plastic wrap to loosen their skins with steam. Wear rubber gloves to avoid staining your hands when peeling the beetroot with a paring knife.

BARBECUE-ROASTED BEETROOT SALAD WITH PEPITAS AND FETA

SERVES: 4
PREP TIME: 30 TO 40 MINUTES

HEAT: INDIRECT MEDIUM HEAT 180° TO 230°C
    (350° TO 450°F)
COOKING TIME: 1 TO 1½ HOURS

4 golden or red beetroots (or a combination of both), about
    1 kg (2 lb) total
Extra-virgin olive oil

DRESSING
2 tablespoons red wine vinegar
1 teaspoon dijon mustard
1 teaspoon runny honey
1 teaspoon ground cumin
¼ teaspoon crushed red chilli flakes
125 ml (4 fl oz/½ cup) extra-virgin olive oil
½ teaspoon sea salt
¼ teaspoon freshly ground black pepper

175 g (6 oz) baby cos lettuce leaves, whole or torn into pieces
4 tablespoons pepitas (shelled pumpkin seeds), toasted
125 g (4 oz) feta or goats' cheese, crumbled

1. Prepare the barbecue for indirect cooking over a medium heat. Brush the cooking grills clean.

2. Trim off the leafy tops and root ends from the beetroots and scrub them under cold water. Lightly brush them with oil. Barbecue the beetroot over *indirect medium heat* for 1 to 1½ hours, with the lid closed as much as possible but turning occasionally, until they are tender with pierced with the tip of a knife. Remove from the barbecue and place the red beetroot and golden beetroot in separate bowls. Cover the bowls with plastic wrap and allow them to stand at room temperature until cool enough to handle. Cut off the ends and remove the skins. Cut the beetroots crossways into 5-mm to 1-cm (¼- to ½-inch) slices and keep the slices in their separate bowls (to keep the red beetroot from dying the golden beetroot red).

3. Whisk or pulse the vinegar, mustard, honey, cumin and chilli flakes together in a bowl or food processor. Slowly drizzle in the oil, whisking until the dressing has emulsified, then season with the salt and pepper.

4. Divide the lettuce and beetroot slices between 4 salad plates and drizzle with some dressing. Garnish each plate with pepitas and cheese. Serve warm.

FENNEL AND FONTINA

SERVES: 4 TO 6
PREP TIME: 10 MINUTES

HEAT: DIRECT MEDIUM-LOW HEAT ABOUT 180°C (350°F)
COOKING TIME: 23 TO 28 MINUTES

3 fennel bulbs
3 tablespoons extra-virgin olive oil
1 tablespoon fresh lemon juice
½ teaspoon sea salt
⅛ teaspoon freshly ground black pepper
125 g (4 oz) fontina cheese or other semi-soft cow's
    cheese, grated

1. Prepare the barbecue for direct cooking over a
medium-low heat.

2. If the fennel stalks have the fronds attached, trim off the
fronds and chop enough to make 2 tablespoons. Cut off the
thick stalks above the bulbs and save the stalks for another use.
Cut each fennel bulb into quarters and then remove the thick
triangular-shaped core. Cut the fennel vertically into 5-mm
(¼-inch) thick slices.

3. Pile the fennel off to one side of a sheet of heavy-duty
aluminium foil, about 60 by 20 cm (24 by 12 inches), leaving
enough foil to completely cover and envelope the fennel. Pour
the oil and lemon juice over the fennel and season with the salt
and pepper. Fold the foil over the fennel and seal the packet
tightly so that no liquid can escape.

4. Barbecue the packet over ***direct medium-low heat*** for
20 to 25 minutes, with the lid closed, until the fennel is barely
tender. Carefully open the packet with tongs and sprinkle the
cheese over the fennel. Barbecue for 2 to 3 minutes, with the
foil packet open, until the cheese has melted slightly. Carefully
remove the packet from the barbecue and garnish with
chopped fennel fronds. Serve warm.

HOW TO BARBECUE FENNEL

1. Cut off the thick stalks and the root end from each bulb,
but reserve some of the fronds for garnish.

2. Cut each bulb lengthways into quarters and cut away nearly
all the tough core.

3. Thinly slice the fennel, then arrange the slices on a large
sheet of foil and coat them with good-quality olive oil.

4. Barbecue the fennel in a sealed foil packet until barely tender. Open the packet and finish cooking the fennel with grated
fontina cheese. Sprinkle with the chopped fronds and serve.

Shelled pistachios and garlic are at the heart of a non-traditional but delicious pesto for coating barbecue-roasted potatoes.

POTATO SALAD WITH PISTACHIO PESTO

SERVES: 4 TO 6
PREP TIME: 20 MINUTES

HEAT: DIRECT MEDIUM HEAT 180° TO 230°C (350° TO 450°F)
COOKING TIME: 10 TO 15 MINUTES
SPECIAL EQUIPMENT: PERFORATED GRILL PAN

PESTO
1 garlic clove
50 g (2 oz) basil leaves
25 g (1 oz) shelled unsalted pistachios
2½ tablespoons mayonnaise
2 teaspoons white wine vinegar
½ teaspoon sea salt
¼ teaspoon freshly ground black pepper

8 waxy potatoes, such as kipfler, each 5 to 7.5 cm (2 to
    3 inches) in diameter, about 1 kg (2 lb) total, scrubbed
    (do not peel)
Sea salt
2 large red or yellow (or 1 of each) capsicums, cored, deseeded
    and chopped into 2.5- to 3.5-cm (1- to 1½-inch) pieces
2 tablespoons extra-virgin olive oil
Freshly ground black pepper
2 tablespoons torn basil leaves, optional

1. Very finely chop the garlic in a food processor. Add the basil and pistachios and pulse until they are finely chopped. Transfer the mixture to a large bowl and mix with the remaining pesto ingredients.

2. Cut each potato into eighths and put them into a large saucepan. Cover with at least 2.5 cm (1 inch) water. Add 2 teaspoons of salt to the water and bring to the boil over a high heat. Reduce the heat to a simmer and cook for 5 to 10 minutes until the potatoes are barely tender.

3. When the potatoes are barely tender, drain them in a colander and return them to the dry pan. Add the capsicum pieces, oil and ½ teaspoon of salt, then toss to coat the vegetables evenly.

4. Prepare the barbecue for direct cooking over a medium heat. Preheat the grill pan over **direct medium heat** for about 10 minutes. When the pan is hot, spoon the potatoes and capsicums on to the pan, spreading them out in a single layer. Barbecue over **direct medium heat** for 10 to 15 minutes, with the lid closed as much as possible but turning occasionally, until the potatoes are seared with golden brown marks on all sides and they are quite tender. Transfer the vegetables to the bowl with the pesto and gently toss to coat the vegetables completely. Allow the potatoes to cool for at least 5 minutes. Season to taste with salt and pepper. Garnish with basil, if desired. Serve warm or at room temperature.

COCONUT-GLAZED SWEET POTATOES

SERVES: 4 TO 6
PREP TIME: 15 MINUTES

HEAT: DIRECT MEDIUM HEAT 180° TO 230°C (350° TO 450°F)
FOR CHARCOAL BARBECUES ONLY
COOKING TIME: ABOUT 1 HOUR
SPECIAL EQUIPMENT: 30-CM (12-INCH) CAST-IRON
     FRYING PAN

4 sweet potatoes

GLAZE
1 can (425 ml/14 fl oz) coconut milk
Finely grated rind and juice of 1 lime
2 tablespoons light brown sugar
15 g (½ oz) unsalted butter
1 jalapeño chilli, very finely chopped
½ teaspoon sea salt

30 g (1¼ oz) coconut flesh, grated

1. Wash and dry the potatoes and then wrap them individually in sheets of aluminium foil.

2. Prepare a bull's-eye fire for a medium heat (see below). When the coals are ready, place the sweet potatoes directly on the charcoal grate resting on the edge of the charcoal. Close the lid and cook for 45 to 55 minutes, turning them occasionally, until the potatoes are soft. To check for doneness, squeeze the potatoes with a pair of tongs.

3. Remove the potatoes from the barbecue and allow them to cool for about 15 minutes before unwrapping them. Slit the skins with a knife and peel off and discard the skins. Cut the flesh into 1-cm (½-inch) cubes. Set aside while you make the glaze.

4. Place a 30-cm (12-inch) cast-iron frying pan over **direct medium heat**. (You can also do this step on the stove top.) Combine the glaze ingredients in the pan and bring the mixture to a simmer, stirring occasionally. Allow the mixture to simmer for 5 to 8 minutes, stirring occasionally, until reduced by half. The glaze will be slightly thick. Remove the pan from the heat and add the sweet potato cubes, gently stirring to coat with the glaze, being careful not to mash them.

5. Toast and brown the coconut for about 2 minutes in a small frying pan over a high heat.

6. Place the potatoes in a serving bowl and sprinkle the toasted coconut over the top. Serve warm.

HOW TO BARBECUE SWEET POTATOES

1. Choose cylindrical sweet potatoes of similar size and thickness so that they cook evenly.

2. Wrap them in foil and lay them against the coals, turning them occasionally.

3. Moisten and flavour the potatoes with a thick glaze based on coconut milk and brown sugar.

4. Garnish with shredded coconut that has been toasted in a frying pan.

HOW TO MAKE FLAT BREAD

1. To make sticky dough easier to handle, add a little oil to the dough and the chopping board.

2. Use a 'bench scraper' (shown here) or a large knife to cut the dough into equal-sized portions.

3. Make 12 equal-sized balls and use your hands to press and stretch each one into whatever shape you like, as long as they are about 8 mm (1/3 inch) thick.

4. Stack the flattened pieces of dough between sheets of baking paper. Make sure every piece of dough has a coating of oil on each side to prevent it from sticking on the barbecue.

BARBECUED FLAT BREAD WITH THREE TOPPINGS

SERVES: 4
PREP TIME: 15 MINUTES
RISING TIME: 1½ TO 2 HOURS

HEAT: DIRECT MEDIUM HEAT 180° TO 230°C (350° TO 450°F)
COOKING TIME: ABOUT 6 MINUTES FOR EACH BATCH
SPECIAL EQUIPMENT: ELECTRIC STAND MIXER

DOUGH
350 ml (12 fl oz) warm water (40° to 43°C/100° to 110°F)
1 sachet instant dry yeast
½ teaspoon sugar
625 g (1¼ lb) strong white flour
3 tablespoons extra-virgin olive oil
2 teaspoons sea salt

1. Combine the water, yeast and sugar in the bowl of an electric stand mixer. Stir briefly and allow to stand for 5 minutes, or until the top surface has a thin, frothy layer. (This indicates that the yeast is active.) Add the flour, oil and salt. Fit the mixer with the dough hook and mix on low speed for about 1 minute or until the dough begins to come together. Increase the speed to medium. Continue to mix for about 10 minutes until the dough is slightly sticky, smooth and elastic. Form the dough into a ball and place in a lightly greased bowl. Turn it over to coat all sides and tightly cover the bowl with plastic wrap. Allow the dough to rise in a warm place for 1½ to 2 hours, until it has doubled in size.

2. Prepare the barbecue for direct cooking over a medium heat.

3. Turn the dough out on to a lightly greased surface and cut it into 12 equal-sized portions, 50 to 75 g (2 to 3 oz) each. Using your fingers and the palms of your hands (oil them, too), stretch the dough to a length of about 20 cm (8 inches). The first stretch will probably shrink back, but continue to pull and stretch using gentle pressure until you achieve the proper length. Add more oil to the surface, as needed, to keep the dough moist and pliable. Stack the pieces of dough between sheets of baking paper.

4. Brush the cooking grills clean. Carefully lay the pieces of dough, a few at a time, over **_direct medium heat_**. Within 1 to 2 minutes the undersides of the dough should crisp, darken and harden, and the tops will puff slightly. Turn them over and continue to cook for about 6 minutes total, turning over every minute, until both sides are dark brown. If desired, keep warm over indirect heat. Serve warm or at room temperature with the topping(s) of your choice.

WHITE BEAN PURÉE WITH ROASTED GARLIC
MAKES: 1½ TO 2 CUPS
PREP TIME: 10 MINUTES

HEAT: INDIRECT MEDIUM HEAT 180° TO 230°C
    (350° TO 450°F)
COOKING TIME: 45 MINUTES TO 1 HOUR

1 small head garlic
2 tablespoons plus 1 teaspoon extra-virgin olive oil
1 can (425 g/14 oz) cannellini beans, rinsed and drained
1 teaspoon finely grated lemon rind
2 tablespoons fresh lemon juice
1 teaspoon sea salt
¼ teaspoon freshly ground black pepper
15 g (½ oz) flat-leaf parsley leaves
2–3 small sage leaves

1. Prepare the barbecue for indirect cooking over a
medium heat.

2. Remove the loose, papery outer skin from a head of garlic
and cut off the top to expose the cloves. Place the garlic on
a large square of aluminium foil and drizzle 1 teaspoon of
the oil over the top of the cloves. Fold up the sides to make a
sealed packet, leaving a little room for the expansion of steam.
Barbecue over **indirect medium heat** for 45 minutes to 1 hour,
with the lid closed, until the cloves are soft.

3. Squeeze the garlic into the bowl of a food processor, being
careful not to add any of the papery skin, then add the beans,
the remaining 2 tablespoons of oil, the lemon rind, lemon juice,
salt and pepper and purée. Add the parsley and sage and
process to give the purée a consistency that resembles the
texture of hummus. If necessary, add additional oil to create a
smoother consistency.

TOMATO TAPENADE
MAKES: 1 CUP
PREP TIME: 10 MINUTES

75 g (3 oz) pitted kalamata olives
75 g (3 oz) oil-packed, sun-dried tomatoes, drained
1 small garlic clove or several roasted garlic cloves
3–4 tablespoons extra-virgin olive oil
15 g (½ oz) basil leaves
2 tablespoons capers, drained
2 teaspoons balsamic vinegar
¼ teaspoon freshly ground black pepper

1. Pulse the olives, tomatoes and garlic in a food processor
several times to coarsely chop them. Add in 3 tablespoons of
the oil and the rest of the ingredients. Continue to purée until
the mixture is well combined. Add the remaining tablespoon of
oil if the tapenade seems too chunky.

BLUE CHEESE-WALNUT SPREAD
MAKES: 1 CUP
PREP TIME: 10 MINUTES

125 g (4 oz) blue cheese, crumbled
50 g (2 oz) unsalted butter, softened
65 g (2½ lb) walnuts, lightly toasted and coarsely chopped
40 g (1½ oz) very finely chopped shallot
1 tablespoon fresh lemon juice
¼ teaspoon freshly ground black pepper
Finely chopped flat-leaf parsley

1. Mix the blue cheese and butter in a blender or using a fork to
form a semi-smooth spread. It's okay if there are some chunks
of blue cheese. Fold in the remaining ingredients,
including parsley to taste.

FRUIT

TECHNIQUES

RECIPES

HOW TO BARBECUE PINEAPPLE UPSIDE-DOWN CAKE

1. Trim about an 2.5 cm (1 inch) from both the top and bottom of a ripe pineapple.

2. Stand the pineapple upright and rotate it as you cut off the tough skin.

3. Go back around the pineapple to trim off the dark 'eyes'.

4. Cut the pineapple crossways into 1-cm (½-inch) slices.

5. Use a paring knife to cut round the core of each slice (on both sides), then remove it.

6. Brush the slices with butter and grill them over a direct medium heat.

7. Combine brown sugar, cream and cinnamon in a 30-cm (12-inch) cast-iron frying pan.

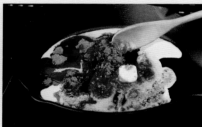

8. Melt the brown sugar mixture over direct medium heat.

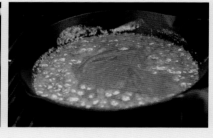

9. When the mixture bubbles around the outer edge, remove the pan from the heat.

10. Very carefully arrange cut pineapple slices in the hot mixture and pour the cake mixture on top.

11. Spread the mixture evenly to the edge of the frying pan.

12. Cook over indirect heat until a skewer inserted in the centre comes out clean. Invert the cake onto a large platter and allow to cool.

PINEAPPLE UPSIDE-DOWN CAKE

SERVES: 6 TO 8
PREP TIME: 30 MINUTES

HEAT: DIRECT AND INDIRECT MEDIUM HEAT 180° TO
    230°C (350° TO 450°F) FOR GAS BARBECUES ONLY
COOKING TIME: 46 TO 58 MINUTES
SPECIAL EQUIPMENT: 12-INCH CAST-IRON FRYING PAN

TOPPING
6 rings fresh (not canned) pineapple, each 1 cm (½ inch) thick,
    peeled and cored
25 g (1 oz) unsalted butter, melted
100 g (3½ oz) dark brown sugar
4 tablespoons double cream
½ teaspoon ground cinnamon

CAKE MIXTURE
150 g (5 oz) plain white flour
1 teaspoon baking powder
½ teaspoon sea salt
¼ teaspoon bicarbonate of soda
150 ml (5 fl oz) buttermilk
2 eggs
1 teaspoon vanilla extract
125 g (4 oz) unsalted butter, softened
150 g (5 oz) sugar

1. Prepare the barbecue for direct and indirect cooking over a
medium heat. Brush the cooking grills clean.

2. Brush the pineapple rings with the melted butter. Barbecue
them over **direct medium heat** for 4 to 6 minutes, with the lid
open and turning once, until nicely marked. Remove from the
barbecue and allow them to cool. Leave one pineapple
ring whole and cut the others in half.

3. Combine the brown sugar, cream, cinnamon and any
melted butter remaining from brushing the pineapple slices
in a 30-cm (12-inch) cast-iron frying pan over **direct medium
heat**. Cook for about 2 minutes until the sugar has melted and
the liquid has started to bubble round the outer edge. Remove
the pan from the heat and place on a roasting tray. Place the
whole pineapple ring in the centre of the pan, then arrange the
pineapple halves around it. Set aside.

4. Mix the flour, baking powder, salt and bicarbonate of soda
together in a large bowl. Whisk the buttermilk, eggs and vanilla
in a separate bowl.

5. Cream the butter and sugar with an electric mixer on
medium-high speed for 2 to 4 minutes until light and fluffy. With
the mixer on low, add the buttermilk mixture and then gradually
add the flour mixture. Blend until smooth, scraping down the
side as necessary. Using a rubber spatula, spread the mixture
evenly over the pineapple slices in the pan.

6. Bake the cake over **indirect medium heat** for 40 to 50 minutes,
keeping the temperature of the barbecue as close to 180°C
(350°F) as possible, with the lid closed, until the top is golden
brown and a skewer inserted into the centre comes out clean.
Wearing insulated barbecue mitts or oven gloves, remove the
cake from the barbecue and allow it to cool at room temperature
for about 10 minutes.

7. Before removing the cake from the pan, run a palette knife
around the edge to loosen it. Place a serving platter, large enough
to hold the cake, over the top of the pan. Wearing mitts, carefully
invert both the pan and platter, and then slowly remove the pan.
Replace any pineapple that has stuck to the bottom of the pan.
Let the cake cool briefly before slicing into wedges and serving. It
is best served warm or at room temperature the day it is made.

FRUIT

HOW TO MAKE CRÈME FRAÎCHE

1. After 8 hours at room temperature, a bit of buttermilk turns double cream into thick crème fraîche.

2. After 24 hours, the same crème fraîche is even thicker and more delicious.

HOW TO BARBECUE APPLES

1. Apple slices coated with butter quickly turn brown and tender on the barbecue.

2. Toss them with caramel sauce before assembling the dessert.

APPLE CARAMEL ON PUFF PASTRY

SERVES: 4
PREP TIME: 20 MINUTES

HEAT: DIRECT MEDIUM HEAT 180° TO 230°C (350° TO 450°F)
COOKING TIME: 8 TO 10 MINUTES
SPECIAL EQUIPMENT: PERFORATED GRILL PAN

1 sheet frozen puff pastry, about 23 cm (9 inches) square, thawed

SAUCE
75 g (3 oz) light brown sugar
125 ml (4 fl oz/½ cup) double cream
50 g (2 oz) unsalted butter

4 granny smith apples, peeled, cored and cut into 1-cm
    (½-inch) thick wedges
50 g (2 oz) unsalted butter, melted
Coarse sea salt, optional
4 tablespoons crème fraîche (recipe follows) or whipped cream

1. Cut 4 rounds from the pastry sheet using a 10-cm (4-inch) biscuit cutter. Prick each pastry round about 12 times with a fork to prevent the dough from rising too much in the oven. Following packet instructions, bake the pastry rounds on a baking sheet until golden brown. Transfer to a wire rack to cool.

2. Combine the sauce ingredients in a small saucepan over a medium heat and cook for 4 to 5 minutes, stirring constantly until the sugar has dissolved and the butter has melted. Remove the pan from the heat and set aside.

3. Toss the apple slices with the melted butter in a large bowl to coat well.

4. Prepare the barbecue for direct cooking over a medium heat. Preheat a perforated grill pan over **direct medium heat** for about 10 minutes. Add the apple slices to the pan and barbecue them for 8 to 10 minutes, with the lid closed as much as possible but turning once or twice, until they are well

browned and tender. Transfer the apple slices to a bowl. Reheat the sauce over a low heat, if necessary, and spoon some of the sauce over the apple slices, gently tossing to coat.

5. To assemble, place each pastry round on a dessert plate. Arrange the apple slices on top of the pastry rounds. Spoon the remaining sauce over the apples, allowing it to run down on to the plates. Sprinkle with a little coarse sea salt, if desired. Finish with a dollop of crème fraîche or whipped cream.

CRÈME FRAÎCHE
MAKES: 275 ML (9 FL OZ)
PREP TIME: 2 MINUTES
STANDING TIME: 8 TO 24 HOURS

250 ml (8 fl oz/1 cup) double cream
2 tablespoons buttermilk

1. Combine the cream and buttermilk in a small bowl. Cover and allow to stand at room temperature for 8 to 24 hours. It can be kept in the refrigerator for up to 10 days.

GINGERBREAD
WITH BARBECUED APRICOTS

SERVES: 12
PREP TIME: 30 MINUTES

HEAT: INDIRECT AND DIRECT MEDIUM HEAT 180° TO
230°C (350° TO 450°F) FOR GAS BARBECUES ONLY
COOKING TIME: 39 TO 41 MINUTES
SPECIAL EQUIPMENT: 23- OR 25-CM (9- OR 10-INCH)
CAST-IRON FRYING PAN

200 g (7 oz) plain white flour
1 teaspoon ground ginger
¾ teaspoon ground cinnamon
¾ teaspoon bicarbonate of soda
¾ teaspoon sea salt
125 g (4 oz) unsalted butter, softened, plus more for the pan
100 g (3½ oz) sugar
1 egg, at room temperature
175 g (6 oz) light molasses
125 ml (4 fl oz/½ cup) hot water
3 tablespoons chopped crystallised ginger

12 firm but ripe apricots, cut in half lengthways and stoned
40 g (1½ oz) unsalted butter, melted
40 g (1½ oz) sugar
1 tablespoon dark rum, optional

12 scoops vanilla ice cream

1. Combine the flour, ginger, cinnamon, bicarbonate of soda and salt in a small bowl. In a separate bowl, beat the butter and the sugar with an electric mixer on high speed for about 3 minutes until the mixture is light and fluffy. Beat in the egg and then the molasses. With the mixer on low speed, gradually add in the flour mixture, scraping down the side of the bowl with a rubber spatula. Add the water and mix until smooth. Stir in the ginger. Lightly butter the inside of a 23- or 25-cm (9- or 10-inch) cast-iron frying pan. Evenly spread the mixture in the pan.

2. Prepare the barbecue for indirect cooking over a medium heat. Brush the cooking grills clean.

3. Barbecue the gingerbread over **indirect medium heat** for about 35 minutes, with the lid closed, until a small skewer inserted in the centre comes out clean. Keep the barbecue's temperature as close to 180°C (350°F) as possible. Wearing insulated barbecue mitts or oven gloves, carefully remove the pan from the barbecue.

4. Gently toss the apricots with the melted butter, sugar and rum in a large bowl. Lift the apricots from the butter mixture, letting the excess butter fall back into the bowl. Barbecue the apricots, cut sides down, over **direct medium heat** for 4 to 6 minutes, with the lid closed as much as possible but turning and brushing the apricots with the butter mixture once, until heated through. Cooking times will vary depending on the ripeness of the apricots.

5. Cut the gingerbread into wedges and serve warm with the apricots. Spoon any remaining butter mixture over the top and serve with ice cream.

HOW TO BARBECUE GINGERBREAD AND APRICOTS

1. Cook gingerbread over indirect medium heat until a small skewer comes out clean.

2. Cut each apricot in half and remove the stones.

3. Toss the apricots in a bowl with sugar and melted butter.

4. Barbecue the apricots, cut sides down first, over direct medium heat, then turn over.

BANANAS FOSTER

SERVES: 6 TO 8
PREP TIME: 10 MINUTES

HEAT: DIRECT MEDIUM HEAT 180° TO 230°C (350° TO 450°F)
COOKING TIME: 2 TO 3 MINUTES

4 firm but ripe bananas
25 g (1 oz) unsalted butter, melted

SAUCE
125 g (4 oz) unsalted butter
100 g (3½ oz) dark brown sugar
¼ teaspoon ground cinnamon
⅛ teaspoon ground nutmeg
125 ml (4 fl oz/½ cup) dark rum
4 tablespoons banana liqueur

Vanilla ice cream

1. Prepare the barbecue for direct cooking over a medium heat.

2. Cut each banana in half lengthways and leave the skins attached (they will help the bananas hold their shape on the barbecue). Brush the cut sides with the melted butter.

Barbecue banana halves in their skins to hold the fruit together. Peel and cut the fruit before adding it to the rum sauce.

3. Brush the cooking grills clean. Barbecue the bananas over **direct medium heat** for 2 to 3 minutes, with the lid open and without turning, until warmed and well marked but not too soft. Remove from the barbecue. Peel the banana halves, cut them into quarters and set aside.

4. To make the sauce, melt the butter in a large frying pan over a medium-high heat. Add the brown sugar, cinnamon and nutmeg, and cook for about 2 minutes, stirring constantly, until it bubbles. Stir in the rum and banana liqueur. Allow the liquid to warm for a few seconds and then carefully ignite the rum with a long match or multi-purpose lighter, then allow the flames to die down. Add the banana pieces and cook over a medium heat for 2 to 3 minutes, or until the bananas curl slightly. Spoon the banana mixture over vanilla ice cream and serve immediately.

FRUIT

BARBECUED BANANA S'MORES

SERVES: 8
PREP TIME: 15 MINUTES

HEAT: INDIRECT AND DIRECT MEDIUM HEAT
ABOUT 200°C (400°F)
COOKING TIME: 15 TO 21 MINUTES
SPECIAL EQUIPMENT: 20- BY 20-CM (8- BY 8-INCH) BAK-
ING TIN SUITABLE FOR THE BARBECUE

CRUST
75 g (3 oz) digestive biscuits, finely crumbled
50 g (2 oz) unsalted butter, melted
1 small egg yolk

15 g (½ oz) unsalted butter, melted
1 teaspoon brown sugar
2 firm but ripe bananas
400 g (14 oz) mini marshmallows
75 g (3 oz) chocolate chips

1. Prepare the barbecue for indirect and direct cooking over a
medium heat.

2. Combine the crust ingredients in a a large bowl and mix
well. Firmly and evenly press the mixture into the bottom of a
20- by 20-cm (8- by 8-inch) baking tin. Barbecue the crust over
indirect medium heat for 6 to 8 minutes, with the lid closed
as much as possible, until firm. Remove the crust from the
barbecue and set aside to cool for about 10 minutes. This will
allow the crust to set.

3. Meanwhile, combine the butter and brown sugar in a small
bowl. Cut each banana in half lengthways and leave the skins
attached (they will help the bananas hold their shape on the
barbecue). Liberally brush the cut sides of the bananas with the
butter mixture.

4. Barbecue the bananas, cut sides down, over **direct medium
heat** for 2 to 4 minutes, with the lid open and without turning,
until they start to soften. Remove the bananas from the
barbecue and allow them to cool briefly, then score the bananas
into bite-sized pieces.

5. Fill the pan with half of the marshmallows, making sure
they cover the bottom of the crust evenly. Next, scoop out
and distribute the banana pieces, followed by the remaining
marshmallows.

6. Barbecue the pie over **indirect medium heat** for 5 to
7 minutes, with the lid closed, keeping the temperature of
the barbecue as close to 200°C (400°F) as possible, until the
marshmallows have puffed up and started to brown. At this
point carefully sprinkle the chocolate chips over the top and
continue cooking for about 2 minutes until the chips appear
glossy and melted. Remove the pie from the barbecue and
allow to cool for 5 minutes. Spoon into small serving bowls and
serve warm.

HOW TO BARBECUE BANANA S'MORES

1. Pour the crumb mixture into a pan, level it out and press it
into the corners with a spatula.

2. Cook the crust until firm. Barbecue the buttered bananas in
their skins so they hold their shapes.

3. Cut the bananas into bite-sized pieces and layer them in the
pan between the marshmallows.

4. During the last couple minutes, sprinkle chocolate chips on
top so they melt into the sweet, gooey marshmallows.

HOW TO PREP PANNA COTTA

1. Sprinkle gelatine over cold water to soften it.

2. Grease the ramekins to help the panna cotta slide out later.

3. Fill the ramekins and chill the panna cottas for at least 8 hours.

4. Very gently separate the chilled dessert from each ramekin with your thumb.

LEMON-BUTTERMILK PANNA COTTA WITH BARBECUED FIGS

SERVES: 6
PREP TIME: 20 MINUTES
CHILLING TIME: AT LEAST 8 HOURS

HEAT: DIRECT MEDIUM HEAT 180° TO 230°C (350° TO 450°F)
COOKING TIME: 4 MINUTES
SPECIAL EQUIPMENT: SIX 175-G (6-OZ) RAMEKINS OR
    CUSTARD CUPS

PANNA COTTA
2½ teaspoons (1 sachet) gelatine
4 tablespoons cold water
250 ml (8 fl oz/1 cup) double cream
100 g (3½ oz) sugar
500 ml (17 fl oz/2 cups) low-fat buttermilk, well shaken
½ teaspoon vanilla extract
1 tablespoon finely grated lemon rind

Sunflower or other vegetable oil

9 ripe figs, about 40 g (1½ oz) each, stalks removed and
    cut in half lengthways
1 tablespoon runny honey
1 bunch of mint, to decorate, optional

1. Sprinkle the gelatine over the water in a small bowl and allow to stand for about 5 minutes until the gelatine softens.

2. Bring the cream and sugar to a simmer in a saucepan over a medium-low heat, stirring to dissolve the sugar. Once the mixture is simmering, remove the pan from the heat and add the softened gelatine, stirring constantly for about 2 minutes until the gelatine has dissolved. Stir in the buttermilk and vanilla. Strain the mixture through a fine sieve into a large glass measuring cup or pitcher, and then stir in the lemon rind.

3. Use a wad of paper towel to completely grease the insides of 6 ramekins. Pour equal amounts of the mixture, about 150 ml (5 fl oz), into each ramekin. Place the ramekins on a roasting tray and loosely cover with clingfilm. Refrigerate the panna cottas for at least 8 hours, or up to 1 day, until chilled and set.

4. Prepare the barbecue for direct cooking over a medium heat. Lightly brush the cut sides of the figs with oil. Brush the cooking grills clean. Barbecue the figs over *direct medium heat* for about 4 minutes, with the lid closed as much as possible but turning once after 3 minutes, until well marked and heated through.

5. To remove the panna cotta from the ramekin, use your thumb to gently press each pudding round its circumference to pull it away from the sides of the ramekin. You may need to go around a couple of times before it totally releases. This works better than running a knife around the inside of each pudding, which could cut into the pudding. Place a dessert plate on top of a ramekin, and invert the plate and ramekin. Shake firmly, and let the pudding fall on to the plate. Repeat with the remaining ramekins.

6. For each serving, arrange 3 warm fig halves alongside the panna cotta and drizzle a little honey on the plate. Decorate with mint leaves, if desired.

Arrange ripe strawberries snugly in a pan and cook them over direct heat so that their juices bubble and thicken with butter, sugar, vanilla and orange liqueur.

FIRE-ROASTED STRAWBERRIES

SERVES: 6 TO 8
PREP TIME: 10 MINUTES

HEAT: DIRECT HIGH HEAT 230° TO 290°C (450° TO 550°F) FOR GAS BARBECUES ONLY
COOKING TIME: 8 TO 12 MINUTES
SPECIAL EQUIPMENT: 20- BY 20-CM (8- BY 8-INCH) BAKING TIN SUITABLE FOR THE BARBECUE

20 to 24 large strawberries, washed and blotted dry
4 tablespoons sugar
½ teaspoon vanilla extract
4 tablespoons orange-flavoured liqueur, or 2 tablespoons water and 1 tablespoon lemon juice
15 g (½ oz) unsalted butter, softened
Vanilla ice cream

1. Hull and trim the stalk end of the strawberries so that they are flat. Combine the berries, sugar, vanilla and liqueur in a bowl and toss to coat.

2. Use the softened butter to generously coat the base and sides of an 10- by 10-cm (8- by 8-inch) ovenproof baking tin or disposable aluminium tin. The tin should be just large enough to hold the berries in a single layer with their sides almost touching (this allows the berries to gently support one another as they begin to soften). Prepare the barbecue for direct cooking over a high heat.

3. Remove the berries from the bowl and line them up so that they fit snuggly, pointing up, in the prepared tin. Pour the contents from the bowl over the berries and cook over **direct high heat** for 8 to 12 minutes, with the lid closed, until they're bubbling and have begun to slump. Cooking times will vary depending on the variety, size and ripeness of the strawberries. Watch closely to catch them before they collapse.

4. Spoon the pan juices over the berries to moisten them, allow them to cool for 5 minutes and then carefully cut them into quarters or leave whole. Ladle the berries and their juices over ice cream.

■■■

The woodsy smoke of charcoal doesn't belong in fruit desserts like this one. Grill them over gas instead.

■■■

FRUIT

HOW TO MAKE SHORTCAKES

1. Mix the butter with the dry ingredients using the back of a fork to create a crumbly mixture. Leave some pea-sized clumps of butter for flaky shortcakes.

2. Add the cream and gently stir the mixture just until it comes together, but don't toughen the dough by overworking it.

3. Turn the dough out on to a lightly floured work surface and pat it to a thickness of about 2 cm (¾ inch).

4. Use a floured biscuit cutter to stamp out smooth rounds.

5. Gently gather the scraps into another single strip of dough.

6. Cut a couple more rounds from the strip.

HOW TO BARBECUE PEACHES

1. Fill the centres of the peach halves with brown sugar and barbecue until the sugar has melted and the peaches are tender.

2. Remove the peaches with a fish slice or spatula. Peel and discard the charred skins and chop the peaches, then serve them with split shortcakes and whipped cream.

PEACH SHORTCAKES

SERVES: 8
PREP TIME: 20 MINUTES

HEAT: DIRECT MEDIUM HEAT 180° TO 230°C
(350° TO 450°F) FOR GAS BARBECUES ONLY
COOKING TIME: 23 TO 30 MINUTES

300 g (10 oz) plain white flour, plus more for dusting
5 tablespoons sugar
1 tablespoon baking powder
½ teaspoons sea salt
125 g (4 oz) unsalted butter, cold, cut into small pieces
125 ml (4 fl oz/½ cup) pouring cream, cold
15 g (½ oz) unsalted butter, melted

250 ml (8 fl oz/1 cup) double cream
1 teaspoon vanilla extract
2 tablespoons icing sugar
4 large firm but ripe peaches, cut in half lengthways, stoned
40 g (1½ oz) light brown sugar
8 mint sprigs, to decorate, optional

1. Preheat oven to 200°C (400°F).

2. Combine the flour, sugar, baking powder and salt in a bowl and blend well. Add the butter and mix with a fork or a pastry blender just until the mixture resembles coarse breadcrumbs. Add the cream and gently stir it in (the mixture will be crumbly), then use your hands to mix the dough quickly and gently in the bowl just until it comes together. Turn the dough out on to a lightly floured work surface. Lightly dust your hands with flour and gently pat out the dough to about 2 cm (¾ inch) thick. Dip a 6- to 7-cm (2½- to 3- inch) round biscuit cutter in flour and stamp out rounds of dough. Gather scraps of dough and pat out, using a light touch so you don't over-work the dough; cut to make a total of 8 shortcakes. Place the shortcakes about 5 cm (2 inches) apart on a baking sheet lined with baking paper. Brush the tops with the melted butter. Bake the shortcakes for 15 to 20 minutes. Set aside to cool.

3. Combine the cream, vanilla and icing sugar in a large bowl and beat just to stiff peaks; do not over-beat. Cover and refrigerate until serving.

4. Prepare the barbecue for direct cooking over a medium heat. Brush the cooking grills clean. Sprinkle the cut sides of the peach halves with the brown sugar. Barbecue the peach halves, cut sides up, over **direct medium heat** for 8 to 10 minutes, with the lid closed, until the sugar has melted and the peaches are softened. Carefully remove from the barbecue and pour the melted brown sugar from the peaches into a medium bowl.

5. Pull the charred skin off the peaches and discard. Cut the peaches into bite-sized pieces and add them to the bowl with the melted brown sugar. Gently toss to coat. Split each shortcake horizontally and top each bottom half with equal portions of the peaches and whipped cream. Add the shortcake tops and decorate with mint sprigs, if desired.

PEAR AND PROSCIUTTO SALAD WITH CHAMPAGNE VINAIGRETTE

SERVES: 4
PREP TIME: 20 MINUTES

HEAT: DIRECT MEDIUM HEAT 180° TO 230°C (350° TO 450°F)
COOKING TIME: 4 TO 6 MINUTES

VINAIGRETTE
4 tablespoons champagne or white wine vinegar
2 tablespoons very finely chopped shallot
1 teaspoon dijon mustard
½ teaspoon sugar
¼ teaspoon sea salt
¼ teaspoon freshly ground black pepper
4 tablespoons extra-virgin olive oil
2 tablespoons toasted hazelnut oil or olive oil

8 paper-thin slices prosciutto
2 firm but ripe corella pears, quartered and cored
500 g (1 lb) rocket or mesclun greens
50 g (2 oz) manchego or parmesan cheese
100 g (3½ oz) skinned hazelnuts, toasted and coarsely
    chopped
Sea salt
Freshly ground black pepper

1. Whisk the vinegar, shallot, mustard, sugar, salt and pepper together in a small bowl. Gradually drizzle in both oils, whisking constantly, until emulsified. Taste, and if the vinaigrette is too acidic, add 1 tablespoon or so of water.

2. Prepare the barbecue for direct cooking over a medium heat. Brush the cooking grills clean.

3. Wrap a slice of prosciutto around each pear wedge, pressing the loose ends of the ham down so the meat stays together. Lightly brush the outside of the wrapped pears with

some vinaigrette and barbecue them over *direct medium heat* for 4 to 6 minutes, with the barbecue lid open and turning as necessary, until the prosciutto is slightly crisp and golden brown and the pears are warmed through.

4. Whisk the vinaigrette again to emulsify the ingredients. Toss the rocket with enough vinaigrette to lightly coat the leaves (you may not need all the vinaigrette) and divide among 4 salad plates. Top each salad with 2 warm pear wedges and drizzle with some additional vinaigrette. Shave wide ribbons of cheese over each salad with a vegetable peeler, then sprinkle with the hazelnuts. Season to taste with salt and pepper. Serve immediately.

HOW TO PREP PEAR AND PROSCIUTTO

1. Quarter each pear lengthways.

2. Trim away the core and seeds.

3. Cut the prosciutto into strips for wrapping round the quarters.

4. Overlap and press each strip of ham on itself so that it stays in place during cooking.

FRUIT

276

HOW TO WRAP BRIE IN VINE LEAVES

1. Overlap rinsed and dried vine leaves, vein-side up, and place the cheese in the centre.

2. Pull the edges over the cheese, overlapping them on top.

3. Create an X with 2 long pieces of butcher's string and put the cheese bundle on top.

4. Wrap the string around the cheese bundle a couple of times, knotting in the centre each time.

VINE LEAF-WRAPPED BRIE WITH GRAPE SALSA

SERVES: 4 TO 6 AS A STARTER
PREP TIME: 15 MINUTES

HEAT: DIRECT MEDIUM HEAT 180° TO 230°C (350° TO 450°F)
COOKING TIME: 4 TO 5 MINUTES
SPECIAL EQUIPMENT: BUTCHER'S STRING

SALSA
1 tablespoon balsamic vinegar
½ teaspoon sugar
150 g (5 oz) seedless red and/or purple grapes, coarsely
    chopped
1 tablespoon chopped mint

6 large vine leaves
1 wheel triple-cream Brie cheese, about 250 g (8 oz)
1 baguette, about 250 g (8 oz), cut diagonally into 1-cm
    (½-inch) slices
1 tablespoon grapeseed oil or olive oil

1. Combine the vinegar and sugar in a small sauté pan over a medium heat. Add the grapes and cook for about 2 minutes, stirring occasionally, to soften them. Transfer them to a small bowl and cover to keep warm. Add the mint just before serving.

2. Prepare the barbecue for direct cooking over a medium heat.

3. Unroll and rinse the vine leaves. Spread out the leaves on a work surface and pat dry with paper towel. Cut off and discard the tough stalks. Overlap 4 vine leaves, vein-side up, into a 23- or 25-cm (11- or 12-inch) circle. Put another leaf in the centre, and then put the cheese on top. Cover the cheese with another vine leaf. Wrap the leaves around the cheese, overlapping them to prevent the cheese from ultimately leaking out. Knot together two 90-cm (3-feet) pieces of butcher's string in the centre. Lay on a work surface in the shape of an 'X'. Set the cheese bundle on top. Bring the string to the top and tie snugly. Wrap the string round the cheese 1 or 2 more times

like spokes on a wheel, knotting snugly in the centre each time. Tuck in any loose leaf edges. Trim the ends of the string.

4. Lightly brush the cheese bundle and bread slices all over with oil. Brush the cooking grills clean. Barbecue the cheese over **direct medium heat** for 3 to 4 minutes, with the lid closed as much as possible but turning once, until each side is soft when gently pressed. Carefully remove the cheese and allow it to rest for about 2 minutes. Meanwhile, barbecue the bread slices over **direct medium heat** for about 1 minute until they are lightly toasted on one side only. By barbecuing only one side of the bread it ensures a nice sturdy base for the melted cheese and salsa.

5. Arrange the cheese and barbecued bread on a serving plate or tray. Cut the string and discard it. Pull the vine leaves open to reveal the cheese inside. Be sure to do this just before serving as the cheese begins to ooze out as soon as you remove the vine leaves. Top the cheese with some of the grape salsa or serve it alongside in a bowl. Use spoons to scoop up cheese and salsa, and place on slices of barbecued bread.

RESOURCES

STAURANT

BAR-B-Q PORK

BARBECUING GUIDES AND TIPS

RECIPES

RUBS

A rub is a mixture of spices, herbs and other seasonings (often including sugar) that can quickly give a boost of flavours to foods before barbecuing. The following pages provide some mighty good examples, along with recommendations for which foods they complement, but dare to be different. One of the steps towards developing your own style at the barbecue is to concoct a signature rub recipe or two. Only you will know exactly what ingredients are blended in your special jar of 'magic dust'.

A word about freshness: ground spices lose their aromas in a matter of months (8 to 10 months maximum). If you have been holding on to a little jar of coriander for years, waiting to blend the world's finest version of curry powder, forget about it. Dump the old, tired coriander and buy some freshly ground. Better yet, buy whole coriander seeds and grind them yourself. Whatever you do, store your spices and spice rubs in airtight containers away from light and heat, to give them a long, aromatic life.

HOW LONG?

If you leave a rub on for a long time, the seasonings intermingle with the juices in the meat and produce more pronounced flavours, as well as a crust. This is good to a point, but a rub with a lot of salt and sugar will draw moisture out of the meat over time, making the meat tastier, yes, but also drier. So how long should you use a rub? Here are some guidelines.

1 TO 15 MINUTES	Small foods, such as shellfish, cubed meat for kebabs and vegetables
15 TO 30 MINUTES	Thin cuts of boneless meat, such as chicken breasts, fish fillets, pork fillet, chops and steaks
30 TO 90 MINUTES	Thicker cuts of boneless or bone-in meat, such as leg of lamb, whole chickens and beef joints
2 TO 8 HOURS	Big or tough cuts of meat, such as racks of ribs, whole gammons, pork shoulders and turkeys

CLASSIC BARBECUE SPICE RUB

MAKES: ABOUT 5 TABLESPOONS

4 teaspoons sea salt
2 teaspoons pure chilli powder
2 teaspoons light brown sugar
2 teaspoons garlic granules
2 teaspoons paprika
1 teaspoon celery seeds
1 teaspoon ground cumin
½ teaspoon freshly ground black pepper

CHICKEN AND SEAFOOD RUB

MAKES: ABOUT 4½ TABLESPOONS

4 teaspoons onion granules
4 teaspoons garlic granules
1 tablespoon sea salt
2 teaspoons chilli con carne seasoning
2 teaspoons freshly ground black pepper

CRACKED PEPPER RUB

MAKES: ABOUT 1½ TABLESPOONS

1 teaspoon whole black peppercorns
1 teaspoon mustard seeds
1 teaspoon paprika
½ teaspoon garlic granules
½ teaspoon sea salt
½ teaspoon light brown sugar
⅛ teaspoon ground cayenne pepper

Crush the black peppercorns and mustard seed in a
spice mill or using a mortar and pestle. Transfer to a
small bowl and combine with the remaining ingredients.

CAJUN RUB

MAKES: ABOUT 3 TABLESPOONS

2 teaspoons finely chopped thyme
1½ teaspoons sea salt
1 teaspoon garlic granules
1 teaspoon onion granules
1 teaspoon paprika
1 teaspoon light brown sugar
¾ teaspoon freshly ground black pepper
¼ teaspoon ground cayenne pepper

PORK RUB

MAKES: ABOUT 2½ TABLESPOONS

2 teaspoons pure chilli powder
2 teaspoons freshly ground black pepper
2 teaspoons sea salt
2 teaspoons ground cumin
2 teaspoons dried oregano
1 teaspoon garlic granules

BEEF RUB

MAKES: ABOUT 4 TABLESPOONS

4 teaspoons sea salt
1 tablespoon pure chilli powder
1 tablespoon onion granules
1½ teaspoons garlic granules
1 teaspoon paprika
1 teaspoon dried marjoram
½ teaspoon ground cumin
½ teaspoon freshly ground black pepper
¼ teaspoon ground cinnamon

FENNEL RUB

MAKES: ABOUT 4 TABLESPOONS

3 teaspoons ground fennel seeds
3 teaspoons sea salt
3 teaspoons pure chilli powder
1½ teaspoons celery seeds
1½ teaspoons freshly ground black pepper

KEY

- RED MEAT
- PORK
- POULTRY
- SEAFOOD
- VEGETABLES

MORE RUBS

SOUTH-WEST RUB

MAKES: ABOUT 3½ TABLESPOONS

2 teaspoons pure chilli powder
2 teaspoons garlic granules
2 teaspoons paprika
2 teaspoons sea salt
1 teaspoon ground coriander
1 teaspoon ground cumin
1 teaspoon freshly ground black pepper

CARIBBEAN RUB

MAKES: ABOUT 6 TABLESPOONS

1 tablespoon light brown sugar
1 tablespoon garlic granules
1 tablespoon dried thyme
2¼ teaspoons sea salt
¾ teaspoon freshly ground black pepper
¾ teaspoon ground allspice

TARRAGON RUB

MAKES: ABOUT 5½ TABLESPOONS

1½ tablespoons dried tarragon
2½ teaspoons sea salt
2 teaspoons freshly ground black pepper
1½ teaspoons dried thyme
1 teaspoon rubbed dried sage, packed

MAGIC RUB

MAKES: 2 TABLESPOONS

1 teaspoon mustard powder
1 teaspoon onion granules
1 teaspoon paprika
1 teaspoon sea salt
½ teaspoon garlic granules
½ teaspoon ground coriander
½ teaspoon ground cumin
½ teaspoon freshly ground black pepper

ESPRESSO-CHILLI RUB

MAKES: ABOUT 4 TABLESPOONS

2 tablespoons dark-roast coffee or espresso beans
2 teaspoons cumin seeds, toasted
1 tablespoon ground ancho chilli powder
1 teaspoon sweet paprika
1 teaspoon sea salt
1 teaspoon freshly ground black pepper

Pulse the coffee beans and cumin seed together in a spice mill until finely ground. Transfer to a small bowl, add the remaining ingredients and stir to combine.

ASIAN RUB

MAKES: ABOUT 5 TABLESPOONS

2 tablespoons paprika
2 teaspoons sea salt
2 teaspoons ground coriander
2 teaspoons Chinese five-spice powder
1 teaspoon ground ginger
½ teaspoon ground allspice
½ teaspoon ground cayenne pepper

KEY	
	RED MEAT
	PORK
	POULTRY
	SEAFOOD
	VEGETABLES

BABY BACK RIBS RUB

MAKES: ABOUT 8 TABLESPOONS

2 tablespoons sea salt
2 tablespoons paprika
4 teaspoons garlic granules
4 teaspoons pure chilli powder
2 teaspoons mustard powder
2 teaspoons freshly ground black pepper

BAJA FISH RUB

MAKES: 4 TEASPOONS

1 teaspoon pure chilli powder
1 teaspoon ground cumin
1 teaspoon sea salt
½ teaspoon ground cayenne pepper
½ teaspoon ground cinnamon

MEXICAN RUB

MAKES: ABOUT 3½ TABLESPOONS

1 tablespoon ground cumin
1 tablespoon light brown sugar
2 teaspoons sea salt
1 teaspoon pasilla or pure chilli powder
1 teaspoon ground coriander
1 teaspoon dried oregano

NEW WORLD RUB

MAKES: ABOUT 2 TABLESPOONS

1 teaspoon garlic granules
1 teaspoon onion granules
1 teaspoon paprika
½ teaspoon cumin
½ teaspoon dried lemongrass
½ teaspoon dried basil
½ teaspoon dried thyme
½ teaspoon sea salt
¼ teaspoon freshly ground black pepper
⅛ teaspoon ground cayenne pepper

BARBECUE CHICKEN RUB

MAKES: ABOUT 3 TABLESPOONS

1 tablespoon smoked paprika
2 teaspoons mustard powder
1 teaspoon sea salt
½ teaspoon garlic granules
½ teaspoon onion granules
¼ teaspoon ground chipotle chilli

LEMON-PAPRIKA RUB

MAKES: ABOUT 2 TABLESPOONS

2 teaspoons smoked paprika
2 teaspoons sea salt
Finely grated rind of 1 lemon
½ teaspoon garlic granules
½ teaspoon freshly ground black pepper

ALL-PURPOSE RUB

MAKES: ABOUT 2 TABLESPOONS

1 teaspoon pure chilli powder
1 teaspoon garlic granules
1 teaspoon paprika
1 teaspoon sea salt
½ teaspoon ground coriander
½ teaspoon ground cumin
½ teaspoon freshly ground black pepper

PULLED PORK RUB

MAKES: ABOUT 6 TABLESPOONS

2 tablespoons pure chilli powder
2 tablespoons sea salt
4 teaspoons garlic granules
2 teaspoons freshly ground black pepper
1 teaspoon mustard powder

MARINADES

Marinades work more slowly than rubs, but they can seep in a little deeper. Typically, a marinade is made with some acidic liquid, some oil and some combination of herbs and spices. These ingredients can 'fill in the gaps' when a particular meat, fish or vegetable (yes, vegetable) lacks enough taste or richness. They can also give food characteristics that reflect regional/ethnic cooking styles.

If indeed your marinade includes some acidic liquid, be sure to use a non-metallic container. This is a dish or bowl made of glass, plastic, stainless steel or ceramic. A container made of aluminium, or some other metals, will react with acids and add a metallic flavour to food.

HOW LONG?
The right times vary depending on the strength of the marinade and the food you are marinating. If your marinade includes intense ingredients, such as soy sauce, a spirit or hot chillies and spices, don't overdo it. A fish fillet should still taste like fish, not a burning-hot, salt-soaked piece of protein. Also, if an acidic marinade is left too long on meat or fish, it can make the surface mushy or dry. Here are some general guidelines to get you going.

15 TO 30 MINUTES	Small foods, such as shellfish, fish fillets, cubed meat for kebabs and tender vegetables
1 TO 3 HOURS	Thin cuts of boneless meat, such as chicken breasts, pork fillet, chops and steaks, as well as sturdy vegetables
2 TO 6 HOURS	Thicker cuts of boneless or bone-in meat, such as leg of lamb, whole chickens and beef joints
6 TO 12 HOURS	Big or tough cuts of meat, such as racks of ribs, whole hams, pork shoulders and turkeys

BEER MARINADE

MAKES: ABOUT 300 ML (10½ FL OZ)

250 ml (8 fl oz/1 cup) dark Mexican beer
2 tablespoons dark sesame oil
1 tablespoon finely chopped garlic
1 teaspoon dried oregano
1 teaspoon sea salt
½ teaspoon freshly ground black pepper
¼ teaspoon ground cayenne pepper

JERK MARINADE

MAKES: ABOUT 250 ML (8 FL OZ/1 CUP)

75 g (3 oz) brown onion, roughly chopped
1 jalapeño chilli, roughly chopped
3 tablespoons white wine vinegar
2 tablespoons soy sauce
2 tablespoons canola or other vegetable oil
½ teaspoon ground allspice
¼ teaspoon garlic granules
¼ teaspoon ground cinnamon
¼ teaspoon sea salt
¼ teaspoon freshly ground black pepper
⅛ teaspoon ground nutmeg

PACIFIC RIM MARINADE

MAKES: ABOUT 500 ML (17 FL OZ)

1 small brown onion, roughly chopped
   (about 150 g/5 oz)
5 tablespoons soy sauce
4 tablespoons fresh lemon juice
4 tablespoons canola or other vegetable oil
2 tablespoons dark brown sugar
2 tablespoons very finely chopped garlic
½ teaspoon ground allspice

KEY	
	RED MEAT
	PORK
	POULTRY
	SEAFOOD
	VEGETABLES

MOJO MARINADE

MAKES: ABOUT 175 ML (6 FL OZ)

4 tablespoons fresh orange juice
3 tablespoons fresh lime juice
3 tablespoons extra-virgin olive oil
2 tablespoons finely chopped coriander
1 tablespoon finely chopped jalapeño chilli,
   including seeds
1 tablespoon very finely chopped garlic
¾ teaspoon ground cumin
½ teaspoon sea salt

LEMON-SAGE MARINADE

MAKES: ABOUT 250 ML (8 FL OZ/1 CUP)

1 tablespoon finely grated lemon rind
4 tablespoons fresh lemon juice
4 tablespoons extra-virgin olive oil
3 tablespoons finely chopped sage
2 tablespoons very finely chopped shallot
2 tablespoons wholegrain mustard
1 tablespoon finely chopped garlic
1 tablespoon freshly cracked black peppercorns

TERIYAKI MARINADE

MAKES: ABOUT 600 ML (21 FL OZ)

250 ml (8 fl oz/1 cup) pineapple juice
125 ml (4 fl oz/½ cup) low-sodium soy sauce
75 g (3 oz) brown onion, finely chopped
1 tablespoon dark sesame oil
1 tablespoon grated fresh root ginger
1 tablespoon very finely chopped garlic
1 tablespoon dark brown sugar
1 tablespoon fresh lemon juice

GREEK MARINADE

MAKES: ABOUT 125 ML (4 FL OZ/½ CUP)

6 tablespoons extra-virgin olive oil
3 tablespoons red wine vinegar
½ teaspoon very finely chopped garlic
½ teaspoon sea salt
½ teaspoon dried oregano
¼ teaspoon crushed red chilli flakes

MORE MARINADES

MEDITERRANEAN MARINADE

MAKES: ABOUT 125 ML (4 FL OZ/½ CUP)

2 tablespoons extra-virgin olive oil
2 teaspoons paprika
1 teaspoon ground coriander
1 teaspoon ground cumin
1 teaspoon garlic granules
1 teaspoon sea salt
¼ teaspoon freshly ground black pepper

SOUTH-WEST MARINADE

MAKES: ABOUT 250 ML (8 FL OZ/1 CUP)

125 ml (4 fl oz/½ cup) fresh orange juice
3 tablespoons extra-virgin olive oil
2 tablespoons red wine vinegar
1 tablespoon very finely chopped garlic
2 teaspoons pure chilli powder
1½ teaspoons dried oregano
1 teaspoon sea salt
½ teaspoon freshly ground black pepper
½ teaspoon ground cinnamon

TEQUILA MARINADE

MAKES: ABOUT 450 ML (16 FL OZ)

250 ml (8 fl oz/1 cup) fresh orange juice
125 ml (4 fl oz/½ cup) tequila
2 tablespoons fresh lime juice
2 tablespoons light brown sugar
2 teaspoons ground cumin
1 jalapeño chilli, cut into 8-mm (⅓-inch) slices

BOURBON MARINADE

MAKES: ABOUT 250 ML (8 FL OZ/1 CUP)

125 ml (4 fl oz/½ cup) bourbon
4 tablespoons tomato sauce
2 tablespoons extra-virgin olive oil
2 tablespoons soy sauce
1 tablespoon white wine vinegar
2 teaspoons very finely chopped garlic
½ teaspoon hot sauce, or to taste
½ teaspoon freshly ground black pepper

HONEY-MUSTARD MARINADE

MAKES: ABOUT 250 ML (8 FL OZ/1 CUP)

125 g (4 oz) dijon mustard
75 g (3 oz) honey
2 tablespoons extra-virgin olive oil
2 teaspoons curry powder
1 teaspoon freshly grated lemon rind
½ teaspoon garlic granules
½ teaspoon sea salt
¼ teaspoon ground cayenne pepper
¼ teaspoon freshly ground black pepper

TARRAGON-CITRUS MARINADE

MAKES: ABOUT 250 ML (8 FL OZ/1 CUP)

4 tablespoons extra-virgin olive oil
4 tablespoons roughly chopped tarragon
Rind and juice of 1 orange
Rind and juice of 1 lemon
2 tablespoons sherry vinegar
2 teaspoons sea salt
1 teaspoon very finely chopped garlic
1 teaspoon grated fresh root ginger
½ teaspoon chilli con carne seasoning
½ teaspoon freshly ground black pepper

KEY

■ RED MEAT
■ PORK
■ POULTRY
■ SEAFOOD
■ VEGETABLES

MONGOLIAN MARINADE

MAKES: ABOUT 300 ML (10½ FL OZ)

125 ml (4 fl oz/½ cup) hoisin sauce
2 tablespoons oyster sauce
2 tablespoons soy sauce
2 tablespoons dry sherry
2 tablespoons rice vinegar
2 tablespoons canola or other vegetable oil
1 tablespoon honey
1 tablespoon very finely chopped ginger
1 tablespoon very finely chopped garlic
½ teaspoon crushed red chilli flakes (optional)

SPICY CAYENNE MARINADE

MAKES: ABOUT 125 ML (4 FL OZ/½ CUP)

4 tablespoons extra-virgin olive oil
2 tablespoons fresh lemon juice
1 tablespoon very finely chopped garlic
2 teaspoons dried oregano
2 teaspoons paprika
1½ teaspoons sea salt
1 teaspoon celery seeds
1 teaspoon ground cayenne pepper

CUBAN MARINADE

MAKES: ABOUT 500 ML (17 FL OZ)

125 ml (4 fl oz/½ cup) fresh orange juice
125 ml (4 fl oz/½ cup) fresh lemonade
65 g (2½ lb) brown onion, finely chopped
4 tablespoons extra-virgin olive oil
2 tablespoons very finely chopped garlic
2 tablespoons dried oregano
2 tablespoons fresh lime juice

CHINESE HOISIN MARINADE

MAKES: ABOUT 175 ML (6 FL OZ)

125 ml (4 fl oz/½ cup) hoisin sauce
2 tablespoons red wine vinegar
1 tablespoon canola or other vegetable oil
2 teaspoons very finely chopped garlic
1 teaspoon very finely chopped fresh root ginger
1 teaspoon hot sauce, or to taste
1 teaspoon dark sesame oil

TANDOORI MARINADE

MAKES: ABOUT 300 ML (10½ FL OZ)

250 g (8 oz) plain yogurt
1 tablespoon grated fresh root ginger
1 tablespoon paprika
1 tablespoon sunflower or other vegetable oil
2 teaspoons very finely chopped garlic
2 teaspoons sea salt
1½ teaspoons ground cumin
1 teaspoon ground turmeric
½ teaspoon ground cayenne pepper

BARCELONA MARINADE

MAKES: ABOUT 175 ML (6 FL OZ)

5 spring onions, cut into 2.5-cm (1-inch) pieces
50 g (2 oz) basil leaves
3 large garlic cloves
2 serrano chillies, roughly chopped
4 tablespoons extra-virgin olive oil
2 tablespoons sherry vinegar
1 teaspoon sea salt
½ teaspoon freshly ground black pepper

Process the ingredients in a food processor or blender for
1 to 2 minutes until a smooth paste forms.

CORIANDER PESTO MARINADE

MAKES: ABOUT 250 ML (8 FL OZ/1 CUP)

2 tablespoons coarsely chopped walnuts
2 garlic cloves
75 g (3 oz) coriander leaves and tender stalks
25 g (1 oz) flat-leaf parsley and tender stalks
½ teaspoon sea salt
¼ teaspoon freshly ground black pepper
4 tablespoons extra-virgin olive oil

Finely chop the walnuts and garlic in a food processor.
Scrape down the sides of the bowl. Add the coriander, parsley, salt and pepper and process until finely
chopped. With the motor running, slowly add the oil to
create a smooth purée.

SAUCES

Sauces open up a world of flavours for barbecuers. They offer us almost limitless ways for distinguishing our food and making it more interesting. Once you have learnt some of the fundamentals about balancing flavours and some of the techniques for holding sauces together, you are ready to develop your own. I've included several styles of sauces on the following pages, some of them featuring a barbecued ingredient or two for greater depth. Find the sauces that suit you and the kind of food you like to barbecue. Return to them a couple times so that you understand how and why they work, then start pushing the parameters. A little more of this. A little less of that. Maybe a few more minutes simmering over the fire. Sauces are playgrounds for discovery. Learn the basics and build from there.

PASILLA BARBECUE SAUCE

MAKES: ABOUT 500 ML (17 FL OZ)

2 tablespoons extra-virgin olive oil
6 garlic cloves, peeled
100 g (3½ oz) red onion, finely chopped
2 dried pasilla chillies, stemmed, deseeded and cut
   into strips
250 g (8 oz) canned tomatoes with juice, diced
250 ml (8 fl oz/1 cup) amber Mexican beer
1 tablespoon apple cider vinegar
1 teaspoon sea salt
½ teaspoon dried oregano
¼ teaspoon freshly ground black pepper

Heat the oil in a small, heavy-based saucepan over a medium heat. Add the garlic and cook for 4 to 5 minutes, turning occasionally, until lightly browned. Add the onion and chillies, cook for about 3 minutes, stirring occasionally. Add the remaining ingredients and bring to the boil, then simmer for 15 minutes. Remove the pan from the heat and allow the mixture to stand for 15 minutes to soften the chillies and blend the flavours. Purée in a blender.

CLASSIC RED BARBECUE SAUCE

MAKES: ABOUT 350 ML (12 FL OZ)

175 ml (6 fl oz) apple juice
125 g (4 oz) tomato sauce
3 tablespoons apple cider vinegar
2 teaspoons soy sauce
1 teaspoon worcestershire sauce
1 teaspoon molasses
½ teaspoon pure chilli powder
½ teaspoon garlic granules
¼ teaspoon freshly ground black pepper

Mix the ingredients together in a small saucepan.
Simmer for a few minutes over a medium heat, and then
remove the pan from the heat.

RED CHILLI BARBECUE SAUCE

MAKES: ABOUT 500 ML (17 FL OZ)

4 dried pasilla chillies, about 20 g (¾ oz) total
2 tablespoons canola or other vegetable oil
125 g (4 oz) tomato sauce
3 tablespoons soy sauce
2 tablespoons balsamic vinegar
3 garlic cloves, crushed
1 teaspoon ground cumin
½ teaspoon dried oregano
¼ teaspoon sea salt
¼ teaspoon freshly ground black pepper

Remove the stalks and cut the chillies crossways into
sections about 5 cm (2 inches) long. Remove most of the
seeds. Warm the oil in a frying pan over a high heat. Add
the chillies and toast them for 2 to 3 minutes, turning
once, until they puff up and begin to change colour.
Transfer the chillies and oil to a small bowl, cover with
250 ml (8 fl oz/1 cup) of hot water and allow the chillies
to soak for 30 minutes. Pour the chillies, along with the
oil and water, into a blender or food processor. Add the
remaining ingredients and process until very smooth.

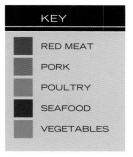

KEY	
	RED MEAT
	PORK
	POULTRY
	SEAFOOD
	VEGETABLES

SASSY BARBECUE SAUCE

MAKES: ABOUT 250 ML (8 FL OZ/1 CUP)

125 ml (4 fl oz/½ cup) water
125 g (4 oz) tomato sauce
2 tablespoons molasses
1 tablespoon white wine vinegar
1 tablespoon dijon mustard
1 tablespoon light brown sugar
2 teaspoons worcestershire sauce
½ teaspoon sea salt
¼ teaspoon hot sauce, or to taste
¼ teaspoon garlic granules
¼ teaspoon freshly ground black pepper

Whisk the ingredients together in a small, heavy-based
saucepan. Bring to the boil over a medium heat, then
reduce the heat and simmer for 10 minutes, stirring
occasionally.

ANCHO BARBECUE SAUCE

MAKES: ABOUT 250 ML (8 FL OZ/1 CUP)

40 g (1½ oz) flaked almonds
2 dried ancho chillies, about 15 g (½ oz) total
6 tablespoons fresh orange juice
40 g (1½ oz) roasted red capsicums from a jar, roughly
    chopped
3 tablespoons tomato sauce
2 tablespoons extra-virgin olive oil
1 tablespoon red wine vinegar
½ teaspoon garlic granules
¼ teaspoon sea salt
¼ teaspoon freshly ground black pepper

Toast the almonds in a frying pan over a medium heat for
3 to 5 minutes, stirring occasionally, until golden brown.
Transfer the almonds to a food processor. Remove the
stalks from the chillies, make a slit down the side of
each one with scissors and remove the veins and seeds.
Flatten the chillies and place them in the pan over a
medium heat. Use a spatula to hold the chillies flat for
5 seconds, then turn them over and repeat for another
5 seconds. Transfer the chillies to a bowl and allow the
chillies to soak in hot water for 15 minutes. Remove the
chillies, squeeze out the excess water and then roughly
chop. (You should have about 4 tablespoons.) Place
the chillies and the remaining ingredients in the food
processor with the almonds. Process to create a
coarse purée.

MORE SAUCES

CREAMY HORSERADISH SAUCE

MAKES: ABOUT 250 ML (8 FL OZ/1 CUP)

175 ml (6 fl oz) sour cream
2 tablespoons prepared horseradish
2 tablespoons finely chopped flat-leaf parsley
2 teaspoons dijon mustard
2 teaspoons worcestershire sauce
½ teaspoon sea salt
¼ teaspoon freshly ground black pepper

Thoroughly mix the ingredients together in a bowl. Cover and refrigerate until about 30 minutes before serving.

CHIMICHURRI SAUCE

MAKES: ABOUT 350 ML (12 FL OZ)

4 large garlic cloves
50 g (2 oz) flat-leaf parsley
50 g (2 oz) coriander leaves
25 g (1 oz) basil leaves
175 ml (6 fl oz) extra-virgin olive oil
4 tablespoons rice vinegar
1 teaspoon sea salt
½ teaspoon freshly ground black pepper
½ teaspoon hot sauce, or to taste

Very finely chop the garlic in a food processor with the motor running. Add the parsley, coriander and basil and pulse to finely chop the herbs. With the motor still running, slowly add the oil in a thin stream and then add the remaining ingredients.

ROMESCO SAUCE

MAKES: ABOUT 175 ML (6 FL OZ)

2 red capsicums
1 garlic clove
25 g (1 oz) whole almonds, toasted
25 g (1 oz) flat-leaf parsley
2 teaspoons sherry wine vinegar
½ teaspoon sea salt
⅛ teaspoon ground cayenne pepper
4 tablespoons extra-virgin olive oil

Grill the capsicums over **direct medium heat** (180° to 230°C/350° to 450°F) for 12 to 15 minutes, with the lid closed as much as possible but turning occasionally, until they are blackened and blistered all over. Place the capsicums in a small bowl, cover with plastic wrap and set aside for about 10 minutes, then remove and discard the skins, stalks and seeds. Finely chop the garlic in a food processor. Add the almonds and process until finely chopped. Add the capsicums, parsley, vinegar, salt and cayenne and process to create a coarse paste. With the motor running, slowly add the oil and process until you have a fairly smooth sauce.

GARLIC AND RED CAPSICUM SAUCE

MAKES: ABOUT 150 ML (5 FL OZ)

1 large red capsicum
4 tablespoons mayonnaise
2½ tablespoons sour cream
1 tablespoon finely chopped basil
2 teaspoons very finely chopped garlic
2 teaspoons balsamic vinegar
¼ teaspoon sea salt

Barbecue the capsicums over **direct medium heat** (180° to 230°C/350° to 450°F) for 12 to 15 minutes, with the lid closed as much as possible but turning occasionally, until they are blackened and blistered all over. Place the capsicums in a small bowl and cover with plastic wrap to trap the steam. Set aside for at least 10 minutes, then remove the capsicum from the bowl and peel away the charred skin. Cut off the top, remove the seeds and roughly chop the capsicum. Place the capsicum in a food processor along with the remaining ingredients and process until smooth. Cover and refrigerate until about 20 minutes before serving.

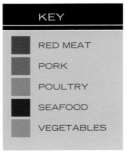

KEY	
	RED MEAT
	PORK
	POULTRY
	SEAFOOD
	VEGETABLES

COOL GREEN CHILLI SAUCE

MAKES: ABOUT 350 ML (12 FL OZ)

3 long anaheim chillies or other mild chillies
3 spring onions, root ends discarded, all the rest
    roughly chopped
15 g (½ oz) coriander leaves and tender stalks
1 small garlic clove
125 g (4 oz) sour cream
125 g (4 oz) mayonnaise
Finely grated rind and juice of 1 lime
¼ teaspoon sea salt

Barbecue the chillies over **direct high heat** (230° to 290°C/ 450° to 550°F) for 3 to 5 minutes, with the lid open and turning occasionally, until they are blackened and blistered in spots all over. Remove the chillies from the barbecue. When cool enough to handle, remove and discard the stalk ends. Use a sharp knife to scrape off and discard nearly all the blackened skins. Roughly chop the remaining parts of the chillies and drop them into a food processor or blender. Add the spring onions, coriander and garlic and process to make a coarse paste, scraping down the side once or twice. Add the remaining ingredients and process for 1 to 2 minutes to create a smooth sauce. If it seems too thick, add a little water. Adjust the seasonings. Cover and refrigerate until about 30 minutes before serving.

TOMATILLO SALSA

MAKES: ABOUT 500 ML (17 FL OZ)

1 brown onion, cut into 1-cm (½-inch) slices
Extra-virgin olive oil
10 tomatillos, husked and rinsed, about 250 g
    (8 oz) total
1 small jalapeño chilli, stalk removed
15 g (½ oz) coriander leaves and tender stalks
1 garlic clove
½ teaspoon dark brown sugar
½ teaspoon sea salt

Lightly brush the onion slices on both sides with oil. Brush the cooking grill clean. Barbecue the onion slices, tomatillos and jalapeño over **direct high heat** (230° to 290°C/450° to 550°F) for 6 to 8 minutes, with the lid closed as much as possible but turning once or twice and swapping their positions as needed for even cooking, until lightly charred. Be sure the tomatillos are completely soft as you remove them from the barbecue. Combine the onion slices, tomatillos and jalapeño in a food processor, along with the remaining ingredients, and process until fairly smooth. Taste and adjust the seasonings.

RÉMOULADE

MAKES: ABOUT 175 ML (6 FL OZ)

125 g (4 oz) mayonnaise
1 tablespoon capers, drained and very finely chopped
1 tablespoon sweet pickle relish
1 tablespoon finely chopped tarragon
2 teaspoons very finely chopped shallot
1 teaspoon tarragon vinegar
1 teaspoon very finely chopped garlic
½ teaspoon dijon mustard
¼ teaspoon paprika
⅛ teaspoon sea salt

Whisk the ingredients together in a bowl. If not using right away, cover and refrigerate for as long as 24 hours.

BALINESE PEANUT SAUCE

MAKES: ABOUT 300 ML (10½ FL OZ)

175 g (6 oz) smooth peanut butter
125 ml (4 fl oz/½ cup) stirred coconut milk
2 tablespoons fresh lime juice
2 teaspoons garlic-chilli sauce, such as sriracha
2 teaspoons fish sauce

Combine the ingredients in a small saucepan over a very low heat and cook for 3 to 5 minutes, whisking occasionally, but do not let the sauce simmer, until the sauce is very smooth. If the sauce seems too thick, whisk in 1 to 2 tablespoons of water.

TOMATO SALSA

MAKES: ABOUT 500 ML (17 FL OZ)

275 g (9 oz) ripe tomatoes, finely diced
65 g (2½ lb) white onion, finely diced and rinsed in a sieve
    under cold water
2 tablespoons finely chopped coriander
1 tablespoon extra-virgin olive oil
2 teaspoons fresh lime juice
1 teaspoon very finely chopped jalapeño chilli (with seeds)
¼ teaspoon dried oregano
¼ teaspoon sea salt
¼ teaspoon freshly ground black pepper

Mix the ingredients together in a bowl. Allow the salsa to stand at room temperature for about 1 hour. Drain in a sieve just before serving.

RED MEAT

WHAT YOU NEED TO KNOW

TASTE AND TENDERNESS ARE TRADE-OFFS

When you pay more for steak, usually you are paying for tenderness. That's why a fillet steak is more expensive than a flank steak, even though the flank steak has more flavour. The pricey and tender steaks, like the porterhouse, the T-bone, the fillet and the sirloin, come from the loin area of a cow, which gets very little exercise while the cow lumbers around. Other steaks, like the flank and the rump, come from parts of the cow that get more of a workout.

FEED MATTERS

It's natural for cows to eat grass. But feeding them grass their whole lives is expensive. It requires moving the animals from pasture to pasture as the seasons change. It's cheaper to herd them in one place and feed them a grain-based diet, which fattens them up faster than grass too, and makes them more tender. Grass-fed cattle are usually leaner and free of the added hormones and antibiotics that grain-fed animals often receive, but the meat is a little tougher and stronger in flavour.

BE A SMART SHOPPER

Whether you shop at a butcher's or a supermarket, it is up to you to know what to look for when buying meat. Be selective and choose the cuts with a coarse marbling or milky white fat. The flesh should be a rich pink or light cherry colour. If you see any with a deep red or brown colour, it could mean those steaks came from older, tougher animals. And the surface should be moist, but not wet or sticky. When you get your purchase home, immediately refrigerate at the bottom of the refrigerator, where there isn't any chance of it cross-contaminating cooked or ready-to-eat foods.

BROWN IS BETTER

Whichever cut of meat you choose, and whatever its quality might be, you'll get the most flavour from it when the surface is cooked to a deep brown colour. When sugars and proteins in the meat are heated by the barbecue, they produce literally hundreds of flavours and aromas. That's why so many recipes in this book involve searing over direct heat. A lot of people will tell you that searing seals in moisture, but that theory has been debunked. Instead, searing develops a layer of incredible flavour and also some nice texture.

Wet meat doesn't sear, it steams, so be sure to pat the surface dry with paper towel before cooking. Salt can also affect searing. I recommend waiting to salt red meat until 20 to 30 minutes before cooking, because, over a longer period of time, salt pulls blood and juices from inside the meat, making the surface wet. Salt does, however, need to go on before cooking. Salt added afterwards doesn't penetrate very well.

CUTS OF STEAK

RIB-EYE / SCOTCH FILLET
A rib-eye steak's abundant internal fat melting into the meat creates one the juiciest steak-eating experiences imaginable. Do yourself a favour: before barbecueing, trim the fat around the perimeter to about 5 mm (¼ inch). That will reduce the chance of flare-ups.

PORTERHOUSE / SIRLOIN
Also known in America as a New York strip, a Kansas City strip, a strip loin, a top loin, a shell steak, a club steak, an ambassador steak…it all depends on where you are and who's talking. Regardless of the name, sirloin's a relatively lean cut with a firmer texture than a rib-eye or fillet, but the flavour is great.

FILLET
Pricey and velvety soft, fillets make a nice splurge for special guests, though it's really the tenderness you are buying. The flavour can be a little underwhelming unless you lightly char the outside with a blazing hot barbecue.

T-BONE
This is the classic American steakhouse steak that features both a sirloin steak and a fillet, separated by a bone. Start these steaks over high heat and finish them on a cooler section of the barbecue so you don't blacken the bone or the meat beside it.

RUMP
These flat, firmly grained steaks bring kebabs quickly to mind because it's so easy to cut them into solid cubes. Pick out the rump steaks with visible marbling and don't take them beyond medium rare.

TRI-TIP
Not widely available, a tri-tip is taken from the sirloin area. It's not so much a steak as it is a skinny roast, but you can cook it like a thick steak. The meat is affordable and very flavourful. Just don't overcook it.

FLANK
You can quickly spot this steak by its flat oval shape and its long, clearly defined grain. It used to be the steak of choice for London broil. Now the flank steak stars in all kinds of barbecue recipes. Minimise the chewy effect of the grain by slicing across it.

SKIRT
Like the flank steak, the coarsely grained skirt steak is cut from the chest area of the animal, so chewiness is an issue. Even so, after barbecueing, it tends to be juicier and richer in flavour than flank steak, especially if you marinate it first.

OYSTER BLADE
Normally you would expect a steak cut from the shoulder to be tough, but the flatiron, a.k.a. a top blade steak, is nestled into a tender pocket of the shoulder area, so it's a surprisingly soft exception to the rule. In some cases you'll need to remove a thin vein of gristle running down the centre of a feather.

TYPES OF RED MEAT FOR THE BARBECUE

Tender cuts for barbecuing	Moderately tender cuts for barbecuing	Bigger cuts for searing and grill-roasting	Tougher cuts for barbecuing
Beef fillet (filet mignon steak) Beef rib steak/rib-eye steak Beef porterhouse steak Beef sirloin Beef T-bone steak Lamb loin chop Veal loin chop	Beef rump steak Beef flank steak Beef hanger steak Beef skirt steak Beef oyster blade steak Veal shoulder blade steak Lamb shoulder blade chop Lamb sirloin chop	Beef whole fillet Beef tri-tip roast Beef rib roast (prime rib) Rack of veal Rack of lamb Leg of lamb	Brisket Beef ribs

HOW TO FREEZE STEAKS

Cutting steaks from a big piece of meat like a porterhouse or a boneless rib roast allows you to make steaks just the right thickness. Barbecue some of the steaks now and freeze the remaining ones for another day. Here's how: the key to freezing a steak properly is to prevent air from touching the surface of the meat. Wrap each steak individually with plastic wrap, not butcher paper or aluminium foil, and seal it as tightly as possible. Place the wrapped steaks in a resealable freezer bag and set the freezer as close to -18°C (0°F) as it will go. The colder, the better. Steaks packaged this way will keep very well for about three months. Label them so that you don't forget when to cook them!

WHEN IS IT DONE?

Recognising the moment when a big piece of red meat has reached the degree of doneness you want is actually quite simple. Stick the probe of an instant-read thermometer into the thickest part of the meat. When the internal temperature is 5 to 10 degrees below what you ultimately want to eat, take the meat off the barbecue. That's because larger pieces of meat retain quite a bit of heat as they 'rest' at room temperature and they continue to cook.

The Food Standards Agency (FSA) approves eating rare steaks and other whole cuts of beef (and lamb), as long as the outsides have been properly sealed. For other beef products, such as burgers, kebabs, sausages and pork, however, the FSA recommends they should be cooked all the way through with an internal temperature of 70°C (160°F) for more than 2 minutes at their thickest part. Rolled joints made from several pieces of any meat, however, should also not be eaten rare, according the FSA guidelines. Most chefs today tend to cook their meats to a lower internal temperature. The chart below gives you some indication of what professional cooks consider the optimum internal temperatures. Ultimately, it is up to you what degree of doneness you choose.

Checking for the doneness of steaks and chops is a little more difficult with an instant-read thermometer because you need to position the sensing 'dimple' of the probe right in the centre of the meat. It's easy to miss the centre and get an inaccurate reading, so I recommend learning to use the 'touch test.' Most raw steaks are as soft as the fleshiest part of your thumb when your hand is relaxed. As they cook, the steaks get firmer and firmer. If you press your index finger and thumb together and press the fleshiest part of your thumb again, the firmness is very close to that of a rare steak. If you press your middle finger and thumb together, the firmness on your thumb is very close to that of a medium-rare steak.

If you are still not sure of the doneness, take the steak off the barbecue and put the best-looking side (presentation side) facing down on a chopping board. With the tip of a sharp knife, make a little cut in the middle so you can see the colour of the meat inside. If the colour is still too red, put it back on the barbecue. Otherwise, get the rest of the meat off the barbecue.

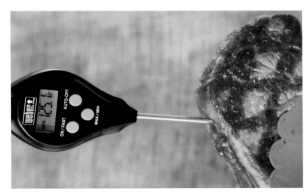

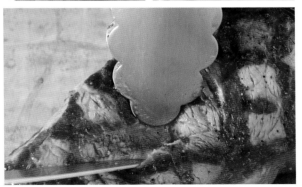

DONENESS	CHEF STANDARDS
Rare	49° to 52°C (120° to 125°F)
Medium rare	52° to 57°C (125° to 135°F)
Medium	57° to 63°C (135° to 145°F)
Medium well	63° to 68°C (145° to 155°F)
Well done	68°C (155°F) +

BEEF BARBECUING GUIDE

The following cuts, thicknesses, weights and cooking times are meant to be guidelines rather than hard and fast rules. Cooking times are affected by such factors as altitude, wind, outside temperature and desired doneness. Two rules of thumb: cook steaks and kebabs using the direct method for the time given on the chart or to your desired doneness, turning once. Barbecue joints and thicker cuts using the indirect method for the time given on the chart, or until an instant-read thermometer reaches the desired internal temperature. Let joints, larger cuts of meat and thick steaks rest for 5 to 10 minutes before carving. The internal temperature of the meat will rise during this time.

BEEF	THICKNESS/ WEIGHT	APPROXIMATE TIME
Steak: sirloin, porterhouse, scotch fillet, rib-eye, T-bone and fillet	1.5 cm (¾ inch) thick	4 to 6 minutes direct high heat
	2.5 cm (1 inch) thick	5 to 8 minutes: sear 4 to 6 minutes direct high heat, grill 1 to 2 minutes indirect high heat
	3 cm (1¼ inches) thick	8 to 10 minutes: sear 6 minutes direct high heat, grill 2 to 4 minutes indirect high heat
	3.5 cm (1½ inches) thick	10 to 14 minutes: sear 6 to 8 minutes direct high heat, grill 4 to 6 minutes indirect high heat
	5 cm (2 inches) thick	14 to 18 minutes: sear 6 to 8 minutes direct high heat, grill 8 to 10 minutes indirect high heat
Skirt steak	5 mm to 1 cm (¼ to ½ inch) thick	4 to 6 minutes direct high heat
Flank steak	750 g to 1 kg (1½ to 2 pounds), 1. 5 cm (¾ inch) thick	8 to 10 minutes direct high heat
Kebab	2.5 to 3.5 cm (1 to 1½ inch) cubes	4 to 6 minutes direct high heat
Fillet, whole	1.75 to 2 kg (3½ to 4 lb)	35 to 45 minutes: sear 15 minutes direct medium heat, grill 20 to 30 minutes indirect medium heat
Minced (ground) beef burger	1.5 cm (¾ inch) thick	8 to 10 minutes direct high heat
Rib roast (prime rib), boneless	2.5 to 3 kg (5 to 6 lb)	1¼ to 1¾ hours indirect medium heat
Rib roast (prime rib), with bone	4 kg (8 lb)	2½ to 3 hours: sear 10 minutes direct medium heat, grill 2⅓ to 3 hours indirect low heat
Strip loin roast, boneless	2 to 2.5 kg (4 to 5 lb)	50 to 60 minutes: sear 10 minutes direct medium heat, grill 40 to 50 minutes indirect medium heat
Tri-tip roast	900 g to 1.25 kg (2 to 2½ lb)	30 to 40 minutes: sear 10 minutes direct medium heat, grill 20 to 30 minutes indirect medium heat
Veal loin chop	2. cm (1 inch) thick	5 to 8 minutes: sear 4 to 6 minutes direct high heat, grill 1 to 2 minutes indirect high heat

Note: All cooking times are for medium-rare doneness, except minced (ground) beef (medium)

LAMB: THE OTHER RED MEAT

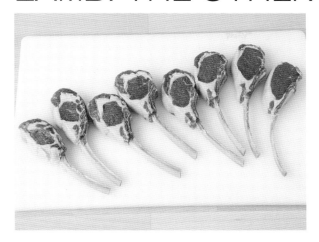

When buying lamb, look for meat that is light red (not too dark) and finely grained (not coarse). The fat should be white (not yellow). Lamb chops cut from the rack are quite flavourful and tender. Be sure to trim the fat close to the meat so you don't face flare-ups. The lamb loin also produces very nice chops, with a little bone in the middle of each one, just like a miniature T-bone steak. Even chops from the sirloin and shoulder areas are tender enough for barbecuing, because the animals are almost always younger than one-year-old when they are brought to market. A leg of lamb opens up lots of possibilities, too, including grill-roasting it over indirect heat or cutting the meat into cubes for kebabs.

LAMB BARBECUING GUIDE

The following cuts, thicknesses, weights and cooking times are meant to be guidelines rather than hard and fast rules. Cooking times are affected by such factors as altitude, wind, outside temperature and desired doneness. Two rules of thumb: cook chops using the direct method for the time given on the chart or to your desired doneness, turning once.

Barbecue joints and thicker cuts using the indirect method for the time given on the chart, or until an instant-read thermometer reaches the desired internal temperature. Let joints, larger cuts of meat and thick chops rest for 5 to 10 minutes before carving. The internal temperature of the meat will rise during this time.

LAMB	THICKNESS/ WEIGHT	APPROXIMATE TIME
Chop: loin, rib or shoulder	1.5 to 3 cm (¾ to 1½ inches) thick	8 to 12 minutes direct medium heat
Leg of lamb, boneless, rolled	1.25 to 1.5 kg (2½ to 3 lb)	30 to 45 minutes: sear 10 to 15 minutes direct medium heat, grill 20 to 30 minutes indirect medium heat
Leg of lamb, butterflied	1.5 to 1.75 kg (3 to 3½ lb)	30 to 45 minutes: sear 10 to 15 minutes direct medium heat, grill 20 to 30 minutes indirect medium heat
Rib crown roast	1.5 to 2 kg (3 to 4 lb)	1 to 1¼ hours indirect medium heat
Minced (ground) lamb burger	1.5 cm (¾ inch) thick	8 to 10 minutes direct medium heat
Rack of lamb	500 to 750 g (1 to 1½ lb)	15 to 20 minutes: sear 5 minutes direct medium heat, grill 10 to 15 minutes indirect medium heat

Note: All cooking times are for medium-rare doneness, except minced (ground) lamb (medium).

PORK

PORK BARBECUING GUIDE

The following cuts, thicknesses, weights and cooking times are meant to be guidelines rather than hard and fast rules. Cooking times are affected by such factors as altitude, wind, outside temperature and desired doneness. Two rules of thumb: cook chops and bratwursts using the direct method for the time given on the chart or to your desired doneness, turning once. Barbecue joints and thicker cuts using the indirect method for the time given on the chart, or until an instant-read thermometer reaches the desired internal temperature. Let joints, larger cuts of meat and thick chops rest for 5 to 10 minutes before carving. The internal temperature of the meat will rise during this time.

PORK	THICKNESS/ WEIGHT	APPROXIMATE TIME
Bratwurst, fresh		20 to 25 minutes direct medium heat
Bratwurst, pre-cooked		10 to 12 minutes direct medium heat
Pork chop, boneless or bone-in	1 cm (½ inch) thick	5 to 7 minutes direct high heat
	1.5 cm (¾ inch) thick	6 to 8 minutes direct high heat
	2.5 cm (1 inch) thick	8 to 10 minutes direct medium heat
	3 to 3.5 cm (1¼ to 1½ inches) thick	10 to 12 minutes: sear 6 minutes direct high heat, grill 4 to 6 minutes indirect high heat
Fillet	500 g (1 lb)	15 to 20 minutes direct medium heat
Loin roast, boneless	1.25 kg (2½ lb)	40 to 50 minutes direct medium heat
Loin roast, bone-in	1.5 to 2.5 kg (3 to 5 lb)	1¼ to 1¾ hours indirect medium heat
Pork shoulder, boneless	2.5 to 3 kg (5 to 6 lb)	5 to 7 hours indirect low heat
Minced (ground) pork burger	1 cm (½ inch) thick	8 to 10 minutes direct medium heat
Ribs, baby back	750 g to 1 kg (1½ to 2 lb)	3 to 4 hours indirect low heat
Ribs, spareribs	1.25 to 1.75 kg (2½ to 3½ lb)	3 to 4 hours indirect low heat
Loin ribs, country-style, boneless	750 g to 1 kg (1½ to 2 lb)	12 to 15 minutes direct medium heat
Loin ribs, country-style, bone-in	1.5 to 2 kg (3 to 4 lb)	1½ to 2 hours indirect medium heat

WHEN IS IT DONE?

The Food Standards Agency recommends that pork should be cooked to an internal temperature of 70°C (160°F), but most chefs today cook it to 65° to 67°C (150° to 160°F), when it still has some pink in the centre and all the juices haven't been driven out. Of course, the doneness you choose is entirely up to you.

The pork chop on the left, with raw meat in the centre, is clearly undercooked. The chop on the right, with a dry, grey appearance, is overcooked. The chop in the middle, with a little bit of pink in the centre, is cooked to 65°C (150°F), which is just right in my opinion. See how the meat gives a little under pressure.

BABY BACK RIBS VERSUS SPARERIBS

Despite the big differences in the size of baby back ribs and spareribs, they are really just two pieces of the same slab of meat. Baby back ribs (bottom of photo) are cut from the top of the ribcage, near the backbone. Spareribs (top of photo) are cut from the bottom of the ribcage, and sometimes they include the brisket, which is a bony piece of meat that hangs from the bottom. The further down the ribcage you go, the meatier the ribs get. That is essentially why spareribs take longer to cook.

WHAT IS A SHINER?

A shiner is an exposed bone on a rack of ribs. It is what unfortunately happens when a butcher cuts too close to the bone. Ribs should be meaty all over, so if you see a rack with shiners at the market, look for something better. Also avoid all ribs with dry edges or yellowish fat. And know that fresh ribs will almost always yield better results than previously frozen ribs.

TYPES OF PORK FOR THE BARBECUE

Tender cuts for barbecuing	Moderately tender cuts for barbecuing	Bigger cuts for searing and grill-roasting	Tougher cuts for barbecuing
Rib chop Loin chop Centre-cut chop Fillet (whole or in medallions)	Sirloin chop Shoulder blade steak Ham steak	Rack of pork Centre rib roast Centre loin roast Cured ham Country-style ribs	Baby back ribs Spareribs Shoulder

POULTRY

WHAT TO LOOK FOR IN CHICKEN

Chicken is chicken, right? Not exactly. Most supermarkets carry big national brands, or sometimes supermarkets put their own brands on these mass-produced birds raised in cages. They are low in fat, they cook quickly and they are pretty tender, however their flavour is pretty darn bland. Fortunately, the barbecue provides just what they need. With a little oil, some seasonings and maybe a sauce, they are very good on the barbecue.

Today we are seeing more and more premium chickens available, and usually they are worth their higher price, though not always. Typically, these chickens are from old-fashioned breeds known more for their flavour than their plump breasts and perfectly even shape. Often called 'free-range' chickens, they have access to the outdoors, or at least the freedom to wander indoors. The exercise contributes to firmer, more flavourful meat. Check them out. Any chickens you buy should have skins that fit their bodies well, not spotty or shrivelled or too far overlapping. The colour of the skin says little

about quality, but the smell of a chicken will tell you everything you need to know about freshness. If it smells funny, don't buy it.

How chickens are processed can also affect the quality. Some producers submerge their chickens in chlorinated iced water, which works quickly, but often the process means that the chickens absorb some water to chill them. Another process involves spraying the chickens with chlorinated water and then sending them though long tunnels filled with cold air. The air-chilled chickens absorb less water, which is good. Who wants to pay extra for iced water?

Some chickens, even when they have been properly chilled, carry upsetting bacteria like salmonella. There is no sense in rinsing raw chickens prior to cooking. That would only raise the chances of spreading bacteria around your kitchen. Simply cook your chickens properly and all the dangerous bacteria will be killed.

WHEN IS IT DONE?

The Food Standards Agency recommends cooking poultry until the internal temperature reaches 70°C (160°F), however my recipes give you an internal temperature of 74°C (165°F) with tender, succulent results. Keep in mind that in whole birds the internal temperature will rise 5 to 10 degrees during resting.

Check the thigh meat by inserting the probe of a thermometer into the thickest part (but not touching the bone). If you don't have a thermometer, cut into the centre of the meat. The juices should run clear and the meat should no longer be pink at the bone.

POULTRY BARBECUING GUIDE

The following cuts, weights and cooking times are meant to be guidelines rather than hard and fast rules. Cooking times are affected by such factors as altitude, wind and outside temperature. Two rules of thumb: cook boneless poultry pieces using the direct method for the time given on the chart, turning once. Barbecue whole poultry and bone-in poultry pieces using the indirect method for the time given on the chart or until an instant-read thermometer reaches the desired doneness. Cooking times are for an internal temperature of 74°C (165°F). Let whole poultry rest for 5 to 10 minutes before carving. The internal temperature of the meat will rise by 5 to 10 degrees during this time.

POULTRY	WEIGHT	APPROXIMATE TIME
Chicken breast, boneless, skinless	175 to 250 g (6 to 8 oz)	8 to 12 minutes direct medium heat
Chicken thigh, boneless, skinless	125 g (4 oz)	8 to 10 minutes direct high heat
Chicken breast, bone-in	300 to 375 g (10 to 13 oz)	30 to 40 minutes indirect medium heat
Chicken pieces, bone-in leg/thigh		30 to 40 minutes indirect medium heat
Chicken wing	50 to 75 g (2 to 3 oz)	18 to 20 minutes direct medium heat
Chicken, whole	1.75 to 2.2 kg (3½ to 4½ lb)	1 to 1½ hours indirect medium heat
Turkey breast, boneless	1.25 kg (2 lb 12 oz)	1 to 1¼ hours indirect medium heat
Turkey, whole, unstuffed	5 to 6 kg (10 to 12 lb)	2½ to 3½ hours indirect low heat
	6.5 to 7.5 kg (13 to 15 lb)	3½ to 4½ hours indirect low heat
Duck breast, boneless	300 to 350 g (10 to 12 oz)	9 to 12 minutes: grill 3 to 4 minutes direct low heat, grill 6 to 8 minutes indirect high heat
Duck, whole	2.5 to 3 kg (5½ to 6 lb)	40 minutes indirect high heat

SEAFOOD

TIPS TO PREVENT STICKING

CLEAN COOKING GRILLS
Use a stainless-steel bristle brush to get the grates really clean.

A LITTLE OIL
Coat the fish on all sides with a thin layer of oil, but don't grease the grills.

HIGH HEAT
Fish comes off the grate after a delicate crust of caramelisation develops between the flesh and grate. That requires heat, usually high heat.

A LOT OF PATIENCE
Leave the fish alone. Caramelisation happens faster when the fish stays in place on the hot grate. Keep the lid down as much as possible and turn the fish only once.

GOOD TIMING
The first side down on the grills will be the side that eventually faces you on the plate. Cook it a few minutes longer than the second side and it will release more easily and look fabulous on the plate, with picture-perfect grill marks.

HOW TO REMOVE FISH FROM THE COOKING GRILLS
If the fillets have skin attached, cook the skin side last. When each fillet is ready to serve, slide a spatula between the skin and flesh and then lift each fillet, leaving the skin behind.

 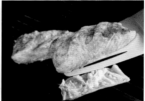

WHAT TO LOOK FOR IN FISH

The first thing to know is that firm fish and seafood are easiest to barbecue. The meatier they are, the better they hold together as they cook and as you turn them over. Many tender fish work nicely, too. Though they require a little more care. The chart below features many of your widely available choices. Feel free to substitute within the categories. If you find two fish with similar sizes and textures, just replace one for the other.

TYPES OF FISH FOR THE BARBECUE

Firm fillets and steaks	Medium-firm fillets and steaks	Tender fillets	Whole fish	Shellfish
Swordfish	Monkfish	Bream	Red snapper	Prawns
Tuna	Halibut	Whiting	Sea bass	Scallops
Salmon	Mahi-mahi	Trout	Grouper	Lobster
Grouper	Mackerel		Bluefish	Oysters
Squid	Sea bass		Mackerel	Mussels
Flathead	Red snapper		Trout	Clams
	Perch		Bream	
	Barramundi		Flathead	
			Whiting	

WHEN IS IT DONE?

Overcooking fish is a crime. With almost every kind of fish, you should get it off the barbecue before it flakes by itself. You are looking for an internal temperature of 52° to 55°C (125° to 130°F), but that's tough to measure with fillets or steaks, so rely on the internal appearance (the whitish colour of the fish should be opaque all the way to the centre), as well as the times given in the recipes and in the chart below.

SEAFOOD BARBECUING GUIDE

The following types, thicknesses, weights, and cooking times are meant to be guidelines rather than hard and fast rules. Cooking times are affected by such factors as altitude, wind, outside temperature and desired doneness. The general rule of thumb for barbecuing fish: 4 to 5 minutes per 1 cm (½ inch) thickness; 8 to 10 minutes per 2.5 cm (1 inch) thickness.

FISH	THICKNESS/ WEIGHT	APPROXIMATE TIME
Fish, fillet or steak Includes halibut, red snapper, salmon, sea bass, swordfish and tuna	5 mm to 1 cm (¼ to ½ inch) thick	3 to 5 minutes direct high heat
	1 to 2.5 cm (½ to 1 inch) thick	5 to 10 minutes direct high heat
	2.5 to 3 cm (1 to 1¼ inches) thick	10 to 12 minutes direct high heat
Fish, whole	500 g (1 lb)	15 to 20 minutes indirect medium heat
	1 to 1.2 kg (2 to 2½ lb)	20 to 30 minutes indirect medium heat
	1.5 kg (3 lb)	30 to 45 minutes indirect medium heat
Prawn	40 g (1½ oz)	2 to 4 minutes direct high heat
Scallop	40 g (1½ oz)	4 to 6 minutes direct high heat
Mussel (discard any that do not open)		5 to 6 minutes direct high heat
Clam (discard any that do not open)		6 to 8 minutes direct high heat
Oyster		2 to 4 minutes direct high heat
Lobster tail		7 to 11 minutes direct medium heat

VEGETABLES

COOK WHAT'S GROWING AT THE TIME
Vegetables in season locally have big advantages over whatever has been shipped from across the world. They are riper, so they taste better. That means you can cook them simply with great results.

EXPOSE AS MUCH SURFACE AREA AS POSSIBLE
Cut each vegetable to give you the biggest area to put in direct contact with the cooking grills. The more direct contact, the better the flavours will be. For example, choose capsicums with flat sides that you can easily slice off the core. The flatter the sides, the more surface area will caramelise on the hot cooking grills.

USE THE GOOD OIL
Vegetables need oil to prevent sticking and burning. Neutral oils like canola oil will do the job fine, but an extra-virgin olive oil provides the added benefit of improving the flavour of virtually every vegetable. Brush on just enough to coat each side thoroughly but not so much that the vegetables would drip oil and cause flare-ups. Season the vegetables generously with salt and pepper (some of it will fall off). For more flavours, marinate the vegetables at room temperature for 20 minutes to an hour in olive oil, vinegar, garlic, herbs and spices.

WHEN IS IT DONE?

I like firm vegetables, such as onions and fennel, to be somewhere between crisp and tender. If you want them softer, cook them a few minutes longer, although watch them carefully for burning. The barbecue intensifies the sweetness of vegetables quickly and that can lead to burning. Cut the vegetables as evenly as you can. A 1 cm (½ inch) thickness is right for most of them.

VEGETABLE BARBECUING GUIDE

Just about everything from artichokes to tomatoes tends to cook best over direct medium heat. The temperature should be somewhere between 180° and 230°C (350° and 450°F). If any parts get a little too dark, turn the vegetables over. Otherwise turn them as few times as possible.

VEGETABLES	THICKNESS/SIZE	APPROXIMATE TIME
Artichoke (300 to 375 g/10 to 13 oz)	whole	14 to 18 minutes: boil 10 to 12 minutes; cut in half and grill 4 to 6 minutes direct medium heat
Asparagus	1-cm (½-inch) diameter	4 to 6 minutes direct medium heat
Beetroot (175 g/6 oz)		1 to 1½ hours indirect medium heat
Butternut pumpkin (750 g/1½ lb)	halved	40 to 60 minutes indirect medium heat
Capsicum	whole	10 to 15 minutes direct medium heat
Carrot	2.5 cm (1-inch) diameter	7 to 11 minutes: boil 4 to 6 minutes, grill 3 to 5 minutes direct high heat
Chilli, sweet	5-mm (¼-inch) slices	6 to 8 minutes direct medium heat
Eggplant	1-cm (½-inch) slices	8 to 10 minutes direct medium heat
Fennel	5-mm (¼-inch) slices	10 to 12 minutes direct medium heat
Garlic	whole	45 to 60 minutes indirect medium heat
Mushroom, portabello		10 to 15 minutes direct medium heat
Mushroom, shiitake or button		8 to 10 minutes direct medium heat
Onion	halved	35 to 40 minutes indirect medium heat
	1-cm (½-inch) slices	8 to 12 minutes direct medium heat
Potato	whole	45 to 60 minutes indirect medium heat
	1-cm (½-inch) slices	14 to 16 minutes direct medium heat
Potato, new	halved	15 to 20 minutes direct medium heat
Spring onion	whole	3 to 4 minutes direct medium heat
Sweet corn, husked		10 to 15 minutes direct medium heat
Sweet corn, in husk		25 to 30 minutes direct medium heat
Sweet potato	whole	50 to 60 minutes indirect medium heat
	5-mm (¼-inch) slices	8 to 10 minutes direct medium heat
Tomato, garden or roma	halved	6 to 8 minutes direct medium heat
	whole	8 to 10 minutes direct medium heat
Zucchini	1-cm (½-inch) slices	3 to 5 minutes direct medium heat
	halved	4 to 6 minutes direct medium heat

FRUIT

Barbecuing fruit is much like barbecuing vegetables. Select fruit that's ripe (or almost ripe) and firm, because it will soften on the barbecue. Also, because of its texture, it's a good idea to watch fruit carefully while barbecuing and to turn it occasionally. The sweet succulence of most fruits turns golden brown and delicious on the barbecue, but if left too long in one place, golden brown can turn to black and bitter. To check the colour and doneness, slide a thin spatula or spatula gently under the fruit and slightly lift.

Warm fruit off the barbecue needs only a scoop of ice cream or frozen yogurt to seal a meal with style. Or use the barbecued fruit to accompany a shortbread biscuit, a wedge of gingerbread or a slice of Madeira

cake. Fruit served like this shows all your guests that you've developed the techniques to barbecue almost anything, from starters to desserts.

FRUIT BARBECUING GUIDE

The following types, thicknesses and cooking times are meant to be guidelines rather than hard and fast rules. Cooking times are affected by such factors as altitude, wind and outside temperature. Barbecuing times for fruit will depend on the ripeness of the fruit.

FRUIT	THICKNESS/SIZE	APPROXIMATE TIME
Apple	whole	35 to 40 minutes indirect medium heat
	1-cm (½-inch) slices	4 to 6 minutes direct medium heat
Apricot	halved, stone removed	6 to 8 minutes direct medium heat
Banana	halved lengthways	6 to 8 minutes direct medium heat
Nectarine	halved lengthways, stone removed	8 to 10 minutes direct medium heat
Peach	halved lengthways, stone removed	8 to 10 minutes direct medium heat
Pear	halved lengthways	10 to 12 minutes direct medium heat
Pineapple	peeled and cored, 1-cm (½-inch)	5 to 10 minutes direct medium heat
Strawberry		4 to 5 minutes direct medium heat

BARBECUE MAINTENANCE

A little TLC is all it takes to ensure that you get years of use from your barbecue. Maintenance is the key (consult the owner's manual that came with your barbecue). Each time you use the barbecue, remember to clean the cooking grills. With the barbecue on high (either right before cooking or right after), brush the cooking grills with a long-handled, stainless-steel brush. Be sure to get in between the grills with your brush, too.

MONTHLY MAINTENANCE PLAN FOR GAS BARBECUES

1. When your barbecue is warm, but not hot, use a wet, soapy sponge or cloth to wipe the inside of the lid. This will help keep natural carbon build-up from accumulating inside the lid.

2. Remove the grills and brush the metal bars that shield the burners. A good brush, like the one you use to brush the cooking grills, will work well. This will help to eliminate flare-ups. (If you barbecue often, like I do, you may need to do this a little more frequently than once a month.)

3. Gently clean the burner tubes with a steel brush. Brush side-to-side along the burner tubes and take care not to damage the openings themselves by brushing too hard.

4. Use a plastic putty knife or spatula to scrape the grease from the bottom of the barbecue. If your barbecue has a collection tray, scrape the bits into it, then dispose of the contents of the collection tray.

5. Wash the inside of the barbecue with warm, soapy water. Take care not to get water in the burner tubes.

6. Reassemble, wait a month, and repeat.

MONTHLY MAINTENANCE PLAN FOR CHARCOAL BARBECUES

1. When the barbecue is cold, remove the ash from the bowl. Because the ash naturally contains a small amount of moisture, it is important to get the ash out of the bowl each time you use it and before storing your barbecue. If your barbecue has an ash catcher, empty after each use.

2. Wipe the inside of the bowl with a warm, wet sponge. This will help to keep natural carbon build-up from accumulating inside your barbecue.

MONTHLY MAINTENANCE PLAN FOR ELECTRIC BARBECUES

1. When your barbecue is warm, but not hot, use a wet, soapy sponge or cloth to wipe the inside of the lid. This will help keep natural carbon build-up from accumulating inside the lid of the barbecue.

2. Remove the grills. Use a plastic putty knife or spatula to scrape the grease from the bottom of the barbecue. If your barbecue has a collection tray, scrape the bits into it, then dispose of the contents of the collection tray.

3. Wipe the inside of the barbecue with a warm, damp sponge, being very careful not to get the heating element wet.

SELECTING YOUR BARBECUE

One of the most valuable skills a good cook learns is the art of substitution. Tuna fillets, for instance, can substitute for mahi-mahi in a pinch, and a T-bone steak will work nicely in place of a porterhouse. When it comes to barbecues, however, there simply is no substitute for quality. After all, the one thing every meal you prepare from this book will have in common is your barbecue.

WHAT TO LOOK FOR IN A GAS BARBECUE

1. Check out the construction and durability. A barbecue is an important purchase and you will own it for years to come. Since most barbecues are kept outside and exposed to the elements, they need to be well made and durable. If you choose a stainless-steel barbecue, look for heavy-gauge construction that will ensure the barbecue will last more than a season or two. A porcelain-enamel finish will also hold up well. Carefully check out the corners to make sure there are no sharp edges. Size up the fit and finish. If a barbecue's doors or frame are misaligned, it may be a reflection of poor design.

2. Lift the lid and kick the tyres. The inner workings and construction of a barbecue are more important than how the barbecue looks on the outside. Lift the lid and see how the barbecue opens and closes. It should have a tight fit and the barbecue shouldn't feel wobbly when you open it. Look for heavy-duty cooking grills that will hold up to years of use.

3. Look at burner placement. Uneven heat is a barbecuer's worst nightmare. A well-designed gas barbecue will have burners placed evenly across the cooking box. Angled metal bars will cover the burners, directing drippings away from the flames and minimising flare-ups. These bars also serve to distribute the heat evenly across the entire cooking surface.

4. Give yourself room. The cooking grill needs to be big enough to handle the amount food you like to cook, and remember, many recipes call for both direct and indirect heat. Be sure you have the room to move your food from direct to indirect heat any time.

5. Don't be blinded by BTUs. It's a common belief that more is better when it comes to BTUs. Not necessarily so. BTU stands for British Thermal Unit. It's a measure of how much heat it takes to raise one pound of water by one degree Fahrenheit. A gas barbecue burning 35,000 BTUs per hour should reach a searing temperature of around 290°C (550°F), no problem. Unless your cooking area is large, you should be fine with a barbecue with a BTU rating of 35,000 to 40,000 BTUs. More than that and you may be wasting energy.

6. Don't overlook the basics. One of the most important things you should consider when buying a gas barbecue is where the grease and debris will go. Grease is combustible and if it is not channelled away from the inside of your barbecue it could lead to some serious flare-ups. A well-designed system should include a removable grease tray that is accessible from the front of the barbecue. The drip pan itself should be at least a couple of centimetres (inches) deep and should come with disposable liners to make clean-up easier.

7. Be critical of the bells and whistles. These days, many barbecues come with nice added features, such as a side burner or a rotisserie. These options can improve your barbecuing experience, if they are done well. Make sure the side burner has adequate power to do the job or it may be a waste of money. It should also have a hinged cover so that you don't lose valuable cooking space when the burner is not in use. An added benefit of a hinged cover is that it can act as a windshield, improving the burner's performance. If you are buying a barbecue with a rotisserie, check out the motor. A wimpy motor will lead to wimpy performance. You will need a heavy-duty motor to turn larger items like turkey and leg of lamb. And check out the heft of the spit. Again, it needs to be strong enough to hold larger items and should have strong forks to hold the meat in place. Finally, look at the position of the rotisserie. Is the motor or the spit over the side burner? If so, you'll limit your ability to use it when you are rotisserie cooking.

WHAT TO LOOK FOR IN A CHARCOAL BARBECUE

1. Go for one with a lid. Open barbecues, such as hibachis, are fun to use but the design limits your flexibility. Buying a barbecue with a lid broadens your options. When you buy a charcoal barbecue, make sure it has a well-fitting lid, with top and bottom vents for airflow. The lid effectively turns the barbecue into an outdoor oven capable of both direct and indirect cooking. The vents allow you to control the temperature inside.

2. Make sure it's built to last. A good charcoal barbecue should last for years. Look for solid construction and a durable porcelain-enamel finish over thick-gauge metal.

3. Look for great grills. Your charcoal barbecue should have thick, durable grates. Either heavy wire or stainless steel work well. For the serious barbecuer, I recommend a hinged cooking grill that allows you to add more coals while cooking. My favourite way to prepare the Thanksgiving turkey is on my charcoal barbecue, and a hinged cooking grill allows me to easily add coals each hour to maintain even heat.

4. Make sure clean-up is easy. Charcoal is going to produce ash, which can be a mess to clean-up. Therefore I recommend you choose a charcoal barbecue that is designed with a system to push ash from the bottom of your barbecue into a removable ash catcher. After all, the easier it is to clean your barbecue, the more you're going to use it.

SAFETY

GENERAL NOTES

1. Always read your owner's manual prior to use.

2. Barbecues radiate a lot of heat, so always keep the barbecue at least 1.5 m (5 feet) away from any combustible materials, including the house, garage, deck rails and so on. Combustible materials include, but are not limited to, wood or treated wood decks, wood patios or wood porches. Never use a barbecue indoors or under a covered patio.

3. Keep the barbecue in a level position at all times.

4. Use proper tools with long, heat-resistant handles.

5. Don't wear loose or highly flammable clothing when barbecuing.

6. Do not leave infants, children or pets unattended near a hot barbecue.

7. Use insulated barbecue mitts or oven gloves to protect hands while cooking or adjusting the vents.

GAS BARBECUE SAFETY

1. Always keep the bottom tray and grease catch pan of your gas barbecue clean and free of debris. This not only prevents dangerous grease fires, it deters visits from unwanted animals. (A sprinkle of cayenne pepper is another safe way to discourage animals.)

2. If a flare-up does occur, turn off all burners and move food to another area of the cooking grill. Any flames will quickly subside. Then light the barbecue again. Never use water to extinguish flames on a gas barbecue.

3. Do not line the funnel-shaped bottom tray with foil. This could prevent grease from flowing into the grease catch pan. Grease is also likely to catch in the tiny creases of the foil and start a fire.

4. Never store propane tanks or spares indoors (that means the garage, too).

Keep a fire extinguisher handy in case of a mishap.

5. For the first few uses, the temperature of a new gas barbecue may run hotter than normal. Once your barbecue is seasoned and the inside of the cooking box is less reflective, the temperature will return to normal.

CHARCOAL BARBECUE SAFETY

1. Charcoal barbecues are designed for outdoor use only. If used indoors, toxic fumes will accumulate and cause serious bodily injury or death.

2. Do not add charcoal starter fluid or charcoal impregnated with charcoal starter fluid to hot or warm charcoal.

3. Do not use gasoline, alcohol or other highly volatile fluids to ignite charcoal. If using charcoal starter fluid, remove any fluid that may have drained through the bottom vents before lighting the charcoal.

4. Do not use a barbecue unless all parts are in place. Make sure the ash catcher is properly attached to the legs underneath the bowl of the barbecue.

5. Remove the lid from the barbecue while lighting and getting the charcoal started.

6. Always put charcoal on top of the charcoal grate and not directly into the bottom of the bowl.

7. Do not place a chimney starter on or near any combustible surface.

8. Never touch the cooking or charcoal grate or the barbecue to see if they are hot.

9. Use the hook on the inside of the lid to hang the lid on the side of the bowl of the barbecue. Avoid placing a hot lid on carpet or grass. Do not hang the lid on the bowl handle.

10. To extinguish the coals, place the lid on the bowl and close all of the vents (dampers). Make sure that the vents/dampers on the lid and the bowl are completely closed. Do not use water as it will damage the porcelain finish.

11. To control flare-ups, place the lid on the barbecue and close the top vent about halfway. Do not use water.

12. Handle and store hot electric starters carefully. Do not place starters on or near any combustible surfaces.

13. Keep electrical cords away from the hot surfaces of the barbecue.

FOOD SAFETY TIPS

1. Wash your hands thoroughly with hot, soapy water before starting any meal preparation and after handling fresh meat, fish and poultry.

2. Do not thaw meat, fish or poultry at room temperature. Thaw them in the refrigerator.

3. Use different utensils and preparation surfaces for raw and cooked foods.

4. Wash all plates and cooking utensils that have come into contact with raw meats or fish with hot, soapy water and rinse well with hot water.

5. When resting meats at room temperature before barbecuing, note that room temperature is 18° to 20°C (65° to 70°F). Do not place raw food in direct sunlight or near any heat source.

6. Always barbecue minced (ground) meats and poultry to at least 70°C (160°F), the internal temperature recommended by the Food Standards Agency.

7. If a sauce will be brushed on meat during barbecuing, divide the sauce, using one part for brushing and the other for serving at the table. Vigorously boil marinades that were used for raw meat, fish or poultry for at least 30 seconds before using as a baste or sauce.

PROPER BARBECUING FORM

1. Trim excess fat from steaks and chops, leaving only a scant 5-mm (¼-inch) of fat, which is sufficient to flavour the meat. Less fat is a virtual guarantee against flare-ups and makes clean-up easier.

2. A light coating of oil will help brown your food evenly and keep it from sticking to the cooking grills. Always brush or spray oil on your food, not the cooking grills.

3. Keep a lid on it! A Weber® barbecue is designed to cook foods with the lid down. Keeping the lid on allows heat to circulate, cooking food evenly and without flare-ups. Every time you lift/open the lid, except when instructed to in a recipe, you add extra cooking time.

4. Take the guesswork out of barbecuing. Use a thermometer and a timer to let you know when it's time to take food off the barbecue. Checking meats for internal temperatures is the best way to determine when food is properly cooked or when done is about to become overdone.

5. Use the right utensils. Long-handled tools and long insulated barbecue mitts or oven gloves protect you from the heat. Use forks only to lift fully cooked foods from the barbecue and tongs or turners to turn them (forks pierce food and flavourful juices are lost).

6. Remember that cooking times in charts and recipes are approximate and based on 20°C (70°F) weather with little or no wind. Allow more cooking time on cold or windy days, or at higher altitudes, and less in extremely hot weather.

INDEX

TECHNIQUES

RECIPES

TEACHING THEATRE ONLINE

Step-by-step lesson plans for
virtual theatre camps and classes.

WRITTEN & COMPILED BY
Amanda Broadfoot

www.bbbpress.com

ISBN: 978-0-578-73618-1

Published by Beat by Beat Press
www.bbbpress.com
Copyright © 2020 Beat by Beat Press

TABLE OF CONTENTS

Table of Contents | Teaching Theatre Online

About the Author

Amanda Broadfoot is the managing director of Making Light Productions, a Tallahassee, Florida-based Non-Profit performing arts school with a mission of providing inclusive arts education for kids of all abilities. Amanda fell in love with theatre in the fifth grade when she directed YOU'RE IN LOVE, CHARLIE BROWN during recess. Starting her college career as an actress, she graduated with a degree in creative writing and spent 7 years as a screenwriter in Los Angeles, selling screenplays to actors such as Meg Ryan and Ellen Degeneres. With partner Juliet Yaques, she founded Making Light Productions in 2016, and wrote the children's musical UNDER THE RAINBOW. She lives in Tallahassee with her husband and two kids, one of whom has autism, and she is a passionate advocate for inclusion in the arts.

Introduction

Theatre.

The very word IS the building in which the magic takes place, right? We *perform* "theatre" with our awesome kid casts *in* a THEATER.

As I am writing this, Making Light Productions (our private performing arts school) has just this week finished a 12-month renovation of an on-site small, 75-seat theater. Our final step was installing those 75 seats on raised, stadium risers. I just stared at those beautiful seats and thought, "Will anyone ever sit there?"

Of course they will. But I'm sure every theatre teacher out there has had similar doubts.

For most of us, there has never been any doubt that a theatre program takes place in a theater -- at least, until about March 15, 2020. If you're like me, you went through all the stages of grief:

- Denial: "This virus thing will pass quickly… right?"
- Anger: "What do you mean I have to cancel my show???!"
- Bargaining: "What if I did the show… but with no audience????"
- Depression: "I'm going to sit here sadly, obsessing about the show I didn't have and the budget that has been wasted on that show for which we now have no ticket sales…"
- Acceptance: "Ok, explain Zoom to me…"

Why Is Virtual Theatre Camp a Good Idea?

Part of our challenge, as theatre directors and teachers, is to communicate to parents why virtual theatre camp is a really good idea for their kids.

1. First, don't call it "virtual theatre camp." I'm serious. At this point, parents -- and many of you are among them -- have had so many negative experiences with the words "virtual learning" and "online school" that "virtual camp" sounds to their ears like "nonsense camp." Virtual learning was thrust upon teachers and students across the country -- many of whom had no preparation or background in technology -- and the results have run the gamut from incredible innovation to … well, "nonsense school."

   So we don't want to be connected to that. Consider other names for your camp like "Leland Lake Elementary Theatre Project" or "The Spotlight Connected Camp" or the "The Leon County Applause TV Channel!" Look for something that communicates the positives of online performing arts -- rather than highlighting the fact that it's not "real" camp:

2. Now that we've named it something better, let's communicate how important it is to have a sense of structure and stability for kids in these uncertain times. Their world has been turned upside down, and having something they can count on, at a specific time each

day, with a specific group of people, is grounding and healthy for most children. Also, theatre helps them connect with joy in their lives through their love of performing arts.

3. <u>The technical skills of learning in this environment are LIFE skills</u> -- virtual learning is not going away! Self-taping, editing, and mastering Zoom, YouTube and other platforms will make sure they can participate in whatever form learning takes in the future. What if your rehearsal space suffers hurricane damage, or was overbooked by the debate team, or undergoes renovation (wouldn't that be nice!)? Your program will be ready for whatever is thrown at it!

4. Being able to "enter" their home space <u>allows teachers to support them in unprecedented ways</u> -- we can help them set up their rehearsal space for success.

5. For parents, let's be honest -- <u>it's super CONVENIENT</u>! Do not discount how easy it is for parents to get kids "to rehearsal" when that rehearsal takes place in their living room. No more conflicts with commutes or multiple drop offs - this is a theatre rehearsal that can be done any time from any location with Internet access.

6. <u>It's safe</u>. There is a lot of conflicting medical advice out there right now, and we will likely be living with uncertainty for a while. But one thing we know is that virtual learning will be available to us, even if another lockdown is ordered, even if schools close again. And in virtual theatre class, there is no chance of infection.

7. Depending on how you do it: <u>Video analysis - recording themselves and rewatching with an instructor - builds great skills in objectively analyzing and improving their own performance.</u> This is optional for our online model but can be very powerful for motivated performers.

How Virtual Camp Works

(Remember, don't call it "virtual camp!")

No one wants to sit in front of a Zoom screen for hours on end. A virtual camp platform will need to take into account the fact that kids are kids. They need to move. They need to talk. Their attention wanders. They need to stay engaged. Some of them like to perform for their friends -- but not all of them. They get TIRED.

We think a 2.5 hour virtual musical theatre camp can be successfully accomplished with the following schedule:

15 minutes initial meeting
45 minutes ACTING
45 minutes DANCE
45 minutes MUSIC
30 minutes share / closing meeting

*Optional: 45 minutes of art/stagecraft -- if you have an instructor who could coordinate with your theatre curriculum to teach costume design, set/scene design, prop making, etc., this can add a wonderful component to your camp that also doesn't require kids to "stare at a screen" the entire time. (See below for curriculum ideas.)

Setting Up Your Classes

Before you do anything else, make sure you have a Zoom account without a time limit. You can sign up for a paid account or you may be eligible for free time-limit removal. Learn more about that here: https://bit.ly/3e8VxoD

Zoom Breakout Sessions (multiple instructors available)

No one wants to be in one giant Zoom class for any length of time -- neither teachers nor students. Ideally, if you start with a large group (15+ students), you can then use Zoom's "breakout sessions" feature to send students to small group instruction. Imagine your main Zoom meeting as the "assembly hall" where everyone meets, and the breakout rooms as individual classrooms for music, dance, acting, etc.

You can find a link to a tutorial about creating and managing breakout sessions here: https://bit.ly/38HRtee

So, for instance, one group of 6-10 kids might be scheduled for the acting block (see below) with one instructor, while another group of 6-10 is scheduled for dance/movement and another 6-10 is scheduled for music. At the end of each block, they rotate to their next subject. At the end of a camp day, they will have rotated between all three areas of the "triple threat" instruction and come together again as a large group where they can share their favorite part of the day and those who wish can perform for everyone.

This model requires an instructor for each "classroom" and the "assembly hall" which you can also use as a classroom. If someone loses their connection to the Zoom meeting, they will rejoin the "assembly hall" and then the Meeting Host can send the student to the appropriate breakout session. If you don't have the budget to hire additional teachers, consider recruiting some volunteers: Motivated and skilled parents would likely be willing to help, especially if this is a fundraiser for the program. Also, many older teens -- some of whom had their musicals canceled this past year -- are eager for theatre of any kind right now!

One Zoom Meeting (one instructor available)

If you are a single-teacher studio or class and no additional instructors can be recruited, you'll be limited to hosting one group at a time. Please consider having multiple small groups at various times of the day, rather than trying to instruct more than 10 students at a time in a Zoom session. For instance, you could have one camp from 10 AM-12:30PM and a different group from 1:30 PM - 4:00 PM each day.

Helping Kids Feel Connected in Zoom

Chances are you have a few kids that might feel lost in the crowd in a Zoom Meeting. Don't ignore this! A major contributor to that student being present is the relationships with you and the other students. In person they could raise their hands or otherwise get your attention, but this is harder in Zoom when everyone's movement is confined to the same little rectangle. Fortunately Zoom has ways to help!

- Open the Zoom meeting a few minutes early so the students can chat with each other, just like they would in an on-site class.
- In-Meeting Chat – We recommend leaving this option enabled, especially for the kids who are unlikely to speak out during class. Kids are used to chatting and gaming at the same time and you will be pleasantly surprised at their multitasking abilities. Some of our most valuable insights into how students are faring were gleaned from their chats. However, we recommend monitoring the chat stream just in case the language becomes inappropriate. Learn more about Zoom In-Meeting Chat here: https://bit.ly/2Z7MMai
- Raise Hand – We mentioned raising hands a moment ago and thanks to the "nonverbal feedback" in Zoom, we can still raise hands! Set expectations for students to "raise their hand" just like they would in in-person class and then call on students as you normally would. Learn more about Zoom Reactions here: https://bit.ly/2VYGYxT

Nothing takes the place of being mindful of who is participating and who is quiet, so you may want to keep a scratchpad nearby to note who has had a chance to speak and who hasn't.

Virtual Instruction Blocks

A suggested cycle for each class block of the following - not necessarily in this order but utilizing some of these for each session:

1. **Warm up/Listen/Watch (15 minutes)**
   This is a great place to share your screen, show a video and/or a script. This is also a good time for some tidbits of theatre history, music theory, or dance terminology. (See the appendix for some pre-screened history/technique/theory links appropriate and engaging for kids.) If you have a script of a scene to read through, you can share your screen through Zoom and kids can take turns reading parts, without having to have a printed copy of the text.

   In addition, I ask that my students keep a notebook, and for each cycle of our classes, there is ONE FACT that they will record in their notebooks. Just one. Anybody can write down one thing. That means that at the end of each day, they will have *at least* three facts about music, dance and theatre that they have committed to memory -- and at the end of a week, that amounts to 15 important facts. Parents tend to see facts as "take away value" -- and more importantly, it has been scientifically proven that facts build confidence. The more a child KNOWS, the more confident they feel. While they can't all hit a "high C" in vocal class, they can all memorize the note names on the treble clef, review the titles of Shakespeare's comedies or understand french terms used in ballet.

2. **Discuss (5 minutes)**
   After everyone has experienced the media, have a list of prepared questions about the subject -- and VERY IMPORTANT, a list of kids' names so that you can call on those kiddos who don't necessarily push themselves forward. I had one kiddo who said "I feel like I'm not there" in Zoom meetings, because everyone else is clamoring forward and making a noise and he tends to be more quiet. It's easy for the quiet kiddo to get lost in the Zoom crowd. This discussion should be preparation for the next phase...

3. **Practice (away from the screen) (10 minutes)**
   Make time AWAY from the screen a part of each class block. However, the teacher is always "on call" to assist if the child is struggling. Having pre-recorded materials that they can work through is helpful for this time -- for instance, you can share a link to a private YouTube playlist where you have recorded some choreography and assign them specific steps to rehearse. You can email a PDF of a monologue or share a poetry worksheet that prompts them to write their own song lyrics.

4. **Perform for friends (15 minutes)**
   This is a great place to teach kids to provide FEEDBACK.   You could be as formal as providing a pre-printed rubric for scoring various aspects of the performance -- or as informal as asking kids to take it in turn to comment with two positive bits of feedback and one bit of constructive criticism.

Performances

Live Performance vs. Pre-Recorded

As you are planning your curriculum, it's important to think about how you want to present the final performance because that will impact your rehearsal plans. There are a couple of ways to approach the performance for the online theatre camp/class:

1. All live Zoom instruction with live performance at the end of the week
2. Live Zoom instruction but kids submit videos that will be edited together into a final performance

We have provided a checklist in Appendix D that will help you plan and provide the right information to parents about the performance.

All Live Zoom Instruction and Performance

The upside to this approach is that truly all you need is a Zoom connection and a group of kids. Even if you've never Zoomed, their website has easy-to-follow tutorials on getting started, scheduling Zoom sessions, using breakout sessions, managing chats, etc.

In this model, you will spend most of the camp week prepping your kiddos to perform live on Zoom at a designated time at the end of the week. You could either schedule that to happen during the last hour of your regularly scheduled camp -- or plan a special time for the performance after camp (leaving you with all your rehearsal time) and allowing you to combine groups. For instance, if you had a morning camp group and an afternoon camp group, they could join together for a 6 PM Zoom performance.

For our purposes, we are going to present this curriculum as though you are performing your show during the last hour of camp on Friday. (If you would like information on how to use Zoom to stream your performance live on Facebook, you can find a tutorial here: https://bit.ly/2CeXJ0I)

I have seen powerful live Zoom performances of dance solos, musical theatre solos and acting monologues and scenes.

YOUR. STUDENTS. CAN. NOT. SING. TOGETHER. OVER. ZOOM.

I cannot reiterate this strongly enough. The technology doesn't exist. The delay makes every attempt to make music together a complete train wreck.

All those videos you've seen of bands seemingly playing together over Zoom, choirs seeming to sing together? It's all edited together after the fact. That kid that got the cast of Hamilton to sing to her? Totally edited together after the fact. I promise you.

That being said, a live Zoom performance -- a play reading, a dance solo, a musical theater number -- can work very successfully. There is something to be said for the nervous energy that accompanies that live performance - it's closer to the reality of a live, in-person theatre performance... with a few additional anxieties. Could the Internet fail? Yes. Could a student's iPad go dead during a performance. Yep. I've totally had that happen. Could someone's mom bring them a plate of spaghetti for dinner right before they are supposed to start singing??? YES. YES, THAT HAPPENED.

So even if you choose to go this route, I would suggest having a backup plan. What happens if a student's internet fails? What happens if the teacher's Zoom connection conks out?

Communicate ahead of time with your parents that "in the unlikely event of technical problems, we will allow all students to submit pre-recorded performances which we will post on our website/FB page/Instagram TV/etc."

To get parents excited about the show on Friday, tell them where they can find a social media post about the Zoom program that they can share on their own social media pages! Make sure they do NOT publicly share any Zoom links or passwords, as those should only be shared privately with family and friends.

Live Zoom Instruction with Pre-Recorded Performance

In this model, we complete instruction live on Zoom, just as above, but have students record videos at home and submit those to the teacher to be edited together for a final performance. For teachers with experience in even basic video editing, this can be a fun option.

(If you don't have experience, there are tutorials for everything on YouTube, and this is a fun thing to learn in your extra quarantine time, but don't expect to pick it up overnight. If you consider yourself somewhat technically proficient and have about a week, you could pick up all the skills you need to edit together a professional-looking showcase using a program as easy as iMovie for iPad.)

Nothing would change during your camp rehearsal/instruction time, using this model. However, you would need to communicate certain things to your students and their parents:

- Deadline for submitting videos (give yourself plenty of time)
- How to submit videos ... Most big video files can't be sent via email or text. Options:
    - You could have them upload the videos to Google Drive and share the link with you. Then you could move their video to the folder you've designated for the showcase.
    - You could create a Google folder and give all the students "editing" privileges to submit directly here. HEADS UP: If they have "editing" privileges, they can accidentally delete other files from the folder, so just be aware.
    - We like WeTransfer.com because it allows the student to "email" the video without using their email program. They don't even need a WeTransfer account -- just go to the WeTransfer.com website, enter the email address to which they would like to send and select the file from their hard drive.
    - There is no "magic bullet" for slow internet. If their connection is slow, no matter what system you use for submitting the videos, it's going to take a long time. If they complain about how long it is taking, suggest that they go into their camera's settings and change the "record video" rate to "720p," which will make the files smaller.

- The date of the performance and where it will be published: Facebook, website, YouTube, etc. Make sure that if you plan to share a performance online, you have received signed permission from the parents to do so. (We make a blanket publicity / photo permission a part of registration process for camps, classes and lessons. If a parent has an issue with image use / distribution, we are happy to figure out a way to accommodate their wishes.)

Sample Curriculum

Before your camp week starts, be sure to communicate frequently with parents, telling them how to log on (Zoom ID and password), as well as how the schedule will work, what materials - if any - kids will need, what kind of space they need in their home, etc. Will you be using music tracks during the week that they will need to access from a Google Drive or YouTube playlist? Or a pdf of a script(s)? If so, share that with parents and ask that they show their kids how to access it from their device.

One helpful pre-camp step for us is to send out a questionnaire, asking parents about things such as experience (in dance, theatre, music), special areas of interest, challenges (learning challenges, for instance, or diagnosed attention issues), or mobility restrictions.

To get them excited about camp, you might announce specific "dress up days" for each day -- a theme around which they can build a costume and pick a Zoom background. We have suggested themes for each day :) I also like to choose my own Zoom background from a famous musical for each day and have the kids guess the musical -- and then we talk briefly about that show.

Week 1: Broadway Variety Show

MONDAY

Welcome Meeting (15 Minutes)

The first day's morning meeting is going to be a little bit longer, because it is going to be a little bit about Zoom training -- which sounds awful, so let's call it… a "virtual scavenger hunt!" Believe me, spending a few minutes training the kids on where to find important controls on Zoom will endear you to parents forever.

It's probably going to take a few minutes for everyone to get logged on, call roll, and ensure your entire variety show cast is online. When everyone has arrived, tell them how the camp is going to work, how the schedule will run each day, and what kind of performance you are working towards at the end of the week. Then let each student introduce themselves and answer a fun question (favorite musical or movie or TV show, for instance). It might also be fun to play an applause sound effect after each introduction and let your "cast" each take a bow.

This way, they can practice unmuting themselves and re-muting and everyone gets a chance to talk. Let them practice turning their video on and off, selecting "Speaker View" (so that the person talking is biggest on their screen) and how to "pin speaker" if, for instance, they want the dance teacher to remain largest on screen the whole session. You, as the Meeting Host, can also choose on whom the students should focus by choosing to "Spotlight" them in Zoom. This meet and greet time will also give you a chance to see who has challenges with technology, who might be dealing with a slow internet connection, who is shy, who is a talker, etc.

If you're going to use Zoom breakout sessions, this would be a great time to practice with the kids: You create the rooms and assign a teacher and students to each room. The students can practice "accepting" the breakout session, going into that room, and then coming back to the main room. You could even make a "scavenger hunt" out of it: When they go into a room you have assigned them, they will see that teacher and guess what musical his/her Zoom background is from. When they've visited all three rooms, they will have finished the scavenger hunt!

This is also a good session to discuss the "Zoom rules" for your class. You can decide what boundaries you are going to set, but here are a few suggested topics to discuss:

- Are you going to enable the chat feature? If so, what is OK/Not OK to say in chats?
- We stay muted until we have to ask a question -- not because we don't want everyone to talk but even a little bit of background noise can be distracting.
- How to ask a question: physically raise your hand or use the "virtual hand-raising" feature on Zoom.
- Your video stays ON during class, unless you're asked to turn it off - but iPads do not go to the bathroom with you (yep, it has happened).

At the end of the session, assign students to breakout sessions OR start your first curriculum block, depending on the structure of your camp. If students are going into breakout sessions, make sure teachers and students know what time to return to the main session to be reassigned.

Acting (45 Minutes)

Acting is one of the branches of the performing arts that is most easily adapted to the online format. Sound delays -- which create major challenge in group music --- have minimal effect on scene work, and the time we can't spend on blocking (because there's only so far you can travel on the Zoom screen), we can devote to characterization, facial expressions, pacing of a scene, diction, etc.

ACTIVITY: Name Game
Purpose: To learn names and something about each player. To understand how to pantomime and communicate ideas.
1. Everyone's video is on and the teacher has a list of names.
2. As each player's name is called, that player unmutes themselves and will say their first name and pantomime a gesture for each syllable in their name. The action should be simple and can demonstrate a hobby, interest, or something that they do everyday. Example: I say "Pam-e-la" and gesture a paddle stroke on each side of my body (one stroke per syllable, on my left-right-left side) to show I like to canoe.
3. Each player individually says their name while demonstrating the gesture then all together the group repeats the name and gesture.
4. Repeat the process so everyone shares their name and gesture.
5. Let any player up for the challenge demonstrate the name and gesture of every person in the group. This can be done in the same session if time allows or at a later session.

ACTIVITY: Share your screen - History
This is a fun and really well-done YouTube video with a short history of the theatre, created by a student actor, using Lego and stop-motion animation: https://youtu.be/CpgAJNNypSg

DISCUSSION: What Is Acting?
What different kinds of acting did the students see in the video? What kinds of acting have they done? What is different about acting on a Zoom screen and acting on a stage? How is acting

for Zoom like other forms of acting -- like TV or movies? (Try to make sure everyone gets a chance to participate in the conversation.)

Define the following words (consider placing these definitions in a document that you share on screen):
- Monologue: a long speech by one actor in a play or movie
- Scene: part an act in a play during which the action takes place in a single place without a break in time
- Play: a piece of writing which can be seen at a theatre or on TV, or heard on the radio. Plays often show conversations between people. A play is usually watched, rather than read.
- Musical: a type of theatre, which usually includes singing, dancing and acting.

ACTIVITY: Slow Motion Emotion
- Ask three students to "take the stage" (they leave their video on and everyone else turns their video off).
- Use your chat to send a PRIVATE MESSAGE to each student with their assigned emotion. Ask them to give you a thumbs up when they have it.
- As you slowly count down from 10 to 1, they are to gradually put that emotion in their faces.
- Have the class guess which emotion they chose and reflect on what gave away that emotion.
- Repeat this activity until everyone who wishes gets a chance to play.

Discussion: What did we learn? How do our faces change as we reflect emotion? Which emotions are harder? Which are easiest to show?

ACTIVITY: Scenes and Monologues
Explain that in the show on Friday, each student will have the option of performing in a scene or performing a monologue. Let them know that you will select and share monologues and scenes from which they can choose and they will be available online (Google Drive folder, uploaded to private Facebook group, emailed out, etc.) Let them know you will have "auditions" in class the next day.

- Share the monologue "Spell" and ask for a volunteer to read and perform. (Beat by Beat Press has provided this monologue for free at the back of this book in **Appendix C: Sample Scenes & Monologues**. It is from *Fantasy Monologues for Young Actors* by Douglas M. Parker which can be purchased in its entirety here: https://bit.ly/3f6WrDz)
- Share the scene "Clubhouse" and take volunteers to read for Devon, Dale and Dylan. (Beat by Beat Press has provided this scene for free at the back of this book in **Appendix C: Sample Scenes & Monologues**. It is from *Contemporary Scenes for Young Actors* by Douglas M. Parker which can be purchased in its entirety here: https://bit.ly/3edabLC)

Discuss the character in the monologue: Is he/she happy about their magic skills? How old do you imagine that they are? How would the monologue be different if she were very young vs. very old? How would the monologue be different if she were angry? Sleepy? Nervous? A robot? Speaking in slow motion? If time allows, let various actors try a few lines of the monologue or scene, directed to reflect a specific emotion in the characters.

Dance/Movement (45 Minutes)

While dance online doesn't look exactly like dance in the studio or on the stage, there are some powerful technology tools that can really help young dancers learn and improve. A lot of kids -- *I'm looking at you, you adorable self-conscious teenagers* -- feel shy about dancing, especially if they don't have a background in the discipline and they're learning alongside more experienced students. Pre-recorded choreography videos, accessible to all campers offline, allow them to practice and develop skills in the privacy of their own homes.

ACTIVITY: Dance Stretch and Warmup
If you don't have a "go to" stretch that you use in your classes, this quick uptempo warmup is good for all ages and experience levels: https://bit.ly/2O6mdMv

EXPLORE: Dance & Movement in Musicals
- Have the class take a seat.
- Remind the students that musical theatre is a "heightened" form of telling stories, and one tool that adds to this heightened form is dance.
- Share your screen and select "Share whiteboard." Draw the three steps of emotion in musical theatre. (alternatively, you can use a pre-drawn image and just share that with students, but it's kind of fun for them to watch you draw in real time :)
- Explain that all movement in musical theatre has a purpose. It can: 1. Express emotion 2. Advance the plot 3. Give deeper understanding of character/conflict
- Ask for students to give examples of how each purpose might be used.
- Consider showing a video of the opening dance sequence of West Side Story: https://bit.ly/31WZIS9
- Have the class describe the action and how they knew what was happening. This is an example of using dance to further the plot.
- Explain that standing motionless may be appropriate in dramatic plays and film/TV, but in musicals having some sort of purposeful action/movement is almost always a stronger choice. It helps punctuate emotions, and can bring new perspectives to character relationships.

ACTIVITY: Practice Creating Choreography
Today we're going to learn how to build movement that accompanies a certain number of counts of music. We're going to start with 8 counts.
- Without music, teacher claps and counts for 8 beats.
- While muted, have students clap 8 beats.
- Next, they will clap for 4 beats and march for 4 beats.
  (We keep everyone muted because the sound delay will make it sound like a train wreck when in fact, everyone is probably keeping time with the instructor just fine. Don't stress if it looks to you like they're out of sync - it's just the technology lag in action.)
- Next practice marching for four beats and then step-touch L, step touch R for the remaining four beats.

- OPTIONAL: If you feel comfortable teaching basic dance steps, discuss that there are certain building blocks of musical theatre dance that you can master and start to incorporate into your choreography. One of the most basic is the jazz square. You can find a video tutorial here: https://bit.ly/2Zfm7bP
- Finally, ask the students to walk away from the screen and practice 8 counts and then return to the screen at a designated time to share what they've learned. Stay "on call" in case they need some help!

Music (45 Minutes)

Talk to your students about how vocal warmups, exercises and rehearsals are different in the virtual world. We can't sing in unison together, but we can still sing and learn a lot about music and musical theatre.

ACTIVITY: Exploring Stage 1 - Breathing on the Floor
Everyone is muted, but they can hear you and you can see them.
- We're going to begin by focusing on Stage 1, creating the air, or breathing. Great vocal sound begins with great breath control.
- Ask the students to find a place on the floor where they can lie down on their backs comfortably.
- Tell them to relax their shoulders and head, and to take deep breaths.
- What part of your body moves when you take a deep breath? The belly! That muscle directly below your rib cage that is expanding in and out is called the "diaphragm." When singing correctly air should always be coming from your diaphragm. It should constantly be expanding and compressing.
- Have them take a deep breath and let out an "Ooooooooh" from high to low. They should feel their diaphragm getting smaller as they let out the sound.
- Now have them try the same thing without moving their bellies. Notice the change in sound quality? Notice the strain in your throat? This is the incorrect way to sing. This is how you end up losing your voice!

VOCAL WARMUP: Ready to Sing!
- Tell the class to take a seat. We're now going to further warm up our voices.
  - Explain proper singing position: Sitting at the edge of the seat, with their back up straight. Have everyone give it a try. Tell them from now on whenever you call out "Ready to Sing!" this is the position they should take.
- Make a quick game out of this: Tell the class to sit like they are lazy on the couch at home watching TV. Then say "Ready to Sing!" and watch as they pop up into position. Repeat a few times between "lazy on the couch" "or couch potato" and then "Ready to Sing!"
- Compliment them on how professional they look!
- Instruct the class: When I say "go", using the sound "Ahh", I want you to sing from your highest note all the way down to your lowest note in 10 seconds. Ready...go! Do it with them, counting down with your fingers 10 to 1. For the first round, everyone is muted except the teacher, but they are practicing along with you. Then call on certain students,

unmute them and have them demonstrate the practice -- everyone else is still practicing too, but muted. (Only one person's sound should be live at a time!)

- You can joke they sort of sound like a robot powering down. =)
- Tell them we're going to do it again, but this time in only 5 seconds. Ask for a volunteer to demonstrate.
- Then in 3 seconds. Ask for volunteers to demonstrate.
- Have the students place their hands on their stomachs and shout "Ha!" Explain that this is where the "good air" for singing comes from. They should feel their bellies bounce.
- Introduce Vocal Warmup #1 an arpeggio on the word "Ha!" (**Appendix E: Music Cue 01:** https://bit.ly/MusicCue01)

DISCUSSION: Friday Performance

Let the students know that during the Friday performance, everyone who wishes will be allowed to sing a vocal solo. You can either provide them with a list of songs/links from which they can choose (YouTube has a plethora of musical theatre karaoke tracks that are appropriate for kids and kid voices) or you can have them choose one and give a deadline for this song to be screened/approved.

IMPORTANT NOTE: Any accompaniment track *must* be played on the student's end of the connection. Each soloist will have to have access to their solo track and should practice playing the track and singing with it (this may require them to have more than one device, so that they can keep the Zoom connection/camera open and play the music).

Even if a student prefers not to sing a solo in the performance on Friday, let them know that you would still like them to choose a song to work with this week!

LEARN A SONG: "My Treehouse" from THE MOST EPIC BIRTHDAY PARTY

Throughout the week, students will learn to read a musical score by learning a solo song as a group. Again, we are NOT going to attempt to sing this song together live, but by using this sheet music, we can teach students important things about acting the song, music theory, and most importantly, being able to take a piece of sheet music and know how to follow it.

- Share the "My Treehouse" sheet music (**Appendix F: Sample Songs.** This song is from Beat by Beat's *The Most Epic Birthday Party Ever* by Betina Hershey and Denver Casado. Learn more about this musical here: http://bit.ly/18Kpx0Y)
- Demonstrate where the VOCAL line is located and where the instrumental music is located. I like to teach my students to locate the treble clef and then "count treble clefs" -- which is important when they start to decipher songs with parts. In this case, the first treble clef line is always theirs and the one beneath is the one for the piano/instruments.
- Play the vocal track (**Music Cue 02:** https://bit.ly/MusicCue02, share your screen) and use your cursor to follow along on the vocal line.
- For the amount of time left, take the song in phrases and utilize "call and response" technique to teach the melody: "First, you listen as I sing. My turn: 'Just me up here in my tree house. Not much to fear in my treehouse.' Now your turn... Billy, can you sing that back to me?" And you unmute Billy and he sings that phrase -- but SO DOES EVERYONE ELSE, just muted. And everyone gets a chance to sing unmuted at some point in the song as you repeat this process: "my turn" and now "your turn" to sing.

- OPTIONAL: Tell them that the instructors will hold "auditions" for someone to sing this particular song in the showcase. You could even let kids and teachers vote on the best performance.

Closing Meeting (15 Minutes)

On the first day, this final meeting should really be a celebration: Have a little freeze dance party… let everyone describe their favorite part of the day…

One of my students' favorite things is getting to choose the dress-up theme for the next day, so you can make that part of the final meeting.

Every final meeting should include some kind of performance. There won't be time for everyone to perform a solo, but keeping a list so that you know who has had a chance to solo, and then letting everyone else perform their jazz square, or a scene they rehearsed, will make the final meeting something everyone looks forward to.

Discuss any issues that cropped up during the day, any instructions on at-home practice and encourage everyone to be back for virtual rehearsal on Tuesday!!

TUESDAY

Welcome Meeting (15 Minutes)

It's Day 2 of your online theatre project, and no doubt, your students are popping up and excited to show you their new Zoom backgrounds, tell you about songs they would like to sing or scenes they would like to perform. It's important to surrender to a little bit of chaos at the beginning of these large group meetings; they're excited to see each other. They need this controlled cacophony in their lives (I'll admit: I will miss that "mute all" button a bit when we go back to in-person rehearsals).

It's also important for us to look for that student who's not necessarily piping up and pull them into the conversation with some open-ended questions like "Who has done something cool this week they would like to share?" Or "Who has a pet who would like to join us for our welcome meeting?" As bedlam ensues, they will connect with their joy for being together -- and be more ready to settle down after a few minutes.

AFTER the joyful intro, it's time to get down to business: Mute everyone but show them how they can silently express their support for something by waving their jazz hands. Practice this by announcing, "Welcome to Day 2 of the Broadway Variety Show!" and have them respond by waving their jazz hands (that's also a great time to take a screenshot "cast photo" of the group!).

This might be a good time to review some of the important rules, particularly anything that posed a problem on Day`1: Do students need to be gently reminded about good chat behavior? Do we need to talk about what to do if your Internet knocks you out of the Zoom session? If students will need to have materials -- paper, pencils, access to music tracks or scripts -- this is a good time to double check they have those.

Acting (45 Minutes)

WARMUP: Drama Game - One Word Story
- In in-person classes, we do this seated in a circle, but you can facilitate this in the virtual world by making a list of everyone in the class, and sharing it on your screen.
- Have each student find their name on the list.
- Then explain the rules of the game:
- The first person on the list says a single word to begin a story.
- The next person says another word, then the next person says another word, continuing down the list.
- The goal to tell a coherent story, one word at a time.

DISCUSSION: Auditions
Announce which scenes your class will be performing for the Friday show and that today you are going to hold "auditions" at the end of class. (Any age-appropriate scene with two or three

characters at a time can work. Consider checking out Beat by Beat's Contemporary Scenes for Young Actors (https://bit.ly/3edabLC) or Group Scenes for Young Actors (https://bit.ly/3etXbkQ) to use for this purpose.)

ACTIVITY: Scenes and Monologues
Share your screen, and read through a different scene and monologue than yesterday, accepting volunteers for roles -- ideally, students who didn't get the opportunity to perform the day before.

Next, tell them that they have 10 minutes to practice with the text on their own before auditions. Again, stay available on screen in case a student needs help with a word, character, etc. Tell them they do NOT have to memorize for this audition, but just to study until they feel ready to audition with either a monologue or as part of a scene. Let them know that your casting decisions will be announced at the Welcome Meeting on Wednesday. Then give them a time to return to their Zoom screens for auditions.

ACTIVITY: Auditions
Make sure that everyone knows that just because they don't read for a particular character today, or audition for a certain scene or monologue, that doesn't mean that they aren't in consideration for that role. Talk about what you're looking for: expression, diction/articulation, characterization. Explain that this is not a reading contest.

Use the remaining acting class time to audition your actors and make notes on strengths/ challenges of different performers. Consider sharing a rubric with your cast and letting them make private notes as well, learning to look for particular strengths in a performer. At the end of auditions, if time allows, you can ask them to share their favorite moments of the auditions they watched.

Dance/Movement (45 Minutes)

Because of the lags and delays in sound caused by technology, dancing together is really difficult -- and that's if you discount the challenges of dancing in kitchens, around pets and over furniture. However, we're going to prepare a dance "informance" for our parents for Friday -- performance + information we have learned ABOUT performance = INFORMANCE. So as your students learn more about dance and choreography, they are going to demonstrate those dance steps and share the facts they've learned with their audience. But first, we have to warm up...

ACTIVITY: Dance Stretch and Warmup
If you don't have your own favorite dance warmup to do, this fun dance/PE warmup is fun for all ages and abilities. Let kids know to do as much as they can manage -- and that you'll share this video for them to do at home with family members or pets if they want to get better at it: https://bit.ly/2CdSJJM

DISCUSSION: What Is an Informance?
Talk to your cast about what an informance means. Explain that they're going to teach their parents, siblings and friends about what they have learned about musical theatre dance on

Friday, demonstrating dance steps and explaining terminology for the show. Explain that everyone who wishes to will be able to demonstrate one dance step and then show their own sixteen counts of choreography -- either with or without music to accompany them. If there is music in the Friday show, each student will need to play their own music on their end. (See **Appendix B: Musical Theatre Tracks for 16-Count Choreography**.)

ACTIVITY: Copycat Dance
- Have all the students stand up.
- The teacher starts clapping a steady beat (or plays a metronome).
- Choose one student to be the leader. Ask them to begin some simple repetitive dance movement. It could be marching, waving one arm, nodding the head, etc., as long as it is in time with the beat.
- After performing the movement for at least eight beats, that student then chooses someone from the group and calls out his or her name.
- The chosen student then copycats the movement for at least 8 counts, and then takes over as leader. The initial leader student freezes as the new leader continues.
- The new student must now change the dance move slightly, then repeat the process again, choosing a new student.
- Continue until everyone has had a chance to be the leader.
- Calm the energy of the class by doing some breathing/stretching exercises.

ACTIVITY: Review and Learn
- Review Jazz Square that we learned on Monday. https://bit.ly/2Zfm7bP
- Practice marching 4 beats and adding a 4-beat jazz square at the end and repeating that sequence several times. Let several students demonstrate their ability to do this. If they are able to play a track from their own device to dance to, "One" from A CHORUS LINE works well with this (https://bit.ly/3edcoXq). (But remember, each student will need to be able to play their own music for the movement/music to appear to match.)
- Now it's time to learn a new fundamental musical theatre dance step, the Kick Ball Change! If you don't feel comfortable demonstrating this step yourself, you can watch this simple tutorial: https://bit.ly/2CcEq8h
- Explain that the "ball" in the kick-ball-change is referring to the ball of your foot, and this step is really just a fancy way to march: If you're standing on your left foot, kick with the right, then step back with your right foot and shift your weight on to it. Then step on your left again. You could also call the Kick-Ball-Change the "Left-Right-Left" or "Right-Left-Right" step!

How many students can demonstrate (on your clapped beat) 8 counts of marching, followed by a jazz square for four counts and a four-count kick-ball-change to finish?

Explain that dance steps don't have to be complicated to help tell the musical theatre story.

EXPLORE: Relax and Watch
Reminding the students of the three steps of the musical theatre "emotional staircase" - speaking - singing - dancing, show this clip from *Newsies* of "Seize the Day:" https://bit.ly/3gzW9Fq
- Ask them to stay seated during the speaking.

- Stand up when the singing begins.
- Clap along when the dancing begins!

Music (45 Minutes)

Tell everyone to sit lazy in their chairs like they're watching TV at home. Then command, "Ready to Sing!" Did they remember how singers get ready? As students for a list of reminders for singers. Some correct answers:
- Sitting up straight
- Back away from the chair
- Feet flat on the floor
- Chin straight (head tilted neither down or too far back)

EXPLORE: Discuss and Understand
To demonstrate what happens when your body is in the wrong position for singing, have the students tucks their chins all the way to their chests and attempt to breathe and sing. Then drop the head all the way back, staring at the ceiling. What happens to the singer's airway?

Now ball up in the chair, completely slumped down. Is it easy to breathe? Now stand up and attempt to take a deep breath. Is that easier?

This fun video does a great job of explaining the role the diaphragm plays in the process of breathing - and SINGING: https://bit.ly/3gGvreA

ACTIVITY: Vocal Warmups
Begin with gentle breathing exercises and Vocal Warmup #1 that we learned yesterday, an arpeggio on the word "Ha!" [**Appendix E, Music Cue 01:** https://bit.ly/MusicCue01]

Introduce Vocal Warmup #2: Me May Mo. [**Appendix E, Music Cue 03:** https://bit.ly/MusicCue03]

Discuss the role that vowels and consonants play in singing: We actually sing the VOWELS, while the consonants "pinch" the sound in different ways, creating words. Without consonants, no one would understand what we were singing.

Demonstrate trying to sing the first line of "My Treehouse" with no consonants. Sounds really silly right?! We practice exercises like tongue twisters to warm up our "articulators" so that we are ready to sing really clearly.

ACTIVITY: Tongue Twisters
Everyone has their favorite tongue twisters and kids love them. Start by speaking the phrase: "Mama made me mash my M & Ms. Oh my!" Start very slowly and work to get a little faster each time. Have everyone practice together while muted and then take volunteers to unmute and say the phrase very quickly and articulately.

Next, teach them the melody to the tongue twister, Vocal Warmup #3 [**Appendix E, Music Cue 04:** https://bit.ly/MusicCue04]. Again, use "call and response" singing, demonstrating the warmup a capella and then calling on the students in term to demonstrate their mastery of it. You can also add a hand movement to this one, pounding one fist into the palm of the other hand as you "mash the M & Ms."

REVIEW AND DISCUSS: "My Treehouse"
With everyone muted, play the vocal track of the song "My Treehouse" and have everyone sing along. After the song ends, ask what they know about the character of Skylar based on this song. About how old do they think she is? Could this character be played by a boy? Why or why not? How does this character feel right before she starts singing? While she's singing? Has her emotional state changed during the song?

AUDITIONS: "My Treehouse"
Ask who would like to try to sing the new song, "My Treehouse" as a solo. Make sure they have access to the track to play on their side -- OR they can sing a capella. [The Accompaniment Track to "My Treehouse" can be found on **Music Cue 05: My Tree House Accompaniment:** https://bit.ly/MusicCue05]

Before closing out music class, ask how many students would like to sing a solo in the Friday show. If they have not already, have them submit their song choices to you. They can send their selections by chat and then you can have a list at the end of the day by copying and pasting the chat log. (It's a good idea to review the day's chat at the end of day anyway; you never know what surprises you might find!) Do they need help finding an accompaniment track? Do they wish to sing a capella?

Ask that they come prepared to sing their song for the class on Wednesday, when you will be learning about "acting the song."

Closing Meeting (15 Minutes)

ACTIVITY: Celebrate
As kids come in to the main Zoom room from breakout sessions -- or just settle down for the end of the day, play a celebration song for everyone to move to for a few minutes -- like the Kidz Bop version of "Celebration": https://bit.ly/3e6pHcg

SHARE
Call on each student - and staff member -- to share their favorite moment of the day, a fact they learned, or demonstrate a dance step.

PREPARE
Make sure everyone knows what they need for the next day. If they're going to sing a solo in the Friday showcase, they should send you the name of the song and a link to the accompaniment track (if they have one). Let them know that you will announce casting for the scenes and song on Wednesday morning!

After Camp on Tuesday

Tonight is casting time! A fun way to make sure every performer has a significant contribution to the variety show on Friday -- and to build in some transition time between performances -- is to create some narration to link performances together. For instance, have one student introduce the Acting portion of the show with a line like, "This week we learned about acting. We learned that monologues are speeches made by one character, and that scenes involve more than one character in the same location. Our first scene is 'Clubhouse,' starring..."

Now that you've cast the scenes, heard each of your performers sing, seen them dance, draft an order of the show. How long will you need to schedule for the performance? Will it take place during the camp day or at a designated time afterwards?

Optional Fundraising Ideas

- Each student will have the option to sing a solo in the Friday performance. There won't be a lot of one-on-one rehearsal time during the group classes, but you can offer to your students' parents to schedule a private lesson with a solo vocalist after camp hours.
- While there probably won't be a physical program book for your show, if you have the resources and skills, you could create a "good luck slide show" to play on Zoom prior to the performance. Slide shows are fairly easy to create with any number of free apps available for Macs or PCs. Just have the parents send you their favorite performer's photo and a message. And let them know how the funds will be used: "The proceeds from these Good Luck ads will fund costumes for our fall 2020 musical..."

WEDNESDAY

Welcome Meeting (15 Minutes)

Let's kick off our Wonderful Wednesday with a celebration song. "Best Day of My Life" Dance-Along from KidzBop works well for this: https://bit.ly/38HXVBY)

As kids begin logging on this morning, share your screen, have this song playing and send them a message in the chat to dance along. That frees you up to manage the participants (letting them in the Zoom session) and to answer any parent questions that tend to come up at the start of the day.

It's time to announce casting! Prepare a drumroll sound effect before your share on your screen a printed cast list with an order of the show. Remind everyone to respond with happy jazz hands! In addition to the acting scenes, choose a student or students to demonstrate each of the dance steps you'll teach this week, and announce which student has been chosen to sing "My Treehouse" for the show. And let all the students know that they will get a chance to rehearse their songs in music class over the next two days and receive feedback from the instructor.

Acting (45 Minutes)

WARMUP: A Sense of Place
Now that everyone has been cast in a scene, we can start developing our characters. It's important for each scene to have a strong sense of PLACE.
- Have the students close their eyes and imagine they have been playing in the snow for a very long time.
- What does it feel like? Ask them to put that feeling in their whole bodies; their shoulders, faces, backs, hands and toes.
- Are your feet a little wet? Are your fingers numb? Are you shivering?
- Tell them a snow storm has just picked up and the snow is lashing at their faces. Put it in your body.
- Finally you walk into a warm cabin. There's a fire burning. You take off your big, damp jacket. Someone hands you a cup of hot chocolate. You start to feel warmth in your whole body as you sit down by the fire.
- Tell them to open their eyes.
- What did it feel like going from one environment to another? How did it change your body?

DRAMA GAME: Two Person Environment
- Give the students 30 seconds to quietly think of a specific environment. (i.e. The circus, a football game, detention, etc.)

- Choose a student to begin, and everyone else's video is turned off except for this one student. He instantly begins to act within the environment he thought of. For instance, if he's at the movies, he might stare up, as if at a screen, while he mimes eating popcorn.
- When another player becomes aware of what the environment is, they give you a virtual "raised hand" through Zoom and you call on the next player and ask them to turn on their video and unmute themselves.
- Player 2 then says one line of dialogue to Player 1, Player 1 responds, then the scene is over and they turn their video sound off and you call on the next Player 1 to start a new scene.
- FOR EXAMPLE: Player 1 turns on his video and immediately begins wiping his brow from sweat. Player 2 turns on her video and looks equally hot and exhausted, and tries to pour the last drops of water from her canteen into her mouth. Player 2 says "I don't know how you convinced me to go on this hike through the Sahara Desert." Player 1 says, "Well, you said you wanted a vacation in the sun!" Scene is over.

DISCUSSION: What Works Best?

Have a conversation about the kinds of movements, expressions and stage business that really work in the virtual environment. How might you do a scene differently if you were all in the same room?

Take each scene or monologue scheduled for the show one at a time and have a similar discussion: Where are the characters located? What kinds of costumes/props/set pieces will be needed? Encourage the kids to be creative with what they have around the house, but not worry about getting too elaborate. We have specifically chosen scenes that won't require any expensive costumes -- and backdrops can literally be your Zoom background! Characters in the same scene can share the same Zoom background.

For instance, if you're performing the scene "Clubhouse" from *Contemporary Scenes for Young Actors*, just search for "Clubhouse" or "Treehouse" in Google images and find an image that the cast can agree looks like the kind of clubhouse where Devon, Dylan and Dale would be meeting! Then share that image with all three cast members and let them practice making that their Zoom background.

REHEARSAL: Scenes and Monologues

Give each student 10 -15 minutes to rehearse their scenes and monologues on their own. Let them know that they don't have to be fully memorized for Friday but the closer you are, the more effective your scene will be -- and the more fun it is to act. Set a time for everyone to meet back at the screen for a run-through.

As they move away from their screens to rehearse, let them know that you are available to meet with each one to discuss characterization, performance, etc. for a couple of minutes individually.

When they come back for the run-through, practice everyone turning off their screens, except the cast member for that scene. Everyone should select "Speaker View" which makes the person speaking pop up the largest on screen in Zoom. At the end of the scene, practice each one of them taking a bow. (If they say "thank you" right before their bow, that will make them pop up as the "Speaker" in Speaker View.)

Dance/Movement (45 Minutes)

ACTIVITY: Dance Stretch and Warmup

If you don't have a favorite dance warmup, this up-tempo, 3.5-minutes Zumba-based warmup is a lot of fun for kids and accessible to everyone. Tell them this is just about warming up their bodies -- technique is not important, just do what they can, and if they need to stop, just keep marching in place! https://bit.ly/3edRBTL

ACTIVITY: Review and Perform

Let's review the steps we have learned so far! Ask for volunteers to demonstrate the Jazz Square and the Kick Ball Change. Before they perform, have them say, "Next I would like to show you the [Kick Ball Change / Jazz Square]," so that they can practice their informance teaching skills. Take a few minutes to make sure everyone has mastered these steps.

Would anyone like to show off 8 counts of choreography using the steps we have learned so far? "Better When I'm Dancing" from the Peanuts movie can add some fun to this exercise. If you share this link in the Zoom chat, they can each play it from their own device: https://bit.ly/2BIL1aR

EXPLORE: History of Dance

Let everyone breathe for just a moment as they watch a video on 110 Years of popular Dance -- this fun video has every dance from The Charleston to the Harlem Shake -- encourage them to try, if they wish, to dance along! https://bit.ly/2CcEK6Z

After the video, ask who can remember the names of five different dances?
- Black Bottom
- Texas Tommy
- Lindy Hop
- Moonwalk
- Mambo
- East Coast Swing
- Rock and Roll
- Go Go Dancing
- Disco
- Breakdancing
- Hip-Hop
- Jumpstyle
- Zumba
- Rumba
- Electro Dance
- Gangnam Style

Can you think of other styles of dance NOT included in this video? (Ballet, tap, modern, etc.)

LEARN: Step-Touch and Pivot Turn

Today, we are going to learn two more fundamental musical theatre dance steps: step-touch and pivot turn. The pivot turn is going to be the most challenging, for sure, so we will start with the step-touch. If you don't feel comfortable teaching these steps, these easy tutorial videos can help:

Step-Touch
https://bit.ly/31WaPdZ

Pivot turn
https://bit.ly/31WaQi3

Start with no music. Just break down each step slowly. It's important that the focus is on your voice and your movements and not background noise distractions. So everyone stays muted as we learn choreography; it's important to "Spotlight" (controlled by Meeting Host) or "Pin Speaker" (controlled by Meeting Attendee), keeping the teacher's image largest on the screen at all times.

After the students have mastered the new steps, add in a slow clap so that they can perform the parts of each step on the beat. Finally, try a song like Kidz Bop's version of "Old Town Road" (https://bit.ly/3iHMJcR) which has a pretty slow beat (start at about :28 because the intro is long). A slower tempo allows students to master dancing with the beat without getting lost.

Optionally, see if the class can now choreograph 16 counts using any/all of the steps we've learned so far: marching, jazz square, kick-ball-change, step-touch, or pivot turn. After demonstrating what that might look like, give everyone a few minutes to come up with their own 16 count sequence before coming back to the screen to perform for the group.

Music (45 Minutes)

Today's focus is on "acting the song." Explain that over the next two days, everyone will get a chance to perform their song for the group and give feedback to their friends.

ACTIVITY: Vocal Warmups

After some deep breathing and a reminder about getting "ready to sing," choose any of our previous vocal warmups to sing. Let a student suggest a favorite tongue twister or choose one of ours:
- Mommy made me mash my M&Ms
- Super duper double bubble gum
- Chester cheetah chewed a chunk of cheap cheddar cheese

ACTIVITY: Personalize the Song

A first step to having students give an authentic performance is finding a way for them to personally connect with the song.
- Ask one brave student to "take the stage" and guide them through a series of questions to help them find a personal connection with the song, "My Treehouse."

- Here's an example of some guided questions:
  - Have you ever been excited about a big event, but you were disappointed because it didn't go as planned?
  - What did it feel like?
  - If you're upset, do you have a place you like to go to? What place? Why? How does it make you feel to be there?
  - Have you ever felt jealous of someone?
  - How do you calm yourself down if you feel angry?
  - What's been the best birthday you've ever had? The worst?
- Have them perform "My Treehouse" with that new connection. (Remember, they must play the audio backing track on their end -- or sing a capella.)

Explain that every song tells a story, and the person singing is a character. Sometimes, like with Skylar in "My Treehouse," the story and the context are obvious. We have a lot of information about Skylar. The same is true of most musical theatre songs. But even if your song is a pop song with little "back story," you can look at the text and create a backstory for this character.

Take Rachel Platten's "Fight Song" -- which, in my studio, was every other tween/teen girl's go-to vocal solo about 3-4 years ago. Let's look at the lyrics of the first verse and chorus:

> *Like a small boat*
> *On the ocean*
> *Sending big waves*
> *Into motion*
> *Like how a single word*
> *Can make a heart open*
> *I might only have one match*
> *But I can make an explosion*
> *And all those things I didn't say*
> *Wrecking balls inside my brain*
> *I will scream them loud tonight*
> *Can you hear my voice this time?*
> *This is my fight song*
> *Take back my life song*
> *Prove I'm alright song*
> *My power's turned on*
> *Starting right now I'll be strong*
> *I'll play my fight song*
> *And I don't really care if nobody else believes*
> *'Cause I've still got a lot of fight left in me*

Ask one of the students to read the lyrics as though they are a text monologue without music. Who could suggest a setting for where this "scene" takes place? Maybe it's a school in the middle of a desert town and she's dreaming about the ocean because that seems so far away. Has she been bullied? Has that ever happened to you? Something happened to inspire this song, and it doesn't matter whether the performer and Rachel Platten have the same backstory in mind, as long as the lyrics mean something very specific to the singer and they can convey that meaning through their performance.

Rehearse and Feedback

As time allows, let as many soloists perform their songs for the group as possible. Ask listeners to look for emotional connection in the performance of the song. Each listener should be prepared to contribute two of their favorite things about a performance and one area they think the performer can improve. Discuss the importance of learning to give and receive criticism. Explain that anyone who doesn't perform today will have the opportunity on Thursday.

Closing Meeting (15 Minutes)

ACTIVITY: Stop/Go/Sing/Dance

Let's play a unique game of freeze dance. Choose a song that the group knows at least the chorus to. You will play this song from your device, with everyone else muted. You'll need three pieces of colored construction paper: Red, Green and Purple.

Explain when you hold up the Green paper for the camera, they dance. When you hold up the Red paper, they stop. When you hold up the Purple paper, they sing. If you hold up Purple and Green, they have to sing AND dance! You can add variations to this by adding a Blue for hopping on one foot, and Orange paper for clapping -- and complicate it by picking up two or three colors at the same time: Can they sing, clap and hop at the same time?!

SHARE

At the end of a few rounds of this game, allow everyone - including any staff members - to share their favorite part of the day, one at a time, and encourage them to practice their scenes, monologues, songs, and dance steps at home.

Also, let them know that tomorrow is a "dress rehearsal," meaning that if they are using a costume (or particular outfit) or prop for their performance(s), to bring those to perform for the group tomorrow!

After Camp

Tonight, take a look at the run of your show -- do you need to make any changes? Do any students need help finding accompaniment tracks? You might need to track down Zoom background images for the show's scenes and monologues. You'll need time to practice with the students how to change their background, mid-show on Friday, to fit the performance. You could choose a uniform, standard red curtain theatre background to be the default for the group to use during singing or dancing - when they don't need a specific background for a scene.

Note any changes on your show order. At what point do you need to prompt a singer to prepare their backing track? At what point should everyone in a particular scene change their background? This will be a part of Friday's "tech rehearsal," but it's a good idea to make those notes now.

THURSDAY

Welcome Meeting (15 Minutes)

It's Day 4 of the Broadway Variety Show!! Once again, play some music as everyone is logging on.

Welcome everyone back to the Broadway Variety Show and explain that today is "Dress Rehearsal Day" - does everyone have everything they need to run through their performance(s)? Explain that in Broadway shows, a dress rehearsal is when everyone gets DRESSED in their costumes and performs the show, before the show is open to the public. That way, if there are any problems with a costume or prop, the cast and crew can find out before the performance.

Acting (45 Minutes)

Today as we rehearse our scenes, we're going to pay special attention to our facial expressions and our "stage business." Explain that, generally speaking, "blocking" is what we call it when an actor moves from one place to another on stage. "Stage business" is what happens after you get there -- for instance, he might cross stage left, then pick up a letter and open it. Blocking is how we would describe the crossing, but what he does with the letter is "stage business." We might not be able to do much blocking in our virtual scenes, but let's look out for opportunities to incorporate stage business that might help to tell the story.

WARMUP: Let's Eat!
Everyone's video is on, but they are muted. Explain that as you call out a food, they are to mime chewing that particular food or substance. A few items you could include:
- bubble gum (1 piece, 2 pieces, 3 pieces)
- super sticky taffy
- really hot pizza
- carrots
- teeny tiny pretzels
- stale licorice

Can anyone think of some other things that would require you to chew differently? How would eating an ice cream cone look differently than eating a hot dog? What about drinking different things -- how would someone hold and drink from a soda? Now what about a coffee cup?

DRAMA GAME: Three Objects
- Select one student and private message them through Zoom with a "where" environment. For instance, "the kitchen" or "the bedroom" or "a cafe."
- Their goal is to enter the stage, mime interaction with 3 specific objects in that environment, then exit. (For example, if the environment is "bedroom": Player enters,

goes to the closet to pull out a hat, goes to the dresser to put on a belt, then looks at herself in the mirror, then exits, etc.)
- There should be no talking in the scene.
- The class must try to guess what the environment is and what three objects were used.
- Repeat as time allows.

Rehearsal/Run-Through

The majority of our Acting Class time today will be spent running through the scenes and monologues for the performance. Explain to the cast that they will be documenting -- on their scripts if they have a printed copy, or in a notebook -- important information such as stage business, facial expressions (when they're important to the story), set or costume changes -- anything that they might need for the show.

It's important for the rest of the group to practice being good audience members as each group or solo performs. Tell them to make notes on aspects of the performances that they really enjoyed, those things that needed work, and any ideas they might have for bringing a scene to life.

Don't forget to practice taking bows!

Discussion

What worked best? Allow each student to practice giving specific and encouraging critiques of the performance. Explain that "I think you could speak a little more slowly in the beginning" is helpful and specific but "I didn't like it" doesn't give a fellow performer much to work with. The same goes for positive criticism: "Good job" is nice, but not particularly helpful. "I thought it was very funny when your eyes got really wide after you read the letter" is specific and helpful -- that tells the actor that moment worked for the audience, so she might make a note to repeat that in the next performance.

Dance/Movement (45 minutes)

WARMUP: My Name Is a Dance

Instead of using a video or music to warm up today, we're going to do some creative movement: We're going to spell our names with our bodies and turn that into a dance! If your name is Bob, it'll be a short dance, so maybe do the first AND last. But the Maximillians in the class are going to be exhausted by the time they get to "N." Demonstrate this process by spelling out your own name using your body; show them it doesn't have to be perfect or readable. Our goal is to make unusual shapes with our bodies, to force them into positions we might not comfortably use in dance -- and to create continuous movement so that our name becomes a dance. Give kids 5-10 minutes to work on this and then ask for volunteers to demonstrate their "name dance."

Watch and Discuss

Everyone can now relax for a few minutes! Even though our focus has been on jazz dance fundamentals this week, there are all kinds of musical theatre dance. Has anyone in the group studied tap dance? It has a lot in common with jazz dance steps -- every step we've learned so far could be part of a tap dance as well, with the difference, of course, being the sound made by the taps on the ball and heel of the tap shoe.

42nd Street is a famous musical that uses tap dance to tell the story. Tap dance was very popular in musicals of the 1930s and 1940s especially. Before watching this next scene, explain that the characters in this scene of *42nd Street* are auditioning to be dancers in a Broadway show: https://bit.ly/3ealaEK

A few questions for discussion:
- What makes tap dance fun to watch? (Students might mention how synchronized the dancers are or the sound of the dance.)
- Did you learn anything about the characters from this dance? Who was in charge? Who was kind of pushy?
- What elements of the story were you able to figure out from this one dance sequence?

Review
Let's review the steps we've learned. Ask for volunteers to demonstrate each step and ask them to introduce the step right before they perform it, just as they will in the show:
- Jazz Square
- Kick-Ball-Change
- Step-Touch
- Pivot Turn

DANCE AND LEARN: The Grapevine
Today we're going to learn another fundamental dance step: the Grapevine. If you don't feel comfortable teaching this step, check out this easy to follow tutorial from YouTube: https://bit.ly/2Dr1wc5

The most common error on this step happens when kids step in front instead of back. But other than that, it's a pretty foolproof dance move. Practice moving toward the right and then perform the grapevine back to the left. Once everyone has it on both sides, try performing the step on the beat: Clap out a steady, slow beat and have each dancer perform the grapevine for you.

Now it's time to put it all together! Have the students choose any or all of the steps we've learned this week and create 16 counts of choreography to share with the class. Give them a specific time to come back and demonstrate their work for the class!

MUSIC (45 minutes)

At today's music dress rehearsal, we're going to explore "acting the song" further, and we're going to discover what our musical theatre characters really WANT. Every protagonist -- the star of the story -- wants something, and what they want is the driving force behind the whole story.

WARMUP: 10 Dollars, Please

- Tell the students that one by one, they are going to try and convince you to lend them 10 dollars.
- But every so often your "character" is going to change.
- Begin as their best friend, choose a student to start, and say Go!
- When you say the next student's name, they take over and begin to ask you for 10 dollars.
- Every so often you'll change your character.
- Here is a list of characters you can become: I am now…
  - your younger cousin in kindergarten
  - your father
  - your favorite teacher
  - your least favorite teacher
  - your 85-year old grandma
  - your angry older brother
  - a stranger
  - your worst enemy
  - your crush

What was that warmup like? What did you notice? How did your tactic change based on who you were speaking to?

When performing a song, two of the most important questions you can ask are:
1. What do I want?
2. Who am I speaking to?

We're going to focus on these two questions today, but first, let's warm up our voices.

Vocal Warmup

Begin by getting "Ready to sing!" Then do some gentle breathing exercises before further warming up the voice with Vocal Warmup #4: Bumblebee [**Appendix E, Music Cue 06:** https://bit.ly/MusicCue06].

Follow this warmup with a favorite tongue twister. Here are a few more favorites:
- Red Leather, Yellow Leather
- These sheep shouldn't sleep in a shack Sheep should sleep in a shed.
- Betty bought butter but the butter was bitter, so Betty bought better butter to make the bitter.

OPTIONAL: Watch and Discuss

Depending upon how much time you have left and how many solo songs you need to rehearse today, you can include this 7-minute light-hearted video which explains the "I Want Song" and its purpose in musical theatre. The best way to use this is to share your screen, but be prepared to stop the video occasionally to elaborate on concepts or point out important concepts. For instance, "Did you hear how many times the actual words 'I want' were used in songs in the intro?" or to talk a little bit about Greek theatre and the invention of the protagonist. https://bit.ly/2W1tuBp

Rehearse

Let each remaining student (who didn't get to sing for the group the day before) rehearse their solo song for the performance. Before they sing, have them discuss their character: Who is singing? Who are they singing to? What does this character want more than anything else?

Remind the audience to keep their feedback to two positive and specific supportive comments and one specific constructive bit of criticism.

Closing Meeting (15 Minutes)

Play some music as everyone is coming back to the main room together and getting settled down -- this Olivier Awards performance of "A Chorus Line" is all about a cast rehearsing, entering a beautiful London theatre and getting ready to perform and sets the mood perfectly: https://bit.ly/2VWIv8z

After everyone is present and accounted for, pull up a rundown of the performance order for the next day and share that screen with your cast. Go through each act and discuss any details, challenges or costume/set changes. Confirm that everyone has everything that they need: props, accompaniment tracks, etc. and that they know how to handle the technical requirements for each act:

- Do they know how to change their Zoom screen mid-show if needed?
- Do they know how to access any tracks and have a device to play them on from their end?
- Do they know when to turn their video on/off during the performance?

Let them know that you will have one final run-through of the show, from beginning to end, the next morning.

To get everyone excited about the Friday show, let everyone practice taking a bow after their name is announced -- tell them to be as elaborate with the bows as they like!

After Camp

Now is a great time to send out invitations to the show tomorrow! If you're going to use Zoom to go live on Facebook, Instagram or YouTube, promote that to all your followers. If you're going to invite viewers directly into the Zoom session, make sure parents know attendance is limited (most accounts allow up to 100) and they should approve additional attendees with you before sharing the Zoom link and password with other family and friends. The last thing you want is for a performer to be unable to log on because the meeting fills up!

Email a copy of the run of the show to all parents and/or share it in a private Facebook group. Make sure all parents know what each child needs to have access to before the show tomorrow: costume pieces, props, Zoom background, accompaniment tracks, etc.

FRIDAY

Welcome Meeting (30 Minutes)

It's show day!! Choose some opening music to set the scene like "Another Op'nin', Another Show" from *Kiss Me, Kate*: https://bit.ly/2VYObOt

Today's morning meeting will be a little longer, but when everyone gets logged in, get them immediately up on their feet and go ahead and warm up...

ACTING WARMUP: Shake It Out
- First, have everyone stand up.
- Explain that the students are to as a group count down from 8 while shaking out each of their limbs (In this order: Right arm, Left arm, Right leg, Left leg). Then they will count down from 7, then 6, etc. until they reach 1.
- They should do this getting increasingly louder and louder.

So it will go like this:

> ALL CLASS
> Right arm: "8, 7, 6, 5, 4, 3, 2, 1!"
> Left arm: "8, 7, 6, 5, 4, 3, 2, 1!"
> Right leg: "8, 7, 6, 5, 4, 3, 2, 1!"
> Left leg: "8, 7, 6, 5, 4, 3, 2, 1!"
> Right arm: "7, 6, 5, 4, 3, 2, 1!"
> Left arm: "7, 6, 5, 4, 3, 2, 1!"
> Right leg: "7, 6, 5, 4, 3, 2, 1!"
> Left leg: "7, 6, 5, 4, 3, 2, 1!"
> Right arm: "6, 5, 4, 3, 2, 1!"
> ...etc. until....
> Right arm: "1!"
> Left arm: "1!"
> Right leg: "1!"
> Left leg: "1!"

After the acting warmup, explain the schedule for the day: a series of warmups and then straight into a final run through of the show. After the run-through, there will be about 30 minutes for everyone to have a bathroom break, get organized and get ready before the performance!

VOCAL WARMUP
Choose 1 articulation warmup and 2 vocal warmups from previous lessons.

DANCE WARMUP
If you don't have a favorite dance warmup, this jazz dance warmup will get everyone moving: https://bit.ly/3iKWMhB

Final Dress/Tech Rehearsal: 1 Hour
Use the first hour after the morning meeting for a run-through of the program. Keep an eye out for sound or lighting problems. For instance, if a student's light source is behind them, it might throw them in shadow, but that can be easily adjusted. It's a good idea to test out the Facebook Live connection, which you can do by going live for a couple of minutes at the beginning of the rehearsal and having the whole cast wave as you tell everyone to stay tuned for the show at the scheduled time.

Another tip: Record the final rehearsal on Zoom! That way, if for some reason the internet connection fails during the live performance, you'll have a pre-recorded rehearsal that you can share!

Break: 15 Minutes
Let the cast have a 15-minute break after rehearsal to regroup, reorganize and get ready for the show.

Pre-Show Warmup/Checklist: 15 Minutes
Make sure everyone has a run of the program available on their end. Have them check that their devices are charged, and that they have access to any music tracks they need.

Then tell them some jokes. I'm serious. It's really weird to be "backstage," nervous -- and technically all on your own. If we were in the theater together, they would have their fellow cast members to lean on, but everyone is kind of isolated with their nerves. So let's make them laugh.

Tell them it's an acting exercise and that they aren't allowed to laugh…

- An actor I know fell through the floor recently. It's just a stage he was going through. [insert rim shot sound effect]

- Knock knock!
  Who's there?
  Stephanie!
  Stephanie who?
  Stephanie-six trombones led the big parade!

- Why is a piano so hard to open? Because the keys are on the inside!

- How many dancers does it take to change a light bulb?" Five! … Six! … Seven! … Eight!

Ask if anyone else has a theatre, dance or music joke to share. Then when everyone in the group is either smiling or groaning, have everyone turn off their video. Let them know that you will call on them to turn it on when it is time to perform. Tell them that they can still have access to you and ask any questions via chat.

Create a document on your computer that says, "Please turn off your video, mute your volume and select 'Speaker View' on Zoom!" Then share that screen, so that any visitors who enter the Zoom session will see that message and know what to do. One minute before the performance time, turn off the screen sharing, go live on FB or YouTube if you are doing that, and address the audience(s).

IT'S SHOWTIME!

Begin your program by welcoming everyone, whether they're viewing on Facebook or as a part of the Zoom audience. Talk to them about how proud you are of these amazingly innovative young performers who have chosen to learn and perform and create together, even with all the challenges they've faced.

Explain to the audience that part of what they will see is an "informance" which will share a little bit of information about what the students have learned this week as they studied acting, music and dance. Everyone will need to keep their video screens off and sound muted, but we will provide an applause track for every performer to express what we know that they're feeling. They can also send chat messages after each performance ("Way to go!") -- but please do hold those to the end of the performance.

You are the emcee of the show, and you will announce each performer, giving them a few moments to turn on their video and sound, etc. You can even remind the next couple of acts that they should be getting ready. No one will mind this more informal approach to narrating the show. Nor will they mind the occasional technical problem -- just stay lighthearted about it and the audience will as well.

At the end of the show, announce each performer and let them take their own bow. Just a reminder: if everyone selects "Speaker View" and each performer says "Thank you" as soon as you call their name, they will appear larger than everyone else long enough to take a bow before you call the next name.

Have the last word! Thank everyone for coming to the show and let them know where they can find a recording of the performance if they would like to view it again later (they will!). Now is an awesome time to tell them about your upcoming plans for programming -- whether online or in person -- and to invite them to sign up for the next show!

WEEK 2: Improv, Script Writing & Radio Plays

Before Camp

Before your camp week starts, be sure to communicate frequently with parents, telling them how to log on (Zoom ID and password), as well as how the schedule will work, what materials - if any - kids will need, what kind of space they need in their home, etc.

Let them know that you will be performing a live Zoom radio play on Friday, during the last hour of camp. Share the link to the play with them and ask that students either print the script at home or have it open on a separate device for rehearsal.

MONDAY

Morning Meeting (30 Minutes)

Welcome to "Not Necessarily on Stage!" Week of our Online Theatre Project! Today's morning meeting will last a little longer than most days, because it will take some time to acclimate new students to this virtual format. Once again, I recommend playing some fun music in the background and encourage kids to sing and dance along, as you manage the participants in the room and answer texts from parents who can't find the Zoom password or are having connection problems.

When everyone has arrived, tell them how the camp is going to work, how the schedule will run each day, and what kind of performance you are working towards at the end of the week. This week is about all kinds of acting that might not take place on a stage -- and we are going to create our own scripts! At the end of the week, we are going to stage a live performance, which will include new plays that the students have written, improv games AND a live radio drama!

At this point, explain that before it was possible to transmit video images into people's homes, radio dramas provided weekly mystery stories, science fiction, dramas, comedies that families gathered around and LISTENED to. The actors used their voices only, and sound effect artists were extremely important to the process, creating sounds like footsteps, doors opening and slamming, hoofbeats of horses, gunfire for Westerns, spaceships taking off -- you name it.

Next, let each student introduce themselves and answer a fun question (like a favorite musical or movie or TV show, for instance). It might also be fun to play an applause sound effect after each introduction and let your "cast" each take a bow.

This way, they can practice unmuting themselves and re-muting and everyone gets a chance to talk. Let them practice turning their video on and off, selecting "Speaker View" (so that the person talking is biggest on their screen). You, as the Meeting Host, can also choose on whom the students should focus by choosing to "Spotlight" them in Zoom. This meet and greet time will also give you a chance to see who has challenges with technology, sound, lighting, who might be dealing with a slow internet connection, who is shy, who is a talker, etc.

If you're going to use Zoom breakout sessions, this would be a great time to practice with the kids: You create the rooms and assign a teacher and students to each room. The students can practice "accepting" the breakout session, going into that room, and then coming back to the main room. You could even make a "scavenger hunt" out of it: When they go into a room you have assigned them, they will see that teacher and guess what musical his/her Zoom background is from. When they've visited all three rooms, they will have finished the scavenger hunt!

This is also a good session to discuss the "Zoom rules" for your class. You can decide what boundaries you are going to set, but here are a few suggested topics to discuss:

- Are you going to enable the chat feature? If so, what is OK/Not OK to say in chats?
- We stay muted until we have to ask a question -- not because we don't want everyone to talk but even a little bit of background noise can be distracting.
- How to ask a question: physically raise your hand or use the "virtual hand-raising" feature on Zoom.
- Your video stays ON during class, unless you're asked to turn it off - but iPads do not go to the bathroom with you (yep, it has happened).

At the end of the session, assign students to breakout sessions OR start your first curriculum block, depending on the structure of your camp. If students are going into breakout sessions, make sure teachers and students know what time to return to the main session to be reassigned.

Improv/Theatre Games (45 Minutes)

(Many of the improv activities and lessons in this unit are adapted from Teaching Improv: The Essential Handbook (https://bit.ly/3fsZXYZ) written by Mel Paradis, which includes 16 lesson plans and 114 improv activities for traditional classroom teaching.)

Begin the class by sharing a numbered list of students' names; everyone should either write out this list or print it. Everyone is assigned a number. They should know who is before and after them. This will serve as our virtual "circle," because there are some improv games we would like to flow as smoothly as if we were standing in a circle (without having to call out a student's name each time), and you can't control the order in which Zoom windows appear on everyone's screens.   But if everyone knows their order in the line, you can do progressive games as though you were standing in a circle.

Practice each student counting aloud their numbers in order, and then #1 starting over after the end of the list, making a virtual "circle." Run through the numbers two or three times.

DISCUSS: What is improv?
What is improv? Has anyone ever seen an improv show? How is it different from other forms of acting? (Some might mention having seen Saturday Night Live.)

Other possible answers:

- Acting without a script
- Playing games where you get suggestions from other people
- Scenes where you create everything as you go along
- Sometimes serious, but most of the time associated with comedy

Here is a clip kids will enjoy from "Whose Line Is It Anyway?" that uses improv and music: https://bit.ly/2WiVSzj.

Write these rules of improv in a document and share the screen with your class:

Rules of Improv
1. Teamwork and Trust
2. Make Associations
3. Yes…and
4. Listen
5. Relate
6. Be Honest
7. Be in the Present
8. Tell a Story
9. Develop Relationships

Tell them we will uncover the importance of each of these rules as we move through the week. Keeping these rules in mind will help them to develop their improv skills.

ACTIVITY: Warmup: 10% More
- The teacher starts a small physical motion and sound.
- #1 accepts the small motion, repeats it AND magnifies it 10%.
- For instance, if the teacher starts with a small wave and a quiet "hey," #1 will make the wave a little larger and might say, "heeey."
- #2 makes the wave larger and extends out the "heeeeeey."
- This goes around through the group with the motion and sound getting bigger and bigger.
- After it goes through the group once or twice, start a new sound and motion and pass it around the circle in the other direction.

Game Debrief: Did the progression feel natural? Was there a moment where it jumped more than 10%? Successful improv scenes move in small increments. You will lose your audience if you take too big of leaps.

DISCUSSION: Yes, And...

> *"Just say yes and you'll figure it out afterwards."*
> -Tina Fey, The Second City and Saturday Night Live

In improv we take what was presented before us, say "yes" to it and then heighten it.
- Heightening is adding information that raises the stakes in a scene and makes it more interesting.
- As things get heightened, it makes for better scenes and that is where the humor lies.
- If we negate what is said or presented to us, then our scene partner is not going to trust us AND the scene will go nowhere.
- Call on one student and and ask them to say the line "That is a beautiful dress you're wearing" to you.
- Once they say the line, reply: "This isn't a dress. It's a baseball uniform."
- Does this feel like a good way to start a scene? No. I just blocked, or denied their offer to me.
- How would you feel if you were in a scene and your partner blocked your offer? Let's try this again.
- Cue the student to say the line, "That's a beautiful dress you're wearing." Reply, "Thanks, I think it is pretty too."
- This is slightly better - I "Yes-ed" the statement, but did not AND it as well. The scene didn't go anywhere. Let's give this one more try...
- Cue the student to say one more time "That's a beautiful dress you're wearing."
- Reply with "Thanks it is going to look beautiful on my wedding day."
- Now I "Yes, And"-ed - I have accepted the statement and jumped to a "logical" step. I associated a dress with a wedding. This scene is now a bride trying on wedding dresses.
- It is our goal to always accept what is offered, and then heighten it. This is what we'll be practicing today.

ACTIVITY: So I'll
- Choose two students. Everyone else's video is turned off so the focus can be on the performers "on stage."
- Give the actors a starting prompt, such as "It is a rainy day."
- Students take turns accepting the statement said by their partner, then adding "So I'll..." and taking the story to the next logical step.
- Before adding to a statement, students repeat what their partner said.

Example:
- Student A: "It is a rainy day, so I'll pull out my umbrella."
- Student B: "What you're saying is 'you'll pull out your umbrella,' so I'll open the door for you." Student A: "What you're saying is 'you'll open the door for me,' so I'll go for a walk."
- Let this go for 3-4 minutes.

  Repeat the process with additional scenarios:
  - It is snowing outside.

- It's very crowded in this room.
- I'm very hungry.
- There's a shark in the water!

Script Writing (45 Minutes)

DISCUSSION: What is a script?

Scripts are different from books, short stories, magazines, newspapers. What makes a script different from these other kinds of writing? Some possible answers:
- Scripts have characters who speak to each other, unlike magazines and newspapers.
- Scripts are meant to be performed.
- Scripts can be turned into plays or movies or TV shows.
- Scripts have a story or plot.

A script is a way to tell a story that is meant to be performed. It will have characters, one or more of whom are the PROTAGONIST (usually the "good guy"), often an ANTAGONIST (usually the "bad guy"), a PLOT (the action of the story) and a SETTING (when and where the story takes place).

Talk about each of these fairy tale stories and identify the PROTAGONIST, ANTAGONIST, PLOT and SETTING:
- Cinderella
- Little Red Riding Hood
- Jack and the Beanstalk
- Aladdin

ACTIVITY: Script Read

Share your screen where you have loaded the script for "Ghosts" (**Appendix C**, from *Contemporary Scenes for Young Actors*). Point out where the characters' names are located, the scene descriptions, the dialogue. Explain that this is the way that the page is laid out for a stage play. TV, film, commercial and radio scripts are laid out differently (we will take a look at each throughout the week).

Read through the scene, taking volunteers from class.

Questions for discussion:
- Who are the characters?
- What is the plot?
- What do the main characters want?
- What is stopping them from getting it?

Talk about the difference between an external struggle -- like two people fighting against each other -- and an internal struggle -- like someone battling with their own fear. In this case, the big obstacle is not another person or being but the characters' own ideas.

ACTIVITY: Away from Screen

Tell the students that they are going to spend a little time away from the screen now, thinking specifically about characters. Tell them they can choose any fairy tale they know and answer these questions about the main characters:

- PROTAGONIST ("Good Guy")
  - What does he/she want?
  - What stands in their way?
  - What are this character's strengths?
  - What are this character's weaknesses?
  - Who wants to help the protagonist achieve their goal (supporting characters)?

- ANTAGONIST ("Bad Guy")
  - How does the bad guy try to keep the protagonist from achieving their goal?
  - What are this character's strengths?
  - What are this character's weaknesses?
  - Who wants to help the antagonist achieve their goal (supporting villains)?

Let them know that if they get stuck on a question, you are available for them to come back to the screen and ask for help at any time.

After everyone has chosen a story and written down their answers, go around the group and ask them to share their thoughts about the protagonist and antagonist of each story. Does anyone disagree? (There isn't a right or wrong answer and share examples of stories -- like the Three Bears -- where it's hard to pin down.)

Final question for discussion: How would each plot be different if written from the ANTAGONIST'S point of view? For instance, we could imagine the story of Jack and the Beanstalk from the point of view of the giant: This kid invades his house and steals his stuff!

Let the group know that tomorrow we are going to outline the plots of our own plays! Students' homework is to think of a famous fairy tale that they would like to turn into a play. They can tell it traditionally -- from the point of view of the same main character they've always heard. OR they can switch up the story and focus their play on the Big Bad Wolf in Red Riding Hood or the Golden Goose in Jack and the Beanstalk.

Voice Acting (45 Minutes)

Welcome everyone to voice acting class today by using a funny accent. Ask them if any of them can do any impressions (Spongebob, Bugs Bunny, the Queen of England, etc). Tell them one of the cool things about voice acting is that one actor can play a whole bunch of different characters

Then get everyone on their feet and tell them we're going to warm up our voices. Yep, this may not be voice class, but our voices are still being used and still need to be warm.

ACTIVITY: Warm Up
- Explain you're an engineer who's going to create a roller coaster that their voice will take a ride on.
- Give the class the first note to start on and have the entire class "move" their voices up and down the roller coaster (you can choose any vowel sound).
- As you raise your hand up or down, their voices need to follow your hand's movements.
- Your roller coaster could start very low and make a slow climb upwards, fall quickly or even do loop-de-loops!
- After you've directed them a few times, ask for a volunteer to be "train engineer."

(OPTIONAL: You can also use the virtual "white board" feature under the Zoom "share screen" option and draw the roller coaster rises and falls. The kids LOVE to take over the virtual white board, so your roller coaster engineers will be super excited to engineer their own designs for everyone to sing.)

ACTIVITY: Tongue Twisters
- Unique New York
- Three free throws
- Red Leather, Yellow Leather
- Silly Sally swiftly shooed seven silly sheep The seven silly sheep Silly Sally shooed Shilly-shallied south

Try repeating the tongue twisters normally and then call on various cast members to say the line "like a baby," "like an old man," "like a robot," etc.

DISCUSSION: What is voice acting?
Explain to the students that before there was film and television, radio was the center of family entertainment and everything from the news, to soap operas to sci-fi and mystery programs were acted out in sound. What the actors looked like made no difference, as long as they could sound like the characters they were portraying -- from Little Orphan Annie to the Lone Ranger. They didn't need costumes because no one could see them.

Even Superman! Share your screen with this Superman radio drama script: https://bit.ly/3haJZU7

[We are using this Superman Radio Hour episode as an example in this curriculum but there are a TON of old radio scripts out there to choose from. Some companies have even produced new ones just for children. I think it's fun to produce one ourselves that was actually on the radio at one time. Whichever one you choose to produce, look for ones with lots of opportunities to incorporate characters with different voices and all kinds of sound effects!]

As you share the script on screen, show the students where to find the name of the episode, the character names, the stage directions. Explain that "FX" refers to "sound effects" which helped to tell the story -- especially for a superhero like Superman. And that every radio show started and ended with commercials -- which we are familiar with in modern programs too. These early radio shows were more likely to have a single sponsor for a whole program and the Narrator or Announcer who helped tell the radio story ALSO very often read the commercial script -- it would be like if Baby Yoda had to walk out at the beginning of The Madalorian and tell everyone how much he enjoyed Cheerios before starting the TV show!

FOLEY ARTISTS are special sound effects creators who make the sound effects that tell the story -- they were every bit as important to radio dramas as the other characters. The foley artist's feet would create the footsteps that the listener thought were Clark Kent's feet walking into his office -- or the phone ringing sound or the door opening and closing. Check out this video of a modern-day foley artist sharing a few tips! https://bit.ly/32iRjsf

WATCH AND LISTEN: Radio Drama
Superman Radio Hour Recording, Episode "Dr. Dahlgren's Atomic Beam Machine"
https://bit.ly/3euPDyk

Start this video at the 14:09 mark (there is another episode of Superman right before our episode). Explain that we are going to perform this radio drama for our show on Friday! We will play and/or create our own special effects live, as well as cast the show. Tell the kids that auditions will be tomorrow. No one has to memorize the script, but all characters will need to be very comfortable with the material by then.

Also, each actor will need to either print out a copy of the script OR have the script on another device for the show, so that you won't have to share the script on screen during the performance. For instance, they could Zoom on a laptop and pull up a copy of the script on an iPad.

Pay attention to where the sound effects are located and the various ways the actors change their voices: accents, muffling, moving away from the mic to give the impression of distance, etc. Can you tell how they create the sound effects?

Closing Meeting (15 Minutes)

Play some celebration music as the students settle down for the end of their first day, and encourage them to move along. I love the KidzBop version of "Celebration:" https://bit.ly/3esWlVJ

GAME: Alien, Tiger, Cow
- Everyone in the group stands.
- Everyone needs to have Zoom on the Gallery View so that all players can be seen at once.
- On the teacher's count of 3, the players have the choice of being one of three things (i.e. rock, paper or scissors):
  - Alien, Tiger or Cow
    - **ALIEN** – players hold their fingers up to their head like antennae and say "Bleep, bleep, bleep."
    - **TIGER** – players throw their hands out like claws and say "Roooar!"

- **COW** – players put their hands on their tummies with fingers sticking out like udders and say "Mooo!"
  - Whichever one of these things is the minority of the group, those players must turn off their video -- they are "out" for this round. (If there are 4 Aliens, 7 Tigers, and 3 Cows, the Cows are the minority and turn off their video.)
  - It's against the rules to change your character!
  - Continue until there are only 1 or 2 players left.
    <u>Variation:</u> A different goal to playing this game is for everyone to become the SAME character (no elimination). Obviously it will take a few turns for this to happen. Let the players organically try to figure it out.

Thank everyone for a great day and find out if there are any questions. Encourage them to think of fairy tales for their scripts and to read through the episode of Superman again if they have a chance.

Take suggestions for tomorrow's dress-up theme (unless you have pre-chosen and pre-announced those themes) and let the kids vote on their favorite! Some of our favorites: superheroes, favorite musical theatre character, favorite fairytale character, FOOD! (we had one kiddo turn herself into a plate of spaghetti with her mother's yarn :), animals, and magical beings.

TUESDAY

Morning Meeting (15 Minutes)

This morning's celebration song is "Walking on Sunshine!" (https://bit.ly/308EoXo) As everyone logs on, checks in and sends any questions they may have via chat, encourage the rest of the group to move and sing along with the music.

Welcome everyone to Day 2 of "Not Necessarily On Stage!" Today's word of the day is ENSEMBLE. Explain that an ensemble is a group of performers who works together, trusts each other and creates together. Each member of an ensemble is equally important. To illustrate that fact and celebrate our creativity, let's tell a story together.

WARMUP: Drama Game - One Word Story
Share the class list on which every student is assigned a number (from Improv class) -- this is their number for this game:
- #1 says a single word to begin a story.
- #2 says another word, then the next person says another word, continuing down the list.
- The goal to tell a coherent story, one word at a time.

Now it's time to either break students up into breakout sessions or begin your first curriculum block...

Improv / Drama Games (45 Minutes)

Review
Who remembers the definition of improv? What are the rules of improv that we discussed yesterday?

In case they don't remember or need a visual reminder...

Rules of Improv
1. Teamwork and Trust
2. Make Associations
3. Yes…and
4. Listen
5. Relate
6. Be Honest
7. Be in the Present
8. Tell a Story
9. Develop Relationships

Why is it important to LISTEN when you're performing improv? Why is it important to tell a story -- as opposed to just making a lot of random silly sounds?

ACTIVITY: Rumors
- Start with everyone on the Speaker View on Zoom (this setting makes the person speaking appear bigger than the other members of the group, which works well for this activity}.
- Call on a student to begin the game. This student calls on another student of their choice and says to them, "[Student's name], did you hear about…" (insert the name of a famous person, an object, or a place).
- That student then accepts the offer and creates a ridiculous rumor.
- Example:
  - Student A: "Student B, did you hear about the President of the Student Council?"
  - Student B: "Yes, she was impeached after no one showed up for the Homecoming Parade that she planned!"
  - Student B picks another student and asks them about a new rumor ...
- Example:
  - Student B: "Did you hear about chicken noodle soup?"
  - Student C: "Yes, I heard that everyone in the cafeteria got food poisoning from it!"
- Continue through the group.

Game Debrief: Was it easier to come up with an opening statement or the heightened reply? Why?

Watch and Learn
Play this clip from the television show, "Whose Line Is It Anyway" in which they play an improv game called "Hollywood Director." https://bit.ly/2ZsoMif

Let's talk about the rules of improv and how we saw them played out in this game. (It might even be helpful to re-run the clip and stop and start it to discuss what you see):

Teamwork and trust are apparent. These actors have worked together for years and it's clear to see that they trust one another's instincts and respect their creativity. And obviously, they are telling a story! Let's talk about the relationships they create between the characters -- who are the characters and what do they do to develop their connections? Let's talk about "Yes...and" - The skit was funny enough the first time, but they HEIGHTENED the humor when they did what in the game? What might have happened if they hadn't been LISTENING?

ACTIVITY: Improv Exercise - Two-Headed Interview
- Choose two students to turn on their video and everyone else's video is off (this just makes it easier for these two students to know to whom they are speaking).
- These students are partners, and these partners will be giving an interview as a "two-headed" person.
- Each head can speak one word at a time. One person says a word and the other person adds the next word to the sentence, etc.
- Get a suggestion from the class of an expertise.

- The class asks questions about that topic for the two-headed people to answer. Try and avoid simple yes or no questions.
- Example: Experts on making ice cream. Question from the class: "How do you decide what flavor of ice cream to make?"
  - Partners A (Alternating one word at a time): "We" "think" "that" "every" "day" "a" "new" "flavor" "should" "be" "made." "We" "choose" "the" "flavor" "by" "looking" "out" "the" "window" "and" "seeing" "what" "is" "there."
- Choose a new pair of actors, a new expertise and a new question.
- After several rounds of the game this way, take it up a notch. Now we have a new two-headed person and both heads say the same word AT THE SAME TIME as they answer the questions.
- These partners must watch each others' lips to say the same words together.
- Example: Experts on making ice cream. Question from the class: "How do you decide what flavor of ice cream to make?"
  - Partners B (speaking simultaneously): "Weeeee llliiiike tooooo loooook iiiin ouuuur rrrrreeeeeefrigerator to seeee wwwwhaat fooooood iiiis thhhhere."
- Each round may go for a few questions then give new students a chance to play. Both sets of partners must listen but they will be listening in different ways:
  - One Word at a Time: Avoid too many "ands" and "because" or the answer will lose focus.
  - Speaking Simultaneously: One person should be the leader and the other follows. Make sure you change up the leadership.

Game Debrief: Was it easier to speak simultaneously or one word at a time? Why? How did you listen to your partner? How did you decide who would take the lead and who would follow?

Watch and Learn
As a reward for their great ensemble work, share this video of the cast of IMPROVAGANZA playing the Two-Headed Interview game, and be prepared for some hysterical laughter: https://bit.ly/2ZsoMif

Could they identify a leader/follower in the simultaneous speaking duo? Where were the 10% more moments? And the "Yes and--" moments?

Script Writing (45 Minutes)

DISCUSSION: Protagonists and Antagonists
Welcome to Day 2 of Playwriting! Who can explain the difference between a protagonist and an antagonist? Ask how many of the students have selected a fairy tale that they would like to turn into a play. Allow as many as would like to share their ideas for plays.

If anyone hasn't chosen a fairy tale at this point, let them know that you can help them decide on one when the next activity begins.

ACTIVITY: Away from Screen - Who, What, When, Where
Next we are going to take our fairy tale idea and create an outline for our script.

We are going to answer three questions:

1. **WHO:** We need a PROTAGONIST and an ANTAGONIST for our play. Also, we need to identify the SUPPORTING characters. For example, in the traditional story of Cinderella, the protagonist is Cinderella, antagonist is the Wicked Stepmother and supporting characters include the Prince, the Fairy Godmother, the Wicked Stepsisters, and other people at the ball.

2. **WHAT:** What does the protagonist want? What is the obstacle that keeps her/him from getting it? Cinderella wants to go to the ball, but her Wicked Stepmother and Stepsisters try to destroy her chances. So then what happens? The Fairy Godmother appears. How does it end? She and the Prince get married.

3. **WHERE/WHEN:** What is the setting for the show? This is only as important as it affects the story. Cinderella was originally written in the 1600s in France, but could it be set in England in the 1800s? Absolutely. More importantly, it takes place in a manor house and at a castle ball, at a time when people still used horses and carriages as a means of transportation.

Now ask each of your students to spend 15 minutes crafting their initial outline of character (who), plot (what), and setting (where). Make sure they know what time to come back to the Zoom meeting. And let them know that, should they get "stuck," you are available to help them with their writing.

Any students who have not yet chosen a fairy tale are invited to sit with you until they decide on a story that they feel excited to write. Ask them about their favorite childhood stories. You might get some that flatly refuse to choose a fairy tale, insisting on superheroes or Pokemon and that is totally fine. As long as they are writing out a who/what/where/when outline.

ACTIVITY: Share Time
Allow each student to share their who/what/when/where. As each student shares their idea for a play, ask them what kind of scenes they think are important to the story. For instance, with Cinderella, we know that we need a scene that shows her finding out about the ball, a scene where she is told she can't attend the ball, a scene with the Fairy Godmother, a scene at the ball... how many scenes can they immediately think of that MUST be a part of their story.

ACTIVITY: Devising a Scene
Explain that one of the ways to write scenes for a play is to gather some actors, give them a scenario (characters, intention, setting) and let them improvise the scene.

- Take one of the suggested scenes from one of the student works, and choose student actors (not the playwright) to play those parts. For instance, we might have a Cinderella and a couple of wicked stepsisters.

- After they have finished improvising, ask the young playwright how close this came to her vision. Even if it was vastly different, are there any elements of that improvised scene that she might use in her play?

Voice Acting (45 Minutes)

Explain that today is the day we are going to audition for roles in our Superman radio play! But first, we need to warm up our voices, bodies and acting skills...

WARMUP: 30 Seconds of Character
- Have everyone pick a character with a distinct voice in their head. This could be a southern belle, Forrest Gump, a valley girl, Arnold Schwarzenegger, a New York cop, etc. It's OK for multiple students to play the same character.
- Tell the students to then pick a creature of fantasy, such as a dragon or unicorn.
- Give the class 30 seconds where they all simultaneously, in character, give a monologue about the creature.
- Example: (spoken in an Arnold Schwarzenegger voice) Unicorns are the most magical creature in all of the world. In fact I know that they are not imaginary. I have a pet unicorn that I keep in my bedroom. When I get home from school we go on a bike ride. The unicorn runs in front. If it is dark out, I put a light on his horn and it helps me stay safe…

How did that go? Was it hard to stay focused? Were you able to stay in character? If not, why not? If we try to talk over our scene partners or conversely, if our scene partner never stops yapping, we can't listen.
- Try the warmup again, but this time going down the list of students so that only one person speaks at a time.
- Each student should allow the speaker about 30 seconds of monologue. At this time, the new student begins to speak and the previous student should stop and listen. Encourage students to feed off the same energy of the previous speaker.

ACTIVITY: Auditions
Explain that today we're going to hold auditions for our radio play, "Superman: Dr. Dahlgren's Atomic Beam Machine." We're only going to use three passages from the script for auditions, but we're going to do these three characters in three different ways:
1. With a big announcer voice;
2. As a small, shy child; and
3. As someone who is sinister and evil.

Even though this won't be the way we ultimately perform the show -- the announcer WILL likely have an announcer voice and the Mask will sound sinister and evil, but no one will sound like a baby! - our goal today is to see how flexible you are with doing different characters with your voice. Also, we'll be auditioning everyone's EVIL LAUGH - MWAHAHAHAAHAHAHA!

There are several more characters who are in the show and will be cast, but whose lines aren't a part of the audition today. Also, several of our actors will be working as "foley artists," creating sound effects for the show.

Does anyone have any questions?

Here are our audition characters:

- ANNOUNCER:
  And now, Superman, amazing figure from another world with powers and abilities never before realized by mortal men… When we last saw Superman, in his disguise as young Clark Kent, reporter for the Daily Planet, he and his editor, Perry White, had just received a warning telephone message from a mysterious voice which identified itself as The Yellow Mask.

  In exactly twenty-four hours, said The Mask, the Daily Planet would be blown to a thousand fragments. Horror-stricken, Kent and his chief stared at each other in the humming office. Then, pandemonium!

- DAHLGREN:
  Certainly, Professor Schmidt. Unlimited power for destruction. Which is why I am determined to keep the discovery a closely guarded secret. In the world today, my friend, there is destruction enough. Men are at one another's throats like dogs gone mad. No, I will never be a party to war and bloodshed. Ah, but come, I waste time. Into this room, Professor. Er, don't brush against the metal-work.

- MASK:
  Beyond the reach of the police, I assure you. I have laid my plans with great care, Doctor. First, I shall destroy the building which houses one of your great newspapers, because a reporter on that paper foiled my plans in the West and succeeded in jailing two of my men. When that is done, I will go about the task of creating for myself the position I rightfully deserve -- Emperor of the World! And now, I must go.

- [EVIL LAUGH]

Read through each of the passages one time for them. Then ask them to spend 10 minutes rehearsing the passages with different voices: big announcer voice, small shy voice and evil voice. Let them know what time to come back to the screen for auditions.

Auditions
Use the remainder of the class time for auditions. Sharing your screen with the list of student names, start with #1 and ask them to read one or more of the passages in the three different voices. At the end of each reading, ask them to give you their best evil laugh!

Closing Meeting (15 Minutes)

It's time to celebrate and "Make Some Noise!" (https://bit.ly/3j09JEd) As the kids come into the final meeting play this celebration song and encourage them to dance along for a few minutes.

Congratulate everyone on their hard work as an ENSEMBLE today, and let them know that casting for our radio play will be announced the following morning at the Welcome Meeting.

Next, ask for volunteers who would like to share their favorite part of today. Favorite moment in improv? Playwriting? Voice acting? Anything they learned today that they would like to talk about?

Finally, share your OWN favorite moments of the day, being as specific as possible. Kids respond well to the knowledge that the grownups are paying attention and take them seriously as performers. A statement like "I loved how Jocelyn surprised me with her evil laugh in voice acting today - I really believed in her as the evil scientist!" goes a long way to reinforcing brave choices and encouraging creativity.

After Camp

It's time to cast the radio show! I would recommend casting main roles AND understudies. And then each of the understudies can also be a foley artist and help create the sound effects for the show.

WEDNESDAY

Welcome Meeting (15 Minutes)

It's Hump Day! Welcome to Day 3 of "Not Necessarily On Stage!" Today's word is CONFIDENCE, and we are going to start with a Dance Along all about that: https://bit.ly/3gWN0Hm So as the students start logging on, encourage them to sing and dance along, because today we're going to be brave and confident and proud of ourselves -- if they don't feel like dancing, they can draw a picture that suggests CONFIDENCE while we're waiting for everyone to arrive...

DISCUSSION: Confidence
Today's word is CONFIDENCE -- why is confidence important in performing?

It's time to announce casting for the radio play! Cue up a drum roll sound effect, and share your copy of the cast list. Explain that every single player is very important and none more so that our sound effect artists.

Wish everyone a great Wednesday and send them off to their breakout sessions or start your first curriculum block...

Improv / Theatre Games (45 Minutes)

DISCUSSION: Confidence in Improv
Briefly review the rules of the improv class and discuss how some of those rules will help you build confidence as a performer… How important is trust in confidence? Do you have more confidence in your performance if you trust the people around you? How can everyone's honesty help build confidence? Talk about "being in the present" -- what does that mean? It takes confidence to be in the present -- to not worry about what happened in the past or what might happen in the future but to react IN THE PRESENT.

ACTIVITY: Drama Game: Three Objects
- Ask all students to stand, but not to get too far away from the camera. The goal is that they will have enough environment to act in, but not be so far away that their movements will be unrecognizable. A waist-up level in the Zoom screen should be sufficient.
- Through the Zoom chat system, privately message a selected student with a "where" environment written on it.
- Their goal is to enter the stage, interact with 3 specific objects in that environment, then exit. (For example, if the environment is "bedroom": Player enters, goes to the closet to pull out a hat, goes to the dresser to put on a belt, then looks at herself in the mirror, then exits, etc.)
- There should be no talking.
- The class must try to guess what the environment is and what three objects were used.
- Continue until everyone has a chance to participate.

Some potential environments: kitchen, bathroom, doctor's office, photo studio, cockpit of plane, beach, church, park, grocery store, barbecue, etc.

WATCH AND LEARN: New Choice
https://bit.ly/2CwDH1S

Discussion questions: Did you see how much these characters had to stay IN THE MOMENT to immediately respond with a "new choice?" How would the performance have been different if there was a pause after each time the host demanded, "New choice!" and before that choice was made?

ACTIVITY: Martha Game
- Everyone's video is turned off.
- Choose a location and ask the first five students on your student list to participate in the next scene.
- Each student will turn on their video, one at a time, and announce that they are an object found in the environment.
- The fifth student turns on his video and plays a character found in that environment. For example, at the beach:
  - First student enters and says, "I am a beach chair" and lays down like a beach chair.
  - Next student enters and says, "I am an umbrella" and becomes an umbrella.
  - Third and fourth students become a wave lapping up the beach and a sea gull eating trash.
  - The fifth student enters as an ice cream vendor.
- The teacher clears the stage, with the phrase "Scene!"
- Run several more rounds with different locations.
- Game Debrief: How did we do as a class creating honest environments? Did anything stick out or distract from the environment?

Script Writing (45 Minutes)

DISCUSSION: Conflict
Let's dive into an important element of storytelling: Conflict. What is conflict? See what kind of answers the students give and how well they understand this idea.

If you took a famous story and took away the conflict, there would be no excitement or interest in what happened. Imagine the story of Cinderella: Cinderella wants to go to the ball. Everyone in the house says, "Great! You should! Here's a great dress!" They get ready and go to the ball together. The prince and Cinderella dance and decide to get married and everyone is happy for them.

Literature and film conflict is often broken down into the categories that begin with "man versus…"
- Here are some examples of these. Read a few of the examples and discuss:
- Man versus Self: Harry Potter: Hallows or Horcruxes?

- Man versus Man: Hunger Games: Katniss killing other tributes.
- Man Versus Society: The Grinch against the Whos.
- Man Versus Nature: Hatchet: Brian versus the elements post plane crash; animal attacks, tornado, finding food, etc.
- Man Versus Technology: Terminator and Westworld: Man versus Robots
- Man Versus Fates/Gods/Supernatural: Lord of the Rings: Frodo struggles against the eye of Mordor to follow his destiny and destroy the ring.

These are examples of BIG conflicts.

WATCH AND LEARN: Conflict

https://bit.ly/32tZQsP

This video used The Hunger Games to illustrate Man Vs. Society because Katniss was opposed to what her society was doing. But she was ALSO in a Man vs. Man conflict because she had to literally fight against other human beings to save her own life. She was ALSO frequently in a Man Vs. Nature and Man Vs. Technology fight. The best stories will have more than one conflict for the character but one of them will be most important and will lead to the greatest change in the character.

ACTIVITY: Write a Scene

Without worrying too much about formatting (how the story is laid out on the page), we're going to write one scene from our fairy tale play. This should be a scene that involves the major conflict in the story. Let's look at each play that you've chosen to write and collaborate together on choosing a conflict to illustrate with a scene.

Let each playwright pitch their story to the group and if they know already, tell you which scene they would like to work on. If they have difficulty determining the central conflict in the story, open it up to group discussion and ask the students to make suggestions to their fellow writer.

For instance, the story of Cinderella could include a scene between Cinderella and her stepmother (man vs. man). The story of Aladdin could include a scene in which Aladdin has to decide whether or not to be brave and tell the truth. Even though he might be talking to the genie, the conflict happens inside himself (man vs. self).

There are a few important rules to writing a scene for a play:

1. A scene takes place in one location and one moment in time. Even though you occasionally see years of time passing before your eyes in musical montages in movies and TV shows, that doesn't happen on stage. We are capturing one event in one place and one time.
2. Scenes involve things we can SEE and HEAR. What do the characters say and what do they do? We don't usually have thoughts in a play -- unless the character is "thinking out loud." For instance, Aladdin might pace back and forth and talk about his dilemma.
3. Something should CHANGE for the main character by the end of the scene. At the beginning of a scene, for instance, Cinderella is excited about the invitation to the ball. Then her stepmother comes in and tells her she can't go, and so she ends the scene feeling sad.

4. Scenes are about obstacles and conflict. Just like the play as a whole is about a BIG want and a BIG conflict, each scene has its goal and obstacle as well. The overall goal of Cinderella is to be free of her wicked stepmother and live happily ever after. In one scene, though, her goal is to go to the ball and the obstacle to that is her stepmother says she can't.

Ask your students to spend 15 minutes working on their scene. Let them know when to come back to the Zoom meeting and that you are available on screen at any time that they need help. If students need help getting started, meet with them one or two at a time to kick off their projects.

If there is time left at the end of class, after the writing exercise, allow some of the authors to read their work. Let them know that anyone who didn't get to read from their play today will get that opportunity on Thursday.

Voice Acting (45 Minutes)

As the class comes into voice acting today, play these sound effects and look up and around as though you expect to see Superman flying around your room:
https://bit.ly/3j1QgD0

Then play this sound effect and pretend to answer the phone:
https://bit.ly/3iZUM4Z

YOU (answering the phone): "Oh, it's time for class to start? Great! We'll get started!"

Today we're going to learn about Sound Effects and then focus on rehearsing our play for the performance on Friday. There are many different fun ways to create sound effects. A performer who creates sound effects is called a "foley artist." In the beginning of radio and stage, a "foley table" was where all the elements for creating live sound effects were kept: chains to rattle, miniature doors to close, boxes of gravel to walk on to create outdoor footsteps. Today, foley artists are still used in film and TV shows...

WATCH AND LEARN: Sound Effects
https://bit.ly/3eqJEe8

Vocal Warmup
Choose three of your favorite tongue twisters and practice saying them normally, as though you're very sad, as though you're fighting back laughter and as though you're angry. Here are a few to start:

- How much wood could a woodchuck; chuck if a woodchuck could chuck wood
- Mix a box of mixed biscuits with a boxed biscuit mixer
- Toy boat. Toy boat. Toy boat.

ACTIVITY: Read Through

Now that everyone has been assigned a role, we will attempt to read through the episode of Superman. As we arrive at a sound effect, we will assign it to one of our foley artists and briefly discuss how best to make that sound effect. Some will be live and some will be pre-recorded.

Remind everyone of the casting of the show, and ask them to either pull out their printed scripts or open the script on another device. The cast should make notes on their script about when they should turn on their video and unmute themselves (unless you or a staff member will be controlling that). Encourage them to use big, dramatic voices, to articulate clearly and to take their time with the dialogue.

Assign each sound effect to a particular foley artist (you can do that as you read through the script). It is recommended that they record these sounds separately on a separate device so that they don't have to worry about YouTube commercials or cueing them up during the live performance. Using their phone's memo recording app, they can play the YouTube track, record it and name it with the name and number of the sound effect in the script. Then when their moment comes to play the sound effect, they just have to hit PLAY on the right track. (It is not necessary to use EVERY sound effect that they mention in the script.)

Sound effects:
- Sirens - pre-recorded https://bit.ly/3j3ZCyk
- Footsteps - perform live if possible
- Machine whirring -- COULD be recorded, if one of the foley artists would like to try to record a blender or other object in the home. But if not, you can use this pre-recorded sound: https://bit.ly/2OBR5Vr
- Glass breaking - https://bit.ly/38UcimC
- Running Footsteps - LIVE
- Noisy Newsroom - https://bit.ly/38X6E3c
- Window opening and closing (could be recorded in foley artist's home or use this YouTube sound): https://bit.ly/308Ftyq
- Phone rings (old fashioned) and pickup: https://bit.ly/3erfVBF
- Phone hang up (the hang up happens about halfway through this track): https://bit.ly/3h1FET8
- Door opens and closes: https://bit.ly/3fozvQl
- Superman flying: https://bit.ly/32nPjzj

If any of our foley artists are planning to create their own sound effects at home (like footsteps, doors closing, etc.), they should consider that "home work" and bring those effects to class tomorrow.

OPTIONAL: Sound Effect Improv Game

This hilarious video shows performers trying to create sound effects vocally for a narrated story on the show "Whose Line Is It Anyway?" https://bit.ly/2CdTtie
Did the players make any sound effects that were really believable? Did you notice how the narrators changed the story to make the sound effects believable?

Closing Meeting (15 Minutes)

As everyone comes in and settles in for our final meeting, play some fun uptempo music like this version of "Uptown Funk": https://bit.ly/3erglYL Once everyone is back in the main room, fade out the music and ask everyone to stand up.

ACTIVITY: Relating Circle
- Have everyone stand up.
- The teacher makes a strong character statement.
- The students think of characters who would be related to your character.
- As students come up with ideas they should unmute themselves, and in character, deliver a response. (Novice students should state who they are before delivering their line. Advanced students do not need to do this step.)

    Example: Teacher Statement: I was elected student body president!
    - Possible student reactions:
        - The Best Friend: I am so excited for you!
        - A student who lost: Oh, good for you, Mike (said through gritted teeth).
        - Coach: I hope this isn't going to take too much time away from your football practice!
    - Continue for a few rounds with different situations.

Remind everyone they need to be able to pull up the script for the radio show on a separate device for the next two days, so they won't need to read off your shared screen. (When you share your screen, their faces are obscured, which won't work for the performance.) They can print it out, if they have that capability, or open it on a tablet.

Finally, it's time to share a few of our favorite things… going down the list of students, ask them about their favorite moments of the day. If they would like to reflect on their confidence, this would be a great time for this. What makes them feel more or less confident?

As always, close with some of your specific favorite moments of the day. Were there any student breakthroughs that really inspired you? Reinforce those moments when you know that students made brave choices today. And tell them that one way to build confidence is to keep practicing that skill. So with that in mind, we will see you on Thursday!

THURSDAY

Welcome Meeting (15 Minutes)

Today's word is CONNECTION. Play "This Is Me" as everyone is logging on and encourage them to sing along: https://bit.ly/2Zq24r8

DISCUSSION: Connection
What do we mean by CONNECTION in theatre? What kinds of connections do we experience? Discuss each of the following:
- The connection we have as a cast;
- The connection between characters;
- The connection between the cast and the audience;
- The connection we have as a theatre community, with other performers, most of whom we don't even know, who perform in theatre around the world; and
- The connection we have with the people who came before us, who paved the way for us.

WARMUP: Shake It Out
- First, have everyone stand up.
- Explain that the students are to as a group count down from 8 while shaking out each of their limbs (In this order: Right arm, Left arm, Right leg, Left leg). Then they will count down from 7, then 6, etc. until they reach 1.
- They should do this getting increasingly louder and louder.

So it will go like this:

    ALL CLASS
    Right arm: "8, 7, 6, 5, 4, 3, 2, 1!"
    Left arm: "8, 7, 6, 5, 4, 3, 2, 1!"
    Right leg: "8, 7, 6, 5, 4, 3, 2, 1!"
    Left leg: "8, 7, 6, 5, 4, 3, 2, 1!"
    Right arm: "7, 6, 5, 4, 3, 2, 1!"
    Left arm: "7, 6, 5, 4, 3, 2, 1!"
    Right leg: "7, 6, 5, 4, 3, 2, 1!"
    Left leg: "7, 6, 5, 4, 3, 2, 1!"
    Right arm: "6, 5, 4, 3, 2, 1!"
     …etc. until….
    Right arm: "1!"
    Left arm: "1!"
    Right leg: "1!"
    Left leg: "1!"

After everyone is warmed up, send them to their various breakout sessions or begin your first curriculum block.

Improv / Theatre Games (45 minutes)

DISCUSSION: Connections

How does having a connection help performers on stage? Think about people who have been really good friends for a very long time, people who have spent so much time together that they can finish each other's … sandwiches. Isn't it easier to perform improv with someone whose behavior is more predictable to you? Now imagine having to perform improv along someone you despise, someone that, perhaps, you're in the middle of a really big fight with. How would that impact your ability to perform alongside them?

ACTIVITY: Drama Game: Gibberish Interpreter
- Everyone's video is off except for two students that you call on to start.
- Ask those two students to turn on their video.
- One will speak gibberish, and the other will "translate" the gibberish into English.
- Give the gibberish student a specific situation to talk about, or take suggestions from the class. (i.e. You have just won the world's biggest hot dog eating contest and are telling us all about it.) The gibberish speaker should speak only one line at a time, using as much physicality as he/she can.
- Then the interpreter will mimic the motions and translate the phrase into English.
- Encourage the gibberish speaker to be very specific in his/her intention and actions.
- Encourage the interpreter to think very carefully about trying to make the gibberish make sense.
- After a while, allow the class to act as the "press" and ask questions. (They should do this one at a time as you call on them, to keep noise to a minimum. YOU: "Becky from the New York Times, you had a question about the hot dog contest?" And then Becky unmutes herself before asking her question.)
- Repeat the game with other actors.

ACTIVITY: Watch and Learn

Take a load off and get ready to laugh with this improv game from an episode of "Whose Line Is It Anyway" in which they play the game "New Choice." Pay particular attention to the way the relationship between the actors changes throughout this silly scene. Where do they "Yes and--" each other? Where do they give it (at least) 10% more? https://bit.ly/32inU1m

ACTIVITY: Two-person Scenes

Improv scenes often start with strong initiation statements. These statements tell us who the characters are, where they are and what they are doing. The following elements are super important to every improv scene:

Qualities of Great Improv Scenes
1. Location
2. Strong Initiation
3. Relationship

4. Conflict

We're going to take a look at some scenes that work and some scenes that don't and discuss why / why not. Tell the students to imagine that these are improv scenes that are being made up as the actors perform.

Everyone turns off their screens except for the two actors you call on to read Mom and Matilda...

<u>TWO-PERSON SCENE 1: Good Two Person Scene Script</u>

MOM: (Hold a plate and fork. Chew and swallow a piece of cake). Matilda, this is the most delicious cake you've ever baked!

MATILDA: Mom, I'm so glad you like it. I'm really scared that I'm not going to win the baking battle.

MOM: Oh, I don't think you have a chance to win the baking battle. This cake doesn't taste that good, but it is way better than the last two cakes you baked. Those were totally inedible.

MATILDA: (Take cake plate from mom. Scrape the cake in the garbage and start washing the dish). You are the worst mom ever! You don't support me in anything I do.

MOM: Not true honey. (Walk over, take the plate from Matilda and start drying it). I supported you when you wanted to be a ballerina. (Continue to wash the dishes).

MATILDA: You told everyone we knew not to go to the recital because it was going to be terrible.

MOM: Well sure, but I showed up to support you.

After the scene, have everyone turn their video back on but stay muted for discussion until called. If they want to answer a question or make a comment, they can raise their hand and you can call on them to unmute themselves. Or you can unmute them after you call on them.

<u>DISCUSSION: Why did this work?</u>

- Let's talk about the initiation, or beginning of the scene. This one has Strong Initiation: We know what the character is doing and we know the scene is going to involve cake (though as we see the scene goes beyond the cake). Matilda's mom is already in the middle of eating the cake.
- Location: Kitchen, demonstrated through eating and then later through washing dishes
- Relationship: Mother/Daughter
- Conflict: Matilda doesn't feel her mom supports her

Now have everyone turn off their screens except for the two actors you call on to read Charlie and Bob...

TWO-PERSON SCENE 2: Missing: Strong Initiation That Starts in the Middle of the Action
(Both characters should be sitting doing nothing).

CHARLIE: Nice day.

BOB: Yes, it is pretty.

CHARLIE: I love being on the river.

BOB: Charlie, this ain't gonna work. (Pantomime reeling in a fishing line with no fish. Continue unsuccessfully fishing for the next few lines).

CHARLIE: It ain't my fault you forgot to pack the worms, Bob. (Pantomime rowing a boat through the end of the scene).

BOB: Dad told me that you packed the worms and I was supposed to bring the poles.

CHARLIE: Well dad told me that I was supposed to bring the poles and YOU were going to pack the worms. (Put down fishing pole).

BOB: But you DIDN'T pack the poles, I did.

CHARLIE: I just thought you were being an overachiever.

BOB: This is pointless. (Put down fishing pole). Hand me a sandwich.

CHARLIE: Oh I'm hungry too. Please tell me you made peanut butter and jelly.

BOB: You were supposed to pack the worms AND the lunch, Charlie.

CHARLIE: No, I was supposed to pack the poles and load the boat.

BOB: But I loaded the boat AND packed the poles!

CHARLIE: I just thought you were being an overachiever.

(Screens back on, everyone stays muted until called on)

DISCUSSION: What worked and didn't work.
- What was missing? Strong Initiation. The beginning of the scene is a bit lame and gives the audience nothing to ground themselves. Starting with the line "nice day" gives us very little to go on. We don't know who, where or what. If they had started rowing the boat from the first line of the scene, that environment work would have made for a strong initiation.
- Location: on a row boat in the river
- Relationship: brothers

- Conflict: Charlie didn't do anything he was supposed to, so they are missing half of what they need.

(Video goes back off except for the students you call on to portray Naomi and Levi...)

TWO-PERSON SCENE 4: Missing: Relationship

NAOMI: I can't believe how huge this big top is! (Look around in awe).

LEVI: This IS the Greatest Show on Earth!

NAOMI: Come on. Let's sneak behind the curtains.

LEVI: I don't think we are supposed to go back there. We could get into trouble.

NAOMI: Who cares. We might get a chance to see a clown or even walk on the tightrope.

LEVI: Whoa whoa whoa...trying to see a clown is one thing, but walking on the tightrope? That is just stupid.

(All screens back on, everyone stays muted until called on)

DISCUSSION: What worked and didn't work.
- Missing: Relationship.We are unclear of how Levi and Naomi know each other. Adding in a line, such as "Mom will be mad" or "We need to stay with our class" gives us a point of connection. It's hard for the audience to care about the relationship between characters until we know how they're connected.
- What are some other ways that relationship could be established?
  (There is a status play going on here that could be played further. Naomi could take on more control with Levi reluctantly and nervously following her).
- Location: The circus
- Strong Initiation: This initiation lets us know the location. They are already walking around the tent.
- Conflict: Naomi wants to break the rules and Levi is a rule follower

Script Writing (45 Minutes)

ACTIVITY: Read Aloud
Start off our Thursday scriptwriting class with asking who has a scene from the day before that they would like to share with the class.
- Spend the first part of class letting them read their work out loud and discussing the ways that they have shown conflict, character and setting within their scene.
- Allow listeners to give feedback -- two positive and specific comments and one bit of constructive critique.

DISCUSSION: The Plot Mountain

Explain to the class that now that they've written a scene, they have the building blocks of a play. A play is built on a series of scenes, woven together by the protagonist's main goal and need to overcome their greatest obstacle.

Share your screen's virtual white board and draw a basic "mountain." Explain that the plot -- the backbone of the story of the play -- is like a mountain. It has a beginning (write "beginning" on the bottom left of the mountain), a middle (write "middle" at the peak of the mountain) and of course, an ending (write "ending" at the bottom right of the mountain).

In the beginning, we have to "set up" the story, introducing the main character(s) and main conflict(s). This is when we learn who Cinderella is, where she lives, what her obstacles to happiness are. We meet her mean stepmother and stepsisters and see how hard she works.

About halfway up the left side of the mountain, some "inciting event" occurs that could change our main character's situation. For Cinderella, the invitation to the ball arrives! But for every positive event, there is an obstacle to follow. Her stepmother won't let her go. But then close to the peak of the mountain, she discovers she has a fairy godmother who makes all things possible. BUT there's a catch: She has to be home by midnight.

At the peak of the mountain is the climax of the story. Cinderella goes to the ball, but nearly doesn't make it home in time. Then we move down the other side of the mountain much faster: events start happening quickly to take us up to the end: The prince announces a nationwide search to find the owner of the glass slipper; he finds Cinderella's house with her sociopathic family. He's eventually reunited with our protagonist and they live happily ever after.

Hopefully, our students will write stories in which their protagonists take a lot more action to improve their own lives than poor, passive "Someday My Prince Will Come" Cinderella, but the story works for the sake of illustration.

The important takeaways from this discussion:

BEGINNING: Set up of characters, main goal and main conflict. An "inciting event" takes place to set the story in motion.

MIDDLE: This is where the climax happens -- the stakes are really high: It looks like the protagonist might finally get what she wants. Right after this, an "all is lost" moment tends to happen when it looks like it's game over for the protagonist.

END: "Bad guys close in" but in comedies and/or romances, they don't win. In Shakespeare, the woman wearing men's clothing is happily revealed and everyone gets married. In Disney movies -- well, it's pretty much the same thing. There are a lot of weddings at the ends of plays and movies. But the important thing is the main character's goal has been reached -- or not.

ACTIVITY: Outlining Your Plot

Ask each young playwright to draw the plot mountain and make notes of where important story points should take place:

- What should happen in the beginning of your story?
- Which characters do you need to introduce?
- What is your inciting event?
- What happens at the climax?
- What happens between the climax and the end of the story?
- Do bad guys close in -- or does the cavalry come to the protagonist's rescue?
- Does she figure out how to solve her own problem? Who helps her?
- What does the final scene of the play look like? (Who is there and how do you show that the goal is achieved or not achieved?)

Ask your students to step away from their screens and work on their outline for 15 minutes. Once again, make sure they know what time to come back to the screen. And if they need help figuring it out, let them know that you're always available to them.

Important note: There are no right or wrong ways to annotate the "Plot Mountain." Sometimes kids get too fixated on exactly what is supposed to be written exactly where. This is just a tool to help with the writing of the rest of the play and ANYTHING on it could change -- and usually does during writing the play -- at any time.

Voice Acting (45 Minutes)

Today is our "dress rehearsal" for our show -- but of course, we don't have to have costumes in a radio play. However, if the students want to wear costume pieces to help them get into character, that can be a lot of fun: a fedora for the guys, a Superman T-shirt - if our hero has one, a lab coat for the scientists. But again, not necessary.

Warmup
Before we start, let's build our CONFIDENCE in our ability to work as an ENSEMBLE with a strong CONNECTION. This is a variation on the One-Word Story:
- First, share the list of student names/numbers on your screen, so that everyone knows the order in which they speak.
- The group stands and everyone unmutes themselves.
- Going through the list in order, each player says one word at a time, building upon one another to collectively create a phrase that sets a challenge for today's work (or positively reflecting on today's activity).
- When the group collectively feels that the phrase is complete, they raise their hands in the air and shout, "Yes!"
- Then a new phrase begins where they left off.
- Example: For the start of a session:
    "Today…we…will…listen…and…work…together."
    ALL: "Yes!"
- For the end of a session:
    "I…learned…to…never…turn…my…back…to…the…audience."
    ALL: "Yes!"
- Variations:

- ○ Consider allowing the kids to come up with their own affirmative phrase instead of "Yes!" (i.e. Whoohoo! Totally! You got it dude! etc.)
- ○ Instead of going in order, consider letting kids add words randomly in a "give and take".

ACTIVITY: Rehearsal

The main focus today's class is running through the whole script and trying to incorporate the sound effects as smoothly as possible. Did anyone bring in sound effects that they created at home?

Ask the cast to pull up the script on their separate device or bring out their printed copy, so that you can still see all the performers. Ask everyone to make sure they're on "Speaker View." Depending on your cast, you can either leave everyone unmuted (remind them to stay very quiet) or you or another staff member can control muting and unmuting performers as their characters enter the scene.

At the end of the rehearsal, let everyone practice taking their bows!

BOW PROCESS:
- Everyone places their Zoom settings on Speaker View.
- After you call each student's name, they unmute themselves, say, "Thank you," which makes them the "Speaker" and makes their window come up largest on the screen.
- Then they can bow and mute themselves again as you call the next performer.
- This will take a little practice for it to run smoothly.
- You can use an applause track, but if you do that during a live Zoom session, use the Gallery View setting on Zoom. Because if the applause sound is coming from your computer, Zoom will consider you to always be the speaker and therefore, always be the biggest image in Speaker View. With Gallery View, at least everyone will be the same and they can bow individually or as a group.

Closing Meeting (15 Minutes)

As students settle down for the final meeting of the day, play some upbeat music like "Can't Stop This Feeling" from Trolls: https://bit.ly/308q9BY . Encourage everyone to move around, because they've likely been sitting for a little while.

After everyone is settled in, ask if anyone has questions about the show tomorrow. Remind them that they all need to have their scripts available, either on a separate device or printed out. They need to have all their notes for the production too. Foley artists need to have easy access to their sound effects.

Let them know that the schedule for tomorrow will be a little bit different, as we will be doing a final run through of the show and a performance, so other classes will be shorter.

Next, let everyone share their favorite part of the day and end on a high note before the big show!

After Camp

Do you have all your ducks in a row for the performance tomorrow? Remember if you would like information on how to use Zoom to stream your performance live on Facebook, you can find a tutorial here: https://bit.ly/2ZtSrHG .

That way, people can watch without you having to share your Zoom ID and password, and without you having to worry about audience members' sound interrupting your show. But then again, what would live theatre be without the occasional phone ringing or adorable crying baby? In Zoom performances, though, you also have to consider barking dogs, lawnmowers, and toilets flushing!

FRIDAY

Morning Meeting (15 Minutes)

IT'S SHOW DAY! And today's word is CELEBRATION! Choose some opening music to set the scene like "The Greatest Show" from *The Greatest Showman*: https://bit.ly/2C18mVm

Today's schedule will be a little different, but when everyone gets logged in, get them immediately up on their feet and go ahead and warm up...

ACTING WARMUP: Shake It Out
- First, have everyone stand up.
- Explain that the students are to as a group count down from 8 while shaking out each of their limbs (In this order: Right arm, Left arm, Right leg, Left leg). Then they will count down from 7, then 6, etc. until they reach 1.
- They should do this getting increasingly louder and louder.

So it will go like this:

> ALL CLASS
> Right arm: "8, 7, 6, 5, 4, 3, 2, 1!"
> Left arm: "8, 7, 6, 5, 4, 3, 2, 1!"
> Right leg: "8, 7, 6, 5, 4, 3, 2, 1!"
> Left leg: "8, 7, 6, 5, 4, 3, 2, 1!"
> Right arm: "7, 6, 5, 4, 3, 2, 1!"
> Left arm: "7, 6, 5, 4, 3, 2, 1!"
> Right leg: "7, 6, 5, 4, 3, 2, 1!"
> Left leg: "7, 6, 5, 4, 3, 2, 1!"
> Right arm: "6, 5, 4, 3, 2, 1!"
> ...etc. until....
> Right arm: "1!"
> Left arm: "1!"
> Right leg: "1!"
> Left leg: "1!"

After warmup, explain to them that today we are CELEBRATING all their hard work and progress! Schedule-wise we're going to do shorter Improv and Script-Writing classes today to make sure we have time for our rehearsal and show at the end of the day. Now is a great time to make sure everyone has everything they need -- scripts, sound effect tracks, devices are charged, etc. -- and to ask if there are any questions about the performance. Assure them that they are ready and that they have come so far as a cast in one short week.

<u>SHOW DAY REMINDER:</u> Ask everyone if their devices are CHARGED. Zoom sucks battery power, so if they are on a portable device, keep it plugged in all day! In fact, if an iPad goes completely dead, for many it's impossible to run Zoom while charging because Zoom uses power faster than most chargers can charge. I say all this to just reiterate the importance of MAKING. SURE. DEVICES. ARE. CHARGED. I'm going to put in reminders about this all day long!

REFLECTION: We are CELEBRATING!
- Since it will be such a busy day, let's spend a little bit of time reflecting on what we've learned and how our ideas about theatre have changed this week.
- Has anyone changed their ideas about WHERE theatre can take place? "Not Necessarily The Stage" is about realizing that, as Shakespeare said, "All the world's a stage..." That includes your living room, the Zoom screen, your front yard, a shopping mall, the top of a cafeteria table...
- Has anyone discovered a passion for playwriting?
- What has improv class done to change your impressions of acting and performing?
- What have you learned about building an ensemble?

Improv / Theatre Games (30 Minutes)

Welcome to our last day of Improv! Today we are going to get in as much practice as we can in our shorter time...

WARMUP: Alphabet Group Story
- Begin by sharing the list of student names/numbers.
- Everyone starts muted and unmutes themselves as their number comes up. (We don't want to have to call out names in between sentences.)
- The goal is to tell a coherent, group story (similar to One Word Story) one sentence at a time. (Each student adds an entire sentence to the story.)
- The twist is that each new sentence must start with the next letter of the alphabet.
- Get a suggestion for the story.
- Example suggestion: vacuum cleaner
  - Teacher: "Alastair was known throughout his school as the human vacuum cleaner."
  - Student A: "Boys and girls alike were amazed by his ability to inhale food."
  - Student B: "Chewing was not something Alastair needed to do."

Let's try an old favorite and see if it's any easier on Friday than it was on Tuesday:

ACTIVITY: IMPROV EXERCISE: Two-Headed Interview
- Choose two students to turn on their video and everyone else's video is off (this just makes it easier for these two students to know to whom they are speaking).
- These students are partners, and these partners will be giving an interview as a "two-headed" person.
- Each head can speak one word at a time. One person says a word and the other person adds the next word to the sentence, etc.

- Get a suggestion from the class of an expertise.
- The class asks questions about that topic for the two-headed people to answer. Try and avoid simple yes or no questions.
- Example: Experts on making ice cream. Question from the class: "How do you decide what flavor of ice cream to make?"
  - Partners A (Alternating one word at a time): "We" "think" "that" "every" "day" "a" "new" "flavor" "should" "be" "made." "We" "choose" "the" "flavor" "by" "looking" "out" "the" "window" "and" "seeing" "what" "is" "there."
- Choose a new pair of actors, a new expertise and a new question.
- After several rounds of the game this way, take it up a notch. Now we have a new two-headed person and both heads say the same word AT THE SAME TIME as they answer the questions.
- These partners must watch each others' lips to say the same words together.
- Example: Experts on making ice cream. Question from the class: "How do you decide what flavor of ice cream to make?"
  - Partners B (speaking simultaneously): "Weeeee llliiiike tooooo looooook iiiin ouuuur rrrrreeeeeefrigerator to seeee wwwwhaat fooooood iiiis thhhhere."
- Each round may go for a few questions then give new students a chance to play. Both sets of partners must listen but they will be listening in different ways:
  - One Word at a Time: Avoid too many "ands" and "because" or the answer will lose focus.
  - Speaking Simultaneously: One person should be the leader and the other follows. Make sure you change up the leadership.

<u>SHOW DAY REMINDER:</u> Once again, ask everyone if their devices are CHARGED. Zoom sucks battery power, so if they are on a portable device, keep it plugged in all day!

Final Rehearsal (30 Minutes)

We're going to schedule our final rehearsal for the show right after Improv class, because the kids should be high energy and ready to perform now! However, you could easily schedule this at the beginning of the day or right before the performance. (But I find that most young performers lose their "mojo" if they rehearse a show and then go directly into performing.)

Give everyone a few minutes to gather their materials, any costume pieces that they choose to wear (optional - again, this is theatre for the ears and ears can't see your costumes), and tracks or materials for sound effects.

<u>A word about the technical side of this production:</u>

You know your cast well enough now to know how well they handle being unmuted and staying quiet. Some kiddos, bless them, seem to make noise even when sitting still, and Zoom is designed to pick up all the sounds. If you have some sound-makers in the group, I would recommend controlling the sound yourself and muting/unmuting characters as they enter/exit the scene. If you use the Superman script, you can unmute small blocks of characters at a time. For instance, Dahlgren and The Mask have a lengthy scene, followed by a lengthy scene between Clark Kent and Perry White. Alternatively, you could have them unmute themselves when it's time for them to speak or create sounds. But if it's possible for everyone to stay quiet, in a quiet room, it's a lot easier to just unmute everyone throughout the performance.

I would also recommend using the Gallery View for this production, instead of Speaker View. Because this is an audio production, it doesn't really matter WHO is speaking, and it can get confusing if we are supposed to believe Clark Kent is walking down a hallway but the foley artist is the one that is expanded on the screen (if you were in Speaker View), making the walking sound with his feet.

This is a great time for you to test your Facebook Live or YouTube Live connection, by going Live for just a few minutes to remind your viewing audience that the show is coming up.

Also, PLEASE RECORD THE DRESS REHEARSAL. Zoom gives you the option to record your sessions and this way, if something goes wrong with the Live performance, you'll have this recording to upload later.

Script Writing (30 Minutes)

<u>SHOW DAY REMINDER:</u> **Once again, ask everyone if their devices are CHARGED.**

DISCUSSION: Next Steps
The goal of this week has been to teach our young playwrights a process they can use to transform their ideas into plays. We've learned about the elements of a play: the characters, the plot, the setting. We've learned how to outline the structure of the plot. And we've learned how to write a scene.
- What has been the most fun part of playwriting?
- What has been the hardest?
- Was there any part of the process that surprised you?

ACTIVITY: Finishing the Play
This will take a while - quite a bit longer than 30 minutes. Writing a play very rarely happens in a week, and we won't finish today, but we will finish learning how:

- The next step in finishing the play would be to take our plot structure -- our "Plot Mountain" from yesterday -- and use it to generate as many ideas for scenes as we possibly can. I like to use index cards - one for each scene idea -- because I can move them around if I decide to change the order of something in my story. Another option is to use the Sticky Notes app on your computer, then share your desktop and move/add sticky notes as needed. I'll be referring to index cards from this point on but either one will work.

  Let's go back to Cinderella:

- Open up your shared screen virtual white board and show them the image of the Plot Mountain with the Cinderella story plotted on it.

- Looking at my Plot Mountain, I can instantly see that I need a scene between Cinderella and her ~~wicked stepmother~~ fairy godmother, a scene between Cinderella and her fairy godmother, a scene of Cinderella at the ball, a scene when the prince comes to the house and a wedding scene.

- Each one of those scenes goes on a separate index card. Now obviously, I need a lot more scenes than that, but those are scenes that I definitely want in the play. I might only write a few words on the index card, if I don't know a lot about what happens in that scene yet. But if I have a lot of ideas about a particular scene, I might make notes on the card about how it starts, what the conflict is in that scene and how it ends.

  [If possible write each of those scene ideas on an index card and mount them in order on a wall or a white board behind you that the class can see. Remember, you'll have to turn off your wacky Zoom background in order for them to see anything in your actual background!]

- Once I've made an index card for every scene I can think of, I lay them out -- on the floor or a table or tape them to the wall (ruins the paint and drives my husband crazy!) -- in order. And then I ask myself, what needs to happen between this scene and the next scene? Is there one scene or more missing? If so, I make note of those scenes on separate index cards and place them in order.

  [Have the kids suggest scene ideas that might fill in the gaps in the Cinderella story. Remind them that a staged scene must take place in the same place and time -- and include only those plot elements we can actually do in the real world - thinking, "I'll let the prop department figure out how to make that pumpkin transform into a carriage" might come back to bite you later.]

- I repeat this process until I have a card for every scene that I believe should be in the show. Then I pick up the first card and start writing that scene. Scene after scene after scene: I figure out who is in it, how to start the scene, what the central conflict is, and how that conflict is or isn't resolved by the end of the scene.

  [Choose a card and ask the kids if we have enough information to write the scene: Do we know all the characters? Do we know the central conflict? Do we know how the scene begins? How about an ending? Will this scene advance the plot and change something for one or more characters in it?]

MOVING FORWARD:

- Tell them that after you repeat that process with every scene in your play -- and this could take weeks or even months -- you have a first draft of your show! And that is REALLY cause to celebrate! (Of course, this is a very simplified, one-week "quick-start approach to playwriting inspired by Beat By Beat's wonderful, in-depth course for teaching playwriting to kids called Teaching Playwriting: The Essential Handbook! https://bit.ly/2ZtZzE9)

- And then you start rewriting. Let trusted readers -- people who care about you but who will be both supportive AND honest with you -- read the first draft and give you feedback.

- One of the most fun steps near the end of the process is when you feel the play is ready, you can ask for volunteers and stage a reading of your show, casting various actors in the roles and letting them read the script aloud. Nothing is more satisfying to a playwright than hearing the lines that they slogged over in their own room read aloud by actors.

ACTIVITY: It's a Scene Storm!

Students should use the rest of class time to generate as many scene ideas for their plays as possible. They can just write them out as a list or if they have access to index cards, practice writing one scene per card and putting them in order. If they reach the point where they can't think of a single additional scene -- or they just get bored with that process -- pull out one of the cards and start writing that scene. Select the card that you have the most detail about -- the card for the scene that you can "see" most clearly. Before you start writing, you should know who is in that scene and its central conflict. When you finish writing that scene, you'll have a pretty good idea if you need a scene AFTER that one, or if you need to change the scene before it in some way.

If one or more of the students quickly reaches the point in which they feel like they have EVERY scene for their play, ask them to use their cards or their list of scenes to summarize their story to the class. Does anyone in the class feel like there is a scene, moment, or character missing?

BREAK (5 Minutes)

Give students a bathroom / water break and ask them to rejoin you for warmups in 5 minutes! I've listed this as an essential part of the schedule because there's nothing worse than being in the middle of a Zoom performance and instead of a "Superman," you're looking at an empty chair, because Superman is in the bathroom.

Remind them to gather their materials, including their scripts, and get set up for the show.

SHOW DAY REMINDER: You know what I'm going to say already. Are those devices charged? Trust me when I say there is one kid who thinks "7% is FINE."

WARMUP (10 Minutes)

Is everyone ready? We'll begin by using our breath to calm down ...

WARMUP: Exploring Breathing on the Floor

Everyone is muted, but they can hear you and you can see them.

- We're going to begin by focusing on Stage 1, creating the air, or breathing. Great vocal sound begins with great breath control.
- Ask the students to find a place on the floor where they can lie down on their backs comfortably.
- Tell them to relax their shoulders and head, and to take deep breaths.
- What part of your body moves when you take a deep breath? The belly! That muscle directly below your rib cage that is expanding in and out is called the "diaphragm." When singing correctly air should always be coming from your diaphragm. It should constantly be expanding and compressing.
- Have them take a deep breath and let out an "Ooooooooh" from high to low. They should feel their diaphragm getting smaller as they let out the sound.

WARMUP: *Character Tongue Twisters*

Today we're going to warm up our articulators -- those parts of our vocal instrument, like our lips and our tongue -- with tongue twisters but we're going to speak them in various characters:

- Cooks cook cupcakes quickly
  - As Clark Kent (pretty normal)
  - As Superman's announcer (big voice)
  - As The Mask

- A bragging baker baked black bread
  - As Lois Lane (the reporter on the scene)
  - As a surprised observer (like the one who spots Superman in the sky!)
  - As a terrified victim of the Mask

SHOWTIME! (20 - 30 Minutes)

Begin your program by welcoming everyone viewing on Facebook or another platform. Talk to them about how proud you are of these amazingly innovative young performers who have chosen to learn and perform and create together, even with all the challenges they've faced.

As your cast takes their places, you (or another cast member) can set the scene like this:

Intro
"Radio drama - or radio theatre - is a dramatized, purely acoustic performance, broadcast on radio or published on audio media. With no visual component, radio drama depends on dialogue, music and sound effects to help the listener imagine the characters and story. This week we've learned to use our voices to create characters -- and our imaginations and various household items -- to create the multitude of sound effects that build this world.

Radio drama achieved widespread popularity within a decade of its initial development in the 1920s. By the 1940s, it was a leading international popular entertainment. So we ask you to sit back and relax as we transport you back in time -- the year is 1940 and families around the country are gathering around the radio to hear the next installment in the story of the Man of Steel..."

<u>The Show Begins!</u>
Don't freak out if there are technical glitches during the run of the program. As long as you stay lighthearted about it, so will your viewing audience. There is a lot of grace for the people who entertain us right now, and everyone is familiar with the unpredictability of the Internet.

At the end of the show, let each of the performers take a bow, while you run a pre-recorded applause track.

Have the last word! Thank everyone for coming to the show and let them know where they can find a recording of the performance if they would like to view it again later (they will!). Now is an awesome time to tell them about your upcoming plans for programming -- whether online or in person -- and to invite them to sign up for the next show!

Chapter Sources:

Many of the improv activities in this chapter were inspired by material original found in *Teaching Improv: The Essential Handbook* (https://bit.ly/3fsZXYZ) written by Mel Paradis, which includes 16 lesson plans and 114 improv activities for teaching short form improv to middle and high school studentsk

WEEK 3: Super Summer Actor's Studio

Before Camp

Before your camp week starts, be sure to communicate frequently with parents, telling them how to log on (Zoom ID and password), as well as how the schedule will work, what materials - if any - kids will need, what kind of space they need in their home, etc.

Create a list of all campers and assign each one a number. This is a list you will refer to throughout the week and share with the students. It will be particularly helpful in your Improv class -- we can't physically create a circle in the same room, but if everyone knows their number on the list, then you can play improv games during which you don't want to have to call each student's name and interrupt the game play.

Let parents know that our actors will be performing scenes live on Zoom on Friday. If possible, please print the scenes (that you will send them in an email), but if printing isn't a possibility, please open the scene on a second device, so that their primary device can be used for Zoom without interference.

MONDAY

Welcome Meeting (30 Minutes)

Welcome to the Summer Actor's Studio! Today's Welcome meeting will be a little longer (we've shaved 5 minutes off each of the other classes to accommodate the extra time) as we get trained on using Zoom in the classroom setting.

We'll begin with some upbeat celebration music to start the day, because 1. It will take a little longer today for everyone to get online the first time and 2. People who are online -- especially parents of your students -- are likely to have some questions.

Try this version of "Make Some Noise" -- it has the added benefit of being a "dance along" video, which means there is an activity for the kids, even if you need to handle a parent or student question. If you have a more experienced student in the mix, ask if they will lead the way by singing and dancing while you're otherwise occupied: https://bit.ly/3j09JEd

Once everyone is safely online, this is a great time for everyone to introduce themselves and answer a question: How much experience have they had with acting? Who are their favorite actors? Why do they want to learn to act? Call on each student on your list, and ask that they unmute themselves and share their perspective.

Let them practice turning their video on and off, selecting "Speaker View" (so that the person talking is biggest on their screen). This meet and greet time will also give you a chance to see who has challenges with technology, sound, lighting, who might be dealing with a slow internet connection, who is shy, who is a talker, etc.

Talk about how the week will work -- how many of them have been doing school on Zoom? Have any of them participated in an online performance before? Explain that each day we will rotate between three classes -- Acting the Scene, Acting the Song and Acting in Improv -- and on Friday we will do an online performance LIVE via Zoom!

If you're going to use Zoom breakout sessions, this would be a great time to practice with the kids: You create the rooms and assign a teacher and students to each room. The students can practice "accepting" the breakout session, going into that room, and then coming back to the main room. You could even make a "scavenger hunt" out of it: When they go into a room you have assigned them, they will see that teacher and guess what musical his/her Zoom background is from. When they've visited all three rooms, they will have finished the scavenger hunt!

This is also a good session to discuss the "Zoom rules" for your class. You can decide what boundaries you are going to set, but here are a few suggested topics to discuss:

- Are you going to enable the chat feature? If so, what is OK/Not OK to say in chats?
- We stay muted until we have to ask a question -- not because we don't want everyone to talk but even a little bit of background noise can be distracting.
- How to ask a question: physically raise your hand or use the "virtual hand-raising" feature on Zoom.
- Your video stays ON during class, unless you're asked to turn it off - but iPads do not go to the bathroom with you (yep, it has happened).

At the end of the session, assign students to breakout sessions OR start your first curriculum block, depending on the structure of your camp. If students are going into breakout sessions, make sure teachers and students know what time to return to the main session to be reassigned.

Acting the Scene (40 Minutes)

DISCUSSION: What is a scene?
- Who can define a scene?
- How is it different from a play?
- How is it different from a short story? From a news story? From a mime?
- Can a mime be in a scene? (Sigh. Yes.)
- Can one person be a scene?

- What is a drama?
- What is a comedy?

A scene is like a mini play. Scenes are also the building blocks of a play. A scene has a beginning, middle and end, just like a play, but very often a scene ends in a way that asks more questions than it answers.

Scenes are built around CHARACTERS and what those characters want. Because people are different, their goals and objectives are different - and sometimes those differences cause conflicts. And conflicts between characters are the heart of SCENES.

WARMUP: Drama Game: Human Barometer
Tell the students that they are going to be a human barometer. As you ask questions, they're going to decide how much they agree or disagree.
- Standing up tall with both arms in the air overhead is *agree 100%*.
- Sitting on the floor is *disagree 100%*.
- They can be anywhere in between (half-standing, on their knees, standing but without raising their arms, etc.).
- Demonstrate something you completely agree with -- and something you halfway agree with and what that looks like.
- Encourage the students to be as truthful as they can.
- Check out the list below for suggested statements.

SUGGESTED STATEMENTS:
- Breakfast is the best meal of the day.
- Math is my favorite class.
- I like pineapples.
- I get scared very easily.
- I'd like to be famous one day.
- I like sports.
- Stealing is wrong.
- I'd like to live in another country.
- [_____] is the best drama teacher ever.
- I like the rain.
- I watch TV every night.

REFLECTION
- What did you notice?
- Is everyone in this room very similar in regards to their likes and dislikes? Was there a big range?
- On Wednesday, we are going to perform this exercise again but with our characters from our scenes, instead of our own opinions!

ACTIVITY: Slow Motion Emotion
- Ask three students to "take the stage" (they leave their video on and everyone else turns their video off).

- Use your Zoom chat to send a PRIVATE MESSAGE to each student with their assigned emotion. Ask them to give you a thumbs up when they have it.
- As you slowly count down from 10 to 1, they are to gradually put that emotion in their faces.
- Have the class guess which emotion they chose and reflect on what gave away that emotion.
- Repeat this activity until everyone who wishes gets a chance to play.

ACTIVITY: Cold Read

For this unit, you will need four or five 2-person scenes appropriate for your age group that you will hand out and revisit each day. Keep these handy for each class. If you're in need of scenes to use, I recommend Beat by Beat's *Contemporary Scenes for Young Actors* (https://bit.ly/ 3edabLC) which has over 30 high quality drama and comedy scenes that are appropriate for this age group. Below are the specific scenes I have found to work well from that collection, and I will be referencing them throughout the rest of the unit the illustrate the exercises. However feel free to replace these scenes with any others you already own:

Recommended Scenes from *Contemporary Scenes for Young Actors:*
- 2-Person Drama - "Ordinary"
- 2-Person Comedy - "Lemonade"
- 2-Person Comedy - "Art"
- 2-Person Comedy - "Knowledge"
- 2-Person Comedy - "Canada"

Tell the class this week, we will rehearse two-person scenes, which we will then perform live on Zoom on Friday at the show. Today, we will do a "cold read" of these scenes. Tomorrow, we will "audition" for roles in one of these scenes and Wednesday morning, I will announce casting for our show!

- Share your screen with the cast - let them know that while they won't need to memorize everything by Friday (though they can if they feel motivated!), they will need to either print their scene or open it on a separate device.
- Ask for 2 volunteers to read each scene.
- After each scene, ask the students who the characters are? Can they identify what each character wants. Do those goals and objectives help create conflict in the scene? Where is the scene set?

Tell them that while costume requirements on each of these scenes is minimal, we can have fun with our Zoom backgrounds, using lemonade stand images for the background of that scene, a matching outdoor background for "Art," the inside of a school bus for "Knowledge," etc.

Acting the Song (40 Minutes)

As the students settle down for the new class, sing every word you would typically speak as you instruct them for a few minutes, in order to illustrate the fact that musical theatre actually delivers information through song. Every singer is telling a story on stage. And this week we're going to learn how to tell that story, but first, we need to warm up our voices...

ACTIVITY: Vocal Warmups

Talk to your students about how vocal warmups, exercises and rehearsals are different in the virtual world. We can't sing in unison together, but we can still sing and learn a lot about music and musical theatre. Find out how many of them have music experience, can read music, play an instrument, etc. Because that will influence your instruction -- and also tell you a lot about what brings them to the class.

ACTIVITY: Exploring Stage 1 - Breathing on the Floor

Everyone is muted, but they can hear you and you can see them.

- We're going to begin by focusing on Stage 1, creating the air, or breathing. Great vocal sound begins with great breath control.
- Ask the students to find a place on the floor where they can lie down on their backs comfortably.
- Tell them to relax their shoulders and head, and to take deep breaths.
- What part of your body moves when you take a deep breath? The belly! That muscle directly below your rib cage that is expanding in and out is called the "diaphragm." When singing correctly air should always be coming from your diaphragm. It should constantly be expanding and compressing.
- Have them take a deep breath and let out an "Oooooooh" from high to low. They should feel their diaphragm getting smaller as they let out the sound.
- Now have them try the same thing without moving their bellies. Notice the change in sound quality? Notice the strain in your throat? This is the incorrect way to sing. This is how you end up losing your voice!

ACTIVITY: Vocal Warmup - Ready to Sing

- Tell the class to take a seat. We're now going to further warm up our voices.
- Explain proper singing position: Sitting at the edge of the seat, with their back up straight. Have everyone give it a try. Tell them from now on whenever you call out "Ready to Sing!" this is the position they should take.
- Make a quick game out of this: Tell the class to sit like they are lazy on the couch at home watching TV. Then say "Ready to Sing!" and watch as they pop up into position. Repeat a few times between "lazy on the couch" "or couch potato" and then "Ready to Sing!"
- Compliment them on how professional they look!
- Instruct the class: When I say "go", using the sound "Ahh", I want you to sing from your highest note all the way down to your lowest note in 10 seconds. Ready...go! Do it with them, counting down with your fingers 10 to 1. For the first round, everyone is muted except the teacher, but they are practicing along with you. Then call on certain students, unmute them and have them demonstrate the practice -- everyone else is still practicing too, but muted. (Only one person's sound should be live at a time!)
- You can joke they sort of sound like a robot powering down. =)
- Tell them we're going to do it again, but this time in only 5 seconds. Ask for a volunteer to demonstrate.
- Then 3 seconds. Ask for volunteers to demonstrate.

- Have the students place their hands on their stomachs and shout "Ha!" Explain that this is where the "good air" for singing comes from. They should feel their bellies bounce.
- Introduce Vocal Warmup #1 an arpeggio on the word "Ha!" [**Appendix E, Music Cue 01:** https://bit.ly/MusicCue01]

DISCUSSION: Friday Performance

Let the students know that during the Friday performance, everyone who wishes to will be allowed to sing a musical theatre vocal solo. You can either provide them with a list of songs/links (See Appendix A) from which they can choose (YouTube has a plethora of musical theatre karaoke tracks that are appropriate for kids and kid voices) or you can have them choose one and give a deadline for this song to be screened/approved.

Does anyone already know if they would like to sing a solo and if so, what song they would like to sing? (I would suggest sticking to musical theatre songs for this showcase, simply because there's more to ACT as Eliza Doolittle in "Wouldn't it Be Loverly" than there is in Miley Cyrus singing "Wrecking Ball," but at the end of the day, I would rather the kiddo connected with a piece of music than force them to sing something they didn't like, especially in a short-term situation like camp.)

Even if a student prefers not to sing a solo in the performance on Friday, let them know that you would still like them to choose a song to work with this week so that they can practice discovering their character and bringing him or her to life on stage.

IMPORTANT NOTES: Any accompaniment track *must* be played on the student's end of the connection. So each soloist will have to have access to their solo track and should practice playing the track and singing with it (this may require them to have more than one device, so that they can keep the Zoom connection/camera open and play the music).

ACTIVITY: Learn a New Song - "More Like Me"

Explain that today we're going to introduce a song that they may or may not have heard before -- it's from the musical, *The Grunch*. Through this song, we're going to learn more about reading a score, finding character clues in the text of the lyrics, and proper vocal technique.

- Set up the scene so the students understand the character: Rudy Grunch HATES the drama club, because they always steal his thunder. He wants more people at school to "be like me" and love chess club and soccer. During this song, he's imagining a world without the drama club and cooking up a scheme to rid himself of them forever (insert maniacal laughter).
- Share the lyric sheet [**Appendix F**] with the group while you play the track: https://bit.ly/3h32WYJ or [**Music Cue 07: More Like Me Vocal Track:** https://bit.ly/MusicCue07]
- Read the lyrics like they are a character's spoken monologue.
- What does this character want? (Hint: More people to be like him.)
- Switch to sharing the sheet music onscreen and demonstrate where the VOCAL line is located and where the instrumental music is located. I like to teach my students to locate the treble clef and then "count treble clefs" -- which is important when they start to decipher songs with parts. In this case, the first treble clef line is always theirs and the one beneath is the one for the piano/instruments.

- Play the track (share your screen) and use your cursor to follow along on the vocal line.
- For the amount of time left, take the song in phrases and utilize "call and response" technique to teach the melody: "First, you listen as I sing. My turn: 'First a crowd rushing up, to find out who's been cast, as if nothing else matters at all.' Now your turn… Billy, can you sing that back to me?" And you unmute Billy and he sings that phrase -- but SO DOES EVERYONE ELSE, just muted. And everyone gets a chance to sing unmuted at some point in the song as you repeat this process: "my turn" and now "your turn" to sing.
- We are going to use "More Like Me" for illustration purposes throughout the week, but you can change it up and use any sheet music that you own, if you would like, to teach various principles, utilizing the call-and-response method of online vocal teaching.
- OPTIONAL: Tell them that the instructors will hold "auditions" for someone to sing this particular song in the showcase. You could even let kids and teachers vote on the best performance.

ACTIVITY: Watch and Learn
Elise Blake performs "Quiet" from *Matilda*: https://bit.ly/3ftNzYF

REFLECTION
- What does this character want? (Hint: Quiet.)
- How can you tell what she wants?
- How does the singer use her whole body to tell the story?
- Did you notice that she doesn't move around any further than what you can do in a Zoom background? So limited movement doesn't necessarily impact the actor's ability to tell the story.

Improv / Theatre Games (40 Minutes)

(Many of the improv activities and lessons in this unit are adapted from *Teaching Improv: The Essential Handbook* (https://bit.ly/3fsZXYZ) written by Mel Paradis, which includes 16 lesson plans and 114 improv activities for traditional classroom teaching.)

DISCUSS: What is improv?
What is improv? Has anyone ever seen an improv show? How is it different from other forms of acting? Any students who were with you the week before will have a lot to say about this -- let them talk. If they're excited enough about improv to come back this week, their excitement will be infectious for some of the newer students.

Some potential answers to discuss:
- Acting without a script;
- Playing games where you get suggestions from other people;
- Scenes where you create everything as you go along; and
- Sometimes serious, but most of the time associated with comedy.

Again, continuing students will have heard about the rules of improv already, but reshare those for the benefit of the newbies and to remind the one-week veterans. Write these rules of improv in a document and share the screen with your class:

Rules of Improv
1. Teamwork and Trust
2. Make Associations
3. Yes…and
4. Listen
5. Relate
6. Be Honest
7. Be in the Present
8. Tell a Story
9. Develop Relationships

Today we're going to focus a lot on #8 -- using improv to tell a story. Let's start by warming up…

ACTING WARMUP: Tug of War with the Invisible Man
Ask each student to plant their feet and pretend to have a tug of war with someone offscreen.

- As you watch the group, you can tell instantly through this exercise who really enjoys improvisation and who, if anyone, is uncomfortable without a script.
- Tell them that a second person just joined the other side, and now the rope is being pulled twice as hard.
- Now a THIRD person has joined the contest on the other side! You're losing ground!
- Oh my goodness, they all let go of the rope! (Be careful!)

REFLECTION: By "adding another tugger" to the other side, we heightened the improv scene in a very simple way, which makes it more interesting for the viewer. What are some other ways we could have developed the story of the Tug of War Contest?

WATCH AND LEARN: Secret (Priests in Church)
Explain that part of the fun for an audience in watching improv is seeing a performer accept the unexpected and then create a scene with that unexpected material:
https://bit.ly/2ZrDt4Z

DISCUSSION: In this case, the actor's were handed a scenario (a secret in a confessional) but they didn't know which way the story would go until they heard their scene partner speak. In what ways did they heighten the scene for one another during the game?

DISCUSSION: Yes, And…
"Just say yes and you'll figure it out afterwards."
-Tina Fey, The Second City and Saturday Night Live

In improv we take what was presented before us, say "yes" to it and then heighten it. (Returning students from last week will be familiar with this concept, but it's so crucial that it's worth explaining again for the rest of the class and we're going to change up the demo, so it won't be a complete repeat for anyone returning.)

- Heightening is adding information that raises the stakes in a scene and makes it more interesting.
- As things get heightened, it makes for better scenes and that is where the humor lies.
- If we negate what is said or presented to us, then our scene partner is not going to trust us AND the scene will go nowhere.
- Call on one student and and ask them to say the line "Your puppy is so cute" to you.
- Once they say the line, reply: "This isn't a puppy. It's a rock."
- Does this feel like a good way to start a scene? No. I just blocked, or denied their offer to me.
- How would you feel if you were in a scene and your partner blocked your offer? Let's try this again.
- Cue student to say the line, "Your puppy is so cute." Reply, "Yes, he is."
- This is slightly better - I "Yes-ed" the statement, but did not AND it as well. The scene didn't go anywhere. Let's give this one more try...
- Cue student to say one more time "Your puppy is so cute."
- Reply with "Yes, and he's going to be a champ in the Westminster Dog Show!"
- Now I "Yes, And"-ed - I have accepted the statement and jumped to a "logical" step. I associated a dog with a competition. This scene is now a dog and his owner trying to win a championship.
- It is our goal to always accept what is offered, and then heighten it. This is what we'll be practicing today.

ACTIVITY: Drama Game - Sausage
Let's practice using focus and teamwork to help us "stay in character" on stage.
- Select two students to keep their video on. Everyone else turns theirs off.
- "Student A" will face "Student B" and ask him/her a question. No matter the question, "B" must keep a straight face and answer "sausage." They can use different intonation -- and aggressive "SAUSAGE!" if they're passionately answering a question; a meek and shy "sausage," a questioning, "Sausage?" to indicate they aren't really sure.
- After eight questions -- or when one of them breaks character -- they will switch off their video and two new actors are selected.

  EXAMPLES:
  A: What's that hanging from your ear? B: Sausage.
  A: What's your sister's name? B: Sausage
  A: How old are you? B: Sausage.

You can can create a series of scenarios as well:
- A detective questioning a suspect;
- A journalist interviewing a big celebrity; or
- A kid meeting and getting to know a new kid at school.

Remember, the questioner uses regular language and the answerer must answer with "sausage," but stay in character!

Closing Meeting (15 Minutes)

Congratulations on a great first day! Play some celebration music like one of my favorites with a great message for young performers, "Raise You Up" from *Kinky Boots*: https://bit.ly/30cRu5Z

After everyone has arrived from breakout sessions, bathroom/water breaks/etc., ask them about their first day of the Actor Workshop. If there's a returning student, ask them to contribute their feedback on how it's different this week. Most importantly, give all the kids a chance to talk to you and each other about their day, their dreams, their frustrations. In virtual education, it's important to stop every once in a while and just connect with the kids. Zooming can be exhausting, and perhaps even a reminder of what they're missing. Help facilitate the kind of chat that naturally occurs at in-person classes and rehearsals.

Encourage them to read through the scenes again tonight for auditions tomorrow. Remind them to select a musical theatre song to study this week and perhaps perform on Friday -- and to let you know if they need help finding a backing track. Also, remind them that they will need to play the track from THEIR end during rehearsals and the performance in order for their vocals to match up with the track to listeners.

One of our favorite online closing rituals: I say, "Look at the amazing performers on your screen in front of you that you have the privilege of working with. Give them all a round of applause!" And because they're all muted, they silently clap "around" in a circle to represent their "round" of applause for each other.

TUESDAY

Welcome Meeting (15 Minutes)

It's Day 2! It's audition day and three days until our show. As students log on and get settled, play some inspiring music -- like "How Far I'll Go" from *Moana*: https://bit.ly/32fPoVo

Tell the students that today is all about getting INSPIRED and ask them to sing along -- while you answer questions and get everyone sorted out to start the day successfully. Remind them that while the "start the day" music is playing, they can always send you questions via Zoom chat.

Once everyone is ready to go, let them know that we're going to complete auditions today for the scenes in acting class. Talk a little bit about auditions and find out what, if any, experience your students have had with auditions. For some of them, it represents exciting opportunities -- and for others, they have experience with disappointment. If possible, share an experience from your own audition history. While everyone may not get the role that they think they want right now, everyone who wants one WILL get a role and through the process of connecting with your character, you will come to appreciate that role more than you can possibly imagine right now.

DISCUSSION: Setting Intentions

Today in our morning meeting, let's also talk a little bit about setting intentions. Explain that when we state out loud what our intention is for the day, it helps us to stay on track. Ask for suggestions on what the intention should be for today. Is it "Stay focused?" "We are a team?" Some of these other ideas for intention are inspired by the rules for improv:

- Actors are honest on stage.
- Stay in the moment.
- Focus, focus, focus.
- Tell the story.
- I am strong and creative.

Whatever you choose as a group for today's intention, have everyone stand, take several deep breaths as they think about this intention and visualize it playing out in classes today. On your cue -- even though they are all muted -- they will open their eyes and state the intention for the day out loud.

Acting the Scene (45 Minutes)

Today in Acting the Scene we will be conducting auditions, so double check that all the students either have a printed copy of the script or another device on which they can view it. (You don't want to have to share your screen during auditions, because then it will be difficult for scene partners to see each other).   But first, we warm up…

ACTING WARMUP: Shake It Out
If you have returning students this week, choose one of them to lead the classic whole-body acting warm up, "Shake it Out," today.

- First, have everyone stand up.
- Explain that the students are to as a group count down from 8 while shaking out each of their limbs (In this order: Right arm, Left arm, Right leg, Left leg). Then they will count down from 7, then 6, etc. until they reach 1.
- They should do this getting increasingly louder and louder.

So it will go like this:

> ALL CLASS
> Right arm: "8, 7, 6, 5, 4, 3, 2, 1!"
> Left arm: "8, 7, 6, 5, 4, 3, 2, 1!"
> Right leg: "8, 7, 6, 5, 4, 3, 2, 1!"
> Left leg: "8, 7, 6, 5, 4, 3, 2, 1!"
> Right arm: "7, 6, 5, 4, 3, 2, 1!"
> Left arm: "7, 6, 5, 4, 3, 2, 1!"
> Right leg: "7, 6, 5, 4, 3, 2, 1!"
> Left leg: "7, 6, 5, 4, 3, 2, 1!"
> Right arm: "6, 5, 4, 3, 2, 1!"
> …etc. until….
> Right arm: "1!"
> Left arm: "1!"
> Right leg: "1!"
> Left leg: "1!"

VOCAL WARMUP: Tongue Twisters
Explain that actors need to warm up their bodies and their voices, particularly their articulators. Tongue twisters -- even the silliest -- help us to do that.

- Unique New York
- Three free throws
- Red Leather, Yellow Leather
- I thought a thought
  But the thought I thought
  wasn't the thought I thought I thought

ACTIVITY: Auditions
Begin with a brief discussion about the audition process:
- Take your time: Too often our nerves cause us to rush our lines during auditions. Slow down, and you will immediately improve your performance.

- Be open to trying new things: Today you may be asked to read a line or a character in a particular way. Whether here today or in another audition, your director wants to see that you can take direction.
- Have fun. If you feel yourself getting tense, take a breath and remind yourself that EVERYONE here wants you to succeed and you WILL succeed! Everyone will receive a role and this process is just to help us more carefully fit roles to students.

Ask if there are any particular roles that specific actors would really like to read. Are there any that anyone really does not want? Can they explain why? (These kinds of conversations are helpful, because it will inevitably lead to a conversation about acting. "I don't want to play a mean character," will allow you to discuss how the bad guys are frequently the most memorable characters and by doing a really good job as the BAD guy, you can actually help illustrate what GOOD looks like in the world.)

For the remainder of class time, run the scenes, asking for volunteers, and stop them frequently, asking them to read a line differently, in a silly voice or while moving around the room, louder, softer, faster, slower. In addition to casting scenes, we're trying to teach them how to take direction.

REFLECTION: The Audition Process

How did they feel the audition process went? What was their favorite part? The most challenging part? (Someone will likely bring up acting online and how technology makes it weird/awkward. If so, spend a little time talking about the strengths of technology and what we CAN do successfully -- facial expression, articulation, taking our time with the scene, etc.)

Acting the Song (45 Minutes)

ACTIVITY: Vocal Warmups

Begin with gentle breathing exercises and Vocal Warmup #1 that we learned yesterday, an arpeggio on the word "Ha!" [**Appendix E, Music Cue 01:** https://bit.ly/MusicCue01]

Introduce a new Vocal Warmup #2 [**Appendix E, Music Cue 02:** https://bit.ly/MusicCue02]

Discuss the role that vowels and consonants play in singing: We actually sing the VOWELS, while the consonants "pinch" the sound in different ways, creating words. Without consonants, no one would understand what we were singing.

Demonstrate trying to sing the first line of "More Like Me" with no consonants. Sounds really silly right?! We practice exercises like tongue twisters to warm up our "articulators" so that we are ready to sing really clearly.

ACTIVITY: Tongue Twisters

Everyone has their favorite tongue twisters and kids love them. Start by speaking the phrase: "Mama made me mash my M & Ms. Oh my!" Start very slowly and work to get a little faster each time. Have everyone practice together while muted and then take volunteers to unmute and say the phrase very quickly and articulately.

Next, teach them the melody to the tongue twister Vocal Warmup #3 [**Appendix E, Music Cue 04**: https://bit.ly/MusicCue04]. Again, use "call and response" singing, demonstrating the warmup a capella and then calling on the students in term to demonstrate their mastery of it. You can also add a hand movement to this one, pounding one fist into the palm of the other hand as you "mash the M & Ms."

DISCUSSION: "I Want" Songs
Review with the students what an "I Want" song is and how it is used in musical theatre. Also, define a protagonist and an antagonist. Can an antagonist -- the "bad guy" -- have an I Want song? Of course! Those are some of the best songs in musical theatre. Does anyone know "You'll Be Back" from *Hamilton*? That's a bad guy that wants something very specific from all his subjects -- for them to obey him. There's "Poor Unfortunate Souls" from *The Little Mermaid* and "Little Girls," sung by the horrible Ms. Hannigan in *Annie*.

"More Like Me" is an "I Want" song from an antagonist!

ACTIVITY: Sing "More Like Me"
Before we sing the song, who can describe what Rudy Grunch wants and why he wants it? Some acceptable answers:
- He wants friends.
- He wants the school to himself.
- He wants to get rid of the drama club.
- Because he is lonely.
- Because his feelings were hurt that no one came to his chess competition.
- Because he's jealous.

Play the song from your computer [**Music Cue 07:** https://bit.ly/MusicCue07] and share your screen showing the sheet music [Appendix F]. All the students are muted, but invite them to sing along in their own space.

DISCUSSION: The Emotional Staircase
- Remind the students that musical theatre is a "heightened" form of telling stories, and one tool that adds to this heightened form is singing.
- Share your screen and select "Share whiteboard." Draw the three steps of emotion in musical theatre. (Alternatively, you can use a pre-drawn image and just share that with students, but it's kind of fun for them to watch you draw in real time. 😊)
- Explain that all songs in musical theatre have a purpose. They can: 1. Express emotion 2. Advance the plot 3. Give deeper understanding of character/conflict
- At the point that a character starts singing, we've taken another step up the emotional staircase for some reason -- the emotion has been HEIGHTENED.

WATCH AND LEARN: "Memory" From CATS
Ask your students to watch this performance of "Memory" from the Broadway production of *CATS* (not the movie). https://bit.ly/2ZqBHkE

How does the singer use her facial expressions to tell the story? How much does she move? Watch when she changes her focus by shifting her eyes and body?

ACTIVITY: Marking Your Music
When we get ready to act out a musical theatre song, we have to do a little "homework." If you can print out the sheet music, you can mark up your sheet music ahead of time to reflect your work on this activity and show the students your marked up paper.

Acting the song process:

- What is <u>happening</u> to my character in the story right now?
- How does he/she <u>feel</u>?
- Where are the different "<u>thoughts</u>" in this song?
- Where does the <u>music change</u> noticeably?
- Where are my different <u>focus points</u>?

When you're acting the song in musical theatre, it's very important to know what has happened just before the song. Where is the character? What has inspired them to start singing? There has been some "heightening" of emotion to inspire singing; what happened?

With *The Grunch*, Rudy has just experienced the rest of the cast sing about their love of theater -- that has caused him to sing his angry response and cook up his evil plan in "More Like Me." Ask if one or more of the students would like to share their song choice and talk about what is happening to their character and how they feel.

Next, let's take a look at the <u>different thoughts</u> in the song and underline them.

"First a crowd rushing up to find out who's been cast as if nothing else matters at all" is one thought. That thought is followed by another, separate thought: "Then a gasp and a shriek as they find out at last they got in and then faint in the hall."

In the next phrase two things happen:
- Rudy's thought process changes -- he's now imitating one of the theatre kids.
- AND the key changes in the music. You can see it on the sheet music, but you can also hear this happen.

(I like to use sheet music because there are so many visual cues in the music, and I like to teach kids to decipher sheet music, so that it doesn't intimidate them. But if anyone does feel intimidated by the sheet music, or doesn't have access to it, they can still do this exercise just looking at lyrics.)

"Oh I dreamt about this the whole summer and at last I am finally a star. I'm so glad I got cast, oh I'm having a blast!" is all one new thought -- it might even be sung in a completely different voice!

"Don't you find their exuberance bizarre!" is another completely new thought and a response to what was just sung.

If you just stood in one place staring straight ahead for the entire beginning of the song -- four separate thoughts -- it would actually be pretty difficult to know much about the character.

Through this process, we go through the entire lyrics sheet or sheet music, underlining the various thoughts and musical changes until we get to the end of the song with this process, so that we can break down the song into manageable chunks. Once we've broken the song into those chunks, we're going to work with each chunk individually and bring it to life.

AWAY FROM SCREEN ACTIVITY: Thinking about THOUGHTS

Give the students 5-10 minutes to think about their songs for Friday, and (they don't need sheet music, lyric sheets are fine) spend a few minutes looking for and marking complete thoughts. Explain that there is NO wrong way to do this -- as long as they understand their character's thought process, it works. This is just a tool to help them tell the story through song.

When they return, ask them to share their work with the class and what they have learned about their characters.

Improv / Theatre Games (45 Minutes)

WARMUP: Drama Game - One Word Story
- In in-person classes, we do this seated in a circle, but you can facilitate this in the virtual world by making a list of everyone in the class, and sharing it on your screen.
- Have each student find their name on the list.
- Then explain the rules of the game:
- The first person on the list says a single word to begin a story.
- The next person says another word, then the next person says another word, continuing down the list.
- The goal is to tell a coherent story, one word at a time.

DISCUSSION: Guessing Games
Guessing games are some of the most fun to watch as an audience and can be some of the most stressful, but exciting to perform in as an improv actor. Guessing games require using all the improv rules that we have learned:
- We need teamwork to help the guesser out.
- Associations are how we come up with hints.
- We accept the suggestions we are given and run with them (Yes, and).
- It is essential to listen and relate to those giving clues.
- We must be honest and clear with our clues or they will not be guessed.
- A big part of being in the present is working with objects and the environment.
- We tell stories through our clues.
- Finally, we can use relationships as a way to bring clarity to the characters we are representing.

ACTIVITY: What's My Job
- Ask everyone to set their Zoom view to Speaker View.

- Make sure everyone is muted except one student who "takes the stage."
- This student pantomimes actions performed in a specific job while explaining the action in gibberish.
- The class guesses the job via chat.

Example:
- Short Order Cook - flipping pancakes and cracking eggs into a pan while explaining in gibberish "Blah blue blah goo bah, dah da."
- Go through the list, allowing each student a turn.
- Guessing alternative: When the class thinks they know the job, have them write the answer on a piece of paper or a dry erase board and hold it up to the camera.

Game Debrief: What was successful, what was not? Where did we see teamwork used? How did we see storytelling illustrated?

DISCUSSION: Clear Goals
Just like acting a scene from a pre-written play, actors of improv make their characters interesting by making it clear what their characters WANT. Every character should have a goal. Has anyone seen an infomercial? Let the kids mention infomercials they might have seen: Veggie Bullet, ShamWow, etc.
What is the goal of the host of the infomercial? To sell something, right? It's a really clear goal, easy for the viewer to understand. They have other, secondary, goals:
- To explain what the product is (it can't be too complicated).
- Make the audience believe it's a good value.
- Be entertaining (no matter how good the product, boring hosts don't sell products).

Let's watch a game based on infomercials...

WATCH AND LEARN: Infomercial
This is a "parody" of an infomercial -- meaning that it assumes that everyone understands how infomercials work so that they can make fun of it, and it will be funny to everyone. It only works if people understand what a REAL infomercial looks like and how this is different.
https://bit.ly/3etMRcX

DISCUSSION: What made this funny? Where did you see the rules of improv in action?
Teamwork? Yes, and? Associations? How did Colin deal with the problem of just not knowing how to use a prop? (He just made a joke about having no idea what to do and went on.)

ACTIVITY: Sell Me Something
Each of you is going to create a product -- real or imaginary -- and improv your own infomercial about it. We're going to take 15 minutes AWAY FROM SCREEN to grab something from your house -- a shampoo bottle, a jar of something, an item of clothing, a toy -- and create an infomercial for it.

The only rule is YOU HAVE TO TRANSFORM THE OBJECT. You can't advertise its original purpose. For instance, if you choose one of your sister's stuffed animals, you can't be selling a stuffed animal but "The world's easiest pet!" A bottle of shampoo could become an invisibility potion. A jar of peanut butter could become scented Playdough or a new kind of cosmetic. (But get permission from parents before taking something from the house.) We're going to develop these infomercials and use two or more of them in our show on Friday!

Give students about 15 minutes to develop their products. Eventually, they can make their own labels, props, etc., but the purpose today should be to focus on convincing the audience of the product's merits. So think of at least 5 reasons why the audience should want to buy this product. Some ideas:

Solves a problem (like bad breath or blotchy skin):
- It's cheap!
- It's faster/bigger/smaller than competing products. (a piece of candy becomes the world's smallest phone, a pillow becomes the world's largest marshmallow, etc.)
- It will make you the envy of your neighbors.

ACTIVITY: Sell Me Something, Part 2
If time allows, give each student 30 seconds to pitch their product, infomercial style. They could even have fun with adding the "legalese" speed-talking at the end. Tell everyone who doesn't get an opportunity today to keep working on their scenes and we will start with more demos tomorrow!

Closing Meeting (15 Minutes)

What a terrific Tuesday! As students are coming in from breakout sessions or returning from bathroom breaks, play some inspiring celebratory Broadway music, like this remake of "You're Never Fully Dressed Without a Smile" from the 2014 movie version of *Annie*:
https://bit.ly/3j1RNZM

After everyone is ready to close the day, ask if anyone has any questions about the classes, performance on Friday, etc.

Remind them that casting for the scenes will be announced in the morning. Also, we'll be demo-ing our imaginary products in improv class and choosing the best scenes to be a part of the Friday show. Then ask everyone to give some thought to their songs, their character's "I Want" moments and how to tell their story on stage.

Finally, ask everyone to stand up. Remind them of the intention we set this morning. Ask them to close their eyes and silently think for a moment of all the ways we were faithful to that intention. Then, when you're ready, count to three, have everyone open their eyes and state that intention again together.

See you on Wednesday!!

After Camp

It's casting time! You probably have a good idea of which of your actors will be best cast in different parts -- who is naturally funny? Who can give weight and focus to the dramatic scene? Also make notes about any costume pieces or props that you might want them to locate around their homes, if possible. Finally, what backgrounds might you use for each scene in Zoom? Locate some appropriate images, so that you can share them with their actors and each partner set will have a matching background for their scene -- their own virtual set! Showing those to the students tomorrow will help them get excited about the performance.

Prepare a cast list -- a document you can share on your screen -- and a drumroll sound effect ready for your casting announcement.

WEDNESDAY

Welcome Meeting (15 Minutes)

It's the start of a Wonderful Wednesday! As your class gets logged on, play this "Wednesday Wake-up" from *Singin' in the Rain*, "Good Morning:" https://bit.ly/2WlrwMi

When everyone is settled in, parent questions answered and technological issues handled, play your drumroll sound effect and share your screen with the cast list on it. After everyone is aware of which role they will be acting, it will be fun to share the background images you have chosen for each scene.

DISCUSSION: Setting intention for the day. What does the ensemble feel should be their focus today? Teamwork? FOCUS? Creativity? Choose a general theme, but not the wording of the intention yet.

ACTIVITY: Setting Intention
- Have everyone stand.
- Share your screen with the list of names of students so that they know the order in which they will speak.
- One word at a time, one word per student, you will build an intention statement based on the theme you have chosen for the day.
- When you're done, you can edit it if it's gotten a little long and unwieldy. About ten words is plenty.
- Then have everyone close their eyes, focus on that intention and on the count of three, open their eyes and everyone makes that statement aloud together.

Acting the Scene (45 Minutes)

DISCUSSION: Friday Performance
Today we begin rehearsals of our scenes for the show on Friday as a cast. Does anyone have any questions about the show or the casting?

WARM-UP: Drama Game: Stop, Go, Jump! (modified for virtual theatre)
- Tell the students to "take the stage." (From this point on "stage" will refer to their playing area at home.)
- When you say GO, they are to walk around the stage trying to fill up all the space, not leaving any gaps.
- When you say STOP they should stop. Try this out a few times.
- Now when you say CLAP they should clap, when you say JUMP they should jump. Try this out a few times, then mix it in with GO and STOP.

- When you say KNEES they should bend over and put their hands on their knees, when you say SKY they should reach up toward the sky. Try this out, mixing it in with the previous commands.
- After they've gotten the hang of this, kick it up to Level 2: They are now to do everything in exact opposite. STOP means GO, GO means STOP, CLAP means JUMP, JUMP means CLAP, KNEES means SKY, SKY means KNEES.
- Try out this new level for a while, slowly at first, then increasingly faster.

REFLECTION
- Why do you think we played this game?
- What skills were we working on?
- As an actor, you're going to be required to do things that sometimes feel unnatural, to step outside your comfort zone, and to always be focused and listening for direction. This helps prepare us for that.

ACTIVITY: Second Read-Through
Before we move further on developing our scenes, we're going to do a "table read," with everyone reading the characters' for which they've been cast. For example, my scenes would be:

- 2-Person Drama - "Ordinary"
- 2-Person Comedy - "Lemonade"
- 2-Person Comedy - "Art"
- 2-Person Comedy - "Knowledge"
- 2-Person Comedy - "Canada"

Make sure everyone has either a printed copy of the script or a separate device on which to view the script -- so that they can still see their fellow actors on screen. Ask them to locate a pencil/pen and if they don't have a printed script, a notebook on which they can make notes about their scene.

As you finish each scene, question the actors:
- Who is your character (name, approximate age, etc.)
- What does your character want?
- How does your character feel?

Ask them to take notes about these answers -- as well as any notes you might have about costume pieces or props that you might want them to locate around the house.

WARMUP: Drama Game: Human Barometer
Today we're going to repeat the "human barometer" game, but with our characters in mind -- not our own feelings. Clearly you don't have the answers to all these questions in your script, but take your best guess.

For instance, if I were to state "I like lemonade," the characters in the scene "Lemonade" would likely agree 100% -- but how does the older brother in *Ordinary* feel about lemonade? Maybe if he's your character, you imagine he also loves lemonade -- in fact, lemonade was something he

REALLY missed when he was deployed in Afghanistan. Coming up with "backstory" like that helps you develop your character.

As you ask questions, the students will decide how much their characters agree or disagree.
- Standing up tall with both arms in the air overhead is *agree 100%.*
- Sitting on the floor is *disagree 100%.*
- They can be anywhere in between (half-standing, on their knees, standing but without raising their arms, etc.).
- Demonstrate something you completely agree with -- and something you halfway agree with and what that looks like.
- Encourage the students to be as truthful as they can.

Some suggested statements:
- I'm very smart.
- I'm very kind.
- I'm really good at making money.
- I'm a creative person.
- I make friends easily.
- Breakfast is the best meal of the day.
- Math is my favorite class.
- I get scared very easily.
- I'd like to be famous one day.
- I like sports.
- Stealing is wrong.
- I'd like to live in another country.
- I watch TV every night/

After the barometer exercise, ask the students if they imagined any backstory for their characters based on a question that they had to guess to answer.

AWAY FROM SCREEN: ACTIVITY: Social Media Profile
These days we put our entire personal lives on social media. We're going to develop our own characters by imagining them on Facebook, Twitter and Instagram.

Share your screen with the following activities on it:

- FACEBOOK profile:
  - Age:
  - Gender:
  - Place of Birth:
  - Hair Color:
  - Eye Color:
  - Height:
  - Hobbies/Interests:
  - Favorite Music:
  - Favorite Movie:
  - Your biggest dream:

- o Your biggest fear:
- o Someone you look up to:
- o Your deepest secret:
- o Your best friend:
- o If you had a day to do whatever you could, what would you do?

- TWITTER: What are your character's last three Tweets? Did he/she share news? Retweet a celebrity's tweet? Make a strong political statement?

- INSTAGRAM: Describe the last five photos that your character shared on Instagram. A selfie in the lemonade stand? A photo of their dog? A group photo with friends? If so, who was in the photo?

Give them about 15 minutes to write down as much as they can brainstorm about their character. Tell them this exercise is designed to be a character development prompt and in NO WAY do you think they're going to fill out everything right now. But see where the ideas take you -- especially if there are any ideas about this character's background that will help you approach your scene.

REFLECTION: Character Development

Invite the student to discuss what they've learned about their characters during this process. Did anyone come up with an interesting backstory for their character? The students who seem most engaged and inspired by this activity should be allowed to run part or all of their scenes again with this new character development in mind.

Question the other students: Could you see a change in their performances? How did understanding their characters better improve their performance?

Acting the Song (45 Minutes)

Welcome everyone to Acting the Song by first making sure they are "Ready to sing!" Then lead them through some gentle breathing exercises -- "In through the nose, exhale through the mouth 5-4-3-2-1" is a good way to get everyone focused.

ACTIVITY: Vocal Rollercoaster

- Explain you're an engineer who's going to create a roller coaster that their voice will take a ride on.
- Give the class the first note to start on and have the entire class "move" their voices up and down the roller coaster (you can choose any vowel sound).
- As you raise your hand up or down, their voices need to follow your hand's movements.
- Your roller coaster could start very low and make a slow climb upwards, fall quickly or even do loop-de-loops!
- After you've directed them a few times, ask for a volunteer to be "train engineer."

(OPTIONAL: You can also use the virtual "white board" feature under the Zoom "share screen" option and draw the roller coaster rises and falls. The kids LOVE to take over the virtual white board, so your roller coaster engineers will be super excited to engineer their own designs for everyone to sing.)

VOCAL WARMUP: Can You Help Me Clean My Room?
- This singing warm-up asks singers to warm up their voices singing ascending and descending fifths.
- First, demonstrate for them: One group sings, "Can (G) you (G) help (G) me (G) clean (G) my (G) room (C)?" (GGGGGGC)
- Group 2 responds with: "Oh (C) NO (G) I (G) won't (C)!" (CGGC)
- Then you play the fifth a half a step higher for them, and they repeat the call and response.
- Ask two students to unmute themselves. They will be the leaders of Group A and Group B.
- Divide the rest of the group into Groups A and B, but only the leaders will be unmuted.
- Tell the entire group to put all their acting skills to the test as they either PLEAD for help with their room or REFUSE to help.
- After you repeat this a few times and advance several half steps with the exercise, flip the groups and allow Group B to plead for help and Group A to refuse as you come back down the scale. Choose a different leader for each group. Stress the importance of acting the "song."

LISTEN AND LEARN: Song Performance
Ask for a few students to each perform their solo songs. (Remember, they must play a track -- if there is one -- from their side in order for their vocals and the music to match up for listeners.) After each student performs, ask for feedback in the form of "two specific positive responses and one piece of constructive criticism."

ACTIVITY: Changing Focus Points
Ask for everyone to pull out their notes from the day before, where they underlined complete thoughts in either their lyric sheet or their sheet music. Now that we've marked up our script, we can start looking for ways to change focus points. Focus points are quite literally where you are focusing your energy and attention. We will get into the reason for doing this further in upcoming classes but for now, demonstrate how this works by playing and singing "More Like Me" and changing your focus -- with a slight shift of your head/eyes -- with each new thought. Remind them that too much movement, unless it helps tell the story of the song, can be distracting.

AWAY FROM SCREEN: Ask the students to spend 5-10 minutes away from the screen, working with their lyric sheet or sheet music and practicing shifting focus with each new thought. Tell them that this kind of movement should be just as planned and intentional as choreography or blocking.

LISTEN AND LEARN: Song Performance
Once again ask for a few students to each perform their solo songs in the time remaining.

Remind them that they can virtually "clap" for each performance by waving their jazz hands. 😌

After each student performs, ask for feedback in the form of "two specific positive responses and one piece of constructive criticism." How did their focus shift? Did it seem natural and driven by character choices and new thoughts?

Improv / Theatre Games (45 Minutes)

WARMUP: Alphabet Group Story
- Begin by sharing the list of student names/numbers.
- Everyone starts muted and unmutes themselves as their number comes up. (We don't want to have to call out names in between sentences.) If you have a quiet and not very large group, they can all stay unmuted.
- The goal is to tell a coherent, group story (similar to One Word Story) one sentence at a time. Each student adds an entire sentence to the story.
- The twist is that each new sentence must start with the next letter of the alphabet.
- Get a suggestion for the story.
- Example suggestion: vacuum cleaner
  - Teacher: "Alastair was known throughout his school as the human vacuum cleaner."
  - Student A: "Boys and girls alike were amazed by his ability to inhale food."
  - Student B: "Chewing was not something Alastair needed to do."

If the story gets too off the rails or completely silly, you can call "Scene!" and start again.

DISCUSSION: Are we becoming better listeners? How is the activity more successful if you listen and build on the sentence of the student before you? We're going to play one more improv game before moving on to our infomercials...

ACTIVITY: Party Quirks
This is the quintessential improv guessing game!
- Ask three volunteers to unmute themselves.
- The rest of the class will be muted "guessers" this round, writing their answers on a piece of paper and holding it up to the camera when the time comes.
- The four "contestants" are quirky party guests arriving at a party.
- The teacher plays the "host" of a party who welcomes and interacts with each guest.
- Tell them the order in which they will arrive (1, 2, 3, 4).

Choose three "types" ahead of time and share it with the class so that the guessers have an idea of what they are looking for. Through direct private message in the Zoom chat (make sure you are interacting ONLY with that actor!), send each of your three actors their character. (As skill improves, allow them to generate their own -- within the boundaries of the types). A few options:
- Celebrity with a new job (Arnold Schwarzenegger as a zoo keeper)
- Superhero with a fear (Wonder Woman who is afraid of cats)
- Animal with a talent (elephant who can spin plates)

The game begins with the host miming opening the door and saying, "Welcome!" to the first guest.

- The first guest "enters" in character, dropping hints as to their character.
- After a few lines of dialogue, the next guest comes to the door and the host and new guest interact.
- Finally, the last guest enters.
- All guests and hosts should interact with each other, but not speak over each other. (Remember this is a group scene).
- As soon as the audience guesses who a guest is, they will write it on a piece of paper and hold it up to the screen.
- Game ends when the last guest is figured out.
- If the class cannot figure out who someone is, the teacher can "knock on the door" and enter as a delivery person, dropping as many hints as they can.

ACTIVITY: Infomercial Time!

Allow the class a few minutes to gather their resources for their infomercials.   Remind them that they must keep their character's intention -- to SELL this product -- forefront in their improv. Each student will get a chance to present their product... but we have a TWIST:

- The first time through, they should use only gibberish to introduce and demonstrate their product.
- Remind them that their intention for each gibberish statement should be clear -- to surprise the audience, to show a feature of the product, to give information, to list side effects and disclaimers, etc.

REFLECTION: After everyone has had a chance to present their product using only gibberish, ask for feedback -- what worked in the scene? Was it important to the audience to see a change in facial expression? How did voice intonation play a part? What parts were hard to understand?

Repeat the activity, but this time, allow each student to use real words to "sell" their product. Remind them that their monologue about the product should remain FOCUSED on at least 5 reasons why the audience should want to buy this product. A reminder of some ideas:

Solves a problem (like bad breath or blotchy skin).
- It's cheap!
- It's faster/bigger/smaller than competing products. (a piece of candy becomes world's smallest phone, a pillow becomes world's largest marshmallow, etc.)
- It will make you the envy of your neighbors.

PRESS CONFERENCE: After each product is presented, if time allows, choose one of the students to be a "reporter" who can ask the presenter one question about the product.

Closing Meeting (15 Minutes)

Let's celebrate the close of a Wonderful Wednesday with a song and dance break!

GAME: Stop/Go/Sing/Dance

Let's play a unique game of freeze dance. Choose a song to which the group knows at least the chorus. This Kidz Bop version of "Party in the USA" usually works: https://bit.ly/3fuRi8m

You will play this song from your device, with everyone else muted. You'll need three pieces of colored construction paper: Red, Green and Purple.

Explain when you hold up the Green paper for the camera, they dance. When you hold up the Red paper, they stop. When you hold up the Purple paper, they sing. If you hold up Purple and Green, they have to sing AND dance! You can add variations to this by adding a Blue for hopping on one foot, and Orange paper for clapping -- and complicate it by picking up two or three colors at the same time: Can they sing, clap and hop at the same time?!

DISCUSSION: Intention

How did our intention work out for the day? Encourage kids to talk about specific examples of when they saw the intention successfully play out in class. I love this exercise (starting/ending the day with intention) because when the kids get in the habit of looking for opportunities for Teamwork, Creativity, Honesty, Relationship, Focus, they start to see them everywhere.

Before you close, have everyone restate the intention together and then give each other a "round of applause!"

After Camp

Tonight is the night to come up with a program for your show. You could go class by class, or sprinkle scenes, infomercials and songs through the program. I prefer the latter, because I think attention is better if we're constantly surprising people. A few thoughts:

- How many songs will you include?
- How many infomercials?
- What props, costume pieces, backing tracks, etc. do you still need for the performance.

THURSDAY

Welcome Meeting (15 Minutes)

It's time to kick off a Thrilling Thursday! Dress rehearsal day deserves a high energy kick off for our morning. May we suggest something like "My Shot" (clean lyrics version) from *Hamilton*? https://bit.ly/2OlZsEn

DISCUSSION: Thrilling Thursday
- After welcoming everyone, point out that "My Shot" is another "I Want" song. Hamilton wants to NOT "throw away his shot," so what he wants is to grab every opportunity, he is ambitious and WANTS to get ahead in the world.
- Walk everyone through the program for the Friday show, and explain that today is our "dress rehearsal." In each class, we will warm up and run through each of the performances with any costume pieces, backing tracks, props or scene backgrounds that we plan to use.

ACTIVITY: Setting Intention
Today ask everyone to stand up and close their eyes. Think about their individual "I Want." Instead of a group, today we're going to set our individual intentions. After they've had a minute to visualize their individual goals, call on each student and ask them to complete the sentence:

TEACHER: "Julie. 'I want…"
JULIE: "To stay focused. I want to stay focused."

Then move on to the next student, until each student has had a chance to state their intention for the day. Ask them to spend a minute focusing on that intention at the beginning of each class.

Acting the Scene (45 minutes)

Ask everyone to lie on the floor. Spend one minute breathing slowly and thinking about their individual intention. When you're ready for them, ask everyone to stand.

ACTIVITY: Warmup
- Tell the kids to make their faces as big as they can for 5 seconds.
- Then tell them to make their faces as tiny as they can for 5 seconds.
- Tell them to stand up tall, pull their shoulders back and relax them, put their hands on their stomachs, take a big breath in then say "Ha! Ha! Ha!"
- They should feel their bellies bouncing.
- This is where the strength of our voice comes from. Practice a few times.
- Say the following commands loudly and precisely:
- Repeat after me: "Articulate!" (Articulate!)

- "Exaggerate!" (Exaggerate!)
- "Project your voice!" (Project your voice!")
- Repeat.

ACTIVITY: Drama Game: Vocal Exaggeration Circle

Let's focus on exaggeration.
- Everyone is standing, video on, with their volume on, but remind them NOT to speak until it's their turn. Share your screen with a numbered list of students so they know in which order they speak (and you don't have to call names in between).
- Choose a phrase from the list below (simple tongue twisters) and have the kids choose an emotion. "Unique New York. Sad."
- Each player is going to say this phrase going down the list; however the phrase is going to get more and more exaggerated - both volume and emotional level - as it progresses.
- For each new phrase start at a different point on the list and "circle back." For instance, the first time, you might start with Student Number 1 being the smallest voice/emotion and Student Number 10 being the most exaggerated. Next time, start with Student Number 5 being the smallest, and by the time you go through the end of the list and start over, Student Number 4 will be last and the most exaggerated this round.

Exaggeration Phrases:
- Unique New York
- World wide web
- I was born on a pirate ship
- The lips, the teeth, the tip of the tongue
- A horse, a horse, my kingdom for a horse

DISCUSSION: Character Development

Ask the students to pull out the notes they made about their characters yesterday and spend a few minutes studying them. Would anyone like to discuss some new choices they've made for their characters based on this study?

Preparation: After the discussion, give them a couple of minutes to pull together whatever materials, costumes, props they need for their scenes, as well as change their Zoom backgrounds to the setting you have chosen for them. Remind them that if they aren't memorized, their script should be on a separate device or printed out so that they can still see their scene partner.

ACTIVITY: Dress Rehearsal

Run through each scene without interruption. All video is off and students are muted EXCEPT for the actors in the scene - Teacher is muted and video off as well. Tell students to choose Speaker View so the actor who speaks will become momentarily larger on screen.

REFLECTION: If time allows, ask for feedback from both the performers and the audience members for each scene on how well it went. What worked? Where could we improve? How does the actor's focus point (where the eyes and energy are focused) help or hinder the storytelling?

Acting the Song (45 Minutes)

As your students enter the classroom, ask them to spend a silent minute or two, concentrating on their intention they created and committed to this morning.

VOCAL WARMUP: Ready to Sing/Breathe
- Is everyone "Ready to sing!?" Give them some gentle reminders about posture, head placement, placing their feet on the ground (if sitting), etc. One thing about online classes is that kids [AND THEIR TEACHERS] can quickly get physically and emotionally exhausted. We can use breathing exercise to release some of that pent-up tension:
- Slowly lift arms overhead on the inhale: 1-2-3
- Slow release of the breath and lower the arms on the exhale: 1-2-3-4-5-
- Next move to 3 counts of inhale, 7 counts of exhale.
- Then three counts of inhale, 10 counts of exhale.

Tell them that breath is our fuel as singers, and learning to control it and release it as and when you need it ensures that we get good "gas mileage" from our fuel and have breath when we need it!

VOCAL WARMUP: Bumblebee
Play the track for Vocal Warmup #4: Bumblebee **[Appendix E, Music Cue 06:** https://bit.ly/MusicCue06**]** and while muted, have the students sing along. Keep repeating as the music moves up half a step for 4 or 5 repetitions.

WATCH AND LEARN: Mr. Cellophane
Watch this performance of the incredible Nigel Planer singing "Mr. Cellophane" from *Chicago*. Watch for his shifts in focus. This is not a high movement/dancey song. But it is SO moving. It's a song about a person who feels he's invisible, that no one in his life notices or cares about him. (For those who don't know, explain that "cellophane" is something transparent.) As you watch, raise your hand silently every time you see a shift in focus...
https://bit.ly/3emXb6o

DISCUSSION: Acting the Song
Ask your students to pull out their notes on character motivations, complete thoughts and focus points that they've developed over the past two days. How has this study helped them better understand their character? How has this understanding influenced how they perform the song? Have the audience members noticed stronger characters emerge from their friends' study of their characters in each song?

ACTIVITY: Dress Rehearsal
Run through each student's song, without pausing for input or comment before the end. All video is off and students are muted EXCEPT for the singer in each act -- Teacher is muted and video off as well. Tell students to choose Speaker View so the singer is larger on screen than the rest of the class.

REFLECTION: If time allows, ask for feedback from both the performers and the audience members for each song on how well it went. What worked? Where could we improve? How does the actor's focus point (where the eyes and energy are focused) help or hinder the storytelling of the song?

Improv / Theatre Games (45 Minutes)

As everyone enters the virtual classroom for improv, ask them to spend a few moments thinking about their intention that they set this morning and how that intention will help them in improv class.

ACTIVITY: Drama Game - Gibberish Interpreter
To warm up our improv muscles, let's revisit an improv game we have done in past improv classes:
- Ask two students to turn on their video and sound -- everyone else is muted with screens off.
- One of our actors will speak gibberish, and the other will translate the gibberish into English.
- Give the gibberish student a specific situation to talk about, or take suggestions from the class. (i.e. You have just won the world's biggest hot dog eating contest and are telling us all about it.)
- The gibberish speaker should speak only one line at a time, using as much physicality as he/she can.
- Then the interpreter will mimic the motions and translate the phrase into English.
- Encourage the gibberish speaker to be very specific in his/her intention and actions.
- Encourage the interpreter to think very carefully about trying to make the gibberish make sense.
- After a while, allow the class to act as the "press" and ask questions.

OTHER SCENARIOS:
- A scientist explaining her recent discovery of a 2nd moon
- A pop singer giving a press conference after falling asleep during his concert performance
- A child describing what it was like getting her first cavity
- A chef explaining how to cook his favorite meal, candy spaghetti (or anything else!)
- A farmer explaining how to milk a cow in record time

ACTIVITY: Drama Game - Gibberish Interpreter Infomerical Edition
Repeat the gibberish activity, but this time, pair students up and have the "owner" of the product (who invented it and has said product on his screen) be the gibberish speaker and the interpreter is another student. It doesn't matter if the interpreter remembers what the product is/ does. They should interpret it as best they can -- it's also fine if the gibberish speaker reacts flabbergasted or irritated at being interpreted incorrectly. After they finish about a minute of the scene, let them switch and the interpreter becomes the gibberish speaker and presents his/her own product, with the former gibberish speaker becoming the interpreter.

REFLECTION: Infomercial Gibberish
What did they learn about their infomercial scenes from this exercise? Is the movement the actor is using helping to tell the story and explain the product? What moments drew a laugh? Where did the scene pair use good teamwork?

ACTIVITY: Infomercial Run-Through
Allow each student to present their infomercial to the class. Run through all the scenes, without interruption this time, and after all students are finished, if time allows, ask for feedback.

Closing Meeting (15 Minutes)

As students settle down for the final meeting of the day, play some upbeat music like this virtual performance of "You Can't Stop the Beat" from *Hairspray*: https://bit.ly/3fwoFl3 Encourage everyone to move around to their own beat!

After everyone is settled in, ask if anyone has questions about the show tomorrow. Explain the schedule for the next day, and share the program order onscreen. Explain that the schedule will work differently tomorrow, to have time to run through the show from top to bottom before the performance. So other classes will be shorter.

Remind them that they all need to have their scripts available, either on a separate device or printed out, if they aren't memorized. Run through a checklist of costumes, props, etc. Make sure everyone knows when to change their Zoom backgrounds.

Vocalists need to make sure their backing tracks are easily accessible. They can also use a special Zoom background for their performance, as long as they know how to easily change back and forth between that and the one they will use for their scene and/or infomercial.

REFLECTION: Intention for the Day
How did their individual intentions play out during the day? Did everyone feel successful at performing as they intended to do? Why or why not? Encourage them, and let them know that their intentions are designed to help them focus, not to set unrealistic expectations. "Stay focused" is a great reminder during the day, but EVERYONE struggles with focus at times. Everyone.

THE BOW: Ask the students to smile at their fellow cast members, appreciate them for who they are and give them a "round of applause!"

After Camp

Do you have all your ducks in a row for the performance tomorrow? Remember if you would like information on how to use Zoom to stream your performance live on Facebook, you can find a tutorial here: https://bit.ly/2ZtSrHG. That way, people can watch without you having to share your Zoom ID and password, and without you having to worry about audience members' sound interrupting your show.

FRIDAY

Welcome Meeting (15 Minutes)

It's Show Day!! Get students excited about how performing artists people can be, even while socially distancing, with this amazing parody of the song "Dancing Queen": https://bit.ly/2Ordbto Ask them to sing and dance along to the music.

Today's morning meeting will be a little longer, but when everyone gets logged in, get them immediately up on their feet and go ahead and warm up...

ACTING WARMUP: Shake It Out
- First, have everyone stand up.
- Explain that the students are to as a group count down from 8 while shaking out each of their limbs (In this order: Right arm, Left arm, Right leg, Left leg). Then they will count down from 7, then 6, etc. until they reach 1.
- They should do this getting increasingly louder and louder.

So it will go like this:

> ALL CLASS
> Right arm: "8, 7, 6, 5, 4, 3, 2, 1!"
> Left arm: "8, 7, 6, 5, 4, 3, 2, 1!"
> Right leg: "8, 7, 6, 5, 4, 3, 2, 1!"
> Left leg: "8, 7, 6, 5, 4, 3, 2, 1!"
> Right arm: "7, 6, 5, 4, 3, 2, 1!"
> Left arm: "7, 6, 5, 4, 3, 2, 1!"
> Right leg: "7, 6, 5, 4, 3, 2, 1!"
> Left leg: "7, 6, 5, 4, 3, 2, 1!"
> Right arm: "6, 5, 4, 3, 2, 1!"
> ...etc. until....
> Right arm: "1!"
> Left arm: "1!"
> Right leg: "1!"
> Left leg: "1!"

After the acting warm-up, explain the schedule for the day: a series of warmups and then straight into a final run through of the show. After the run-through, there will be about 30 minutes for everyone to have a bathroom break, get organized and get ready before the performance!

VOCAL WARMUP: Breath Control
- Slowly lift arms overhead on the inhale: 1-2-3
- Slow release of the breath and lower the arms on the exhale: 1-2-3-4-5-
- Next move to 3 counts of inhale, 7 counts of exhale.

- Then three counts of inhale, 10 counts of exhale.

VOCAL WARMUP: Bumblebee
Play the track for Vocal Warmup #4: Bumblebee **[Appendix E, Music Cue 06:** https://bit.ly/MusicCue06] and while muted, have the students sing along. Keep repeating as the music moves up half a step for 4 or 5 repetitions.

VOCAL WARM UP: Can You Help Me Clean My Room?
- Lead the vocal warm-up "Can You Help My Room" from **Page 111.**

ASK EVERYONE IF THEIR DEVICES ARE CHARGED. **You will see me ask this more than once. Zoom eats batteries faster than a 13-year-old with a pizza.**

Final Dress/Tech Rehearsal: 1 Hour

Use the first hour after the morning meeting for a run-through of the program. Keep an eye out for sound or lighting problems. For instance, if a student's light source is behind them, it might throw them in shadow, but that can be easily adjusted. It's a good idea to test out the Facebook Live connection, which you can do by going live for a couple of minutes at the beginning of the rehearsal and having the whole cast wave as you tell everyone to stay tuned for the show at the scheduled time.

Another tip: Record the final rehearsal through Zoom! That way, if for some reason the internet connection fails during the live performance, you'll have a pre-recorded rehearsal that you can share!

Break: 15 Minutes

Let the cast have a 15-minute break after rehearsal to regroup, reorganize and get ready for the show. DEVICE CHECK: **HOW ARE THOSE DEVICE BATTERIES LOOKING???**

Pre-Show Warmup/Checklist: 15 Minutes

Make sure everyone has a run of the program available on their end, marked with when they need to change their Zoom background, cue music tracks for their solos, grab props or costume pieces, etc.

Then tell them some jokes. I'm serious. It's really weird to be "backstage," nervous -- and technically all on your own. If we were in the theater together, kids would have their fellow cast members to lean on, but everyone is kind of isolated with their nerves. So let's make them laugh.

Tell them it's an acting exercise and that they aren't allowed to laugh...

- What is the "bare minimum?"

One bear. (It's a joke you really have to HEAR to appreciate - LOL!)
- What do you call a magic dog?
  A Labracadabrador.
- What's orange and sounds like a parrot.
  A carrot. (Get it?? A parrot/A carrot??? Another sound joke. I swear, it's an actual joke.)

Ask who else has some silly jokes -- ALL G RATED PLEASE (Whatever you're imagining, yes, that has happened and that's why I remind them of this.)

One Minute to Showtime!

It's time to go LIVE on Facebook (or YouTube or Instagram -- wherever you're hosting your broadcast). Use the Zoom chat to call "Places!"

It's Showtime!

Begin your program by welcoming everyone, whether they're viewing on Facebook or as a part of the Zoom audience. Talk to them about how proud you are of these amazingly innovative young performers who have chosen to learn and perform and create together, even with all the challenges they've faced.

Explain to the audience that this week the students have learned about acting from a script, acting a song, and improv acting. Explain that through their improv commercials, these creative performers also developed their own products and infomercials to sell them, and you will see some of those through the performance.

You are the emcee of the show, and you will announce each performer, giving them a few moments to turn on their video and sound, etc. You can even remind the next couple of acts that they should be getting ready. No one will mind this more informal approach to narrating the show. Nor will they mind the occasional technical problem -- just stay lighthearted about it and the audience will as well.

At the end of the show, announce each performer and let them take their own bow. Just a reminder: if you select "Speaker View" and each performer says "Thank you" as soon as you call their name, they will appear larger than everyone else long enough to take a bow before you call the next name.

Have the last word! Thank everyone for coming to the show and let them know where they can find a recording of the performance if they would like to view it again later (they will!). Now is an awesome time to tell them about your upcoming plans for programming -- whether online or in person -- and to invite them to sign up for the next show!

WEEK 4: All About Arts

This week's curriculum is NON-performance based, for those groups who wish to have one week of online curriculum without the pressure or the technological demands of a performance. However, it's easy to add a performance if you would like one, turning the material from this week into an "informance" and letting the students demonstrate to their parents what they've learned this week.

Before Camp

Communicate with parents, welcoming them to this exciting week, and include all the relevant information about Zoom ID and password, meeting times, etc. Also, give them a list of any supplies you would like the students to have available to them this week: paper, pencils, scissors.

Recommend that each student download, if possible, a free piano app on their device. There are dozens of them out there! Also, see if they can locate something on which the kids can make RHYTHM (don't say the word drums to parents -- they may have been locked in their homes with their kids for months and the thought of adding drums to that equation just sounds cruel). A box, upside down small trash can, or even a desk or table will work.

Also, ask them to assemble, in the student's workspace, at least eight small, circular markers. By this, I mean M&Ms, coins (pennies and/or dimes work best), or just small circular pieces of paper.

MONDAY

Welcome Meeting (15 Minutes)

Welcome!! Set the upbeat tone for the start of your amazing week of performing arts by playing this "It's Only the Theatre for Me" from *The Grunch*: https://bit.ly/32heEe3

We begin with some upbeat celebration music to start the day, because 1. It will take a little longer today for everyone to get online the first time and 2. People who are online -- especially parents of your students -- are likely to have some questions.

Once everyone is online, ask each student to introduce themselves and answer a question: What areas of the performing arts have they had experience with? What is their favorite kind of music? What about dance? Call on each student on your list, and ask that they unmute themselves and share their perspective.

Let them practice turning their video on and off, selecting "Speaker View" (so that the person talking is biggest on their screen). This meet and greet time will also give you a chance to see who has challenges with technology, sound, lighting, who might be dealing with a slow internet connection, who is shy, who is a talker, etc.

Talk about how the week will work -- how many of them have been doing school on Zoom? Have any of them participated in an online performance before? Explain that each day we will rotate between three classes -- Theatre, Music and Dance.

If you're going to use Zoom breakout sessions, this would be a great time to practice with the kids: You create the rooms and assign a teacher and students to each room. The students can practice "accepting" the breakout session, going into that room, and then coming back to the main room. You could even make a "scavenger hunt" out of it: When they go into a room you have assigned them, they will see that teacher and guess what musical his/her Zoom background is from. When they've visited all three rooms, they will have finished the scavenger hunt!

This is also a good session to discuss the "Zoom rules" for your class. You can decide what boundaries you are going to set, but here are a few suggested topics to discuss:

- Are you going to enable the chat feature? If so, what is OK/Not OK to say in chats?
- We stay muted until we have to ask a question -- not because we don't want everyone to talk but even a little bit of background noise can be distracting.
- How to ask a question: physically raise your hand or use the "virtual hand-raising" feature on Zoom.
- Your video stays ON during class, unless you're asked to turn it off - but iPads do not go to the bathroom with you (yep, it has happened).

At the end of the session, assign students to breakout sessions OR start your first curriculum block, depending on the structure of your camp. If students are going into breakout sessions, make sure teachers and students know what time to return to the main session to be reassigned.

Theatre (45 Minutes)

ZOOM BACKGROUND: Choose an image of an ancient Greek Theatre.

ACTIVITY: Name Game
Let's learn names and something about each player! In the process, we'll also start to understand how to pantomime and communicate ideas.
- Everyone's video is on and the teacher has a list of names.

- As each player's name is called, that player unmutes themselves and will say their first name and pantomime a gesture for each syllable in their name. The action should be simple and can demonstrate a hobby, interest, or something that they do everyday. Example: I say "Pam-e-la" and gesture a paddle stroke on each side of my body (one stroke per syllable, on my left-right-left side) to show I like to canoe.
- Each player individually says their name while demonstrating the gesture then all together the group repeats the name and gesture.
- Repeat the process so everyone shares their name and gesture.
- Let any player up for the challenge demonstrate the name and gesture of every person in the group. This can be done in the same session if time allows or at a later session.

ACTIVITY: Slow Motion Emotion
- Ask three students to "take the stage" (they leave their video on and everyone else turns their video off).
- Use your Zoom chat to send a PRIVATE MESSAGE to each student with their assigned emotion. Ask them to give you a thumbs up when they have it.
- As you slowly count down from 10 to 1, they are to gradually put that emotion in their faces.
- Have the class guess which emotion they chose and reflect on what gave away that emotion.
- Repeat this activity until everyone who wishes gets a chance to play.

DISCUSSION: What Is Theatre?
What is theatre? What makes a good actor? Why do we want to become actors in the theatre? Ask the students if they can describe what theatre is:
- How is it different from reading a book?
- How is it different from watching a movie?
- Theatre is the art of telling stories through live acting.
- We train to be good actors because we want to be the best we can at connecting with an audience to tell stories.

Share your screen and choose the virtual white board option. Draw a picture of a large stick figure on the board. Ask the students to list what they think makes a good actor. As you receive suggestions, write them down with arrows pointing from the stick figure.

Some of the suggestions you should receive:
- Can play different characters
- Can speak loudly and clearly
- Works together well
- Funny
- Can take directions
- Doesn't goof off (focused), etc.
- Add any items they missed.

Our work from here on out will be on exploring and developing the skills necessary to be a great actor; to best act out stories and connect with an audience.

We're going to start at the start -- where theatre began...

WATCH AND LEARN: Masks in Ancient Theatre
https://bit.ly/2AYZTRZ

DISCUSSION: Why did performers in ancient theatres wear masks? Some possible answers:
- Ritual
- They were really far away from the audience
- The actors played more than one character

How would wearing a mask make your job as an actor easier? How would it make it harder? Explain that actors had different masks to show different emotions for the same character.

AWAY FROM SCREEN ACTIVITY: Make Masks
Today we're going to make simple theatre masks:
- We need two sheets of paper, preferably a little heavier stock, but any paper can work.
- Each mask will have two sides: The first is HAPPY on one side and SAD on the other. The second is SURPRISED on one side and ANGRY on the other side.
- Demonstrate masks you have made and show them how, for instance, you drew an open mouth to show surprise and maybe furrowed eyebrows to show anger.
- If students want to, they can place their masks on sticks (even pencils or pens taped to them can work for our purposes), but sticks are not necessary.
- Give the students 15 minutes to complete this activity, and let them know that you will be online and available if anyone needs any help at any point.
- Make sure they know what time to come back to the screen.

ACTIVITY: Acting With a Mask
- When the students return, have them show off their masks that they've made. Tell them to get them masks ready as you narrate a story. As you get to a point where the emotion changes, they will flip the mask -- or pick up a different mask -- and put it into place.
- Narration 1: "One beautiful morning, Riley decided to walk to school. (HAPPY MASK) The sun was shining, the birds were singing and he knew it was going to be a great day. Suddenly, out of nowhere, in a puff of smoke, a wizard appeared! (SURPRISED MASK) …"
- Next call on one student to unmute himself and continue the story with one sentence. The only requirement is that they change the emotion from SURPRISED to something else by a twist in the story.
- Continue until all the students get a chance to continue the story, changing the emotion as they go.

Narrate one sentence at a time -- each new student has to narrate a sentence that would cause the reaction of the next emotion.

AT HOME CHALLENGE: Today's optional challenge in acting class is to write a new short story in which emotions change every sentence or two.

Music (45 Minutes)

ACTIVITY: Write What You Hear

As students come into music class, for about two minutes, play some classical music. (Like this Mozart track: (https://bit.ly/32j7pSS). Ask them to listen intently and "write what you hear" -- just one word at a time. How would they describe the music in one word? What images come to mind? For instance, one might write "calm, water, piano, sleepy," while another student might write, "fairies, magic, high, slow."

DISCUSSION: What Is Classical Music?

Ask if anyone can explain what they think of when they hear the term classical music. Do they know the names of any classical composers? Has anyone studied classical music -- maybe in piano or violin lessons? How is it different from pop music?

How we use the term "classical music" refers to two different things:
- Refers to a specific time period - 1700s and 1800s - when music was composed by people like Mozart, Haydn and Beethoven. This period came between the Baroque period before it and the Romantic period after it.
- Most of us are more familiar with using the term "classical" to just mean western concert music. This is music we're used to LISTENING to (as opposed to dancing or singing to).

ACTIVITY: Watch and Learn

Music Theory -- Learn to Read Music (https://bit.ly/3eAlo8p)
If you aren't comfortable introducing music theory, you can share this video. It's a very engaging way to introduce a subject that kids can sometimes find a little dry. I find it effective to stop the video at various points, ask if it's making sense, if kids have questions and maybe re-explain the concept.

WRAP UP:
- Written music is a musical script telling a performer what to play and when.
- Music is written on a five-line staff.
- The higher the note on the staff, the higher the pitch we play or sing.
- Written music also shows us how fast or slow to perform each note of music.
- There are seven notes in the musical alphabet: A through G. The pattern repeats.
- A quarter note is worth one beat, a half note two beats, a whole note four beats and an eighth note gets half a beat.
- Written music is divided into chunks called "bars" or "measures" by bar lines.
- The time signature describes the rhythm and tells us how many beats are in each bar.

ACTIVITY: Rhythm Lesson

Today we're going to focus on rhythm. If the students have an area or object on which to make rhythm, have them get that now.

- Share your screen and open up the virtual white board option. (You can also do this on a real handheld white board and hold it up to the screen but the virtual white board is usually fun for the students.) You can also share a visual like this one: https://bit.ly/2ZpuYaO

- Briefly draw and review the various note values:
  - Quarter note receives one beat.
  - Half note receives two beats.
  - Whole note receives four beats.
  - Eighth note gets half a beat.
- But that doesn't mean much until you actually put it into practice. Pull up some of your favorite note value practices.
  - I like this one, based on food: https://bit.ly/32gUjFH
  - And for your more advanced students, here's a COVID-19-specific one: https://bit.ly/2WfdZ96
- Explain the rhythm values, have the students tap out the rhythms (while muted) and while they are saying the words:
  "Ice / Cream / Ham / Bur-ger/ Av-o-ca-do/Toast…"
- Next, write or type several easy food words on the white board and ask students to take a second (while muted) and see if they can work out the rhythm. More advanced students can write out the rhythm in notes. Words like:
  - Apple
  - Watermelon
  - Orange
  - Blackberry
  - Mango
  - Kiwi Fruit
- When they're ready, call on them one at a time and ask them to tap or clap out the rhythm. After they've successfully performed it, show them what the rhythm looks like in notation.
- Show how you can do the same thing with superheroes:
  - Superman
  - Batman
  - Wonder Woman
  - Iron Man
- Finally draw some simple rhythm patterns and ask them to generate words and phrases that fit those rhythms.

VOCAL WARMUP: Breath Control

Explain that we're going to sing a little every day. And we'll start with our breath. Explain that every voice needs breath, because it's like fuel for our singing engine. By breathing in through our nose and out through our mouths, we are warming up the air before it enters our body and then that warm air helps to warm up our vocal instrument:

- Slowly lift arms overhead on the inhale: 1-2-3
- Slow release of the breath and lower the arms on the exhale: 1-2-3-4-5-
- Next move to 3 counts of inhale, 7 counts of exhale.
- Then three counts of inhale, 10 counts of exhale.

VOCAL WARMUP: Powering Down

- Instruct the class: When I say "go", using the sound "Ahh", I want you to sing from your highest note all the way down to your lowest note in 10 seconds. Ready…go! Do it with them, counting down with your fingers 10 to 1. For the first round, everyone is muted except the teacher, but they are practicing along with you. Then call on certain students, unmute them and have them demonstrate the practice -- everyone else is still practicing too, but muted. (Only one person's sound should be live at a time!)
- You can joke they sort of sound like a robot powering down. =)
- Tell them we're going to do it again, but this time in only 5 seconds. Ask for a volunteer to demonstrate.
- Then in 3 seconds. Ask for volunteers to demonstrate.
- Have the students place their hands on their stomachs and shout "Ha!" Explain that this is where the "good air" for singing comes from. They should feel their bellies bounce.

LEARN A SONG: "Simple Gifts"

You can choose any song for this section, but I have chosen Simple Gifts because of its tie-in with classical music (Aaron Copeland used the melody in his classical composition, *Appalachian Spring*, from the 1940s.)

- Use a "call and response" technique to teach vocal music this week:
  - "First it's my turn" - and the teacher sings "Tis the gift to be simple tis the gift to be free… -- Now Kate, can you sing that back to me?" And Kate unmutes herself and sings the short phrase back to you. Repeat until everyone who wishes gets a chance to sing.
  - If you have boys going through a voice change, use this opportunity to show them how an octave works and how they can sing the same note an octave lower.

Piano accompaniment for "Simple Gifts": https://bit.ly/3fwLTho
Animated sheet music for "Simple Gifts": https://bit.ly/2Wl3GjR

NOTE: The animated sheet music is a fun way to show them music theory in action. You can use this, stop the video occasionally and point out terms and concepts they have learned today:

- Treble clef
- Time signature
- Notes/note values
- Bar lines
- Etc.

AT HOME: Rhythm Challenge

The challenges are something extra that your students can do at home. Have them copy down a simple rhythm notation that you display, and at home, their goal is to find as many words and phrases as they can to match that rhythm. If you have a small prize you could give away at the end of the week, you could make every completed challenge another entry into the drawing for the prize - maybe a T-shirt from your school, a Starbucks or iTunes gift card, a piece of sheet music or whatever you think is most motivating to your students.

Dance (45 Minutes)

ZOOM BACKGROUND - Choose a beautiful ballet image like this one from the Russian Ballet Theatre's *Swan Lake*: https://bit.ly/32lrCYb

As students come in, tell them where the image is from and who the characters are in the ballet. If you need a little reminder of the plot, Wikipedia has you covered: https://bit.ly/3j2SFNR

WARMUP: Creative Movement
Ask everyone to stand up tall. Tell them they're going to use their bodies to make letters.
- Practice first by everyone trying to make an A. Let them know that it's OK if it isn't perfect.
- Now an O and an S. They can create these letters from any position: standing, sitting, lying down.
- Next, tell them to take a few moments to practice spelling their names with their bodies. As best they can, try to connect the letters -- so rather than making an A, stopping and then making an M, let the movements flow together.
- Ask for volunteers to demonstrate their body name spelling.
- Tell them, "Guess what? You just choreographed a dance!"

DISCUSSION: What is dance? What is ballet?
- Dance is just sequences of human movement. Sometimes those movements are planned --or "choreographed" -- and sometimes they aren't. It's still dance, whether you're on a stage or dancing in the shower.
- There are many different types of dance -- how many can the students name?
  - This week, we're going to study the following:
  - Ballet
  - Jazz
  - Tap
  - Hip-Hop
  - Line-Dancing/Disco
- Did you know there is archaeological evidence (cave drawings) that shows dance happening 9,000 years ago?!
- The Greeks and Romans used dance in their celebrations, rituals and yes, on stage in their plays.
- Today's focus is on Ballet -- who here has studied/is studying Ballet? What do you know about it? How is ballet different from other forms of dance? Let's learn a little more...

WATCH AND LEARN: History of Ballet
https://bit.ly/2ZvaqOh

Fast Facts:
- Ballet began in Renaissance Italy as a way for people to interact at parties!
- It started to look more like the ballet we know in the court of King Louis 14th.
- King Louis 14th danced in a lot of ballets himself!
- He founded the Royal Academy of Dance in 1661.

- That school established the 5 positions of ballet that we still use today.

ACTIVITY: Five Positions of Ballet
For more than 350 years, ballerinas and danseurs have been learning the same 5 positions of the hands and feet. (If you don't feel comfortable teaching these five positions, there's an easy to follow tutorial here: https://bit.ly/3fFgau8)

- The barre: Tell them that dancers in ballet class use a barre, but they can use the back of a chair or the edge of a table for balance.
- If you have any experienced ballet dancers in the group, have them help you demonstrate the movements. Some of the kids newer to dance may feel awkward and self-conscious about this. Tell them that you aren't expecting them to be perfect at the steps you learn today, but only to have a better appreciation for the art form when they see it done really well in the future.

ACTIVITY: Three Ballet Movements
Explain that French is the language of ballet -- just as we learn Italian terms in music. And today we are going to learn three French words and their corresponding movements:

- *Plié* means "to bend" in French and refers to a specific kind of turned-out knee bend that is used in ballet. (https://bit.ly/32iQi3K)
  - A Demi Plié (literally means "half" plié) is a smaller movement, not so deep.
  - A Grand Plié is a full plié in which the thighs end up parallel to the floor.
- *Tendu* means "to stretch" in French, because you are stretching out your leg as you point. (https://bit.ly/2WiQhlZ) The working leg is extended along the floor until only the tip of the toe remains touching the floor. You can tendu to the front, either side or directly behind you!
- *Relevé* means "to rise" in French, because it's the act of rising up on your toes. Beginners in ballet are just rising up onto the ball of their foot NOT trying to go "on pointe." (https://bit.ly/3fwNm7o)

Have the kids attempt each movement without a lot of pressure to do it correctly. Remind them, though, that in ballet, posture is SUPER important and everything is performed "lifted" as though a string was attached to their chests and pulling them straight up from there.

Finally, to test the vocabulary more than the dance skill, try calling out different movements and see if they can remember:
- 1st position
- Relevé
- 5th position
- Tendu - Right side
- Demi plié
- Fourth position

No doubt they will be giggling and falling over, particularly if you call out the movements faster and faster!

Before you dismiss, wow the students with these "Hardest Ballet Moves" performed by experienced dancers at the Washington Ballet: https://bit.ly/3j2UfPN

AT HOME CHALLENGE: Describe the Ballet
With parent permission, watch a ballet on YouTube, like *Swan Lake*, *The Nutcracker* or *Sleeping Beauty* and describe five things:
- Your favorite costume
- Your favorite set piece
- The music
- The story of the ballet
- The characters

Closing Meeting (15 Minutes)

Congratulations on a Marvelous Monday All About Arts! As the students come in, play some celebratory music, like "Welcome Home" from *James and the Giant Peach*: https://bit.ly/3iZ7bWW

SHARE: Use the rest of the class today to share. Allow each student -- and staff member -- to share their favorite part of the day.
- Would anyone like to share a rhythm challenge?
- Would anyone like to show off their masks to the class?
- Who can demonstrate the five positions of ballet?

AT HOME CHALLENGE: Create a Costume
Remind the students of the At Home Challenges you've already announced and offer another one: Tomorrow is Shakespeare Day in theatre class, so special prizes for the students who can assemble, from stuff in their house, a costume for a character from a Shakespearean play. Tell them that Shakespeare had any of the following characters in his shows:
- Kings and Queens, princes and princesses, lords and ladies
- Ghosts
- Magicians
- Fairies
- Fools
- A man with a Donkey head
- Witches
- Wizards
- Soldiers
- Priests
- Maids
- Servants
- Minstrels
- And LOTS of women disguised as men (who were really young men, but we'll explain all that tomorrow…)

TUESDAY

Welcome Meeting (15 Minutes)

ZOOM BACKGROUND: Choose a beautiful set design from a Shakespearean company -- be sure to make time to tell kids about the play ("Midsummer" and "Tempest" always have beautiful images) and the company/designers involved in the photo you use.

Welcome back to a terrific Tuesday. A special thanks to a clearly awesome English teacher named Mrs. Barnaby for this amazing lyric video of "Welcome to the Renaissance" from *Something Rotten*, a great way to kick off today. Encourage kids to sing along as you share your screen with the video and lyrics: https://bit.ly/3h1s7uq

RECOGNIZE any students who have shown up in costume!! Don't forget to take a screenshot of your Zoom background with everyone smiling for the camera! And definitely have everyone POSE and count to three for that photo. "Candid" Zoom shots don't work: You'll inevitably catch a couple of nose explorers and 75% of the kids will look miserable -- even when you know they're happy!

SHARE: Does anyone have any results from home challenges they would like to share? Allow a few students to share their theatre, dance, music or closing meeting challenges.

Theatre (45 Minutes)

ZOOM BACKGROUND: You can use the same Shakespearean background as the Welcome meeting.

WARMUP ACTIVITY: Change
When everyone arrives for theatre, ask everyone to give you a thumbs up if they can see you. Give it a second to make sure everyone is looking at you and when you get all the thumbs up, turn off your video screen. While your video is off, change one significant thing -- maybe put on a hat or even change the Zoom background.

When you turn the video back on, see if anyone instantly mentions the change. If they don't, ask, "Do you notice anything different?" Let them guess.

Then ask for a volunteer to repeat the process, turning off their video and making a change for someone to guess.

DISCUSSION: Focus and Attention to Detail
- How does this game apply to being an actor?
- When can focusing on our surroundings help us in theatre?
- What happens if we aren't focused and don't notice details?

- Discuss situations like listening for our entrance cues, realizing when a prop isn't where it's supposed to be, countering when someone upstages us, etc.
- We must train ourselves to notice the little things. These little things will add up to help us create unique characters.

ACTIVITY: Home Challenges
Who wrote a story for masks that they would like to share? Remember, the emotion needs to change every sentence or two!

WATCH AND LEARN: Shakespeare
Today we're going to learn a little bit about one of the most famous playwrights in history, William Shakespeare. We cannot possibly scratch the surface of Shakespeare in 45 minutes, but we hope to instill in students an interest in the subject and also teach them a little bit more about Shakespeare's life and how he wrote.

THE LIFE OF SHAKESPEARE: https://bit.ly/2OrcO29
Fast Facts:
- Shakespeare was born in Stratford-Upon-Avon, England, in 1564.
- When he moved to England, he was part of an acting company called Lord Chamberlain's Men.
- Shakespeare wrote comedies, tragedies and histories.
  - Comedies like *A Midsummer Night's Dream*, *Twelfth Night* and *Much Ado About Nothing*.
  - Tragedies like *Romeo and Juliet* and *Hamlet*.
  - Histories like *Julius Caesar* and *Henry V*.
- Most of his plays were performed at the Globe Theatre.
- He died in 1616.

DISCUSSION: What Is a Play?
Yesterday we learned about the beginnings of theatre. After the ancient Greeks and Romans used theatre for rituals, to teach history and to entertain, theatre evolved. And we can still read their plays today. Shakespeare's plays are very different but they all share a few things in common. What makes a play a play?
- Characters
- Story/Plot
- Setting
- Stage
- Costumes

ACTIVITY: Iambic Pentameter
- Shakespeare's plays were actually written as poetry. That's right. He didn't just tell stories that were sometimes six hours long, he also wrote them in poetry:
- He wrote in a form called "iambic pentameter:"
  - An "iamb" is a foot or beat of poetry with an unstressed syllable followed by a stressed syllable.
  - Speak and clap the following from *A Midsummer Night's Dream*:
    "eNOUGH, eNOUGH, my LORD you HAVE eNOUGH."

- ○ "eNOUGH" represents one foot of poetry, or one iamb.
  - ○ When you have five of those in a row, you have iambic pentameter.
- Share your screen with the students and share these lines from Puck's, the fairy Queen's favorite, monologue:

<u>PUCK:</u>
my MIStress WITH a MONster IS in LOVE.
near TO her CLOSE and CONseCRAted BOWER.
while SHE was IN her DULL and SLEEPing HOUR.
a CREW of PATCHes, RUDE mechANiCALS,
that WORK for BREAD upON aTHENian STALL,
were MET toGETHer TO reHEARSE a PLAY.

- Explain that Puck is reporting back to Oberon, the King of the fairies -- with whom Titania is having a little fight -- that she has fallen in love with the donkey-headed character, Bottom -- it's a trick he helped Oberon play on Titania.

- Now explain to them that despite the meter of the poetry, actors do NOT deliver their lines in that rhythmic way. Play this audio recording of the same monologue so that they can hear how it comes to life: https://bit.ly/3fu4cDP

- Explain that it's important to know the CONTEXT of this speech and a little about Puck's character:
  - ○ He's a trickster and joins whichever side suits him best and looks like the most fun. He plays Oberon against Titania and vice versa. Has anyone known "friends" like that? Who just enjoy stirring up trouble?
  - ○ He's telling this story to his king, and WANTS to entertain and please him.

- Who would like to take a shot at delivering these lines like a trouble-making trickster? Let each student who wishes read the lines, keeping in mind what the character wants -- the listener's (Oberon's) delight and appreciation of his devilish work...
  - ○ Can they say it while smiling widely through every line?
  - ○ How does it change if you recite the lines while frowning?
  - ○ Ask one student to recite them like a bored servant.
  - ○ Another to read like they're SUPER excited.
  - ○ Another to read like they're worried they're about to get in trouble.

- This is a scene that Puck plays with Oberon, the fairy king. What do you think Oberon's reaction will be? After they respond with their ideas, tell them that Oberon literally says to Puck, "This couldn't have worked out any better!'

AT HOME CHALLENGE: *Let's Get Iambic*
Write four or more lines of iambic pentameter about something in your home. Remember, it's ten syllables per line with every other syllable stressed like:

i HAVE a CAT whose NAME is MISter CAT.
he LIVES inSIDE a SHOE he CALLS a HAT.

whenEVer HE eMERGes FROM this CAP.
he WANTS right THEN to SIT upON my LAP.

You do not have to make the stressed syllable in all caps, but it may help with your writing to underline the stressed syllables as you go.

Music (45 Minutes)

ZOOM BACKGROUND: Choose something quintessentially jazz, like this image of the Cotton Club: https://bit.ly/2Cu7kkp

ACTIVITY: Write What You Hear
Play this music as students come in: https://bit.ly/2B2iZ9Q and ask them to write down what they hear. Just one word at a time. It might be "fast," "fun," "piano," etc." What images do they see in their minds? (It's a seven-minute version of "Ain't Got A Thing" so you probably want to fade it out before the end.)
SHARE: After the song ends, ask the students to share what they wrote down.

ACTIVITY: Home Challenges
Display the rhythm that you sent home as a challenge and ask who would like to demonstrate they can play it.

WATCH AND LEARN: History of Jazz
Check out this animated history of jazz: https://bit.ly/3frVfe4

Fast Facts:
- Jazz music began in America over 100 years ago.
- Jazz almost always includes improvisation.
- Jazz is an American form of music.
- Jazz music has a feeling or a flavor that we call "swing."

ACTIVITY: MUSIC THEORY - Reading the Treble Clef
Today we're going to learn a little more about how to read music.
- Review: Yesterday we learned note values and a little bit about what the music staff looks like. The site, GlobalGuitarNetwork.com has this helpful visual: https://bit.ly/3040bzq
  - Quarter note
  - Half Note
  - Whole Note
  - Eighth Note
- We also learned that the notes live on a staff of five lines and four spaces -- and that pitch (how high or low a note is) corresponds to how high or low it is on the staff.
- We learned that there are just seven notes in the musical alphabet -- who can remember them?
- Share your screen and select "virtual white board." Draw a very basic staff and direct the students to do the same on their paper.

- Draw the notes on your staff with their letter names as you play each note on the piano (or piano app).
- Explain that there are simple tricks to learning the line notes and the space notes on the staff -- we all have our favorites. This image has a simple and clear explanation: https://bit.ly/2Oonqi7

ACTIVITY: Note Speller

- Direct the students to grab a blank sheet of paper and something to write with. (preferably blank white copy paper and not pre-lined. Also, grab their circular "notes" (M&Ms, coins, dried beans or scraps of colored paper, etc.).
- Ask them to draw five lines on the paper, wide enough apart that their notes can fit in the spaces.
- Keeping your staff on the white board as a reference ask them to spell out the following words on the staff, using their circular "notes:"
  - CAB
  - FACE
  - CAGE
  - EGG
  - What other words can they come up with?

VOCAL WARMUP: Breath Control

Explain that we're going to sing a little every day. And we'll start with our breath. Explain that every voice needs breath, because it's like fuel for our singing engine. By breathing in through our nose and out through our mouths, we are warming up the air before it enters our body and then that warm air helps to warm up our vocal instrument:

- Slowly lift arms overhead on the inhale: 1-2-3
- Slow release of the breath and lower the arms on the exhale: 1-2-3-4-5-
- Next move to 3 counts of inhale, 7 counts of exhale.
- Then three counts of inhale, 10 counts of exhale.

VOCAL WARMUP: Hello / Goodbye

- This warmup is sung on a descending fifth on the way up and an ascending fifth on the way back down.
- Beginning on the middle E, sing "HEL - LO" (E down to A) and then advance half a step singing, "HEL-LO" (F down to B-flat). And so on up the scale for four or five repetitions until you decide to descend.
- On the descent, sing "GOOD-BYE," with the first syllable being the lower note in the fifth and the second syllable a fifth above, as in GOOD-BYE (C up to G), GOOD-BYE (B - F#), GOOD-BYE (Bb - F) and so on.

LEARN A SONG: Don't Mean a Thing

Again, you can use any jazz standard during this section, if there's one you prefer, but I chose "Don't Mean a Thing" because it's a song about how much the singer loves jazz. 😄 A few reminders:

- Use a "call and response" technique to teach vocal music this week:

- "First it's my turn" - and the teacher sings "'It don't mean a thing if it ain't got that swing.' Now it's your turn -- Jason, can you sing that back to me?" And Jason unmutes himself and sings the short phrase back to you. Repeat until everyone who wishes gets a chance to sing and/or you make it through the whole song.
  - Encourage them to use their own nonsense words during the scatting part of the song!
  - Everyone should sing along, muted, even when the one singer is unmuted. So that they're learning and singing the entire song and not just one phrase.
- Animated sheet music: https://bit.ly/3emZ9Uk
  - You can use the animated sheet music video to point out where the notes go up and down
- For another fun take on this song, check out this a capella group: https://bit.ly/3euUq2M

AT HOME CHALLENGE: *Jazz Playlist*
With parent permission, create a playlist of five more jazz songs you enjoy.

Dance (45 Minutes)

ZOOM BACKGROUND: Use an iconic Fosse Jazz image like this one - https://bit.ly/2ZqFTks

WATCH AND LEARN: *History of Dance*
As students enter, show them this brief "History of Dance," which begins in the 1920s with the Jazz Age. https://bit.ly/3fuSNDN

WARMUP: *Creative Movement*
Explain that today we're going to warm up by doing a dance with just one part of our bodies at a time. From your computer, play some jazz class music like "Putting on the Ritz:" https://bit.ly/2Cvr7zY and ask the students to perform a dance using:
- Just their pointer fingers! And then…
- Their right elbow!
- Their head!
- Their knees!
- Their shoulders! … then start combining --
- Shoulders and knees!
- Head and pinkie fingers!
- Hips and elbows, etc.!

DISCUSSION: *What Is Jazz Dance?*
How many students have experience with jazz dance? Are any students returning from our first week when we learned a little Broadway jazz every day? Some important points:
- Jazz dance became popularized along with jazz music in the past century.
- Until some time in the 1950s, when people said "jazz dance," they were referring to "tap dance" because tap was one of the most popular forms of dance frequently performed to jazz music. But these days jazz and tap mean two different things.
- Jazz and ballet have a lot in common. In fact, the five feet/arm positions in jazz are very similar to those we learned in ballet.

- Jazz dancers usually wear special jazz shoes -- but those aren't required. (If possible, demonstrate a pair of jazz shoes and explain how these soft/flexible shoes are helpful.)
- Famous jazz dance choreographers include George Balanchine, Jack Cole, Jerome Robbins and Bob Fosse.

ACTIVITY: Learning Jazz Dance

The best way to understand jazz is to experience it. Unlike ballet, the language of jazz is English, reflecting its American roots. While jazz dance has special terms, they're names like "Jazz Square, Step Touch, Kick-Ball-Change," etc.

Through this next part, if you have experienced students, recognize their skill and ask them to help you demonstrate the movements.

- Who can show me what "**Jazz Hands**" look like? Explain that this movement is more than just open hands -- they should stretch all the way through every finger. This movement should reflect energy. So whenever I call, "Jazz Hands!" immediately show me your energy!

- **Jazz Square -** A very popular step in jazz dance is the jazz square. If you don't feel comfortable teaching this step, you can find a tutorial here: https://bit.ly/2OoYVl0
    1. Cross right foot over the left leg and plant the foot.
    2. Step back with the left foot.
    3. Bring the right foot parallel with the left.
    4. Step forward with the left.
    5. Repeat.
- Once the students can comfortably complete this step, reverse the process and do it on the other side:
    1. Cross the left foot over the right and plant the left foot.
    2. Step back with the right foot.
    3. Bring the left foot parallel with the right.
    4. Step forward with the right.
    5. Repeat
- Now ask them to perform a jazz square with jazz hands.
- More advanced students can alternate their jazz hands up and down as they complete the square: Step across (Jazz hands up), Step back (Jazz hands down), Step side (Jazz hands up again), step front (jazz hands down).
- **Step Touch -** This is an easy one! Just step to the right with your right foot and then bring your left foot over to meet it. Then step left with your left foot and bring your right foot over to meet it.
    - Once the students can comfortably step touch, add jazz hands to the step touch.
    - Challenge: Who can lift just their right arm up as they step right and their left arm up as they step left?
    - Now let's practice 8 counts of step touch, followed by a slow 8-count jazz square jazz square!
- **Pivot turn** (Tutorial: https://bit.ly/31WaQi3)
    Another important step in jazz and tap is the pivot turn:
    - Step forward with your right foot.

126

- Releve slightly on the balls of your feet, and pivot on the balls of your feet 180 degrees. (Your feet have not left the ground since you planted your right foot.) Then pick up your right foot, step forward again, and repeat the process: Raising up on the balls of your feet and pivoting until you're facing front again.
- Now try to reverse the process and do it on the left side!

AWAY FROM SCREEN: Dance Practice
Have them spend about 10 minutes practicing these steps and trying to put them into combinations. You could play some good jazz dance music for them, like Beat By Beat's "Jazz Hands:" https://bit.ly/2ZrBPQS Let them know that you're available to assist them if they need help and make sure they know what time to come back to the screen.

PERFORM: Playing your favorite jazz dance music, let them take turns performing the combinations they've created.

AT HOME CHALLENGE: Choreograph Yourself
Choreograph one minute of music -- any song you like -- using all three of the dance steps we learned today. You can use other dance moves as well, but you have to incorporate step touch, pivot turn and the jazz square.

Closing Meeting (45 Minutes)

As the students are returning to the main room from breakout sessions or bathroom breaks, demonstrate how jazz music and dance come together, by playing this iconic performance of "Sing, Sing, Sing" from the 1998 Tony Awards: https://bit.ly/3etzppd

SHARE
It's been a full and Terrific Tuesday! Give each student a chance to share their favorite part of the day. Some other prompts:

- Did they learn anything new about jazz music? About Shakespeare?
- Would anyone like to demonstrate their favorite dance move?

AT HOME: Costume Challenge
Let them know that tomorrow we're going to learn a lot about Rock and Roll so of course, their at-home costume challenge is to put together an outfit representing their favorite rock star!

WEDNESDAY

Welcome Meeting (15 Minutes)

- **ZOOM BACKGROUND:** Pick something that says "Rock and Roll" today, like this image from Elvis Presley's *Jailhouse Rock*: https://bit.ly/2DlymFp
- **BACKGROUND MUSIC:** To keep the kids engaged until you have everyone logged on and questions answered, play this clip from *Hairspray*: https://bit.ly/3eu35m0
- Recognize everyone who showed up in costume! Let them tell you which rock and roll star they are. Don't forget to take a screenshot of your Zoom background with everyone smiling for the camera!

ACTIVITY: Home Challenges
Who has completed a challenge from yesterday that they would like to share with the group? (Limit performances to one per student)
- Acting: Writing in iambic pentameter.
- Music: Jazz Playlist
- Dance: Choreograph one minute of music

Theatre (45 Minutes)

ZOOM BACKGROUND: For theatre class, try something improv-related like this image: https://bit.ly/32jjtUm

HOME CHALLENGES: Iambic Pentameter
Did anyone (who didn't share in the Welcome Meeting) create four lines of poetry they would like to share with us? If there are some who would be willing to share further, ask them if you could share their work on your school's Facebook page or in a blog post on your website to show the public what you guys are working on.

WATCH AND LEARN: Questions Only
Today we're going to learn about a kind of theatre called "improvisation." This is a kind of acting where instead of using a script, the actors make up the characters and story as they go. Let's watch an example from a show called "Whose Line is it Anyway?"
https://bit.ly/2ZsGkuP

Discussion: How did each actor who entered the story develop and change the plot, the characters, the setting? After the first couple were announced, how did we know who was who as the actors entered the scene? What was your favorite part?

WARMUP: Alphabet Group Story (modified for virtual theatre)
- Begin by sharing the list of student names/numbers.

- Everyone starts muted and unmutes themselves as their number comes up. (We don't want to have to call out names in between sentences.) If you have a quiet and not very large group, they can all stay unmuted.
- The goal is to tell a coherent, group story (similar to One Word Story) one sentence at a time. Each student adds an entire sentence to the story.
- The twist is that each new sentence must start with the next letter of the alphabet.
- Get a suggestion for the story.
- Example suggestion: drive-in movie theaters
    - Teacher: "Angela was so excited to go to the drive-in movie."
    - Student A: "But little did she know, this movie theater was cursed!"
    - Student B: "Caused by the fact that the movie theatre was built on a Native American cemetery, the curses caused moviegoers to go crazy."

If the story gets too off the rails or completely silly, you can call "Scene!" and start again.

In that improvisation, the only tools we had were our words, our imaginations and our teammates. Next we're going to perform an exercise where we take words away from one of our teammates:

ACTIVITY: Drama Game - Sausage
Let's practice using focus and teamwork to help us "stay in character" on stage.
- Select two students to keep their video on. Everyone else turns theirs off.
- "Student A" will face "Student B" and ask him/her a question. No matter the question, "B" must keep a straight face and answer "sausage." They can use different intonations -- and aggressive "SAUSAGE!" if they're passionately answering a question; a meek and shy "sausage," a questioning, "Sausage?" to indicate they aren't really sure.
- After eight questions -- or when one of them breaks character -- they will switch off their video and two new actors are selected.

    EXAMPLES:
    A: What's that hanging from your ear? B: Sausage.
    A: What's your sister's name? B: Sausage.
    A: How old are you? B: Sausage.

You can can create a series of scenarios as well:
- The host of a game show asking a contestant trivia questions;
- A job interview; or
- A teacher trying to find out who stole her candy bar.

Remember, the questioner uses regular language and the answerer must answer with "sausage," but stay in character!

DISCUSSION: Rules of Improv
If you have any returning students, ask them if they can remember any of the rules of improv.

Rules of Improv
1. Teamwork and Trust
2. Make Associations

3. Yes…and
4. Listen
5. Relate
6. Be Honest
7. Be in the Present
8. Tell a Story
9. Develop Relationships

How important is TEAMWORK when we do something like tell a one-sentence story? What would happen if the third student in line just said, "And everyone died. The end." (I used to have one kiddo in class who did that EVERY. TIME.)

How does it help the scene to develop the relationships? Imagine if the couple on the screen said first thing, "Well, goodbye…" and just walked off stage. That's kind of funny in that it's unexpected, but it's a lot more entertaining to see their relationship develop -- and as we get to know them, how they interact and develop relationships with other characters.

BE IN THE PRESENT reminds us not to spend too much time in our heads planning. The point of improv is to be spontaneous and react in the moment.

ACTIVITY: Questions Only
We're going to do our own version of the Questions Only game:
- The setting is WIZARD OF OZ.
- Everyone turns off their video except two selected actors
- One actor will play DOROTHY and her partner is the SCARECROW.
- Interact ONLY in question form. When one actor forgets to answer with a question, the teacher calls "Scene!" Then that actor will turn off his video and you will select another actor to enter the scene and play the next character:
    - Glinda the Good Witch
    - Wicked Witch of the West
    - Cowardly Lion
    - Tin Man
- If they struggle to come up with questions, tell them to remember their question words: How, Why, Who, Where, When, Which, What, etc.

AWAY FROM SCREEN ACTIVITY: Scavenger Hunt
We're going to locate some props for the kids to use in the next improv, but don't tell them that's what they're doing. Just give them this list of things to find at home and no more than five minutes to find what they can and come back (if they don't find all five, it's fine):
- One bottle of something (shampoo, for instance)
- A pet or a stuffed animal
- A shoe
- Something green
- Something that plugs in

ACTIVITY: Props

- Ask each student to randomly select one of the objects and hold it up to the screen so you can see it (this is so they can't change when you tell them what you want them to do with it!) Now they're going to SELL this object to the rest of the cast in a 30-second infomercial. The only rule is they can't call it what it actually is. If they pick up a shoe, for instance, they'll have to sell it as a phone or a paperweight or anything except a shoe.
- Call on the students individually to unmute themselves and begin their infomercial. Call "Scene!" when they've used up their 30 seconds.
- After everyone has had a chance to do an infomercial, ask them to pick up another prop and show it to you. This time, they're going to have 30 seconds to convince everyone that this is their new best friend: "I know he looks like just a shampoo bottle, but he's actually HILARIOUS -- and an excellent cook!" Start with someone this time who had a lot of time to prepare for the last improv.
- Repeat the process and have them hold up one more prop. When you call on them, they have to turn this item into an item of clothing. If it already is an item of clothing -- like the shoe, for instance, or a green shawl -- they have to wear it in a different way.

REFLECTION: Improv vs. Scripted Acting

How is acting in improv different from acting from a script? Are there things you learned in improv that you could also use when developing a character from a script?

AT HOME CHALLENGE: New Scenarios

Develop five new scenarios for Questions Only -- like Wizard of Oz or Frankenstein's Castle. We will use the best ones in class later this week!

Music (45 Minutes)

ZOOM BACKGROUND: You could use an image from the movie musical *Grease* like this one: https://eonli.ne/2DEfDut

WRITE WHAT YOU HEAR: Rock Around the Clock

Play "Rock Around the Clock," and let the kids, once again, write one word at a time, how they would describe the music. What images come to mind? What instruments do they hear?

HOME CHALLENGES: Jazz Playlist

Did anyone create a playlist of jazz songs they like? Give them a chance to discuss their favorites.

WATCH AND LEARN: Rock and Roll

https://bit.ly/3eo4hHK

FAST FACTS:

- Rock started as a combination of blues, R&B, electroboogie and jazz.
- First #1 hit: Rock Around the Clock.
- Rock was the first style of music to specifically appeal to listeners under the age of 18.

- The 1950s are seen as the beginning of the popularity of rock and roll -- a genre which continues to be popular today.

LEARN A SONG: *Rock Around the Clock*
- Using the sheet music to the song, 'Rock Around the Clock," use call-and-response singing to teach the students the song, one at a time, phrase by phrase. (Downloadable/ printable music is available from multiple sources: MusicNotes, SheetMusicDirect, etc.)
- You can also purchase a digital version of this sheet music from VirtualSheetMusic.com (about $8) and play and share this version with students, allow you to do further score study: https://bit.ly/30dEOff .
- Karaoke Track: https://bit.ly/30eblMu (remember, if you play the track from your end, you'll need to keep the kids muted. However, you can share the link to the track via Zoom chat and they could each individually play the track on their device and sing (solo) unmuted.

ACTIVITY: Lyric Lab
Let's read through the lyrics of "Rock around the Clock." Pick a student to read the intro, as though it were a poem not a song, and then a different student to read each subsequent verse.

INTRO
One, two, three o'clock, four o'clock, rock
Five, six, seven o'clock, eight o'clock, rock
Nine, ten, eleven o'clock, twelve o'clock, rock
We're gonna rock around the clock tonight

VERSE 1
Put your glad rags on and join me, hon'
We'll have some fun when the clock strikes one
We're gonna rock around the clock tonight
We're gonna rock, rock, rock, 'til broad daylight
We're gonna rock, gonna rock, around the clock tonight

VERSE 2
When the clock strikes two, three and four
If the band slows down we'll yell for more
We're gonna rock around the clock tonight
We're gonna rock, rock, rock, 'til broad daylight
We're gonna rock, gonna rock, around the clock tonight

VERSE 3
When the chimes ring five, six and seven
We'll be right in seventh heaven
We're gonna rock around the clock tonight
We're gonna rock, rock, rock, 'til broad daylight
We're gonna rock, gonna rock, around the clock tonight

VERSE 4
When it's eight, nine, ten, eleven too
I'll be goin' strong and so will you
We're gonna rock around the clock tonight
We're gonna rock, rock, rock, 'til broad daylight
We're gonna rock, gonna rock, around the clock tonight

VERSE 5
When the clock strikes twelve, we'll cool off then
Start a rockin' round the clock again
We're gonna rock around the clock tonight
We're gonna rock, rock, rock, 'til broad daylight
We're gonna rock, gonna rock, around the clock tonight

DISCUSSION:
Rhyme is the repetition of sounds at the ends of words. Let's ignore the intro for now and take a look at the last word in each line of verse 1:

- In Lines 1 and 2: "Hon" and "One" rhyme.
- In Lines 3, 4, and 5 "Tonight," "Daylight" and "Tonight" again.
- We're going to call the "one" rhymes A, and the "ight" rhymes B. So we can see that the rhyming pattern - or "rhyme scheme" -- for this song is AABBB.
- Let's check the other verses and see if they fit this pattern. (They do.)
- Finally, let's go back and take a look at the first line of the intro:
  - "One, two, three, o'clock, four o'clock rock --"
  - Clock and rock rhyme and that's an example of INTERNAL rhyme. Can you see any other places in the song with internal rhymes?

Let's take a look at another song we've learned, "Simple Gifts" and examine the rhyme scheme:

'Tis the gift to be simple 'tis the gift to be free (A)
'Tis the gift to come down where we ought to be, (A)
And when we find ourselves in the place just right, (B)
'Twill be in the valley of love and delight. (B)

When true simplicity is gained,
To bow and to bend we shan't be ashamed,
To turn, turn will be our delight,
Till by turning, turning we come 'round right.

- How would you describe this rhyme scheme?
- Point out the fact that the first two lines rhyme the "EE" sound and the second two rhyme the "IGHT" sound in the first version, which means we have an AABB rhyme scheme.

HOME CHALLENGE: Lyric Lab
Look at the lyrics of two more songs and see if you can work out the rhyme scheme.
Some possible suggestions:
- Jailhouse Rock

- Great Balls of Fire
- Hound Dog

Dance (45 Minutes)

ZOOM BACKGROUND: Choose something to celebrate tap, like this image from *42nd Street* -- https://bit.ly/32hHifd

No tap shoes are required for today's lesson on tap, but if students' have tap shoes, they can feel free to wear them, of course! The steps we've chosen to introduce today are picked because they don't actually require taps to get a lot out of the lesson. 😌

Make sure everyone has plenty of room to move around. And let's go straight into the warmup...

WARMUP: Jazz Dance
We're going to warm up our bodies today with a jazz dance warmup. If you don't have a favorite warmup, this one from Dancer's Feed YouTube Channel is an easy one that's accessible to anyone, regardless of dance experience:
https://bit.ly/3h1sOnw

HOME CHALLENGE: Choreograph Yourself
Does anyone have some choreography they put together at home that they would like to share with the class? Remember if they are going to use music, they'll need to play it on their end in order for their movements to match up with the music.

WATCH AND LEARN: Tap Dance
Check out this video on the origins of tap dance: https://bit.ly/2C0ArvX

Fast Facts:
- Tap is a true American art form.
- Tap dancing started in what is now Chinatown in New York City.
- Tap was a combination of African dances and Irish jigging.
- Improvisation is an important part of tap.
- Tap appeared in films even before they had sound.
- Other cultures and dance styles are still being integrated into tap.

DISCUSSION: Who has experience with tap dance? Who has seen tap dance in person?

REVIEW: Jazz Steps
Start by reviewing Jazz steps from yesterday -- they also work in tap!
- Step touch
- Jazz Square
- Pivot turn
Who can put them together into a combination?

ABOUT TAP SHOES - A tap shoe has two taps: A ball tap and a heel tap. And the steps that we execute in a tap shoe are designed with the sounds of those two taps in mind. Imagine tap dancing as playing drums with your feet.

- Imagine you have a tap under the ball of your foot (unless you're wearing actual tap shoes!) Lift the ball of your foot off the ground and tap that front tap against the floor for 8 beats. It's like you're waving "goodbye" with just your foot. Repeat that with the other foot.
- The next important tap step we're going to learn is a SHUFFLE. A shuffle is the foundation of so many important tap steps as we will see and it's VERY easy to learn. You're basically just standing on one leg and swinging the other foot forward and backward while brushing the floor.
  (Tutorial: https://bit.ly/2ZuZtMG)
- Who is ready to try a SHUFFLE HOP STEP? Remember a HOP stays on the same foot. In tap, a LEAP is the way we describe jumping from one foot to the other.
  (SHUFFLE HOP STEP Tutorial: https://bit.ly/2ZqgNST)

- Still building on our SHUFFLE, we're now going to learn a SHUFFLE BALL CHANGE. For those who are returning students or have experience with jazz dance, you'll recognize the BALL CHANGE. It works the same way in tap that it does in jazz dance -- it just makes a little more music!
  (SHUFFLE BALL CHANGE Tutorial: https://bit.ly/3fuftE8)

AT HOME CHALLENGE: 24 Counts
Once again, we're going to challenge the students to put the steps we've learned -- both jazz and tap -- into a 24 count combination, with or without music. Recommend to them that they do the movements SLOWLY if they're new to them. Also, let them know where you will post the tutorials for them to re-watch. (A private facebook group, website, YouTube playlist, etc.)

Closing Meeting (15 Minutes)

ZOOM BACKGROUND: Choose something tap related to get them excited about this potential new dance passion they discovered today - https://bit.ly/3j2GKzO

CELEBRATION: As the students come in, play this rousing performance form *42nd Street*'s performance from the Olivier Awards: https://bit.ly/309EuxN

SHARE: Allow each member of the group and members of staff to share their favorite part of the day. Did anyone learn a surprising fact? Did anyone master a new skill they want to show off? (If you have witnessed one student have a breakthrough or accomplish something today, this is a great time to recognize their achievement -- whether that achievement is mastering a tap step or just being willing to try something brand new. Both are worthy breakthroughs!)

AT HOME COSTUME CHALLENGE: Tomorrow we have a couple of exciting costume options! Announce that we'll be studying musical theatre in theatre class and in dance… it's DISCO! So they can choose from either 1. Favorite musical theatre character OR 2. 1970s disco style!

THURSDAY

Welcome Meeting (15 Minutes)

- **BACKGROUND MUSIC:** Statistics suggest that approximately 98% of your students (and their parents) will be obsessed with *Hamilton*, and this clip from the Tonys has the bad words bleeped out: https://bit.ly/2WIN7V7
- **ZOOM BACKGROUND:** How about something from *Hamilton* to celebrate musical theatre day? https://bit.ly/30dF9P3
- Don't forget to recognize everyone in costume and get a group photo! Let everyone who came as a favorite musical theatre character share who they are.
- **HOME CHALLENGES:** Does anyone have any results from yesterday's home challenges that they would like to share with the group? Again, just allow one from each student to manage the time in Welcome Meeting -- let them know that they will get to share the rest of their challenges in those classes.
  - ACTING: Improv - New scenarios for Questions Only
  - MUSIC: Comparing rhyme schemes in different song
  - DANCE: 24 counts of jazz/tap choreography

Acting (45 Minutes)

ZOOM BACKGROUND: See which of your students can guess which musical this image is from: https://bit.ly/2DHKmqE

HOME CHALLENGES: Ask again for any more suggestions for the "Questions Only" game, and choose the best ones to run that improv game again.

ACTIVITY: Questions Only
Using scenario suggestions from the students, run the game that we played yesterday again. (See Wednesday Acting for rules of the game.)

DISCUSSION: What Is a Musical?
- Ask who knows the three elements of musical theatre:
  - Singing
  - Dancing
  - Acting
- Share your screen and select "virtual white board" (You can also do this on a regular white board and hold it up to the screen, but that can be awkward.)
- Straw the Emotional Staircase of Musical Theatre:
  - Step 1: Speaking
  - Step 2: Singing
  - Step 3: Dancing

- Whenever the plot of the musical takes the emotion up a notch, we take another step up the emotional staircase.
- Ask if they can name examples of musical theatre scenes they know that begin with talking, then singing begins and finally the cast starts dancing.

ACTIVITY: *Climbing the Staircase*
- Play this clip from *The Grunch*: "We're Gonna Write a Musical" (https://bit.ly/38VQvuG) Explain that the kids have just found out that they have no funds to license a musical this year and so they're going to have to write their own. This song also serves the purpose of explaining the important plot points of a musical.
- While the cast is speaking, everyone stays seated.
- When the singing begins, they stand up.
- When the cast starts dancing, the students should move around the room!

WATCH AND LEARN: *The Broadway Book Musical*
Fast Facts:
A "book" musical is a work of musical theatre with three parts:
- A book, or script, with dialogue
- The music, arranged for instruments
- The lyrics to the songs

But did you know that musical theatre wasn't always like that?
https://bit.ly/32iY5hF

ACTIVITY: Freeze Frame Song
- All students are unmuted with video on.
- All students walk around their space for about a minute, until you call FREEZE!
- They should each freeze in an action pose, like they're in the middle of doing something specific.
- When you call their name they should unfreeze by singing one line that fits with their action. For instance, if I'm frozen into a pose like I'm swinging a golf club, I might sing the line, "How can I get a hole in one when there's a hole in my heart?!"
- The students will then guess that the singer was golfing.
- When students are unfrozen, they should mute themselves. But then they can help guess the actions of the next students to be unfrozen -- through Zoom chat.

ACTIVITY: Emotional Staircase Improv
Give a funny improv example of moving up the emotional staircase: talking, then singing, then dancing. For example …
- You're watching TV with your friend to see if you've won the lottery (speech).
- The numbers are being drawn and you sing that this could finally be your chance (sing).
- You win the jackpot (dance!).
- Ask for volunteers, 2 at a time, to turn on their video and improv their own progression up the staircase.
- Everyone but those two actors has sound and video off.
- Provide them with specific conflicts or ask the class for suggestions:
  - Class starts in 5 minutes and your homework is due but you haven't even started yet.

- ○ You're lost in the woods and it's going to start raining.
- ○ You're the cleaner for the space shuttle and you accidentally got locked in when it's about to take off.
- Students should begin by talking, then singing, then dancing as the emotional level rises.
- Sound on Zoom can cut out if two people are talking at the same time, so they should pay close attention to each other and try to only sing or talk when the other is finished with a phrase.
- Choose two more performers and run the exercise again.

REFLECTION: How did it feel as a performer? As an audience member?

HOME CHALLENGE: One-Man Show
Develop a "mini one-man show": create an improvised scene, based either in reality or fantastical, in which you illustrate the Emotional Staircase by starting with a little monologue, followed by a few lines of a song, to which you then begin dancing.

Music (45 Minutes)

ZOOM BACKGROUND: Something from the musical Bright Star would be appropriate today - https://bit.ly/3gXH0ht

WRITE WHAT YOU HEAR: Folk Music
As the students come in play a piece of famous folk music, like "The Wreck of the Edmund Fitzgerald" -- this performance by Gordon Lightfoot from 2000 is very moving: https://bit.ly/3esklZ7
Once again, have them record one word at a time what the music makes them feel. What images do they see? What instruments do they hear?

REFLECTION: Allow them to share their thoughts about this sad song. And tell them the story of the song. (If you're not familiar with the story, you can find the Wikipedia summary here: https://bit.ly/2CARDrw)

DISCUSSION: Home Challenges
Did anyone have some song lyrics they analyzed for rhyme schemes that they would like to discuss today?

DISCUSSION: What Is Folk Music?
- Explain to the students that folk music is the music of a people or a culture.
- The term "folk music" comes from the German word "Volksmusik" which literally means "The people's music."
- There is folk music that is so old that no one knows who composed it. (Play a clip of this recording of "Shenandoah" - https://bit.ly/2ZpG13E)
- Ask if the students can think of other old folk songs they know, so old that they have no composer… some possible answers:
    - ○ "Oh My Darling Clementine"
    - ○ "Yankee Doodle"

○ Spirituals like "Go Down, Moses" or "Swing Low, Sweet Chariot"
- Traditionally, folk music has an oral history, and so the melodies and lyrics are passed down from generation to generation.
- There is folk music that is newer but written by composers to sound a lot like older folk music, like "The Wreck of the Edmund Fitzgerald."
- Folk music tends to deal with history, with protest, with tragedy.

ACTIVITY: Lyrics Lab

Let's look at the lyrics to "Oh My Darling Clementine".

In a cavern, In a canyon, (A)
Excavating for a mine, (B)
Dwelt a miner forty-niner, (C)
And his daughter Clementine. (B)

Chorus:
Oh my darling, Oh my darling, (A)
Oh my darling Clementine, (B)
You are lost and gone forever, (C)
Dreadful sorry Clementine. (B)

Light she was and like a fairy, (A)
And her shoes were number nine; (B)
Herring boxes, without topses, (C)
Sandals were for Clementine. (B)

(Repeat chorus)

Drove she ducklings to the water,
Every morning just at nine;
Hit her foot against a splinter,
Fell into the foaming brine.
(Repeat chorus)

Ruby lips above the water,
Blowing bubbles, soft and fine;
But Alas! I was no swimmer,
So I lost my Clementine.

- Point out the ABCB rhyme scheme and that in the verse, the "C" line also has an internal rhyme: miner/forty-niner and in verse 2, boxes / topses (thought that is a truly terrible rhyme.)
- Like "The Wreck of the Edmund Fitzgerald," this song is also about a tragedy. What has happened? What do we know about Clementine?

ACTIVITY: Vocal Rollercoaster
- Explain you're an engineer who's going to create a roller coaster that their voice will take a ride on.
- Give the class the first note to start on and have the entire class "move" their voices up and down the roller coaster (you can choose any vowel sound).
- As you raise your hand up or down, their voices need to follow your hand's movements.
- Your roller coaster could start very low and make a slow climb upwards, fall quickly or even do loop-de-loops!
- After you've directed them a few times, ask for a volunteer to be "train engineer."

(OPTIONAL: You can also use the virtual "white board" feature under the Zoom "share screen" option and draw the roller coaster rises and falls. The kids LOVE to take over the virtual white board, so your roller coaster engineers will be super excited to engineer their own designs for everyone to sing.)

VOCAL WARMUP: Can You Help Me Clean My Room?
- This singing warm-up asks singers to warm up their voices singing ascending and descending fifths.
- First, demonstrate for them: One group sings, "Can (G) you (G) help (G) me (G) clean (G) my (G) room (C)?" (GGGGGGC)
- Group 2 responds with: "Oh (C) NO (G) I (G) won't (C)!" (CGGC)
- Then you play the fifth a half a step higher for them, and they repeat the call and response.
- Ask two students to unmute themselves. They will be the leaders of Group A and Group B.
- Divide the rest of the group into Groups A and B, but only the leaders will be unmuted.
- Tell the entire group to put all their acting skills to the test as they either PLEAD for help with their room or REFUSE to help.
- After you repeat this a few times and advance several half steps with the exercise, flip the groups and allow Group B to plead for help and Group A to refuse as you come back down the scale. Choose a different leader for each group. Stress the importance of acting the "song."

LEARN A SONG: The Water Is Wide
- "The Water is Wide" can be traced back to a Scottish folk song from the 1600s!
- Using your preferred arrangement of the song (the sheet music is available from literally everywhere), teach the vocal line to the students with the "call and response" technique, in which everyone gets to sing a phrase unmuted.
- This is also a lovely song to introduce harmony. Show how everyone doesn't sing the same note all the time. (The animated sheet music, stopped in the harmony parts, can be helpful with that.)
- Animated Sheet Music Video: https://bit.ly/3epEY8l
- To demonstrate how beautiful this song can be when sung in harmony, play this version from a Lilith Fair performance: https://bit.ly/32fToFo

AT HOME CHALLENGE: Write a Verse
Write at least one verse and chorus that either tells a story or protests an injustice (serious or funny). Explain your rhyme scheme.

Dance (45 Minutes)

ZOOM BACKGROUND: I don't think it gets much better than this Saturday Night Fever image: https://bit.ly/38TeoTV

WARMUP: Get Ready to Disco Dance
- Make sure everyone has plenty of room to move as we warm up, because today we are going to MOVE! If you have your favorite version of a disco dance warmup, by all means go for it, but if not, may I recommend a little "Dancing Queen?" (https://bit.ly/3gZFM5n)
- Make sure the kids know that the important thing is just to keep moving. They will pick up the steps as we go because it keeps repeating!

DISCUSSION: Home Challenge
Does anyone have some choreography that they worked on at home, combining jazz and tap steps that they would like to demonstrate? Remember, if they play music for their movement, they will need to do so from their side of the connection.

WATCH AND LEARN: Saturday Night Fever
This scene is a fun way to introduce disco to the students. Explain that this film, *Saturday Night Fever*, was based on a magazine article that came out at the time about the disco lifestyle and featured a character very much like the star of the movie, who saw disco as his way out of his mundane life: https://bit.ly/3j5KArF

ACTIVITY: Let's Learn The Hustle!
The Hustle is one of the most popular disco line dances, and gets played at pretty much every wedding since Saturday Night Fever came out. If you don't know The Hustle, this tutorial is a lot of fun: (https://bit.ly/3j0Y7AX) The dance teacher in this one moves pretty quickly, though, and the students -- particularly those new to dance -- will likely need the steps broken down a lot more slowly.

ACTIVITY: Dance to the Music
- When everyone can comfortably complete the movements four times and make it all the way around and back to their starting position, try performing the dance to the original music from Van McCoy: https://bit.ly/3fsNB3j (I would start the track at :33 because there's a loooooong intro.)
- Or you can use the same moves with the "Electric Slide:" https://bit.ly/38YkCla
- Or "Dancing Queen!" https://bit.ly/2OreJUp

HOME CHALLENGE: Hustling at Home
Can you "Hustle" to one of the following songs:
- "All Night Long" by Lionel Richie

- "Girls Just Wanna Have Fun" by Cyndi Lauper
- "Poker Face" by Lady Gaga

Closing Meeting (15 Minutes)

ZOOM BACKGROUND: Keep the Saturday Night Fever Background, play "Dancing Queen" and see how many of the students will celebrate their newfound disco moves.

SHARE: Let everyone share their favorite moment of the day. Let them know that tomorrow is our last day, and our CLOSING MEETING will be extra long tomorrow while we have a Pajama Jam Party! We'll have a karaoke party -- so everyone find their favorite karaoke track that they would like to sing (remind them they will need to play the music from their end). Everyone can either wear their pajamas the whole time or change before our closing meeting.

HOME COSTUME CHALLENGE: Tomorrow's costume is a choice of either fantastic pajamas OR your favorite musical theatre character.

FRIDAY

Welcome Meeting (15 minutes)

- **ZOOM BACKGROUND:** How many students can recognize "In the Heights?" https://bit.ly/2Zu4J2Z How many have seen it?
- **BACKGROUND MUSIC:** https://bit.ly/3euW8RK
- As soon as everyone has logged on, let's take a look at those costumes and get a group photo!
- **DISCUSSION**: How many students have completed home challenges they would like to share with the group? Allow a maximum of one per student and let them know that the rest can share in their classes.
- Remind everyone that our individual classes will be shorter today to save time for our Pajama Jam at the end of the day, when we are going to give everyone a chance to sing, dance, tell jokes, whatever feels like a Celebration!

Theatre (35 minutes)

ZOOM BACKGROUND: An option from the Broadway production of *Matilda* - https://bit.ly/3j5pDNu

DISCUSSION: How many students recognize the musical? How many students know which Matilda song is being sung in this image?

WATCH AND LEARN: Musical Theatre Mashup
https://bit.ly/2WiOgwy This is a fantastic mash-up / history of musical theatre performed by the Spirit Young Performers Company. Ask the kids, as they watch the video, to comment in the chat if they've seen a particular musical and where they saw it.

DISCUSSION: HOME CHALLENGES
Does anyone have an "emotional staircase improv" that they would like to share with the class? Allow each student to unmute themselves and present their scene.

ACTIVITY: Slow Motion Pantomime
- In this activity we're going to let the music affect how we perform an action on stage.
- Play the music clip: Theme from *2001 A Space Odyssey* (https://bit.ly/2Wj6RJ4)
- Explain that each student has to come up with a very boring task (washing a window, doing the dishes, making a bed, weeding the garden, etc.).
- The goal is for the actor to create an overly dramatic, epic scene in slow motion that centers around that task. The scene should have a beginning, middle, and end.
- This is a silent scene that will be accompanied by the music you are hearing now.
- You have five minutes to work on this.

- Have each student turn off their video while they work out their scene (so we can't see what they're doing.
- Play the music as they work.
- After five minutes, ask everyone to come back and turn on their video.
- Call on the students one at a time to present their scenes.
- Allow the students to present their scenes, commending those that are focused and have a clear beginning, middle and end.

ACTIVITY: Students' Choice
For the final activity today, let the students choose their favorite game or exercise. If its not unanimous, ask for a chat vote.

Music (35 minutes)

ZOOM BACKGROUND: https://bit.ly/30ootV9
How many students have seen *Mary Poppins* on stage? Have any been in it? How is the stage show different from the movie?

WRITE WHAT YOU HEAR: Musical Theatre Mashup
Today's "Write What You Hear" will be a little different as we listen to another musical theatre mash-up. It's not a test, so it's TOTALLY OK, if they don't know the name of the musicals in the mashup. Just write what they hear: which instruments, accents, foreign languages, harmony, actors they recognize, etc. Write what images come to mind, and IF they recognize a musical write that down as well. (Don't share your screen today, since this is about listening.)
https://bit.ly/2OIZuMx

REFLECTION: Let each student share what they wrote down that they heard in the video. In return, share with them the "answers:" the names of each music and the three actors' names who performed them all. Did anyone recognize Lin Manuel Miranda and Mary Poppins herself, Emily Blunt?

ACTIVITY: Music Game - Send the Clap
- Explain to everyone that in music, DYNAMICS refer to how loud or soft a song or part of a song is. Dynamics can affect the mood of a song -- and a scene -- dramatically. Explain that soft sounds are referred to as "piano" while we describe loud music as "forte" (pronounced FORtay).
- Ask everyone to stand - everyone's video AND sound should be on, so they will need to stay focused and quiet.
- Let them know that you will clap once to begin the game. Another person will then clap either loud or softer than you, and another person will do the same after them.
- There are two major challenges to this game:
  - Try not to clap at the same time as another person.
  - Don't wait too long between claps. Eventually we should be able to naturally build both a rhythm and a dynamic ebb and flow.
- Tell the class you'd like to send the clap through the group again, but this time you want it to begin as piano, and gradually end as FORTE! (from quiet to loud)

- Repeat, but this time the opposite - gradually from FORTE! to piano
- Depending on the level of your students and available time, you could introduce the terms for fast and slow, and incorporate them into the commands for this activity:
  - Fast = Vivace (pronounced: vee-VAH-chay)
  - Slow = Adagio (ah-DAH-gee-o)

DISCUSSION: Home Challenges
Did anyone write a protest or story-based folk song that they would like to share with the class?

FINAL ACTIVITY: Student's Choice
Is there a particular song or vocal warmup that the class would like to perform on our last day of music class?

Dance (30 minutes)

ZOOM BACKGROUND: In honor of the *Hamilton* choreography we'll be learning about today - https://bit.ly/2Or2YNQ

DISCUSSION: Home Challenges
Has anyone learned to Hustle to another song? Allow each student who has practiced to present their song. If they wish to have music with their choreography, remind them that they need to play it from their end.

WARMUP: Hip Hop
If you don't have a favorite hip-hop dance warmup, this one is safe and effective for all dance skill levels: https://bit.ly/2CaeTwP

WATCH AND LEARN: The Choreography of Hamilton
(https://bit.ly/2Orf4Xb) The choreographer of Hamilton is Andy Blankenbuehler. He has been nominated for a Tony five times for his choreography and has won three times: for *Hamilton*, *In the Heights* and *Bandstand*. Today, we're going to watch him explain his thinking behind the choreography of *Hamilton*. The purpose of this video is to show students how much careful thought goes into every choreography choice in musical theatre and how you can use movement to convey strong ideas and emotion -- no matter how easy the dancers make the movements look. Unlike other videos we have watched, encourage the students to stand up and try and copy his moves as he breaks them down.

REFLECTION: How has hearing from the choreographer changed your impression of the dancing in *Hamilton*?

ACTIVITY: Review the Hustle
Let the students choose their favorite Hustle track and rehearse the song together!

Break (5 Minutes)

Allow the students a five-minute break to change into PJs, visit the restroom, grab party snacks, etc.

Closing Meeting (45 Minutes)

ZOOM BACKGROUND: Something festive from Broadway is called for, like this beautiful background courtesy of the Broadway show, *Moulin Rouge* - https://bit.ly/3foF8hr

BACKGROUND MUSIC: https://bit.ly/38HXVBY - As the students come in, have something upbeat like this "Best Day of My Life" dance-along playing.

PRIZE TIME: Once everyone has joined the party, pull the name out of the hat and/or announce the Challenge winner (if you're offering a prize)!

KARAOKE PREP: Find out how many kids want to sing karaoke, just so you can get an idea of how much time it will take. And remind them of your rules about language/content/etc. of their karaoke choices. (You can also ask them to send you their links ahead of time to approve if you have concerns.) Finally, make sure everyone knows that they will have to play the tracks from their end.

SHARE: Before we get into the karaoke solos, give everyone their last opportunity to share their favorite moments from the week. Be sure to end with yourself and make a point of telling them specifically how much this week has meant to you and when/where you would love to have them in your class again.

ACTIVITY: Let's Hustle!
One more time -- let's play our favorite "Hustle Song" and dance together.

ACTIVITY: Karaoke Time
Introduce each singer and let everyone give jazz hands or a "round of applause" (muted clapping in a circle). Only the singer will be unmuted. Remind everyone else to clap with their jazz hands and send positive encouragement via chat. Tell them that using Speaker View will make sure each performer appears larger on their screen.

Give the students a 10-minute warning before the end of class. Before the last song, tell them again how much you appreciate their being with you in this virtual classroom all week.

End on an emotionally powerful song, like a group singalong of "Seasons of Love" from *RENT*: https://bit.ly/2OqvqPO

OPTIONAL: Record the Zoom karaoke session and share it with the students from a private Google Drive after the week is over. This also gives you another chance to communicate with them and let them know you're still thinking of them.

Appendix A: Solo Vocal Songs for Kids Ages 8-14

- "My Treehouse" from THE MOST EPIC BIRTHDAY PARTY

- "More Like Me" from THE GRUNCH

- "Seize the Day" from NEWSIES

- "Happiness" from YOU'RE A GOOD MAN, CHARLIE BROWN

- "In Summer" from FROZEN

- "Tomorrow" from ANNIE

- "Maybe" from ANNIE

- "You're Never Fully Dressed Without a Smile" from ANNIE

- "Neat to be a Newsboy" from WORKING

- "Part of Your World" from LITTLE MERMAID

- "Naughty" from MATILDA

- "Quiet" from MATILDA

- "Proud of Your Boy" from ALADDIN

- "Beautiful City" from GODSPELL

- "Wouldn't It Be Loverly" from MY FAIR LADY

- "Simple Joys of Maidenhood" from CAMELOT

- "You'll Be Back" from HAMILTON

- "Razzle Dazzle" from CHICAGO

- "I Want to Be a Producer" from THE PRODUCERS

Appendix B: Musical Theatre Tracks for 16-Count Choreography

"One" from a Chorus Line:
https://bit.ly/3edcoXq

"Happy" by Pharrell Williams
https://bit.ly/3979ZwR

"Hard Knock Life" from Annie
https://bit.ly/2Zql2ww

"Better When I'm Dancing" from the Peanuts Movie
https://bit.ly/2BIL1aR

Appendix C: Sample Scenes & Monologues

SPELL

(NOTE: Although the monologue calls for a ruler, if you don't have a ruler handy, a pen or pencil will do. Just be sure to change the words in the monologue accordingly.)

If you believe in something enough, that makes it real. I know that for a fact, because I believe it a lot. Palm reading is real. ESP is real. Magic for sure is real.
(Hold up book.)
See this? It's a book of magic spells from forever ago. Like 1990. Maybe even 1980. It says you need a magic wand to make the spells work, but I'm pretty sure that any kind of stick will do it. Because I believe that a lot.
(Hold up ruler.)
See this? I stole this ruler from my brother. It's like fifteen years old and has a lot of power. I think. Probably. OK, now watch. This is a spell for weather.
(Clear your throat. Be sure to use big, "magical" gestures when casting the spell.)
Clouds - gather overhead.
Skies darken.
Sun go dead.
Air, thicken – turn to black.
Winds roar.
Clouds crack.
Foul breezes howl and blow.
Thunder growl.
Tempest grow.
Earth shake and lightening flash.
Trees break and mountains crash.
Whirlwind shatter, scream and spin.
Lightening, thunder, rain – BEGIN!
(Look around and listen for several moments for any sign of a storm.)
Darn it! Darn it! That always happens.
(Look at your "wand," then throw it on the ground.)
I need to get a better ruler.

CLUBHOUSE

(Scene for three people.)

(DEVON, DALE and DYLAN are old friends.)

DEVON: OK, I call this meeting of the Thursday Afternoon Super Exclusive Club to order. Does anyone want to second that?

DALE: *(Enthusiastically.)* I will! I will!

DEVON: Awesome. The totally first ever meeting of the Thursday Afternoon Super Exclusive Club is now in session.

DYLAN: *(Raising hand.)* Will there be food?

DEVON: Did you bring any food?

DYLAN: No.

DEVON: Then no, Dylan, there won't be any food.

DYLAN: *(Sulking.)* Fine.

DEVON: Now, the first order of business should be . . .

DALE: *(Cutting DEVON off. Enthusiastically.)* I second that!

DEVON: Thank you, Dale, but I haven't said anything yet. The first order of business should be . . .

DYLAN: *(Cutting DEVON off.)* Why do you get to decide what the first order of business is?

DEVON: Because I'm the president.

DYLAN: No you're not. This is the first meeting. We need to hold elections.

DALE: Is somebody going to bring food next time?

DEVON: OK, Dylan, fine. I nominate myself for president.

DALE: I second that!

DYLAN: OK, then I nominate me for president. *(DYLAN looks at DALE for a moment, waiting.)* Dale?
DALE: What? . . . Oh . . . I second that!

DEVON: *(To DYLAN.)* Dale can't second the nomination of two different people.

DYLAN: Who says?

DEVON; It's the rules.

DYLAN: We don't have any rules yet, 'cuz we haven't voted on anything.

DEVON: Well, we can't vote on anything if we don't have any rules.

DALE: Yeah! No rules, rules!

DYLAN: I move that anyone can second anything they want.

DALE: I second that!

DEVON: Fine. All in favor raise your hand.

> (*DEVON looks at DALE, shakes head, and silently mouths the word, "No." DALE and DYLAN raise their hands.*)

DYLAN: Yes! The motion passes. Anyone can second anything, so we're both running for president.

DEVON: (*Rolling eyes.*) Fine. All in favor of me being president, raise your hand. (*DEVON and DALE raise their hands.*) That's two. Aaand all in favor of Dylan being president? (*DYLAN and DALE raise their hands.*) Dale, you can't vote for two different people

DALE: Why not?

DEVON: It's the rules.

DALE & DYLAN: (*Together.*) There are no rules!

DEVON: You know what? This is a worthless club. I quit.

DYLAN: Fine! We don't need you anyway. (*DEVON exits.*) I hereby declare myself president of the Thursday Afternoon Super Exclusive Club.

DALE: I move that we should both bring food next week and we have to eat everything we ·bring.

DYLAN: I second that. (*DALE and DYLAN raise their hands, then quickly look around for any other votes.*) Done.
DALE: Devon is crazy. This is definitely not a worthless club. This club is awesome!

DYLAN: I'll second that.

> (*DALE and DYLAN raise their hands, then quickly look around for any other votes. DALE and DEVON look at each other and smile.*)

DALE: Yeah!
-   *END SCENE -*

GHOSTS

(Scene for two people.)

NOTE: *Although it is stated that the two characters in the scene below are lying in bed, if preferred, the scene can be presented with both actors standing (as though they were lying in bed) or with both actors in chairs (as though lying in bed). Similarly, the sheets mentioned can be real or imaginary.*

(It is the middle of the night. RILEY and KELLY are sleeping in twin beds in the same room. After a moment, RILEY stirs, then opens eyes and sits up.)

RILEY: *(To KELLY.)* What was that?

KELLY: *(Waking up.)* What?

RILEY: That noise.

KELLY: *(Sitting up.)* What noise?

> *(RILEY and KELLY listen for a moment, then are suddenly visibly startled as they hear the noise again.)*

RILEY: That one!

KELLY: Whoa!

RILEY: *(A little frightened.)* It's probably nothing, right?

KELLY: Yeah it's probably…

> *(RILEY and KELLY hear the noise again and jump.)*

BOTH: Whoa!!

KELLY: You should go downstairs and look.

RILEY: No you should.

KELLY: No you should.

> *(RILEY and KELLY look at each other.)*

RILEY: OK, we both will.

> *(RILEY and KELLY hear the noise again and react even more startled and frightened.)*

BOTH: WHOA!!!

RILEY: OK, we'll both stay up here.

KELLY: It's probably safer under the covers.

> *(RILEY and KELLY lie back and pull the their blankets up to their chins.)*

RILEY: Yeah.

KELLY: It's probably even safer all the way under.

RILEY: Yeah. *(RILEY and KELLY go all the way under the covers.)* Do you feel safer?

KELLY: *(From under the covers.)* No.

RILEY: Me neither.

> *(BOTH come out from under the covers.)*

KELLY: You know what? I'm sick of this. I'm sick of being scared.

RILEY: Yeah?

KELLY: Yeah. And I'm gonna do something about it. *(Loudly.)* Come and get me!

RILEY: What!?!?

KELLY: *(Louder.)* Come and get me!

RILEY: Dude! Be quiet!

KELLY: *(Even louder.)* COME AND GET ME!!!

RILEY: *(Frantic.)* Get *her/him*! Get *her/him*!

> *(BOTH look around, waiting. Several moments pass.)*

KELLY: Do you feel safer?

RILEY: No. Do you?

KELLY: *(Uncertainly.)* . . . Sure. Yeah.
RILEY: *(Faking it, but badly.)* Yeah - me too.

KELLY: So we should get some sleep, right?

RILEY: Yeah. Sleep.

KELLY: *(Still sitting up in bed.)* Totally ready for this.

RILEY: *(Still sitting up in bed.)* Yeah. Totally.

KELLY: OK then. *(Faking a yawn.)* G'night. *(Remains sitting up.)*

RILEY: Yeah. *(Faking a yawn.)* G'night. *(Remains sitting up.)*

  (RILEY and KELLY continue to sit up in bed, staring rigidly ahead, waiting.)

-         *END SCENE -*

This scene is from Beat by Beat's
*Contemporary Scenes for Young Actors (*https://bit.ly/3edabLC*)*
By Douglas M. Parker.

Appendix D: Video Preparation Checklist

Basic video preparation checklists for live Zoom performances and recorded performances. You'll see that recorded performances have more things to check off but the amazing trade-off is almost absolute control over the end result. Recorded performances edited together are, as of this writing, really the only way to give the appearance of ensemble singing; you won't be able to do this live.

Item	Live Zoom Performance	Recorded Performance
Lighting – Make sure lighting is good from behind the camera; don't sit/stand in front of a window.	☐	☐
Sound – Make sure the mic on your device is picking up sound the way you intended and isn't picking up vibrations from speakers or instruments.	☐	☐
Background – Don't be upstaged by what's behind you. Make sure household members know you're recording. Turn off ceiling fans – they are so distracting in a video!	☐	☐
Internet Speed – If you have doubts about the quality of your internet connection during a Zoom Meeting, sit as close as possible to your router or use an ethernet cable to connect your computer to your modem.	☐	
Using Virtual Backgrounds - Have fun with Zoom virtual backgrounds if appropriate.	☐	
Playback Device and Earbuds – If you are performing in a virtual ensemble, you'll need one device to record yourself and another device and earbuds to play back your guide track.		☐
Green Screen (optional) - If you will be using iMovie or other video-editing software, use a green or blue screen/ sheet/wall so a "set" can be added in later!		☐

Item	Live Zoom Performance	Recorded Performance
File Size – If you have doubts about your ability to upload the very large video file you're about to record, consider changing your device's camera settings to 720p. This will still give you decent quality but with a moderate video size.		☐
Uploading Video Files – Have a couple methods available because when it comes to all the variables of internet and devices, one size does not fit all. Email and text apps will usually not accommodate the size of a video file but here are a couple of great options: • Wetransfer.com – no sign-in needed and no file size limit. The sender just enters your email address and you'll receive notification once the file is uploaded. • Google Drive – most people have a Google sign-in and this has been a great back-up for us on the few occasions when people were not able to upload to wetransfer.com. Facebook groups are great for communication but don't use them for sharing videos meant for a performance. You cannot download others' videos from Facebook. We tried screen-capturing Facebook videos but the quality was massively degraded.		☐

Appendix E: Vocal Warm Ups

VOCAL WARM-UP #1: Ha Ha Ha (Music Cue 01)

Ha ha ha ha ha ha ha.　　Ha ha ha ha ha ha ha.

Keep repeating a half-step higher, 4 or 5 more times.

VOCAL WARM-UP #2: Me May Mo (Music Cue 03)
VOCAL WARM-UP #3: M&Ms (Music Cue 04)

Me___ May___ Mo Oh oh.　　Me___ May___ Mo Oh oh.

Keep repeating a half-step higher, 6 or 7 more times.

VOCAL WARM-UP #4: Bumblebee (Music Cue 06)

Ma-ma made me mash my M & M's. Oh my!　　Ma-ma made me mash my M & M's. Oh my!

Keep repeating a half-step lower, 6 or 7 more times.

Bum - ble - bee___ Bum - ble - bee___ Bum - ble - bee___ Bum - ble - bee.

Bum - ble - bee___ Bum - ble - bee___ Bum - ble - bee___ Bum - ble - bee.

Keep repeating a half-step higher, 4 or 5 more times.

Appendix F: Sample Songs

MY TREEHOUSE
From *The Most Epic Birthday Party Ever*

SKYLER:
When I was 8 and was afraid to go to my first piano recital, I hid in this treehouse. I felt safe.
When I was 10 and my dad yelled at me for lying, this is where I ran to. I felt protected.
And now that I'm 12, and everyone has left me on my birthday...well, what better place to be?

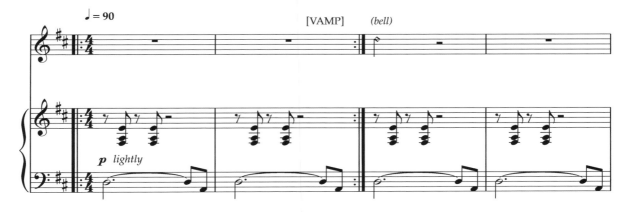

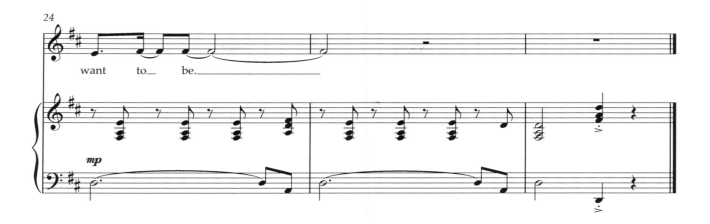

Lyrics by Betina Hershey, Music by Denver Casado

My Treehouse - Lyrics

SKYLER

When I was 8 and was afraid to go to my first piano recital, I hid in this treehouse. I felt safe. When I was 10 and my dad yelled at me for lying, this is where I ran to. I felt protected. And now that I'm 12, and everyone has left me on my birthday...well, what better place to be?

Just me up here in my tree house
Not much to fear in my tree house
I'm all alone
But I feel like I belong here

Just me and leaves in my tree house
A calming breeze in my tree house
It may sound simple
But I cant do much wrong here

'Cause in my tree
Freedom reigns
So much to see
Above the plains
Just little me
No one complains

So safe and sound in my tree house
I won't be found in my tree house
Unless I want to be

MORE LIKE ME

From *The Grunch*
Lyrics by Betina Hershey, Music by Denver Casado

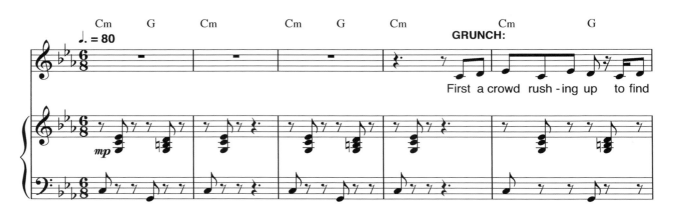

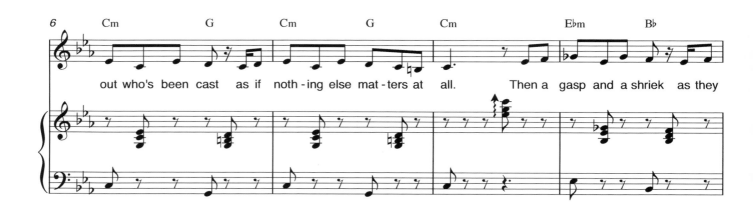

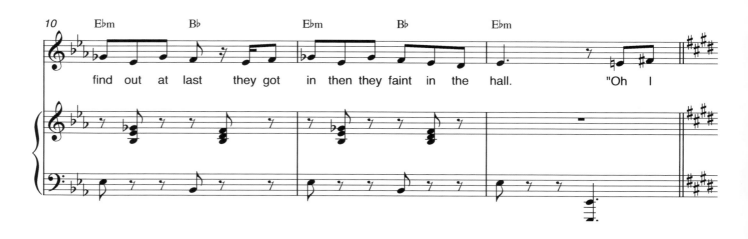

MILLS: I still don't understand why you're so angry...isn't your aunt a theatre critic in New York?

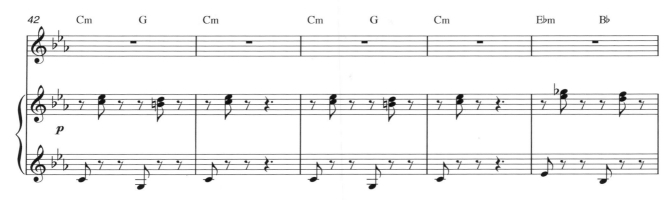

GRUNCH: That's the other side of the family...wait a second...Mills, you're brilliant!!!
I can use her to ruin the musical forever!

MILLS: What?!

GRUNCH: Yes...I'll get my aunt to come see the musical, and somehow,
someway, I'll make sure they get the worst review ever! I've got it...

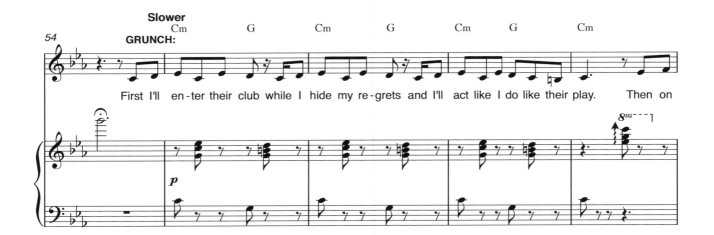

First I'll en-ter their club while I hide my re-grets and I'll act like I do like their play. Then on

More Like Me - Lyrics

GRUNCH
FIRST A CROWD RUSHING UP TO FIND OUT
WHO'S BEEN CAST
AS IF NOTHING ELSE MATTERS AT ALL
THEN A GASP AND A SHRIEK AS THEY
FIND OUT AT LAST
THEY GOT IN. THEN THEY FAINT IN THE
HALL

(Mockingly)
"OH, I DREAMT ABOUT THIS THE WHOLE
SUMMER
AND AT LAST I AM FIN'LLY A STAR.

MILLS
I'M SO GLAD I GOT CAST
OOH, I'M HAVING BLAST!"

GRUNCH
DON'T YOU FIND THEIR EXUBERANCE
BIZARRE..!!!!

THEY TAKE OVER THE GYM AND THE
HALLS AND THE YARD
AS IF NOBODY ELSE NEEDS THE SPACE
THEY THINK EVERYONE'S GLAD BUT
THEIR LOGIC IS MARRED
EVEN IF IT'S JUST ME THEY DISPLACE

"OH, I LOVE MY WHOLE CAST AND
DIRECTOR
YES, I FEEL LIKE WE'RE REALLY A TEAM

MILLS
EVERY DAY WE REHEARSE
MEMORIZING EACH VERSE"

GRUNCH
IT'S ENOUGH TO MAKE ME WANNA
SCREAM
AHHHHH!

APPLE *(popping head onstage)*
Hey, you have a really powerful voice, you should join
the school musical!

*(GRUNCH stomps toward APPLE which scares her
away.)*

GRUNCH
Out!

MILLS
I sill don't understand why you're so angry..isn't your
aunt a theatre critic in New York?

GRUNCH
That's the *other* side of the family...wait a second...Mills,
you're brilliant!!! I can use her to ruin the musical
forever!

MILLS
What?!

GRUNCH
Yes...I'll get my aunt to come see the musical, and
somehow, someway, I'll make sure they get the worst
review ever! I've got it...

FIRST I'LL ENTER THEIR CLUB WHILE I
HIDE MY REGRETS
AND THEY'LL THINK THAT I DO LIKE
THEIR PLAY
THEN ON OPENING NIGHT I'LL HAVE
HIDDEN THEIR SETS
AND HAVE TAKEN THEIR COSTUMES
AWAY!

AND MY AUNTIE WILL HATE THEIR
PERFORMANCE
YES, SHE'LL CRUSH THE WHOLE GROUP
WITH HER INK
I'LL HAVE DONE THE SCHOOL RIGHT
I WILL SHOW THEM THE LIGHT
YES, I'LL SHOW THEM THAT MUSICALS
STINK!

I'LL HAVE WON! THEY'LL GO HOME AND
STOP DREAMING
AND THE NEXT YEAR WILL BE SO SERENE
NO MORE PLAY, NO MORE SONG
NO MORE CLUB TO BELONG
THE WHOLE SCHOOL WILL BE MUCH
MORE LIKE ME!
THE WHOLE SCHOOL WILL BE MUCH
MORE LIKE ME!

Appendix G: Music Cues List

Music Cue 01: Vocal Warm-Up "Ha Ha Ha" (https://bit.ly/MusicCue01)

Music Cue 02: My Treehouse Vocal Track (https://bit.ly/MusicCue02)

Music Cue 03: Vocal Warm-Up "Me May Mo" (https://bit.ly/MusicCue03)

Music Cue 04: Vocal Warm-Up "M&Ms" (https://bit.ly/MusicCue04)

Music Cue 05: My Treehouse Accompaniment Track (https://bit.ly/MusicCue05)

Music Cue 06: Vocal Warm-Up Bumblebee (https://bit.ly/MusicCue06)

Music Cue 07: More Like Me Vocal Track (https://bit.ly/MusicCue07)

Music Cue 08: More Like Me Accompaniment Track (https://bit.ly/MusicCue08)

About Beat by Beat Press

Beat by Beat Press is the world's fastest growing publisher of contemporary new musicals and teaching drama resources for young actors. The materials are created by a team of professional playwrights and arts educators in New York City and Los Angeles. Since 2011, Beat by Beat materials have been used in over 100 countries and have been translated into 5 different languages.

Other Resources from Beat by Beat Press

Learn more and discover over 150 free drama games at
www.bbbpress.com.

Printed in Great Britain
by Amazon